PERSONAL BALANCE SHEET

Assets	Five years ago	TODAY	Five years from now
Cash in bank			
Life insurance (paid-in value)			
Annuities (cash value)			
Real estate			
Furniture			
Automobile (trade-in value)			
Money due from others			
Other assets (cash value)			
Security investments:			
Government bonds			
Corporate bonds			
Stocks			
TOTAL ASSETS			

Liabilities			
Bills payable			
Loans payable			
Unpaid mortgage			
Other debts			
TOTAL LIABILITIES			
TOTAL ASSETS			
LESS TOTAL LIABILITIES			
NET WORTH			

PERSONAL FINANCE

Sixth Edition

PERSONAL FINANCE

JEROME B. COHEN, Ph.D.
Professor of Finance and Dean (Emeritus)
Bernard M. Baruch College
The City University of New York

1979 **RICHARD D. IRWIN, INC.** Homewood, Illinois 60430
Irwin-Dorsey Limited Georgetown, Ontario L7G 4B3

End paper forms courtesy of
Merrill Lynch, Pierce, Fenner, & Smith.

© RICHARD D. IRWIN, INC., 1954, 1958, 1964, 1972, 1975, and 1979

ISBN 0-256-02154-6
Library of Congress Catalog Card No. 78–70948
Printed in the United States of America

1 2 3 4 5 6 7 8 9 0 K 6 5 4 3 2 1 0 9

LEARNING SYSTEMS COMPANY—
a division of Richard D. Irwin, Inc.—has developed a
Programmed Learning AID
to accompany texts in this subject area.
Copies can be purchased through your bookstore
or by writing PLAIDS,
1818 Ridge Road, Homewood, Illinois 60430.

Preface

This is the Sixth Edition of *Personal Finance,* or the 25th anniversary edition of my first (1954) volume. That it has stood the test of the years so well is, I think, not a testimony to my writing style, but rather to the drama of the stirring economic and financial events that have characterized the period.

The tempo of change has accelerated so much in the last few years that any book dealing with personal finance quickly becomes outdated, necessitating revision, updating, and in due course, a new edition.

Inflation has hit harder and harder. It doesn't seem to abate or diminish. The dollar in your pocket now buys only half as much as it did only a dozen years ago.

The "rule of 72" shows how powerfully inflation compounding works. Simply divide any rate of inflation into 72. The answer is the number of years it will take to cut the purchasing power of the dollar in half. Over the past ten years we have had an average annual inflation rate of about 6.5 percent.

Double digit inflation is with us once again, along with fiscal deficits, the declining value of the dollar internationally, a stock market which was lower last year than it was ten years ago. The cost of mortgage interest is now over 10 percent in most sections of the country.

As upsetting as today's prices and trends are, what you can expect to pay in the year 2001 (at only a 6 percent inflation rate) is astonishing. An income of $45,000 a year in 2001 will buy no more than $10,000 does today. The average new house will cost $171,000. An economy car (the smallest compact) $17,000, annual tuition at a private college will run about $16,000.

Coffee, if you can still stand the expensive taste, will sell at about $8.50 a pound, ground beef at about $4.60. Your luncheon hamburger will cost $6.60–$7.00 each, a tube of toothpaste $2.50, a head of lettuce about $2.60, and bus fare $2.20 per ride.

Headlines tell the bitter story:

"Inflation Pinches Everyone"

"Economy Seen Changing Many Lifestyles Sharply"

"The High Cost of Living It Up"

"Inflation Is Cruel to the Already Poor"

"Middle Income: The Fun's Gone— Low Income: Getting by Becomes Still More Difficult"

"The Squeeze on the Middle Class"

"Even the Well-to-Do Begin to Feel Inflation's Bite"

"Is Inflation Chewing up Your Plans for the Future?"

"Have Homeowners Really Beaten Inflation?"

A new lifestyle has been emerging in the United States, a revaluation of beliefs and norms, stimulated by the pressure of financial change. There has been a weakening of family ties. The number of nonfamily households has doubled in a little over two decades. The divorce rate has also doubled. As we approach zero population growth, geriatrics is becoming more important than pediatrics, and nursing homes more numerous than day care centers.

Traditional personal financial problems have changed drastically over recent years.

You will face a host of perplexing financial choices over the next 40 or 50 years. Whether you handle them poorly or competently will go far toward determining the quality of your lifestyle.

If the following pages have any value, the measure of their worth will be the degree to which they will help you to reason wisely, to understand, and to come to sensible decisions on the host of financial dilemmas which will confront you.

Since most of us have no funds to administer before we start earning an income, this book begins with an examination of income and occupation, the determinants of whatever financial lifestyle you can achieve or enjoy.

Next, attention is shifted to basic expenditures that usually consume the major share of total income. We have become more aware of consumer fraud and rip-offs and consumer protection is now receiving the increasing legislative attention needed. We turn our attention next to the tax bite which each year seems to grow larger and larger.

The remainder of the volume is devoted to that residual segment of resources, small though it may be, which can provide comforts, satisfactions, and security beyond the basic needs. At first this segment may be a mere emergency fund of dollars to fall back on in case of need. A combination of some of these surplus dollars and borrowing may bring the benefit of extra goods and services.

As the savings grow, you normally think of the advantages of insurance, a home of your own, and the need for retirement income when earnings cease.

Social security provides a base for life insurance programming, as well as for annuity and pension planning. Health care has become terribly important and costly. Automobile insurance, if you can get it, is more and more expensive. If you are fortunate in accumulating modest or even immodest surpluses, you have an investment problem on your hands and ultimately, since you can take nothing with you when you depart this life, the matter of the fair disposition of your accumulation must also be faced. This in brief, is the order followed in the development of this text.

A substantial upheaval has shaken the consumer's world over recent years. New and interesting developments have come so fast that a whole new body of laws and protective measures have been originated, ranging from the new federal Consumer Product Safety Commission and the Truth in Lending and the Fair Credit Reporting laws to the Automobile Consumer Action Panels (Auto CAPs), the federal Warranty Standards Act, the Security Investors Protection Act, the Real Estate Settlement Procedure Act, no-fault divorce, and no-fault automobile insurance. There is a new awareness of the rights of and responsibilities to consumers. No longer does the caveat emptor (buyer beware) philosophy prevail. Consumer agencies have received recognition and achieved maturity. We have endeavored to capture and portray both the facts and the atmosphere of these developments. This new edition therefore reflects important developments in many fields ranging from consumer credit protection to health care to tax matters to investment innovations.

All facts and figures throughout the text were updated. Yet this book is about 250 pages shorter than the Fifth Edition.

A new first chapter, entitled Changing Life Styles, designed to reflect the new social and economic developments of the last decade, has been added.

There is a new factual section on consumer frauds and rip-offs as well as a review of the programs suggested or adopted to protect and help the consumer.

Several chapters have been consolidated, emphasizing the expanded treatment of automation and new savings opportunities and reflecting the increased competition between commercial banks, savings banks, savings and loans, and credit unions for the favor of the bank customer.

The latest in credit history reporting (a change in terminology and forms), scoring, and all the new federal legislation and enforcement procedures in this field, especially the activities of the Federal Reserve and the Federal Trade Commission in relation to the individual creditor and/or borrower are explained. A special section is devoted to equal credit opportunities for women.

The Tax Act of 1978 and the new Social Security legislation have been fully incorporated and discussed.

The Health Care chapter is presented from the personal viewpoint, highlighting the twin problems of increasing costs and the need for expanded care.

New studies of the skyrocketing cost of home ownership and the latest types of "variable mortgage" and "flexible payment plans" are reviewed and analyzed.

Comparative shopping for insurance policies and the new forms of adjustable life policies receive expanded coverage.

The entire chapter on wills, estates, and trusts has been rewritten in the light of the Tax Act of 1978 which, along with the Tax Act of 1976, drastically changed gift and inheritance tax substantive and reporting procedures.

A new Investment Alternatives chapter has replaced the previous Introduction to Investments chapter. Since over the last decade there has been disillusionment with investment in common stock (more losers than holders of gains) owners of surplus funds have turned to numerous alternative forms of investment, such as real estate, money market funds and investments, tax exempts, short term bills and notes, and "collectibles." The advantages and disadvantages of these alternatives, in the light of investor requirements, are examined.

A new chapter entitled, Managing Your Investments has replaced two former chapters. This new chapter discusses the criteria and time which the investor will need if, he or she wishes to personally manage the funds as compared to relying on professional management services.

The new edition also includes some two dozen appropriate cartoons from *The Wall Street Journal,* designed to add a note of levity to complex and sometimes perhaps somber personal finance problems.

This text is designed for college use, essentially for a one-semester course, be it quarter, trimester, or semester. It may, however, easily be adapted to a two-semester course by the simple expedient of spending one session discussing the principles of a given topic and the following session on the case-problem material on that topic given in part at the end of each chapter and at greater length in a new and expanded teacher's manual. The case problems represent, as closely as possible, real-life situations and may, therefore, play a vital part in courses utilizing this text. Objective tests for each chapter will be found in the teacher's manual.

April 1979   JEROME B. COHEN

Acknowledgments

The range of topics covered in this volume is so diverse, detailed, and practical that it was essential to consult numerous experts. While any errors that remain are the author's responsibility, the assistance rendered by the writings and the cooperation shown by those versed in the various specialized topics is gratefully acknowledged. Hundreds of requests have gone forth for permission to use the fruits of their labor. Practically without exception it has been granted enthusiastically. So many experts in their own specialties have given advice or constructive criticism that it is impossible to mention them all in the brief space available here, much as one should like to do it. Some of them, however, have provided such substantial help that specific acknowledgment must be made.

I am especially indebted to:

Mr. Fred C. Cohn, President, Johnsons' Charts Inc.

Dr. William Freund, Vice President and Chief Economist of the New York Stock Exchange

Dr. Allan O. Felix, Director of Education of the New York Stock Exchange

Mr. Joseph Naar, Director of Public Relations of the Conference Board

Mr. Yale Hirsch, the Hirsch Organization

Mr. Fabian Linden, Director of Consumer Research of the Conference Board

Prof. Joseph M. Belth, Graduate School of Business, Indiana University

Dr. S. Lees Booth, Senior Vice President of National Consumer Finance Association

Mr. Forest Bicknell, Chief of the Applications and Payments Branch; Mr. Jim Brown of *HEW News* of the Social Security Administration, Washington, D.C.; Mrs. Bernice Bernstein, Director of the New York Regional Office; and Mr. Morris Ordover, Director of Information of the New York Regional Office of the Social Security Administration.

Mrs. Solidelle Wasser of the Bureau of Labor Statistics, U.S. Department of Labor (New York)

Dr. Elmer Harmon, Senior Vice President and Mr. Wayne Gottlieb, Assistant Vice President of the Bowery Savings Bank

Mr. Arnold Kaufman, Editor, *The Outlook,* Standard & Poor's Corp.

Dr. Robert Ortner, Vice President and Economist of the Bank of New York

Ms. Beulah Land of the Bureau of the Census, U.S. Department of Commerce

Mr. Vernon G. Phelps, Assistant Vice President of the Government Employees Insurance Company

Mr. Jerome Sterling, President, M. C. Horsey & Co.

Mrs. Joan Scott, CLU of Teachers Insurance & Annuity Association of America

Ms. Ann. V. Galvin, Vice President of the Anchor Corp.

Mr. David T. Wendell, Vice President, David L. Babson & Co.

Mr. Joseph G. Bonnice, Assistant Vice President of the Insurance Information Institute

Mr. Eugene P. Starr of Pacific First Federal Savings, Tacoma, Washington

Dr. Dana H. Danforth, President of Danforth Associates

Mr. Richard Rush, Editor, *Art Investment Report*

Mr. Kenneth D. Campbell of Audit Investment Research

Dr. Paul M. Horvitz, Director of Research, Federal Deposit Insurance Corp.

Mr. Seymour Klein, Vice President, Advest Corp.

Mrs. Joyce E. Bryant, Director of Money Management Institute, Household Finance Corporation

Dr. Frank S. Endicott, Emeritus Director of Placement, Northwestern University

Mr. William H. Detlefsen, Manager, Associated Credit Bureaus Inc.

Mr. Gibbs McKenny and Mr. George Thomsen of *Taxes & Estates*

Mr. Raymond F. De Voe, Jr. of Loeb Rhoades, Hornblower

Mr. Louis Crown of the Midpeninsula Health Service

Mr. Norman Guess, Vice President, Dartnell Corp.

Mr. William Walpole of Blue Cross-Blue Shield Association

Prof. Grant J. Wells of Ball State University and Prof. Russell L. Ogden of Eastern Michigan University for constructive and helpful suggestions

Mr. Robert A Driscoll and Mrs. Rosemarie Shomstein of the American Council of Life Insurance

Mrs. Betty B. Peterkin, Food Economist, Research Division, U.S. Department of Agriculture

Ms. Sally Reed, Director of Information, Louis Harris & Associates Inc.

Mr. Ben Rudolph of Jacobs & Jacobs, Insurance

Dr. U. Grant, National Center for Educational Statistics, Office of Education, U.S. Department of Health, Education and Welfare

Mr. Jeffrey Cohelan, Executive Director, Group Health Association of America, Inc.

Mr. Frederick P. Groll, Chief Statistician, Merrill Lynch, Pierce, Fenner, & Smith

Mr. Alain Farhi, Specialist, Commodity Division, Merrill Lynch, Pierce, Fenner, & Smith, Inc.

Naturally, on investments, I have had the supportive advice and suggestions from my co-authors of *Investment Analysis and Portfolio Management:* Dr. Edward Zinbarg, Senior Vice President in charge of common stock investment, Prudential Insurance Company of America, and Mr. Arthur Zeikel, President and Chief Investment Officer of Merrill Lynch Asset Management Inc. Thanks also to Mrs. Linda Lo Monaco Vulpi of Merrill Lynch Asset Management Inc. for providing needed materials.

To my daughter Carla, my very real thanks for furnishing insights and clarifications regarding the changing behavior patterns and values of her generation.

For Ms. Mina S. Cohen a separate paragraph of appreciation and gratitude is required. While her contributions are not reflected in gross national product data, without her talents as an extraordinary researcher, and without her indomitable drive and perseverance, the complete revision and updating of this book would not have occurred.

J. B. C.

Contents

part one

PLANNING YOUR LIFESTYLE

1

Changing Lifestyles—New Consumer Attitudes and Choices

All things must change, to something new, to something strange.

LONGFELLOW

The old order changeth, yielding place to the new.

TENNYSON

Our society has changed perceptibly over the last decade. Old traditions of social order and a work ethic eroded. The Weathermen, the Black Panthers, the Gray Panthers, many of the young, the old, the poor, the women, the handicapped, and almost everyone else who felt disadvantaged became militant in the 60s.

Family ties have loosened. The status of women has altered drastically. They are staying single longer, marrying—if at all—later. Forty-nine percent of all wives work, and the percentage is rising. The divorce rate has risen rapidly. The birthrate has fallen sharply. Many women are just not having children. The Census Bureau reported that by 1978 the number of men and women living together—out of wedlock—had reached about 2 million.

The Birthrate

If the declining birthrate continues, our population will decrease by about 17 percent per generation. To a self-centered generation seeking current personal satisfaction and pleasure, children were too difficult to cope with, too time-consuming, too costly, and largely unrewarding psychologically, according to critics.

A growing acceptance of the concept of zero population growth was another cause of the declining birthrate. Partly offsetting these trends, however, were sudden spurts in births as wives in late marriages or those who had postponed motherhood felt that time was pressing and that they might regret missing a significant experience. In addition, there is the instinct to continue the race by self-replacement.

The Divorce Rate

The divorce rate continues to rise. If the trend continues, for every two marriages there will be a divorce. There were 84 divorced persons for every 1,000 persons in an intact marriage in 1977, as compared with only 35 per thousand in 1960. The dramatic upsurge in divorce has been a relatively recent development. In the late 70s, in addition to the 8 million divorced persons, there were another 3.8 million who were "separated." Nonfamily households continued to increase, and the average household size continued to decline.

The Trend to Singles

More young people remained single. The proportion of women in their early 20s who had never married increased by more than one half between 1960 and 1977. In 1978, *45* percent of all women 20 to 24 years old had not married, as compared with *28* percent in 1960. A definite pattern of postponing first marriages developed among young adults.

The youngsters of the postwar baby boom began to come of age in 1965 at the rate of about 4 million a year. Past generations of young people had lived with their parents until they married. Americans, however, are marrying later these days,

and today some 48 million adults—about 30 percent of all Americans, over 18—are unmarried. Almost half of the women between 20 and 24, and two thirds of the men, are still single.

Only 10 of each 1,000 people in the country get married each year, and the Census Bureau expects the marriage rate to stay low for years. It estimates that one third of all persons between 25 and 35 "may eventually marry but end their first marriage in divorce." Almost half of those who divorce and remarry may have their second marriage end in divorce, too, according to the Census Bureau.

"How large a minority live as unmarried couples?" a recent study asked.[1] The answer given was:

As with so many other statistics, this one can be expressed in a wide range of proportions, depending on the base that is used. The more narrowly one defines the base, the larger the proportion of unrelated adults of opposite sex who may be shown as living together informally. Some of the most relevant examples for demonstrating the width of the range are shown in Table 1–1.

Many of the recent developments relating to marriage and living arrangements in the United States appear to have resulted in contradictions. The increasing postponement of marriage should mean that more young people are mature at the time of marriage and therefore more capable of maintaining stable marriages, but more of those who marry are becoming divorced. One interpretation is that even more would be ending their marriages in divorce if the age at marriage had not been rising. Probably in no small measure because of the increasing availability and use of effective means of contraception, more persons are experimenting in premarital (and intermarital) intimacy, often living as unmarried couples.

Moreover, a growing proportion of di-

[1] Paul C. Glick and Arthur J. Norton, "Marrying, Divorcing, and Living Together in the United States Today," *Population Bulletin,* vol. 32, no. 5 (October 1977), p. 33, Population Reference Bureau, Inc., Washington, D.C.

TABLE 1–1
Proportion of Adults Living as Unmarried Couples: United States, 1977

Unit of Comparison	Total (millions)	Unmarried Couples*	
		Millions	Percent of total
Total population	216.0	1.914	0.9
Unmarried adults	52.63	1.914	3.6
Divorced men	3.17	0.171†	5.4
Divorced men under 35	1.3	0.085†	8.3
Total households	74.14	0.957	1.3
Couple households	48.43	0.957	2.0
Two-person households	17.81	0.753	4.2
Husband or man under 25	3.3	0.248	7.4
Husband or man 35 to 44	9.37	0.090	1.0
Husband or man 65 and over	6.79	0.085	1.3

* According to an even later Census Bureau report (1978), the proportion of households maintained by never-married single persons climbed to 11 percent as the number of households grew to 76 million.
† Estimated for all such men on the basis of data for those in two-person households.
Source: Paul C. Glick and Arthur J. Norton, "Marrying, Divorcing, and Living Together in the United States Today," *Population Bulletin,* vol. 32, no. 5 (October 1977), p. 33, Population Reference Bureau, Inc., Washington, D.C.

vorced men and women are not remarrying. As a consequence, instead of four of every five divorced persons eventually remarrying, the proportion may soon fall to only three of every four. To some extent such a development may mean that more persons who lack the inclination and requirements for living as happily married persons are choosing to remain unmarried.

Close to 40 percent of all marriages of young adults are likely to end in divorce.

Both the increase in divorce and the increase in living together without being married are consequences, to a large extent, of the relaxation of social pressures against such actions. More permissive behavior means greater choice of life-styles and more flexibility in the development of individual potentialities. But it comes at a price.[2]

No-Fault Divorce   California became the first state to legalize no-fault divorce in 1970. Today

the 50 states and territories have no-fault divorce laws. When couples ask for a no-fault divorce, the judgment is not a divorce granted to one or the other, but a dissolution of the marriage "without

"My principal objection to his lifestyle is that he's leading it here!"

Reprinted by permission *The Wall Street Journal*

---

[2] *Time,* November 27, 1978, p. 75, in an article entitled "America's New Manners" says the Census Bureau calls them "Partners of the Opposite Sex Sharing Living Quarters or Poss LQs."

blame," though the court may consider the need and the responsibility of one party or the other in approving custody, property and financial arrangements, or other terms of settlement. Recently, the number of divorces in America in one year passed the 1 million mark for the first time, according to the National Center for Health Statistics. That is more than double the divorces recorded in 1965. The proportion of children under 18 raised in one-parent households climbed from 9 percent in 1948 to about 18 percent in 1975, and is still rising.

The Census Bureau says that in the past seven years the number of people living alone grew by 43 percent, while the number of households with both husband and wife grew by only 6 percent.

Some of the trends behind these cold statistics include: later marriages and child bearing, rising divorce rates, a widening gap between male and female life expectancies, and the increasing ability and desire of the young and the elderly to live alone.

Even the U.S. Court of Claims in a recent tax ruling "noted that changing mores have made cohabitation without marriage acceptable" and said that young people could now "enjoy the blessings of love while minimizing their forced contribution to the federal fisc."[3]

The *National Observer* of May 30, 1977, said, "Whatever you call it, countless unwed couples, from celebrities to college students, to professionals, to widowed pensioners, are bringing new dimensions and respectability to a lifestyle that has been condemned and romanticised, outlawed and tolerated since the adoption of monogamy as the accepted way of life." With the growth of the "meaningful relationship," new questions of etiquette and of property and legal arrangements have arisen.

Articles on the legal side of living have appeared because legal matters change when "mingles" are involved. For example, there are no legal restrictions against an unmarried couple opening a joint bank account. Two different names can appear on an account and no one will object, so

"**What kind of marriage did you have in mind? Open marriage? Conventional marriage? Trial marriage?**"
Reprinted by permission *The Wall Street Journal*

long as there is money in the account to cover all withdrawals. A drawback you should think about, however, is that one of you may decide to split and draw out most, or all, of the money in the account without the other's agreement. Lawyers caution, as does the coauthor of the handbook *Super Tenant,* single clients not to lie about their relationship and not to sign a lease that limits use of the apartment to a "tenant and immediate family." "A red flag should go up when you see that," the lawyer said.[4]

Buying a house requires special contracts and the clarification of many points in advance. Who gets the property if there is a split? If one dies? A bank, however, may not refuse to grant a mortgage because the applicant couple are not married. New life styles must somehow deal with the established financial order.

Instant Marriages: "I Do without Ado"

"I do" does not have to be in writing, the California Supreme Court ruled. The Court bowed to contemporary mores by holding that an agreement be-

[3] *New York Times,* June 13, 1978.

[4] Georgia Dullea, "A Legal Guide to Cohabitation," *New York Times,* June 8, 1977.

tween an unmarried man and woman to share property acquired while living together is valid and binding.

In rapidly increasing numbers, Californians are choosing to wed in ceremonies that are sometimes called instant marriages. They are taking advantage of a procedure that was originally intended to accommodate unmarried couples who had been living together for a number of years, perhaps bearing children, and now want to legalize their relationship secretly in a state that does not recognize common-law marriage.

The state's confidential marriage act provides for a procedure that has few of the encumbrances of the traditional marriage license, requiring only that a couple complete a certificate costing $5 at one of the 200 wedding chapels scattered throughout the state or at a church. There is no blood test with its three-day wait and no public record of the marriage. The only way the certificate can be seen is through a court order or on the request of one of the spouses; in any event, the date of the marriage remains secret since the certificate does not contain it. The confidential marriage isn't new, but the fervor for it is. Confidential marriages have been possible in California since 1877, when the law establishing the procedure was enacted. Few couples knew about it then, however, and in 1971 a minor revision to the old law—wedding certificates had to be filed with the county clerk instead of with one's church—set off a wave of publicity by the state's wedding chapels, which began to advertise instant marriages as if they had just been invented.

The Uncertain Status of the 18-Year-Old

Life is now more complicated than it once was for the 18-year-olds.[5] Legal rights are still uneven for those who some years ago were given or promised the "privileges" of adulthood. In some areas 18-year-olds are being called for jury duty; in other areas they are not. Some landlords require that parents cosign leases for a separate apartment for a teenage daughter or son. The availability of credit

---

[5] For more information, see "What's 'of Legal Age'?" *Changing Times,* October 1978.

may differ from city to city, bank to bank, store to store. Perhaps nowhere is there more confusion than in the restrictions on the sale of alcoholic beverages. An 18-year-old may be hired as a topless dancer in a nightclub, but she may not be allowed to buy a drink there.

The one adult privilege that is now uniform for 18-year-olds in all 50 states is the right to vote in all elections, but the percentage of 18-year-olds who vote is less than their percentage of the total voting population. Many problems of 18-year-olds come from a lack of financial independence.

Census Finds Big Boost in Unwed-Couple Tally

WASHINGTON—The government confirmed what a lot of people thought: There's been a big increase in the number of couples living together who aren't married.

The Census Bureau said there were 660,000 households last year of two unrelated persons of the opposite sex. That's up from 327,000 in 1970.

The bureau said that some of these households could be a bachelor and his maid, or an elderly woman and a college student who is renting out a room. It didn't provide further statistical breakdowns, except to say that 460,000 of these households last year were "headed" by men and 200,000 by women.

There were 72.9 million households in the country last year overall.

Wall Street Journal, February 9, 1977.

Vast Changes in Education

Total educational enrollment remained stable despite fewer elementary school students. Elementary school enrollment, which, of course, is compulsory, dropped in recent years because of the declining births in previous years. The number of children enrolled in elementary school in 1977 was nearly 5 million (about 14 percent) lower than in 1970.

High school enrollment has increased by 7 percent since 1970, though not for the last few years, and unless there is a sudden change in the dropout rate, high school enrollment will soon begin to decline.

Illiteracy has dropped sharply. For all Americans the rate is now a mere 1 percent. The proportion of all high school graduates going on to college has risen steeply, from 43 percent in 1950 to 61 percent at present.

Enrollment rates are higher for black students than for white students in low-income families and especially in middle-income families, according to a recent federal study.[6] A total of 27 percent of all adults ages 18–24 are in college, and 10.7 percent of them are black.

Although the white proportion of the college population fell, the number of whites in college rose. White male enrollment fell to 47 percent from 58 percent a decade ago, while white female enrollment climbed from 36 percent to 40 percent. The number of black college students grew during that decade from 282,000 to 1,062,000.

This report, in a follow-up study of high school graduates of 1972, found that financial aid was an incentive that persons of all races and all ability levels needed in order to graduate and not withdraw midway.

From 1947, when 271,186 bachelor's and first professional degrees were conferred, the number more than tripled by 1975, to 978,849 degrees. The number of doctoral degrees conferred rose from 3,989 in 1947 to 34,083 in 1975.

From 1947 to 1965, a generation of 73 million babies was produced. What that baby boom did to the national life and the consumer economy was sensational. Couples moved from apartments to small houses, then to still larger homes. The housing industry expanded sharply, as did foodstuffs, clothing, furniture, automobiles, home appliances, and medicines, producing in turn a boom in the basic industries, such as steel, machine tools, and building materials. As a result of the baby boom, spending by and for children assumed major importance in the economy all the way from cradle

to college diploma, as parents struggled to satisfy the "needs and wants" of their offspring. *"1947–1977"* was indeed a "youth-oriented and youth-dominated society."

Crosscurrents of Population Change

Before the 1970s the metropolitan areas and the suburbs showed the most rapid population gains. It became an accepted cliché that the *"inner cities"* were in decline and that the "upwardly mobile" were moving out. Although this trend is continuing, the reverse is happening, too.[7] Now, population in the nonmetropolitan areas is also climbing and at a rate double that of the flow toward the urban areas. The migrants are heading particularly to the fast-growing rural counties in the sunbelt states: Texas, Florida, California, Arizona, New Mexico, Utah, Oklahoma, Georgia, and North and South Carolina. They include retirees relocating to warmer climates, young homesteaders trying their hand at farming for the first time, and corporate middle managers between 30 and 50 years of age changing their lifestyle.

Typically, the last have at least $40,000 or $50,000 to sink into businesses that they buy for between $75,000 and $150,000 (they borrow the difference), 90 percent of which are inns, restaurants, small motels, and other franchise operations. They come disillusioned by the depersonalization of working for large corporations, coupled with the desire to work for themselves. It's a matter of being able to take the credit for their own successes and the blame for their own failures. No one comes to make money, they say, but to escape "the rat race." A Conference Board study analyzing the opportunities for prime investment in rural America concludes that "these areas offer a narrow range of job opportunities."

"Urban dwellers who think that, by moving to a rural area, they can exchange a high standard of living for an idyllic existence are likely to be sadly disappointed. Perhaps at the end of World

---

[6] National Center for Educational Statistics, Washington, D.C., June 1978.

[7] Source: "Population Profile of the United States," *Current Population Reports,* Series P-20, no. 324, April 1978, Washington, D.C.

War II, there still remained some local markets, isolated from the national economy, particularly in the Old South. These have disappeared, however, and work today is just as demanding and competitive in rural America as in urban America."[8]

Women in the Work Force

In contrast, as if to confirm that this is an era of change and nonconformity, childless young professional couples with combined incomes in the $50,000 range are moving back to the cities. "If you're *not* going to have four kids or three kids or even two kids, what's the point of living in the suburbs? It's very hard for career women to find jobs out there."[9]

The trend toward women working outside the home began building in the 50s and exploded in the 70s and has now reached almost one in two. For the last couple of years, American women have been pouring into the nation's offices, stores, and factories at rates surpassing all projections made by the Department of Labor. Even where there are school-aged children, the number of working wives has doubled in the last 25 years.

Major factors cited by economists to explain the influx of women into the work force include inflation, which gave rise to the two-paycheck family; the divorce rate, which made many mothers the family breadwinner; and the women's movement, which spurred housewives to economic independence. In growing numbers, wives went to work either to help finance large families or to escape them. A second income frequently meant the difference between poverty and an adequate standard of living. The second income also often sought to achieve a college education for the children or the purchase of a one-family home—both of which are almost impossible today for many one-income families.

_____

[8] *Across the Board,* Conference Board, New York, April 1978.

[9] Comment by Prof. Eli Ginzberg, Columbia University economist and chairman of the National Commission for Manpower Policy.

A complicating development is the rising tension between blue-collar wives who need to work in order to supplement the family income and prosperous working wives who want to work. Resentment exists on both sides. Low-income wives fear that the others are taking jobs from those who need them. Well-to-do wives want a sense of professional satisfaction and appropriate pay from their work, and don't see why they should stay at home just because their husbands have a good income.

Increasingly, families in which a couple earns substantial salaries, such as $45,000–$50,000 combined, decide not to have children. By combining their incomes, they can lead the good life from a very early stage, which would not be possible if the wife withdrew from the labor market because she wanted to raise two or three children. Thus professional couples and affluent families are tending to have fewer or no children.

The future, however, is not all that perfect for the professional couples. Difficulties appear as career advancement for each may pull each to different geographic areas. A growing but still limited number of employers help the spouse of the transferred employee find a new job. Opportunities for promotion may become limited, or family relationships may be strained by separation and its related problems. Sacrifice by either or compromise, with neither achieving the desired goal, is more likely. It's the exceptional couple that can manage the reality of "equality."

Changing Attitudes toward Jobs and Careers

Many former radicals or dropouts have "made it." Women as well as men are climbing up the corporate ladders and getting ahead in law, advertising, architecture, and other professions. At the same time, many persons place work and material success lower on their scale of priorities than might have been true 20 years ago. Career switching is on the rise. As many as one third of all American workers may change their careers over a five-year period.

Today, young men and women, more often than not, expect the job to accommodate personal and family priorities—not the other way around, as in the past. Young lawyers are not hesitant to arrange for time of their own to pursue socially oriented legal activities. Working mothers demand time off to visit their children's nurseries and day-care centers. Promising young executives reject transfers that may be unsettling to the family—even if this means turning down a promotion. Symbolic of the changed thinking is the new corporate fringe benefit that Procter and Gamble Company offers both the men and the women who work for it. Both or either now have the option of taking a six-month "child care leave" when they adopt or have a baby.

Management practices are changing to reflect the dual job holding of today's married couples. Personnel arrangements are made now that would have been unthinkable in the past. A competent but pregnant employee of Prudential Insurance Company no longer need fear a maternity leave and no job at its end. Today she can pick up assignments to work on at home while she is a new homebound mother and thus keep her career on the track. Today's two-income couples, finding themselves with more money to spend and less time in which to spend it, are seeking such benefits as more flexible working hours rather than the more traditional benefits.

Flexitime doesn't shorten the working day, but it lets workers set their own starting time, and it allows a lunch schedule that gives employees the opportunity to arrange personal business. Several states even have projects in which two workers share one job, one salary, and one set of benefits, giving each worker the flexibility for part-time work and other interests. For example, a lawyer employed by a state worked part time and then because his wife also worked, their joint income provided for their needs while he developed a private practice as an attorney.

Our Age Is Showing

At the turn of the century, there were 3.1 million Americans aged 65 or older. That represented 1 out of every 24. Now more than 23 million are in this age bracket—about one in nine. By the end of the century, there will be 30.6 million Americans aged 65 or older. That means one in eight. Put another way, in 1970 the median age was just under 28, in 1978 it was 30, and by the turn of the century it will hit 35. The U.S. population is growing older, as the number of older Americans has increased more than three times as fast as the rest of the population.

Today 1 in every 8 females in the United States is 65 or older, compared with 1 in every 11 males. As we approach the year 2000, geriatrics will become more important than pediatrics, and nursing homes more numerous than child care centers.

As older Americans have demanded improved benefits, payments to them and their dependents or survivors have quadrupled in the last ten years. According to the Senate Committee on Aging, a typical family head 65 or older averages an aftertax income of $5,764, compared to $10,728 for those younger than 65. To attain that average, there will be a goodly number of elderly living comfortably, but there will also be an equally large number who are trying to pay rent or household expenses and to buy food and other necessaries, and are barely managing on a subsistence budget. Medical costs will keep soaring, too, and the elderly get proportionately three times as much health care as do younger citizens. Already, people 65 and older consume half of the tax-supported health expenditures, although they total only one tenth of the population. Who will pay these bills? Americans who are working. Since the political clout of the elderly may increase with their numbers, intergenerational conflict is a possibility.

The Impact of Singles as Consumers

The housing industry probably more than any other has felt the impact of single living. Since the enactment of the Equal Credit Opportunity Act, single women have become the fastest-growing segment of the home-buying market. "SSWDs Don't Need Pampers" was a subhead of a *Wall*

Street Journal article.[10] The story describes the different lifestyle of the "single, separated, widowed and divorced." Living alone increases their need for people—hence more travel, more money spent on entertaining, more dining out. Busy at work during the day, they depend on hiring services to do the many chores that make living comfortable. Both appliances and food containers need to be scaled down for this market. On the other side of the coin, singles of all types are buying large homes for investment, renovating, and just living. Town houses appeal. In the center of urban activity, and using sweat equity to offset a lack of cash, these houses can seem a bargain. The privacy and lack of house maintenance make condominiums attractive—especially to those with limited leisure time and a zest for a leisure activity.

Singles may have less money than couples, but they can spend all of it on themselves. Specialty cars, tape decks, and custom-designed musical equipment satisfy their yearning for the best.

Manufacturers of all types of consumer goods are eager to attract this easy-spending market. The National Association of Appliance Manufacturers regrets that "people who live alone buy refrigerators at only half the rate of the population in general, and washers and dryers at about one quarter of the rate." Manufacturers are producing cooking appliances that "grill one sandwich, slow-cook one serving of stew and fry one plate of french fries." Some of the merchandising aspects may seem absurd, but the SSWDs are an attractive and unique market. The furniture-rental business is growing faster than ever. Among the beneficiaries of the one-person households are restaurants. A study of spending patterns by family size found that the average person who lives alone spends almost as much on restaurant meals as married couples do, and just a bit less than a family of three. Working wives are regarded as a reason for the decline in the supermarket industry and the rise of the fast-food chains.

[10] June Kronholz, "On Their Own—A Living-Alone Trend Affects Housing, Cars, and Other Statistics; Singles Like Condominiums, Town Houses, Mustangs; a Problem in Appliances—SSWDs Don't Need Pampers" *Wall Street Journal,* November 16, 1977, p. 1.

Securities analysts are enthusiastic about the future of food-processing concerns that play to the singles market. Campbell Soup Company's Soup-for-One and Green Giant Company's Casseroles are already fixtures on the supermarket shelves. The firm that designed the Soup-for-One advertising campaign sees singles as having further impact on advertising. "One of the old rules of television commercials was that a woman had to wear a wedding ring to show that she had buying power. That's gone by the wayside."

Singles find urban living attractive in its proximity to work, entertainment, sports, movies, theaters, concerts, and ethnic diversity. Urban slums are being revitalized by affluent singles seeking urban excitement and convenience. Growing numbers of young people are forgoing marriage and children, and are not overly concerned about good schools or any schools. For example, they purchase more luxury items than do traditional families, since they have no child-rearing expenses.

Self-Oriented Parents

Even among people who choose to have children, there has been a change in values. Recent studies have found that large numbers of parents are self-oriented and are reluctant to make sacrifices for their youngsters. Today, advertising caters to such attitudes. Many ads now tend to focus on the individual rather than on the family.

The "Me" Generation

For many young people the pursuit of happiness has become the dominant preoccupation. For many, it means self-indulgence. For others, the goal is self-understanding.

One article begins, "Many of America's young adults have found new heroes—themselves." Glittering discos, sex clubs, singles apartments, and a seemingly endless variety of techniques for baring their psyches enable young people to celebrate themselves in what a leading writer called "The ME Decade of Self-Gratification and Self-Improvement." A psychologist at MIT says, "Forget about the future, do things now, do them today. That is what television says to people." Many bestselling books sound a similar theme, telling people they should be *Looking Out for No. 1* and *Winning through Intimidation.* A New York department store even opened a "Self Center."

Singles Are Trend Setters

Bicycles, blue jeans, ceramics, antiques, work shirts, and skateboards are "in"—or were at the time this was written, but may not be now. Along with long hair and beards, some of these came from the youth movement of the 1960s. Now BMWs are in, Cadillacs are of questionable taste, commune living—once "in"—is dead.

Status and custom vary from section to section of the country and change fast. In some urban centers town houses, season opera tickets, Persian rugs, private club membership, co-ops, bathroom telephones, and customized vans are "in," while in other centers discos, jogging, personal wine cellars, condos, faded jeans, pottery making, transcendental meditation, and EST are "in."

Merchants feel the effect of changing moods, tastes, and needs. Market expectations for toys and infant wear need revision. Gerber Products, which at one time was prosperous producing baby food only, saw its market diminish by 50 percent when the baby boom ended. It therefore turned to a greatly expanding market—the over 65 group. Both the baby group and the over 65 group were similar in that they had few usable teeth and couldn't chew for the most part. So Gerber put out a product line for senior citizens. It paid off handsomely.

Population Changes and Consumer Demand

By 1985, 7½ million families will be headed by persons aged 25–44 who, as the fastest-growing group at that time, will possess tremendous purchasing power. By that year, according to the Conference Board "the income of that group will have risen 80 percent, and it will account for half of all consumer spending." The members of this group are a prime market for home furnishings and other big ticket consumer items, such as autos. Moreover, the styles both in goods and advertising that are likely to appeal to them will probably be far differ-

ent from the appeals that caught their interest when they were younger.

Changing the Way We Live and Play

In the 60s, to show their disaffection with the establishment, young executives sat around offices in shirt sleeves. Suit coats were hanging off in a corner. But attitudes, styles, and tastes change, and in the late 70s the well-dressed young executive wore a tailored, tight-waisted, continental styled suit, coat, *and vest.*

Leisure is one of America's biggest industries. We do a great many individual things—but we somehow all seem to be doing them at the same time. Tennis? Scheduled into a slot? No spur-of-the-moment whim easily translated into a vacant court. Jogging? Rarely alone in serene contemplation. More likely in a pack of fellow joggers—willingly or not. Spend a fortune on mobile homes or vans to camp out luxuriously? You drive for hours to find a rural retreat to park. You acquire own boat at last! Where can you find a place to berth it? And of course there are the endless glacier-like "parking lots"—of our highways slowly moving cars filled with people seeking pleasure.

American leisure tastes range from expensive to simple. Over the last ten years, "spectator sports watching" jumped from $668 million to $15 billion, while flowers, seeds, and potted plant expenditures rose from $1.3 billion to $3.4 billion.

So many people are affluent today that it's not easy to see the disturbing undertones of inflation and energy eating into the seemingly pleasurable scenes. If food and rent and heating fuel cost so much more, then fuel for cars or boats or camping vans will necessarily have to be limited.

People of retirement age make up an increasingly important market. For example, those retired people who have both the income and the leisure to enjoy luxury items travel more than the members of other age groups. They also represent a major market for medicinal products, both ethical and proprietary. They tend illogically to prefer brand name items and are heavy purchasers of pills and prescriptions. But inflation is pulling many of them down and turning their retirement into a bitter experience.

The Impact of High Prices on Lifestyles

Even with the average wage at a new high, polls indicate that most families "feel poor" after coping with living costs that have risen by 92 percent over the past dozen years.

People on fixed incomes find that their living standards go down rapidly. Family incomes which have failed to rise faster than the level of prices strain many household budgets to the breaking point.

As inflation pressures increase, more people than ever before have been teaming up to buy their food in bulk from farmer's markets and cooperatives. Used clothes have become acceptable, even chic. Families are spending more time in public parks, camping out, and fishing instead of pursuing more expensive pastimes. Men and women who have never picked up a tool before have been changing the tires and the oil and doing the repairs on their own autos. Car pools have sprung up in many areas.

In mid-1978, double-digit inflation reappeared as the Consumer Price Index soared to an annual rate of 10.8 percent. The chairman of the Administration's Council on Wage and Price Stability called the return of double-digit inflation a "disaster." "Inflation Is Altering Most Lives in the United States," the *New York Times* stated in a feature article which reviewed the reactions and methods of individual cases in adjusting to and coping with inflation.[11] A Conference Board survey confirms that "A large number of Americans report a decline in their standard of living during the past year, and many say they are cutting back on their buying in order to cope with inflation."

Families whose heads were under 35 apparently have fared better than those 55 and over. About 30 percent of the under-35 families reported that they were better off now than a year ago, compared with only 10 percent of the families whose heads were 55 and over. The survey also found that only 17 percent of the families earning $25,000 and over said that they had a lower living standard now than a year ago, compared with nearly 25 percent of the families earning less than $15,000.[12]

Are Consumers Growing Spending Shy?

Of those polled by the Conference Board survey, 62 percent said that one of the ways in which they were coping with higher living costs was to buy less. Cutbacks in purchasing were reported in all age groups and in all income classes. "Many families are attempting to balance their budget by substituting less costly for more expensive items. . . . The single major exception is strong demand for automobiles—but with higher prices scheduled for new models, some families appear to be buying now on the assumption that a penny 'spent' is a penny earned."

The vast majority of those who curtailed their buying also cited other steps that their families were taking to cope with inflation. While about 40 percent of those polled said that salary increases were helping to offset rising living costs, over 30 percent said that they were dipping into their savings to make ends meet, and 14 percent said that the effects of inflation were being eased because an additional member of the family was working. About 9 percent said that they had been forced to borrow to meet higher living costs.

Perhaps the most effective way to economize on a permanent basis is reported by an accounting supervisor in Texas. He explains, "If I see something I want, I'll go and buy it. So now I've stopped reading the ads in the papers. I deliberately ignore them. And I don't go to the stores as often. I find that I save lots of gasoline and money that way."

According to a Louis Harris survey, Americans are now convinced that not only have important changes in their lifestyles already occurred but that even more important changes are likely to happen in the next 20 years.[13]

Among the major lifestyle changes that Americans expect are a reduced consumption of products. This reflects the belief held by 84 percent of the population that most people buy much more

---

[11] "Poll Shows Majority of Americans Altering Life because of Inflation," *New York Times,* June 5, 1978.

[12] Source: "Double-Digit Inflation Again," *Across the Board,* Conference Board, October 1978.

[13] Louis Harris & Associates Survey, September 1978.

TABLE 1–2
Major Lifestyle Changes Expected by Americans

Recently the Harris Survey asked: "Here are some common aspects of present lifestyles in this country. For each, would you tell me if you think it is going to become more popular, less popular, or remain at just about the present level of popularity."

	More Popular (percent)	Less Popular (percent)	Remain at Present Level (percent)	Not Sure (percent)
Self-service gasoline stations				
Total public	67	9	19	5
18–29 age group . . .	69	8	22	1
Wearing jeans				
Total public	42	18	36	4
18–29 age group . . .	45	14	38	3
Do-it-yourself repairs and construction				
Total public	83	4	11	2
18–29 age group . . .	84	4	11	1
Long hair for men				
Total public	7	71	16	6
18–29 age group . . .	9	63	23	5
Fast-food restaurants				
Total public	65	10	22	3
18–29 age group . . .	59	13	26	2
Informal manners				
Total public	48	17	28	7
18–29 age group . . .	44	16	35	5
Unisex clothing				
Total public	33	28	26	13
18–29 age group . . .	41	26	26	7
Widespread psychological counseling				
Total public	58	10	19	13
18–29 age group . . .	58	13	19	10
A high rate of divorce				
Total public	61	14	21	4
18–29 age group . . .	63	15	18	4
Small families				
Total public	76	7	13	4
18–29 age group . . .	79	8	11	2

Reproduced with permission of Louis Harris & Associates Inc. Released September 18, 1978.

than they need. Among the most affluent group—those who earn $25,000 or more annually—63 percent admit that they buy much more than they need. This shift away from the consumption of greater and greater quantities of goods is reflected in a number of changes that people now see taking place.

The Harris Survey sums up by saying:

People feel that there likely will be far less emphasis on the acquisition and consumption of material possessions in future years. The top five items of which people feel they now make excessive purchases that turn out to be a "waste of money" are clothing; cars;

small kitchen appliances, such as broilers, pan fry equipment, vacuum cleaners, hamburger presses, toasters, ovens and cookware; gadgets of many types and varieties, and junk food.

It seems that self-dependence will be a mark of the lifestyle of the future, although such aids as fast-food restaurants will help to ease the burden of keeping house. The fact that people also expect to see more broken marriages and more psychological counseling indicates that the problems of people living with each other are expected to increase. The implication is that an era with greater emphasis on humanity will not necessarily result in improvements in interpersonal relationships. However, young people would hastily add that facing up to their problems may make for healthier living than in the past.

Conclusion

Sometimes quietly and sometimes noisily, American society is in the midst of change. The shifts that are taking place raise issues affecting policies toward education, housing, marriage, the family, social and sexual mores, investment, taxation, and retirement. They point toward new public pressures on government policy, new programs, new attitudes, new trouble, and new achievements.

From swinging singles to meaningful relationships, from youthful rebellion against accepted social canons and mores to a disdain of marriage in its legal form, millions of young, unmarried Americans refusing to add to the population, seeing no percentage in raising children and then getting divorced, have turned to new and different ways of life, with startling impact on the American economy.

But now, except for the effects of inflation, it looks as if the pendulum has begun to swing back slightly. Students are studying once again, instead of rebelling against authority. JDs and MBAs are boasting of the new-high starting salaries they are getting, seemingly unconcerned that inflation and taxes are putting real income back a decade or so.

Inflation has probably done more to undermine the morale of the middle class and to disrupt tradi-

tional social mores in the United States than either long-standing poverty or the newer affluence.

Even on a no-frills budget, it is estimated that it costs an American family $32,000 to raise one child to age 17 and then add another $12,000–$24,000 for a college education. By 1985, the $32,000 may rise to about $44,000, and the $12,000–$24,000 to $20,000–$40,000. Little wonder, then, that some families have stopped having three or four children and that others are refraining from having any children at all. Inflation raises a question in the minds of many of whether a nonworking wife can be afforded today. More than half the wives are now in the labor force, largely because of inflation.

There is an old Chinese curse, "May you live in changing and interesting times." It seems to have been visited upon this generation.

SUGGESTED READINGS

Ashley, Paul P. *Oh Promise Me But Put It in Writing: Living Together Agreements without, before, during and after Marriage.* McGraw-Hill, New York, 1978.

"America's New Manners," *Time* Magazine, November 27, 1978, pp. 64–76.

Business Week. "Americans Change," Special Report, February 20, 1978.

Glick, Paul C., and Norton, Arthur J. "Marrying, Divorcing, and Living Together in the United States Today," *Population Bulletin,* vol. 32, no. 5 (October 1977), Population Reference Bureau, Inc., Washington, D.C.

Juster, F. Thomas (ed.). *The Distribution of Economic Well-Being.* National Bureau of Economic Research, Studies in Income and Wealth, no. 41. Published for the NBER by Ballinger Publishing Co., Cambridge, Mass., 1977.

U.S. Commerce Department. *Social Indicators: Selected Data on Social Conditions and Trends in the United States.* Washington, D.C.: Bureau of the Census, 1977. Issued annually.

Sternlieb, George, and Hughes, James W. *Current Population Trends in the U.S.* New Brunswick, N.J.: Center for Urban Policy Research, Rutgers University, 1978.

APPENDIX—RAISING CHILDREN IN A CHANGING SOCIETY

Perhaps one of the best views on changing mores can be seen through the eyes of parents. The examples in this appendix are taken from a study of American families in different sections of the country. The summary shows the differences as well as the similarities between the *New Breed* of parents and the *Traditionalists.**

Overview and Summary

American families are divided between the belief in traditional and in new values, but they are surprisingly united in their decision to pass on traditional values to their children.

This is the major theme of this study of American families and how they are raising their young children in a period of changing social values. The study documents and illuminates several dominant trends in child raising in America today.

The New Breed

There is a New Breed of parents today, representing 43 percent of all fathers and mothers of children under 13 years of age.

New Breed parents tend to be better educated and more affluent. They represent the "haves" rather than the "have-nots." New Breed parents have rejected many of the traditional values by which they were raised: marriage as an institution, the importance of religion, saving and thrift, patriotism, and hard work for its own sake. And they have adopted a new set of attitudes toward being parents and the relationships of parents to children. New Breed parents question the idea of sacrificing in order to give their children the best of everything and are firm believers in the equal rights of children and parents.

Compared to previous generations, the New Breed parents are less child-oriented and more self-oriented. They regard having children not as a social obligation but as one available option which they have freely chosen. Given the chance to rethink their decision, nine out of ten would still decide to have children.

The Traditionalists

By contrast, there are the Traditionalists who still represent the majority of all parents (57 percent). Traditionalists continue to support the basic values by which they were raised, but they, too, have been influenced by the new values and are trying to reconcile these newer concepts with older theories and beliefs. As parents, Traditionalists are stricter disciplinarians and more demanding of their children than New Breed parents. And while Traditionalists have a certain nostalgia for the simplicity of the past, they are not prepared for the same kind of self-sacrificing approach to child raising common in their parents' time. They do not believe that parents should stay together just for the sake of their children. And they do believe that parents are entitled to lives of their own even if it means spending less time with the children.

---

* The material in this appendix has been drawn from *The General Mills American Family Report, 1976–1977,* "Raising Children in a Changing Society," conducted by Yankelovich, Skelly and White, Inc., © General Mills, 1977. Reproduced with the permission of the General Mills Company.

Today's Parents

The New Breed—43 Percent	The Traditionalists—57 Percent
Not important values	*Very important values*
Marriage as an institution	Marriage as an institution
Religion	Religion
Saving money	Saving money
Patriotism	Hard work
Success	Financial security
Characteristics and beliefs	*Characteristics and beliefs*
Parents are self-oriented—not ready to sacrifice for their children	Parents are child-oriented—ready to sacrifice for their children
Parents don't push their children	Parents want their children to be outstanding
Parents have a laissez-faire attitude—children should be free to make their own decisions	Parents want to be in charge—believe parents should make decisions for their children
Parents question authority	Parents respect authority
Parents are permissive with their children	Parents are not permissive with their children
Parents believe boys and girls should be raised alike	Parents believe boys and girls should be raised differently
Parents believe their children have no future obligation to them	Parents believe old-fashioned upbringing is best
Parents see having children as an option, not a social responsibility	Parents see having children as a very important value

*What Both Groups
Teach Their Children*

Duty before pleasure

My country right or wrong

Hard work pays off

People in authority know best

Sex is wrong without marriage

Source: *The General Mills American Family Report, 1976–1977,* "Raising Children in a Changing Society," conducted by Yankelovich, Skelly and White, Inc., © General Mills, 1977.

CASE PROBLEMS

1 James Moulton and his wife, Susan, are young teachers, although she has not taught since their daughter, Helen, was born several years ago. The family is "struggling" on James's $16,000-a-year salary, spending almost $20 a month more than he is making. Their home, which cost $27,000, needs about $10,000 in repairs and improvements, much of which James could do if he had the time. Susan wants to return to teaching and knows of an $11,000 substitute position that she can get nearby. They are hesitant, weighing the numerous advantages and disadvantages. *(a)* Discuss the pros and cons. *(b)* How does this couple exemplify today's trends?

2 Jeanne Green and Robert Green both have successful careers—she as assistant to a vice-president in public relations; he in the advertising department of a large manufacturing company. In their four years of marriage each of them has changed jobs twice, moving upward. This last year has been difficult because they have lived in two cities, 125 miles apart. Their joint income of $38,000 and their personal career progress are satisfying, but problems are being created by their weekend marriage, with its double housing, high telephone bills, and expensive commuting costs, as well as the physical and emotional toll that it is taking.

Either or both of them can find jobs in the same city at lower salaries and with less opportunity for advancement. Jeanne and Robert are fearful about their long-distance marriage, and they puzzle over who should make the career sacrifice or whether both should. They are also fearful about the possible effects of such a job change on their marriage and their living standards. Faced with the same problems, what would you decide? What financial and personal factors should enter into this decision?

3 Jennifer Williams, a divorcée after nine years of marriage, is self-supporting. She is employed in an executive position in a city government planning job, but she is not protected by civil service.

She lives in a fashionable condominium, travels a good deal, and spends very freely on clothes and comforts. She frequently works a ten-hour day, and she often attends evening meetings.

The psychic jolt of her divorce has made her fearful about being "on her own" and about trying new sources for the investment of any savings. She has, however, put $1,000 into a Women's Savings and Loan Association as a commitment.

What do you think of her lifestyle? What are the weaknesses in this seemingly comfortable situation?

4 Explain several ways in which the changing lifestyles of the 70s have been reflected in the changing statistics and have helped to change those statistics. In what way or ways do you find that you personally, are typical or not typical of the new life styles expressed in these new statistics?

5 Dave Sherman believes in the now of living. As a chief personnel officer making $27,000 a year in a large insurance company, he should be able to afford that philosophy comfortably. Yet he is deeply in debt. Although single, he owns a large heavily mortgaged house, which he bought for investment. The taxes on it are high. He owes money to department stores, credit card companies, and the bank. But he owns the latest stereo and sports equipment and a new car, and he has a very large wardrobe. He is a careful comparison shopper and gets the best value for his dollar, and he does not see why he shouldn't spend that dollar on what he wants. What are the obstacles to the continuation of his lifestyle?

2

Careers and Income

You have only one life to live, but if you play your cards right, one is enough.

W. C. FIELDS

Experience keeps a dear school, but fools will learn in no other.

POOR RICHARD'S ALMANACK

You have already made the first wise decision in managing your personal finances. You are in college, and experts estimate that the college graduate will receive more income during a lifetime than will the average high school graduate. There is a very high positive correlation between years of education and average lifetime earnings.

Income and Occupation

From the standpoint of maximizing income it still pays to go to college, despite doubts raised recently. This can be seen in the following listing of the mean annual income of all heads of households in the United States:

Elementary School	Less than eight years	$ 8,774
	Eight years	$10,636
High school	One to three years	$12,358
	Four years	$16,079
College	One to three years	$17,918
	Four years or more	$25,132

19

Education makes a difference in lifetime income. According to the most recently available data, during their working lifetime holders of college degrees can expect to earn about three times the total likely to be earned by those who had little schooling.

The conclusion that college leads to increased income and increased lifetime satisfaction has been challenged in a book called *The Over-Educated American,* published in July 1976 and written by Richard B. Freeman of the Department of Economics, Harvard University. Freeman points out that higher education expanded dramatically throughout the 1950s and 1960s. The number of college students tripled; the number of B.A.'s increased by 91 percent; the number of M.A. and Ph.D. recipients jumped more than threefold. State and local governments created hundreds of new public colleges, junior colleges, and community colleges. By 1970, nearly half of all Americans of college age were enrolled in colleges and universities.

For the mid-1970s the study paints a very different picture of the college graduate in the labor market. Newspapers reported new college graduates having difficulty in obtaining college level jobs. Prospective schoolteachers found positions in elementary and secondary schools scarce. Doctoral graduates also faced a severe shrinking academic job market. The English and History Ph.D.'s were particularly hard hit. In some graduate areas such as Physics, the situation deteriorated to virtually crisis proportions. Degree recipients in the first half of the 1970s in many fields had to accept salaries at rates of pay below those of their predecessors and often in less desirable jobs different from their fields of study.

In November 1975 a large headline in the *New York Times* asked, "Is the Value of a College Education Declining?" This appeared to be a temporary viewpoint, however, for by the late 1970s the situation was again favorable, outlets for college graduates were again promising, and the salaries that they were earning over a lifetime were expected to be substantially higher than those of high school graduates.

People receiving their college degrees over the next ten years should remain at an economic advantage, according to a Conference Board analysis and study.[1]

Occupation and education have a good deal to do with income level. Generally speaking, it appears that heads of low-income families have had little formal education or training and are mainly unskilled workers, whereas heads of upper-income families have had much more formal education, and this seems to have led them into either business or the professions. "Average family income tends to rise as the educational attainment of the head increases," according to the U.S. Census Bureau.

"We should all be concerned with the future," Charles F. Kettering once advised, "because we will have to spend the rest of our lives there." Personal finance is meaningful only if there is an adequate income to manage. If you pursue your present course, you are probably well on your way to a higher income bracket.

There is a school of thought, of course, that discounts the value of a college education and emphasizes experience. "Schooling and education are not synonymous: the educational content of time spent at school ranges from superb to miserable," according to one expert, who added, "Moreover, school is neither the only, nor necessarily the most important, training ground for shaping market productivities." College does, however, guide millions toward satisfying goals.

While a college education has many rewards other than monetary benefits, these should not be overlooked. A higher percentage of young people are going to college these days, and of those who graduate many are going on to advanced degrees. Getting your college degree is step one in sound personal finance. Step two is tied in very closely— deciding what career or profession to pursue as your lifework. That's almost as hard as paying for college these days.

Fewer young people will be entering the labor market in the next decade due to the declining birthrate. The number aged 14 to 24 will taper

---

[1] See Leonard A. Lecht, "Grading the College Diploma," *Across the Board,* Conference Board, New York, April 1977.

off by two thirds during the 1970s. Between 1975 and 1985, some 2 million jobs will have opened to college graduates because of educational upgrading. These are some of the conclusions of the Conference Board study.

Choosing a Career

If you are undecided about your career, you may benefit from consulting the *Occupational Outlook Handbook,* issued every two years by the U.S. Department of Labor, Bureau of Labor Statistics. It is a prime source of career guidance information. For each of hundreds of occupations that are discussed, the *Handbook* describes: what the work is like; the personal qualifications, the training, and the educational requirements needed for the occupation; the working conditions usually found on the job; the average earnings; the job outlook and prospects; the chances for advancement; and where to find additional information.[2]

Even more relevant is the *Occupational Outlook for College Graduates.* The latest edition of this volume contains a guide to career opportunities in a broad range of professional and related occupations. In the same fashion as the larger volume, it provides a wealth of information on education and training requirements and prospective earnings, a brief summary of expected changes in the U.S. economy, and an analysis of the overall supply and demand situation for college graduates through the mid-1980s.

The *Handbook* provides a summary of expected annual job openings through 1985 for selected occupations and are estimated on the basis of long-term employment growth and the need to replace workers who leave the labor force because of death, retirement, or other reasons. Some condensed examples follow.

Accountants—employment, 865,000; annual openings, 51,500. Employment expected to increase about as fast as average as managers rely

more on accounting information to make business decisions. College graduates will be in greater demand than applicants who lack college training. The demand will exceed the supply.

Chemists—employment, 148,000; annual openings, 6,300. Employment expected to grow about as fast as average as a result of increasing demand for new product development and rising concern about energy shortages, pollution control, and health care. Except for positions in colleges and universitites, good opportunities should exist.

College and university teachers—employment, 593,000; annual openings, 17,000. Despite expected employment growth, applicants will face keen competition for jobs. The best opportunities are expected in public colleges and universities. Persons who do not have a Ph.D. will find it increasingly difficult to secure a teaching position.

Economists—employment, 115,000; annual openings, 6,400. Employment expected to grow faster than average. Master's and Ph.D. degree holders may face keen competition for college and university positions but can expect good opportunities in nonacademic areas.

Lawyers—employment, 396,000; annual openings 23,400. Employment expected to grow faster than average in response to increased business activity and population. However, keen competition is likely for salaried positions. The best prospects for establishing new practices will be in the small towns and the expanding suburbs, although starting a practice will remain a risky and expensive venture. Initial starting salaries in large corporations are expected to continue to grow sharply.

Health services administrators—employment, 160,000; annual openings, 16,000. Employment expected to grow much faster than average as quantity of patient services increases and health services management becomes more complex.

Home economists—employment, 141,000; annual openings—for the latest figures, write to American Home Economics Association, 2010 Massachusetts Avenue, N.W., Washington, D.C. 20036. Thousands of home economists are employed in college teaching; the federal government, including the Federal Extension Service, employs additional

---

[2] See *Occupational Outlook Handbook,* Bureau of Labor Statistics, bull. no. 1955, 1978–79 edition, 840 pages. A hardbound copy is available for $11; a softbound copy may be purchased for $8.

thousands, as does private enterprise. Keen competition for jobs will exist through 1985, but the limited supply of home economists turned out each year by the universities is *not* likely to meet the full demand, and the present level of salaries, ranging from $11,500 to $20,400, is expected to rise across the board.

Secondary school teachers—employment, 1,111,000; annual openings, 13,000. Keen competition expected due to declining enrollments coupled with large increases in the supply of teachers. More favorable opportunities will exist for persons who are qualified to teach mathematics, the natural and physical sciences, and vocational subjects.

Social workers—employment, 330,000; annual openings 25,000. Employment expected to increase faster than average due to the expansion of health services, the passage of social welfare legislation, and the potential development of national health programs. The best opportunities are expected for graduates of master's and Ph.D. degree programs in social work.

Pointers on working for the federal government appear in the Winter 1978 issue of *The Occupational Outlook Quarterly,* published by the Bureau of Labor Statistcs, U.S. Department of Labor. The special 64-page issue explains how the federal hiring system works, gives suggestions on filling out job applications, tells how people are selected for jobs, and lists nearly every professional entry job in the federal civil service system.[3]

Average Income in the United States

Perhaps it would help if you knew what the income of the average family and person in the United States is. Then you can judge your own position and outlook. The U.S. Bureau of the Census reports on incomes of families, of unrelated individuals, and of households. It answers such questions as: How many families are there in each

"Do you have any qualifications other than good vibes?"

Reprinted by permission *The Wall Street Journal*

income bracket? What is the average annual family income? How does family income vary according to urban and rural residence, major source of earnings, color, size of family, type of family, age of head of family, and number of children?

Of the 57.2 million families in the United States, 12.8 million, or almost 23 percent, received incomes of $25,000 or more in 1977. If we define the middle class as those having incomes between $10,000 and $25,000, we thus include about 50 percent of the population. Families having net incomes between $5,000 and $10,000 amounted to about 18 percent of the total families, while about 5.3 million families (9.3 percent of the total) had incomes well below the poverty line. The median income for all families in 1977 was $16,009; the mean income was $18,264.[4] (See Table 2–1.)

---

[3] *The Occupational Outlook Quarterly* is a career guidance magazine that is published four times a year. It is available from the Superintendent of Documents, Washington, D.C. 20402. The price is $4 for a one-year subscription—or $1.50 for a single issue.

[4] "Median income" may be defined as that income below which (and above which) half of all the units fall. The median is not affected, as is the arithmetic mean (sometimes simply called the "average"), by a few high-income or low-income units.

TABLE 2–1
Families and Unrelated Individuals by Total Money Income in 1977 (families and unrelated individuals as of March 1978)

Total Money Income	Families		Unrelated Individuals	
	Number (thousands)	Percent Distribution	Number (thousands)	Percent Distribution
Total	57,215	100.0	23,110	100.0
Under $2,000	1,134	2.0	2,255	9.8
$2,000 to $2,999	920	1.6	2,887	12.5
$3,000 to $3,999	1,533	2.7	2,905	12.6
$4,000 to $4,999	1,756	3.1	1,912	8.3
$5,000 to $5,999	2,031	3.5	1,760	7.6
$6,000 to $6,999	2,116	3.7	1,430	6.2
$7,000 to $7,999	2,094	3.7	1,261	5.5
$8,000 to $8,999	2,117	3.7	1,138	4.9
$9,000 to $9,999	2,026	3.5	1,019	4.4
$10,000 to $10,999	2,132	3.7	1,020	4.4
$11,000 to $11,999	1,966	3.4	720	3.1
$12,000 to $12,999	2,313	4.0	736	3.2
$13,000 to $13,999	2,038	3.6	592	2.6
$14,000 to $14,999	2,103	3.7	567	2.5
$15,000 to $15,999	2,310	4.0	478	2.1
$16,000 to $16,999	2,053	3.6	417	1.8
$17,000 to $17,999	1,948	3.4	346	1.5
$18,000 to $19,999	3,855	6.7	455	2.0
$20,000 to $24,999	7,962	13.9	587	2.5
$25,000 to $49,999	11,326	19.8	527	2.3
$50,000 and over	1,482	2.6	99	0.4
Median income	$16,009	—	$5,907	—
Standard error	$57	—	$45	—
Mean income	$18,264	—	$7,981	—
Standard error	$58	—	$56	—

Source: U.S Department of Commerce, Bureau of the Census, Consumer Income Series P-60, no. 116, July 1978.

In 1977, 2.6 percent of all families had incomes over $50,000. The Census Bureau survey also indicated that there were about 25 million persons below the poverty level in 1977, amounting to almost 12 percent of the U.S. population. The poverty threshold for a nonfarm family of four at that time was placed at $6,191.

As measures of central tendency medians and averages, of course, conceal fundamental differences in their components. For example, the average income of nonfarm families was considerably higher than that of farm families. Marked differences characterized the income levels of white and nonwhite families. For the country as a whole, the median income of white families was higher than that received by nonwhite families.

Household Income

Income statistics are also collected in terms of households by the Census Bureau. The number of households in 1977 totaled 76 million. What makes a household different from a family? Household income is different from family income because it includes not only the income of all the related persons in the household but also the income of

"I know he should learn the value of a dollar, but I hate to disillusion him."

Reprinted by permission *The Wall Street Journal*

any unrelated persons in the household. It also covers the income of one-person households. Thus, a family is essentially a sociological unit, whereas a household is a basic economic unit. Between 1967 and 1977, there was a shift toward smaller households and the relative number of households headed by women increased. The average size of households is declining due both to the falling birthrate and to the increasing proportion of both young adults and older adults who are living alone.[5]

_____

[5] The Bureau of the Census has been criticized for its selection of terms. "Head of family" or "head of household" has been a particular target. In its very careful way, the Census Bureau at first announced: "However, recent social changes have resulted in a trend toward recognition of more equal status for all members of the household (or family), making the term 'head' less relevant in the analysis of household and family data." Later the Census Bureau announced: "In the 1980 Census, the Bureau of the Census plans to discontinue the use of the terms 'head of the household' and 'head of family.' Instead, 'householder' will be designated as the household reference person. The householder is to be the first adult household member listed in the census question-

The income of the 76 million households averaged $16,100 in 1977, according to a Census Bureau survey. Nonfarm households, comprising 96 percent of the total, averaged $16,168; farm households, $14,111. Households headed by males made up almost 74 percent of the total and averaged $18,689, while households headed by females averaged $8,489.

Household income tends to rise until the head of the household reaches late middle age and to decline thereafter. In 1977, mean income (that is, the total income of the group divided by the number in the group) rose from $10,494 for households whose head was under 25 years of age to $21,537 for households headed by a person between 45 and 54 years of age, then declined to $9,309 for households whose head was 65 years of age or older. (See Figure 2–1.)

Education is one of the most important determinants of the level of household income. The largest single group is that in which the householder had only completed high school. In 1977 this group (one third of all households) had a mean income of $16,079, whereas the college graduates (17 percent of all households) had a mean income of $25,132. The lowest in the scale were those who did not even graduate elementary school, with a mean income of $8,774.

Differences in the characteristics of households are most pronounced at the high and low parts of the income distribution. Households with incomes of less than $5,000 tend to have few members, to live in small towns and the open country, and to be headed by persons 65 or more years of age. Retired persons, unskilled workers, widows, and students are most frequently found at this income level. Households with high incomes ($25,000 or more) are relatively larger in size, live in metropolitan areas, and are most frequently headed by persons between 35 and 64 years of age who are self-employed, in a managerial position, or in a profession. All of these trends and facts are clearly shown in Table 2–2.

_____

aire. The instructions call for listing first the person (or one of the persons) in whose name the home is owned or rented).

FIGURE 2–1
Money Income of Households, 1977

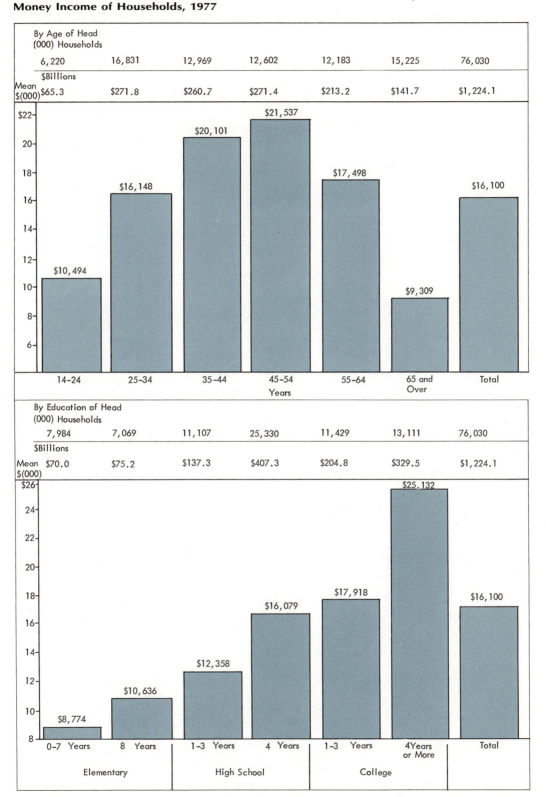

Sources: U.S. Department of Commerce; and *Finance Facts Yearbook.*

TABLE 2–2

Selected Characteristics of Households—Households by Total Money Income in 1977 (numbers in thousands; households as of March 1978)

SELECTED CHARACTERISTICS	TOTAL	UNDER $4,000	$4,000 TO $6,999	$7,000 TO $9,999	$10,000 TO $11,999	$12,000 TO $14,999	$15,000 TO $17,499	$17,500 TO $19,999	$20,000 TO $24,999	$25,000 TO $29,999	$30,000 TO $49,999	$50,000 AND OVER	MEDIAN INCOME VALUE (DOLS.)	MEDIAN INCOME STANDARD ERROR (DOLS.)	MEAN INCOME VALUE (DOLS.)	MEAN INCOME STANDARD ERROR (DOLS.)
ALL HOUSEHOLDS. . .	76 030	9 356	9 686	8 902	5 491	8 149	6 563	5 323	8 758	5 542	6 655	1 604	13 572	52	16 100	49
TYPE OF RESIDENCE																
NONFARM.	73 505	8 921	9 304	8 604	5 302	7 896	6 340	5 174	8 561	5 383	6 473	1 549	13 648	53	16 168	50
FARM	2 524	435	382	299	189	254	223	149	197	159	182	55	11 536	405	14 111	414
INSIDE METROPOLITAN AREAS.	51 369	5 679	6 072	5 704	3 520	5 305	4 429	3 651	6 226	4 194	5 295	1 293	14 611	106	17 137	89
1,000,000 OR MORE. . .	29 706	3 149	3 458	3 137	1 941	2 856	2 536	2 066	3 697	2 506	3 473	889	15 266	109	17 857	121
INSIDE CENTRAL CITIES	12 337	1 840	1 884	1 569	924	1 245	967	741	1 274	675	954	264	11 875	198	14 922	177
OUTSIDE CENTRAL CITIES	17 369	1 309	1 573	1 568	1 017	1 610	1 569	1 324	2 424	1 832	2 519	625	17 564	165	19 941	161
UNDER 1,000,000. . . .	21 663	2 530	2 615	2 567	1 579	2 449	1 893	1 586	2 529	1 688	1 823	404	13 792	131	16 150	129
INSIDE CENTRAL CITIES	10 577	1 574	1 471	1 336	801	1 180	815	706	1 066	711	742	174	12 226	163	14 870	187
OUTSIDE CENTRAL CITIES	11 086	956	1 144	1 231	778	1 269	1 078	880	1 463	977	1 081	230	15 327	157	17 371	176
OUTSIDE METROPOLITAN AREAS	24 660	3 677	3 614	3 198	1 971	2 845	2 134	1 672	2 532	1 348	1 359	311	11 861	123	13 939	108
REGION																
NORTHEAST.	17 173	2 004	2 168	1 894	1 146	1 782	1 481	1 265	2 125	1 280	1 608	420	14 232	130	16 680	114
NORTH CENTRAL.	20 239	2 283	2 482	2 248	1 401	2 164	1 893	1 427	2 446	1 625	1 871	400	14 270	133	16 474	112
SOUTH.	24 316	3 522	3 261	3 087	1 860	2 646	1 977	1 675	2 503	1 578	1 745	463	12 407	94	15 069	105
WEST	14 301	1 547	1 776	1 673	1 084	1 557	1 212	957	1 685	1 059	1 431	321	13 980	131	16 627	123
RACE AND SPANISH ORIGIN OF HEAD*																
WHITE.	66 934	7 334	7 980	7 626	4 805	7 274	5 959	4 862	8 088	5 204	6 255	1 545	14 272	60	16 729	54
BLACK.	7 977	1 869	1 560	1 170	607	749	502	411	535	270	272	32	8 422	113	10 791	96
SPANISH ORIGIN	3 304	470	554	509	331	388	289	183	290	126	147	16	10 647	187	12 565	194
MARITAL STATUS AND SEX OF HEAD																
MALE HEAD.	56 731	3 309	5 261	5 895	4 071	6 492	5 657	4 767	8 108	5 232	6 401	1 539	16 368	56	18 689	59
MARRIED, WIFE PRESENT. .	47 357	1 624	3 803	4 599	3 267	5 405	4 847	4 201	7 402	4 841	5 944	1 423	17 568	58	19 834	65
MARRIED, WIFE ABSENT . .	1 331	270	202	184	99	154	116	69	93	57	77	10	10 148	292	12 724	360
WIDOWED.	1 513	458	336	195	76	97	73	74	75	51	58	21	6 565	238	10 648	320
DIVORCED	2 246	291	287	289	212	290	223	181	197	110	123	44	12 331	189	14 549	276
SINGLE	4 283	666	634	627	417	546	398	242	341	172	199	41	10 844	133	12 893	174
FEMALE HEAD.	19 298	6 048	4 425	3 008	1 420	1 657	905	557	650	310	253	65	6 326	59	8 489	58
MARRIED, HUSBAND ABSENT.	2 401	815	663	376	168	151	81	43	52	17	27	8	5 530	131	7 251	145
WIDOWED.	8 483	3 372	2 100	1 070	447	542	293	181	242	113	94	28	4 995	62	7 496	85
DIVORCED	4 347	869	858	804	455	535	291	165	186	91	77	16	8 600	117	10 159	132
SINGLE	4 066	991	804	757	350	429	241	168	170	88	55	14	7 932	126	9 506	124
RELATIONSHIP TO HEAD																
ALL MEMBERS RELATED. . .	72 821	9 177	9 351	8 464	5 234	7 753	6 259	5 076	8 335	5 288	6 338	1 547	13 503	55	16 043	51
ALL MEMBERS UNRELATED. .	2 356	142	278	337	197	300	212	182	298	174	201	34	14 156	258	16 584	252
SOME MEMBERS UNRELATED .	853	38	57	101	59	96	92	66	125	80	115	23	16 939	453	19 598	483
AGE OF HEAD																
14 TO 24 YEARS	6 220	1 015	1 083	1 171	664	844	538	336	385	117	64	2	9 571	109	10 494	88
25 TO 34 YEARS	16 831	1 027	1 431	1 971	1 530	2 383	2 031	1 597	2 399	1 259	1 066	140	15 075	68	16 148	82
35 TO 44 YEARS	12 969	669	925	1 026	771	1 420	1 373	1 157	2 113	1 450	1 651	414	18 076	117	20 101	128
45 TO 54 YEARS	12 602	812	862	990	703	1 117	1 050	989	1 927	1 429	2 192	531	19 377	158	21 537	138
55 TO 64 YEARS	12 183	1 390	1 463	1 346	869	1 288	973	835	1 377	956	1 305	380	14 311	141	17 498	142
65 YEARS AND OVER. . . .	15 225	4 445	3 921	2 398	954	1 097	598	409	557	330	377	137	6 347	56	9 309	82
SIZE OF HOUSEHOLD																
1 PERSON	16 715	5 822	3 625	2 401	1 221	1 408	856	444	445	227	190	79	5 905	54	8 206	68
2 PERSONS.	23 334	1 886	3 474	3 368	1 850	2 804	2 019	1 672	2 638	1 501	1 707	416	13 072	85	15 638	84
3 PERSONS.	13 040	793	1 059	1 395	978	1 518	1 317	1 082	1 978	1 212	1 433	275	16 367	115	18 406	117
4 PERSONS.	11 955	449	739	878	752	1 321	1 274	1 123	2 038	1 412	1 570	400	18 657	125	20 703	132
5 PERSONS.	6 356	240	419	450	390	623	650	612	1 046	662	1 013	250	19 064	176	21 382	181
6 PERSONS.	2 723	98	204	231	149	268	253	240	392	321	459	110	19 077	294	21 800	304
7 PERSONS OR MORE. . . .	1 906	70	167	181	151	207	194	151	221	208	283	75	17 266	332	20 578	344
EDUCATIONAL ATTAINMENT OF HEAD																
ELEMENTARY: TOTAL	15 054	4 123	3 391	2 201	1 045	1 223	833	625	763	445	355	49	7 014	70	9 648	73
0 TO 7 YEARS.	7 984	2 507	1 846	1 149	523	596	385	281	352	181	147	17	6 316	87	8 774	91
8 YEARS . . .	7 069	1 616	1 545	1 052	522	627	344	344	411	264	208	32	7 914	109	10 636	114
HIGH SCHOOL: TOTAL . . .	36 436	4 026	4 663	4 626	2 958	4 302	3 448	2 778	4 315	2 560	2 452	309	13 229	69	14 945	57
1 TO 3 YEARS.	11 107	1 874	1 937	1 632	946	1 178	852	687	970	503	475	55	10 226	110	12 358	92
4 YEARS . . .	25 330	2 153	2 726	2 995	2 012	3 124	2 596	2 091	3 345	2 058	1 977	253	14 604	92	16 079	70
COLLEGE: TOTAL	24 540	1 207	1 632	2 075	1 488	2 625	2 282	1 920	3 680	2 537	3 848	1 246	18 660	105	21 772	108
1 TO 3 YEARS.	11 429	770	1 024	1 253	836	1 375	1 182	894	1 709	991	1 141	256	15 862	111	17 918	125
4 YRS OR MORE	13 111	437	608	823	653	1 250	1 100	1 026	1 971	1 546	2 707	990	21 513	148	25 132	165
TENURE																
OWNER OCCUPIED	49 398	4 197	4 941	4 766	3 098	5 020	4 448	3 976	6 916	4 695	5 879	1 463	16 404	67	18 680	66
RENTER OCCUPIED.	25 013	4 737	4 447	3 923	2 259	2 980	2 003	1 268	1 725	800	738	132	9 522	65	11 371	60
OCCUPIER PAID NO CASH RENT	1 619	423	298	214	133	149	112	79	117	47	37	9	8 108	274	10 434	238

* Persons of Spanish origin may be of any race.
Source: Current Population Reports, Consumer Income, Series P-60, (no. 116, Washington, D.C., July 1978).

Upper-, Middle-, and Lower-Income Groups—Some Contrasts

The nation's income elite—the top 20 percent of all families in earnings—now numbers more than 11 million, according to a Conference Board study.[6] These families earn a minimum of $25,000, have an average income of $33,000 a year, and account for more than 40 percent of the country's buying power.

Over the last two decades there have been some dramatic shifts in the country's upper-income group, as can be seen in Figure 2–2. An extraordinary 77 percent of these families have at least two people in the labor force, up from 64 percent two decades ago. Almost 33 percent have three or more family members working, compared to 20 percent two decades earlier.

The analysis also finds that more and more upper income families are middle-aged and college-educated, hold professional or administrative jobs, and live in the suburbs and the sunbelt states.

The age mix of the richest one fifth of U.S. fami-

_____
[6] Source: Fabian Linden, ''The Society of The Affluent,'' _Across the Board,_ Conference Board, New York, February 1978.

lies has changed somewhat. About 33 percent of the families are between 45 and 54, an increase of 5 percent since the mid-50s, while those over 65 decreased slightly.

Nearly 36 percent of these upper-income families hold a college degree. (The national figure is 16 percent.) The proportion of upper-income families engaged in the professions or technical occupations has jumped from about 18 percent in the mid-1950s to about 28 percent today. Managers and administrators now comprise 30 percent of the top-income group, compared to an earlier 25 percent.

The top-income group has also become more geographically dispersed. The shift among affluent families has been to the South and Southwest. The proportion of top-income families living in the Northeast has declined somewhat, and in the Far West it has also dipped slightly. Over half the affluent families live in the suburbs, only 26 percent in large cities.

Although 13 percent of the families in the nation are headed by women,—only 3 percent of the most affluent families are headed by women. Blacks and other minorities account for only 5 percent of top-income families, while heading more than 11 percent of all the country's families; however, blacks

FIGURE 2–2
Families by Income Class (based on 1975 dollars)

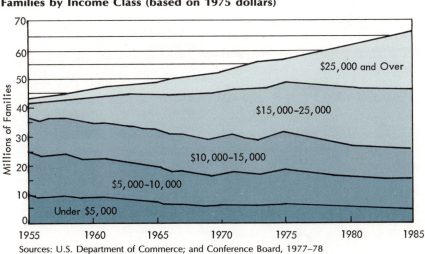

Sources: U.S. Department of Commerce; and Conference Board, 1977–78

and other minorities represented only 2 percent of the top-income group in the mid-1950s.

The Pinch on the Middle Class

Incomes have doubled over the past ten years, but inflation has cut into that increase deeply. It now costs about $47,000 to buy a new house, which had cost about $25,000 in 1967.

A new car costs on the average about $5,500—up from $3,200 in 1968. The expense of a college education has risen to $4,000–$7,000 for a single year, or $16,000–$24,000 for a four-year degree course. In many cases, the wife has gone to work to help meet expenses. Then the family becomes subject to higher-bracket tax rates. A middle-income family earning from $10,000 to $25,000 per year notes that millions of lower-income families qualify for special tax breaks, and government transfer payments (for instance, supplemental social security and public assistance, food stamps, and subsidized housing).

On the other hand, many people at the top of the income ladder are in a position to take advantage of loopholes, and pay on the average a smaller percentage of income tax. Taxes and inflation continue to pinch and frustrate the middle class.

A middle-class family that had a 1960 pretax income of $15,000 would have had to pay $2,357 in income taxes and would have had a remaining purchasing power of $12,643. To achieve the same purchasing power in 1978, the middle-class family would have needed a pretax income of $34,065. Of this, taxes would have absorbed $6,642 and loss of purchasing power due to price increases would have taken another $14,780, leaving an effective residual purchasing power of $12,643. In other words, the middle-class family earning a pretax income of $15,000 in 1960 would have had to earn $34,065 in 1978 to achieve the same purchasing power as 1960's $15,000 of pretax earnings.[7]

_____

[7] See "The Two Way Squeeze, 1978," *Economic Road Maps,* nos. 1828 and 1829, Conference Board, New York, April 1978.

Inflation has been taking a heavy toll, cutting the purchasing power of the dollar. The CPI rose far more rapidly in the eight years 1970–78 (73 percent) than it did over the whole ten-year period of 1960–70, when the increase was 31 percent.

You can see that as this middle-income family's earnings rose to keep pace with inflation, its higher income propelled it into higher tax brackets. Thus, as the family attempted to raise its income to hold its own against inflation, its higher income led to higher federal income and social security taxes. The middle-income family has been fighting a losing battle against inflation, the higher costs of everything, and the more it appears to succeed in keeping its head above inflation, the higher its taxes have risen.

The Lower-Income Group

About 25 million persons, or 12 percent of the population, are below the low-income level. The federal government has set the low-income level (poverty level) at $6,191. The Census Bureau establishes a definition of poverty that is adjusted to reflect changes in the cost of living as measured by the Consumer Price Index. Households are classified as "poor" if their total money income falls below specified levels.

The U.S. poverty level is adjusted from year to year to reflect changes in the Consumer Price Index (CPI). For millions of families, where the poverty line is drawn is a key factor in determining whether or not they will receive aid from the government. When the poverty index is revised upward, as it was in 1978 to $6,191 from $5,850 for the nonfarm family of four, this does not automatically add legions of people to the welfare roles. The poverty line helps determine eligibility for such programs as:

1. *Head Start*—provides enrichment for preschoolers from culturally deprived backgrounds.
2. The Comprehensive Employment Training Act (CETA).
3. Food stamps.
4. Community Action programs.

If the Consumer Price Index rises 3 percent or more in the specified base period, this will trigger an automatic increase in social security and supplementary security payments.

The farm family poverty level is set lower than the urban family level. Poverty is most widespread among the aged, blacks, households headed by women, and persons with little schooling. According to a Labor Department survey[8] of persons who live in poverty areas, the unemployment rate in nonmetropolitan areas is half that in metropolitan areas.

The poverty rates among most population groups declined between 1959 and 1976. For example, the poverty rate for whites declined from 18 percent to 9 percent and that for blacks declined from 55 percent to 31 percent. In 1959, one third of the aged were poor; this proportion declined to 15 percent in 1976. The largest decline in the number of low-income elderly took place during the period 1969 to 1976, when substantial increases in social security benefits were enacted.

A long-range study that has monitored the economic ups and downs of 5,000 American families for a decade has concluded that poverty is far less persistent and yet much more widespread in American life than most would have thought. The study paints a fluid picture, with people and families slipping in and out of poverty fairly often.

Probably the largest factor underlying changes in economic status is change in family composition. Divorce, new children, and other such domestic changes often result in dramatic shifts in well-being, particularly for women and children. For example, a third of the women who were divorced and not remarried fell below the poverty line, even counting alimony, child support, and welfare payments, whereas only 13 percent of divorced men suffered this fate.[9]

---

[8] A poverty area is defined as one in which at least one fifth of the residents have incomes at or below the poverty level.

[9] Robert Reinhold, "Poverty Is Found Less Persistent but Wider Spread than Thought," *New York Times,* July 17, 1977. See also Irwin Garfinkel and Robert Haveman, *Earnings Capacity, Poverty, and Inequality* (New York: Academic Press, 1977).

According to a study on poverty, it is not the verbal classification, but living in an entirely separate economy, that results as a family "ceases merely to have a low income but becomes poor." For example, the poor may have to have a car in areas badly serviced by mass transportation and remote from jobs, because there is no other way to get to work, and this need seemingly conflicts with the necessity of buying food economically or of getting medical help.

When the poor patronize local food establishments—which they do out of loyalty, proximity, and the need for credit, or because of their inability to leave the neighborhood—they pay more. Inadequately educated, the poor rarely read a paper and don't see where sales are advertised, and thus they pay higher prices, further reducing their living standard.

Thus, "poor families are forced to adopt technologies appropriate to the nonpoor. And as a consequence, they are made even poorer." A "discretionary luxury" such as a telephone is not really a luxury in a society where daily living needs require one and where being without one makes a person not merely poor, but isolated as well. The study's conclusion is that "it is better to be poor in a poor society than in a rich one." To be without education and therefore poor is to be alienated from society, because progress, information, skills, and techniques not shared have been made commonplace by technology.

Women in the Labor Force and in the Professions

The growth of the labor force has risen dramatically, principally as a result of the rise in the number of women who are pursuing a paycheck. In the 1950–75 period, some 6.8 million more women than men entered the labor force. According to the Department of Labor, the trend toward a relatively larger labor force containing an increasing proportion of women is expected to continue. From 1975 to 1990, about 2.0 million more women than men are expected to enter the labor force. Of all women 16 or older, 51.4 percent are expected

"No, I'm not a career girl. Are you a career boy?"

Reprinted by permission *The Wall Street Journal*

to be in the labor force by 1990. (See Figure 2–3.)

These projections reflect a number of fundamental social and economic changes, including the opening of new opportunities for women, the inability of many families to manage with only one breadwinner, and the trend toward earlier retirement among male workers. In light of such trends, the ability of the economy to expand in a noninflationary manner to provide jobs for those who want them becomes a matter of prime concern.[10]

In banking and insurance companies, women account for 50–80 percent of their labor force, but in utilities they are only 30 percent according to a 1978 Conference Board study entitled "Women and Employee Benefits." This study notes the changing trend toward unisex in corporate fringe benefits and analyzes recent leading court decisions on the subject.

"Why So Few Women Have Made It to the Top," *Business Week* noted recently:[11]

"In most companies, despite a decade of Government affirmative action programs, steady pressure by corporate women's organizations, the top woman is still indisputably middle management."

That is one conclusion of an attempt to discover how far up the corporate ladder women have climbed in the past ten years. *Business Week* asked 43 corporations, chosen for their preeminence in 13 major industries, to identify their top-ranking women. Only seven of those corporations—General Motors, J. C. Penney, Georgia-Pacific, General Mills, Federated Department Stores, General Electric, and General Foods—named women who by any stretch of business definition could be called top management. The largest group of companies named women with titles such as assistant general counsel, research manager, or advertising director, earning salaries of $20,000 to $50,000—clearly middle management. And more than a quarter of the companies, including Chrysler, Beatrice Foods, and Procter & Gamble, declined to name anyone at all. If anything, the *Business Week* survey may have overstated women's corporate progress in general.

A study released at the same time by the Conference Board found that women had moved fastest in the biggest companies, the group analyzed by *Business Week*.

In summary, a quick comparison of the top titles in top companies today and ten years ago reveals that:

> Women have moved into middle management in companies that had no women there in 1968.
>
> Women have moved further up the ladder in many companies where they had already achieved middle-management status.
>
> Women have made the jump onto at least the lower rungs of top management in just a handful of companies.
>
> Women have not gone very far in most companies, especially middle-sized and small firms.

Women and Middle Management

Historically, women have advanced in the corporation as specialists, such as lawyers, chemists,

---

[10] "Women Swelling the Labor Force," *The Outlook,* Standard & Poor's, October 18, 1976.

[11] "The Corporate Woman," *Business Week,* June 5, 1978, pp. 99–102.

FIGURE 2–3
Women Accounting for Most Labor Force Growth

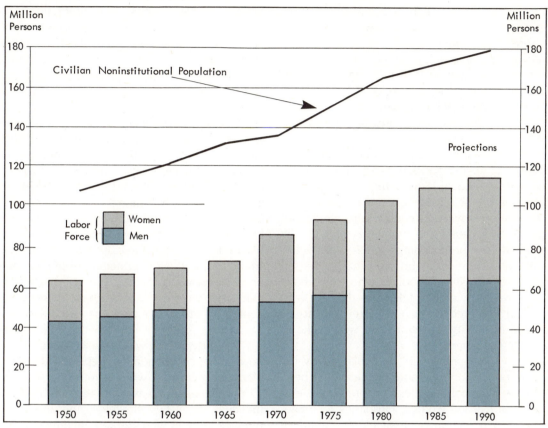

Source: *The Outlook,* Standard & Poor's, October 18, 1976.

or home economists. The result is apparent today. Eleven of the women identified as top-rankers hold law degrees. Not one holds an MBA. The surge into university business schools that has equipped so many young women with their traditional pass-port to corporate promotion has occurred too re-cently to produce current candidates for top jobs.

A decade of change, then, has moved some women to middle management—the $50,000-a-year job—but very few women to really top man-agement—above $100,000.

Educated women are working in greater num-bers than ever before. The higher a wife has climbed the educational ladder, the more likely she is to work—half of the wives with a college degree are in the labor force as against one fifth of the wives with less than five years of schooling.

According to government statistics, one out of six working women is in a profession. The Labor Department forecasts that employment will grow by 18 percent by 1985. In the period from 1960 to date, women's share in accounting has grown from 16.5 percent to 27.5 percent; in college teach-ing, from 23.9 percent to 31.7 percent; in publish-ing as editors or reporters, from 36.6 percent to 44.9 percent. Women lawyers and judges in-creased from 3.5 percent to 9.5 percent, women physicians from 6.9 percent to 11.2 percent, and management jobs are 25 percent female—double the past rate.

Pay inequalities between men and women are complicated and are changing slowly under pressure. One salary study shows that women who are senior engineers earn 25 percent less than men while today's woman entrants into engineering are offered an average of several hundred dollars more than men. Women architects earn a third less than men. Colleges pay women professors an average of 17.5 percent less than men.

Professional women claim acceptance on a basis of equality of ability, not because of the laws enforced by the Equal Employment Opportunity Commission prohibiting sex bias, or because without women employees a federal grant would not be given, or because one woman is individually exceptional. The proportion of wives with higher educational attainments who work has increased while those with less schooling who work have remained relatively constant. Moral—the man who marries an educated woman is more likely to be supported in the style to which he would like to become accustomed.

Some of this increase can be explained by the growth of population. But more significant has been the change in social attitudes concerning the employment of married women. Husbands no longer consider it a reflection on their earning ability if their wives have a paying job, and the earnings of such married women have contributed to higher standards of living, including the rise in home ownership and the increase in the number of college-educated youth.

Changing jobs and geographic location had always been a handicap for women, but today if relocation is part of advancement, it is regarded as discrimination for management to assume that a woman will not accept a transfer. Women have become more willing to be mobile, and management is increasingly going out of its way to accommodate two careers in a family, even to the extent of job hunting for the other spouse—if management desires the talents of one of them.

New federal legislation has strengthened the enforcement of provisions which prohibit sex discrimination. Firms holding federal contracts are required to develop written affirmative action plans for recruiting, hiring, training, and promoting women, and this is having an impact on the hiring policies of companies which are beginning to expand executive opportunities for women.

Wage Differentials

The wage gap between white workers and black workers in the United States has narrowed substantially in recent years, and the gap between black women and white women, has about disappeared, the Rand Corporation said in a study made public in May 1978. Black men's average salaries, however, are still only three fourths those of white men. Increased and improved education has made blacks more competitive in the job market, the study said, and is the principal reason for their improving average income. Another major factor is that wage rates in the South have increased in recent years at a faster pace than the national average, as the South has become more industrialized.

The study, which was commissioned by the National Science Foundation, reported that in 1955 black women who worked full time earned only 57 percent as much as white women who worked full time. By 1975, however, the average wage of black women who worked full time was 97 percent that of white women. The gap between white and black male workers had also narrowed, but not by nearly so much. In 1975, black men who worked full time earned 63 percent as much as white men who worked full time. By 1975, their pay averaged 77 percent of the pay of whites, the study concluded.

An indication of the growing equality in income of the blacks in the United States can be seen in the 34 percent increase of blacks living in the suburbs over the period from 1970–1977, as reported by the Census Bureau. The census figures show 28 percent of black families received $15,000 or more in annual income in 1977. These trends may be attributed in part to the increase of the number of black professionals in the labor force.

Most women's earnings tend to lag behind those

of men in the same occupational group, the difference worsens at the lower end of the income scale. In the professional and technical jobs, Labor Department reports indicate that full-time women workers receive 73 percent of men's pay. In the clerical jobs they receive 64 percent and in sales jobs 45 percent of the income earned by men doing the same work.

College Graduates and the Professions

Clearly, college graduates predominate among upper-income families and spending units, and the heads of the upper-income groups tend to be either professionals or in business. College graduates fill the ranks of the professions. The professions as a group have been expanding rapidly and will probably continue to grow. A major reason for the increase in the total number of workers in professional and related occupations has been the recent development and expansion of newer professional fields.

The number of bachelor's degrees granted in the health professions has shown the most notable growth in the past ten years. The trend is expected to continue throughout the next ten years, with the number of degrees likely to reach over 69,000 in 1985–86. Other fields expecting a significant increase in the number of degrees granted in the next ten years include the computer and information sciences, public affairs and services, architecture and environmental design, communications, and the biological sciences.

Bachelor's degrees conferred in mathematics and statistics and in education have shown the sharpest decline. The number of degrees in mathematics and statistics has dropped from a high of 27,442 in 1969–70 and is expected to continue, to decline, reaching 14,000 in 1985–86.

Educational degrees are expected to drop 25,000 by 1985–86.

Other fields expected to show decreases during the next ten years are the social sciences, foreign languages, and the humanities, while the most significant increases are expected to occur in the

TABLE 2–3
Earned and Projected Degrees, by Level, 1965–1986

Level of Degree	1965–66	1975–76	1985–86
Bachelor's	520,000	909,000	953,000
First professional .	31,000	59,000	72,000
Master's	141,000	316,000	405,000
Doctorate	18,000	35,000	42,000

Source: *Projections of Educational Statistics to 1985–86,* U.S. Department of Health, Education, and Welfare, National Center for Education Statistics (Washington, D.C.: U.S. Government Printing Office, 1977).

health professions and in business and management.

The number of doctorates is expected to remain constant or to increase slightly, with psychology and computer science systems directors showing a large increase. New programs are being developed in health resources administration and these programs are becoming most popular since there is a growing unsupplied need for competent and efficient hospital administrators. (See Table 2–3 for the overall forecast.)

What the Professions Pay

Not all professions pay equally well. Medicine and law provide the highest average income. Teachers and the clergy get the least. Business and engineering lie in between. Of course, some corporation executives get handsome incomes running into six figures, but these are the fortunate few—the exceptions, not the average. A survey of administrative salaries in leading corporations by the Dartnell Corporation of Chicago placed the average executive compensation at the levels shown in Table 2–4.

Business now pays extremely well for needed specializations, as well as for MBA graduates of leading business schools. A Harvard MBA has been called the "Golden Passport." Starting salaries for Harvard Business School graduates (average first-year income) hit the $25,000 mark for the first time in 1978 (earlier figures were $22,595 in 1977, $20,769 in 1976, and $19,183 in 1975). The most

TABLE 2-4

COMPENSATION MODEL

AVERAGE TOTAL COMPENSATION ($000)/ANNUAL SALES VOLUME

President vs. Subordinate Management Positions (65)

Annual Sales Volume Position	Under $5 million %	Comp.	$5-25 million %	Comp.	$25-50 million %	Comp.	$50-100 million %	Comp.	$100-250 million %	Comp.	$250-500 million %	Comp.	$500 million-$1 billion %	Comp.	Over $1 billion %	Comp.
Chief Executive Officer	100	$48	100	$60	100	$96	100	$95	100	$125	100	$153	100	$168	100	$255
Chief Operating Officer	75	36	83	50	81	78	65	62	95	119	72	110	82	138	126	324
Chief Administrative Officer	49	23	64	39	51	49	57	54	56	70	51	79	39	65	40	103
Executive Vice President	62	30	76	46	63	60	63	59	68	85	60	92	59	99	54	137
Financial Vice President	52	25	57	35	53	50	53	50	56	70	45	68	47	78	52	134
Legal Vice President	NA	NA	51	31	36	34	37	35	45	56	41	63	42	70	45	114
Marketing Vice President	63	30	58	35	54	51	53	50	48	60	35	54	39	65	37	94
Manufacturing Vice President	58	28	59	36	51	49	50	47	47	59	39	60	44	74	33	84
Administrative Vice President	39	19	44	26	43	42	42	40	39	49	32	50	38	64	34	88
International Vice President	NA	NA	62	38	56	54	75	72	56	69	47	72	58	98	27	68
Acquisitions/Mergers Executive	NA	NA	60	36	NA	NA	NA	NA	50	63	41	62	37	62	28	70
Research Vice President	71	34	61	37	NA	NA	61	58	45	56	35	53	35	58	57	129
Industrial Relations Vice President	80	38	55	33	42	40	47	44	36	45	35	54	35	59	34	86
Engineering Vice President	59	28	52	31	61	59	46	43	43	54	42	65	32	53	26	66
Treasurer	56	28	45	27	45	43	39	37	32	40	39	59	30	51	29	75
Controller	42	20	42	25	33	32	33	31	34	43	35	53	28	47	32	82
General Sales Executive	56	27	48	29	39	37	41	39	33	42	36	55	33	56	22	55
Public Relations Executive	35	17	NA	NA	NA	NA	NA	NA	26	33	22	34	24	41	21	53
Secretary	32	16	38	23	33	32	32	31	31	39	33	50	37	61	28	70
Advertising Executive	NA	NA	45	27	30	29	33	31	29	36	25	38	29	48	19	48
Manufacturing Executive	63	30	42	25	41	39	36	34	33	41	31	48	30	51	22	55
Tax Executive	NA	NA	NA	NA	NA	NA	29	28	26	32	20	31	21	36	21	54
M.I.S. Executive	NA	NA	38	23	NA	NA	40	38	31	39	29	45	29	48	22	56
E.D.P. Executive	40	19	38	23	25	24	29	28	26	32	24	36	20	34	17	44
Medical Director	NA	NA	NA	NA	NA	NA	NA	NA	22	27	24	36	22	37	23	59
Personnel Director	31	15	32	19	24	23	26	25	23	29	24	36	21	35	17	44
Purchasing Executive	40	19	33	20	27	26	32	30	25	31	27	42	27	45	14	35
Plant Manager	48	25	40	24	30	29	28	27	28	35	29	44	22	37	15	37
Labor Relations Director	NA	NA	NA	NA	NA	NA	40	38	26	33	24	37	28	47	17	44
Director Human Resources	NA	NA	NA	NA	NA	NA	NA	NA	NA	NA	21	32	21	36	15	39
Materials Manager	35	17	32	19	24	23	28	27	22	28	22	33	NA	NA	13	34
Research Manager	31	15	43	26	30	29	40	38	31	39	20	30	27	46	20	51
Top Government Affairs Executive	NA	NA	NA	NA	NA	NA	58	55	34	43	28	43	46	78	31	80
Top Tax Executive	NA	NA	NA	NA	NA	NA	40	38	30	37	22	34	27	45	23	58
Long-Range Planning Executive	NA	NA	60	30	NA	NA	NA	NA	38	47	35	53	33	55	23	58

TABLE 2–4 (continued)

Annual Sales Volume	Under $5 million		$5-25 million		$25-50 million		$50-100 million		$100-250 million		$250-500 million		$500 million -$1 billion		Over $1 billion	
Position	%	Comp.	%	Comp.	%	Comp.	%	Comp.	%	Comp.	%	Comp.	%	Comp.	%	Comp.
Chief Engineer	54	26	45	27	36	35	36	34	27	34	22	33	NA	NA	20	51
Audit Manager	44	21	40	24	30	29	24	23	22	28	18	28	18	30	15	37
Product Manager	54	26	38	23	33	32	28	27	28	35	20	30	23	38	13	33
Industrial Relations Director	NA	NA	33	20	23	22	NA	NA	27	34	25	38	NA	NA	17	44
Public Relations Manager	NA	NA	28	17	NA	NA	NA	NA	28	35	17	26	12	20	15	37
Research Section Head	NA	NA	38	23	29	28	36	34	23	29	21	32	22	37	16	42
General Accounting Manager	31	15	30	18	21	20	26	25	22	27	18	27	16	27	14	36
Management Development Director	NA	NA	NA	NA	NA	NA	29	28	26	33	15	23	20	34	11	29
Regional Sales Manager	50	24	43	26	30	29	33	31	27	34	22	33	21	35	14	35
Production Planning Manager	46	22	33	20	24	23	22	21	22	28	15	23	18	31	16	41
Market Research Manager	NA	NA	32	19	26	25	27	26	21	27	15	23	20	34	13	33
Advertising Manager	NA	NA	32	19	19	18	22	21	16	20	16	25	NA	NA	12	NA
Industrial Engineering Manager	NA	NA	32	19	23	22	26	25	22	27	19	29	NA	NA	15	39
Systems & Procedures Manager	33	16	28	17	21	20	26	25	20	25	18	27	15	25	12	31
Engineering Section Head	44	21	38	23	32	31	33	31	26	32	22	33	NA	NA	15	38
Traffic Manager	NA	NA	32	19	21	20	19	18	23	29	16	24	20	34	15	37
Wage & Salary Manager	NA	NA	28	17	16	15	24	23	21	26	14	22	19	32	13	32
Quality Control Manager	42	20	32	19	22	21	31	29	22	27	17	26	16	27	14	36
Training Director	NA	NA	30	18	15	14	25	24	19	24	16	25	15	25	9	24
Manager Customer Relations	35	17	33	20	19	18	27	26	18	23	15	23	20	33	11	28
Employee Relations Manager	NA	NA	28	17	15	14	23	22	19	24	16	25	16	27	13	32
Sales Promotion Manager	NA	NA	NA	NA	27	26	23	22	18	23	13	20	17	29	14	36
Credit & Collections Manager	31	15	28	17	19	18	22	21	22	27	15	23	16	27	16	41
District Sales Manager	35	17	40	24	32	31	29	28	22	27	19	29	15	26	11	29
Office Services Manager	31	15	27	16	16	15	20	19	15	19	14	22	13	22	12	31
Plant Engineering Manager	NA	NA	33	20	26	25	19	28	25	31	20	30	NA	NA	13	32
Cost Accounting Manager	31	15	30	18	21	20	23	22	21	26	14	22	15	25	12	31
Director Consumer Affairs	NA	NA	NA	NA	NA	NA	NA	NA	NA	NA	17	26	NA	NA	15	38

Total compensation—salary, bonus, deferred compensation, and director's fees.
Percent—computed on chief executive officer's position at 100 percent.
Source: 12th Biennial Survey by J. Paul Steinbrink, Dartnell Corp., 4660 Ravenswood Ave., Chicago, Ill 60640.

"Having rejected the older generation's money values, you should *love* the salary on *this* job."

Reprinted by permission *The Wall Street Journal*

recent survey of business school graduates' later earnings, showed that students who had graduated ten years earlier were then making an average of $56,000 a year.

"My Son, the MBA: A one time rarity, the Master of Business Administration Degree, has become the U.S. second most popular graduate degree.[12]

This year an estimated 550 schools will hand out some 32,000 MBAs, more than five times as many as in 1964, surpassing by perhaps 2,000 the number of law degrees granted and double the number of engineering degrees. The leader had been education, with about 125,000 master's degrees a year, but this number can be expected to fall off.

"They Can't All Be CEOs," *Forbes* remarked. Although they may be good managers, their salaries are still below those of younger doctors. As salaries have risen, MBA degree programs have proliferated.

The problem is really very simple, Arch Patton, recently retired director of McKinsey & Co., concluded: "What it boils down to is that an MBA doesn't guarantee success in business, but success in business is getting increasingly harder to achieve without an MBA. The younger people will have

to get the degree." Patton declared: "Competition for jobs among younger people will be sensational. The MBA is becoming a kind of union card for jobs you could have gotten a few years ago with only a bachelors' degree or a high school diploma."

The Best Paying Professions

The best-compensated professions are probably medicine, law, and dentistry, followed by accounting, engineering, computer systems designing and programming, marketing, health care administration, and finance and financial management.

A recent study by *The Council on Wage and Price Stability* found that the earnings of doctors are higher than those of any other major professional group. The study said that in 1976, the median net income of physicians was $62,800, or roughly twice the median net income of lawyers and dentists. Physicians' fees went up by 9.3 percent in 1976, 50 percent more than other consumer prices. Expenses, however, are high, and doctors earning $100,000 a year are unhappy about their high costs and their alleged "low net." Malpractice insurance, they say, runs as high as $5,000 a year for surgeons. Some $100,000-a-year doctors claim that they net only $15,000 to $20,000 a year.[13]

The study of physicians' fees concludes: "Median physicians' income at $63,000 in 1976, is higher and has risen faster than incomes of other high income professions. Moreover, the high level of physicians' income appears to be substantially above what is required to elicit an adequate supply of physicians."[14]

Dentists have been striving in recent years to close the gap between their incomes and those of doctors. The *Wall Street Journal* reports that the dentists have been about 80 percent successful.[15] Its headline reads: "Job Hazard: Dentists Grow Richer but Feel the Pressure; Suicide Rate

---

[12] *Forbes,* March 1, 1977, p. 41.

[13] *New York Times,* May 15, 1978.

[14] *Physicians: A Study of Physicians' Fees,* Council on Wage and Price Stability, Washington, D.C., March 1978, pp. 92–93.

[15] Janice C. Simpson, *Wall Street Journal,* December 17, 1976.

is High, Some Good Dentist Traits May Foster Depression.'' The story reads in part:

> PALO ALTO, CALIF.—A root canal follow-up, one denture adjustment, one extraction, three crown fittings, five routine checkups and two last-minute emergency cases. The daily schedules taped to the cabinets in dentist Leroy Lucas's four color-coordinated treatment rooms are full, as usual.
>
> Dr. Lucas sees 13 patients this day. That is a formidable caseload, but it is far from his record of 25, and it isn't nearly so impressive as the 30 or so patients some of his colleagues manage to squeeze in.
>
> Such volume is one reason dentists' net income has soared to an average of $35,000 a year. . . .
>
> There are many reasons for the increase in patients. New high-speed drills and other sophisticated equipment save time. Two or more treatment rooms, plus a crew of dental assistants and hygienists who perform routine chores, allow the dentist to move continuously from patient to patient. The spread of dental insurance has brought in more business.

In contrast there is a growth of low cost dentistry in shopping malls across the country.

There are now about 500,000 lawyers in practice in the United States. According to the American Bar Association, lawyers are being admitted at the rate of about 35,000 annually and some 120,000 more attending law schools are now in the pipeline. This would sound like trouble ahead for our lawyers, but our society seems to get more litigious with each passing year.

One consultant points to a developing legal caste system. ''Ten years ago,'' he says,

> just about any graduate of a decent law school could find a position in law but no more. Now, almost all the jobs in the large big-city firms and the federal government are going to graduates in the upper third of their classes at about 20 top law schools and the top few kids at the regional schools. They're the Brahmins, and they are doing great. Starting salaries are averaging about $20,000 a year and go as high as $28,000.

> The middle caste is made up of lower ranking graduates of the top-20 law schools and people in the upper third of their classes in the regionals. They usually can find something but at less than top dollar. Just about everyone else is getting to be an untouchable. Their starting salaries are as low as $700 a month and if one of them turns down a job, two others are there to take it. The consultant said that the most widely used avenue of escaping the caste system is solo practice and the statistics back him up.[16]

With the recent removal of restrictions on fee advertising, legal clinics are appearing, offering legal services at rates far below what had been previously customary.

In a competitive world, no matter which career is selected, the best-trained person is usually more successful—and someone multitrained has even more marketable skills. The job-hunting graduate whose career choice and preparation can fill the needs of the economy at the time is in demand.

Conclusion

The facts presented in this chapter and the additional data available in the sources here utilized should make it possible for you to estimate how much you can expect to earn in a given occupation. Obviously, if you are equally capable of being either a college professor or a doctor and you choose to be the former, you may be sacrificing about $800,000–$1,000,000 of income over your working lifetime.

Although the particular profession or career you choose may have definite attractions for you, you should be aware of the basic financial limitation or advantage and weigh clearly in your own mind all of the relatively favorable and unfavorable aspects, not neglecting the financial factor. You should, of course, not be unmindful of aptitudes and of nonmaterial and spiritual values in making your choice. As you will see in the subsequent pages of this book, there are a great many expenses

---

[16] See ''Going It Alone,'' *Wall Street Journal,* June 2, 1978, pp. 1 and 3.

you will encounter over a lifetime, and as you strive to surmount each financial hurdle, you may some day come to regret that you selected a field of endeavor which yields only two thirds, or a half, of the reward of another and perhaps, on reflection, equally attractive lifetime career.

A pioneering study on the average American "in pursuit of happiness" concluded that happiness depends on the "positive satisfactions" in life. Not unexpectedly, higher income was found to be a "positive satisfaction" and thus closely correlated with happiness.

To those who are so fortunate as to still have the choice of their life's work before them, considerations such as those described in this chapter should be useful in helping to eliminate some of the haphazard guesswork and error involved in the difficult and basic decision of choosing an occupation for the rest of their lives. If the perplexities of the choice tend to get you down, do not be discouraged. Remember, "No matter how the statistics are grouped and regrouped, they always lead to just one conclusion: the financial success of the college man is a truly impressive thing."

In addition, as the Carnegie Commission on Higher Education noted, "Going to college—any college—does give to the individual a chance for a more satisfying life and to society the likelihood of a more effective community."

SUGGESTED READINGS

Council on Wage and Price Stability. *Physicians— A Study of Physicians' Fees.* Washington, D.C.: Executive Office of the President, March 1978.

Freeman, Richard B. *The Over-Educated American.* New York: Academic Press, 1976.

Juster, F. Thomas (ed.). *The Distribution of Economic Well-Being.* National Bureau of Economic Research, Studies in Income and Wealth, no. 41. Published for the NBER by Ballinger Publishing Co., Cambridge, Mass., 1977.

————. *Education, Income, and Human Behavior.* A report prepared for the Carnegie Commission on Higher Education and the National Bureau of Economic Research. New York: McGraw-Hill, 1975; $17.50.

Morgan, James N. (ed.), and the staff of the Economic Behavior Program. *Five Thousand American Families—Patterns of Economic Progress.* Vols. 1–5, 1974–77. Ann Arbor: University of Michigan, Institute for Social Research, 1978.

U.S. Department of Commerce. *Household Money Income and Selected Social and Economic Characteristics of Households.* From *Current Population Reports—Consumer Income.* Series P-60, Washington, D.C.: Bureau of the Census, annual.

————. *Money Income and Poverty Status of Families and Persons in the United States:* From *Current Population Reports—Consumer Income.* Series P-60, Washington, D.C.: Bureau of the Census, annual.

U.S. Department of Labor. *Occupational Outlook Handbook.* Bull. no. 1955. Washington, D.C.: Bureau of Labor Statistics. Latest edition Bull. 1955–32, 1978–79; $8 per copy; paperback.

————. *Occupational Outlook Quarterly.* Washington, D.C.: Bureau of Labor Statistics. Mail orders to Superintendent of Documents, Government Printing Office, Washington, D.C. 20402. Issued four times a year; $4 for a one-year subscription.

CASE PROBLEMS

1 Donald has a real aptitude for science. He also has a very well organized mind. Donald is having difficulty in deciding whether to become *(a)* a chemist, *(b)* a physicist, *(c)* a chemical engineer, or *(d)* an electrical engineer. Help him develop all the relevant facts on the four alternative fields in order to make a decision. (The Engineers Joint Council is located at 345 East 47th Street, New York, N.Y. 10017, as is The American Institute of Chemical Engineers. The National Society of Professional Engineers is located at 2029 K Street, N.W., Washington, D.C. 20006; the American Chemical Society at 1155 16th Street, N.W., Washington, D.C. 20036; and the American Institute of Physics at 335 East 45th Street, New York, N.Y. 10017.) Donald thought he might also consider the less traditional but growing field of health administration. To have more input, he should write the director of each hospital in his area.

2   Phil is majoring in political science and thinks he wants to go on to law school. He wonders whether it makes any difference which law school he enters and what he can expect to earn as a young attorney. He also wonders whether he should take a first job as a junior in a large law office or apply to the legal department of a large corporation or try for a government position. Help him develop the relevant facts. (The American Bar Association is located at 1155 East 60th Street, Chicago, Il 60637.)

3   Rita argues that an amazing social revolution has occurred in the United States in the last 25 years, that the income gap is narrowing, and that there is now a much more equitable distribution of income. Dick, whose family runs a retail business in a coal-mining town, argues that there is still unequal sharing of income and wealth and that the rich are getting richer. With whom do you side in this debate? Develop the relevant facts to support your side of the argument.

4   Robert Armstrong, an economics major, is graduating college this June. He is looking for a career that won't make him rich but holds promise of providing a pleasant quality of life. He is equally interested in the variety of fringe benefits corporations today provide—and in the security that the civil service offers through examination and promotion. He has been told that fringe benefits can add up to almost as much as half of salary. He needs to know which offers more fringe benefits as well as greater promotional opportunities. What factors would make a job especially attractive and which ones would you consider unimportant?

5   Pete and Sylvia Robinson, in their mid-20s, are facing problems of income, status, and career choice. Pete rose to captain in the Air Force after graduation from college. Today he is a junior accountant earning $11,500, working in a large commercial firm, sharing a small office with another employee. He is depressed by the monotony—working with numbers instead of people, confined to his office, and supervised closely. As an officer he had supervised 45 people. He is thinking of journalism as a stepping-stone to public relations, but he does not like job hunting—and any change will lower the family income, at least temporarily. Sylvia was an English major in college and had been contributing $7,500 earned as a bank teller before the recent birth of their son. This income, unsatisfactory as it was will now be lost for a while. Sylvia is also thinking of training for other work. What do you think they should do?

Planning Your Spending

What does Grandpa know about hardships?
He only did without things. . . . He never had
to pay for them!

ROYAL BANK OF CANADA

To paraphrase "You can't take it with you," it's also true to say, "You can't keep it either." Taxes and dollar depreciation take their toll. As you can see from Figure 3–1, the $25,000-a-year man of 1960 had to earn $58,522 in 1978 to maintain the same standard of living.

Unfortunately for most Americans, rising prices and rising taxes have become a way of life. We live in an era of inflation. You have to be over 40 to remember a year in which the price level declined. Since 1970, prices have risen 73 percent. The steady erosion of the value of money shows no sign of ending. But it can be fought. The new inflation fighting guide with more than 140 helpful suggestions may be obtained from the Consumer Information Center (see page 57, footnote 12).

Inflation is personal. If you remember paying 25 cents for a hot dog, then you can feel inflation when you pay 80 cents for a smaller hot dog. The *New York Times* cost 3 cents in 1948, 20 cents in 1978. A ticket to a Broadway musical was $6 in 1948, $15 in 1978. A movie admission rose from 95 cents in 1960 to $4 in 1978.

A Trivia Index[1] of little-noticed everyday items

---

[1] Issued by Loeb Rhoades, Hornblower and Company. Courtesy Raymond F. De Voe, Jr.

FIGURE 3–1
The Two-Way Squeeze, 1978

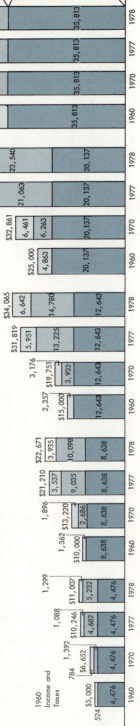

Pretax Income in 1970, 1977, and 1978 Necessary to Equal 1960 Purchasing Power

	$3,000	$5,000	$10,000	$15,000	$25,000	$50,000	$100,000
1960 PRETAX INCOME	3,000	5,000	10,000	15,000	25,000	50,000	100,000
Less: Federal income and social security taxes	126	524	1,362	2,357	4,863	14,187	40,038
Equals: Income after tax	2,874	4,476	8,638	12,643	20,137	35,813	59,962
1970 PRETAX INCOME	4,090	6,652	13,220	19,751	32,861	65,979	127,302
Less: Federal income and social security taxes	322	784	1,896	3,176	6,461	19,028	48,692
Less: Lost purchasing power since 1960	894	1,392	2,686	3,932	6,263	11,138	18,648
Equals: Income after taxes in 1960 dollars	2,874	4,476	8,638	12,643	20,137	35,813	59,962
1977 PRETAX INCOME	6,037	10,246	21,210	31,819	54,359	110,185	201,621
Less: Federal income and social security taxes	157	1,088	3,537	5,951	13,159	36,912	78,939
Less: Lost purchasing power since 1960	3,006	4,682	9,035	13,225	21,063	37,460	62,720
Equals: Income after taxes in 1960 dollars	2,874	4,476	8,638	12,643	20,137	35,813	59,962
1978 PRETAX INCOME	6,473	11,007	22,671	34,065	58,522	118,482	216,553
Less: Federal income and social security taxes	239	1,299	3,935	6,642	14,845	40,804	86,495
Less: Lost purchasing power since 1960	3,360	5,232	10,098	14,780	23,540	41,865	70,096
Equals: Income after taxes in 1960 dollars	2,874	4,476	8,638	12,643	20,137	35,813	59,962

Federal income and social security taxes are computed for a married couple, only one of whom works, with two children. No allowance is made for any other taxes. Calculations use the tax laws in effect each year, with 1977 income tax laws assumed to apply in 1978. On the basis of Internal Revenue Service data, tax-deductible items are assumed to equal certain percentages of pretax incomes: 20% in 1977 and 1978, 17% in 1970, 14% for incomes of $5,000 or less. For 1977 and 1978, maximum tax on "personal service" income is calculated assuming such income is 70% of gross income at the higher income levels. Inflation is calculated on the basis of the Consumer Price Index, with a 6% rise assumed from 1977 to 1978.

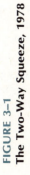

Source: *Economic Road Maps*, Conference Board, nos. 1828–29, April 1978.

"I finally taught my son the value of a dollar. Now he wants his weekly allowance in Swiss francs."

Reprinted by permission *The Wall Street Journal*

(71 in all), slowly rising in price, has a dramatic impact when you become aware of it. A sampling of ten items on the index follows:[2]

	1974 Price	1978 Price	Percent Change
Your weight and fortune (scale)	$0.01	$0.05	+400
Coca-Cola (can)	0.20	0.40	+100
New heels (Drago)	2.00	4.50	+125
Band-Aids (100)	1.13	1.98	+75
Burger King cheeseburger	0.40	0.53	+33
Baskin Robbins cone	0.30	0.50	+67
Slice of pizza	0.35	0.50	+43
Pack of M&M's	0.12	0.25	+108
Kleenex (packet)	0.10	0.20	+100
Local movie	3.00	4.00	+33
Postage stamps	0.08	0.15	+88

---

[2] Note that the price of postage stamps increased to 15 cents after the Trivia Index was published.

To clinch the point: That Baskin Robbins ice-cream cone that rose 67 percent between 1974 and 1978 rose 900 percent for many people alive today who paid five cents for an ice-cream cone in 1942.

If you are not afraid of a look into the future, you may be either fascinated or mesmerized by the possibilities ahead, as seen in Figure 3–2.

The Consumer Price Index

When dependents are included, the incomes of more than half of the U.S. population are pegged to the CPI. More than 50 million people (33 million social security beneficiaries, 9 million wage earners under union contracts, military and federal civil service retirees, postal workers) receive automatically escalated payments based on the CPI. Private contracts ranging from alimony to leases are affected by the index. It sets allowances for 19.5 million people who receive food stamps and 25.2 million beneficiaries of school lunch programs, as well as poverty norms and manpower training.

The CPI is widely accepted as a reliable measure of the purchasing power of the dollar. The base year is 1967—set at 100. If, for example, in 1977 there is a CPI reading of 184.60, this means that an item costing $18.46 in that year cost $10 ten years ago. Critics have argued that the shift of the base period masks the real inflation. One study[3] "calculates that the dollar of 1913 could now buy $6.25 of goods and services—or if 1935–39 still equaled 100, the index would be over 420." Figure 3–3 illustrates the annual percentage change in the CPI by category over the years.

Over the years, consumer spending patterns have changed, but the weights for categories had remained fixed. Figure 3–4 shows the CPI market basket for three different indexes (one old and two new) with relatively different shares of the major expenditure groups. The old CPI was supposed to be phased out in July 1978, but since it is tied to so many contracts and is strongly favored by the

---

[3] *Barron's,* February 20, 1978.

FIGURE 3–2

Living costs: 2001 A.D.

Manplan Consultants of Chicago has prepared a research report on what it will cost to live in the year 2001. The following table (taken from the report) shows what you can expect to pay for basic items—only 23 years from now—at various rates of inflation:

If your present income is $10,000 and your basic living costs are as listed below, income projections at 6%, 10% and 12% levels of cost-of-living increases show what income would be required in the year 2001 simply to maintain your present position.

LIVING COST CALCULATION—2001

Column No. 1	2	3	4	5	6
Item	Percent Cost	$ Cost	6%	10%	12%
Rent	20	2,000	8,600	21,660	33,700
Food	20	2,000	8,600	21,660	33,720
Clothing	15	1,500	6,450	16,245	25,290
Utilities	3	300	1,290	3,249	5,100
Health Care	7	700	3,010	7,581	11,900
Auto	10	1,000	4,300	10,830	16,860
Household Upkeep	10	1,000	4,300	10,830	16,860
Entertainment	10	1,000	4,300	10,830	16,860
Savings	5	500	2,150	5,415	8,430
Totals	100.0	$10,000	$43,000	$108,300	$168,000

How to calculate your own costs:
1. Prepare a percentage item breakdown of your own expense items, income & costs as in Columns 1, 2 and 3 above.
2. For 6% inflation rate, multiply each dollar amount by 4.3 and place in Column 4.
3. For 10% inflation rate, multiply each dollar amount by 10.83, and place in Column 5.
4. For 12% inflation rate, multiply each dollar amount by 16.86, and place in Column 6.

Source: *Consumer News,* Office of Consumer Affairs, Department of Health, Education, and Welfare, March 15, 1978.

unions, this is not happening as planned. The two new consumer price indexes include an increase in the market basket sample from 400 items to several thousand, a 30 percent increase in the retail establishments sample, an increase to 28 in the number of cities included, and an increase in the number of localities where prices are collected from 56 to 85.

One of the new indexes is an update of the old one—reflecting, with revised weights, the spending patterns of urban wage earners and clerical workers (40 percent of the population). The

FIGURE 3–3
Average Annual Percent Change in the CPI (by major category)

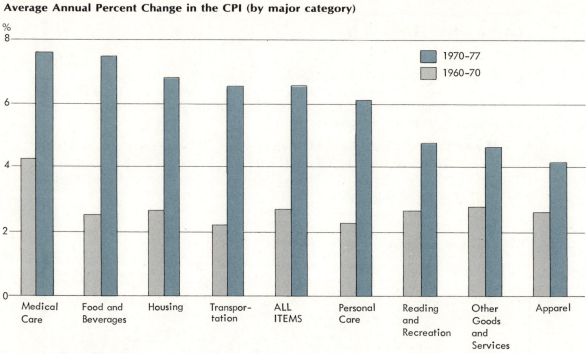

Source: The Conference Board.

completely new index for all urban consumers (80 percent of the population) covers the spending patterns of professionals, retirees, and the self-employed and unemployed, as well as wage earners and clerical workers.

The revised market basket for both new monthly indexes will give less weight to food, increase the housing share, and double the transportation share.

Electronic calculators, jeans, panty hose, tennis equipment, CB radios, and microwave ovens will be newly included. The price data collected every month will depend on which of the variety of models, sizes, and styles sell best in the particular retail outlet designated in a point-of-purchase survey of 20,000 families. From then on, that item will be priced in that store. Some establishments will be designated as all urban or wage earner, depending on how they were selected. More than half of the goods and services will enter both indexes. The

Bureau of Labor Statistics plans to issue the two new indexes for 2½ years and if they turn out similarly to keep only one.

The BLS hopes to revise the indexes quarterly, beginning in 1980—to keep pace with changing consumer patterns. The two new indexes are based on a 1972–73 spending survey—already outdated, since that period preceded the oil embargo that quadrupled petroleum prices.

If you can figure your own CPI you can tell whether your spending is inflationary compared to the urban price index where you live. Citibank of New York[4] explains how to do so. You add your canceled checks or stubs or receipts for each of the BLS categories in the CPI. Divide the spending in each category by the grand total, which will give you each category's percentage of the total.

---

[4] *Consumer Views,* published by Citibank, June 1978.

FIGURE 3–4
Comparing the CPI Market Basket

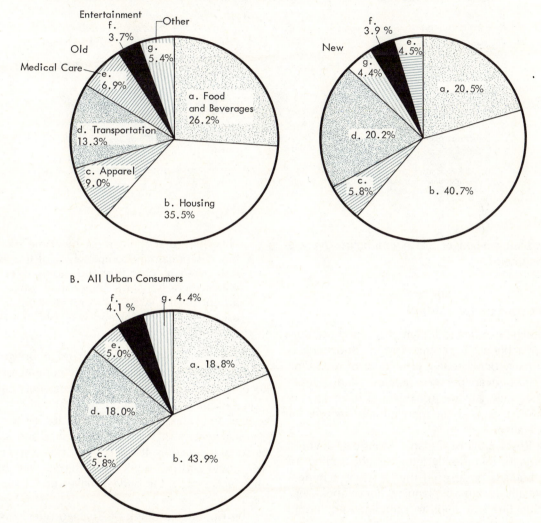

A. Urban Wage Earners and Clerical Workers

Entertainment f. 3.7%
Other
g. 5.4%
Old
Medical Care e. 6.9%
d. Transportation 13.3%
c. Apparel 9.0%
a. Food and Beverages 26.2%
b. Housing 35.5%

New
f. 3.9%
e. 4.5%
g. 4.4%
a. 20.5%
d. 20.2%
c. 5.8%
b. 40.7%

B. All Urban Consumers

f. 4.1%
g. 4.4%
e. 5.0%
a. 18.8%
d. 18.0%
c. 5.8%
b. 43.9%

Note: All items = 100 percent.
Source: The Conference Board.

For instance, if your total entertainment spending was $300 and your total spending was $5,200, then entertainment was 5.8 percent of your total spending. If you live in Chicago, you multiply 175.5 (the entertainment index for that area) by 5.8 percent = 101.79, for your own entertainment index.

Add all seven categories similarly computed, and you have your own CPI. If it is higher than that of the BLS, then your spending is more than the average, and you fall into the highest inflation category. If you make budget cuts in your above-average spending items it will help you save more

TABLE 3–1
Urban Prices Indexes

	Chicago	Detroit	Los Angeles–Long Beach	New York–New Jersey	Phila-delphia
All items	187.3	190.2	189.6	193.5	190.8
Food and beverages	205.0	198.6	198.5	203.0	205.8
Housing	185.8	192.0	199.3	195.6	192.7
Apparel and upkeep	145.2	147.9	145.8	157.1	143.0
Transportation	183.5	180.7	182.3	197.5	188.1
Medical	219.3	249.9	214.4	228.3	235.6
Entertainment	175.5	174.8	163.3	183.5	172.4
Other	181.1	180.4	174.6	187.6	180.7

All figures are expressed as a percentage of the 1967 base of 100. Figures are for April 1978.
Source: Bureau of Labor Statistics, and *Wall Street Journal,* June 19, 1978.

money than will budget cuts in your below-average spending items.[5]

The Purpose of a Budget

A budget is a financial plan. Too often the purpose of a budget is misunderstood. Budgeting is not a dreary bookkeeping procedure of recording the details of every penny expended. Many people have assumed it to be just this and have quickly grown tired of keeping mountainous records of petty details.

The Royal Bank of Canada, Montreal, devoted a number of its monthly letters to the subject of family budgets. It stressed the fact that a budget is essentially a matter of planning, not of bookkeeping. Budgeting is a guide to spending and should not be looked upon as an inflexible pattern into which every penny of expenditure has to be fitted. The bank advised the family not to

> get into the habit of staying home at night, trying to find a missing 23 cents. No one can hope to budget 100 percent accurately, and only foolish persons try. With all his wizardry at mathematics, Einstein could never make his bankbook balance. Let us agree quite

cheerfully that there must be some money that disappears as completely as if the mice had eaten it. One husband, going over his wife's records, came, every little while, on an entry: ''HOK $1.50'' or ''HOK $3.'' He asked what it meant and was told ''Heaven Only Knows.''

Mindful that most people abandon budgeting when it becomes a matter of penny-hunting record keeping, the bank suggests an extra category called ''OIL'' in the budget, amounting to about 2½ percent of the total. It states: ''That's for oil for the troubled waters. It will cover mistakes and saves personal headaches. It will cover the $10 you lend to a friend and never get back; the $5 you spend on impulse when the budget makes no allowance for it.''

The Continental Bank of Chicago offers similar advice. It says that you can go too far with money management. The reckless spender who keeps no financial records winds up with no money—but the man who knows his balance sheet by heart and keeps records on every transaction usually has no fun. The bank suggests an annual spending plan with a priority system for both essentials and the most ''meaningful'' extras to be organized on a monthly spending basis subject to a review every few months.

---

[5] *Wall Street Journal,* June 19, 1978.

"We've done it again. We've disposed of all our disposable income."

Reprinted by permission *The Wall Street Journal*

Even Thoreau in the pastoral peace of Walden discovered that he needed a financial plan. In his book *Walden,* he itemized his expenses during one eight-month period and found that they totaled $61.99, while his income from farming and odd jobs was only $36.78, and he sadly concluded that his net loss came to $25.21. He was still part of a money economy.

No family ever has enough money. A budget is simply an application of willpower to the management of personal finances. It is a plan for spending, not simply a record of expenditures. It is designed to keep you out of financial trouble, to help you live within what—in terms of your wants and desires—is always an inadequate income. It enables you to set priorities in spending and to plan to get the most out of your money. If you were given $400,000 tomorrow, you would think very carefully about how best to use it—whether to spend or invest—and, if the choice were the former, on what. You would do some planning about the disposal of the $400,000. Well, if you average $10,000 a year in earnings between the ages of 25 and 65, you will control the spending of $400,000. Even though you obtain the money over

a period of time, it would be well to ponder and plan its disposal, just as you would if you received it all at once.

It is not essential to budget, of course. If you live within your income easily, satisfy all your needs and wants, and manage to save in the bargain, then budgeting may be a waste of time for you. Some bright, competent people do their financial planning in their heads and do not stop to put it down on paper to see how it shapes up. But many people (and all responsible governments and successful business firms) estimate their income in advance and carefully plan its disposal—on paper. Budget forms create a support system. Because it brings one face to face with reality, the process may not be a pleasant one; but it is better to face facts ahead of time and trim your wants to your income. Some people find this process too onerous. They are the ones who went to debtors' prisons hundreds of years ago and who today have their cars repossessed, their furniture taken back. They pay extra and heavy charges to loan companies, have their salaries garnisheed and their property, if any, attached, and generally slip in and out of side doors to elude creditors' subpoenas and judgments.

Budget planning makes one think about alternatives in spending. The process of choosing makes you a wiser purchaser, although it may make you a sadder one, too. For example, is it more fun to entertain frequently or to be well dressed? Is labor-saving household equipment more important than the convenience of an automobile? Are temporary luxuries more to be desired than the security of a growing savings account? If drawing up a budget shows you that you may have to make such choices (and this irritates and aggravates you), do not blame it on the budget. Blame it on your income, because that is the real cause of your annoyance and frustration. It is not large enough to meet all your needs. The budget lets you see this fact ahead of time. If you wait to find it out through the spending process, you will be more annoyed later.

A Gallup Poll found that four out of every ten American families keep budgets; and of those that do, one out of three said that they failed to stay

"But in the past three years you've doubled your income, so actually we're no worse off than we were before."

Changing Times, the Kiplinger Magazine

within them. Gallup interviewers found that nearly half of all persons who have had a college education keep a budget, as compared to less than one third of persons whose education did not extend beyond grade school. This tends to indicate that people with larger incomes and higher standards of living use budgets more frequently than those who live in more modest circumstances. The two principal reasons given for not keeping a budget were "Not enough money, all spent anyhow" and "Don't need one, can live within means." Those who gave the first reason clearly misunderstood the purpose of budgeting and obviously would benefit from financial planning.

The Components of a Budget

The components of a budget are determined wholly by the needs of the individual or the family for which it is devised. For example, a college student's budget categories will differ considerably from those of a head of a family.

A budget for a college student might have the following breakdown:

A. Income.
   1. From parents.
   2. From odd jobs during spring and fall semesters.
   3. From summer work.
   4. Loans or grants.
B. Expenditures.
   1. Tuition.
   2. Fees.
   3. Books.
   4. Room and board.
   5. Clothing, including laundry and cleaning
   6. Transportation or automobile upkeep.
   7. Medical and dental care.
   8. Donations.
   9. Dues (fraternity, clubs, class).
   10. Newspapers, magazines, postage, and cigarettes.
   11. Recreation and dates.

A budget for a head of a family might be divided into the following categories:

A. Income.
   1. From regular employment—salary or wages.
   2. From additional employment or commissions.
   3. From dividends, interest, or rent.
   4. From bonuses, gifts, government, or other allowances.
B. Expenditures.
   1. Savings.
   2. Taxes.
   3. Repayment of debts or installment payments.
   4. Food.
   5. Rent or mortgage payments.
   6. Household operation—utilities, supplies.
   7. Clothing, including laundry and cleaning.
   8. Insurance.
   9. Home furnishings and household equipment.
   10. Medical and dental care.
   11. Contributions, gifts, subscriptions.
   12. Transportation or automobile expenses.
   13. Advancement.
   14. Personal allowances.
   15. Entertainment.
   16. Miscellaneous (OIL or HOK).

How to Budget

Clearly the point of departure in budgeting or financial planning is to estimate your annual income from all sources and then to see how well or poorly it covers your estimated annual expenses. If it is apparent that your income will not cover them, then you can seek to increase your income or find ways and means of cutting expenses, or preferably do both.

You may possibly wish to keep records temporarily for two reasons. You may not be able to estimate one or another of the categories of proposed expenditures precisely enough in drawing up your original budget plan and may therefore wish to keep a record for a week or a month to see what that category of expenditure actually totals as a means of making a more exact annual or pay period estimate. Or, having drawn up your financial plan (budget), you may wish to check your ability to apply it by keeping an actual record of expenditures as a means of seeing how well you were able to conform to your financial plan.

How can you engage in budgeting without bookkeeping? Very simply. Once you have drawn up your annual financial plan, break it down on a per payday basis, and then set up a plan for spending for each pay period. When the paycheck is cashed, put the cash in different envelopes, one for rent, one for food, and so on, with the amounts determined by the plan. Then, as you spend over the pay period, there is no need to keep a record of expenditures. If one envelope is consistently exhausted before the end of the period (the food envelope, for example), you can either draw from the savings envelope to cover the deficit, thus saving less than you had planned, or you might try to reduce your expenditures for food by buying cheaper cuts of meat, for example, or by eating hamburger rather than steak.

Another useful arrangement is to have your monthly paycheck sent to your bank and to use checks to pay for all important expenditures. When the checks are returned by the bank with your statement, you can sort them out, total each category, and thus see whether you kept to or exceeded your plan. If you like to operate on a cash basis, you can use the envelope method; if you prefer to use a bank, then you can your use checking account to test your budget and eliminate the deadly record keeping which scares so many people away from budgeting.

Another method of budgeting without paper-

work uses two separate checking accounts.[6] Check account 1 is used to pay recurring monthly expenses and household operating accounts. The paychecks go into account 1 at the beginning of each month. Money not needed for household expenses goes into account 2. In account 2, funds accumulate for anticipated expenditures that occur at less frequent intervals—and for specific long-range goals.

It's important that account 1 have a realistic amount in it—a figure of household costs taken from the records of what was actually spent.

To set up account 2, it is necessary to establish what the annual costs are for the "big items" and then to prorate those amounts over a 12-month period. The sum required is set aside each month, and it is there in account 2 when due. Income from other sources goes into account 2 and is identified—on the deposit slip—for the particular fund within the account. The amounts in both accounts can be flexible as to need—and if too much is in either, it can be siphoned off into a savings account. The only accounting separate from stubs and deposit slips is a summary sheet that keeps track of the funds in account 2. At the end of the year two statements are needed: (1) the actual spending in each category—which serves as a target also for the following year, and (2) a statement of net worth—to see whether the year's efforts netted growth. It would work equally well, if not better, if account 2 were a savings account earning interest.

You have to identify your needs and priorities to make satisfying spending decisions. You are not expected to conform to a budget determined by "average spending patterns," but those averages allow you to see whether your style of living fits your pocketbook and also whether some of your expenses could be tailored to enable you to enjoy your lifestyle more thoroughly. It pays to observe what others do, because this indicates what is pos-

---

[6] "One Family's Budgeting Plan—It's Easy and It Works," *Changing Times, the Kiplinger Magazine,* July 1977.

sible. You can't have everything you want—as you know—even with credit. The whole purpose of the budget is to keep track of what you are doing and what you have to do—and what you want to do.

You may live in an area where prices are rising slower than the national average. Prices don't move at the same pace everywhere. Your spending pattern may have changed. Your costs may be less than you had assumed they would be, and a "new look" at your budget might disclose an unsuspected source of funds.

These days personal financial planning is very popular—especially among the upper-income managerial levels. Most of the financial planning consultants advise that you pay yourself first, that saving precede both inescapable expense and discretionary spending. That advice is of benefit at all income levels. Regularly saving part of aftertax income will enable you to buy a big-ticket item faster. It will also cushion the pain of sudden unexpected expenditures. It can be put into some investment that will make your money work for you.

Managing your money is what budgeting is all about. Most people—even those with good incomes—who turn to family debt counseling services have to do so—because they don't manage their money. Their debts become overpowering. Especially hard to handle are the "big" items, such as insurance premiums, mortgage payments, or the installment financing of a car. If you break down those big sums into manageable 12-month parts, putting aside a proportionate sum each month against the date of reckoning, you will be able to manage that once- or twice-a-year payment with less difficulty.

Budget Forms

A considerable number of budget forms have been devised to meet varying situations. One of the most comprehensive series of budget forms, designed to emphasize the planning function, is published by the Money Management Institute of Household Finance Corporation, a large consumer finance company. These forms are found in a booklet entitled *Reaching Your Financial Goals.*[7]

There are many other sources of budget forms for every need and purpose. The New York Life Insurance Company publishes an excellent *Family Finance Record Book*. The National Consumer Finance Association has a family budget plan called "Budgeting without Bookkeeping." The American Council of Life Insurance publishes what it calls "The Family Money Manager." The U.S. Department of Agriculture has *A Guide to Budgeting for the Family* which includes work sheets (Home and Garden Bulletin no. 108). There are also *A Guide to Budgeting for the Young Couple* (Home and Garden Bulletin no. 98)—Figure 3–5 shows one of its work sheets—and *A Guide to Budgeting for the Retired Couple* (Home and Garden Bulletin no. 194).

SUGGESTED EXPENDITURE PATTERNS

Urban Family Budgets at Three Economic Levels

You may also find it helpful in your own financial planning to know the current estimates for three hypothetical annual family budgets prepared by the Bureau of Labor Statistics. These budgets reflect the assumptions made about the manner of living at three income levels—lower, intermediate, and higher. They do not represent how families of this type actually do or should spend their money. Each year's update of these consumption budgets is estimated by applying price changes for each main

---

[7] This company also publishes a *Money Management Booklet Library* which includes 12 booklets, among which are: *Your Food Dollar, Your Clothes Dollar, Your Housing Dollar, Your Home Furnishings Dollar, Your Health and Recreation Dollar, Your Shopping Dollar, Children's Spending, Your Automobile Dollar, Your Equipment Dollar, Your Savings and Investment Dollar,* and *It's Your Credit—Manage It Wisely*. Information concerning these may be obtained by writing to Money Management Institute, Household Finance Corp., Prudential Plaza, Chicago, IL. 60601.

FIGURE 3–5
Budget Guide for the Young Couple

Item	Jan.	Feb.	Dec.	Total
Total money income				
Major fixed expenses:				
Taxes:				
Federal				
State				
Property				
Auto				
Rent or mortgage payment				
Insurance:				
Medical (including prepaid care)				
Life				
Property				
Auto				
Debt payments:				
Auto				
Other				
Savings for:				
Emergency fund				
Flexible expenses:				
Food and beverages				
Utilities and maintenance (household supplies and services)				
Furnishings and equipment				
Clothing				
Personal care				
Auto upkeep, gas, oil				
Fares, tolls, other				
Medical care (not prepaid or reimbursed)				
Recreation and education				
Gifts and contributions				
Total				

Source: *A Guide to Budgeting for the Young Couple,* Consumer and Food Economics Institute, Science and Education Administration, U.S. Department of Agriculture.

TABLE 3–2
Summary of Annual Budgets for a Four-Person Family at Three Levels of Living, Urban United States, Autumn 1977

	Lower Budget	Intermediate Budget	Higher Budget
Total budget	$10,481	$17,106	$25,202
Total family consumption	8,657	13,039	17,948
Food	3,190	4,098	5,159
Housing	2,083	4,016	6,085
Transportation	804	1,472	1,913
Clothing	828	1,182	1,730
Personal care...............	282	377	535
Medical care	980	985	1,027
Other family consumption	489	909	1,499
Other items	472	763	1,288
Social security and disability	632	961	985
Personal income taxes	720	2,342	4,980

Note: Because of rounding, sums of individual items may not equal totals.
Source: Bureau of Labor Statistics.

class of goods and services to the previous year's budget.

How much income does it take for a four-person family to maintain an adequate but modest standard of living in the United States? The "Urban Family Budget," developed by the Bureau of Labor Statistics of the U.S. Department of Labor, shows the average annual budget cost for a hypothetical family of four—husband, wife, a son aged 13, and a daughter aged 8—to be $10,481 a year at a lower level, $17,106 at an intermediate level, and $25,202 at a higher level (see Table 3–2). Living in a metropolitan area cost a lower-budget family 8.6 percent more than living in a nonmetropolitan area, an intermediate-budget family 14 percent more, and a higher-budget family 19.7 percent more.

Family living expenses, including food, housing, clothing, transportation, and medical care, came to 82.5 percent of the total budget at the lower level. The remaining 17.5 percent covered gifts and contributions, occupational expenses, life insurance, and social security and personal income taxes. Consumption costs represented 76 percent of the intermediate budget and 71 percent of the higher budget.

"I'll have to re-check these items. You've got the price stickers all tear stained."

Reprinted by permission *The Wall Street Journal*

The cost of all food outlays (at home and away from home) was 30 percent of consumption costs at the lower level, 24 percent at the intermediate level, and 20 percent at the higher level. Similarly, medical care took 9.3 percent of the lower-level consumption costs, but only 5 percent and 4 percent of consumption costs at the intermediate and higher levels, respectively. Total housing costs (including not only shelter costs but also the cost of house furnishings and household operation) reversed this pattern. At the lower level, where shelter was provided by a rented dwelling unit, housing absorbed 19.8 percent of all consumption costs. It absorbed 25.6 percent at the intermediate level and 24 percent at the higher level. Roughly the same proportion (8–9 percent) was spent on clothing and personal care at all three levels, and for transportation the differences between the levels were very small.

Differences in Living Costs among Urban Areas

Area cost indexes not only represent different price levels but also include regional variations in consumption patterns, climate, modes of transportation, facilities, and taxes, as can be seen in Table 3–3.

Various sources have suggested different annual spending patterns. For example, the Pacific First Federal Savings and Loan Association publishes a slide rule "Family Budget Guide." You set the scale to the column showing your gross monthly income and the number in your family. Then you read across to find suggested spending patterns. For example, if your family consists of a husband, a wife, and one child, the patterns suggested at different levels of income may be seen in Table 3–4. The suggestions cover families of two to four members.

TABLE 3–3
Cities Ranked by Annual Costs of Family Budgets

High Urban U.S., $26,000	Intermediate: Urban U.S., $17,600	Low: Urban U.S., $10,800
1. Anchorage	1. Anchorage	1. Anchorage
2. Honolulu	2. Honolulu	2. Honolulu
3. New York	3. Boston	3. San Francisco
4. Boston	4. New York	4. Boston
5. San Francisco	5. San Francisco– Oakland	5. Seattle
6. Buffalo	6. Buffalo	6. New York
7. Milwaukee	7. Milwaukee	7. Los Angeles– Long Beach
8. Washington, D.C.	8. Washington, D.C.	8. Washington, D.C.
9. Minneapolis– St. Paul	9. Minneapolis– St. Paul	9. Portland, Me.
10. Philadelphia	10. Hartford	10. Philadelphia
11. Los Angeles– Long Beach	11. Philadelphia	11. Champaign– Urbana
12. Detroit	12. Portland, Me.	12. Hartford
13. Baltimore	13. Detroit	13. Baltimore
14. Champaign– Urbana	14. Cleveland	14. Chicago
15. Green Bay	15. Chicago	15. Buffalo
16. Cleveland	16. Champaign– Urbana	16. Milwaukee
17. Hartford	17. Seattle	17. San Diego
18. Chicago	18. Baltimore	18. Cleveland
19. San Diego	19. Los Angeles	19. Minneapolis– St. Paul
20. Portland, Me.	20. Green Bay	20. Detroit

TABLE 3–4
The Family Budget Guide (three in family)

	Gross Monthly Income											
	$500	$600	$700	$800	$900	$1,000	$1,700	$1,200	$1,300	$1,400	$1,500	$1,600
Federal withholding tax	9.00	25.50	39.30	60.90	75.30	96.90	111.30	135.60	153.20	180.40	200.40	230.40
Social security and medicare ..	30.25	36.30	42.35	48.40	54.45	60.50	66.55	72.60	78.65	84.70	90.75	96.80
Net monthly income	460.75	538.20	618.35	690.70	770.25	842.60	922.15	991.80	1,068.15	1,134.90	1,208.85	1,272.80
Food	110.60	126.50	139.15	149.20	154.05	169.80	175.20	188.40	216.85	230.35	245.40	258.40
Shelter	92.15	105.50	114.40	126.40	123.20	155.80	166.00	178.50	181.60	192.95	205.50	216.40
House operation	46.50	53.80	68.00	72.50	107.80	105.30	124.50	133.90	128.15	136.20	145.10	152.70
Clothing	34.10	39.80	40.20	42.15	46.30	54.80	64.55	69.40	85.45	90.80	96.70	101.80
Transportation	74.65	92.60	105.10	124.35	146.35	147.50	156.70	168.60	170.90	181.50	193.40	203.65
Personal	79.70	93.10	111.30	131.90	138.65	144.90	161.45	173.60	197.60	209.95	223.65	235.50
Savings	23.05	26.90	40.20	44.20	53.90	65.70	73.75	79.40	87.60	93.15	99.10	104.35

Source: Pacific First Federal Savings and Loan Association, P.O. Box 1257, Tacoma, WA. 98401, 1978.

Food Groups in the New Consumer Price Indexes

Food is much less important in the two new consumer price indexes, due to changes in family incomes and buying patterns between 1960–61 (the basis for the old index) and 1972–73 (the basis for the new indexes). The new indexes report prices for the entire month rather than three days in the first full week of the month. There is also more complete coverage of items within food categories in the new indexes—and different weights for individual items as well as food groups. With that in mind, the comparison in Table 3–5 nonetheless shows a change in the importance of food in the index.

Reprinted by permission *The Wall Street Journal*

These yardsticks serve only as models. Individual variations are not only necessary but desirable, since few families are exactly like the average at a given income level. Costs of living in different communities vary and must be taken into account. Any financial plan, therefore, must be personal and individual. What may be satisfactory for one person may prove disturbing to another. The important thing is to have a plan—one that is flexible and that fits into your scheme of living.

FOOD

Food expenditure declines proportionately with higher income. As earnings rise, consumers spend relatively less for basic necessities and are able to purchase proportionately more of comforts, luxuries, and nonessentials. But the explosive rise in food prices has hit low- and middle-income families, distorting budgets and causing hardship.

France to Free the Price of Bread after 187 Years

PARIS—French bread, which may have helped start the French Revolution, is to be freed of price controls—for the first time since the revolution.

Announcing the liberation of the French loaf after 187 years, Finance Minister René Monory said the controls would be ended Sunday.

Bakers seemed to take the news with mixed feelings. This may start a price war, said one Paris baker. Another said he would welcome competition. Mr. Monory said bakeries would be required to display their prices clearly, to protect consumers. Currently, the price is the equivalent of about 29 cents for a nine-ounce loaf.

Just before the French Revolution, the rising price of bread caused unrest in Paris and prompted Marie Antoinette's famous remark, ''Let them eat cake.''

Bread costs were among the grievances that sparked the revolution.

The Wall Street Journal, August 10, 1978.

Consumer Lifestyles and Food Shopping Behavior

A study by the Department of Agriculture indicated three ''basic profiles of shopping behavior.'' The efficient shopper (32 percent of the sample)

TABLE 3–5
Food in the Consumer Price Indexes

| | New Indexes | | Old Index |
	All Urban Households	Wage Earner and Clerical Households	Wage Earner and Clerical Households
All foods as percent of total	18.8	19.3	24.0
As percent of all food			
Food at home	69.1	69.9	78.0
Food away from home	30.9	30.1	22.0

Source: National Food Review, U.S. Department of Agriculture, April 1978.

used price as a dominant factor, expended a minimum of time on shopping, kept within a budget, and bought extra quantities of food at a lower price to save time and money. The careful shopper (the smallest type—18 percent of the sample), aware of nutritional information labeling and additives, took advantage of advertised specials and did comparison shopping. The third type (the largest—39 percent of the sample) spent more time on shopping, bought favorite brands even though more expensive, experimented with new food products, and looked for satisfaction from food preparation.

Another source[8] describes Mrs. Average Housewife as spending 17.4 percent of the family budget on food and taking extra care to maintain a moderate standard of living. According to the *Progressive Grocer* ("42nd Annual Report of the Grocery Industry," April 1975), two thirds of the 500 shoppers surveyed always read the weekly ads, "as a guide both to specials and to stocking up on essential groceries; 44% of them had increased their use of coupons, and at least 1/3 used unit pricing." Seventy-five percent claimed that they always made shopping lists, and 37 percent were choosing house brands as opposed to national brands.[9]

[8] Jennifer Cross, *The Supermarket Trap* (Bloomington: Indiana University Press, 1976).

[9] A recent "blind" test conducted at Temple University's School of Business Administration found that only one respondent in five could identify a favorite peanut butter and there was only 23 percent accuracy for margarine and cola. Such results indicate that without advertising, loyalty to national brands would diminish.

Most sources indicate that there is no "average" shopper, but the consensus is that most shopping is done once a week, preferably on weekends, takes about a half hour, and is often impulse buying, especially if the family does it together.

The working woman is not as bargain-conscious as she might be—trading time for money—and is more partial to convenience foods because they save energy (her own).

Home economists claim that food costs can be cut and the diet would still provide adequate nutrition if inexpensive sources of protein were more frequently used.[10]

Food consumption has declined somewhat, but allocation of food dollars tended to fall into the same patterns over the years; one third to meat

[10] See *Family Food Buying—A Guide for Calculating Amounts to Buy,—1977—Comparing Costs,* Home Economics Research Report no. 37, Science and Education Administration, U.S. Department of Agriculture, available from the Superintendent of Documents. For further information, see:

Consumer Leaflet 18, "Cut Food Costs When You Shop." Free from Mailing Room, Building 7, Research Park, Cornell University, Ithaca, N.Y. 14850.

Family Economics Review, a quarterly report on current developments in family and food economics, Consumer and Food Economics Research Division, U.S. Department of Agriculture, Federal Center Building, Hyattsville, MD. 20782.

Your Money's Worth in Foods, 28 pp., free from the Office of Communication, U.S. Department of Agriculture, Washington, D.C. 20250.

and meat alternates and half to fresh foods such as eggs, milk, vegetables, fruit, poultry and seafood. There has been an increase in purchases of prepared and partly prepared mixes and slightly less for milk, bread and cereals.

Shopping Lures and Safeguards

The Supermarket Layout Ever wonder why milk and bread, which are fairly constant purchases, are either in the back of the supermarket or deep inside the aisles? It's planned so that on your way to them you will see as many displays and items and thus do much impulse buying.

The floor layout is planned to lead the shopper into as many areas of the store as possible, to attract the shopper to departments that carry a generally higher profit margin than the groceries in the center maze, such as produce, meat, baked goods, and frozen foods. An industry periodical notes that even at the regular price special displays sell as well as those offering reduced prices. It is also a "fact" that eye-level shelves attract more purchasing. "Tests have shown that the same four items sold 63 percent more during a two-week period when they were raised from waist to eye level and 78 percent more when they were raised from floor to eye level. Conversely, as they were moved down progressively from eye to floor level, sales dropped substantially."[11]

Shoppers buy more if they come without lists and are accompanied by children and spouse. Each minute that the shopper takes beyond a half hour, it is thought, adds 50 cents to the bill.

Checkout Scanners Mixed reactions have greeted the computers that read the parallel black lines on cans and boxes as each can or box is passed over a scanner at the checkout counter. The computers speed checkout lines, but since the laser devices can tally prices without ringing up each price, their use may eliminate the practice of stamping the price on each package—to the disadvantage of the consumer.

The high-speed printing machine connected with the scanner provides an itemized record, including tax and price, making it easier for the customer to check. The new system benefits the supermarket by providing better monitoring of its price and inventory and by cutting operating costs. It enables the supermarket to improve its market research strategy and to assess changing consumer demands. But consumer groups fear that the high cost of installation and maintenance will be passed along in prices to the customer.

Labeling, Unit Pricing, Dating, and Grading Product information listing net contents, ingredients according to predominance by weight, and the name, address, and zip code of the manufacturer, packer, or distributor has long been customary. Because of a growing insistence on more information, manufacturers now also give the number and size of servings in the container; storage and cooking recommendations; nutrient information; U.S. RDAs; the vitamin, mineral, calorie, protein, fat, and carbohydrate content; and the drained weight.[12]

The popular response to the recent nationwide interagency public hearings indicates a prevailing attitude that consumers are entitled to know more about the contents of the food they eat. Most consumers want fuller disclosures about ingredients, such as specific rather than general sources of fats, oils, and sweeteners. Among the issues of great concern are stricter regulation of fortified foods to avoid disguising the real nutritional value and the need to require producers to differentiate between imitation food products and the traditional ones— at least in name.

---

[11] Cross, *Supermarket Trap,* p. 73.

[12] The Food and Drug Administration, the Dept. of Agriculture, and the Federal Trade Commission have launched a nationwide campaign to get consumer views on food labeling. For booklet, write Dept. 703-F, Consumer Information Center, Pueblo, Co. 81009. For issue paper, write Bureau of Foods, Food and Drug Administration, 200 C St., S.W., Washington, D.C. 20204.

Unit Pricing The variety of cans, packages, and containers can leave a shopper befuddled as to contents and weight. If cookies can be cushioned against breakage by much paper, and frankfurters can be stretched by "extender," and spaghetti with meatballs and sauce will have more meat than will spaghetti with sauce and meatballs, how can the shopper know what has been bought? Unit pricing provides some help in comparative judgments. If the stores mark packages with the unit price as well as the total price, or post the unit prices on a shelf, there will be more truth in packaging. Checking the price per ounce, per pound, or per pint makes it possible to achieve considerable savings by finding the most economical brand and size.

Dating Most packages have a concealed code showing date, time, and place of manufacture and the date when the firm's representative should pull the packages from the shelves. How do *you* know whether what is inside a package is fresh and how long it can be safely kept? Twenty states have open dating laws, but most of these laws cover only easily perishable items, such as bread and milk. Federal Food and Drug Administration regulations require that dates and batch numbers be used in case recalls are necessary. The codes used by 84 food manufacturers were studied by the New York State Consumer Protection Board and published in a booklet made available to the public. For examples of how to read the codes, see Figure 3–6.[13]

Grading Meat grading (in categories such as prime, choice, and good) is a voluntary service paid for by meat-packers. Meat need not be graded at all. Meat inspection is mandatory, and federal inspectors decide whether a cut of meat is wholesome and accurately labeled. The use of USDA (U.S. Department of Agriculture) grade standards and inspection service is voluntary. But most canned and frozen fruit and vegetables are packed and priced according to their quality even though a grade is not shown on the label. The USDA Grade

B and C are acceptable quality for table use, cooking and casseroles, sauces and puddings. Grade C products may have less uniform size, color, texture, and maturity. The standard minimum specification for generic food items is USDA Grade C.

Convenience Foods A convenience food is usually regarded as a packaged instant meal, ready to eat or ready to heat and serve. Because of its processing, a convenience food requires little, if any, at-home preparation.

Frozen foods are the fastest-growing convenience products in the field. Canned dinners of specialty foods include sauces in a packaged convenience concept—the skillet dinner or casserole. Dried and dehydrated foods, packaged mixes, as well as freeze-dried, are in packaged instant meals. Since there are more working women than full-time housewives, time and work pressures upon the homemaker with dual "job" requirements necessitate decisions on the differential in time and cost between convenience or processed food forms and their home-prepared or fresh counterparts. The use of convenience and processed foods raises a number of questions.

Cost comparisons must take account of additional ingredients if these are required and of mixing, cooking or baking equipment if it is included. If a convenience food is reasonable in price for one or two persons, does it become expensive if it is intended for use by a large family? Not every convenience food is more expensive. Selective shopping would show that fresh oranges for juice usually cost more than the frozen concentrate and that frozen french fried potatoes are less expensive than french fried potatoes prepared from fresh potatoes. A careful cost comparison study[14] reports that "nearly all the frozen, chilled, or ready to serve baked goods, were more expensive than preparing them from recipes or mixes. Better than half the products made from a complete mix were less expensive than their home prepared counterpart."

---

[13] For a free copy of the code-breaking booklet *Blind Dates,* write New York State Consumer Protection Board, 99 Washington Ave., Albany, N.Y. 12210.

[14] Economic Research Service and Agricultural Research Service, U.S. Department of Agriculture. The detailed procedure is described in *Family Economics Review,* Winter 1976.

FIGURE 3–6
How to Read Coded Packaging Dates

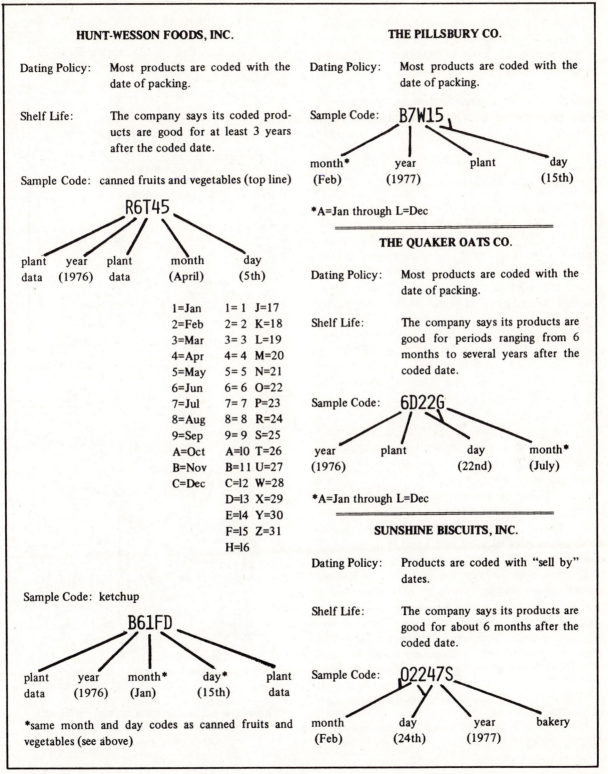

HUNT-WESSON FOODS, INC.

Dating Policy: Most products are coded with the date of packing.

Shelf Life: The company says its coded products are good for at least 3 years after the coded date.

Sample Code: canned fruits and vegetables (top line)

R6T45

plant data | year (1976) | plant data | month (April) | day (5th)

1=Jan	1= 1 J=17
2=Feb	2= 2 K=18
3=Mar	3= 3 L=19
4=Apr	4= 4 M=20
5=May	5= 5 N=21
6=Jun	6= 6 O=22
7=Jul	7= 7 P=23
8=Aug	8= 8 R=24
9=Sep	9= 9 S=25
A=Oct	A=10 T=26
B=Nov	B=11 U=27
C=Dec	C=12 W=28
	D=13 X=29
	E=14 Y=30
	F=15 Z=31
	H=16

Sample Code: ketchup

B61FD

plant data | year (1976) | month* (Jan) | day* (15th) | plant data

*same month and day codes as canned fruits and vegetables (see above)

THE PILLSBURY CO.

Dating Policy: Most products are coded with the date of packing.

Sample Code: B7W15

month* (Feb) | year (1977) | plant | day (15th)

*A=Jan through L=Dec

THE QUAKER OATS CO.

Dating Policy: Most products are coded with the date of packing.

Shelf Life: The company says its products are good for periods ranging from 6 months to several years after the coded date.

Sample Code: 6D22G

year (1976) | plant | day (22nd) | month* (July)

*A=Jan through L=Dec

SUNSHINE BISCUITS, INC.

Dating Policy: Products are coded with "sell by" dates.

Shelf Life: The company says its products are good for about 6 months after the coded date.

Sample Code: 02247S

month (Feb) | day (24th) | year (1977) | bakery

Source: *Blind Dates: How to Break the Codes on the Foods You Buy,* a study conducted and published by the New York State Consumer Protection Board, June 1977.

Of the 37 vegetable convenience products studied, 16 single-ingredient canned or frozen items were cheaper than fresh or home-prepared items except for 6 vegetables during their growing season. Otherwise, of the 162 convenience foods studied, only 36 percent had a cost per serving lower than that of their home-prepared or fresh counterparts.

The Influence of New Lifestyles

Eating Out One out of every three food dollars goes to food eaten away from home—a tremendous growth since the 60s. Fast-food restaurants have been patronized most frequently (at least once a week), especially by younger households whose members are under 50 years of age. Their share of the away-from-home market more than doubled in the last ten years. During the same period, conventional restaurants, lunchrooms, and cafeterias lost 6 percent of the "eat out" share of the total market, which, however, had expanded tremendously for everyone. The rise in working wives and the resultant growth in family income found the fast-food establishments a welcome place for modest price, relaxed eating for parents and kids. A Consumers Union study showed that a hamburger, french fries, salad, and milk shake provide a well-balanced meal.[15]

The over-60 American mostly favored the restaurant where the main course was under $5, and only about a third of the respondents in this age group reported that they had been to a fast-food place in a year.[16] Expensive restaurants were found to be most popular with the 25–50-year-olds surveyed and less popular with the old or the young.

To remain competitive and keep costs down, restaurants have turned increasingly to centrally prepared frozen foods that are thawed, boiled in a pouch, or heated in a microwave oven. This has led to calls for "truth in menus," as customers won-

[15] *National Food Review,* U.S. Department of Agriculture, January 1978.

[16] Economic Research Service, U.S. Department of Agriculture, September 1977.

A Civil War Memo of a Once-Famous Restaurant.

✕DELMONICO'S✕
RESTAURANT.
494·PEARL·STREET.

BILL OF FARE.

Cup Tea or Coffee,	1	Pork Chops,		4
Bowl " "	2	Pork and Beans,		4
Crullers,	1	Sausages,		4
Soup,	2	Puddings,		4
Fried or Stewed Liver,	3	Liver and Bacon,		5
" " Heart,	3	Roast Beef or Veal,		5
Hash,	3	Roast Mutton,		5
Pies,	4	Veal Cutlet,		5
Half Pie,	2	Chicken Stew,		5
Beef or Mutton Stew,	4	Fried Eggs,		5
Corn Beef and Cabbage,	4	Ham and Eggs,		10
Pigs Head " "	4	Hamburger Steak,		10
Fried Fish,	4	Roast Chicken,		10
Beef Steak,	4			

Regular Dinner 12 Cents.

Smith & Handford Printers 23 and 25 Dey St. N. Y.

"There's a lot more food mixed with the additives in this one."

Reprinted by permission *The Wall Street Journal*

der about "homemade" soup, "Idaho" potatoes, "fresh" fish, and "blueberry" pie.

Supermarkets Face the Challenge To meet the competition of fast-food dining out, supermarkets have increasingly offered both "in store eating places" and prepared hot "takeout food." While these services have made some supermarkets more elaborate, others offer the alternative "simple mart"—no frills, discounts, and generic labeling—to blunt the edge of rising prices.

Generic Labeling These plain-label items carry a lower government grading and are sold in plain wrappers at prices about a third below those of national brands and between 10 and 20 percent below those of the house brand. They are usually displayed loosely in big bins, giving the shopper both "choice" satisfaction and the chance to "shop down" in price.

Consumer News has compared generic items with house and national brands in an A&P food store in the Washington, D.C., area. Two samples from this comparison are: an unbranded fabric softener (64 oz.) costs 59 cents compared to the house brand at 69 cents and the national brand (Downey) at $2.13; macaroni and cheese (7½ oz.) sold unbranded at 27 cents, the house brand at 30 cents, and the national brand (Kraft) at 39½ cents.[17]

Three other studies enlarge upon this limited sample, whose results can be seen in Table 3–6. The Progressive Grocer study, in February 1978, compared a shopping list of 30 food and new food items in a midwest chain. Consumer Reports, in June 1978, used 16 food items in an eastern food chain for its study. The U.S. Department of Agriculture did a telephone study which questioned a number of retailers, 15 chains, and 3 wholesalers.

Generic products were first introduced in late 1977 in Chicago and have spread throughout the country. By mid-1978, over 100 firms carried generics, usually between 25 to 50 of the 100 items available. Virtually all firms carry some type of canned corn, peas, beans, fruit juices, tomato prod-

---

[17] *Consumer News,* Office of Consumer Affairs, July 15, 1978.

TABLE 3–6
Average Savings on Generics

Study	Over Store Labels	Over National Labels
USDA estimates from telephone survey	15	25
Consumer Union study	19	30
Progressive Grocer study	20	39

Source: *National Food Review,* Economics, Statistics and Cooperative Service, U.S. Department of Agriculture, September 1978.

ucts, and packaged macaroni and cheese dinners. Among non-food generic items, paper goods are the best sellers, followed by laundry items. Unfortunately, most stores bunch their generic products making price comparison with the other store items more difficult.

Coupons, Stamps, and Games Promotions

Coupons are popular and are used by nearly four out of every five families under the impression that their use reduces price. Their use is higher among middle-income groups and among families with high grocery bills and reflects attempts to combat the sharp rise in food prices. Heavy promotional efforts by manufacturers and retailers have increased the available numbers of coupons and the volume of consumer interest. Coupons can be hedged around with small-print limitations and short expiration dates. The average face value of manufacturers' coupons has risen to about 15 cents per coupon. Manufacturers have been finding coupons an effective tool for increasing sales and introducing new products.

Stamps have become less popular, but are still a habit with many consumers who will shop anywhere to get them. Although marketing studies in this area are still inconclusive, a growing belief voiced by some consumers is that stores offering stamps charge higher prices.

Premiums of the kind that attempt to keep the

customer coming back each week to complete the encyclopedia or the set of dishes, join with sweepstake games or jingle contests and prizes that supermarkets hope will attract the loyalty of the customer. While it would be difficult to figure to what extent the consumer foots the bill, none of these extras decrease the cost of food.

Consumer Self-Help

Studies have documented the savings in purchasing store brands compared to nationally advertised brands and the economy in buying large or medium sizes in preference to small sizes. Although consumers are patronizing supermarkets for their best buys and discounts, they are also forming thousands of neighborhood food-buying cooperatives to enjoy the advantages of volume shopping. A co-op can save almost 40 percent in food prices. Co-ops can be found among the prosperous and the poor, working out of settlement houses, health stores, churches, and Y's. Co-ops usually require work time to help order, buy, and pack food. Usually the more time you spend, the less money it costs. There are membership fees, rules about shopping hours, and procedures on payment. Markup varies among co-ops, as does the type of produce bought.

Farmers' Markets

High food prices anger the consumer, who blames the farmer. The farmer, however, gets only one third of the food dollar; the rest is divided among processors, shippers, and retailers. A revival of farmers' markets and produce road stands has been widespread, stimulated by consumer unhappiness with prices and by the federal government's contribution of funds to help the states develop direct farm-to-consumer marketing programs under the Direct Marketing Act. Some farmers also open their farms to the public to pick produce directly at low prices. This appeal of fresh produce at prices lower than those of the retail stores draws the consumer, while the farmer benefits from prices higher than those he would get from the wholesaler.

Do the Poor Pay More?

The answer would seem to be yes. In inner cities or remote rural areas where only the small "Mom and Pop" store or the "convenience" store is available, prices are much higher and choices limited. Fewer items, lack of specials, and limited fresh produce characterize the small independents. Limited mobility often prevents either the poor or the elderly from taking advantage of giant supermarket chain store shopping.

For those handicapped by age or lack of education, the difficulties of comparative shopping are increased because they cannot read labels and small print or are confused by multiple sizes, grades, and unit pricing. However, a study by the Department of Agriculture failed to show that the relatively low-priced foods rose more rapidly in price than did the higher-priced foods.[18] At different periods since 1967, both groups alternated or rose at the same time.

Those food chains operating in disadvantaged areas have higher labor costs, more frequent turnover of staff and employees, higher insurance costs, and less space, resulting in a 2–3 percent higher operating cost—and less profit.

The complaint that supermarkets charged more in low-income areas and raised prices on days that relief checks and social security checks were cashed has been investigated by several federal surveys, which found no basis for the charges. Evidence to the contrary gathered by citizens' groups and newspapers support the charges. The evils of short weighting and misleading advertising of "specials" that were actually higher priced or not available have been found to be more prevalent. The FTC accepted agreements from four supermarket chains that had been cited that they would provide means for achieving increased availability of specials advertised (or rain checks) and more accurate pricing of sale items. They also agreed to comply with a July 1971 Federal Trade Commission rule concerning retail food store advertising and market-

---

[18] *National Food Situation,* Economic Research Service, U.S. Department of Agriculture, June 1977.

ing practices.[19] The FTC has also undertaken a study of the economic impact of enforcing this rule in order to determine the level of benefits to be derived by consumers and the actual costs that would be borne by industry.

On the basis of a four-year study of food prices and pricing policies of major food chains in 32 cities and a two-year evaluation of the data, leading economists from the University of Wisconsin testified before the Joint Economic Committee to the following conclusions.[20] These allegations were heatedly denied by industry spokesmen.

1. A long-term trend toward larger and fewer stores and increased concentration exists in grocery retailing.
2. The prices of nationally branded food items averaged 12 percent higher than those of store brands.
3. Chain profits are higher in markets where few stores exist.
4. A food chain's profits are higher in areas where it is dominant than in areas where it does not control a major share of the market.
5. In one large Eastern city—where market concentration was excessive, with just two food chains dominating—consumers paid 6.9 percent more for food at retail.

Food Stamps

The Food Stamp Program is available to those at the current poverty line. In determining eligibility, income is computed by subtracting a $60 standard deduction and a 20 percent deduction from earned income to cover taxes and social security deductions. Family assets of $1,750 are excluded, but an automobile which has a market value above $4,500 is included unless it is used in the process of earning a living.

Students must register for part-time work in order to qualify.

There is no longer a cost for food stamps. The impact of food stamps on food expenditures will be mixed, because only a limited amount of the stamps must be spent on food purchases. The use of the rest is discretionary and can go toward such items as sodas, electric lights, and soap.

CLOTHING

Trends

Changing lifestyles have focused on clothing as a vehicle of self-expression. Status symbols in clothing change, and today's emphasis on more casual living clothes costs less than formal suits and dresses. Even though clothes are becoming fashionable again, they weigh less heavily on the budget because fashion does not dictate so completely anymore and traditional clothes are required on fewer occasions.

Expenditures

The percentage of disposable income spent on clothing has been rising over recent years. Historically, clothing prices have influenced purchases. When price increases exceed 5 percent, spending tends to fall off. If you check Table 3–7, you will see that while the percentage of change was gradual each year, the increase between 1970 and 1977 totaled almost 33 percent. Per capita expenditure for clothing and shoes was about 152 percent higher in 1977 than in 1960. This is attributed to a combination of factors: two thirds of the increase was caused by a rise in the level of prices and one third by increased buying.[21] The latter is thought to be a result of rising incomes as well as a change in the population mix.

The Influence of the Life Cycle

There is a larger proportion of persons in the 18–44 age group. This age group buys more clothing, in part because it is the most fashion-con-

[19] Notes from the Joint Economic Committee, Congress of the United States, April 26, 1977.

[20] *FTC News Summary,* Federal Trade Commission, Washington, D.C., May 10, 1977.

[21] *Family Economics Review,* Winter–Spring 1978, Consumer and Food Economics Unit, U.S. Department of Agriculture.

TABLE 3–7

U.S. Consumer Price Index Comparison of Percent Change for All Items and for Food and Apparel, 1970–1978

	Percent of Rise for All Items	Food	Percent of Rise for: Apparel and Upkeep
1970–71	4.3	3.0	3.2
1971–72	3.3	4.3	2.1
1972–73	6.2	14.5	3.7
1973–74	11.0	14.4	7.4
1974–75	9.1	8.5	4.5
1975–76	5.8	3.1	3.7
1976–77	6.5	6.3	4.5
1977–78	7.7	10.8	3.5
Total percent rise			
1970–77	56.1	67.3	32.8
1970–78	68.0	84.0	37.5

Source: Bureau of Labor Statistics, Department of Labor.

"I'm going back to plain white shirts! I can't make co-ordinate decisions this early in the morning!"

Reprinted by permission *The Wall Street Journal*

scious, but mainly because its needs are greatest. It is during this period that school, careers, dating, and sports require clothing to meet the occasion. Population projections indicate that in the early 80s there will be a continuation of a population mix having the greatest proportion of persons in the high clothing expenditure category, after which the size of this group is expected to level off.

Everyone is aware of the clothing needs of the growing child. On the other hand, the over-65 age group who have retired from the work force and whose physical activity decreases spend less on clothes than formerly. This age group, which is gradually increasing, has lessening budgetary needs for clothing than the other age groups.

The Care of Clothing

An FTC staff report[22] proposed revisions to the Care Labeling Rule enacted in 1972, including new

[22] *FTC News Summary,* Federal Trade Commission, June 16, 1978—of 453-page report by the FTC's Bureau of Consumer Protection.

definitions to clarify such terms as *machine-wash, hand-wash,* and *dry-clean.* The report noted that "lack of care instructions on various products has frequently caused consumers to make erroneous assumptions about proper care, to their detriment. Similarly, incomplete, inaccurate or unclear care instructions often have caused consumer confusion with resultant damage or impairment to the labeled products because of improper care." The chemical origin of so much of our clothing complicates its care and cleanliness.

Sizes

There is no national sizing standard for clothing for women and girls. The U.S. apparel industry consists of over 11,000 manufacturers, each of which sets size and measurement terms.

The last time American body sizes were measured in a broad sample was in a program done by the Department of Agriculture in 1930. In 1971, the Department of Commerce released a study entitled "Body Measurements for Sizing Women's Patterns and Apparel," based on figures submitted to the National Bureau of Standards by trade associations, manufacturers, and retailers. Critics of the study note that no one actually went and took measurements of a cross section of the population.

Glamour Magazine ran a chart comparing the Commerce Department measurements for a 9/10 size dress with those of several well-known manufacturers and showed how each of these varied. Children's size 4 is not the same in the 1–4 size group as in the 3–6X size group. Women's clothing is classified by such terms as *misses, juniors, petites,* or a combination of them. Although there are sizes within each group, variation as to waist, hip, or bust measurement depends on the manufacturer. By contrast, men's clothing sizes relate to specific measurement—trousers are marked according to waist measurement; shirts are sized according to collar size and sleeve length.

What does this have to do with a budget? Higher-priced clothing has more material because those who pay more are also willing to pay for alterations so that a garment fits. A woman buying an inexpensive dress will take a larger size to compensate for the skimpiness—and loses overall fit. Confusion over sizes complicates the purchase of clothing. If time is money, shopping and returning can cost more than it should in transportation, packing, effort, and dollars.

HOUSING AND HOUSEHOLD OPERATION

Costs

Since there is a detailed chapter on the costs, problems, and varieties of housing (Chapter 9), this section will cover only a general budget overview of housing expenses.

Today housing and household operation costs exceed the cost for food. They take more than one third of the family dollar. Household operations can be divided into the following proportions:

furniture and appliances, $2\frac{1}{3}$ percent; utilities and telephone, $6\frac{2}{5}$ percent; other supplies and furnishings, almost 6 percent. Homeowner expenditures have risen more rapidly than rental payments.

Rising new-home prices and soaring mortgage rates seem to have become accepted in the light of probable demand. Around age 30 is regarded as the prime home-buying time, and there are 32 million now of that age compared to the 23 million that were in that group in the 60s and the 42 million expected in the 80s. The first-time buyer, especially the young, face particular difficulties in this period of rising prices, rising mortgage interest rates, and rising homeowner operation costs. The average price of a new house is now $65,000, risen from $37,000 in 1973.

The first-time buyer must stretch for the down payment (10%) higher than last year and three fifths higher than the levels common in 1973) because he has no equity from the profitable sale of a former home to provide the funds. A two income family makes it more possible for the first time buyer to finance the purchase of a home. The old rule of thumb about committing 25 percent of family income to housing is being exceeded by two out of every five home buyers. Of first-time home buyers, 29 percent made down payments of 10% or less, which necessitated an extra large mortgage at very high interest rates, and requiring payments that will take an excessive share of their income.

To ease this burdensome debt, graduated-payment mortgages are now being offered. They provide lower than usual monthly payments during the first five years and increase as the income of the young family is expected to rise. Also increasing is the length of the mortgage loan which eases the current monthly cost. While the total cost after 26–27 years is greater, it seems a less pressing problem than now.

Maintenance Costs   But mortgage debt must be budgeted—whatever the type of mortgage—variable interest, graduated, or conventional. Taxes must be paid. The taxpayer revolt, whose rumblings have been heard everywhere, indicates that the cost is painful. Taxes must be budgeted.

Repairs and home improvements are ever with

the homeowner. They must be budgeted, or your equity in your house diminishes.

Fuel Costs Fuel costs have been rising faster than in the past. Even though a kindly bank offers a special lower interest loan for insulation and an interested government offers tax credits, there are fuel costs, and they must be budgeted. If environmentalists make coal mining or wood burning more difficult in order to clear the air, fuel costs will rise even higher for the cleaner fuel—and those costs must be budgeted.

Property Taxes Aside from mortgage payments and fuel costs, property taxes are a substantial housing expense. In the past, as well as today, assessments have not always been equitable and homes have usually been undervalued. As communities struggle for more tax money, homeowners find their property tax bill jumping. Since reappraisals are a seemingly unobtrusive way for local governments to raise taxes without the approval of the voters, and to benefit from increases in the market value of property, there has been a nationwide pattern of local reassessment and a concurrent citizens' tax revolt. All states currently give property tax breaks to the elderly, veterans and their surviving dependents, and low-income homeowners.

LEISURE

Increasingly regarded as a necessity rather than a luxury, the leisure and travel market has grown steadily. Even during the 1972–74 period of declining economic activity and recession, pleasure travel increased. As family income rises above $15,000, the amount spent on travel increases. Those in the middle to upper middle class and the very affluent are in the high travel spending range—as are the well-to-do over 55 years of age.

Those 25–44 years of age account for the largest expenditures for leisure. They comprise 25.1 percent of the population and earn 44 percent of the income. Projections expect this market to double by 1985. Increased income, more vacation time, job pressures, and changing lifestyles—all place a new emphasis on leisure activities. Money they spend for sports equipment increases as interest rises, and spending for better quality equipment takes place.

The length of the workweek has remained fairly stable since 1975, but vacation periods and paid holidays have increased. Three- and four-week paid vacations are becoming more acceptable, as is the trend toward dividing vacation time into different seasons.

EDUCATION

Former low outlays on education shown in average consumer expenditure figures reflect the fact that Americans pay for elementary and secondary school education—and, to a limited extent, higher education—through taxes rather than private outlays. Putting a son or daughter through college these days, however, is likely to involve considerable expense and strain on the budget.

In the last ten years the cost of a public college education has jumped 74 percent and at a private college 77 percent.

Lack of endowment money adds to the tuition cost per student and limits the financial aid that a college can offer. Since 1970, tuition at Boston University (limited endowment funds) has increased 141 percent, while that at Harvard and MIT (two very well endowed institutions) has risen 85 and 88 percent, respectively.

Since you are already in college, is this painful subject less painful to you? No—because tuition fees are rising yearly and the problem of finding the money to continue college may depend on family resources, tuition aid, or loans, or a combination of all three. Since each of these sources is under high pressure today, the problem of financing and budgeting your funds is undoubtedly constantly with you.

Financial Aid

A growing number of institutions are developing plans to protect students against tuition increases in the course of their education. One university offers an entering freshman a guarantee of no increases if the four years of tuition are paid in advance. Freshmen can even borrow from the university at 9 percent to do this, and need only repay within eight years.

Another university adopted three separate plans:

1. A guarantee to freshmen of no increase in their sophomore year and "only modest increases" in their last two years.
2. An undergraduate who returns each semester receives a $50 credit per semester toward the senior year.
3. A 50 percent tuition reduction to the brothers and sisters of full-time undergraduates.

The College Board's Scholarship Service notes that financial aid is available to help defray costs. Students, including many from middle-income families, may qualify for financial aid and should apply

"A college education will add thousands of dollars to your income—which you'll spend sending your son to college."

Reprinted by permission *The Wall Street Journal*

for funds to help them attend colleges that they may not be able to afford on their own.

Colleges offer aid to maintain their "student mix." They do not want an entire student body of any one income level, nor do they want to frighten away capable students who fear the high costs. They have adopted a variety of procedures to help the middle-income student who has difficulties in qualifying for loans or aid on a means test basis and whose parents have hardship in financing the costs.

Tuition-Paying Parents

Middle-class parents feel that the wealthy can handle increased costs by writing a check and that poor students can get scholarship and loans, while they can't do either. The public debate over whether college costs have risen more than after-taxes income or whether other family priorities are competing for the family dollar does not alter their feeling of financial pressure. The College Scholarship Service and the American College Testing Service require financial data from parents before they determine how much aid will be given and how much the family should be expected to contribute. The funds that can come from the student's part-time employment may be included in the financial picture.

Loans and Grants

Basic Opportunity Grants make funds available to eligible students—those enrolled at least half time in a program of study which is six months in length or longer. The financial officer of the college has the forms that determine your eligibility.

Students whose families have incomes of up to $26,000 are eligible. The grants run from $200 to $1,800 a year. They vary according to a family's assets and education costs. A family with income above $26,000 might qualify if it has several children and unusual expenses.

The *Guaranteed Student Loan Program* enables you to borrow directly from a financial institution such as a bank, a credit union, or a savings and loan association. The rules are complex, but essentially they permit undergraduates to borrow from $2,500 a year to a total of $7,500 at no more than 7 percent interest. Graduates or professional students may borrow up to $15,000 (including money borrowed as an undergraduate). The federal government will pay the interest until after the student has left college. The loan must be repaid. Repayment must begin between 9 and 12 months after graduation, and must be completed within ten years. There is no income limitation on participation in this program.

The *National Direct Student Loan* (NDSL) is for students who need a loan to meet educational expenses. They may borrow a total of $2,500 if they are enrolled in a vocational program or have completed less than two years toward a bachelor's degree; or a total of $5,000 if they have completed two years of study toward a bachelor's degree; or $10,000 for graduate study. Repayment begins nine months after leaving school, and the loan must be repaid within ten years, during which time there is a 3 percent interest payment charge on the unpaid balance. Application is made through the college financial aid officer. There are cancellation provisions to attract borrowers to go into certain fields of teaching or military duty.

The *College Work Study* (CWS) *Program* provides a job opportunity to supplement other income. The college financial adviser determines the students to be employed and the suitable jobs, which may be as much as 40 hours weekly while classes are in session.

A private government-sponsored agency called *Sallie Mae* (the Student Loan Marketing Association) provides a secondary market for government-insured student loans issued by financial institutions. Sallie Mae lends money back to the holders of student loans so that they can make more student loans. It also buys loans outright with no strings attached. Proceeds from loans that Sallie Mae makes must go back into the student loan program within a year. This procedure increases the availability of money for loans.

State Aid Each of the states has its own plan for providing guaranteed student loans, made available through private lenders for fixed amounts for study at acceptable institutions. The interest and principal to be repaid beginning several months after studies are completed. The maximum repayment period is usually not more than 10 years, and the maximum period for a loan is normally not more than 15 years. Special consideration is given to those whose adjusted family income is under $20,000.

Professional Schools (Health) A new program of insured loans for students in the medical professions will make funds available for study in schools of medicine, osteopathy, dentistry, veterinary medicine, optometry, podiatry, public health, and pharmacy.

Established under the Health Professions Educational Assistance Act of 1976 and patterned after the existing Guaranteed Student Loan Program (GSLP), the program is administered by the Office of Education's Bureau of Student Financial Assistance.

Loans up to $10,000 a year—for a combined total of $50,000—are insurable for all but pharmacy students, who are limited to $7,500 a year and a total of $37,500. The funds may be used only for education expenses, such as tuition, fees, books, and laboratory equipment.

As in the GSLP, the loan principal is provided by nonfederal sources, including commercial lenders, educational institutions, state agencies, insurance companies, and pension funds.

Unlike the GSLP, this program provides no interest subsidies. Therefore, from the time the loan is made, students will pay interest compounded semiannually at a rate not to exceed 10 percent of the unpaid balance of the loan.

Borrowers will not be required to begin repayment of the principal for 9 to 12 months after they cease training, and then they may take up to 15 years to repay. The payments will be deferred for any additional full-time study and for up to three years of internship or residency training.

The three-year deferment also applies for service

as a full-time volunteer in the armed forces, the Peace Corps, the National Health Service, or other specified programs.

Cancellation of both principal and interest to a maximum of $10,000 a year is allowable for borrowers who enroll in the National Health Service Corps and for those who practice their professions in areas where there is a shortage of health manpower. The law provides stiff penalties for failure to meet obligations under a cancellation agreement.

A student may not receive a loan if he is in default on a Guaranteed Student Loan or a National Direct Student Loan or if he owes a refund on a Basic or Supplemental Educational Opportunity Grant at the school he is attending.

Default   The large sums of student loan money in default are resulting in countermeasures by the government. Although limited by concern over violations of the federal Privacy Act, HEW is searching for defaulters through a computer survey of federal government employees and the use of HEW loan officers and private collectors. New York State's highest court declared that a loan made under the National Direct Student Loan Program was exempt from discharge of debt proceedings and could be recovered by the state even though a petition of bankruptcy was approved.

The rise of student debt raises fear about some negative effects. If a graduate of a medical or law school has a huge debt to repay, the incentive to accept public health or public law practice becomes minimal because a lucrative private practice offers an easier path to more quickly wipe out obligations. Among the solutions suggested are a lengthening of the payback schedule, as well as graduated payments to make public service more attractive.

MEDICAL AND PERSONAL CARE

Hospital costs have risen at the rate of 15 percent a year in recent years. Doctors' fees rose 50 percent more than other consumer prices. The BLS annual budget for a four-person family at different levels of living in the urban United States in autumn 1977 showed that for the lower-budget family medical care took 10½ percent of the total budget and that for the higher-budget family it took 24½ percent. The medical care costs include family membership in a group hospital and surgical insurance plan, a specified number of visits to physicians, provisions for dental and eye care, and prescriptions. The higher budget also provides for major medical insurance coverage. Although the cost of drugs has risen less than the other parts of the medical bill, a 22 percent increase for an item in fairly frequent use does not help the budget. A single cobalt treatment costs $50—a series of these is needed for cancer therapy. When the President of the United States cited a hospital bill for $2,330.99, covering the one day cost of repairing three teeth injured in a boy's fall, headlines highlighted the current excessive medical costs.

Of course, these are not your medical costs—but they are noted here as both a guide and a warning that with costs so high and steadily rising, even health insurance will not completely cover all medical expense. Provision for health care is an essential budget item, but is only mentioned here because it will be covered in detail in Chapter 8.

YOUR AUTOMOBILE

Is a car a necessity or a luxury? A recent Labor Department study reports that the average American family spends about 20 percent of its money for transportation, which is just about as much as the average family spends for food. It may not be the same family, but the statistic makes a dramatic point. In 1947, 56 percent of householders owned one or more cars. Thirty years later, 82 percent of householders had one or more cars.

Perhaps one of the most striking observations that emerged from the Bureau of Labor Statistics budget studies is that the average family, and especially the lower-income family, tends to spend almost twice as much on automobile operation and upkeep as on medical care and more on automobile operation than on clothing. Increased home owner-

FIGURE 3–7
The Automobile Dollar

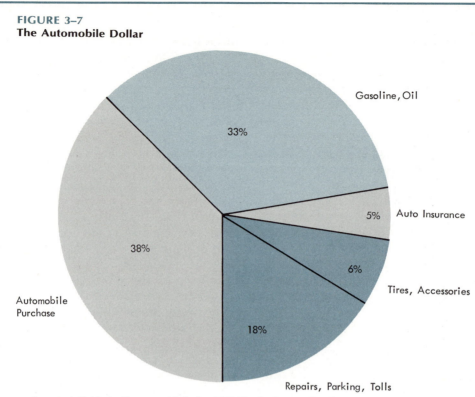

Source: *A Guide to Consumer Marketing* 1977–78, Conference Board.

ship and the growth of suburban living have greatly extended the use of automobiles.

Your purchase of a car is probably the second largest expense you will have. Estimating its total cost won't be difficult if you use the detailed work sheet published by Cornell University.[23]

Using unconventional methods, you can buy any standard American car at $125 over the dealer's cost by using a car brokerage firm. One firm, Car-Puter (operating out of Brooklyn, New York), offers two complementary services, car brokerage and a cost information service (cost $10 + $1 postage), which is an up-to-date computer printout of what the car and the options you want cost the dealer. It also gives you the manufacturer's sug-

gested retail price. The difference between the dealer's cost and the suggested retail price ranges between 10 percent and 26 percent. A midwestern firm, Nationwide Auto Brokerage (Southfield, Michigan), has a cheaper computer printout service ($3.95) and suggests that you pick up the car in Detroit. Delivery will cost an extra charge of $120 and $165.

Automobile Loans

What you pay for credit depends on where you get it and on the financing plan you use. For the use of $2,000 for two years, your cost might vary from $127 to $684—or from a 5 percent (available on some insurance loans) to a 30 percent APR. (Annual Percentage Rate)

As you can see from Figure 3–8, banks finance 58.3 percent of the auto loans; credit unions, 23.15

---

[23] "Costs of Car Ownership," *Consumer Close-ups,* Cornell University, Cooperative Extension State University of New York, Department of Consumer Economics and Public Policy, April–May 1978. Also see *Consumer Reports,* April 1978.

FIGURE 3–8
Share of Auto Loan Market by Selected Lenders

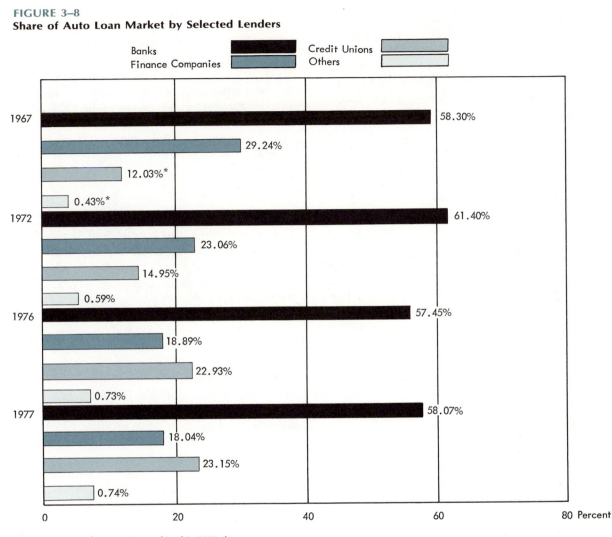

Banks Credit Unions
Finance Companies Others

1967	58.30%	
	29.24%	
	12.03%*	
	0.43%*	
1972	61.40%	
	23.06%	
	14.95%	
	0.59%	
1976	57.45%	
	18.89%	
	22.93%	
	0.73%	
1977	58.07%	
	18.04%	
	23.15%	
	0.74%	

0   20   40   60   80 Percent

* Estimates with categories combined in 1976 data.
Sources: Federal Reserve Bulletin; and Credit Union National Association, *Credit Union 1978 Yearbook.*

percent; and finance companies, 18.04 percent. Since 1972, credit unions have surpassed finance companies in this field, offering lower financing charges.

Credit rates are lower on loans available directly from lending institutions than on dealer-arranged loans. Dealer participation may be necessary if consumers with marginal credit are to secure financing for a major purchase such as a car, because the dealer assumes the risk of loss in case of default. His participation is included in the finance charge.

The longer you owe money, the more you have to pay. A two-year loan of $3,000 at 11 percent APR would cost $355.68; a three-year loan at that rate would cost $535.74; and for a four-year loan, you would pay $721.68. By this time your car has depreciated considerably. If you trade your car before it is fully paid, you lose equity in reverse ratio

	Three-Year Loan	Four-Year Loan
Total financed	$5,976	$6,144
Interest charge	$1,076	$1,229
Net amount borrowed	$4,900	$4,915
Annual interest rate	13.38%	11.40%
Monthly payment . .	$166	$128

to the number of payments left. The less equity, the more financing your new car will require.

From another and different angle, as inflation decreases the value of your money, the dollars you will use to repay the loan will be more plentiful. Thus a longer-term loan may be easier to repay, since it is a fixed dollar commitment over time. You might also consider that if you have accumulated savings, it is less expensive to finance a car purchase by using the savings rather than a loan.

Despite these facts, four-year car loans are popular. The major reason is the lower monthly payment, as the accompanying comparison of two Citibank loans indicates. The higher prices for cars and/or the desire to buy "more" car has created the need for longer-term loans.

A new trend toward five year loans is developing, just as the four year loan has taken hold. A 12 percent interest rate on a $7,500 loan would cost $201.99 a month on a four year loan and $171.52 on a five year loan. However, the total cost of the five year loan is $2,791 compared to $2,195 on the four year loan.

The Cost of Operating a Car

Both the U.S. Department of Transportation and the Enviromental Protection Agency of the H.E.W. issue annual information on the cost of operating a car that is useful to the car owner or the prospective car buyer. Both emphasize fuel costs but differ from an annual estimate done by the Hertz Car Leasing Division in their interpretation of depreciation and the method of figuring financing costs. The American Automobile Association's annual

Your Driving Costs also stresses fuel consumption and in addition separates variable costs from fixed costs as can be seen in Figure 3–9.

Insurance premiums have become a fast rising expense. High insurance rates have made Boston the most expensive city in the nation in which to drive a full-sized car. According to the 1977 edition of *What It Costs to Run a Car,*[24] New York, Chicago, Los Angeles, Providence (Rhode Island), Worcester (Massachusetts), and Miami follow closely.

Mileage

A survey conducted by National Family Opinion, Inc., of Toledo, Ohio, for the Conference Board found that if they were faced again by a gas shortage, 38 percent of those asked felt that they could not reduce their present driving mileage; 22 percent said that they could cut back between 10 percent and 20 percent; and an additional one out of every five families said that they could reduce their driving by 20 percent or more.

The more money a family has, the more it can lower its driving. Families earning more than $20,000 a year feel that they can cut back by an average of 12 percent, while it is less than 10 percent for those earning under $10,000 a year. The higher-income families spend twice as much on gasoline. Lower-income families, older families, and blue-collar families do more essential driving and less leisure driving. Since such families are less able to cut back, they will be hard hit by increased oil costs, which their budgets are least able to bear. A number of respected sources say that a "tune-up" saves both gasoline and money, and suggest that if your gas mileage is usually 15 miles to the gallon and you drive 10,000 miles a year you may save between $30 and $107 a year by keeping your car in tune; if 20,000 miles, an annual saving of $61–$213 is possible. A U.S. Department of Transportation survey showed that all cars operated at less miles per gallon at 60 miles per hour than

[24] *Wall Street Journal,* June 6, 1977. Periodic survey of the Auto and Travel Club of the Automobile Legal Association.

FIGURE 3–9
Your Driving Costs

The National Average

Here is a breakdown of national average costs computed by Runzheimer and Company for a 1978 Chevelle, eight-cylinder (305 cu in.) Malibu Classic four-door sedan with standard accessories, automatic transmission, power steering, power disc brakes, and radio, driven up to 15,000 miles per year. All insurance is based on a pleasure use category in which the vehicle is driven less than ten miles to or from work and there is no youthful operator.

Variable Costs	*Average per Mile*
Gasoline (unleaded) and oil	3.89 cents
Maintenance	1.10 cents
Tires	0.66 cents
	5.65 cents

Fixed Costs	*Annually*
Comprehensive insurance ($100 deductible)	$ 57.00
$250 deductible collision insurance	138.00
Property damage and liability ($100/300/25M)	229.00
License, registration, taxes	74.00
Depreciation	894.00
	$1,392.00
	(or $3.81 per day)

While some fixed costs are the same even if the car remains parked in the garage, the more you drive the less the per mile cost will be. Conversely, a reduction in mileage will raise the per mile cost.

Add-ons

Air conditioning: 0.2 cent per mile and 20 cents per day.

Depreciation for excess mileage: $39 per thousand miles over 15,000 annually. (The $894 is an average based on trade-in at the end of four years or 60,000 miles, whichever comes first. This is the period during which the car is expected to deliver the greatest economy.)

Financing: The total amount of interest computed on a daily basis.

Average Annual Driving Costs

Based on the figures above, the average motorist driving 10,000 miles a year would pay:

10,000 miles @ 5.65 cents	565.00
365 days @ $3.81	1,392.00
	$1,957.00
	(or 19.6 cents per mile)

The same person driving 20,000 miles a year would pay:

20,000 miles @ 5.65 cents	$1,130.00
365 days @ $3.81	1,392.00
5,000 miles @ $39/Thousand	195.00
	$2,717.00
	(or 13.6 cents per mile)

Figures for low-cost and high-cost areas apply to small towns or rural locations and to large metropolitan areas, respectively.

FIGURE 3–9 *(continued)*

	Low-Cost Area		High-Cost Area	
	Per Day	Per Mile	Per Day	Per Mile
Subcompact (4 cyl)	$2.83	3.90¢	$5.09	4.90¢
Compact (6 cyl)	2.98	5.00	5.21	5.95
Intermediate (8 cyl)	3.09	5.10	5.85	6.60
Standard (8 cyl)	3.53	5.35	6.67	6.70

"Per day" costs include $100 deductible comprehensive, $250 deductible collision, $100/300/M public liability, $25M property damage, state taxes, registration fees, and depreciation. All insurance is based on a pleasure use category in which the vehicle is driven less than ten miles to or from work and there is no youthful operator.

"Per mile" costs include gas, oil, maintenance, and tires.
Based on 10,000 miles annually, the total costs are:

	Low-Cost Area	High-Cost Area
Subcompact	$1,423	$2,348
Compact	1,588	2,497
Intermediate	1,638	2,795
Standard	1,823	3,105

Thus, the per mile costs are:

	Low-Cost Area	High-Cost Area
Subcompact	14.2¢	23.5¢
Compact	15.9	25.0
Intermediate	16.4	28.0
Standard	18.2	31.1

Rule of Thumb

With gasoline becoming more and more expensive, it may be well to remember that for every ten-cent-per-gallon increase in the price of gas, the per mile cost of running a car increases by one cent if the car delivers 10 miles per gallon or one-half cent if the car delivers 20 miles per gallon.

Source: *Your Driving Costs,* 1978, American Automobile Association, 8111 Gatehouse Road, Falls Church, VA. 22042.

at 50 and still less at 70 miles per hour. The average increase in fuel consumption when speed rose from 50 to 70 was 30.53 percent, and the 10-mile-per hour increase in speed from 60 miles per hour to 70 showed a proportionately greater increase of 17 percent in fuel consumption.

In what was probably its last fuel mileage list to be published in this form, the Environmental Protection Agency listed the diesel-powered Volkswagen Rabbit as providing the best fuel economy (41 miles per gallon) and the Dodge Colt for the best-rated gasoline-powered car. (30 miles per gallon). The EPA's testing procedures have been criticized because they do not reflect actual driving conditions. Unlike in past years, The EPA now gives miles per gallon for overall use (city) rather than separate mileages for city and highway driving.[25] Most car owners do not achieve the levels reported in the tests.

[25] The EPA Annual Gas Mileage Guide is available from Consumer Information Center, Pueblo, CO 20585—free.

Federal legislation requiring cars to average 19 miles per gallon in 1979 and 20 by 1980 practically mandates the development of minicars and subcompacts to lessen the weight of cars in order to achieve compliance with these fuel efficiency standards. In designing and building cars, companies must meet 50 NHTSA safety standards plus 15 related regulations. The controversial air bag phase-in has been ordered, starting in 1982, and air bags may be in all 1984 models.

Consumer Tire Guide, a publication of the Tire Industry Safety Council (published in cooperation with other organizations, including the National Highway Traffic Safety Administration), tells you how to maintain your tires for maximum safety and economy. It tells you how to "read" a tire's sidewall and describes the types of car tires. Free single copies are available from the Tire Industry Safety Council, Suite 766, National Press Building, Washington D.C. 20004; telephone 202-783-1022.

Used Cars

A new car depreciates 30 percent the first year, 58 percent the second year, and 78 percent by the end of the third year. A good used car, depreciated in price, should be a good buy. How do you know the car is "good" unless you are knowledgeable or you can bring along an expert?[26]

For the last few years, the FTC has held lengthy hearings on proposals requiring used car dealers to certify the mechanical and safety conditions of the car before sale, as well as what warranty protection exists. A car would have to have a sticker with a checklist covering items established by the Department of Transportation to assure safe operation. For mechanical problems, the list would be similar to the one used by Wisconsin, the only state which has mandatory inspection for used cars. The dealer would note "OK" or "Not OK." If the

prospective buyer still bought, it would be with full knowledge. If, however, an item had passed inspection and later was found to be defective, the buyer had whatever rights to take action that the state law provided. The sticker must also disclose the past use of the car and reveal whether the car had been "flooded" or "wrecked." These regulations are not yet effective.

A Wisconsin study found that those with annual incomes under $6,000 paid almost 5 percent more for an equivalent car than those making $12,000–$18,000 a year and almost 10 percent more than those earning over $24,000 a year. It also found that people buying from dealers paid 10 percent more for equivalent autos than those people buying from individuals.[27]

The Motor Vehicle Information and Cost Savings Act requires that sellers of used cars give buyers a signed statement that includes the odometer mileage at the time of sale. It is illegal to change the odometer reading. State attorneys general are authorized to sue on behalf of customers who have been gypped by crooked mileage readings. If the state wins, the buyer can collect triple damages.

Repairs

Consumer complaints about the high cost of auto repairs were investigated in a study of car repair shops in Dallas. What should have been a $1 charge for replacing a distributor rotor of a 1969 Mustang ranged from $54 for an unneeded valve job to a dozen other variations up to $130. Only one mechanic properly replaced the faulty distributor rotor and charged its true cost of $1. When questioned on why he didn't even charge for his labor, he replied, "It didn't hardly take any time."[28]

Since that study the Dallas Department of Consumer Affairs has enforced an auto repair ordinance that prosecutes offenders and has recovered, ac-

---

[26] "Which Cars Keep Their Value Best?" *Money,* August 1978.

[27] *New York Times,* June 18, 1978. See also *Common Sense in Buying a Safe Used Car,* National Highway Traffic Safety Administration. For this free booklet, write Consumer Information Center, Department 22, Pueblo, CO 81609.

[28] *Wall Street Journal,* April 21, 1971.

TABLE 3–8
Comparison of Auto Repair Costs

Part	1969 Four-Door Standard Chevrolet		1972 Chevrolet Impala Damaged in January 1973		1978 Chevrolet Impala Damaged in January 1978	
	Part Price	Labor*	Part Price	Labor†	Part Price	Labor‡
Bumper	$123.45	$52.50	$160.61	$25.64	$ 445.47	$45.32
Grille	41.35	4.20	65.63	27.40	169.75	26.66
Hood	94.20	18.20	134.04	21.22	229.45	38.66
Front fender	77.10	21.70	166.06	52.16	213.96	62.65
Total cost	$432.70		$652.76		$1,231.92	

† At $8.84 per hour.
‡ At $13.33 per hour.
Source: Institute of Insurance Information 1974, 1978.

cording to city authorities, almost $3,000 for consumers every month.[29] Seventeen states and a number of cities and counties have passed similar legislation, requiring repair shops to be licensed, with the proviso that the license will be revoked or suspended if the shop is found guilty of fraud or misrepresentation. Some laws leave it up to the consumer to ask for a written estimate which must be given on request. Consumer protection and industry experts advise the customer to get a specific breakdown of what operations are included in each repair. "Tune-up" or "winterize" may mean many things. Most laws stipulate that a shop may not exceed a written estimate without getting the permission of the customer. The customer should also have a copy of the work order.

The return of old parts is not an effective guarantee, although some laws require it. If there are no identifying marks, why can't a dishonest mechanic hand over a surplus similar part?

Mechanics may be unable to pinpoint a problem because the complicated technology and modifications in each new model series have left them behind. There is also a reluctance to perform warranty work. Frequently the dealer receives less in reimbursement from the manufacturer than he would charge cash customers for the same work. There

is delay, possibly due to difficulty in getting parts, possibly because the warranty is about to run out. This conflict between dealer and manufacturer is not to the advantage of the car owner.

The U.S. Office of Consumer Affairs reported that in state after state the number of complaints had increased more than sevenfold in the last five years. Shoddy and unperformed work headed the list of complaints. A frequent complaint was that mechanics charged book prices based on work time, when the job probably took much less time. In shops where mechanics were paid by the amount of work turned out, no one wanted to do a difficult job.

The average car owner spends more than $150 a year on car repairs, and "almost 40 cents of every dollar spent on car repairs is wasted."[30] Federal Trade Commission officials estimate that of the $40 billion spent annually on auto repairs, $12 billion goes for unnecessary work. Table 3–8 illustrates what has happened to the cost of necessary repairs.

The limited value of federal standards for car bumpers in the 1978 models can be seen in the following comparative sample of repair costs after

[29] *Wall Street Journal,* September 13, 1977.

[30] Joan Claybrook, head of the National Traffic Safety Administration, before the Senate Commerce Subcommittee, March 22, 1978.

the cars listed were driven into a concrete barrier at a speed of ten miles per hour:

Chevrolet Impala (intermediate)	$ 849
Volvo (compact)	1,306
Plymouth Volare (compact)	789
Ford Pinto	639
Volkswagen Rabbit	1,152

Those who are skilled "do-it-yourself" auto buffs have an alternative to the hassle of car repair shops in the growing number of "rent-a-bay" garages, some of which are independently owned and some are franchised by oil companies. Rentals range between $4 and $7 an hour, including the use of a lift and sometimes the emergency assistance of a mechanic, needed if a repair becomes more complicated than you can handle.

Recalls

In 1977 there was a record number of recalls by manufacturers—12½ million—because of potential hazard. A long and complicated procedure must be completed by the National Highway Traffic Administration before it can order a recall. It must prove beyond a doubt that a defect exists and is safety-related. Most recalls are initiated by automobile companies, which are often stimulated by the pressure of lawsuits.

The National Highway Traffic Safety Administration has a toll-free Auto Safety Hot Line (800-424-9393, Monday–Friday, 8:30 A.M.–5:00 P.M.) that will tell you whether your car or one that you are thinking of buying—new or used—has ever been recalled. If you are reporting a safety problem, be ready to describe the problem and to report the odometer mileage. Know the year, make, and model of the car and its vehicle identification number. All reports are fed into a computer to help identify patterns of failure.

Some problems can't be solved—if your car is a lemon. The operators who answer will know whether a certain make and model has an inherent problem that can't be fixed. If you are no longer under the warranty you are advised to sell. If you call up to ask about that particular car and make—

"It's a lemon. I want to recall the payments."

Reprinted by permission *The Wall Street Journal*

because you want to buy—you will be told that it is a lemon!

Aside from recalling cars, some manufacturers have tried to soothe the customer by extending warranty coverage. Ford has set up on a limited experimental basis a consumers appeals board made up of two "industry" (noncompany) representatives and three "consumer" representatives who are unpaid and whose decision is binding on the dealer but not the customer. Figure 3–10 provides information on another possible way of resolving complaints.

"You're supposed to bring the whole car not just the part being recalled."

Reprinted by permission *The Wall Street Journal*

FIGURE 3–10

Latest AutoCAP locations

Automobile dealers and consumers have been getting together around the country in order to resolve consumer complaints relating to automobiles. These mediators meet regularly and comprise Automotive Consumer Action Panels (AutoCAPs) which have been set up with the help and endorsement of the **Office of Consumer Affairs** (OCA). [OCA has also helped set up these Consumer Action Panels (CAPs) in the furniture, appliance and insurance industries. For details see CONSUMER NEWS: Oct. 15, 1976.]

AutoCAPs consist of a small paid staff and a volunteer panel of auto dealers and consumers who meet—much like a jury—to hear complaints that could not be resolved by consumer contact with dealers or by AutoCAP staff members and to make recommendations. Dealers are under no legal obligation to abide by a panel's recommendations, but enough do to have made the AutoCAP program successful.

Below is the latest list of AutoCAPs which have been set up by state and local automobile dealer associations and consumers. Numerous other dealer associations have set up programs to handle complaints, but only those listed have panels.

In trying to resolve automotive complaints, consumers should first attempt to work out the problem with dealers before contacting an AutoCAP.

For more information on AutoCAPS, contact the National Automobile Dealers Association (NADA) 8400 West Park Dr., McLean, VA 22101; phone 703-821-7070.

Connecticut Automotive Trades Assn.
18 North Main St.
West Hartford, CT 06107

Delaware Automobile Dlrs. Assn.
8 Hillvale Circle
Wilmington, DE 19808

Georgia Automobile Dlrs. Assn.
1380 W. Paces Ferry Rd., Suite 230
Atlanta, GA 30327

Kentucky Automobile Dlrs. Assn.
P.O. Box 498
Frankfort, KY 40601

Greater Louisville Auto Dlrs. Assn.
1103 Heyburn Bldg., 332 W. Broadway
Louisville, KY 40202

Idaho Automobile Dlrs. Assn.
2230 Main St.
Boise, ID 83706

Indianapolis Automobile Trade Assn.
7100 Lakewood Bldg.
Suite 210 E
5987 E. 71st
Indianapolis, IN 46220

Louisiana Automobile Dlrs. Assn.
P.O. Box 2863
Baton Rouge, LA 70821

Greater New Orleans New Car Dlrs. Assn.
811 International Bldg.
New Orleans, LA 70130

Automotive Trade Association
National Capital Area
8401 Connecticut Ave., Suite 505
Chevy Chase, MD 20015

Massachusetts State Auto Dlrs. Assn.
437 Boylston St.
Boston, MA 02116

Michigan Automobile Dlrs. Assn.
1500 Kendale Blvd., P.O. Box 860
East Lansing, MI 48823

Niagara Frontier Automobile Dlrs. Assn.
25 California Dr.
Williamsville, NY 14221

Cleveland Automobile Dlrs. Assn.
310 Lakeside Ave., West
Cleveland, OH 44113

Toledo Automobile Dlrs. Assn.
1811 North Reynolds
Toledo, OH 43615

Oklahoma Automobile Dlrs. Assn.
1601 City National Bank Tower
Oklahoma City, OK 73102

Oregon Automobile Dlrs. Assn.
P.O. Box 14460
Portland, OR 97214

AutoCAP
York County Consumer Protection Office
Courthouse
28 Market St.
York, PA 17401

Texas Automobile Dlrs. Assn.
P.O. Drawer 1028, 1108 Lavaca
Austin, TX 78767

Utah Automobile Dlrs. Assn.
Newhouse Hotel, Box 1019
Salt Lake City, UT 84101

Virginia Automobile Dlrs. Assn.
1800 W. Grace St., Box 5407
Richmond, VA 23220

Source: *Consumer News,* Office of Consumer Affairs, Department of Health, Education, and Welfare, Washington, D.C., September 1, 1977.

Repair Insurance

Some car owners turn to extended warranty or mechanical breakdown insurance. The premiums are high, but less than repairs would cost. Big repairs seem to happen when the warranty has expired! Although the statistics would indicate that such protection is not needed, as a general rule, worry has made a growth industry for insurance companies in this field. Five years ago there were fewer than a half dozen. Today there are more than 270 companies, including the major car manufacturers which offer car insurance repair as an option.

AUTOMOBILE INSURANCE

Next to the home and its contents, the automobile is typically the most expensive family possession. Aside from the original purchase price and the upkeep, the automobile is costly in other ways. Insurance is expensive; repair costs are too high to go uninsured; and the possibility of a disastrous jury award to an injured person is too great not to be covered by liability protection. Those who underinsure risk mortgaging a large share of future earnings to pay increasingly high jury awards. Those who do not insure can be a menace to everyone else. Every state has some form of financial responsibility law which requires a person involved in an automobile accident to furnish proof of financial responsibility up to a certain minimum. Usually this requirement is met by the purchase of liability insurance in the minimum amount set by the state in which your car is garaged.

Some states, such as New York, Massachusetts, and North Carolina, have laws which require that liability insurance be carried as a prerequisite to obtaining license plates and registration for the car. Other states require that a motorist who is uninsured and involved in an accident lose his license, regardless of fault.

The Kinds of Automobile Insurance

The budget share of automobile insurance has remained at about 2.5 percent, and over the last 25 years it has stayed at about two fifths of all property and liability insurance. There have been three times as many deaths from automobile accidents since the 1900s in the United States than from battle deaths in our armed forces during the period from the Revolutionary War to the present. Over half of the automobile accidents occur on weekends. Death struck every ten minutes last year, and every seven seconds someone was injured in an automobile accident.

There are six basic automobile insurance coverages. They are:

1. Bodily injury liability.
2. Property damage liability.
3. Medical payments.
4. Comprehensive physical damage.
5. Collision.
6. Protection against uninsured motorists.

Coverage is decided upon classification of age, sex, marital status, driver training, and how the car is used—its purpose, age, and mileage. The most favored are married people between the ages of 30 and 65 who drive for pleasure or only a short distance to work. While insurance companies favor these refinements, the federal insurance administrator disapproves on the principle that they are a means of isolating risks. Although the states regulate rates, this does not mean that all companies within a state charge the same coverage or provide the same services. Insurance companies compile statistics on claims relating to cars garaged within a rating territory and set their basic rates accordingly.

The six basic automobile insurance coverages are available in many combinations and for varying amounts. Table 3–9 shows what each coverage protects. In some cases the coverages can be purchased separately, but large numbers of owners of private passenger cars prefer a package policy, either in the form of the Family Automobile Policy or the Special Automobile Policy. The Special Policy has a single limit for liability coverage instead of the split method—50/100 of the Family Policy. The Special Package Automobile Policy is cheaper than the Family Policy because it is issued mainly

TABLE 3–9
A Summary Chart of Automobile Insurance Coverages

Coverages	Principal Applications			
	Policy-holder	Other Persons	Policy holder's Auto-mobile	Property of Others
Bodily injury				
Liability	No	Yes		
Medical payments	Yes	Yes		
Protection against uninsured motorists .	Yes	Yes		
Property damage				
Liability			No	Yes
Comprehensive physical damage			Yes	No
Collision			Yes	No

Source: Insurance Information Institute.

to low-risk drivers and because the medical expense coverage is limited in that you can only collect for expenses not covered by any other policy.

There is a new Personal Automobile Policy that may someday replace the other two, if it is successful in Delaware, Florida, and Pennsylvania, where it is now available. This policy is expected to be introduced in other states over the next few years.

Experienced drivers and insurance experts will tell you that the basic coverages of bodily injury and property damage are an absolute must. To be without these is to run the risk of financial disaster. Think of paying a damage award of $250,000 over your lifetime out of your earnings.

Bodily Injury Liability Insurance

This pays for the injury, sickness, disease, or death of others for which you may be legally liable, including claims for damages for care and the loss of services, because of accidents involving your automobile, up to the limits of the policy.

Who is protected? You, all other members of your family, and all those who may on occasion drive your car with your permission. Members of your family are covered even when driving someone else's car, as long as the owner has given them

permission. What is covered? Bodily injury liability insurance provides protection in the form of legal defense when claims or suits are brought against you by or on behalf of people injured or killed by your automobile.

Amounts of bodily injury coverage are usually spoken of in such terms as "ten, twenty," "twenty-five, fifty," or "one hundred, three hundred." These are usually written 10/20, 25/50, 100/300. In each case the first number refers to the maximum, in thousands of dollars, that the insurance company will pay for injury to any one person. The second number is the limit that it will pay for all of the injuries resulting from any one accident. This means that the insurance company agrees to protect the insured up to $10,000 for bodily injuries to or the death of any one person, and, subject to the same limit for each person, up to $20,000 for bodily injuries or death involving two or more persons in a single accident. Premium rates for such protection vary greatly from place to place. In rural areas, where the chances of hitting people are considerably smaller, 10/20 bodily injury liability protection may be obtained for less, whereas in the larger cities its cost may amount to five or six times as much. Often you will hear insurance agents refer to bodily injury and property damage limit, com-

TABLE 3–10
Comparative Automobile Insurance Rates in Five Cities

Coverage Available	New York (Manhattan) A	B	Washington, D.C. A	B	Chicago (Evanston) A	B	Dallas A	B	San Francisco A	B
Bodily injury liability										
$10,000/$20,000	$112.80	$296.10	$ 92.50	$247.90	$ 76.20	$212.80	$ 42.00	$104.00	$127.70*	$356.50*
$20,000/$40,000	141.00	370.20	120.30	322.30	105.30	293.80	55.00	135.00	143.30	400.00
$25,000/$50,000	149.00	391.00	128.70	344.80	114.40	319.30	58.00	144.00	155.80	434.90
$50,000/$100,000	171.50	450.20	150.90	404.40	137.20	383.00	68.00	167.00	186.90	521.60
Property damage liability										
$5,000	58.80	154.40	60.50	162.20	64.60	180.30	54.00	134.00	93.90	262.00
$10,000	61.80	162.30	63.70	170.60	67.80	189.30	57.00	140.00	98.70	275.40
$25,000	63.60	167.00	65.40	175.30	69.80	194.70	58.00	144.00	101.40	283.10
$50,000	66.50	174.60	68.40	183.30	73.00	203.70	61.00	151.00	106.10	296.20
No-fault coverage										
Full basic personal injury protection (PIP)	76.80	201.60								
$200 deductible basic PIP	69.20	181.50			15.60	43.60				
Extended PIP rate per vehicle	†	†								
Additional PIP rate per vehicle	9.00	9.00								
Excess PIP dependents					39.00	39.00				
Excess PIP no dependents					28.90	28.90				
$2,500 PIP							22.00	22.00		
$5,000 PIP							31.00	30.00		
$10,000 PIP							41.00	40.00		
Automobile medical payments										
$1,000	NW	NW	15.70	41.90	10.80	30.20	13.00	14.00	25.80	72.10
$2,000	NW	NW	18.20	48.60	13.40	37.20	NW	NW	27.80	77.40
$3,000	NW	NW	19.40	52.00	14.70	37.20	NW	NW	28.60	79.80
$5,000 extended	1.00	1.00	21.90	58.70	17.20	48.00	17.00	18.00	30.60	85.50
$10,000 extended	2.00	2.00	24.90	61.70	20.20	51.00	22.00	22.00	33.60	88.50
Uninsured motorists										
$10,000/$20,000	3.50	3.50	12.00	12.00	10.00	10.00	5.00	5.00	42.00	42.00
Fire, theft comprehensive										
Nondeductible	NW	NW	21.30	57.00	38.20	106.60	28.00	28.00	36.40	101.60
$50 deductible	75.60	198.50	17.50	46.90	30.80	85.80	20.00	20.00	28.80	80.40
Collision or upset										
$25 deductible	NW	NW	166.10	444.90	134.30	374.90	103.00	271.00	278.30	776.70
$50 deductible	NW	NW	103.80	278.10	83.90	234.20	99.00	259.00	173.90	485.50
$100 deductible	180.00	472.50	83.80	224.50	66.40	185.30	84.00	220.00	138.90	387.60
Towing and labor costs										
$25	5.60	5.60	2.00	2.00	3.90	3.90	2.00	2.00	2.50	2.50

Note: A—for a car driven to and from work with no male drivers under 25; B—for a single 18-year-old male driver with driver training credit having principal use of the car to and from work. All quotations are based on a 1971 Ford Galaxie eight-cylinder, four-door sedan. NW—not written.

* The minimum financial responsibility limit is $15,000/$30,000.

† Included in basic PIP effective December 1, 1977.

Source: Government Employees Insurance Company.

bined as "10, 20, and 5." The first two numbers refer to bodily injury liability and the last one to property damage insurance in thousands of dollars. Actual costs for varying limits for five large cities in the United States are shown in Table 3–10.

It's not uncommon for a jury to award an injured person $60,000—or more. If this happened to you and you had 10/20/5 coverage, your insurance company would pay only $10,000 and you would be personally liable for the remaining $50,000. It doesn't cost very much more in the way of an additional premium to increase your bodily injury coverage. If we assume that 10/20 costs $55, then the comparative cost relationships shown in Table 3–11 would prevail. Note that bodily injury coverage in the third level is five times as great as in the first but that the increase in cost is only $19 a year on each $100 of premium. In the last example, the bodily injury coverage is more than doubled, yet the increase in premium is only $8 more.

Thus the extra protection can be gained at relatively little extra cost. Juries, of course, take no notice of, and are in no way bound by, your insurance limits in any damage suit against you. You may carry 10/20, and a jury may award $50,000 damages, if you gravely injure or cripple someone. The insurance company will pay $10,000 if there is only one person injured. You will have to pay the remaining $40,000 either out of savings or future income. It is thus well worth the small added cost to buy all the bodily injury liability coverage you can afford. According to *Consumer Reports* (June 1977), insurance experts seem to agree that minimum coverage in a Family Policy should be 100/300/25.

TABLE 3–11
Comparative Costs of Bodily Injury Liability Coverage

Assume That	10/20 Costs You	$55
Then	25/50 would cost about	$68
Then	50/100 would cost about	$74
Then	100/300 would cost about	$82

The Cost of Being Young or Different

Automobile insurance rates are based principally on the dollar amount of claims paid out over a period of time. The more insured accidents you and your friends have, the more claims insurance companies must pay. The more claims paid, the higher the cost of your automobile insurance. The highest rate is paid by the unmarried male under 30 years of age who owns or is the principal driver of the car. Compare rates for A and B drivers in Table 3–10. However, if a graduate of a standard driver education course, the driver could save about $55 a year. Drivers aged 20 to 24 were involved in the highest rate of fatal accidents. Interestingly—marriage makes a difference. The young married male pays a lower rate.

The most widely used rating system reduces the cost of auto insurance to young drivers year by year. The cost of insurance varies from group to group, dependent on driving records and the accident rate. Rate discounts are allowed women drivers if they are the only operators resident in their households. In some states, drivers over 65 with good records are eligible for a discount, as are youthful drivers of a family car resident at a school more than 100 miles from home. Safe-driver plans in effect in most states offer a lower rate if everyone in the household who drives the family car has a "clean driving record," which means no serious traffic law violation for the preceding three years and no accident in which you were at fault.

In most states, many companies offer a student who ranks in the upper 20 percent of the class or has a B average or better, a discount of up to 25 percent on rates. Some companies offer a discount to drivers between 20 and 24 if they have successfully completed a driver education course.

Not only youth but motor power adds to cost. The higher performance or "muscle" cars carry a higher premium cost, regardless of the driver's age. With these cars, as a three-year study by Nationwide Insurance found, age made no difference in the number of accidents. The lure of motor power defeated the caution that is said to come with age.

Assigned Risks

Assigned risk plans were originally intended for drivers with bad accident records or numerous traffic violations. In many states these plans have become the only available source of insurance for new drivers and residents of inner-city areas. Applications to the assigned risk pool in New Jersey are up 33 percent; in California, 67 percent; Illinois, 61 percent; and Connecticut, 79 percent.

There has been a growing demand that premiums be based, not on a driver's age, sex, marital status, or address, but solely on the driving record.[31] One company refused to renew a policy of a young Chicagoan because he was living with a girl friend, and referred him to a risk affiliate which charged him $368 more for less coverage. He filed a class action discrimination suit which is now in federal court. A rock musician in Virginia was refused coverage because of his occupation. He complained to his state's insurance commission, which fined the company $1,000.[32]

Group rating is obviously unfair to individuals. A 19-year-old male in Newark, New Jersey, who owns a 1977 Camaro, hasn't had an accident, and drives only ten blocks to work pays an annual premium of $1,888, whereas an older man with the same car and the same coverage who commutes 50 miles daily pays only $321.[33]

Three states now regulate against discrimination. In Massachusetts, after the law was changed, annual premiums for a single man under 25 dropped from $2,200 a year to $800. Massachusetts also has a law that does not allow insurance companies to refuse to sell insurance to anyone who wants it and to put that person in an assigned risk pool.

The high rates in the urban areas are causing a growing number of people to drive illegally without insurance.

A number of states have introduced reinsurance facilities to combat the inequities of the assigned risk pools. A driver can obtain insurance from any company at its regular rate. Then, if the company considers him risky, it places him in such a facility, sharing the cost of his claims with other companies. The inclusion of a person in a reinsurance facility can result from a personal decision of the insurance investigator, be based on unchecked gossip in the community, or be linked to an official blacklist of occupations (including ministers, taxi drivers, beauticians) or of families with a potential youthful driver. It is said that ministers are included because they "drive as if God will provide."

Whom do auto insurance companies rate as the best risks? Managers of wholesale establishments, farmers, finance company employees, teachers, and police officers are listed, in that order of desirability.

Insurance Companies and Lawsuits

The average person involved in an automobile accident is apt to feel helpless. Faced with a possible suit for a staggering sum of money, the problem is how to go about conducting an adequate defense. In such a situation it is comforting to have the protection of liability insurance because the insurance company will defend the insured at its own expense. Since insurance companies are constantly defending suits, they are expert in knowing what to do and which attorneys to engage in order to bring the suits to a successful conclusion.

It is essential to collect the facts when an accident occurs. The obvious items of information are the name, address, and license number of the other driver, as well as the name and address of the car's owner and the registration number of the car. Also important are the names and addresses of passengers, injured or not, and especially of witnesses who might later be hard to find. Time, place, weather, estimate of damage, and details of the accident should be noted immediately. The police officer will make a report, but his name, badge

---

[31] Although insurance companies are divided on dropping these criteria, the rates and ratings procedures task force of the National Association of Insurance Commissioners (state insurance regulators) recommended that they be dropped as classifications for setting rates. A number of states have laws disallowing the use of these classifications in setting auto insurance rates.

[32] *Wall Street Journal,* October 11, 1977.

[33] According to the N.J. Dept. of Insurance, there are 234,360 different prices in the state for minimum coverage required by the state's "no fault" insurance statute. *New York Times,* January 28, 1979.

number, and precinct would be helpful information for corroborative support, if needed.

The defendants must hold themselves ready to appear in court, but every move they make is guided by experienced lawyers provided by the insurance companies; one often feels that this defense is worth the total cost of the insurance.

The insurance company, thus, will pay all legal costs as well as bail bond premiums of up to $200 if you are involved in a bodily injury or property damage suit. A fairly new casualty insurance known as "umbrella" insurance, which is a personal catastrophe liability policy issued on top of basic insurance coverage, became available as escalating jury awards made more people aware of such a need. The underlying insurance and the "umbrella" insurance need not be provided by the same company.

Property Damage Liability Insurance

Property damage liability insurance is your protection against financial loss should your car damage the property of others and should you be held liable. This second important type of automobile insurance pays for damages caused to the property of others, for which you are legally liable, up to the limits of the policy. It includes damage to another automobile, damage to or destruction of another's property of any description, and the loss of the use of the property damaged. It is customary to write property damage and bodily injury liability insurance together.

Bear in mind that damage to your own car is *not* covered under property damage liability.

Both property damage insurance and bodily injury insurance cover you if you are driving someone else's car. They also cover anyone driving your car with your permission. Your policies, of course, cover anyone you invite to ride with you.

Automobile Medical Payments

Under this coverage the insuring company agrees to pay, up to the limits of the policy, medical expenses resulting from accidental injury to you and your immediate family, whether in your car or someone else's or if struck while walking. Passengers and guests riding in your car are covered also. The insurance company agrees to pay all reasonable expenses incurred within one year from the date of the accident for necessary medical, surgical, X-ray, dental, ambulance, hospital, professional nursing, and even funeral services, up to the limits declared in the policy. Payment is made regardless of who is at fault or if no one is at fault. Amounts available range from $500 to $10,000 and apply to each individual injured and the proposed new Personal Automobile Policy will extend payment for up to three years from the date of the accident.

Collision Insurance

Collision insurance provides reimbursement for damage done to *your own automobile* through collision or upset, regardless of who was responsible. It doesn't cover damage done to the other person's car. That's covered by the property damage insurance you carry, assuming that the accident was your fault. Put it this way. If the accident was the other fellow's fault, his property damage insurance will pay your damages. His own collision insurance will pay his own damages. If he had no insurance, your collision insurance can cover your car, but your company has the legal right to proceed against him to recover the sums it paid to you. If the accident was your fault, your property damage insurance pays the other person, and your collision insurance pays you.

Current thinking suggests that in the year when the car is new, you should select a high deductible—$250 or $500—with collision and comprehensive insurance. This will cut the cost of your premiums and will give you reasonably lower cost protection while your car is valuable. After that, you drop collision and comprehensive insurance—bearing in mind that the amount of an uninsured casualty loss in excess of $100 is tax deductible.

Comprehensive Physical Damage Insurance

Careful owners almost always insure their automobiles against fire and theft. The annual premium amounts to only a few dollars. In fact, a comprehensive policy affording protection against malicious damage, vandalism, glass breakage, windstorm, or anything except collision and upset, in addition to fire and theft, can be purchased for $20–$100 per annum, depending on location. Reimbursement is made on the basis of the actual cash value of the vehicle when the loss or damage is incurred. In some of the larger cities, losses to companies on this type of insurance have been so large due to petty thefts and vandalism that a number of the companies have either refused to write such policies for cars that are not garaged or have introduced a $50 deductible clause. If the theft or vandal's damage amounts to less than $50, the car owner cannot collect from the insurance company. This relieves the companies of thousands of small claims which are costly to service and permits them to write the insurance less expensively. If the cost of repairing the damage is more than $50, the first $50 is paid by the insured.

Theft of Your Car

If a theft of personal property occurs when your car keys are in the hands of an authorized parking attendant, you are protected through your homeowner's insurance policy, since it is recognized that garages and parking lots require that you surrender the keys to your car, and under these circumstances your property is not considered unattended. If you leave the car unlocked and unattended elsewhere, you are not protected against the theft of personal property.

If your automobile is stolen, your comprehensive policy will compensate you for the cost of substitute transportation, whether rented car or taxi. Usually you cannot collect more than $10 a day for this, and there is an overall limit. Sometimes companies allow the local car rental rate. The theft of the car must have been reported to the police and, of course, to the insurance company. Your insurance does not cover things you leave in the car—only the car itself or its parts, such as tires or battery.

A flourishing national industry with sources in the big cities and outlets both at home and abroad is auto theft that thrives on professional specialists and efficient organization able to neutralize the manufacturer's safeguards and to fatten on owner carelessness. A million cars are stolen each year. The following excerpt explains in part the rising costs of auto insurance.

Even the thieves are able to justify their work. A veteran, very professional thief who lives in New Jersey reasons, "What I do is good for everybody. First of all, I create work. I hire men to deliver the cars, work on the numbers, paint them, give them paper, maybe drive them out of state, find customers. That's good for the economy. Then I'm helping working people to get what they could never afford otherwise. A fellow wants a Cadillac but he can't afford it; his wife wants it but she knows he can't afford it. So I get this fellow a nice car at a price he can afford; maybe I save him as much as $2,000. Now he's happy. But so is the guy who lost his car. He gets a nice new Cadillac from the insurance company—without the dents and scratches we had to take out. The Cadillac company—they're happy too because they sell another Cadillac.

"The only people who don't do so good is the insurance company. But they're so big that nobody cares *personally*. They got a budget for this sort of thing anyway. So here I am, a guy without an education, sending both my kids to college, giving my family a good home, making other people happy. Come on now—who am I really hurting?"[34]

In more than 48 states, if you buy a secondhand car now you can be reasonably sure you have a clear title to the car, since a certificate of ownership is usually filed with the motor vehicle bureau. If you are in a state that does not require title registration, not only are the premiums for theft loss on comprehensive insurance coverage higher and the percentage of stolen cars recovered much smaller, but you might have unknowingly bought a stolen car and added improvements, and then have absolutely no redress if the car is claimed by its legal

---

[34] *New York Times,* June 20, 1971.

owner. Since the car theft rings operate interstate, such a disaster can also happen within a title-registered state, as the car could have been stolen from a state that has no such law.

Protection against Uninsured Motorists

This coverage applies to bodily injuries for which an uninsured motorist, or a hit-and-run driver, is legally liable. It applies to the policyholder and his family, whether occupying their car or someone else's or while walking. It also applies to guests occupying the policyholder's car. The insuring company agrees to pay damages to injured persons to the same extent that it would if it had carried insurance on the uninsured or unknown motorist.

The advantage of protection against uninsured motorists is immediate payment from your insurance company for hospital bills and medical costs. Assuming that the uninsured motorist is at fault, it may take some time before an agreement can be reached on the amount you should receive for your injury. Furthermore, the uninsured motorist may have little or no property or money and may never be able to pay. The amount of protection you can purchase under this coverage is limited to the liability required under the financial responsibility laws of your state. The cost of this protection is so small that automobile owners who know about it are seldom without it.

No-Fault Insurance

Under our present liability or fault system, each case of property damage or personal injury must be decided on its own merits to determine whose is the legal responsibility for losses suffered. The two-year, $2 million study made by the U.S. Department of Transportation indicates that only 48 percent of seriously injured victims, including fatalities, received some reparation under the fault insurance system. One federal study indicates "that it costs $1.07 to deliver one dollar in benefits under the present system; another that consumers receive only 44 cents in recovery on the premium dollar spent. This cost-benefit ratio is drastically lower

than those of other major forms of insurance." "Fifty-five percent of those who were killed or sustained personal injury in auto accidents received no benefits to themselves or to their estates at all from the automobile tort liability system."

"Out of every personal injury liability insurance dollar, approximately 60 cents goes for operating expenses. The expenses of insurance companies account for 28 cents. Lawyer fees, claim adjustment, and other litigation costs amount to 32 cents, leaving only 40 cents for victims." The average delay between the date of the accident and the final settlement of fault insurance claims for all cases of serious injury and deaths, whether settled in or out of court, is 16 months. The delay problem is most serious in urban areas. Studies show that auto accident cases take 17 percent of the time of judges and contribute greatly to the backlog.

No fault is a term used to describe a system of automobile insurance in which the insuring company pays the policyholder for his own personal or bodily injury, instead of protection against claims made for losses he may cause to others. It does not cover property damage.

The "no-fault" basis eliminates the need to prove the "other fellow" responsible for the accident so that you can collect from him. Under the fault or tort system, if you are even partially to blame, the "contributory negligence" principle prevents you from collecting anything. Under "no fault," each injured person would be compensated partly or completely by his own insurance company, regardless of who is to blame. Under the "fault" system, the company insuring the person who is liable pays damages to the innocent party.

One of the most controversial issues concerns the right to sue for "pain and suffering." These claims over and above medical costs and economic losses form the basis for many auto accident suits and are usually responsible for the most expensive litigation. On one hand, a basic right is limited and so is a legitimate claim for those whose expenses and injuries go beyond those provided for by no fault. On the other hand, litigation is the avenue through which minor injuries have become inflated claims that have been responsible for high insur-

"The Bureau of Labor Statistics reports that 10% of the people are on unemployment, 30% are on welfare and the rest are on tranquilizers."

Reprinted by permission *The Wall Street Journal*

ance premiums. The American Trial Lawyers Association would preserve the right of all "innocent parties" to sue. It also favors a low dollar limitation, if there is to be one, on lawsuits. Advocates of no fault support limiting liability suits for damages to a relatively few most serious cases.

Major variations among the states involve dollar limits on medical and hospital expenses (unlimited in some states), funeral or burial expenses, lost income from earnings, and the amount to be paid a person hired to perform essential services that an injured non-income-producer, such as a housewife, is unable to perform, as well as conditions governing the right to sue, which usually include death, serious injury, and a point at which medical expenses reach a certain amount. Most no-fault laws emphasize prompt payment of claims—usually within 30 days and with a penalty of interest if they are unpaid after that.

A nationwide poll has found that three out of four motorists favor no-fault auto insurance. A Department of Transportation survey of no-fault insurance in 16 states concluded that under no fault:

Benefits are more adequate and equitable.
Payments are more prompt.

There have been fewer court cases.
The cost efficiency of administering auto insurance benefits has improved.

The expected decrease in premiums has not occurred. Instead, inflation has pushed premiums higher—with the blame placed on sharply increasing costs of medical care and auto repair. Federal no-fault legislation would require all states to meet minimum federal plans. In any state that did not, a plan mandated by the federal government would go into effect.

Conclusion

Inflation is personal. Not only are you going to look for ways to make more money, but you must make your choice of where you spend what you have. The care used in that decision is the heart of budgeting. We all must eat, but even in that basic part of a budget, there is wide individual choice in quality, quantity, and source that will determine what proportion of your budget is available for other needs. For you—it could be less food, more car. For another, the choice might be more schooling, less housing. This chapter is about informed choices.

SUGGESTED READINGS

American Automobile Association. *Your Driving Costs.* Obtainable from the Association at 8111 Gatehouse Road, Falls Church, VA 22042; latest annual edition available free.

American Council on Consumer Interests. *Journal of Consumer Affairs.* Official publication of the council, published semiannually by the University of Wisconsin Press.

Bohn, Robert F. *A Budget Book and Much More.* Provo, Utah: Brigham Young University, 1978.

Consumer Expenditure Patterns. Part 1 of two part decennial study, New York: Conference Board, 1978.

Consumers Union. *The Buying Guide—Consumer Reports.* A sample copy of the latest monthly *Consumer Report* will be sent on request by Consumers Union, 256 Washington St., Mount Vernon, NY 10550.

———. *Managing Your Auto Insurance*. Mount Vernon, NY: Consumers Union, June–July 1977.

Cross, Jennifer. *The Supermarket Trap—The Consumer and the Food Industry*. Bloomington: Indiana University Press, 1976.

Ford Motor Company. *Car Buying Made Easier*. Annual edition free by writing to Ford Motor Company, Dearborn, MI 48121.

Insurance Information Institute. *Family Guide to Property and Liability Insurance*. New York, latest edition. A free copy may be obtained by writing to the Institute at 110 Williams St., New York, NY 10038.

Money Management Institute—Household Finance Corporation. Library of 12 booklets on personal and family finance. Address: Prudential Plaza, Chicago, IL 60601; $3.50 per set or 35 cents each.

U.S. Department of Agriculture. *Family Economics Review*. Published quarterly by the Consumer and Food Economic Research Division. A free sample copy may be obtained by writing to Agricultural Research Service, U.S. Department of Agriculture, Hyattsville, MD 20782.

———. *A Guide to Budgeting for the Family*. Home and Garden Bull. no. 108. May be obtained from the Superintendent of Documents, U.S. Government Printing Office, Washington, D.C. 20402.

———. *Helping Families Manage Their Finances*. Home Economics Research Report no. 21. May be obtained from the Superintendent of Documents, U.S. Government Printing Office, Washington, D.C. 20402.

U.S. Office of Consumer Affairs. *A Consumer's Shopping List of Inflation-Fighting Ideas*. Washington, D.C., 1978. A free copy may be obtained from Information Center, Dept. 625G, Pueblo, CO 81009.

CASE PROBLEMS

1 Clara and Edward Fedang have been married six years. They have two children, ages three and five. Ed, an engineer in a large New York City architectural construction firm, earns $18,040 after taxes. Clara's father, who died some 15 years ago, left her an estate with a yearly income of $5,000 after taxes.

Clara and Ed had lived within their yearly income without budgeting, but they had not increased their savings in the last two years. This past winter they enrolled in an adult education course in personal finance. An assignment for one class was to develop a family budget plan. What should their budget include, both on an annual and on a monthly basis?

2 Sue Miller, age 22, has just graduated from a midwestern college. She has accepted a teaching position, to begin in September, in a small town about 50 miles from her home. After taxes and other deductions her pay is to be $10,500 a year.

Sue is planning to share an apartment with another teacher; her share of the rent would be $95 a month, but she is not sure how much food will cost. During her senior year, it was necessary for Sue to borrow $350 (at 6 percent interest) from her college. According to the terms of the loan, the money should be paid back a year after her graduation date. Because her mother recently underwent an operation, Sue must remain at home during the summer and cannot take a summer job.

As a teacher, Sue must buy clothes she did not need as a college student. She is looking forward to buying a car as soon as possible, so that she can make weekend trips home. Being an avid golf enthusiast, she would like to join the local golf club.

How should she budget her income to accomplish what she wants to do?

3 Bob and Janet Atkins have been married for four months. Bob has been employed for a year as an engineering salesman, and Janet has just started to teach, following her graduation from college. Their combined income after taxes is $18,000, and their savings account contains $800. Because of the city's excellent transportation system, Bob did not need a car previously, but he now needs one for periodic sales trips.

How should the Atkins plan the purchasing and financing of their car, keeping the family budget in mind?

4 Sally Pinter, a $9,600-a-year 23-year-old systems control analyst, goes on a weekly evening spending spree. Her husband, Walter, earns

$19,000 as an architect, and as long as cash is paid, he approves. Their joint income paid for their first home, their three-week vacation, and their two color TV sets. They have no insurance, and neither believes in saving very much, because after all they are young and healthy and childless. They scorn a budget or any planning because as long as they do not use credit cards, they feel that they control their financial situation. Discuss and evaluate the pros and cons of this approach.

5 Jonathan West is in his third year at college. For the first time he cannot count on family financing, because severe illness is limiting his parents income. He cannot take a part-time job because he wants to use his spare time to be helpful at home. He is afraid to mortgage his future by borrowing from a bank and facing years of debt, and so he decided to manage carefully on his savings of $7,300. How should he budget to manage all his expenses for this year?

Consumer Rip-Offs and Protection

A sucker is born every minute.

P. T. BARNUM

You can fool some of the people all of the time and all of the people some of the time, but you cannot fool all of the people all of the time.

ABRAHAM LINCOLN

The Consumer

Consumers are of all varieties. There are those who need to stretch food stamps and those who can buy a bottle of wine at auction for $3,816. There are consumers who have so little that they need everything. There must even be a consumer who has everything, because a catalog can offer for sale "the most unredeemably useless product that could possibly exist" and even a "double non-value" size for $8 + $1.25 for postage. There are even consumers who will buy a product called a "solar clothes dryer" anticipating a new gadget of superior design, but actually is only a box decorated with a smiling sun. Inside the box are 15 feet of rope and 15 clothes pins.

Each extreme and all the vast number in between resent not getting their money's worth. However, the old Latin expression *caveat emptor*—"let the buyer beware"—shows that rip-offs have been going on for a long time. In this age of consumerism, some progress has been made to achieve fair value. So much more is needed, a task made more difficult

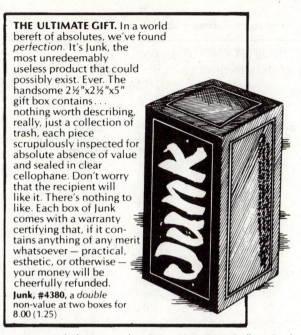

THE ULTIMATE GIFT. In a world bereft of absolutes, we've found *perfection.* It's Junk, the most unredeemably useless product that could possibly exist. Ever. The handsome 2½"x2½"x5" gift box contains... nothing worth describing, really, just a collection of trash, each piece scrupulously inspected for absolute absence of value and sealed in clear cellophane. Don't worry that the recipient will like it. There's nothing to like. Each box of Junk comes with a warranty certifying that, if it contains anything of any merit whatsoever — practical, esthetic, or otherwise — your money will be cheerfully refunded. **Junk, #4380,** a *double* non-value at two boxes for 8.00 (1.25).

Source: Kaleidoscope catalog, Spring 1977, 2201 Faulkner Road N.E., Atlanta, GA 30324.

by the sad reality that 30 percent of adult Americans are "functionally illiterate," according to a University of Texas report funded by the U.S. Office of Education. If it's hard to make change easily, or to understand the significance of the labels required on clothes, or to use unit pricing at the market, or to read an installment contract, how can a sensible consumer judgment be made?

According to one study, there are four consumer types: "the socially integrated consumer, who gives advice and seeks advice from others; the socially isolated consumer, who is just the opposite; the socially dependent consumer, who seeks information but doesn't give advice; and his opposite number, the socially independent consumer."[1] Do you recognize yourself? Or perhaps the distinctions are artificial and the average consumer is all four at different times.

---

[1] *New York Times,* July 26, 1977, quoting from a market researcher whose "Consumer Profiles," meant for marketing companies, are based on a mail sampling of 8,000 that uses the consumer mail panel of National Family Opinions, an Ohio-based opinion poll company.

Consumers go through stages when making a buying decision—awareness, interest, evaluation, and trial. Consumer communication channels which influence that decision can be divided into two groups, those initiated by the marketer (advertising in the media, sales promotion, product publicity, and paid testimonials) and those not initiated by the marketer—such as word of mouth and neutral sources as *Consumer Reports* and comparative shopping.

The Angry Consumer

The rising record of complaints—by letter and phone to business, consumer groups, and federal and state governments—testifies to the increasing outrage felt by consumers. The Office of Consumer Affairs reports that complaints average over 100 a day—30,000 a year. The Consumer Product Safety Commission received 60,000 written complaints last year and 95,000 calls on its "hot line." The Federal Trade Commission and the Food and Drug Administration report a similar number of complaints.

Table 4–1 indicates which industries arouse the most ire. Interestingly, the general public finds banks satisfactory, telephone companies not the most remiss, and have much less interest in nuclear power plants than do consumer activists, who rate all three among the top industries to which attention should be paid. The contrast is especially noticeable in the case of electric utility companies.

A joint study by Ralph Nader's Center for the Study of Responsive Law and Call for Action, a private volunteer organization that operates an action and referral service in 40 cities, states that consumers have problems with one out of four of their purchases and that they report only one third of their problems.

According to the study, those with the lowest incomes saw problems less often than did those with higher incomes and tended to complain less often. Buyers complained most often about expensive items or about items bought on credit and not completely paid for. On inexpensive products consumers merely switch brands. The recommen-

TABLE 4–1
Industries Which Should Receive the Most Attention from the Consumer Movement

Q.22: Which of these industies (HAND RESPONDENT CARD) do you think the consumer movement should give most of its attention to in the future?

	Total Public	Consumer Activist	Government Consumer Affairs	Non-Insurance Regulator	Insurance Regulator	Senior Business Manager	Business Consumer Affairs
				Leaders			
(Sample size:)	(1510)	(217)	(85)	(32)	(33)	(99)	(53)
	%	%	%	%	%	%	%
Food manufacturers	45	64	45	44	21	25	26
Hospitals	44	53	47	69	58	43	40
The medical profession	42	63	58	72	61	39	45
Oil industry	39	65	52	53	39	24	34
Car manufacturers	38	57	48	59	42	19	28
Electric utility companies	37	73	48	56	21	12	26
Pharmaceutical & drug companies	34	56	35	44	30	16	30
Garages and auto mechanics	32	44	60	69	45	44	45
Food stores and supermarkets	29	32	22	16	6	8	15
The advertising industry	28	63	66	41	30	25	28
Homeowners and auto insurance	28	37	28	34	39	17	28
Home building industry	25	38	39	41	15	31	47
Credit loan companies	25	42	45	31	52	29	40
Telephone companies	24	44	34	19	21	6	17
Used car dealers	22	31	54	47	24	26	30
The legal profession	22	39	52	41	52	34	47
Nuclear power plants	19	61	33	22	30	5	19
Mail-order houses	16	23	42	25	12	20	34
Life insurance	16	28	21	25	27	13	11
Electrical appliance manufacturers	16	19	22	9	6	10	11
Department stores	15	11	18	6	6	4	8
Real estate brokers	13	22	28	22	15	13	9
Banks	10	41	22	28	18	5	21
Small shopkeepers	9	8	13	9	9	2	13
Airlines	8	13	16	16	9	2	9
None	1	—	—	—	3	7	4
Not sure	6	—	—	—	3	1	—

Source: *Consumerism at the Crossroads,* Sentry Insurance.

dation of this study may be appropriate, but it will not appeal to the individual consumer. The study suggested that government consumer complaint agencies be aware that they get relatively few complaints and that they should concentrate on general solutions to problems rather than on solving individual complaints.

Rip-Offs

Problems with cars—old and new—and their repair draw the most fire. Frustrations are increased by the fact that the cost of auto insurance has risen an average of 110 percent over the last ten years.

Since cars were discussed in detail in the last

chapter, it would seem adequate to point out that unfortunately this rip-off is not new. Back in 1941, the *Reader's Digest* took a car with a deliberately disconnected coil wire into several hundred garages across the country and found that 63 percent charged for unneeded parts and repairs. Familiar?[2]

The five categories of goods and services that cause the most unhappiness are car repairs, appliance repairs (including the repair of television sets), mail-order items, housing repairs, and toys.

Appliance Repairs

An FTC study compared the relative effectiveness of the procedures used by Washington, D.C., New Orleans, and San Francisco in regulating TV repairs. New TV sets that worked perfectly, except for a single burned-out bulb, were repaired in 20 shops in each city. In Washington, D.C., which had no licensing system, 50 percent of the shops engaged in fraud. The same percentage of fraud prevailed in New Orleans, where a license is required to open a TV repair shop. But in San Francisco, where undercover techniques are constantly used to discover fraud, only 20 percent of the shops were dishonest. In New York City, in a random test of 21 repair shops undertaken by the Consumer Affairs commissioner, 15 percent of the shops gave estimates ranging from $10 to $73.19 to fix sets that experts had predetermined should cost less to repair than a service charge of $15. The $73.19 charge, the commissioner's office said, was for a set with an unplugged cable that simply needed to be reinserted. But the shop's estimate also included two new tubes and renovation of the tuner.

A recent test on air conditioner repairs followed the same scenario. An air conditioner in perfect working order, but with one interior wire deliberately disconnected so that the fan worked but there was no cooling, was taken to 11 repair shops. Three

found the wire, connected it, and charged nothing—or a reasonable service fee. The others, whose prices ranged up to $98, found that the following assorted repairs were needed: gas repair, repair of leak on condenser discharge, replacement of the fan motor, repair of "cracked" tubing leading to the compressor. In one case, the mechanic destroyed the air conditioner by miswiring it and burning it out and the replaced parts that were returned on request were not from the machine that had been brought in to be repaired.

> Major Appliances' Life Expectancies. The U.S. Department of Agriculture has made the following estimates: freezers—20 years; refrigerators—15; gas ranges—13; electric ranges—12; dishwashers—11; automatic clothes washers—11; gas clothes dryers—13; electric clothes dryers—14; black-and-white television sets—11; and color television sets—12. The Federal Supply Service has estimated the life of room air conditioners as seven years, and gas or electric water heaters as ten years.
>
> Source: *Consumer Newsweekly,* July 3, 1978, p. 3.

Bait and Switch

The following three samples of this age-old rip-off are from three different industries.

In testimony before the FTC that led to a consent agreement with Sears, Roebuck & Co., a former salesman described how he would do anything to avoid selling the advertised sale item, because more expensive ones earned a higher commission. He did everything from using the wrong needle on a sewing machine and the wrong brush in a vacuum cleaner to telling the customer that the sale item was not in stock and would take eight weeks for delivery—all in order to switch the customer to a higher priced item—after the sale price had baited him to come in.

Ironically, the same salesman revealed that when he had bought an inexpensive washing machine, it rattled and shook. When the Sears repairman told him that cheap machines vibrate, the

---

[2] Of probable help with the problem is the Transportation Department booklet *Consumer Problems with Auto Repair* (October 1978)—which lists car repair tips, repair laws, and services available in some areas. For a free copy, send postcard to Consumer Information Center, Dept. 704F, Pueblo CO 81009.

salesman bought a better model. Only then did he learn that the shipping bolts had deliberately not been removed from the first machine—the sale machine—so that he would buy a better one.[3]

The Civil Aeronautics Board is investigating whether airlines have attracted customers by advertising discount rates and then since there was limited seating for such special fares, had reservation personnel try to sell fares at the regular rate. Because of complaints, staff members of the board may monitor the airlines by phoning for reservations, posing as customers.

The CAB Office of Consumer Advocate receives thousands of complaints yearly from passengers who have been upset by equipment switching, lost baggage, late flights, confusion over flights, prices, insolvency of tour operators, last-minute cancellations, misinformation, and, most especially, overbooking. Airlines claim that they deliberately overbook on a large scale to compensate for travelers who neither cancel nor keep their reservations.

Both the CAB and the FTC are working on ways to ensure that those promising air travel brochures become real through regulation.[4]

Those who have the facilities to freeze and keep large quantities of meat can take advantage of bulk purchases and save money. But not if the "bait and switch" tactic is used. The FTC filed suit in the U.S. District Court for Colorado against a multistate freezer meat company which according to the charges, advertised attractive low prices to lure customers into their stores where they were switched to higher priced meat.[5] Their advertising also failed to disclose that the advertised meat was untrimmed and would weigh considerably less after trimming. Also sometimes stated and sometimes implied, was the idea that the meat was "prime" or "choice" even though some of the meat was either ungraded or graded less than prime or choice.

Funerals

The saddest rip-off of all takes advantage of the vulnerability of mourners in their weakest moments. In the guise of "grief counseling," funeral directors manipulate families into more expense than they want or need to incur by suggesting that a concern for price shows a lack of respect or affection for the deceased. The FTC, which has been studying the funeral industry for three years and has held 45,000 pages of hearings preparatory to issuing regulations, has found:

1. Misstatements about public health requirements on the need for embalming.
2. Requiring the purchase of coffins to be burned during cremation.
3. Offering funerals as a package and thus hiding individual costs. Even in states such as New York, where itemizing is required, critics say that the same services can be charged for more than once by listing them in overlapping ways.
4. Displaying lower priced coffins in hideous colors or appealing to family pride in order to encourage the purchase of higher priced coffins.

The FTC says that "Americans buy about 2 million funerals a year at an average cost of $2,000, including burial and related expenses. It estimates that adoption of its recommended trade rule could produce savings of up to $1,000 a funeral."[6]

Misleading Advertising

Complaints about questionable advertising practices range from misrepresentation to outright untruth.

The familiar celebrity endorsements of products may have started to decline, thanks to an FTC agreement with a well-known singer. The FTC held that an endorser must verify claims about the product before the first commercial goes on the air—or appears in print—or else risk FTC action. In this case, the singer agreed to contribute to any restitution that the manufacturer had to make for false

[3] *New York Times,* November 3, 1976.

[4] See "Package Tour Bargains That Backfire," *Money,* June 1978, for a number of suggestions for a "travelers' advisory."

[5] F.T.C. News Summary, December 8, 1978.

[6] *New York Times,* June 19, 1978.

advertising. "The endorser may profit from a false advertisement just as much as the manufacturer," said the director of the FTC's Bureau of Consumer Protection, "and thus it isn't unreasonable to obligate him to ascertain the truthfulness of the claims he is paid to make."[7]

A federal judge ordered changes in a TV taste comparison commercial for fried chicken. He ordered the company to remove the statement that the tests were supervised by an independent concern, when, in fact, they were supervised by the company's advertising agency. The lawyer for the company, admitting that the tests weren't backed by scientific evidence, said that the commercials were "puffery." "The public doesn't take advertising so seriously," he said.

Gargle with Listerine?   "Tests made over a 12-year period proved that people who gargled with Listerine full strength twice a day, every day, had fewer colds and milder colds than those who did not."

> According to the FTC's documents, the 12-year tests were conducted during the winters of 1930 to 1942 on two groups of people—those who gargled with Listerine and those who did not. Warner-Lambert conducted the Listerine research on its own factory employees. Employees were allowed to choose which group they would be in. Naturally, the FTC's experts said, those who believed in gargling joined the Listerine group, while those who did not remained nongarglers.
>
> After an FTC complaint, the claims on the Listerine label were softened. "For Bad Breath, Colds and Resultant Sore Throats" became "For Relief of Colds Symptoms and Minor Sore Throats Due to Colds."
>
> Experts also told the FTC that although Listerine does kill germs "by millions on contact," it also leaves millions of other germs still alive.
>
> 93 years after Listerine was first marketed, the FTC charged that claims that the product would cure, prevent, or relieve colds and sore throats and their symptoms were false. After

lengthy hearings, the agency concluded that the company should not only be barred from advertising such claims in the future but required to correct false beliefs created by past advertising. Listerine carried the case to the courts.

A U.S. circuit court of appeal panel ruled that the First Amendment does not prevent the Federal Trade Commission from requiring Warner-Lambert to run corrective ads for Listerine. The FTC order requires that Warner-Lambert state in $10 million worth of ads that "Listerine will not help prevent colds or sore throats or lessen their severity."

The Supreme Court declined to review the case, thus upholding the FTC ruling.[8]

Another old standby, Anacin, unless it wins its appeal against the order of an FTC administrative judge, will have to spend large sums in advertising that it does *not* reduce tension, even though back in 1973 it had stopped making this claim. A 1978 decision held that the "image of Anacin as a tension reliever persisted and the corrective advertising was necessary to change that image." The company was also ordered to disclose in its ads that the product contained aspirin.

TV advertising was found to be "seriously misleading" by a larger percentage (82 percent) than found newspaper or magazine advertising misleading (78 percent) in a study that questioned the general public separately from persons who might be labeled "activist." A harder line was taken toward false or misleading advertisers by the general public than by activists. On the question of preventing advertisers who had been proved to have used false or misleading advertising from advertising for a time, 78 percent of the general public approved, but only 59 percent of the activists. Almost 95 percent of the general public favored corrective advertising by the companies involved.[9]

---

[7] *New York Times,* May 12, 1978.

[8] Summarized from F.T.C. reports.

[9] For an inside picture of how advertising is tailored to the viewer, see the Consumer Survival Kit *New! Improved! and Other Myths: A Look at Advertising,* Maryland Center for Public Broadcasting, Owings Mills, MD 21117.

Mail Fraud

One of the earliest mail frauds involved a guaranteed insect killer. A small advertisement announced:

> New and Different Insect Killer
> Send $1 plus postage
> Results Guaranteed

When you received your package, you found inside two small blocks of wood, with a single paragraph of printed instructions. "Place and hold or pin insect firmly to lower block. Place upper block over insect, lower block and apply pressure. Results Guaranteed."

The U.S. Postal Service is being flooded by thousands of complaints about goods ordered through the mails and not delivered, about promotional schemes that persuade you to send money to make more money and then never happen, or to buy land or gems that will triple in value overnight and turn out to be worthless. It has only 205 inspectors assigned to investigate criminal fraud. Only five lawyers handle the civil violation workload. Even 2,000 arrests and 1,600 convictions are just the tip of the iceberg.

The FTC has begun an investigation into comic book advertising. Big money is at stake. To attract a market of almost 16 million readers between 5 and 17, advertisers pay $12,000 or more a page. Much of the comic and pulp magazine ads, according to the attorney general's office in New York, "is a mixture of self power, get rich quick and miracle weight reduction claims that result in multi million dollar incomes for the promotors. Although the sophisticated reader might not be persuaded, the law says it's to be judged by the audience it is directed at."

One disappointed purchaser ordered 100 little dolls, for $3 plus 50 cents postage and handling charges, from the 100 Doll Co. in East Orange, New Jersey. The dolls had been offered in a Jughead comic book ad which described them as expensively molded in true dimension in genuine styrene and synthetic rubber. The 98 yellow plastic figures 1½ inches high, barely three-dimensional, with hard-to-see features and costumes, bore little resemblance to the advertised details.

Diet remedies are a mail-order regular. A $6.95 purchase from the Ritz Marketing Co., Inc., of Willow Springs, Illinois, of a 30-day supply of Black Beauty diet aid capsules that had been advertised in *Cosmopolitan* magazine brought a preparation containing an appetite suppressant and 250 milligrams of caffeine per tablet—the equivalent of 2½ cups of coffee.

A promoter for the *Ladies' Home Journal* sent out three separate mailings for subscriptions, each time offering the magazine for a bargain rate below a *different* regular annual rate. Depending on which mailing you received, the regular rate was stated as $12.99, $14.97, or $14.99 and the bargain offer was $6.99, $7.97, or $9.99—all of which were higher than the legitimate rate of $4.97 for a year's subscription.

Want to be a Nashville singer or composer? Plan to set poems to music? Cut a record? Unscrupulous operators ripping off aspiring musicians are responsible for the largest number of inquiries to the Nashville/Middle Tennessee Better Business Bureau. The promises of a variety of promotional services which may cost from $3,000–$5,000 lure ambitious musicians by praising their talent and hinting at future riches. A recent F.B.I. investigation of these operators has resulted in an indictment of three people in one company on thirteen counts of mail and wire fraud. More indictments are expected.[10]

The avalanche of mail-order catalogs now descending on homes indicates how lucrative this business has become. The catalogs offer less hassle than personal shopping, large variety, and often less cost because of the lower overhead since the mail-order houses do not need the personnel, displays, or inventory on hand of the retail stores. The legitimate mail-order houses run the gamut.

---

[10] *Consumer News,* December 1, 1978, U.S. Office of Consumer Affairs. You may wish to write for the Music Industry Information Panel's free booklet "What You Should Know about Making a Record in Nashville," available from the Tennessee Department of Consumer Affairs, P.O. Box 40627, Melrose Station, Nashville, TN 37204.

Some offer a large choice of medium-priced, different gadgety objects; others specialize in boating, athletic, or period items; and a few sell unique and very expensive objects. All honor the money back guarantee.

But then so do the promoters, because as an attorney in the Consumer Protection Office of the U.S. Postal Service said, "The failure to give refunds when promised is the quickest way to get a criminal case against you."

The lowest form of mail fraud is that of a commercial company distributing an advertisement on an IBM card in an official-looking envelope on which the term *medicare* appears, implying that the insurance benefits offered in addition to those under the government program are in some way endorsed or approved by the government.

Firms that care about their reputation will do something about a nondelivery if you threaten to notify the postal authorities. The con artist in for a fast dollar will disappear and turn up again in a different guise. Your own guideline should be that if an offer looks too good to be true—don't get involved.

Eyeglasses

A survey conducted by the California Citizen Action Group with the assistance of an FTC grant learned how little the public knew about eyeglasses after asking these questions:

> Lenses for eyeglasses are usually ground to each customer's prescription by persons working in the offices of individual opticians or optometrists. True or False?
>
> It takes at least half a day to prepare and fit lenses to a set of frames. True or False?
>
> Factors such as the strength of correction of a pair of lenses and the quality of the plastic used in them play a large part in determining their cost. True or False?

If you had answered yes, you would have been wrong each time. According to the executive director of the American Optometric Association, single-vision lenses, generally speaking, are mass-pro-

duced by a small number of manufacturers. Most lens cutting is done in large regional or national laboratories that service local opticians. Higher prices are caused by fitting lenses into particular frames—and not by the strength of the prescription or the quality of the plastic. The cost of glasses is related to the location of the retail store and the cost of the frames. The California group found that most glasses can be fitted to the frames in 30 minutes. An FTC staff report found that the average wholesale price of a lens delivered by the manufacturer to a regional laboratory was $3 and from the laboratory to an individual optician or optometrist was under $10.

Witnesses to hearings of the Senate Select Committee on Small Business testified that in New York City, surveys showed that prices of glasses in six neighborhoods varied by as much as 250 percent and that variations ran as high as 300 percent in Ohio and as high as 350 percent in New Jersey.

As a result of hearings, the FTC concluded that it is the lack of information on cost and availability that raises the prices of eyeglasses 25 percent for the consumer, and it favors removing the restrictions on advertising—a move opposed by the state licensing boards.

Removing Professional Restrictions

Most states have licensing boards that regulate professions. It is estimated that the number exceeds 1,500. Illinois, for example, has 32 boards that regulate 100 professions. In almost every state, the members of these boards belong to the profession. Critics charge that the restrictions imposed by these boards tend to raise prices—that the boards are rarely consumer oriented and are casual about consumer complaints. California has broken with the usual practice of self-regulation by the professions, and based on a 1976 law a majority of nonprofessionals have been appointed to most of its 38 boards. The immediate result has been to liberalize regulations and increase competition. In addition, 29 states now have public members on one or more licensing boards. A combination of consumer groups and the state of Maryland is developing a model training program to teach Maryland consumers to be effective representatives on state licensing boards.

The cost of professional services are significantly higher than they would be under effective competition. Entry has been restricted by state regulation and by self regulating boards and agencies drawn from within the professions. One detects a stirring over the last five years to loosen or eliminate the restrictions, increase the supply of professionals, and allow them to compete through advertising.

There have been a series of rulings and consent decrees that have removed restrictions on advertising by lawyers, druggists, and engineers. These decisions have been based on the thinking that, under the First Amendment, the public has a right to commercial information.

Even the sacrosanct medical profession may have to allow advertising of doctors' services and fees if the FTC decision forcing the American Medical Association to "cease and desist" from prohibiting such advertising by physicians is upheld. It is expected that the A.M.A. and its allied societies will appeal to the Supreme Court. The move against the A.M.A. rests upon the anti-trust laws, which can modify or eliminate purely private restrictions.

Land Fraud

The land rush has reached an almost ludicrous pitch. In some areas there are more lots on the market than any conceivable housing demand can justify. New Mexico officials estimate that more than one million acres of the state have been laid out in small lot subdivisions—enough to house eight times the present population if the land was actually developed.

Informed buyers can now avoid buying swampland or cliffs. The federal law that set up the Office of Interstate Land Sales Registration in the U.S. Department of Housing and Urban Development requires companies selling land to register with HUD and give each customer a factual property report on developments, under threat of criminal penal-

ties. A property report similar to a securities prospectus must go to a buyer before sale. There, the buyer will find information on such things as water and sewer availability, existence of liens on the property, number of houses in the development currently occupied, and the type of title the buyer will receive. A seller who fulfills HUD requirements and provides a property report is in the clear, even if the property is worthless. "If you designate the property for what it is," says the head of HUD's Office of Interstate Land Sales Registration, "you can sell it."

New ground was broken and new records set when the Great Western United Corporation agreed to refund almost $4 million to some 14,000 land investors.

The agreement, negotiated by the FTC, reflected complaints by consumers that the company had erroneously told them that the value of the land was sure to increase and that adequate water was available. Not only will a $50,000 penalty be paid, but the company will have to include a statement in all future advertisements, warning that the value of the land in these development projects, is uncertain and telling prospective purchasers, "Do not count on an increase in value."

Home-Related Rip-Offs

Steadily increasing are the complaints about defects in new houses and about problems in repairing older ones. The FTC and one of the nation's largest home builders reached a consent agreement after complaints had been made that the firm had misrepresented the availability of community facilities and schools, the tax burden, and the expected closing costs. In addition, charges were made that the firm did not honor its warranties and failed to make repairs and replacements as promised.

The consent agreement required that the purchasers receive a warranty through HOW (the industry's Home Owners Warranty Program). This seemed to indicate that the industry's promise would be more substantial than the builder's.

Each of the additional requirements in the consent agreement highlights the rip-offs and negative situations that purchasers faced even in dealing with a respected builder.

1. Repairs must be made in a timely and workmanlike manner, and disputes must be settled by arbitration.
2. Changes in specifications connot be made after the plans are filed with the Department of Housing and Urban Development or the Veterans Administration.
3. A house that has major construction defects or does not meet industry standards cannot be sold without taking steps to repair or replace the defective items or to pay the cost of repair.

Solar Schemes

Florida was one of ten states selected by the Department of Housing and Urban Development to participate in a pilot project on the use of solar energy. The state was given 1,650 grants of $400 each to pass on to homeowners who would instal solar-heated water tanks at an average estimated cost of $1,200. Even before the money arrived and could be allocated on a random basis by computer, homeowners received letters from businesses stating that they had signed up with the federal government and could get rebates for their customers.

In Iowa, a firm sold solar collectors for about $250, advertising that two of them would save 20–30 percent on heating costs in an average house. An Iowa court stopped the firm from making such claims and awarded refunds to those who had bought the solar collectors because of the ads.

Consumer Complaints

There are a number of problems which worry consumers greatly. Their primary concerns are the high price of many products, the high cost of medical and hospital care, the poor quality of products, and the failure of many products to live up to their advertising. See Table 4–2 for other important problems that were voiced in the consumer study done for Sentry Insurance.

The Office of Consumer Affairs publishes an annual list of the top 20 consumer complaints it receives—the latest of these lists is reprinted in Table 4–3. Of special interest to the concerned consumer is the comment by the OCA that the top 20 complaints have remained relatively constant—a sad commentary on the lack of progress.[11]

How to Complain

You can start at the bottom—or at the top. Starting at the top may bring faster results. A first possibility is a letter to the *president* of the corporation *by name*. The Standard & Poor's Directory of Corporations, which is to be found in most libraries, will give you the president's name. A second possibility is a letter or phone call to the consumer affairs director of the company involved, providing precise details.

The local Better Business Bureau or the local city, county, or state consumer affairs agency is a possible next step. If satisfaction is still lacking, various federal agencies might help.[12] An independent private agency, Technical Assistance Research Programs Inc., did a follow up assessment on how well 22 federal agencies handled consumer complaints since the original survey of the same agencies in 1975–76. The report was mixed—dramatic improvement in some agencies, "but over a third of the agencies were found to lag significantly in some or many aspects of effective and efficient consumer handling."[13] The consumer advocate of the U.S. Postal Service (for mail frauds) and the consumer advocate of the Civil Aeronautics Board (for airline complaints) are two of the busiest offices.

Under the guidance of the federal Office of Con-

[11] Office of Consumer Affairs, Department of Health, Education, and Welfare, Washington, D.C., March 15, 1978.

[12] See appendix at the end of this chapter for a directory of federal consumer offices. Also, for a free copy of toll-free telephone numbers, send a preaddressed stamped envelope to Ralph Nader—Toll-Free Hotlines, P.O. 19404, Washington, D.C. 20036.

[13] *Consumer News,* U.S. Office of Consumer Affairs, December 1, 1978.

TABLE 4–2
Problems Which Worry Consumers

(Sample size = 1,510)	A Great Deal %	Some- what %	A Little Bit %	Not At All %	Not Sure %
The high prices of many products	77	17	5	1	*
The high cost of medical and hospital care	69	15	6	8	1
The poor quality of many products	48	33	13	6	*
The failure of many companies to live up to claims made in their advertising	44	32	16	7	1
The poor quality of after-sales service and repairs	38	31	14	15	2
The feeling that many manufacturers don't care about you	36	32	19	12	1
Too many products breaking or going wrong soon after you bring them home	35	29	20	15	1
Misleading packaging or labeling	34	29	20	15	2
Not being able to afford adequate health insurance	32	23	12	31	1
The feeling that it is a waste of time to complain about consumer problems because nothing substantial will be achieved	32	27	20	19	2
Not being able to get adequate insurance coverage against an accident or loss	30	23	14	30	3
Inadequate guarantees or warranties	30	31	17	21	2
Failure of companies to handle complaints properly	29	31	19	19	2
Too many products which are dangerous	26	27	22	22	2
The absence of reliable information about different products and services	26	33	22	18	2
Difficulty in getting insurance claims settled fairly	23	19	15	39	4
Not knowing what to do if something is wrong with a product you have bought	21	28	20	30	1
Difficulty in getting insurance claims paid promptly	20	20	17	39	4
The difficulty of choosing between so many products	11	23	25	41	1

Note: Totals may not add to 100% because of rounding.

Source: *Consumerism at the Crossroads,* Sentry Insurance.

sumer Affairs, various industries have organized consumer panels for the resolution of complaints. These include FICAP (Furniture Industry Consumer Action Panel), MACAP (major appliances), CRICAP (carpeting), and AUTOCAP (automobiles).

Various TV and radio programs, as well as a few specialized columns in the newspapers, publicize "action" or "help" centers that respond to letters or phone calls from the public. The results are mixed. If the problem comes from red tape

Major Appliance Consumer Action Panel. MACAP has succeeded in bringing to resolution 84 percent of the more than 26,000 individual consumer appliance complaints addressed to it since its inception in 1970. Of these only about 9 percent were found to be unjustified or unsubstantiated. The vast majority were legitimate appliance problems and were resolved.

Source: MACAP news release, May 22, 1978.

TABLE 4–3

Top 20 complaints

The **Office of Consumer Affairs** (OCA) has compiled a list of the top 20 consumer complaints it received in 1977. The top 20 complaints have remained relatively constant with minor fluctuations over the past 4 years, with only one new complaint making the top 20 in 1977—the "Watches/Clocks" category. Complaints in this area centered on the problems of service, especially when a timepiece has been sent to the manufacturer for repair. Also, many consumers seem to be having trouble with the LED watches.

"Automobile Tires" climbed from 12th place in 1976 to 10th place in 1977, possibly because many new car buyers did not recieve a spare tire with their cars (as a result of a rubber strike in 1976). In addition, there has been an increase in the number of complaints about the quality of original equipment tires.

Here is the 1977 list by rank, category and percentage of total complaints received in each category:*

RANK	CATEGORY	% OF TOTAL
1	Automobiles	21.70
2	Mail order	9.65
3	Business practices	4.98
4	Credit	3.73
5	Appliances	3.38
6	Housing/real estate	2.54
7	Insurance	2.17
8	Food	2.04
9	Travel	2.01
10	Auto tires	1.69
11	Magazines	1.67
12	Advertising	1.64
13	Television/radio	1.61
14	Watches/clocks	1.31
15	Mobile homes/rec. veh.	1.05
16	Utilities	1.01
17	Home repairs	0.09
18	Household	0.08
19	Movers	0.07
20	Medical/dental	0.07

* OCA stresses that it uses these categories in the broadest of terms. OCA is in the process of revising its product classification code to more accurately reflect complaint data received by the office.

Source: *Consumer News,* Department of Health, Education, and Welfare, 1978.

or a computer, it's easy. These centers, often get action on a delayed social security check. But understaffed as they are, most of them respond by form letter or phone, rarely follow up, and publicize the relatively few dramatic successes.

There is always the law—expensive and slow.

The small-claims court is sometimes an answer. It is inexpensive, but even if you win, there are difficulties in collecting.

Consumer Suits

Consumers have received encouragement from Congress to sue manufacturers in antitrust actions for suspected price fixing. The Supreme Court had previously held that since consumers did not buy directly from the manufacturer, but dealt with a middleman, they could not sue. Now state attorneys general and a large number of consumer groups plan class action consumer suits, opening another possible avenue of action to the angry consumer. It is a time-consuming procedure, and if successful, it is more likely to be a victory of principle more than money for the consumer.

Legal Jargon

Consumer grumbling about legalistic double-talk has begun to show results. New York's Citibank simplified its loan form—as you can see from the sample in Figure 4–1. Competitors felt that this was an "idea whose time had come," and a number of other banks followed suit. The idea of simplifying consumer contracts was undertaken by several insurance companies to make it easier for policyholders to understand homeowner coverage. The "plain English" of insurance companies' contracts, however, has to be approved by regulatory commissions in each state in which they operate, before they can become effective. As a result of a 1974 opinion study conducted by Sentry Insurance, which indicated consumer opposition to fine print and hard-to-read-insurance policies, Sentry wrote a "plain talk car policy." The first page of this policy is shown in Figure 4–2.

Federal agencies have also begun revising rules

Citizens'-Band-Radio Rules

Old: "The current authorization, or a clearly legible photocopy thereof, for each station (including units of a station) operated at a fixed location shall be posted at a conspicuous place at the principal fixed location from which such station is controlled."

New: "You must keep your license (or other authorization) in your station records or post it at your station."

U.S. News & World Report, November 7, 1977.

FIGURE 4–1
How Citibank Simplified Loan Form

The translation of Citibank's old loan form has resulted in a legal document that seems almost absurdly simple by comparison. Here are two samples.

Old Form

For value received, the undersigned jointly and severally hereby promise(s) to pay . . . the sum of_____.

In the event of default in the payment of this or any other obligation, or the performance or observance of any term or covenant contained herein . . . or the bank shall deem itself to be insecure . . . the bank shall have the right at its option, without demand or notice of any kind, to declare . . . the obligations to be immediately due and payable.

New Form

To repay my loan, I promise to pay you_____ dollars.

I'll be in default: (1) If I don't pay an installment on time; or (2) If any other creditor tries by legal process to take any money of mine in your possession. You can then demand immediate payment of the balance of this note.

Source: Citibank, New York.

FIGURE 4–2
Your Plain Talk Car Policy

Insuring Agreement

Upon *your* payment of the premiums, we agree that this policy provides the various kinds of insurance *you* have selected as shown on the enclosed declarations page. The declarations page is a part of this policy. This insurance applies only to *car accidents* and losses which occur while this policy is in force. Subject to our consent, *you* may renew this policy. When we consent to renew this policy, *you* must pay the renewal premium in advance. Or, if *you* select a time payment plan, *you* must pay the required down payment in advance.

Cars We Insure

We insure the *car* described on the declarations page and any *car you* replace it with. We'll also insure any additional *car you* acquire if we insure, under this insurance, all *cars you* own. But the replacement or addition is insured only if *you* notify us within 30 days of its acquisition.

We insure any *utility trailer you* own or are using except for collision, comprehensive and rental expense insurance. For collision and comprehensive insurance, the *utility trailer* must be listed on the declarations page and a premium shown for it.

We insure a substitute *car* when the *car* described on the declarations page, or any replacement or addition, can't be used because it's being serviced or repaired, or it's been stolen or destroyed. A *car* owned by *you* or a resident member of *your* family doesn't qualify as a substitute *car*.

We insure other *cars you* use with the permission of the owner. This doesn't include *cars* owned by, or furnished for the regular use of, *you* or resident members of *your* family.

Source: Sentry Insurance.

---

and forms to reduce confusion. HEW has begun a five-year program to rewrite its thousands of rules in understandable English. The example on page 102 of the Federal Communications Commission's simplified rules governing citizens' band radio is certainly more readable than the material it replaced.

One of the difficulties preventing rapid change in this area is the need to find acceptable substitutes for the many words and phrases that are technical terms that have been defined by the courts over the years. Another obvious brake on speedy change is 20,000 pages of federal regulations alone—that are issued yearly.

Senator Proxmire was quoted in a recent issue of *Barron's* as saying:

> Truth in Lending is as sound as it was in 1968. Consumers still want and need usable credit information. But when regulations carrying out the law get so intricate that creditors honestly are not sure how to comply and consumers are faced with disclosure statements three feet long, it's time to take a second look.
>
> Recently, the Federal Reserve Board issued an eight-page proposed regulation, plus an eight-page explanation, all to implement five lines of statutory language. With this kind of regulatory approach, it is no wonder there has been an explosion of lawsuits claiming Truth in Lending violations.

New York State recently adopted a law requiring that consumer contracts dealing with money, goods, and services valued at less than $50,000 be written in "nontechnical language" in "words with common and everyday meanings." Rental contracts, personal loan agreements, and leases are covered, but not such documents as insurance policies. For example, Citibank changed a 117-word paragraph in an application for a loan containing legal gobbledygook into a simple statement of default.

Inability to read the fine print which tended to obscure rather than help, left consumers unprotected and often resulted in the loss of their property under complex repossession clauses.

The new law may still not help very much because it is mainly enforceable through good faith. Good faith could mean just asking the company lawyer to simplify contracts. The maximum penalty for failure to comply is $50. Although consumers may sue for actual money losses without limit, this is not so easy to do.

Keeping Records

Almost as bad as not understanding a legal document is not finding an important paper you need—

for income tax purposes, renewal of a license, a real estate transfer. If the paper is important—and lost or mislaid in stacks of paper scattered in various places—at the least it takes time until you find it, or write the local city hall or health department for a copy.

It's easier to manage your money if you have managed the paper connected with it.

You don't have to keep everything forever. For income tax purposes, a three-year inventory of canceled checks is adequate. The IRS has three years to audit a return unless there is a question of fraud.

A system cuts confusion. You need an active file—current bank statements, recent checks, unpaid bills, recent tax returns. An inactive file of older records can go to the top of the closet or to the basement. You will want to keep important papers in that active file—a list of credit cards (numbers, phone numbers to report loss), employment records, education records, copies of wills, warranties, health records. Records of investment or property ownership, documents of birth and marriage, military service records, signed wills (original at lawyer's), and insurance policies—should be in a safe deposit box. You will have only occasional need for these papers—and they will be safe.

If you need the warranty for the stereo—it's at hand. Is there a question about a department store credit for a returned item?—your proof is within reach. Homeowner's insurance renewal due shortly?—your records will alert you.[14]

Consumer Education

The Sentry Insurance study *Consumerism at the Crossroads,* found that consumer education was regarded as the leading priority for the consumer movement by all groups except top businessmen, who felt that the need for the consumer movement to see both sides of the issues was more important.

There has been renewed interest in establishing consumer education courses for elementary and secondary students. Some states have mandated

[14] For more detail on record keeping, write for the free booklet *Keeping Records—What to Discard,* Consumer Information Center, Pueblo, CO 81009.

such programs. Elsewhere consumer educational units are integrated into other courses, in English, Social Science, or Math.

A test constructed to measure the consumer competence of high school students found that the 500 tested were sadly ignorant in areas of credit. For example, only 15 percent knew that a credit bureau keeps files on customers for business firms that are members of the bureau. A majority thought that credit bureaus decide who gets credit. Some thought credit bureaus made loans to members or kept files on businesses for local banks.

Units developing skills and solving consumer problems are introduced to first and second graders at their level. For instance, a first-grade class began by "playing store" and was introduced to the buyer's problems by the teacher. Sometimes such games are made into skits, for parents to watch—as a way of spreading consumer information into the community.

The Consumer and the Economy

Consumer buying plans have become an eagerly watched economic indicator. The rise and fall of these intentions, especially concerning the spending of their disposable personal income, are carefully charted by several organizations, among which are the Conference Board in New York; the Survey Research Center of Ann Arbor, Michigan; and Cambridge Reports of Cambridge, Massachusetts. Their periodic surveys are given media publicity. Various financial institutions analyze in learned articles the implications of these consumer intentions for the economy. Of considerable interest is the confidence of consumers and their willingness to spend. Indicators have been developed to measure more precisely various aspects of consumer intentions to spend. These indicators have become useful guides in predicting changes in the economy.

The Conference Board monthly surveys are summarized in two indexes—the Index of Buying Plans and the Index of Consumer Confidence. The National Consumer Finance Association has developed Indexes of Consumer Behavior to follow the changing spending patterns.

Some analysts believe that consumers will buy durable goods now to beat tomorrow's inflated price. The Conference Board feels differently.[15] "In real life, only a small number of persons behave that way, mostly in buying high-priced items such as cars and appliances," Fabian Linden, the director of consumer research of the Conference Board, notes. "The vast majority of families experience an erosion of real income as prices escalate, and tend to reduce spending and increase savings as a means of assuring their future ability to secure everyday necessities and meet fixed financial commitments."

The Changing Consumer

No longer passive, today's average consumer—not just the activist who spearheads change—is increasingly unaccepting of misleading advertising, shoddy goods, or inadequate services. An expression of that opinion is seen in Sentry Insurance's latest consumer survey, called *Consumerism at the Crossroads.*[16] The purpose of this study is expressed in the preface:

> Proponents of consumerism generally claim they are providing greater protection for consumers. Businessmen often claim consumerism has brought increased regulations and policies unwanted by most consumers, and—worst—higher costs, which have had to be borne largely by the consumers.
>
> Amid all the controversy, however, the voices of consumers themselves have been heard only rarely, and never in any comprehensive and systematic manner.

Table 4–4 reveals what some of them think.

In reviewing the past decade, consumers felt that their shopping skills had improved (72 percent), that labeling and product information had improved (70 percent), and that product safety had

"Why don't you look at it this way, Mrs. Peters—prices are lower today than they ever will be."

Reprinted by permission *The Wall Street Journal*

improved (60 percent). However, the majority felt that the quality of most products and services had grown worse.

In general, optimism was expressed as to the future. Of those questioned, 76 percent expressed the belief (mixed with hope?) that product information and labeling would improve in the next decade and 71 percent expected their own shopping skills to be better. Although 50 percent thought that product quality would improve, they also expected that products would not last as long as they do now and that it would be more difficult to get things repaired.

The Consumer Movement

The U.S. Chamber of Commerce estimates that some 800 different rip-offs are aimed at the consumer. If you examine Table 4–5 you will see that is the third reason for the growth of the consumer movement. The feeling of not getting your money's worth, along with the poor quality and poor workmanship too often combined with high prices arouses consumer fury. This, in turn, has led to more consumer awareness of the consumer movement which is credited with improving the products

---

[15] Conference Board, Press Release 2841, July 6, 1978.

[16] Conducted by Marketing Science Institute, a nonprofit research organization associated with the Harvard Business School, and Louis Harris & Associates, Inc., 1977.

TABLE 4–4
Some Perceptions of Consumers

Q.4: I am going to read you a number of statements. Please tell me, for each one, which one of the phrases on this card (HAND RESPONDENT CARD) best describes how you feel about it — whether you agree very strongly, agree but not strongly, neither agree nor disagree, disagree but not strongly, or disagree very strongly.

				Leaders			
	Total Public	Consumer Activist	Government Consumer Affairs	Non-Insurance Regulator	Insurance Regulator	Senior Business Manager	Business Consumer Affairs
(Sample size:)	(1510)	(218)	(85)	(31)	(33)	(99)	(53)
	%	%	%	%	%	%	%
Consumers can most effectively voice their discontent with products by not buying them							
Agree	75	59	66	61	72	88	81
Disagree	12	35	25	38	18	9	15
If people are careful and use good judgement, they can still get good value for their money today							
Agree	75	75	91	84	84	99	92
Disagree	14	15	6	9	9	—	4
Many of the mistakes consumers make are the result of their own carelessness							
Agree	69	56	76	71	72	86	83
Disagree	17	31	19	22	12	6	8
Most consumers do not use the information available about different products in order to decide to buy one of them							
Agree	65	67	84	77	78	81	91
Disagree	15	18	2	12	18	10	6
There is generally enough information available for consumers to make sensible buying decisions							
Agree	58	24	42	38	42	82	72
Disagree	27	71	50	55	48	13	23
Most peoples' problems as consumers are among the most nagging and annoying in everyday life							
Agree	53	76	69	83	51	32	53
Disagree	24	10	18	13	24	52	34
Most peoples' problems as consumers are relatively unimportant compared with other problems faced by the average family							
Agree	46	14	23	16	36	44	35
Disagree	30	69	59	68	45	37	53
Consumers don't need any help in looking after their own interests; they are quite able to do it themselves							
Agree	24	8	9	3	3	28	4
Disagree	58	90	87	93	91	57	92

Source: *Consumerism at the Crossroads,* Sentry Insurance.

"About this '101 Tips for Consumers' I bought—there are only 97 tips in it."

Reprinted by permission *The Wall Street Journal*

and services people buy. How the differing groups in the population regard the consumer movement is shown in Table 4–6. Interestingly all elements agree that the consumer movement has kept business on its toes, although they disagree strongly on other aspects of it. Notice in Table 4–7 the consensus that the movement has done some good. According to the poll, no particular group speaks for consumers, but nongovernment consumer activists are seen as most in touch with consumers, and senior business managers least in touch.

Ralph Nader gets much credit for being the catalyst that sparked new growth in the consumer movement, since that first important automobile safety legislation. His principal organization is Public Citizen, a million-dollar tax-exempt group supported by contribution. Under this umbrella are 15 special action groups working for specific goals. There are 75 full-time paid workers and a weekly newspaper column. There have been a number of successes—but in a limited area because of the refusal of the Nader groups to merge with other activist groups.

Consumer Co-ops

With a long history behind it and added strength today, the consumer co-op movement is attempting solutions to problems that laws and regulations have not yet reached. An auto repair shop—which needs capital and has trouble getting it—is one such cooperative. These urban co-ops seek to minimize the cost of the goods that city dwellers buy as well as to improve the availability and the quality of the goods sold.

There are no exact figures on the number of cooperatives in the country, but the accepted estimate is about 3,000 and growing slowly but steadily. It has been felt that the financial help to be offered by the National Consumer Cooperative Bank will encourage the growth of cooperatives. The idea was that the bank would make loans to health, food, or any small business–type cooperative that could become financially self-supporting.

The National Consumer Cooperative Bank was created in 1978 to make loans to all consumer cooperatives that cannot get financing from commercial sources, with 35 percent of the funds earmarked for co-ops to be formed by low-income persons. Within the bank will be an office of Self-Help Development and Technical Assistance to provide technical and research assistance for the developing co-op businesses.

What Does the Public Want?

A survey[17] indicates that the public would support a number of new proposals if these were to be developed:

By a modest majority, 52 percent to 34 percent, the public favors the idea of *a new federal government agency for consumer advocacy.*

72 percent of the public supports a proposal to hold a *major convention every four or five years* at which government, business, and

[17] *Consumerism at The Crossroads,* survey conducted for Sentry Insurance.

TABLE 4–5

Reasons for the Growth of the Consumer Movement

(Sample size:)	Total Public	Consumer Activist	Leaders				
			Government Consumer Affairs	Non-Insurance Regulator	Insurance Regulator	Senior Business Manager	Business Consumer Affairs
	(1510)	(218)	(83)	(31)	(32)	(99)	(52)
	%	%	%	%	%	%	%
Prices are so high that people want to get their money's worth	23	17	16	10	6	15	13
People are tired of poor quality and shoddy workmanship	21	19	14	26	9	14	17
People are dissatisfied and discontent, tired of being cheated and ripped off	14	17	16	23	9	7	15
People are more aware of the consumer movement	13	22	19	10	19	12	15
People want and need organizations to look after their interests	12	4	6	—	6	2	2
People are tired of poor service	6	10	11	16	3	7	8
Big business and manufacturers take advantage of/are not fair to consumers	5	13	8	10	3	5	2
Publicity/advertising/the media	4	5	14	—	3	18	10
Ralph Nader	4	8	10	6	16	10	10
People are buying and spending more	3	2	2	—	—	3	2
Lack of product safety	2	2	1	—	—	1	2
Population is growing	2	—	1	3	—	1	—
Product imports	1	—	—	—	—	—	—
People are tired of worthless guarantees	1	1	—	3	—	—	4
We need it	1	*	—	3	—	—	—
Consumers better educated	—	7	12	6	13	4	19
Consumers have become more active/vocal, organized into groups to demand rights	—	10	7	3	19	6	8
Increased expectations of consumers for better goods/services	—	2	4	—	3	7	12
Consumer groups are effective in getting things done and achieving results	—	3	2	—	9	2	—
Increased number of government agencies to protect and represent consumers	—	1	1	—	3	6	2
Any other answers	12	6	7	13	3	12	19
Don't know	12	—	—	—	—	—	—

Note: Totals add to more than 100% as some respondents gave more than one answer.

Source: *Consumerism at the Crossroads,* Sentry Insurance.

TABLE 4–6

Perceptions of the Consumer Movement and Its Impact

Q.8: I am going to read out some statements which people have made about the consumer movement. Can you tell me how strongly you agree or disagree with each one — whether you agree very strongly, agree but not strongly, neither agree nor disagree, disagree but not strongly, or disagree very strongly?

				Leaders			
	Total Public	Consumer Activist	Government Consumer Affairs	Non-Insurance Regulator	Insurance Regulator	Senior Business Manager	Business Consumer Affairs
(Sample size:)	(1510)	(218)	(85)	(31)	(33)	(99)	(53)
	%	%	%	%	%	%	%
The consumer movement has kept industry and business on their toes							
Agree	77	84	93	87	91	77	80
Disagree	8	8	4	9	6	9	8
The consumer movement has helped a great deal to improve the quality and standards of the products and services people buy							
Agree	69	79	79	75	85	54	66
Disagree	10	10	7	12	9	31	19
Consumers generally make the right buying decisions in terms of their own desires and values							
Agree	61	33	40	28	54	77	57
Disagree	16	48	34	54	27	13	34
Business has too much influence on government policy with regard to consumer affairs							
Agree	53	89	74	72	54	11	19
Disagree	17	9	17	25	27	78	60
Companies would soon go out of business if they did all the things the consumer movement wants them to do							
Agree	35	15	30	25	45	64	63
Disagree	37	76	53	53	42	20	30
The consumer movement makes a lot of charges against companies which aren't justified							
Agree	29	15	33	20	57	84	81
Disagree	42	82	58	51	30	9	17
The activities of the consumer movement will inevitably lead to too much government control over our lives							
Agree	26	5	21	19	33	63	51
Disagree	42	85	68	65	57	25	36
Most people in the consumer movement are more interested in attacking the free enterprise system than in helping the consumer							
Agree	24	5	12	9	15	49	28
Disagree	47	90	75	81	60	31	51
The consumer movement gives a one-sided and unfair picture of what industry and business do							
Agree	21	9	29	28	48	71	55
Disagree	49	83	60	57	42	15	34
The consumer movement seems to be running out of steam							
Agree	15	6	19	22	24	22	4
Disagree	46	82	70	56	57	62	85
The consumer movement is a threat to our free enterprise system							
Agree	13	6	9	—	3	26	17
Disagree	60	92	85	100	82	62	79

Note: Those responding "neither agree nor disagree" and "not sure" are not included in this table.

Source: *Consumerism at the Crossroads,* Sentry Insurance.

TABLE 4–7
The Overall Impact

Q.11: Overall, do you feel that people active in the consumer movement have done a great deal of good, some good, some harm, or a great deal of harm?

			Leaders				
	Total Public	Consumer Activist	Government Consumer Affairs	Non-Insurance Regulator	Insurance Regulator	Senior Business Manager	Business Consumer Affairs
(Sample size:)	(1510)	(218)	(85)	(32)	(33)	(100)	(52)
	%	%	%	%	%	%	%
A great deal of good	16	42	38	16	21	4	17
Some good	67	58	60	78	76	75	75
Some harm	3	*	1	6	3	75	6
A great deal of harm	1	—	—	—	—	12	—
Had no effect (vol.)	4	—	—	—	—	6	—
Not sure	9	*	1	—	—	3	2

Source: *Consumerism at the Crossroads,* Sentry Insurance.

consumer representatives would work out long-term policies in the consumer field.

By 66 percent to 25 percent the public believes that it would be helpful *if every community had a complaint bureau* where complaints against manufacturers, dealers, and salesmen could be dealt with.

By 79 percent to 11 percent the public believes that there should be *a new independent testing center* for evaluating the safety of potentially dangerous products, run by either the federal government or consumer activists, rather than by business.

92 percent of the public believes that *consumer affairs should be a compulsory subject in all high schools.*

Consumer Protection—Federal Agencies

The FTC, as you have no doubt noticed, plays a central part in protecting the consumer. In 1978 the FTC's Bureau of Consumer Protection reorganized its operating divisions. A listing will demonstrate the variety of responsibilities that the FTC handles.

1. *Division of Advertising Practices.* This division has responsibility for programs in advertising monitoring/substantiation, cigarette advertising, health and safety implications in advertising, and children's advertising.
2. *Division of Food and Drug Advertising.* Advertisements for food, over-the-counter drugs, and cosmetics, as well as the trade regulation rule on hearing aids, are handled in this division.
3. *Division of Credit Practices.* All of the Bureau's credit programs, as well as problems arising from the widespread use of credit (such as privacy), are handled here. Included are the creditors' remedies program as well as enforcement of the Equal Credit Opportunity Act, the Truth in Lending Act, the Fair Credit Reporting Act, and the programs on credit billing and consumer leasing.
4. *Division of Professional Services.* Programs involving the delivery and performance of consumer services are located in this division. Those programs include investigations of the funeral industry, prescription drugs, insurance, auto repair, and occupational regulations.

5. *Division of Energy and Product Information.* The bureau's energy programs are located here, as are its packaging and labeling programs and the enforcement of the Textile, Wool, and Fur Labeling Acts and the Hobby Protection Act. The bureau program on disclosure of "inadequacy or risk" in certain products is also in this division.

6. *Division of Compliance.* This division handles the enforcement of FTC trade regulation rules and industry guides, as well as compliance with FTC orders.

7. *Division of Marketing Abuses.* It is principally this division's responsibility to explore future initiatives. Among the programs now located in this division are those covering point-of-sale practices, vocational schools, land sales, business opportunities and franchises, and condominiums.

8. *Division of Product Reliability and Standards.* This division is responsible for the bureau programs on warranties, standards and certification, and the resolution of minor disputes. The standards program will continue to focus on energy issues (other than labeling and advertising) and the development of specific industry or product standards.

Examples of FTC Actions The FTC won a three-year battle with Encyclopaedia Britannica, Inc., and Grolier, Inc. over selling encyclopedias. It ordered Radio Corporation of America, the Ford Motor Company, SCM Corporation, and Standard Brands, Inc., to substantiate their advertisements. Hearings take time; staff survey reports take time, and they are not always effected; but increasingly the FTC has become the protector of "consumers' claims and defenses."

The Food and Drug Administration The FDA is controversial because it is caught between the public demand for new products and industry's desire to sell the products it has developed, on the one side—and on the other side, the concern for public safety.

Sophisticated new methods of detecting potential danger arouse antagonism and fear as they reveal hazards in products long regarded as safe. Under this new awareness, almost everything we eat seems to have become dangerous for one reason or another.

The FDA has been criticized for causing undue alarm and also for taking undue time! The FDA has been taken to court by business, investigated endlessly by Congress, and criticized by both liberals and conservatives. For example, when the FDA sought to set limits on the strength of vitamin and mineral supplements on the basis of evidence that too large amounts of vitamins A and D might be harmful, it took 11 years to put the regulation into effect. Opposed were "believers" in vitamins who claimed that their "freedom" was being violated and pharmaceutical concerns that manufacture vitamins. Lawsuits ended when the Supreme Court supported the FDA position. The opposition then lobbied in Congress and won legislation that nullified the FDA regulation! Almost everything that the FDA does is challenged—and if it doesn't act—it is criticized too.

Under the law drugs must be tested not only for safety but for effectiveness. It has taken the FDA ten years to review the efficacy of 3,500 drugs appearing as 5,800 different formulas. An amendment to legislation passed in 1958 transferred to industry the burden of proving the safety of a chemical—subject to agency review.

The current uproar over cyclamates demonstrates the difficulties. Criticisms were voiced that the company which performed the tests falsified the tests or the results. The average person views as fantasy today's analytic techniques which can detect amounts of contaminants as little as one part per trillion. The publics' love for soft drinks and easy dieting through sugar substitutes adds to its reluctance to accept a seemingly "iffy" conclusion. The FDA's frequent testing and retesting, announcements, and delaying of the implementation of directives added to the uncertainty. In addition, the economic influence of the soft drink industry has probably not remained aloof.

The Commerce Department A different approach is that of the Commerce Department, which is engaged in a program of labeling products to provide consumers with information on the products' performance, such as strength and durability, load capacity, energy usage, and noise level.

The manufacturer develops the information for the labels by conducting tests determined by the National Bureau of Standards. The intent is to provide the buyers with "objectively determined data" at the point of purchase, so that they can decide whether one product is better than another.

The Agriculture Department Previously detailed has been the consumer-oriented activity of the Agriculture Department (see Chapter 3), which is conspicuous in consumer-interest programs.

Warranties

A primary complaint against business is that it is difficult to get defects and problems corrected.

Guarantees and warranties are thought inadequate and not understandable. Evidently the "simple and readily understood language" demanded in the Magnuson-Moss Warranty and Federal Trade Commission Improvement Act has not been achieved, because warranty language has not yet sufficiently shed the legal obfuscations used to protect companies.

Unfortunately for "plain English" the wording of the law itself—as the following sample indicates—provides a poor model:

. . . any warrantor warranting a consumer product . . . by means of a written warranty shall, to the extent required by the (Federal Trade) Commission, fully and conspicuously disclose in simple and readily understandable language the terms and conditions of such warranty.

The act does *not* require manufacturers to give a warranty.[18] However, manufacturers that provide a warranty covering consumer products costing over $15 must:

1. Make the warranty available to you *before* you buy.
2. Must state clearly whether the guarantee is *full* or *limited.*

The Federal Trade Commission, which is responsible for the enforcement of the act, has issued three rules—interpreting the act.[19]

Presale Availability Retailers must display the warranty on or near the products, or the warranty must be available in binders on counters with a sign declaring its availability. Door-to-door sales, mail orders, and catalog sales are covered by rules requiring warranties to be available to shoppers.

Disclosure The warranty must disclose who is covered, what parts are covered, and what the warrantor will pay for and what he will do in case of defect or failure of the product. The warranty must also include the date that it begins, its duration, and information on the existence of any informal dispute settlement mechanism. You should also be told whether you are entitled to additional rights under your state law.

Dispute Mechanisms This rule encourages but does not require warrantors to set up dispute mechanisms before resorting to civil law.

If, however, the warrantor does so, the face of the warranty must disclose:

1. The availability of the mechanism.
2. The name and address and/or the toll-free number of the mechanism.

Such informal procedures may include the Consumer Business Arbitration tribunals established by many Better Business bureaus or the consumer action panels (such as MACAP—Major Appliance Consumer Action Panel) established by industry.

Informal groups must have a majority of public members, a minority of industry members, and be funded in advance, so that a disgruntled company cannot arbitrarily withdraw its financing.

---

[18] For more details, write for *Warranties,* a free pamphlet, Consumer Information Center, Pueblo, CO 81009.

[19] In September 1978 the FTC issued its first Warranty Act Complaint against a major home appliance retailer for failure to abide by its rules.

Implied Warranties   Neither a full nor a limited warranty can deny you your implied warranty rights. Implied rights are created by state law, and all states have them. They mean that a product must do the job it's supposed to do. For example, a reclining chair must recline and a toaster must toast.

Consequential Damages   A company may disclaim consequential damages for either full or limited warranties. If your freezer breaks down and the food spoils, the manufacturer pays—if you have consequential damages.

Warranties are either limited or full—although some products may carry both types. A new car may have a *full* warranty on the *engine* but only a *limited* warranty on the *tires*. (See the accompanying box on Chrysler's warranty.)

Compare warranties before you buy. It may be worth paying more for a product with a better warranty. The warranty choice could be your insurance against a big repair bill.

Consumer Product Safety

Would you believe that for more than three years manufacturers of ladders, representatives of insurance companies, suppliers of raw materials

---

Law Snags Chrysler Plan for "Unlimited" Warranty

DETROIT—Question: When is an unlimited-mileage car warranty not "unlimited"?

Answer: When it's on a Chrysler Corp. automobile.

Chrysler confirmed that it has sent a letter to its dealers advising them against advertising its "12-month unlimited mileage" car warranty as such. Instead, the auto maker said, it told the dealers to advertise it as "the clincher," the name Chrysler gave the warranty when it introduced it last fall.

The warranty hasn't changed—car buyers still are protected for a year regardless of the car's mileage. The law, however, has changed. The Magnuson-Moss Warranty Improvement Act, which went into effect Friday, says that manufacturers must label their warranties as "full" or "limited." Chrysler, with an eye on the law's provision that under full warranties it must give a replacement or refund if warranty repairs don't satisfy a customer, has chosen to designate its warranty as "limited."

And apparently the Chrysler legal staff couldn't live with the word "unlimited" in the warranty ads.

The Wall Street Journal, July 7, 1975.

Warranties

The label **"full"** on a warranty means all of this:

A defective product will be fixed (or replaced) free, including removal and reinstallation if necessary.

It will be fixed within a reasonable time after you complain.

You will not have to do anything unreasonable to get warranty service (such as ship a piano to the factory).

The warranty is good for anyone who owns the product during the warranty period.

If the product can't be fixed (or hasn't been after a reasonable number of tries), you get your choice of a new one or your money back.

A **"limited"** warranty may:

Cover only parts, not labor.

Allow only a pro rata refund or credit (the longer you have had the product, the smaller your refund or credit).

Require you to return a heavy product to the store for service.

Cover only the first purchaser.

Charge for handling.

Reasonable time: The FTC said that the courts would define it. Its thinking is 21 days. State and local laws often provide 30 days. The law is still evolving—for example, the proposed FTC rule concerning used car warranties is still not final.

"If not completely satisfied, return the unused portion of our product and we will return the unused portion of your money."

Reprinted by permission *The Wall Street Journal*

(wood and aluminum), retailers, labor unions, industrial customers, and departments of the federal government have been framing safety rules for the manufacture of ladders? Also involved is the American Standards Institute, a private, nonprofit body that oversees the making of specifications and safety rules for most products in the United States

---

"There ought to be a law"

How many times have you said in frustration "There ought to be a law" when you come across a product which you feel is unsafe? Well, you can do something about it. Especially those products which come under the jurisdiction of the **Consumer Product Safety Commission** (CPSC).

Under Section 10 of the Consumer Product Safety Act, anyone may petition CPSC to issue, amend, or revoke a consumer product safety rule. To make it easier for all concerned, CPSC has issued some guidelines for would-be petitioners:

• A petition must be written in the English language.
• It must include the name and address of the petitioner and indicate the consumer product or products for which a safety rule or a rule change is being sought.
• It must include the facts that establish the rule or rule change sought if necessary. This may include personal experience or medical, engineering, or injury data or research.
• The petitioner must ask the Commission to initiate rulemaking and describe the substance of the proposed rule. A sweeping request for regulatory action will not be sufficient.
• Provide all the information you can. Describe the specific risk of injury; the severity of the likely injury; and the possible reasons for them, such as product defect, a design flaw, or unintentional or intentional misuse.
• If you're seeking an outright ban of the product, you should state why a safety standard would not be sufficient. Also, you should supply other documentation, such as economic and environmental impact, engineering or technical studies, legal analyses, and reports of injuries.

---

and has almost 80 pages of specifications for ladders, updated many times since 1923. Since ladders are responsible for about 80,000 injuries that require hospital treatment each year, the Consumer Product Safety Commission has been responsible for the three-year attempt to make ladders safer. But as one manufacturer said after a two-hour meeting on a 15-word section of the safety code, "Am I in the ladder business, or am I building rocket ships to go to the moon?"[20]

The Consumer Product Safety Commission has jurisdiction over 10,000–12,000 home or recreational product lines that are responsible for a high quota of accidents. Figure 4–3 itemizes the products that appear in the CPSC's current annual list of the ten most dangerous products. The list is complied from a Hazard Index which is weighted for age; both the young and the elderly are especially prone to accidents. Weights are also assigned to emergency rooms in 119 hospitals so that accurate national projections of injury frequency can be made. Over the last few years the agency has supervised new rules for 50 products ranging from

---

[20] *Wall Street Journal,* August 11, 1977.

Safer toys

Consumer Product Safety Commission (CPSC) has issued another in a series of regulations which address hazards that are common to all toys. CPSC's latest regulation prescribes new safety tests for toys and other articles with sharp metal and glass edges that are intended for children up to 8 years old.

This regulation applies to all toys introduced into interstate commerce after March 26, 1979. CPSC has already issued regulations for toys with sharp points, and toys and furniture coated with paint containing more than 0.06% lead. Pacifiers and baby rattles, which have been associated with choking and strangulation, also must comply with certain safety requirements.

In addition to regulations dealing with identifiable hazards, CPSC bans (or recalls) specific, brand-named defective toys on a case-by-case basis.

The new rules for sharp edges do not apply to bicycles or full-sized baby cribs which are covered by separate regulations. Hobby and craft kits or edges on other children's products such as knives and scissors—which must be sharp to function—are also not included.

Details—*Federal Register:* March 24, page 12636; Jan. 7, 1975, pages 1480 and 1488. CONSUMER REGISTER: March 1, 1975. For more information write or call Elaine Besson, Consumer Product Safety Commission, Washington, DC 20207; telephone 301-492-6453.

NOTE: Several years ago CPSC published a hazardous toys list but decided to discontinue it because it was out of date as soon as it was printed. Also, the Commission felt that such a list gave consumers a false sense of security: If a certain toy is not on the hazardous list, it must be safe. Obviously, that is not necessarily the case.

Source: *Consumer Register,* Office of Consumer Affairs, Department of Health, Education, and Welfare, May 1, 1978.

bicycles to aspirin bottles. Each of these is continually updated. (Its number for product-related information, complaints, and accident reports is 800–638–8326.) The monthly magazine *CPSC Memo* is free upon written request to CPSC Memo, Consumer Product Safety Commission, Washington, D.C. 20207.

The Consumer Product Safety Commission either contracts with an independent testing organization to draw up "mandatory" safety standards or lets this be done on a "voluntary" basis by the industry group involved, as in the case of the ladders.

Another example would be the action of the manufacturers of upholstered furniture, who are opposed to the commission's proposed mandatory standards, which they claim would banish popular cotton and velvet upholstery materials in an attempt to reduce fire hazards. The manufacturers complain that not only would the commission's action force a consumer price increase of as much as 27 percent, but that it is powerless to regulate cigarette safety.

They would substitute a program of voluntary self-regulation to reduce or eliminate ignition-prone fabrics at or near surface areas. They claim that this would be 97 percent as effective but only 2.5 percent as costly as the commission's standards.

As part of the campaign to avoid mandatory standards, the upholstery manufacturers staged countrywide meetings to unite the industry in support of a voluntary solution.

The process of setting up safety standards has been very slow; the give-and-take between industry and the commission is time consuming. It was hoped that standards would be set quickly to cover many hazardous situations that are shown in Figure 4–4.

The number of products being recalled is growing rapidly. As many as 25 percent of the country's 500 largest consumer goods companies have been involved in recall campaigns. It is estimated that recalls will continue to total at least 25 million product units a year. Product recalls are being spurred by a trend toward "defensive" recalls (increasingly companies are pulling back products before actual injuries or consumer complaints are reported), by a growing number of product liability actions in the courts, and by the increased activism of government agencies and consumer organizations.

Liability insurance, which has soared because of increasing claims and high dollar awards, is responsible for a crisis feeling because many companies cannot afford insurance at all and others have less coverage than is desired. One company, for example, paid $344 for $1 million of coverage in 1975. Two years later this company, which made cultures used in animal feeds and had no claims against it, was asked by the insurance company to pay a $150,000 premium for $300,000 of coverage along with a $250,000 deductible.

Companies refrain from introducing new products because of insurance costs. Meanwhile, casualty insurance companies, whose reserves are be-

FIGURE 4–4

Priority rankings of consumer products

Consumer Product Safety Commission (CPSC) has announced the products—in order of priority—it hopes to act upon during the next 18 months. All of the products are considered hazardous to some degree.

In addition to the priority products, CPSC will continue to collect and analyze injury data, review consumer complaints, accept petitions and use its authority to deal with substantial hazards under its jurisdiction.

The criteria used by CPSC to rank these priority products included the frequency and severity of injuries; causes of injuries; chronic illness and future injury; cost and benefit of CPSC action; unforeseen nature of the risk; vulnerability of the population at risk; and the probability of exposure to hazard.

The high priority products follow:

1. Asbestos—development of mandatory safety rules covering consumer products containing free form asbestos [see "Consumer Alert" in this issue of CONSUMER NEWS].

2. Power mowers—mandatory safety standard proposal.

3. Gas space heaters—proposed ban of "unvented" types.

4. Communication antennae—possibility of mandatory safety rule and labeling of citizens band base station antennae.

5. Public playground equipment—possible mandatory safety rule.

6. Chlorofluorocarbons—complete labeling of aerosol consumer products containing chlorofluorocarbons and continue cooperation with **Environmental Protection Agency** (EPA) in banning such products.

7. Architectural glazing materials (glass)—certification program to be developed to complement recently completed mandatory standard.

8. Unstable refuse bins—to be banned June 13, 1978.

9. Lead in paint—complete ban on paint containing over 0.06% lead.

10. Baby pacifiers—proposed mandatory safety rule.

11. Baby rattles—possible mandatory safety rule.

12. Sharp points on toys—development of mandatory toy regulations.

13. Methyl alcohol—label antidote instructions on consumer products containing methyl alcohol.

14. Upholstered furniture—possible mandatory safety rule or voluntary standard.

15. Sharp edges on toys—development of mandatory toy regulations.

16. Children's sleepwear enforcement policy—develop better definitions of children's sleepwear under Flammable Fabrics Act.

17. Miniature Christmas tree lights—mandatory safety standard under development through offeror process. National Consumers League is developing the standard and encouraging consumer participation.

18. TV sets—possible development of mandatory safety rule.

19. Aluminum wire—mandatory safety rule or voluntary standard.

20. Ranges and ovens—monitoring of voluntary standards.

21. Skateboards—research to determine feasibility of any regulatory action.

22. Extension cords and trouble lights—possible development of mandatory safety rule.

23. Bicycles—amendment to existing mandatory standard.

24. Matches—completion of mandatory standard rule process.

25. Ladders—monitor development of voluntary standard.

26. Energy conservation devices—research possible hazards and methods for dealing with them.

27. Bathtubs and showers—monitor development of voluntary standard.

28. Smoke detectors—research possible hazards and methods of dealing with them.

Source: *Consumer News*, Department of Health, Education, and Welfare, August 1, 1977.

coming thin, face questioning by state regulatory authorities about these reserves and in turn limit the availability of product liability insurance.

Companies are setting up their own reserves to pay possible damage claims—instead of seeking insurance. There has been a proposal for federal reinsurance, similar to the programs against theft or fire in high-crime areas. Some states are passing legislation that limits the damages if a user has been negligent. Business is trying to protect itself both by redesigning products to reduce hazards and by offering more information teaching buyers how to use products safely.

The White House Office of Consumer Affairs

The influence of this office rises and falls, depending upon the personality of the incumbent and the attitude of the president, who determines its power quotient. It can be a mere public relations office. Or it can display initiative and develop programs that are responsive to the needs of the consumer. It can make its presence felt in representing the consumer point of view on policy decision papers going to the president. It could even, if given the power, be the coordinator of consumer programs in all federal agencies.

Office of Consumer Representation

For many years consumer groups have worked for and failed to win congressional approval for a federal agency that would have legal standing to represent the consumer before other executive agencies and to challenge decisions in court. The agency would not be able to issue any rules of its own. By consolidating the functions of consumer agencies in other executive departments, duplication would be eliminated and the consumer representation would be strengthened.

The opponents of such an agency have insisted that it would be regulatory—even though the bill denied that power—and would add another layer of federal bureaucracy. They have been strong enough to prevent its existence.

State Activity

Increasingly of late, states have passed protective consumer legislation. Many states have set up an office of consumer affairs or a department of consumer protection, and several states have even developed "hot lines," statewide lines that enable consumers to phone their complaints directly to the office of the consumer counsel or the division of consumer protection.

Conclusion

Our awareness of rip-off is so prevalent that it has become an everyday word in the language.

Consumers, both individually and as an organized group, are changing. More knowledgeable and somewhat disillusioned about business and government, they favor many fresh approaches that they hope will get them real value for their money and improve their daily lives.

Consumer choice and decision making are affected by both advertising and pricing policies, and far too frequently by unrealized or only partially realized expectations. Consumer education and consumer protection are decreasing this gap, but as the sampling of rip-offs in this chapter indicates, there is a long way to go. The diligence and concern of the Federal Trade Commission and other federal agencies in interpreting and enforcing the consumer legislation of this decade are improving the consumer's position.

One of the most encouraging developments has been the increasingly accepted recognition by business and government that the consumer has rights.

SUGGESTED READINGS

American Council on Consumer Interests. *Forum.* Write to the council at the University of Missouri, Columbia, MD 65201.

Andreasen, Alan R., and Best, Arthur. "Consumer Complaint—Does Business Respond?" *Harvard Business Review,* July–August 1977.

Consumer Information Center. *Consumer Information Catalog.* Write to the center at Pueblo, CO 81009; published quarterly.

Consumer News. Available from Office of Consumer Affairs, Washington, D.C. 20201. Known as the U.S. Office of Consumer Affairs, since reorganization in October 1978.

Consumer News, Inc. *Help: The Useful Almanac, 1977–78.* Write Consumer News, Inc., at 813 National Press Building, Washington, D.C. 20045; $4.95 postpaid.

Consumers Union. *Annual Consumer Reports Buying Guide.* Available from Consumers Union, 256 Washington St., Mount Vernon, NY 10550.

Epstein, David G. *Consumer Protection.* St. Paul, Minn.: West Publishing Co., 1976. *In a Nutshell* series; paperback.

Federal Trade Commission. *FTC News Summary.* Available from the Commission, Washington, D.C. 20580.

Katz, Robert N. (ed.). *Protecting the Consumer Interest: Private Initiative and Public Response.* Cambridge, Mass.: Ballinger, 1976.

Rosenbloom, Joseph. *Consumer Complaint Guide.* New York: Macmillan, 1978.

_____. *Consumer Protection Guide.* New York: Macmillan, 1978.

Whiteside, Thomas. *Computer Capers: Tales of Electronic Thievery, Embezzlement, and Fraud.* New York: Thomas Y. Crowell, 1978.

CASE PROBLEMS

1   Richard is a strong-minded activist who believes that popular movements can cure existing wrongs. He is torn by an awareness that government agencies have been responsible for much reform. He wants to devote himself to eliminating rip-offs and improve the lot of the consumer. He asks whether he should go into government or into the consumer movement after graduation from college in order to achieve the greater result. How would you answer him?

2   The Petreys went to a discount house to buy their first washing machine. Armed with knowledge about warranties and eager to save money, they were faced by the following choice: one good buy in price had a limited warranty of 90 days on movable parts; a much more expensive brand had a full warranty on the motor and body but for only 30 days.

The Petreys not only find it a difficult choice, but are contemplating going to a "reliable" traditional department store where they will have to pay more for their washing machine. What would you do?

3   Bill and Reta Sonn are discouraged. The new home they had moved into so happily three months ago suddenly seems to be sagging. Cracks are appearing on the walls, and doors don't close. The builder who is completing two more houses in the project keeps saying he will take care of it—but does nothing. In addition, the new expensive chests they bought for the bedroom—but could ill afford—stick and seem warped. They have called the furniture salesman at the department store several times, but can't reach him. What can they do about their problems?

4   After studying the various tables of the Sentry Insurance survey on the consumer movement, how would you report your opinions on the questions asked?

5   The Mitchells are educated, informed—and insecure. Each time a government agency reveals that something is not good or damaging in some food, clothing, drug, or advertised product that they have been accustomed to use all their lives, they stop using it or anything related to it. They feel that it's too limiting to use only natural products, but they don't know what to do? How do you feel about this problem?

APPENDIX

OCA | *directory of federal consumer offices*

A supplement to Consumer News

August 1978

This directory updates and replaces the *Guide to Federal Consumer Services* and was compiled by the Consumer Information Center of the General Services Administration and the U.S. Office of Consumer Affairs of the Department of Health, Education, and Welfare. It is published as a supplement to CONSUMER NEWS, the twice-monthly newsletter of the U.S. Office of Consumer Affairs. Single copies of this directory are available free from the Consumer Information Center, Pueblo, CO 81009. Multiple copies may be obtained free from CONSUMER NEWS, U.S. Office of Consumer Affairs, 621 Reporters Bldg., Washington, DC 20201; telephone 202-755-8830. Boldface directory entries indicate toll-free telephone numbers.

ADVERTISING
Director, Bureau of Consumer Protection, Federal Trade Commission, Washington, DC 20580; phone 202-523-3727.

AIR TRAVEL/ROUTES AND SERVICE
Director, Office of Consumer Protection, Civil Aeronautics Board, Washington, DC 20423; phone 202-673-5937.

AIR TRAVEL/SAFETY
For general information contact the Community and Consumer Liaison Division, Federal Aviation Administration, APA-430, Washington, DC 20591; phone 202-426-8058. For specific safety problems contact the above office marking correspondence APA-100; phone 202-426-1960.

ALCOHOL
Chief, Trade and Consumer Affairs Division, Bureau of Alcohol, Tobacco, and Firearms, Department of the Treasury, Washington, DC 20226; phone 202-566-7581.

ALCOHOLISM, DRUG ABUSE AND MENTAL ILLNESS
Office of Public Affairs, Alcohol, Drug Abuse and Mental Health Service, 5600 Fishers Lane, Rockville, MD 20857; phone 301-443-3783.

ANTITRUST
Bureau of Competition, Federal Trade Commission, Washington, DC 20580; phone 202-523-3601.
Consumer Affairs Section, Antitrust Division, Justice Department, Washington, DC 20530; phone 202-739-4173.

AUTO SAFETY AND HIGHWAYS
Director, Office of Public and Consumer Affairs, Transportation Department, Washington, DC 20590; phone 202-426-4518.

National Highway Traffic Safety Administration; toll-free hotline **800-424-9393**. In Washington, DC call 426-0123.

Associate Administrator for Planning, Federal Highway Administration, Washington, DC 20590; phone 202-426-0585.

BANKS
Federal Credit Unions

National Credit Union Administration, Washington, DC 20456; phone 202-254-8760.

Federally Insured Savings and Loans

Consumer Division, Office of Community Investment, Federal Home Loan Bank Board, Washington, DC 20552; phone 202-377-6237.

Federal Reserve Banks

Office of Saver and Consumer Affairs, Federal Reserve System, Washington, DC 20551; phone 202-452-3000.

National Banks

Consumer Affairs, Office of the Comptroller of the Currency, Washington, DC 20219; phone 202-447-1600.

State Chartered Banks

Office of Bank Customer Affairs, Federal Deposit Insurance Corporation, Washington, DC 20429; phone 202-389-4427.

SUBSCRIPTION INFORMATION

CONSUMER NEWS, published twice a month by the U.S. Office of Consumer Affairs, highlights consumer activities of Federal agencies and explains Government consumer proposals and how consumers may comment on these proposals. A one year subscription costs $6.00. Make checks payable to Superintendent of Documents. Allow six to eight weeks for arrival of first issue.

PLEASE PRINT OR TYPE

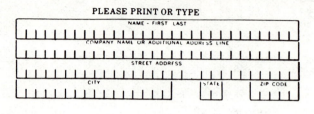

NAME - FIRST LAST

COMPANY NAME OR ADDITIONAL ADDRESS LINE

STREET ADDRESS

CITY   STATE   ZIP CODE

Send Order Form To:

Consumer Information Center
Dept. 016F
Pueblo, CO 81009

BOATING

Chief, Information and Administrative Staff, US Coast Guard, Washington, DC 20590; phone 202-426-1080.

BUS TRAVEL

Consumer Affairs Office, Interstate Commerce Commission, Washington, DC 20423; phone 202-275-7252.

BUSINESS

Office of the Ombudsman, Department of Commerce, Washington, DC 20230; phone 202-377-3176.

Director, Women-in-Business and Consumer Affairs, Small Business Administration, 1441 L St., NW, Washington, DC 20416; phone 202-653-6074.

CHILD ABUSE

National Center on Child Abuse and Neglect, PO Box 1182, Washington, DC 20013; phone 202-755-0593.

CHILDHOOD IMMUNIZATION

Office of the Assistant Secretary for Health, Office of Public Affairs, Washington, DC 20201; phone 202-472-5663.

CHILDREN AND YOUTH

Director of Public Affairs, Office of Human Development Services, Department of Health, Education, and Welfare, Washington, DC 20201; phone 202-472-7257.

COMMODITY TRADING

Consumer Hotline, Commodity Futures Trading Commission, 2033 K Street, NW, Washington, DC. 20581; toll-free hotline in California and states east of the Mississippi, 800-424-9838; states west of the Mississippi except California, 800-227-4428. In Washington, DC call 254-8630.

CONSUMER INFORMATION

For a copy of the free *Consumer Information Catalog*, a listing of more than 200 selected Federal consumer publications on such topics as child care, automobiles, health, employment, housing, energy, etc., send a postcard to the Consumer Information Center, Pueblo, CO 81009.

COPYRIGHTS

Copyright Office, Crystal Mall, 1921 Jefferson Davis Highway, Arlington, VA 20559; phone 703-557-8700.

CREDIT

Director, Bureau of Consumer Protection, Federal Trade Commission, Washington, DC 20850; phone 202-523-3727.

CRIME INSURANCE

Federal Crime Insurance, Department of Housing and Urban Development, PO Box 41033, Washington, DC 20014; toll-free hotline **800-638-8780**. In Washington, DC call 652-2637.

CUSTOMS

Public Information Division, US Customs, Washington, DC 20229; phone 202-566-8195.

DISCRIMINATION

US Commission on Civil Rights, 1121 Vermont Avenue, Washington, DC 20425; phone 202-254-6697.

Equal Employment Opportunity Commission, 2401 E St., NW, Washington, DC 20506; phone 202-634-6930.

For complaints about discrimination in lending practices by financial and retail institutions based on race, color, religion, national origin, sex, marital status, age, or receipt of public assistance, contact the Housing and Credit Section, Civil Rights Division, Justice Department, Washington, DC 20530; phone 202-739-4123. (Also see HOUSING)

DRUGS AND COSMETICS

Consumer Inquiry Section, Food and Drug Administration, 5600 Fishers Lane, Rockville, MD 20852; phone 301-443-3170.

EDUCATION GRANTS AND LOANS

Office of Public Affairs, Office of Education, Washington, DC 20202; phone 202-245-7949. Toll-free hotline for Basic Education Opportunity Grants, **800-638-6700**. In Maryland, call **800-492-6602**.

ELDERLY

Administration on Aging, Washington, DC 20201; phone 202-245-2158.

EMPLOYMENT AND JOB TRAINING

Since nearly all employment and training programs are handled at the state or local levels, check your phone directory under your state government for the Employment Service or under your local government for the mayor's office. If you cannot reach these sources, you can obtain general information by writing to the Employment and Training Administration, Department of Labor, Washington, DC 20213; phone 202-376-6905.

ENERGY

Director, Office of Consumer Affairs, Department of Energy, Washington, DC 20585; phone 202-252-5141.

ENERGY EFFICIENCY

Information Office, National Bureau of Standards, Washington, DC 20234; phone 301-921-3181.

ENVIRONMENT

Office of Public Awareness, Environmental Protection Agency, Washington, DC 20460; phone 202-755-0700.

FEDERAL JOB INFORMATION

Check for the Federal Job Information Center under the US Government in your phone directory. If there is no listing, call toll-free directory assistance at **800-555-1212**, and ask for the number of the Federal Job Information Center in your state. In the Washington, DC metropolitan area contact the Civil Service Commission, 1900 E Street, NW, Washington, DC 20415; phone 202-737-9616.

FEDERAL REGULATIONS

For information on Federal regulations and proposals, the Office of the Federal Register (OFR) is offering, among other services, recorded "Dial-a-Reg" phone messages. Dial-a-Reg gives advance information on significant documents to be published in the *Federal Register* the following work day. The service is currently available in three cities: Washington, DC telephone 202-523-5022; Chicago telephone 312-663-0884; and Los Angeles telephone 212-688-6694.

FIREARMS
(See ALCOHOL)

FISH GRADING

National Marine Fisheries Service, Department of Commerce, Washington, DC 20235; phone 202-634-7458.

FISH AND WILDLIFE

Fish and Wildlife Service, Office of Public Affairs, Washington, DC 20240; phone 202-343-5634.

FLOOD INSURANCE

National Flood Insurance, Department of Housing and Urban Development, Washington DC 20410; toll-free hotline **800-424-8872**. In Washington, DC call 755-9096.

FOOD

Assistant Secretary for Food and Consumer Services, US Department of Agriculture, Washington, DC 20250; phone 202-447-4623.

Consumer Inquiry Section, Food and Drug Administration, 5600 Fishers Lane, Rockville, MD 20852; phone 301-443-3170.

FRAUD

Director, Bureau of Consumer Protection, Federal Trade Commission, Washington, DC 20580; phone 202-523-3727.

HANDICAPPED

Director, Division of Public Information, Office of Human Development Services, Department of Health, Education, and Welfare, Washington, DC 20201; phone 202-472-7257.

HOUSING

Department of Housing and Urban Development, Division of Consumer Complaints, Washington, DC 20410; phone 202-755-5353.

For complaints about housing discrimination call the housing discrimination hotline **800-424-8590**. In Washington, DC call 755-5490.

IMMIGRATION AND NATURALIZATION

Information Services, Immigration and Naturalization Service, 425 Eye St., NW, Washington, DC 20536; phone 202-376-8449.

INDIAN ARTS AND CRAFTS

Indian Arts and Crafts Board, Washington, DC 20240; phone 202-343-2773.

JOB SAFETY
Office of Information, Occupational Safety and Health Administration, Department of Labor, Washington, DC 20210; phone 202-523-8151.

MAIL
Fraud

Check with your local postal inspector about problems relating to mail fraud and undelivered merchandise or contact the Chief Postal Inspector, US Postal Inspection Service, Washington, DC 20260; phone 202-245-5445. (For a listing of regional postal inspectors see CONSUMER NEWS July 15, 1977)

Service

Check with your local postmaster or contact the Consumer Advocate, US Postal Service, Room 5920, Washington, DC 20260; phone 202-245-4514.

MAPS
Public Inquiries Office, Geological Survey, National Center, Reston, VA 22092; phone 703-860-6167.

MEDICAID/MEDICARE
Health Care Financing Administration, Department of Health, Education, and Welfare, Washington, DC 20201; phone 202-245-0312.

MEDICAL RESEARCH
Division of Public Information, National Institutes of Health, 9000 Rockville Pike, Bethesda, MD 20014; phone 301-496-5787.

Center for Disease Control, Attention, Public Inquiries, Atlanta, GA 30333; phone 404-653-3311, ext 3534.

MENTAL ILLNESS
(See ALCOHOLISM, DRUG ABUSE AND MENTAL ILLNESS)

METRIC INFORMATION
(See ENERGY EFFICIENCY, National Bureau of Standards)

MOVING
Interstate Commerce Commission; Washington, DC 20423; toll-free moving hotline **800-424-9312**. In Florida call **800-432-4537**. In Washington, DC call 275-7852.

PARKS AND RECREATION AREAS
National Forests

Forest Service, US Department of Agriculture, Washington, DC 20250; phone 202-447-3760.

National Parks and Historic Sites

National Park Service, Washington, DC 20240; phone 202-343-7394.

Recreation Areas on Army Corps of Engineers Project Sites

Recreation Resource Management Branch (CWO-R), Army Corps of Engineers, Washington, DC 20314; phone 202-693-7177.

Other Recreation Areas

Office of Public Affairs, Department of the Interior, Washington, DC 20240; phone 202-343-3171.

PASSPORTS
For passport information check with your local post office or contact the Passport Office, Department of State, 1425 K St., NW, Washington, DC 20524; phone 202-783-8200.

PATENTS AND TRADEMARKS
Patents

Commissioner, Patent Office, Department of Commerce, Washington, DC 20231; phone 703-557-3080.

Trademarks

Commissioner, Trademark Office, Department of Commerce, Washington, DC 20231; phone 703-557-3268.

PENSIONS
Office of Communications, Pension Benefit Guaranty Corporation, 2020 K Street, NW, Washington, DC 20006; phone 202-254-4817.

Labor Management Standards Administration, Department of Labor, Washington, DC 20210; phone 202-523-8776.

PHYSICAL FITNESS/SPORTS
President's Council on Physical Fitness and Sports, 400 6th St., SW, Washington, DC 20201; phone 202-755-8131.

PRODUCT SAFETY
Consumer Product Safety Commission, Consumer Services Branch, Washington, DC 20207; toll-free hotline **800-638-2666**. In Maryland call **800-492-2937**.

RADIO AND TELEVISION BROADCASTING/ INTERFERENCE

Consumer Assistance Office, Federal Communications Commission, Washington, DC 20554; phone 202-632-7000.

RUNAWAY CHILDREN

The National Runaway Hotline; toll-free **800-621-4000**. In Illinois call **800-972-6004**.

SMOKING

Office on Smoking and Health, 12420 Parklawn Drive, Room 158 Park Building, Rockville, MD 20852; phone 301-443-1575.

SOCIAL SECURITY

Check your local phone directory under US government. If there is no listing check at your local post office for the schedule of visits by Social Security representatives, or write: Division of Public Inquiries, Social Security Administration, 6401 Security Boulevard, Baltimore, MD 21235; phone 301-594-7705.

SOLAR HEATING

National Solar Heating and Cooling Information Center, PO Box 1607, Rockville, MD 20850; toll-free hotline is **800-523-2929**. In Pennsylvania, call **800-462-4983**.

STOCKS AND BONDS

Consumer Liaison Office, Securities and Exchange Commission, Washington, DC 20549; phone 202-523-5516.

TAXES

The Internal Revenue Service (IRS) toll-free tax information number is listed in your tax package and is generally listed in your local telephone directory. If you cannot locate the number, call your information operator for the number for your area. If you wish to write, send the letter to your IRS District Director. Problem Resolution Program (PRP). Offices have been established in each district to solve unique problems and complaints which have not been satisfied through normal channels. Taxpayers may call the toll-free number and ask for the PRP Office.

TRAIN TRAVEL

AMTRAK (National Railroad Passenger Corp.) For consumer problems first try to contact a local AMTRAK consumer relations office listed in your phone directory. If there is not an office near you contact AMTRAK, Office of Consumer Relations, PO Box 2709, Washington, DC 20013; phone 202-383-2121.

TRAVEL INFORMATION

US Travel Service, Department of Commerce, Washington, DC 20230; phone 202-377-4553.

VENEREAL DISEASE

VD toll-free hotline **800-523-1885**. In Pennsylvania call **800-462-4966**.

VETERANS' INFORMATION

The Veterans Administration has toll-free numbers in all 50 states. Check your local phone directory, or call **800-555-1212** for toll-free directory assistance. For problems that can't be handled through local offices, write Veterans Administration, (271), 810 Vermont Avenue, NW, Washington, DC 20420.

WAGES AND WORKING CONDITIONS

Employment Standards Administration, Department of Labor, Washington, DC 20210; phone 202-523-8743.

WARRANTIES

For a problem involving the failure of a seller to honor a warranty, contact the Division of Special Statutes, Federal Trade Commission, Washington, DC 20580; phone 202-724-1100. Or you may contact the FTC regional office nearest you. They are listed in your telephone directory under US Government.

For more information

If you have questions about any program or agency in the Federal Government, you may want to call the Federal Information Center (FIC) nearest you. FIC staffs are prepared to help consumers find needed information or locate the right agency—usually Federal, but sometimes state or local—for help with problems. Each city listed below has an FIC or a tieline—a toll-free local number connecting to an FIC elsewhere. Local listings printed in *italics* are tielines to the nearest FIC.

ALABAMA
Birmingham   205-322-8591
Mobile   205-438-1421

ARIZONA
Phoenix   602-261-3313
Tucson   602-622-1511

ARKANSAS
Little Rock   501-378-6177

CALIFORNIA
Los Angeles   213-688-3800
Sacramento   916-440-3344
San Diego   714-293-6030
San Francisco   415-556-6600
San Jose   408-275-7422
Santa Ana   714-836-2386

COLORADO
Colorado
Springs   303-471-9491
Denver   303-837-3602
Pueblo   303-544-9523

CONNECTICUT
Hartford   203-527-2617
New Haven   203-624-4720

DISTRICT OF COLUMBIA
Washington   202-755-8660

FLORIDA
Fort Lauder-
dale   305-522-8531
Jacksonville   904-354-4756
Miami   305-350-4155
Orlando   305-422-1800
St. Petersburg   813-893-3495
Tampa   813-229-7911
West Palm
Beach   305-833-7566

GEORGIA
Atlanta   404-221-6891

HAWAII
Honolulu   808-546-8620

ILLINOIS
Chicago   312-353-4242

INDIANA
Gary/
Hammond   219-883-4110
Indianapolis   317-269-7373

IOWA
Des Moines   515-284-4448

KANSAS
Topeka   913-295-2866
Wichita   316-263-6931

KENTUCKY
Louisville   502-582-6261

LOUISIANA
New Orleans   504-589-6696

MARYLAND
Baltimore   301-962-4980

MASSACHUSETTS
Boston   617-223-7121

MICHIGAN
Detroit   313-226-7016
Grand Rapids   616-451-2628

MINNESOTA
Minneapolis   612-725-2073

MISSOURI
Kansas City   816-374-2466
St. Joseph   816-233-8206
St. Louis   314-425-4106

NEBRASKA
Omaha   402-221-3353

NEW JERSEY
Newark   201-645-3600
Paterson/
Passaic   201-523-0717
Trenton   609-396-4400

NEW MEXICO
Albuquerque   505-766-3091
Santa Fe   505-983-7743

NEW YORK
Albany   518-463-4421
Buffalo   716-846-4010
New York   212-264-4464
Rochester   716-546-5075
Syracuse   315-476-8545

NORTH CAROLINA
Charlotte   704-376-3600

OHIO
Akron   216-375-5638
Cincinnati   513-684-2801
Cleveland   216-522-4040
Columbus   614-221-1014
Dayton   513-223-7377
Toledo   419-241-3223

OKLAHOMA
Oklahoma City   405-231-4868
Tulsa   918-584-4193

OREGON
Portland   503-221-2222

PENNSYLVANIA
Allentown/
Bethlehem   215-821-7785
Philadelphia   215-597-7042
Pittsburgh   412-644-3456
Scranton   717-346-7081

RHODE ISLAND
Providence   401-331-5565

TENNESSEE
Chattanooga   615-265-8231
Memphis   901-521-3285
Nashville   615-242-5056

TEXAS
Austin   512-472-5494
Dallas   214-749-2131
Fort Worth   817-334-3624
Houston   713-226-5711
San Antonio   512-224-4471

UTAH
Ogden   801-399-1347
Salt Lake City   801-524-5353

VIRGINIA
Newport News   804-244-0480
Norfolk   804-441-6723
Richmond   804-643-4928
Roanoke   703-982-8591

WASHINGTON
Seattle   206-442-0570
Tacoma   206-383-5230

WISCONSIN
Milwaukee   414-271-2273

5

The Tax Bite

Computation of Income Tax: Pauper Work
RALPH NOEL

*I'm proud to pay taxes in the United States.
Only thing is—I could be just as proud for half
the money.*
ARTHUR GODFREY

Mark Twain, once asked what the difference was between a taxidermist and a tax collector, answered, "The taxidermist takes only your skin." We don't know who said that the taxpayer is the only varmint expected to yield a pelt every year, but we do know you'd like to meet the mild little man who walked into the income tax collector's office, sat down, and beamed at everyone. "What can we do for you?" asked the receptionist. "Nothing, thank you," replied the little man. "I just wanted to meet the people I'm working for." If you stop to reflect, you do work for the government three or four months out of every year.

Today the chief source of federal revenue is the income tax. It was originally introduced as a means of helping to finance the Civil War, but in its modern form it dates only from 1913.

Figure 5–1 shows the first Form 1040—on 1913 earnings. As you can see, rates soared to 6 percent in the top bracket, on income of over $500,000. Exemptions—$3,000 for single persons, $5,000 for a married couple. The deductions were very lib-

FIGURE 5–1

Form 1040 for 1913

TO BE FILLED IN BY COLLECTOR.

List No. ....

.... District of ....

Date received ....

Form 1040.

INCOME TAX.

THE PENALTY
FOR FAILURE TO HAVE THIS RETURN IN
THE HANDS OF THE COLLECTOR OF
INTERNAL REVENUE ON OR BEFORE
MARCH 1 IS $20 TO $4,000.
(SEE INSTRUCTIONS ON PAGE 4.)

TO BE FILLED IN BY INTERNAL REVENUE BUREAU.

File No. ....

Assessment List ....

Page .... Line ....

UNITED STATES INTERNAL REVENUE.

RETURN OF ANNUAL NET INCOME OF INDIVIDUALS.

(As provided by Act of Congress, approved October 3, 1913.)

RETURN OF NET INCOME RECEIVED OR ACCRUED DURING THE YEAR ENDED DECEMBER 31, 191....

(FOR THE YEAR 1913, FROM MARCH 1, TO DECEMBER 31.)

Filed by (or for) .... of ....
　　　　　　　　　(Full name of individual.)　　　　　　　　　　　　　　　(Street and No.)

in the City, Town, or Post Office of .... State of ....
　　　　　　　　　　　　　　(Fill in pages 2 and 3 before making entries below.)

1. GROSS INCOME (see page 2, line 12)	$				
2. GENERAL DEDUCTIONS (see page 3, line 7)	$				
3. NET INCOME	$				

Deductions and exemptions allowed in computing income subject to the normal tax of 1 per cent.

4. Dividends and net earnings received or accrued, of corporations, etc., subject to like tax. (See page 2, line 11)	$				
5. Amount of income on which the normal tax has been deducted and withheld at the source. (See page 2, line 9, column A)..					
6. Specific exemption of $3,000 or $4,000, as the case may be. (See Instructions 3 and 19)					
Total deductions and exemptions. (Items 4, 5, and 6)	$				
7. TAXABLE INCOME on which the normal tax of 1 per cent is to be calculated. (See Instruction 3).	$				

8. When the net income shown above on line 3 exceeds $20,000, the additional tax thereon must be calculated as per schedule below:

	INCOME.				TAX.			
1 per cent on amount over $20,000 and not exceeding $50,000....	$				$			
2 " " 50,000 " " 75,000....								
3 " " 75,000 " " 100,000....								
4 " " 100,000 " " 250,000....								
5 " " 250,000 " " 500,000....								
6 " " 500,000								
Total additional or super tax					$			
Total normal tax (1 per cent of amount entered on line 7).....					$			
Total tax liability................................					$			

Source: U.S. Internal Revenue Service.

eral—for example, all dividends were deductible. Instructions took up all of one whole page.

At first, rates were very moderate; but two world wars and the state of the world today have caused the rates to rise to very high levels. The growth in the burden of the personal income tax may be seen from the fact that in 1915 a single person with no dependents, earning $10,000 a year, paid a federal income tax of only $70. In 1929 the tax was $90. Today the tax is approximately $1,216. A married couple with no dependents, earning $10,000 a year, paid $60 in 1915 and $52 in 1929, and pays about $757 today. For the married couple with two dependents, comparable payments on a $10,000 income were $60 in 1915 and $40 in 1929, and are $442 today.

Inflation adds to the real burden of the income tax. If wages are increased to compensate for the loss of purchasing power due to inflation, the taxpayer over time gets pushed into a higher tax bracket under a graduated-rate income tax structure. The Revenue Act of 1978 adopted new tax rate schedules with broader taxable income brackets and reduced tax rates for several income brackets. The widening of the brackets is designed to prevent higher earnings, generally caused by inflationary forces, from pushing taxpayers more quickly into higher tax brackets. For example, a married couple filing a joint return showing a taxable income of $25,000 in 1978 will have a tax of $4,956 before any tax credits. On the same taxable income in 1979, the couples tax before any tax credits will be $4,633 or $323 less than in 1978.

THE FEDERAL INCOME TAX LAW

Since practically everyone who works or has any income is subject to the federal income tax law, it is of the utmost importance that everyone have knowledge of at least its main provisions. Unfortunately, the law has grown so complex that only those persons who devote most of their time and attention to it (tax experts) can really be fully conversant with it; and even they constantly run into troublesome situations in which final decisions must be left to the courts.

Just how complex the federal income tax law has become can be seen from the fact that in a recent year one out of every five of the more than 75 million federal income tax returns filed was in error. Some 14 million returns were incorrect— nine out of ten paid too little; one out of ten paid too much. Approximately $136 million was overpaid; $1.4 billion was underpaid. The Bureau of Internal Revenue has time and staff to examine only a limited number of all returns filed, and it does this largely on a sampling basis—except for the larger returns, all of which are examined. The larger your return, the more likely it is that you will face an audit.

"We're not questioning your tips and donations - it wasn't necessary to bring proof!"
Courtesy of Jeff Keate and Chicago Tribune—New York News Syndicate, Inc.

Any of It Yours?

There's $99.4 million waiting to be claimed at the IRS in the form of 244,803 undelivered refund checks. Eventually the unclaimed checks will be canceled, and the amounts credited to taxpayers' accounts to be applied to next year's tax bill. But if an unclaimed refund can't be returned within two years, the money goes to the Treasury.

The Wall Street Journal, December 13, 1978.

Martinsburg Monsters

Electronic data processing (EDP) has now been extended nationwide. Performing arithmetic checks at speeds of 250,000 numbers and over a second, this electronic computer system detects errors, discloses proper refunds and credits, and maintains a continuing account of your individual tax records. IRS keeps track of you by your tax identification number (social security number). Also, information returns have taken on an expanded role. Banks, brokers, and other businesses paying you $10 or more a year in dividends must report them to the Internal Revenue Service. Each information return contains your taxpayer's identification number.

"Martinsburg Monsters" are what Internal Revenue Service employees call the four huge computers at the National Computer Center at Martinsburg, West Virginia. On these machines are run the magnetic tapes of all the returns received at the Internal Revenue Service's seven regional processing centers. The tax return filed by the taxpayer first goes to one of the seven regional centers, where the most vital information is placed on magnetic tape and then sent to Martinsburg, where for the next three years, before it is stored elsewhere, the taxpayer's return will be sent through the suspicious computers almost 200 times. The computers are programmed to look for errors, odd items, unusual changes, and unlikely comparisons. Any taxpayer whose return is different from others in his class is immediately singled out for special attention. For example, a return listing $6,500 income and $2,000 in payment to charitable organizations is immediately spotted by the computer. If a taxpayer does not earn interest from savings accounts this year after having collected considerable interest for several years before, he too might be singled out. A doctor's return is lined up against the returns of others in the profession to compare incomes, deductions, and expenses. The same is done for returns in other professions. Anything unusual or out of line singles out a return for an audit.

The regional center gets shocks occasionally. In Austin, Texas, it was a quiet afternoon when a shriek pierced the air. A woman employee opened a return and found it soaked in blood (chicken's blood, the supervisor concluded), and the return was processed. Each year the regional centers are flooded with phony or humorous returns (see Figure 5–2), with shirts off taxpayers' backs, with tea bags (symbolic of the Boston Tea Party), and with Band-Aids because it hurts. One Form 1040 was reproduced on a shirt; another was blown up on a six-foot-long piece of butcher paper. One woman sent a lock of hair, saying she felt scalped after filling out the return. And a man included a handful of buttons, because, he said, "You got the shirt last year." One person sent in a comb, explaining that he didn't need it anymore because he had pulled out all his hair while figuring his taxes. One fellow sent along a sandwich bag full of mud, declaring: "This form is as clear to me as this mud."

The Pay-as-You-Go Plan—Withholding

Much of the income tax is collected through the withholding system. Under this system, the employer deducts part of your pay as tax and turns it over to the district director of internal revenue or to a depository bank. The tax owed by you is determined after the close of your taxable year when you file your income tax return. You are then given full credit for the amounts withheld from your pay as shown by your withholding statement (W–2).

Wages subject to withholding include salaries, fees, bonuses, commissions, vacation allowances, and dismissal and severance pay. Certain kinds of income, such as payments for odd jobs and retirement and pension payments, are not subject to withholding. Amounts received as scholarship and fellowship grants are not subject to withholding.

Two things determine how much tax your employer withholds from you. These are the amount of your salary and the number of withholding exemptions you claimed in a statement you are required to file with your employer on a Withholding Exemption Certificate (Form W–4). You are entitled to receive from your employer on or before January 31 *two* copies of a "withholding statement" (Form

FIGURE 5–2

SIMPLIFIED UNOFFICIAL

FORM 1040XX — INDIVIDUAL DEFICIT RETURN

INFERNAL REVENUE SERVICE **1976**

For the year ended December 31, 1976, or any date within the year of the Dragon.

Do Not Write in This Space	**For Net Refunds of not more than $500,000.99**	Write All You Want to Here

Notes: Before preparing this return, read "Ten Years in Stir," by Al Capone. Attach blood sample and note type of cell-block desired:

☐ Color TV ☐ Private ☐ Co-ed ☐ Ward

Print REAL Name, Please, and Address Below

Name_____ Horoscope Sign_____

Address_____ Master Charge No._____

City_____ State_____ Zip_____ Diners Club No._____

Name of your Bookie _____ Phone No._____ Swiss Bank No._____

Filing Status Is this a joint return?_____ Which joint?_____ Living with wife?_____ Why?_____ Did you file a return last year?_____

How much did you file?_____ (If "Same", send copy of last year's return. We don't want to go through all of this again!)

↓

Staple here all W-2's, 1099's, Lottery and Race Track Tickets, 24-column (or less) work sheets

INCOME

1. PAY DAY TOTALS (in dollars, bushels, or services received) . . . . $_____
2. INTEREST (or have you lost it), PHONEY SALES EXPENSE VOUCHERS, KICK-BACKS . . . . . _____
3. STATE LOTTERY, FOOTBALL POOLS, BINGO, Etc. . . . . _____
4. TOTAL INCOME . . . . $_____

DEDUCTIONS (This is the good part. Use your imagination.)

5. CONTRIBUTIONS:

Donations to Political Boondogglers, Election Campaign (If cash, who got it?**) . . . . . $_____
Donation of Personal Papers, Tapes (Be sure to back-date.) . . . . $_____
Hush Money, Slush Funds, Wire Tap Charges, Traffic Tickets . . . . $_____
Donations to Fast Women, Slow Horses, State Lotteries, Punch-and-Miss Boards . . . . $_____
Paid to better poker players, gin players, golfers, bowlers, Las Vegas Trips . . . . . $_____
Office raffles, welcome party, farewell party, get-well party, baby-coming,
baby-not-coming, bachelor dinner, divorce party, any-other-excuse party donations . . . . $_____ $_____

6. DEDUCTIONS:

Business Expenses *(If Entertainment, attach names and phone numbers of
Entertainers) Night Clubbing, Fishing Trips, Booze, Bait. Etc. . . . . . . $_____
Stock Market Losses, Leaky Tax Shelters, Losses of Joint Property thru Divorce . . . . $_____
Lunches, Gifts to Purchasing Agents, Assistants and Secretaries . . . . . . $_____
Alimony, Mother-in-Law, Uncle Jake, Aunt Minnie, Dogs, Cats, Mynah Birds . . . . . $_____
Taxes Paid: City, County, State Income Taxes, Sales Tax, Beer Tax, Thumb Tacks . . . . $_____ $_____

7. COST-OF-LIVING ALLOWANCE: (Take 18% of TOTAL INCOME, Line 4 above) . . . . $_____
8. TOTAL DEDUCTIONS: (Should exceed TOTAL INCOME. If not, start over and use more imagination) . . . $_____
9. LESS TOTAL INCOME: (Line 4 above) . . . . $_____
10. BALANCE OF NET DEFICIT TO BE REFUNDED Stipulate preference:

☐ Food Stamps ☐ Postage Stamps ☐ Lottery Tickets . . . . $_____

GENERAL INSTRUCTIONS

Buy yourself an Excedrin (non-deductible) and hurry to the nearest tax expert. If he won't help, turn him in as an Un-American.

*—See line 17a, section f, paragraph 3.

**—Be sure to answer fully all questions on pages 2, 3, and 7.

AFFIDAVIT

I/we swear we're as confused as anybody by the simplified, simple Form 1040XX. Subscribed and sworn at before me on this_____ day of_____ 19_____.

X_____
Signature

XX_____
Witness (bartender or Sick-iatrist suggested)

↑

Please note: We at PSI are not tax experts. We're as baffled by tax forms and reforms as you are. Our redesigned version of Form 1040 ought to convince you we both need help. Free copies (any quantity if you really want them) are yours. Just call (313) 399-3300, or write to:

PSI PRINTING SERVICE INC., 1451 E. Lincoln, Madison Heights, Mich. 48071

P. S. When it comes to redesigning accounting systems, business forms, bank checks, continuous-style forms . . . we're No. 1. Try us and see.

Source: Printing Service, Inc., 1451 E. Lincoln, Madison Heights, MI 48071.

"Income Tax Guides? Yes, sir—they're over in Section R, between our Greek manuscripts and our books on integral calculus."

Reprinted by permission *The Wall Street Journal*

tax return. The return covers the previous year's income. The declaration estimates the current year's anticipated income. It must be accompanied by your first quarterly installment payment of the estimated tax. Payments are due April 15, June 15, September 15, and January 15.

If you do not expect any considerable change in income from last year to this one, the whole estimating process can be simplified by using last year's income and last year's tax as your current year's estimate. If you do this, you will not be subject to any penalty even though your income and tax finally turn out to be greater than the amounts used in your declaration. Estimates do not have to be absolutely accurate. You are allowed a 20 percent margin of error before a penalty is imposed, and you are given an opportunity to change your estimate from quarter to quarter. If your situation calls for a different estimate (for example, if last year's income was abnormally high), secure a Form 2210 from your district director. It should be of considerable help in making your calculations.

W–2). This statement shows the total wages paid and the income tax and the social security tax withheld, if any, during the previous calendar year. One copy of the W–2 Form should accompany your tax return. The remaining copy is for your personal records.

Declarations of Estimated Tax

Because the withholding tax on wages is not sufficient to keep many taxpayers—particularly business owners, professional people, investors, and landlords—paid up on their income tax, they are required to file a declaration of estimated tax and to make quarterly payments in advance of the annual income tax return.

Normally, you file your declaration (Form 1040 ES) on or before April 15, along with your annual

"Do we get employee's discount?"

Reprinted by permission *The Wall Street Journal*

Can the go-go girls at the Hello Doll bar gyrate around the IRS?

The dancing girls were the main attraction at a North Hollywood, Calif., bar where they performed on a mirrored stage. The bar didn't pay Social Security taxes for them or withhold income taxes from their paychecks because it considered them independent contractors. But the Internal Revenue Service considered them employes and told the bar to pay $32,000 in back payroll taxes.

Whether workers are independent contractors or employes often is determined by how much control the person employing them has over their work. In the case of the dancing girls, a federal court jury was told to consider, among other things, "whether the hirer can control the details of the dancer's performance." The jury was instructed that "if the services rendered are artistic in nature and not subject to control as to how they are to be performed, that is indicative of an independent contractor."

The jurors, all females, apparently didn't find the performances at the Hello Doll bar "artistic in nature," for they found the dancers were employes subject to payroll tax.

Source: *The Wall Street Journal,* August 30, 1978.

Who Must File a Federal Income Tax Return[1]

The minimum income required for a single person or a head of household is $3,300, and for a married couple, under age 65, it is $5,400.

Note that you should file a federal income tax return if you had income tax withheld from your pay but did not have enough to be required to file a return. By filing a return and claiming your personal exemption, you can get a refund, even though you are claimed as a dependent by another taxpayer.

Tax Forms

The two most commonly used forms for individual federal income tax returns are the Short Form

1040A and the regular Form 1040. Most taxpayers have a choice as to which form they use. You may use the Short Form 1040A if all your income was from wages, salaries, tips, dividends, and interest. You may not itemize deductions, however, if you use Short Form 1040A. To itemize deductions you must use Form 1040.[2]

If you file Short Form 1040A, no additional schedules are necessary. If you file Form 1040 you will probably also need one or more of the following schedules:

If you *itemize deductions,* use Schedule A (Form 1040).

Sources of dividends and interest must be itemized in Schedule B.

Profit (or loss) from your business or profession is reported on Schedule C (Form 1040).

Gains and losses on sales or exchanges of property are reported on Schedule D (Form 1040) and Form 4797.

Supplemental Schedule of Income, Schedule E (Form 1040), is used to report income from pensions, annuities, rents, royalties, partnerships, estates, trusts, and small business corporations.

Farm income and expenses are shown on Schedule F of Form 1040.

Income averaging is computed on Schedule G (Form 1040).

If you claim retirement income credit, use Schedule R (Form 1040).

Use Schedule SE (Form 1040) to compute your self-employment tax.

Use Schedule TC—Tax Computation.

---

[1] For further information, see IRS Publication no. 528, *Information on Filing Your Tax Return,* Internal Revenue Service, Washington, D.C. A free copy may be obtained from any local IRS office.

[2] See *Your Federal Income Tax,* Publication no. 17, U.S. Department of the Treasury, Internal Revenue Service, Washington, D.C., latest edition. The pages which follow contain only highlight information current at the time of writing. Necessarily, not all facets, aspects, rules, and regulations are covered. For tax facts, advice, or information, consult the Internal Revenue Service (toll-free phones are listed in *Your Federal Income Tax*) or an attorney or a certified public accountant. The tax regulations are very complex, and they are constantly changing. Consultations with competent sources are essential for up-to-date, accurate information.

TABLE 5–1
1979 Tax Rates

Married Individuals Filing Joint Return or Surviving Spouses

Taxable Income	Tax	% on Excess
$0— $ 3,400	$ —	—
Over 3,400	—	14
5,500	294	16
7,600	630	18
11,900	1,404	21
16,000	2,265	24
20,200	3,273	28
24,600	4,505	32
29,900	6,201	37
35,200	8,162	43
45,800	12,720	49
60,000	19,678	54
85,600	33,502	59
109,400	47,544	64
162,400	81,464	68
215,400	117,504	70

Married Individuals Filing Separate Returns

Taxable Income	Tax	% on Excess
$0— $ 1,700	$ —	—
Over 1,700	—	14
2,750	147	16
3,800	315	18
5,950	702	21
8,000	1,133	24
10,100	1,637	28
12,300	2,253	32
14,950	3,101	37
17,600	4,081	43
22,900	6,360	49
30,000	9,839	54
42,800	16,751	59
54,700	23,772	64
81,200	40,732	68
107,700	58,752	70

Unmarried Individuals

Taxable Income	Tax	% on Excess
$0— $ 2,300	$ —	—
Over 2,300	—	14
3,400	154	16
4,400	314	18
6,500	692	19
8,500	1,072	21
10,800	1,555	24
12,900	2,059	26
15,000	2,605	30
18,200	3,565	34
23,500	5,367	39
28,800	7,434	44
34,100	9,766	49
41,500	13,392	55
55,300	20,982	63
81,800	37,677	68
108,300	55,697	70

Heads of Households

Taxable Income	Tax	% on Excess
$0— $ 2,300	$ —	—
Over 2,300	—	14
4,400	294	16
6,500	630	18
8,700	1,026	22
11,800	1,708	24
15,000	2,476	26
18,200	3,308	31
23,500	4,951	36
28,800	6,859	42
34,100	9,085	46
44,700	13,961	54
60,600	22,547	59
81,800	35,055	63
108,300	51,750	68
161,300	87,790	70

If you use Short Form 1040A you may have the IRS compute your tax. If you use Form 1040, the IRS will figure your tax only if your adjusted gross income is $20,000 or less and was only from wages, salaries, tips, dividends, interest, pensions, and annuities, and you are willing to take the standard deduction. Thus, if you wish to itemize deductions you cannot have the IRS figure your tax for you.

The IRS suggests that you round off numbers in figuring your tax. If your dividends are $150.12, you list them as $150. If they are $150.56, the

"Your return was neat and accurate and indicated that you understood the forms completely . . . what *we* want to know is *how?*"

Reprinted by permission *The Wall Street Journal*

figure becomes $151. It pays to do this because if you are single and your taxable income is $9,951, your tax is $1216, but if your arithmetic can help you lose that $1, your tax will be $1205, or $11 less.

Form W–2 is not a tax return. It is a receipt which shows how much tax has been withheld from your salary, and it must accompany your return as evidence of taxes withheld. If you work for more than one employer during the year you will have more than one Form W–2. Copy B of *each* Form W–2 must accompany your return.

An income tax form is like a laundry list—either way you lose your shirt.

—*Fred Allen*

Married Persons—Joint or Separate Return

Marital status is determined as of the last day of the taxable year. For tax purposes, a person is considered to be married for the entire calendar year if he or she is married on December 31, regardless of the date of the wedding. If you are divorced or legally separated on or before December 31, you are single for the entire calendar year for income tax purposes.

If either the wife or the husband dies before the close of the survivor's taxable year, the survivor is considered, for tax purposes, as having been married for the entire year. Thus, if the survivor did not remarry before the close of the taxable year, a joint return may be filed by the surviving spouse.

In some states, which are known as "community property states" (Arizona, California, Idaho, Louisiana, Nevada, New Mexico, Texas, and Washington), the earnings of a married couple belong one half to the husband and one half to the wife, irrespective of who earned it. If, therefore, a husband and wife in a community property state file separate returns, it is mandatory that each report one half of the combined community income. Taxpayers domiciled in these states have always divided their income for federal income tax purposes.[3]

Although married couples in non–community property states cannot divide their income under state law, they can "split" their income for purposes of federal income taxation in joint returns. This equalizes federal income taxes on married couples in all states.

Married taxpayers may make a joint return and include all the exemptions, income, and deductions of both husband and wife. Even though one spouse has no income, husband and wife may still file a joint return. Ordinarily it will be advantageous, if married, to file a joint return using the "split income" method of computing the tax. It usually results in a lower tax than would result from the use of separate returns. This is because the tax is

---

[3] See IRS Publication no. 555, *Community Property and the Federal Income Tax,* Internal Revenue Service, Washington, D.C. A free copy may be obtained from any local IRS office.

computed at the lower surtax rate which applies to each half of the income rather than at the higher surtax rate which would apply to the combined or total income.

By not hearing a case brought by two Indiana couples in 1978, the Supreme Court left standing a lower court decision that did nothing about the tax laws that cause a married couple who are both working to pay more taxes than two single people earning the same amount and living°together. To diminish the "marriage penalty" for the working couple, Congress figured the exemptions in the 1978 tax law, so as to lessen the disadvantage between their joint return and the return of the single taxpayer. On the other hand, the IRS will not allow a dependency deduction for people who live together.

Divorce, it seems, is a haven for loving couples who hate taxes.

The tax tables don't favor married couples if both partners work. They would pay less if they weren't married. A married couple with $40,000 of combined taxable income—$20,000 from each spouse—pays the IRS $10,700, whether filing separate returns or a joint one. But two single people with like incomes have a total tax bill of $8,884, or $1,816 less than the marrieds.

Some married folks used to get divorced near the end of the year and file as singles, then remarry the first of the next year only to divorce again for tax avoidance. The IRS stopped this marriage-divorce merry-go-round some years ago. But the agency recently ruled that a married couple getting divorced but planning to stay together without remarrying will qualify as single taxpayers. Prentice-Hall, tax publisher, reported the ruling with this comment:

"We won't presume to offer any advice on this one."

Source: *The Wall Street Journal,* September 20, 1978.

Earned Income Credit

Low-income households—with a maximum of $10,000 income and a dependent child or a disabled dependent in the household—may qualify for "earned income credit" of up to $500. The credit is 10 percent of your first $5,000 of income. It is phased out at a 15 percent rate from $6,000 to 10,000 or you can subtract this credit from your tax bill—and get a refund if the credit is larger than the tax. Beginning July 1, 1979, the credit is to be integrated with withholding taxes so that you can elect to have an advance payment of the earned income credit added to your paycheck each pay period. This tax benefit for low-income individuals and the amendment that allows payments to grandparents for the care of their grandchildren eligible for the child care tax credit help the young low-income family.

Unmarried Persons as Heads of Household

If you are not married (or are legally separated) at the end of the taxable year, you qualify as a "head of household," provided that you furnish over half of the cost of maintaining a home which, during the entire taxable year, except for temporary absences, was occupied as a principal residence both by yourself and by (a) any related person for whom you are entitled to an exemption or (b) your unmarried child, grandchild, or stepchild, even though such child is not a dependent. If your mother or your father, or both, qualify as your dependent, and you maintain a home for one or the other or both, it is *not* necessary that you live in the same household to qualify as a head of household. You may live in a separate home and still meet this test. A rest home or a home for the aged qualifies as a household for this purpose.

When to File a Return

For most individuals, April 15 is the date when federal income tax returns must be filed. Returns, in most cases, can be filed at any time after the close of the taxable year up until midnight April 15.

You may receive an automatic two-month extension of time to file your tax return by filling out, in duplicate, Form 4868, "Application for Automatic Extension of Time to File U.S. Individual

Income Tax Return." You are not even required to give a reason.

In filling out Form 4868, you must make a tentative tax estimate for the year. The application must be filed, by the due date of the return, with the Internal Revenue Service Center for your area. You must also make full payment of any tax due with the application for the automatic extension. You cannot request an extension if you use Short Form 1040A when you file your return because there are less paperwork problems. If you need an additional extension beyond the 60 days you must file Form 2688, "Application for Extension of Time to File U.S. Individual Income Tax Return." This will not be granted as a matter of course, and you must have substantial reasons. The form is an extension of time to file but not an extension of time to pay.

If you cannot pay your tax you can file Form 1127, requesting an extension of time, but you must file a return.

How to Claim Your Exemptions[4]

You, as the taxpayer, are always entitled to at least one exemption for yourself. If, at the end of your taxable year, you were blind or were age 65 or older, you get two exemptions for yourself. If you were both blind and age 65 or over, you get three exemptions. You get exemptions for your spouse if the two of you are filing a joint return.

If you were divorced or legally separated at the end of the year you may not claim your former wife's exemption, even if you contributed all of her support.

The allowance for the personal exemption and exemptions for each dependent is currently $1,000. You can claim your personal exemption of $1,000 even if you are the dependent of another taxpayer.

Information Returns

In case you are ever tempted not to report part or all of your income, remember that the Internal Revenue Service has, by statutory authority, many sources which can be checked for information about your income. The "information at source" provision of the Internal Revenue Code requires every individual, partnership, or corporation to report certain payments to the director of internal revenue.

Banks and corporations must send you on Form 1099 a statement of interest and dividends over $10 sent to you over the year—a copy of which is also sent to the IRS.

What Income Is Taxable

If you win the Nobel Prize or the Pulitzer Prize, you won't have to pay tax on the income from it! The law says that all kinds of income are subject to tax, with specific exceptions. This means that all income which is not specifically exempt must be included in your return, even though it may be offset by expenses and other deductions. Exempt income should be omitted entirely from your return.

Examples of income which *must* be reported, in addition to the usual wages, salaries, bonuses, commissions, tips, pensions, dividends, interest, rents, royalties, and profits, include jury duty fees, contest prizes, lottery and gambling winnings, alimony, and all illegal income.[5] It is hard to believe its not "tongue in cheek," but the I.R.S. has issued guide lines for substantiating gambling winnings to prove that there really are losses and that the winnings are not more than claimed. The I.R.S. suggests keeping a diary, just as businessmen do, to record the "date of the wagering activity, the name and address of the gambling establishment, the amounts won or lost, and the names of other persons, if any, who were present with the taxpayer at the gambling place."[6]

These are merely examples. The list is not all-inclusive, since all income, unless specifically exempt, must be reported.

---

[4] For further information, see IRS Publication no. 501, *Your Exemptions and Exemptions for Dependents.* A free copy may be obtained from your local IRS office.

[5] For further information, see IRS Publication no. 525, *Taxable Income and Non-Taxable Income.* A free copy may be obtained from any IRS office.

[6] *New York Times,* September 27, 1977.

You need not report social security, welfare benefits, life insurance proceeds, gifts, inheritances, scholarship grants, veteran payments, or workmen's compensation.

Dividends

Dividends representing distributions of earnings and profits by corporations and associations are taxable income. Those which are merely a return to the taxpayer of part of his investment are nontaxable.

In some cases, a corporation distributes both a dividend and a repayment of capital at the same time. When the mixed distributions are made, the check or notice will usually show the dividend and the capital repayment separately. In any case, you must report the dividend portion as income. If you are the owner of stock held in the name of your broker, the dividend must be reported on your return.

You may exclude from your income $100 of dividends received from domestic corporations during your taxable year. If a joint return is filed and securities are held jointly, $200 of dividends may be excluded. If securities are held individually, each spouse may exclude $100 of dividends received from qualifying corporations, but one spouse may not use any portion of the $100 exclusion not used by the other. For example, if the husband had $200 in dividends and the wife had $20, only a total of $120 may be excluded on a joint return.

Interest

Interest income is usually taxable. You must include in your return any interest that you receive or that is credited to your account (whether entered in your passbook or not) and can be withdrawn by you. All interest on bonds, debentures, notes, savings accounts, or loans is taxable, except for certain governmental issues. For example, interest is fully exempt from tax if it is interest from state and municipal bonds and securities (including political instrumentalities or subdivisions thereof, such

as the Port of New York Authority, the Indiana Toll Road Commission, state industrial development boards, and the Oklahoma County Utility Services Authority).

Business or Profession

Profits from an unincorporated business or profession are taxable to the individual as income and therefore must be included in your personal income tax return.[7] A separate Schedule C, entitled "Profit (or Loss) from Business or Profession," is provided to enable you to subtract your costs from your receipts to arrive at your net profit.

Generally, the costs you can deduct are the ordinary and necessary expenses of doing business— cost of merchandise, salaries, interest, taxes, rent, repairs, and incidental supplies. In the case of capital investments and improvements in depreciable property, such as buildings, machines, fixtures, and similar items having a useful life of more than one year, the law provides an annual depreciation allowance as the method of recovering the original capital cost tax-free. If some of your expenses are part business and part personal, you can deduct the business portion but not the personal portion. For instance, a doctor who uses his car half for business can deduct only half of the operating expenses of the car and take depreciation on only half of the original cost of the car.

A partnership or similar business firm (not a corporation) does not pay income tax in the firm's name. Therefore, each partner must report in his personal tax return his share of his partnership's income and pay tax on it. As a partner, you must include in income on your Form 1040 (Schedule E) your distributive share of partnership earnings, which may be more or less than withdrawals. The partnership is required to file a Form 1065, which is an information return showing the results of its

---

[7] See *Tax Guide for Small Business,* Internal Revenue Service Publication no. 334. It may be obtained from the Internal Revenue Service free of charge. See also IRS Publication no. 463, *Travel, Entertainment, and Gift Expenses.* A free copy may be obtained from your local IRS office.

operations for the taxable year and the items of income, gain, loss, deduction, or credit affecting its partners' individual income tax returns. The partnership pays no income tax unless it has elected to be taxed as a corporation. Your distributive share of the partnership's income is your part of the partnership's business results, whether or not they are distributed to you.

The social security tax for those who are self-employed is reported and paid as part of Schedule C of the personal income tax. The computation of your self-employment tax is made on the separate Schedule C, which, with the attached Schedule SE, should be filed with your income tax return on Form 1040. The self-employment social security tax applies to every self-employed individual if he has at least $400 of net earnings from self-employment in a taxable year.

The Sale and Exchange of Property

If you sell your house, car, furniture, stocks or bonds, real estate, or any other kind of property, the law requires you to report any profit in your tax return. Because of the many special rules for taxing the profit and deducting the loss from such transactions, a special form, Schedule D, is provided. Capital gains and losses will be considered in more detail later.

Annuities and Pensions

The monthly payments you receive from social security when you retire are *not* taxable income, nor are veterans' pensions. If you receive any other kind of pension or annuity, however, it must be reported in Schedule E.

If your pension did not cost you anything and it was fully paid for by your employer, you must pay tax on the full amount you receive each year. If you and your employer each contributed a part of the cost of your annuity or pension and you will recover your contributions completely within three years from the date of your first pension payment, the amounts you receive are *not* taxed as income *until* you have recovered your contribution in full. All amounts received after you have fully recovered your cost are included in taxable income.

If you will not recover your cost within three years after your pension starts, your pension or annuity will be treated under the general rule for annuities.[8]

Rents and Royalties[9]

The term *rents* includes income from real estate and income from any other propery. Royalties are received by authors and composers and for the use of inventions. People owning rented property must incur costs in connection with it. Ordinary expenses and repairs are deductible expenses. Capital expenditures or improvements must be added to the cost of the rented property and depreciated over its remaining life.

If a taxpayer occupies a portion of a dwelling and rents out the rest of it, only those expenses chargeable against the rented portion are deductible. Rents and royalties are reported on Part II of Schedule E of Form 1040. However, if you hold an operating oil, gas, or mineral interest you report gross income and expenses on Schedule C of Form 1040.

Adjusted Gross Income

Some deductions are subtracted from *gross income* to determine the amount of *adjusted gross income*. Other deductions are subtracted only from *adjusted gross income* in arriving at the amount of *taxable income*.

Adjusted gross income is the balance remaining after deducting from *gross income* the following:

1. Expenses of a trade or business.
2. Expenses of a property yielding rents or royalties.

---

[8] IRS Publication no. 575, *Tax Information on Pensions and Annuities.* Free copies are available from local IRS offices.

[9] See IRS Publication no. 550, *Tax Information on Investment Income and Expenses.* A free copy may be obtained from your local IRS office.

3. Expenses of travel, meals, and lodging while away from home at least overnight in the service of one's employer. You may also deduct transportation expenses incurred in connection with the performance of service as an employee even though you are not away from home.
4. Reimbursed expenses (other than those for travel, meals, and lodging while away from home overnight) incurred in the service of one's employer.
5. Allowable losses from a sale or exchange of property.
6. Sick pay, if it is included in your gross income.
7. Sixty percent of the excess of net long-term capital gains over net short-term capital losses.
8. Payments by self-employed persons to retirement plans.
9. Moving expenses incurred as a result of employment.
10. Alimony, by the person who pays it.

The importance of *adjusted gross income* as a factor in determining your tax liability cannot be overemphasized. It is used to determine the limitation on deductions for contributions and medical expenses if you do itemize your deductions.

DEDUCTIONS

The Zero Bracket Amount

The zero bracket amount replaces the percentage standard deduction and the low-income allowance. It is based on your filing status without regard to the amount of your income as follows:

If You Are:	Your Zero Bracket Amount Is:
Married filing jointly or a qualifying widow or widower	3,400
Single or an unmarried head of household	2,300
Married filing separately	1,700

The zero bracket amount is incorporated into the tax tables and the tax rate schedules. You do not deduct this amount when computing your tax unless your itemized amounts are higher than your zero bracket deduction.

There are two ways of taking deductions: (1) you may itemize them, if they are greater than your zero bracket amount, on Schedule A of Form 1040, or (2) you may take the zero bracket amount, which includes deductions.

A husband and wife filing separate returns should use the method of claiming deductions most beneficial to them as a unit, even though it may be less advantageous to one of them. They both must use the same method of claiming deductions. If one itemizes deductions, the other must itemize. If one takes the zero bracket amount the other must too.

Charitable contributions, interest, and taxes of a nonbusiness nature (state income taxes or sales taxes, for example), medical and dental expenses, and certain losses and other expenses may be itemized on Schedule A of Form 1040.

It will usually be to your advantage to itemize your deductions if you are a homeowner paying interest and taxes or if you paid unusually large medical and dental bills during the year, made substantial contributions to qualified charities, paid significant state income taxes, or suffered a major uninsured casualty loss.

How to Figure Depreciation as a Deduction

A professor owns a house or rents an apartment. Because his office space at the university is crowded and congested, he finds that he can get little or no work done at his college desk, so he sets one or two rooms aside in his house as an office where he really accomplishes his research and writing. Many of the expenses connected with the maintenance and operation of this office are tax deductible under recent Internal Revenue Service rulings and court decisions. For example, he can write off (depreciate) his office furniture and equipment and the books he purchased for his research and writing.

In the case of capital investments and improvements in depreciable property having a useful life of more than a year and owned for the purpose of making a profit from rents, royalties, business, or a profession, the tax law provides an annual depreciation allowance as the method of recovering the original capital cost tax-free. This means that you can spread the cost over as many years as the property is expected to be useful. These rules apply to a profession as well as to a business. For instance, a lawyer can deduct the cost of his lawbooks and a doctor can deduct the cost of his instruments *only* through the depreciation allowance.

The first step in figuring depreciation is to determine the useful life of each asset to be depreciated. The useful life of an asset depends on how long you expect to use it; its age when acquired; your policy as to repairs, upkeep and replacement.[10]

"My congratulations, sir, on so ordering your life that everything you do is deductible."
Reprinted by permission *The Wall Street Journal*

How to Deduct Bad Debts

Bad debts not originally created or acquired in a trade or business (nonbusiness bad debts) must be treated as short-term capital losses. They are subject to the limitation on deductions for capital losses and should be reported in Schedule D of Form 1040.

Bad debts, with certain exceptions, are deductible if they become worthless during the year. For a debt to be worthless, it must not only be uncollectible but must also appear to be uncollectible at any time in the future. The taxpayer must take reasonable steps to collect the debt. He does not have to go to court, however, if it can be shown that a judgment, once obtained, would be worthless. If a debtor, as lawyers say, is "judgment proof," then the judgment would be of no value. Bad debts must be shown to have existed in fact and in law. A taxpayer cannot, for example, claim a bad debt deduction for a debt which cannot be enforced in the courts. A gambling debt is a good example of an unenforceable debt.

Advances to relatives to tide them over financial difficulties may not be legally collectible debts, since they may be made without any fixed understanding as to repayment and may therefore be legally considered as gifts rather than loans.[11]

How to Deduct for Contributions

If you itemize deductions, you can deduct gifts to religious, charitable, educational, scientific, or

---

Model Tax Ruling Holds Beauty Is Never Obsolete

WASHINGTON, Nov. 13—The Internal Revenue Bureau told a group of models today that wrinkles were not tax deductible.

The girls had asked the bureau if they could make allowances on their income tax returns for bodily depreciation. They said that they were subject to "age, exhaustion and obsolescence." The bureau replied: "Charm, beauty and talent, while undoubtedly of great value in your profession, are not generally recognized as depreciable for tax purposes. American beauty never becomes obsolete."

---

[10] For more detailed information, see IRS Publication no. 534, obtainable free of charge from the Internal Revenue Service, Washington, D.C. This will also explain "additional first-year depreciation."

[11] For further information, see IRS Publication no. 548, *Tax Information on Deductions for Bad Debts*. A free copy may be obtained from your local IRS office.

literary organizations and organizations for the prevention of cruelty to children or animals, *unless* the organization is operated for personal profit, or conducts propaganda, or otherwise attempts to influence legislation. You can deduct gifts to fraternal organizations if they are to be used for charitable or religious purposes. You can also deduct gifts to veterans organizations or to governmental agencies which will use the gifts for public purposes. The law does *not* allow for gifts to individuals, or to other types of organizations, however worthy.

The contribution deduction is now more complicated than it used to be. In general, contributions to most charities may be deducted up to 50 percent of your adjusted gross income. However, contributions to certain private nonoperating foundations, veterans' organizations, fraternal societies, and cemetery organizations are limited to 20 percent of adjusted gross income.[12]

A contribution may be made in money or property (but not services). If in property, it is measured by the fair market value of the property at the time of the contribution. For example, if you give $50 in old clothes to your church, it's as much a deductible contribution as if you had given cash. Although you can deduct for gifts to the types of organizations mentioned previously, you cannot deduct for dues or other payments to them for which you receive personal benefits.

Interest as a Deduction

In general, interest on indebtedness is deductible if you itemize your deductions. Interest on mortgages, judgments, delinquent taxes, personal loans, and installment payments is deductible. Discount (interest paid in advance by being deducted from principal of the loan) is deductible on a cash basis only when the loan is fully paid, but taxpayers on the accrual basis may take the deductions as they accrue.

---

[12] For further detail, see IRS Publication no. 526, *Income Tax Deductions for Contributions,* Internal Revenue Service, Washington, D.C. Certain limited political contributions may now be deducted under restricted circumstances. See also IRS Publication no. 561, *Valuation of Donated Property.*

Probably the most common type of interest deducted is the interest paid on home mortgages. Monthly mortgage payments usually consist of interest and the repayment of principal. The former is deductible; the latter is not. If your records do not clearly show these two components, ask the lender to give you the exact breakdown. If you prepay your mortgage, any fee charged by the bank

---

Appreciation of New Collectibles Could Mean a Deduction for the Clothes off Your Back

NEW YORK—If you're scraping the bottom of the barrel for a last-minute tax deduction, try this one on for size: a seven-year-old dress, decorated with antique Chinese mandarin badges alone worth $800. Last week, Mrs. Gardner Cowles, wife of the publishing executive, donated the dress to the Staten Island Museum. Mrs. Cowles observes that it was one of her few outfits that has appreciated in value (by 33%) in the wearing.

Donating art that has risen in value long has offered nice tax breaks for well-to-do philanthropists, but actually giving the clothes off your back is a relatively fresh phenomenon. It all has to do with rapid appreciation in the value of collectible clothing and fine fabrics in the past few years. Although it may seem difficult to believe that perishables like fabrics can rise in value, that is just what's happening. Increased demand for the limited supply of fine old fabrics in good condition has caused big price rises in the past few years.

Joseph M. Lesser, vice president of Allied Stores Corp., bought a 19th century Chinese dragon robe last year for $1,200. He is confident that the robe, which has been worn by an empress, would fetch $3,000 today, although it isn't for sale. Mr. Lesser was steered to the robe by the Metropolitan Museum of Art, which hopes that he will donate in some day.

Last Christmas, Dana S. Creel, vice chairman of the Rockefeller Brothers Fund, bought a $350 skirt for his wife featuring a main panel of gold brocade from a Chinese ceremonial robe. "I bought it because it was beautiful and unusual: But a definite factor in my mind was the thought that if and when my wife got tired of it, there would be something reclaimable there," Mr. Creel says.

The Wall Street Journal, June 7, 1975.

"You say you made all these charitable deductions directly to God?"

Reprinted by permission *The Wall Street Journal*

for this privilege is deductible as interest. If you purchase a cooperative apartment, you are entitled to deduct your portion of the interest payments on the indebtedness of the cooperative. Condominium apartment owners may deduct the interest they paid on the mortgage indebtedness of the project allowable to their share of the property.[13]

Taxes as Deductions

Nonfederal taxes are generally deductible. These include state and local income taxes, personal property taxes, and real estate taxes (except those assessed for pavements, sewers, or other local improvements which tend to increase the value of your property). You can deduct state or local retail sales taxes if under the laws of your state they are imposed directly on the consumer, or if they are imposed on the retailer and the amount of the tax is separately stated by the retailer to the consumer.

Taxes chargeable to rents and royalties and taxes on property used in business may be deducted as business expenses in computing adjusted gross income. State income taxes are not deductible in computing adjusted gross income but may be taken

as nonbusiness deductions. Social security taxes paid by an *employer* are deducted as business expenses, but you are not permitted to deduct the social security tax which you pay as an *employee*.

In general, you cannot deduct any federal excise taxes on your personal expenditures, such as taxes on automobiles, tires, cosmetics, airline and railroad tickets, and telephone.

Taxes imposed on a previous owner of a property and paid by the taxpayer as part of the contracted purchase price should be included in the cost of purchased property. Real property taxes and personal property taxes are deductible.

Federal income taxes, customs duties, gift taxes, estate taxes, and excise taxes are not deductible, nor are taxes paid by you for another person.[14]

Casualty or Theft Losses

A personal casualty or theft loss is deductible to the extent that it exceeds $100. This deduction is allowed only to the person who owns the property. Special rules may apply if the property was in a disaster area. Different rules apply for computing a casualty loss deduction on property used for personal purposes and property used for business purposes. A casualty or theft loss on business property or on property held for the production of income is deductible in full, without regard to the $100 limitation.

To have a deductible loss you must have actually sustained one. For example, if a painting that cost you $5,000, but was worth $10,000, were stolen, your deduction would be $4,900, your actual loss less the $100 limitation.

You must be able to prove your loss and show that the amount or the loss is deductible. Sentimental values are excluded from consideration when determining the amount of loss. The amount of the loss to be deducted is measured by the fair market value of the property just before the casualty less its fair market value immediately after the

---

[13] See IRS Publication no. 545, *Income Tax Deduction for Interest Expense.* It is available at your local IRS office.

[14] For further information, see IRS Publication no. 546, *Income Tax Deduction for Taxes.* A free copy may be obtained from your local IRS office.

casualty (but not more than the cost or other adjusted basis of the property), reduced by any insurance or compensation received.[15]

Dental, Hospital, and Medical Expenses

If you itemize deductions, you can take limited deductions for the amounts you paid during the year (not compensated by hospital, health, or accident insurance) for medical or dental expense for yourself, your wife, or any dependent who received over half of his support from you. The limit of deductions for dental and medical expenses is the amount by which they exceed 3 percent of your adjusted gross income.

You may deduct, disregarding the 3 percent limitation, one half of the amount you paid for medical insurance. This deduction, however, may not exceed $150. The balance is added to your other medical expenses and is subject to the 3 percent limitation. Your expenditures for medicines and drugs may be included in medical and dental expenses only to the extent that they exceed 1 percent of your adjusted gross income. Taxpayers and dependents aged 65 or older as well as younger persons are subject to the 1 percent and 3 percent limitations. There is no maximum limitation on your medical expense deduction. Any reimbursement (insurance or otherwise) reduces the allowable deduction.

You can deduct payments to doctors, dentists, nurses, and hospitals. Allowable deductions are limited to expenses which are sustained "primarily for the prevention or alleviation of a physical or mental defect or illness." These deductions include expenses for hospital, nursing, medical, laboratory, surgical, and dental services; eyeglasses; hearing aids; a seeing-eye dog and its maintenance; supplies (including false teeth and artificial eyes and limbs); ambulance hire; and necessary travel for medical care. Medical expenses include sums paid for hospitalization, membership in certain associations which furnish medical service, and clinical care. Premiums for accident and health insurance which indemnifies for the medical care of a specific injury are classed as medical expenses.

Medical expenses also include the cost of installing air conditioning systems, elevators, pools, and other facilities if these are recommended by a physician for medical conditions, to the extent that such improvements do not increase the value of the home; they also include the operation and maintenance costs of such improvements.

Also deductible as medical expenses are food or beverages specially prescribed by a physician (for the treatment of illness and in addition to, not as a substitute for, regular diet). A physician's statement is needed for such deductions.

Burial and funeral expenses are not medical expenses, nor can you deduct as medical expenses the cost of an illegal operation or travel ordered or suggested by your doctor merely for rest or for change.[16]

If medical expenses are deducted in one year and reimbursement is received in a later year, the reimbursement must be reported as income in the year it is received, but only to the extent that the reimbursement equals the deduction. You may not include in medical expenses the cost of toothpaste, toiletries, or cosmetics.

An example will serve to make clear the medical deduction. Assume that your adjusted gross income is $12,000. Your medical expenses for the year total $950. Three percent of $12,000 is $360. The first $360 of your $950 in medical expenses is *not* deductible. The remaining $590 *is* deductible.

The Care of Children and Other Dependents

A taxpayer who maintains a household may claim a deduction of 20 percent for employment-related expenses incurred in obtaining care for a

---

[15] For further information, see IRS Publication no. 547, *Tax Information on Disasters, Casualty Losses, and Thefts.* A free copy may be obtained from your local IRS office.

[16] There are some very elaborate and subtle distinctions between what you may deduct and what you may not deduct. For further detail, see IRS Publication no. 502, *Deduction for Medical and Dental Expenses.* A free copy may be obtained from any IRS office.

child or a disabled dependent to enable the tax-payer to be gainfully employed. In the case of child care, the cost of services outside the taxpayer's home—day-care center expenses, for example— may be claimed. A member of the household who is not a dependent, and is subject to social security deductions from payment may be employed in the care of the child or a dependent.[17] Payments to grandparents for the care of their grandchildren is now allowed.

Her hypoglycemia was stilled by a special diet that made the IRS gag.

Leona had a low-blood-sugar condition known as hypoglycemia. Her doctor told her to eat high quality protein six to eight times a day and avoid processed foods and carbohydrates. Comparing her $3,100 annual food bill with her friends' bills, she concluded that the special diet added 30% to her food costs. So she deducted 30% of her grocery bill as a medical expense.

The Internal Revenue Service found that totally unpalatable. The special foods "satisfied her nutritional needs," were "substitutes for food normally consumed," and thus weren't deductible, the IRS argued. However, the Tax Court declared recently that "an average person doesn't include six to eight feedings of protein a day or exclude all processed foods and carbohydrates." Food or beverages prescribed for medicinal purposes and consumed in addition to normal diet usually qualify as a deductible medical cost, the court said.

Leona could deduct the added expense of "high quality protein foods used as treatment for her disease," the court concluded.

Source: *The Wall Street Journal,* September 27, 1978.

Expenses of Earning Nonbusiness Income

Taxpayers may deduct expenses incurred in earning income from securities and real estate, providing this is not business income. For example, if you subscribe to an investment advisory service such as Standard and Poor's or Moody's, or if you pay a fee to an investment counselor, you may

---

deduct the expense. You may deduct the rental cost of a safe deposit box in which you keep securities but not the cost of a box used merely for jewelry and other valuables.[18]

Expenses for Education

Expenses for education may be deducted if they are primarily for the purpose of: *(a)* maintaining or improving skills required in your employment or *(b)* meeting the express requirements of your employer, or those needed to maintain your salary, status, or employment.

Educational expenses incurred to obtain a new position, to meet minimum requirements, to achieve a substantial advancement in position, or for personal purposes are not deductible.[19] For example, a computer programmer who takes courses to keep abreast of new developments can take a tax deduction for his courses, but the general practice lawyer who takes a graduate degree in taxation, so he can specialize, can't deduct the cost because the IRS claims he is changing his line of work.

If you receive a scholarship or fellowship grant (graduate or undergraduate), you may exclude the amount from your gross income, if you are a candidate for a degree.

If you are a degree candidate, there is no limitation on the amount of fellowship grant or scholarship that may be excluded from your income.

If you are required, as a condition for receiving a scholarship, to agree to work for the grantor after completing your training, the scholarship is considered compensation for future services and thus must be included in gross income.

Alimony Payments

You may deduct from gross income alimony or separate maintenance to your spouse or former spouse without itemizing.

---

[17] For more information, see IRS Publication no. 503, *Child Care and Disabled Dependent Care.* A free copy may be obtained at your local IRS office.

[18] For further information, see IRS Publication no. 550, *Tax Information on Investment Income and Expenses.* A free copy may be obtained from your local IRS office or from Washington.

[19] See Publication no. 508, *Tax Information on Educational Expenses* obtainable free from any IRS office.

You may not deduct payment made to your spouse or former spouse for child support.

Alimony or separate maintenance that you receive is taxable income to you.

However, you may not deduct lump-sum settlements, specific maintenance payments for the support of children, or any voluntary payments not under a court order or a written separation agreement. Any alimony payment for which one spouse is allowed a deduction must be reported by the other spouse as income.

If the total sum of an individual's alimony obligation is specified and the total is payable within ten years, no deduction is allowed. If the pay period is more than ten years, each installment may be deducted, but not more than 10 percent of the total sum may be deducted in any one year. Where no total sum is specified but the court orders periodic payments for life or until the former spouse remarries, the payments are deductible. Obviously, from a tax viewpoint, how alimony payments are to be made is an important consideration.[20]

Automobile Expenses

The expense of running an automobile may be a business expense, a personal expense, or a combination of both. It depends on how the automobile is used. The costs of gasoline, oil, repairs, garage rent, insurance, and any other necessary operation and upkeep expenses are deductible for an automobile used in a trade, a business, or a profession but not for personal use. Deductions are allowable for damages paid as a result of accidents which result from business use, provided, of course, that the taxpayer is not reimbursed by insurance, or otherwise, for the damages for which he is liable. Such deductions are not allowable if the car is used for personal purposes. Depreciation on the cost of an automobile used in a trade, a business, or a profession is also deductible, but it is not deductible if the automobile is used for personal pleasure. Taxpayers who use their automobiles to look after income-producing properties, yielding either rents

or royalties, can deduct their automobile expenses from such income.

If you use your car for both business and personal travel, you must apportion your expenses appropriately. Suppose you are a consulting engineer and that you drove your car 20,000 miles during this year. Upon checking your records, you find that 12,000 miles was for business travel and 8,000 for personal travel. In this case 12,000/20,000, or 60 percent, of the total cost of operating your car may be claimed as a business or employment expense.

A simple alternative method is available for claiming automobile expenses. For the business use of a family car you may take 17 cents a mile for the first 15,000 business miles and 10 cents a mile for any in excess of 15,000. Where you use a car for charitable work or for medical expenses, such as trips to a hospital for treatments, you can claim expenses of seven cents a mile.

As far as personal expenses are concerned, taxpayers who itemize nonbusiness deductions may claim the following nonbusiness automobile deductions:

1. State and municipal property taxes on automobiles.
2. Interest on money borrowed on the security of an automobile.
3. Losses from fire, accident, storm, or theft not compensated for by insurance or otherwise.
4. Annual registration fees.
5. Damages to an automobile not compensated by insurance and not resulting from a willful act of negligence of the taxpayer.
6. State and municipal sales taxes on the purchase of a car, accessories, or replacement parts.[21]

Moving Expenses

If you moved to a new residence because you went to work for a new employer or transferred

---

[20] See IRS Publication no. 504, *Tax Information for Divorced or Separated Individuals.*

[21] For more detail, see *Automobile Income Tax Deductions,* latest annual revision by the American Automobile Association. A free copy may be obtained by writing to the association at 8111 Gatehouse Road, Falls Church, VA 22042.

to a new place of work, you may be able to deduct the cost of the move.

The 35-Mile Distance Requirement   To deduct the cost of moving to a new residence, your new place of work must be at least 35 miles farther from your former home than was your former place of work. For example, if your former place of work was 7 miles from your old residence, your new place of work must be at least 42 miles from your old residence.

The Full-Time Work Requirement   In addition to the 35-mile minimum distance requirement, you must also meet one of the following time requirements.

1. Employees must work full time at least 39 weeks during the 12-month period immediately after their arrival in the general location of their new principal place of work. It is not necessary that you work for one employer for the 39 weeks or that the weeks be consecutive. It is necessary only that you be employed on a full-time basis within the same general commuting area.

2. Self-employed persons will be allowed a deduction for moving expenses if during the 24-month period immediately following their arrival at the new principal place of work, they perform services on a full-time basis for a specified period.

Deductible Moving Expenses   These include the following items:

1. *Travel expenses* (including meals and lodging) for yourself and your family while en route from your old residence to your new residence. Your family includes any member of your household who had your residence as his principal place of abode before the move and who moved to your new residence with you.

2. *The cost of moving household goods* and personal effects of both you and members of your family. This includes the actual transportation or hauling from your old residence to your new one, the cost of packing and crating, in-transit storage, and insurance. The cost of shipping your automobile to your new residence is deductible.

3. *The cost of premove house-hunting trips* (travel, meals, and lodging) after obtaining work.

4. *The cost of temporary quarters* (both meals

and lodging) at the new location of work for up to 30 consecutive days.

5. *The costs of selling your residence* or settling your lease at the old location and purchasing a residence or acquiring a lease at the new location. This includes broker's commissions, attorney's fees, ''points'' (to the extent that they do not represent interest), and other similar expenses incidental to the sale or purchase of a home. A loss on the sale of a residence is not deductible.

Limitations   The deduction for the expenses of house-hunting trips, temporary quarters, and selling your residence—items 3, 4, and 5 above—is limited to $2,500 overall, of which no more than $1,000 may be for house-hunting trips and temporary quarters. For married persons filing separate returns, the limitations are $1,250 overall and $500 for house hunting and temporary quarters.

A self-employed person is not entitled to expense for house hunting or temporary quarters unless he has already made substantial arrangements to begin work at the new location.[22]

Miscellaneous Deductions

Many people pass up tax savings because they overlook obscure deductions, do not know about them, and do not take them. You are going to be paying income taxes for the rest of your life—a good many years—and it will pay you to familiarize yourself with the present-day complications of tax forms and tax rulings as early as possible in your career. Sooner or later, if you procrastinate, you will learn the hard way. It is really much simpler to spend a few hours now and straighten yourself out on a matter which will affect you all your life.[23]

For example, Tom Dobbins came back from two years' service in the Army. He weighed 158 pounds, whereas he had weighed 179 when he was drafted. He gave away all his old clothes to

[22] Moving expenses are discussed in detail in IRS Publication no. 521, *Tax Information on Moving Expenses,* available free by sending a postcard to your local IRS office.

[23] For further information, see IRS Publication no. 529, *Other Miscellaneous Deductions.* A free copy may be obtained at your local IRS office.

the Salvation Army because they did not fit. He could have deducted the fair market value of these, but he did not know that. Then he got a job which required that he furnish small tools and a uniform at his own expense. He could have deducted for this, too, but he did not know that if you work for wages or a salary you can deduct the ordinary and necessary expenses that you incur for your employer's benefit. He joined a union, because he had to as a condition of keeping his job; and he had to pay union dues, which he could have deducted. He had paid a fee to an employment agency for getting him a job, but he did not deduct that either, though he could have. His boss sent him to a neighboring town to do some repair work. He used the company car to get there and back, but he had to stay over two nights. He could have deducted for meals and room, since he was not reimbursed for these outlays; but no one told him, and he had never read anything about taxes.

Generally speaking, if you operate a business or engage in a trade or profession, you can take a lot more deductions than if you are a wage earner. If you are an executive, the cost of a chauffeur to drive your car, used in business, is deductible; but a working wife may not deduct wages paid to a part-time cleaning woman. If you are in business and entertain customers at dinner, you can deduct the cost of the dinner—yours and your customers'—but an allowance paid by a husband to his wife for cooking dinner for him is not deductible, nor is the cost of the dinner. Traveling expenses, such as railroad fares, meals, lodging, and tips, incurred while away from home in the pursuit of your regular trade or business are deductible (in computing your adjusted gross income). But no deduction is allowable for traveling expenses that are personal in nature; this includes commuter's fares and similar costs of traveling between your home and your place of employment or business.

If you own your own home and use it solely as your personal residence, its depreciation, the cost of its restoration by repainting, the cost of insurance, or any loss on its sale represents personal expenses which are not deductible. If you own

the house and rent it for income, all of these expenses are deductible. A vacation home, used partly as an investment, has limited deductions. Even the maintenance costs of idle property, when you are attempting to rent or sell the property, are deductible. If you rent part of your house, you may deduct a proportionate part of the expense of running the house against rental income. If you are in business and your firm pays the expense of a membership in Kiwanis or Rotary, this is deductible; but if you pay your personal dues, they are not deductible. The legal expenses of a business are deductible, but you may not deduct legal fees paid for the preparation of a will or for securing a divorce.

The law specifically provides that no deduction shall be allowed for "personal living or family expenses, except extraordinary medical expenses." They are not part of the cost of operating a business or of producing income from investment property. The basic principle covering deductions applies to all taxpayers: if you seek a deduction you must point to some specific provision of law or regulations authorizing that deduction, and you must be able to prove that you are entitled to the deduction. It is very important to keep records and receipts in case you are called upon for such proof.

CAPITAL GAINS OR LOSSES

In general, capital gains are profits from selling or exchanging any kind of property, except when they are used or held in your trade or business. The capital assets you hold may be of two types: income producing and non–income producing. Stocks and bonds purchased as investments are normally income producing; the house in which you live and your pleasure car are non-income-producing assets. The law requires that you report and pay a tax on any gains from the sale or exchange of either of these two types of capital assets and allows you to claim a loss and deduct in the case of the sale or exchange of income-producing property, such as stocks or bonds, but not in the case of non-income-producing capital assets (such as the home in which you live or the pleasure car you drive). In the latter case, you pay a tax on the capital gain, if any, but can take no deduction for the capital loss, if any.

Accordingly, stocks and bonds are capital assets when held by individual taxpayers but are not when held for sale by a securities dealer. One's personal residence is a capital asset, but houses held for sale by a real estate dealer are not. A pleasure automobile is a capital asset, but one used in business is not.

If a capital asset is held less than a year, the gain or loss resulting from its sale or exchange is short term. In general, any such profit is fully taxable and any loss is deductible in full. If a capital asset is held more than 12 months, the gain or loss resulting from its sale is long term. Short-term capital gains and losses are merged to obtain the net short-term captial gain or loss. Long-term capital gains and losses (taken into account at 100 percent) are merged to obtain the net long-term capital gain or loss.

If the net short-term gain is greater, the excess is fully reported as income. If the result is a net long-term gain, only 40 percent is reported and taxed as ordinary income. The tax on the total gain will not exceed 28 percent. If the result is a long-term loss, you can deduct $2 of net long-term loss to offset $1 of ordinary income—up to $4,000. An excess loss may be carried over and deducted over a period of years until it is exhausted.

Net short-term loss offsets ordinary income dollar for dollar.

Obviously, it pays to hold your securities long enough to establish long-term rather than short-term capital gains, since the tax advantage is considerable. The holding period of 12 months that is needed to establish the long-term gain includes the day of sale but not the day of purchase.

When You Sell Your Home

If you sold your home at a profit, you can avoid paying a capital gains tax if you buy another house to live in within 18 months—or two years if you build a new home.[24]

You are allowed additional time in case of *(a)* construction of a new residence of *(b)* military service. The law takes the position that the new residence is in substance a continuation of your former investment in a home. To the extent that the former residence, however, sells for more than the cost of the new property, the gain is taxable.

A *loss* on the sale or exchange of your residence is *not* deductible and has no effect on the basis of your new residence. If you have more than one residence, only the sale of your principal residence qualifies for the rule allowing postponement of the tax. For example, if you own and live in a house in town and also own a beach house which you use in the summer, the town property is your principal residence; the beach house is *not.*

Persons aged 55 or over can exclude $100,000 of capital gain realized on the sale of a personal residence if it was occupied for three out of the five years preceding the sale. This tax exemption can be used only once in a lifetime. It does not affect the rollover provision that allows a waiver of tax liability on profits from the sale of a home if these profits are reinvested in another home. In this way a taxpayer can actually have a gain of more than $100,000 and pay no tax.

If relocation is job related, a taxpayer can have more than one gainful rollover in an 18-month period and pay no tax.

If you are a tenant-shareholder in a cooperative housing development and use as your principal residence the apartment you are entitled to occupy by reason of your stockholdings, that apartment qualifies as your principal residence. Ordinarily your basis will be the cost of your stock in the corporation, which may include your allocable share of a mortgage (on the apartment building)

---

[24] See IRS Publication no. 523, *Tax Information on Selling Your House.* A free copy may be obtained from your local IRS office or by sending a postcard to Internal Revenue Service, U.S. Treasury Department, Washington, D.C. See also IRS Publication no. 530, *Tax Information on Deductions for Homeowners.* A free copy may be obtained from your local IRS office.

that you are required to pay as a condition of retaining your stock interest. The sale of a condominium apartment is similar to that of a cooperative apartment. As in the case of the "co-op," your basis is your cost, which may also include your allocable share of the mortgage on the entire property, if there is one.

Income Averaging

If your income increases substantially in any given year, it may be to your advantage to compute your tax under the income averaging method. The income averaging method permits a part of the unusually large amount of taxable income to be taxed in lower brackets, thus resulting in a reduction of the overall amount of tax due.

You may choose this method of computing your tax if your averageable income for this computation year is over $3,000 more than 30 percent of the total of your adjusted taxable incomes for your four previous base years.[25]

To figure out whether income averaging will help you—try this.

Add your taxable incomes for the last four years—omitting this year. Multiply by 30 percent, and add $3,000 to that amount. If this year's taxable income is greater, then income averaging is for you.

Cash or Accrual Accounting

Your return must be on a cash basis unless you keep accounts on the accrual basis. "Cash basis" means that all items of taxable income actually or constructively received during the year (whether in cash or property or services) and only those amounts actually paid during the year for deductible expenses are shown. Income is "constructively" received when the amount is credited to your account, or set aside for you, and may be

"Try me. I think I can safely assure you that all those nitty-gritty details will not bore me."

Reprinted by permission *The Wall Street Journal*

drawn upon by you at any time. Thus, such income includes uncashed salary or dividend checks, bank interest credited to your account, matured bond coupons, and similar items which you can immediately turn into cash. The "accrual basis" means that you report income when earned even though it has not been received, and that you deduct expenses when incurred, even though they have not been paid within the taxable period. Most people find it more convenient to use the cash basis.[26]

Examination of Returns

Before your return goes to a computer it gets a check by examiners for obvious errors and omissions at the service center which received the return. The data on your return are then put on tape

---

[25] A complete discussion of income averaging, including a comprehensive example, may be found in IRS Publication no. 506, *Computing Your Tax under the Income Averaging Method,* available free by sending a postcard to your local IRS office.

[26] For further information, see IRS Publication no. 538, *Tax Information on Accounting Periods and Methods.*

TABLE 5–2
IRS Audit Coverage

Type of Return	Number Filed* (millions)	Number Audited† (millions)	Percent Audited
Form 1040, standard deduction	28.46	0.19	0.68
Itemized, under $10,000	12.24	0.42	3.45
$10,000–$50,000	31.17	0.75	2.40
Over $50,000	0.64	0.07	11.35
Businesses			
Under $10,000	4.47	0.14	3.12
$10,000–$30,000	4.59	0.09	2.07
Over $30,000	0.98	0.07	7.36

* Calendar year 1976.
† Fiscal year 1977.
Source: Internal Revenue Service.

and go to the Martinsburg, West Virginia, computer, where the data are entered in your personal "master file." The computer now analyzes your return. Your return may be matched with the appropriate Form 1099 information returns—this is more likely if the company has its data on tapes, less likely if the company's data are on a paper copy of the form you received. Currently, 60 percent of those million information forms are paper slips and 40 percent are on magnetic tape. It costs the IRS $400 to process 100,000 of the latter, and $20,800 to process the same number of paper forms.

The government is allowed (by the applicable statute of limitations) three years from the filing of the return in which to examine it. This general rule is subject to three exceptions:

1. If a fraudulent return is filed, there is no limit to the time which the government may take to examine the return.
2. When no return if filed, the government may at any time levy the amount it determines to be due.
3. If more than 25 percent of the total gross income received is omitted from a return, the government has five years in which to assess a tax or to start court proceedings to collect.

You must keep records to determine your correct tax liability. The law does not require any particular kind of record. Regardless of your bookkeeping system, your records must be permanent, accurate, and complete, and must clearly establish income, deductions, credits, and so on. Receipts, canceled checks, and other types of records are essential for explaining financial transactions.[27]

The Internal Revenue Service divides returns according to adjusted gross income. The computer assigns weights to certain significant items. According to a former commissioner, the computers are programmed to flag returns in which there was "a rather unusual relationship between adjusted gross income on the one hand and a particular deduction or combination of deductions on the other."

Of the 82½ million individual tax returns that the IRS received in 1977, it audited 1.7 million, or 2.11 percent. This was done by a combination of man and computer. Most of the returns selected for audit were preselected by a computer program known as DIF (for Discriminate Function System),

[27] See IRS Publication no. 552, *Record-keeping Requirements and a Guide to Tax Publications.* Free copies are available from the Internal Revenue Service.

which selects returns that have a high probability of error.

Of the taxpayers whose returns are audited, one in four have had their calculations accepted, $\frac{1}{10}$ of 1 percent emerge with more money instead of less, and most owe additional taxes.

Tables that list the average amounts of itemized deductions, such as charitable contributions, taxes, and medical expenses, may be guidelines, but the IRS says that they are misleading if your assume that by staying inside those ranges you escape audit.

If your return is selected for audit, you'll need your records to substantiate it. There are three levels within the Internal Revenue Service at which agreement to the results of an examination may be reached. The first level is an *audit* by an examining officer; the second is a conference with a member of the District Conference Staff; and the third is a hearing with the service's Appellate Division. If you wish, and you should, you may have someone accompany you or represent you at any or all of the levels. If you are not satisfied with the outcome, you may file a court suit, but this is costly. However, if you disagree with an increase in your income tax liability, as indicated in the notice of deficiency, you may ask for consideration of the deficiency by the U.S. Tax Court.[28]

As a last appeal you may file a claim for refund at the U.S. district court or the U.S. court of claims—but only after you have paid the tax.

There is now a Small Case Division of the U.S. Tax Court. If neither the disputed amount of the deficiency, nor any claimed overpayment with respect to it, exceeds $5,000 for any one tax year, you may request that your case be handled in that court under the special procedures provided for small cases. These are simple, expeditious, and informal. However, the decision cannot be appealed.[29]

[28] To obtain a copy of the rules for filing a petition with the court, write to the Clerk, United States Tax Court, Box 70, Washington, D.C. 20044.

[29] See IRS Publication no. 556, *Audit of Returns, Appeal Rights, and Claims for Refund.* A free copy may be obtained by writing to the Internal Revenue Service, Washington, D.C., or from your local IRS office.

The rules are unique and in your favor. No decision can be cited as a precedent in another case. Thus, making a concession to an individual does not raise the specter of having thousands seize upon the concession as a precedent. Since this would cause tremendous loss of revenue, there would be some hesitation before making such a concession.

Penalties

A whole series of penalties are provided for in the tax law. There is a penalty for failing to file a declaration on time. A penalty is imposed if returns are not filed when they are originally due or within a period of extension, deferment, or postponement. A penalty in the form of interest at the rate of 7 percent must be paid on taxes not paid by their due date. There is a penalty for failure to pay a tax on time—5 percent per month of the amount unpaid with a maximum of 25 percent. In addition there is—as in the past—a 7 percent interest penalty. A similar penalty is charged if a declaration is filed but installments are not paid on time. When the taxpayer is able to satisfy the Internal Revenue Service that the delay was not caused by willful neglect but was the result of a reasonable cause, neither of these two penalties is levied.

If the tax is underestimated by more than 10 percent, a penalty may be levied. This penalty is not applicable if the taxpayer applied the current rates and exemptions to an amount not less than the previous year's income. There is, of course, no penalty if the sole reason for underestimation is an increase in tax rates. Severe fines and jail sentences may be imposed by the courts in cases involving large frauds.

Minimizing Taxes

The higher their clients' income, the more numerous are the ingenious techniques that clever tax lawyers devise to enable their clients to minimize taxes. The methods are fascinating to read about, but they can seldom be used by people of moderate income and they are usually of little

"And now, brethren, let us give in accordance with what we reported on Form 1040."

Reprinted by permission *The Wall Street Journal*

use to those who depend primarily on wages or salaries for income.

Just for future reference when you climb up into the $100,000-and-over annual income bracket, let's look at a few of them. First, you can arrange to divide your income among members of your family. How? By gifts, by family trusts, and by family corporations. A married man earning $50,000 pays about $15,500 in taxes. Assume that his father dies and leaves him $50,000 (after estate taxes). If he invests it at 6 percent, he can keep less than half of the $3,000 income he would receive. He

doesn't need the income, and he feels that it would be wasteful to receive it and then have to pay most of it in taxes. He has four children. They are young now, ages one, two, three, and four. Putting all four through college someday, he figures, will cost him about $28,000 each. He decides to create irrevocable trusts of $12,500 for each. Each will receive $750 a year income (at 6 percent) from his $12,500 trust until age 18, when the proceeds of the trusts will be paid to each over a four-year period to finance the costs of a college education. Thus the father, by turning over his $50,000 inheritance to his children in irrevocable trusts, saves the taxes on the annual $3,000 income. Since $750 annually goes to each of the children, they pay no tax on it, because each has a $1,000 exemption. They will remain exemptions for the father, since he will continue to provide more than half of their support.

A device which is now being used by moderate-income families is the bunching of deductions in alternate years. In one year you use the zero bracket amount without itemizing. Deductions are then maximized by bunching into the second year the contributions, doctors' bills, and property taxes which you would normally pay each year. Assume, for example, that you normally give $100 to the Community Chest in December. You postpone this contribution until the next month, that is, January of the following year, and then at the end of the year, in December, you give again as you normally do. Thus in the first year you make no contributions. In the following year you make your donations both at the beginning and the end of the year. By doing this with as many deductions as you can, you maximize your legitimate deductions. It should be noted that a check delivered or mailed in one year (Dec 30th) qualifies as a payment in that year, even if the check is not cashed or charged to your account until the next year.

When you are in the upper brackets, capital gains look much more attractive than income. That's why many a corporate executive prefers a stock option plan to a boost in salary. If the executive is in the 60 percent bracket, a $10,000 increase in salary leaves only $4,000, whereas an ability to buy shares of the company's stock and then sell them in the open market at a $10,000 gain will exclude $6,000 from any tax and leave $4,000 to be taxed at ordinary income rates.

As an actual example, consider the option granted in 1956 to Thomas J. Watson, Jr., the former president of the International Business Machines Corporation, giving him the right, *for 10 years,* to buy a total of 11,464 shares of the company's stock at $91.80 per share. Subsequently the stock soared to $600 per share. Assume that Mr. Watson exercised his rights and bought the 11,464 shares. They would have cost about $1 million. Had he sold them at $600 a share, he would have had a total profit of $5.8 million on which he would have been taxed at the favorable capital gains rate. Had he exercised his rights but not sold the shares and held them until his death, he would not have paid any income or capital gains tax on this considerable profit.

It is to increase the opportunity for capital gains that many corporations in which insiders have large holdings deliberately keep dividend payments low. Plowing back earnings enhances the value of the company's stock and may ultimately mean a handsome capital gain.

Fortune reported that Mrs. Horace Dodge invested the entire estate that her husband left her—$56 million—in tax-exempt state and municipal bonds, and, assuming a return at that time of 3.5 percent, had an annual tax-free income of $1,960,000.

In the past the corporate expense account has often been a favorite device for shifting personal expenses which would otherwise be nondeductible to corporate deductible business expenses. Under the guise of "business," for example, corporate officials have gone to Florida in the winter and to Europe in the summer, to Las Vegas in the spring and to the Bahamas in the fall, and have had their liquor, theater, restaurant, medical, dental, hospital, insurance, pension and annuity, and country club bills paid by their companies. Taxwise, it has paid to be an "organization man." The Internal Revenue Service has been clamping down on these corporate "fringe" benefits.

There are a good many other devices and techniques, but by the time you get to the $100,000 bracket, some of the old loopholes will have been plugged and new ones opened.

Tax Shelters

The standard tax shelter came in for thorough scrutiny and curbing of abuses in the Tax Reform Act of 1976 and was additionally examined and restricted in the Tax Reform Act of 1978. No phrase in the tax lexicon is more controversial. *Tax shelter* is a term loosely applied to any investment that gives the investor an immediate, substantial tax deduction, often much greater than the cash he puts up. The "deductions" shelter his income from other sources by offsetting taxes that he would otherwise pay.

The big deductions resulted from special tax provisions or accounting techniques. For instance, cattle-feeding syndicates could pay in advance (using mostly borrowed money) for a feed supply, thus contriving a year with large expenses but no income. The following year, when cattle were sold, there would be income without expenses. But in theory, at least, the cycle could be repeated, thus postponing the day of tax reckoning.

Tax shelters, now greatly restricted, included oil and gas exploration and development, farming, nonresidential real estate accelerated depreciation, racehorses, master phonograph recordings, movies, and videotapes. These tax-sheltered investments suffered additional blows under the provisions of the Tax Reform Act of 1978, with only residential real estate remaining unaffected.

The "at-risk" rule of 1976, which said that an investor might not take a tax deduction exceeding his actual cash investment, has been extended to virtually all types of tax shelter partnerships and "closely held" corporations. "Closely held" in the 1978 tax law generally means a company that is more than 50 percent owned by five or fewer individuals.[30]

---

[30] "How the New Tax Law Changes Your Investment Planning," *Business Week,* November 13, 1978.

Minimum Tax on Tax Preferences

Earlier tax reform acts attempted to crack down, gently, on the growing tax shelters enjoyed by the wealthy. A congressional study revealed that 301 individuals who reported incomes of at least $200,000 paid no income tax at all. Their number included 56 persons with incomes of $1 million or more. The legislative response was the tax preference provision which imposed a 15 percent minimum tax on certain types of tax-sheltered income. The alternative minimum tax enacted by the Tax Reform Act of 1978 to apply to the untaxed part of capital gains becomes effective on a sliding scale after deductions and a $20,000 exemption. A minimum tax now applies to a number of items that are considered to be of a tax preference nature. Some of the items of tax preference are:

1. *Capital gains.* This is 40 percent of the amount by which your net long-term capital gains exceed your net short-term capital losses for the year.
2. *Accelerated depreciation on real property.* This is the amount of the depreciation deduction during the year on real property that is in excess of the depreciation deduction that would have been allowable had the straight-line method of depreciation been used.
3. *Stock options.* Upon the exercise of a qualified or restricted stock option, the amount by which the fair market value of the stock exceeds the option price at the time the option is exercised is an item of tax preference.
4. *Depletion.* This is the excess of your depletion deduction over the adjusted basis of the property at the end of the year (determined without regard to the depletion deduction for the year).[31]

However, one of the most widely used tax shelters has been left untouched: income from state and municipal bonds is still tax-free.

"What this country needs, besides the spirit of '76, is the income of '66, the prices of '36 and the taxes of '26."
Reprinted by permission *The Wall Street Journal*

Maximum Tax

There is a 50 percent maximum tax which is levied on earned income and limits the rate of tax on the personal service income of high-salaried individuals. Otherwise such taxpayers in a high bracket, would be paying a much larger tax because of the higher rate. *Earned income* is a new tax term that covers salaries, bonuses, and other compensation paid currently, but excludes dividends, and such deferred income as pensions and profit-sharing income.

Conclusion

As you have undoubtedly gathered by now, taxes are a very complicated subject; and, aside from studying the instructions and forms carefully, you should get expert advice if you are in doubt. The Internal Revenue Service offices will be glad to give you help at any time on a specific problem involving your own situation. Visit, phone, or write

---

[31] For further information, see IRS Publication no. 525, *Taxable Income and Nontaxable Income.*

the office. A hypothetical or theoretical question will not be answered, however. If you have a complicated tax situation, you would do well to consult a lawyer or an accountant with experience in handling tax matters. The advice and suggestions you receive may save you time, trouble, and money. Do not ever hesitate, however, to take the deductions and exemptions to which you feel you are really entitled. It is not fraud to become involved in a legitimate disagreement with the Internal Revenue Service. As Justice Learned Hand once held: "Nobody owes any public duty to pay more than the law demands."

SUGGESTED READINGS

American Automobile Association. *Automobile Income Tax Deductions*. A free copy may be obtained by writing to the association at 8111 Gatehouse Road, Falls Church, VA 22042; latest annual edition.

Barnes, Leo, and Feldman, Stephen. *Handbook of Wealth Management*. New York: McGraw-Hill, 1978.

Executive Reports Corporation. *Educator's Tax Desk Manual*. Englewood Cliffs, N.J.; latest edition.

Explanation of the Revenue Act, latest edition, Commerce Clearing House Inc., Chicago, Illinois.

Forbes. "It's April 15, but Don't Shoot the Tax Collector," April 3, 1978.

Internal Revenue Service. *Tax Guide for Small Businesses*. Publication no. 334. Washington, D.C.: U.S. Government Printing Office; latest edition.

Merrill Lynch, Pierce, Fenner & Smith. *Investor's Tax Guide*. A free copy may be obtained by writing to this firm at One Liberty Plaza, 165 Broadway, New York NY 10006; issued annually.

Money. "You and Your Taxes," February 1978; special issue.

Treasury Department, Bureau of Internal Revenue. *Your Federal Income Tax*. Publication no. 17. Washington, D.C.; latest edition. A copy may be obtained by writing to the Superintendent of Documents, U.S. Government Printing Office, Washington, D.C. 20402. There is no charge for this 192-page compendium.

Treasury Department, Bureau of Internal Revenue. *U.S. Income Tax Form 1040 and Instructions for [Year]*. Washington, D.C.; latest year. Free.

Other Internal Revenue Service publications. The publications listed below may be obtained free by sending a postcard to any Internal Revenue office. IRS employees in these offices will also be happy to furnish you with any necessary forms you may need and to assist you if you need any help in the filing of returns.

Publication Number

538	*Accounting Periods and Methods, Tax Information on*
519	*Aliens, United States Tax Guide for*
504	*Alimony Payments, Income Tax Deduction for*
520	*American Scholars in the United States and Abroad, Tax Information for*
556	*Audit of Returns, Appeal Rights and Claims for Refund*
548	*Bad Debts, Tax Information on Deduction for*
535	*Business Expenses, Tax Information on*
503	*Child Care and Disabled Dependent Care*
567	*Civil Service (U.S.) Retirement and Disability Retirement, Tax Advice on*
517	*Clergymen and Religious Workers, Social Security for*
555	*Community Property and the Federal Income Tax*
549	*Condemnations of Private Property for Public Use*
526	*Contributions, Income Tax Deduction for*
542	*Corporations and the Federal Income Tax*
551	*Cost or Other Basis of Assets, Tax Information on*
512	*Credit Sales by Dealers in Personal Property*
534	*Depreciation, Tax Information on*
547	*Disasters, Casualty Losses, and Thefts, Tax Information on*
561	*Donated Property, Valuation of*
508	*Educational Expenses, Tax Information on*
510	*Excise Taxes for 1975, Information on*
501	*Exemptions and Exemptions for Dependents, Your*

CASE PROBLEMS

1 You are a graduate student, and your wife works. There is no convenient day-care center to take care of your little boy during the morning. You don't have any extra money, but you must hire someone, even if this means skimping elsewhere. How do the tax laws help?

2 You bought some stamps years ago when you thought collecting would be an interesting hobby. You have just learned that you can sell them at a good profit. A friend told you that you'd have to pay a tax on the gain unless you had a loss to balance the profit. You wonder whether those 20 shares of Willow Nuclear you bought several months ago that have been declining should be sold. How can you best use the capital gains tax to your advantage?

3 You are married, live in your own home in Baltimore, and work in Washington, D.C. You are to be transferred to Boston in a month. Your wife flew to Boston and found a house to her liking, within your budget, and meeting your requirement that it must be within driving distance. You sold your Baltimore home at a profit. Long-distance movers took care of your furniture and household effects with no problems, and they arrived on time. How does the tax law help you with all these financial arrangements? What tax credit do you get for the use of your car in driving to work?

4   Henry Downs earns $22,000 a year. He supports his mother and contributes to several charities in which he has a strong interest. His medical insurance of $200 did not help very much in covering the costs of his hernia operation. His company's policy paid for the hospitalization, leaving him with $830 of expenses for drugs and doctors. He expects to have less expense next year, as he won't have to pay alimony to his ex-wife, who is remarrying. How do these personal problems affect his income tax?

5   Peter Martin's 1977 income tax was audited, and the examiner disallowed his casualty loss deduction at the amount Peter Martin claimed. The examiner also rejected a number of medical item deductions. What can Peter Martin do, since he feels he was correct in every detail?

part two

PROTECTION OF LIFE AND ASSETS

6

LIFE INSURANCE

A man's dying is more the survivors' affair than his own.

THOMAS MANN

Expectation of Life

Seventy-five years ago, conditions were such that the expectation of life at birth for a male was 48 years and for a female 51 years. The baby born today can be expected, on the average, to live to age 70 if it's a boy, to 77 if it's a girl. Thus, within four generations the expectation of life has risen by about 25 years.

If you are 20 years old now and a male, having survived the extra hazards and perils of the teens, you can expect to live another 52.9 years. If you are a female, you are obviously anything but a member of the "weaker sex." On the average, you can expect to live seven years longer than the average male. Today a woman of 20 can look forward to another 58.5 years. If you reach the age of 60 you are likely to live until 77, if male, and until 82, if female. Major gains in diet and health care, expecially in the prevention and care of heart disease, have since 1960 extended the life expectancy especially of those over the age of 65, who can now expect to live another 16 years. These actuarial data have caused some life insurance companies to cut premium costs.

Sharing Risks by Insurance

Insurance is a plan by which a large number of people, each in some danger of loss, the time of which cannot be foreseen or prevented, are brought together for mutual protection so that when one of the group suffers a loss, it will be made good, partly or wholly, from the contributions of the entire group. In other words, all members of the group contribute small sums regularly and beforehand in order to make good particular losses to the individuals who suffer them

Insurance is possible because of the law of probability and the law of averages. If you toss a penny just once, you have no way of knowing whether you will get heads or tails; but if you tossed it a million times, you could be pretty sure of getting very close to 500,000 of each. Insurance companies have "actuaries," skilled mathematicians who study the proportion of people who die at various ages. These actuaries calculate rates of mortality based on hundreds of thousands of cases, and the results are compiled in mortality tables which insurance companies use as the basis for calculating the rate to charge for insuring any particular person.

Mortality Tables and Premium Rates

A very basic mortality table, the Commissioners Standard Ordinary Table of Mortality, compiled by the National Association of Insurance Commissioners, is based on the experience of life insurance companies. As illustrated in Figure 6–1, the table starts with 10 million people under the age of one and follows them through to age 99. For each year it shows how many of the original 10 million will still be living and how many will die; it calculates the death rate per 1,000 at that age. At age 20 for example, 9,664,994 of the original group are still alive. That year, 17,900 may be expected to die, which means that the death rate is 1.79 per thousand. Thus, 10,000 college students, all age 20, could easily figure out how to insure themselves and what to pay for one year. They can be reasonably certain that 18 of them will die within the year, but of course they do not know which 18.

FIGURE 6–1
The Road of Life

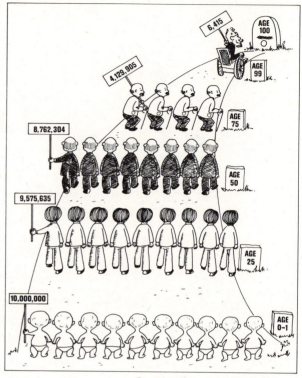

Courtesy Life Insurance Marketing and Research Association, Hartford, Conn.

The story of the road of life is depicted in the CSO Table of Mortality. Visualize 10 million people under age one starting down this road. By age 25, there are 9,575,635 living. By age 50, 8,762,304 remain. Only 4,129,905 are alive at age 75, and there are only 6,415 left at age 99.

If they wanted to be certain that the families of each of the 18 who died would receive a payment of $1,000, they could each (10,000) contribute $1.80, thus establishing a fund of $18,000, out of which $1,000 could be paid to the families of each of the unfortunate 18 who were to die. Each student would be paying for pure protection, and there would be nothing left over from the insurance fund at the end of the year. If the same group, now numbering 9,982, wanted to insure in the same way the next year, from age 21 to age 22, each would have to contribute a little more than the $1.80 of the year before, first, because there would be fewer contributors and second, because more of the contributors will die during the second year—and during each succeeding year. The group left to contribute each year would become progressively smaller, and each year fewer survivors would have to pay steeply increasing amounts. This approximates the simplest form of insurance—term insurance—which will be described later. The rates are low when the average age of the insured is low, but they climb steadily, until old surviving members can hardly pay the premiums.

For example, let us assume that the insurance company has invested the payments (premiums) of the 1,000 20-year-olds at 3.5 percent, thus decreasing the amount that each would have to pay. If a 20-year-old pays $1.73 on that basis, at age 40 he will pay $3.30, and at age 60 the same protection will cost $18.99. The step rate plan is fine for the 20-year-old, difficult for the 60-year-old, and it has only provided a year-by-year protection against death. There are no living benefits. At an increasing cost the step rate premium makes less harsh the fear of dying too soon but does nothing about the fear of living too long.

Do You Need Life Insurance?

Not if you have no one to protect. Not for its forced savings—there are better ways to save. Not because you think or have been told that it's "the thing to do."

But let's assume that you have worked hard month after month, year after year, to achieve your goal of financial independence—to be free of money worries. During this time you have saved some, invested some, married, and have had a child.

What happens if you die before your reach your goal? How except through insurance can your family have an instant estate?

Theoretically insurance can be discussed separately as protection or as saving and investment. Realistically these complement each other—just as talk of sudden death leads to the subject of life expectancy in any discussion of insurance.

What do you want life insurance to do for you? If you are young and have no obligations—not much. Most people buy life insurance to replace some or all of the income that their families would lose if they died. As you go through life, your needs will change. The amount that you can afford now is different from the amount that you will be able to afford when you're at your peak earning years or when you retire.

Who Owns Life Insurance?

Almost everyone sooner or later. The number of people in the United States who own some form of life insurance now totals over 155 million, or two out of three. The size of the average new ordinary life policy is $18,010, and the average amount of life insurance owned per insured family is $39,500.

The amount of insurance purchased annually by women has been increasing at a faster rate than the amount bought by men. The average size ordinary life policy purchased on the life of a woman has also more than doubled in the last ten years. Some insurance companies offer women life insurance policies at rates that they would charge a man who is four or five years younger. Experience statistics favor giving women this advantageous differential because they live longer, and having lower death rates they can be charged a lower rate. As more women take jobs in business and professions they find it important to have adequate protection. Also in families where there are young children, insurance on the wife provides for the high cost of family care that would be required if she were to die.

How Much Insurance Should I Buy?

A student once asked his professor, "Skipping all the details, how much insurance should I carry, and what's the best policy for me?" The professor thought for a moment and then said, "Skipping all details, just tell me when you are going to die and whether you'll have any dependents or not at the time. Then I'll answer your question."

Table 6–1 is Citibank's answer to that question. Its study showed that if a family has an aftertax income of 75 percent of its aftertax income before the breadwinner's death it can maintain its former living standard, but that if it has less than 60 percent it will fare poorly. The "multiples of salary" table enables you to calculate the amount of insurance needed, dependent upon the age of your spouse, the social security benefits you expect, and your desire and ability to provide the 60 percent or 75 percent needed.

If your spouse is 25 years old and you earn $9,000 a year before taxes and you wish to provide 75 percent of your current income if something happens to you, then you must have $36,000 of insurance. Or if your gross income is $30,000 a year, your spouse is 45 years old, and you aim at 60 percent net income replacement, then you need insurance equal to 6.5 times your present gross earnings, or $195,000 in insurance.

If you are wondering why a $15,000 breadwinner who dies leaving a 35-year-old spouse would need insurance equal to 4.5 times gross yearly earnings to provide 60 percent net income replacement and only three times gross earnings if the spouse is 25 years old, the answer lies in social security benefits. The more you get from social security, the less insurance you need. The older the family, the lower the benefits, because the average covered earnings of the past were lower than those of today.

To use the table you multiply the appropriate factor under your income replacement goal by your present gross earnings.

In calculating these multiples, Citibank expected that insurance benefits would be invested to produce, after inflation, a 5 percent return. It also assumed that the principal would be gradually converted to the family's use so that by the time of the surviving spouse's death—based on average life expectancy—it would disappear.

Citibank suggested that if other assets exceed one year's gross income, the amount of insurance needed can be proportionately reduced. If they equal one year's gross income—those assets should be kept for emergencies and funeral expenses.

The Present Value Method Still another method for computing how much insurance you need is the present value method. In estimating your insurance requirements, you must select an interest rate to calculate the present value of the required income. You determine the amount of life insurance required by adding all other available sources, for example, social security, investments, savings, possible inheritance, and the earnings of any adult in the family, and by subtracting that total from the amount needed to maintain the family at its current living standard. You also have figures for the years you need to provide for the dependents in the family.

Assume that your family needs $10,000 a year for ten years after your death. The total needed

TABLE 6–1
The Multiples-of-Salary Chart

Your Present Gross Earnings	Present Age of Spouse							
	25 Years		35 Years		45 Years		55 Years	
	75%	60%	75%	60%	75%	60%	75%	60%
$ 7,500	4.0	3.0	5.5	4.0	7.5	5.5	6.5	4.5
9,000	4.0	3.0	5.5	4.0	7.5	5.5	6.5	4.5
15,000	4.5	3.0	6.5	4.5	8.0	6.0	7.0	5.5
23,500	6.5	4.5	8.0	5.5	8.5	6.5	7.5	5.5
30,000	7.5	5.0	8.0	6.0	8.5	6.5	7.0	5.5
40,000	7.5	5.0	8.0	6.0	8.0	6.0	7.0	5.5
65,000	7.5	5.5	7.5	6.0	7.5	6.0	6.5	5.0

Source: *Consumer Views,* Citibank, July 1976.

would be $100,000. If you select a conservative 5 percent interest rate (savings accounts pay at least that), you can see from the present value table in Appendix A at the end of this chapter that you will need $81,080 of insurance to achieve $100,000. If you fear that inflation will cause your family's income to be less, you can assume a lower interest rate for the present value, say 3 percent. Again consulting the table, $1,000 at 3 percent for ten years equals $8,786. Multiply by 10—$87,860 is the amount of life insurance you need to achieve $10,000 a year for ten years. Through the courtesy of Professor Joseph Belth, an acknowledged expert in the insurance field, four ways of coping with the problem are shown in Appendix A.

How Much Life Insurance Is Enough? You can answer this question with common sense if you examine your needs. In fact, you can list those needs and come to a pretty definite answer. Figure 6–2 will help. Naturally, a college student at 18 or 20 isn't thinking about death, and consequently your first and most immediate need may not even occur to you. It's—

1. *Cleanup Expenses.* The high cost of your dying will hit your family. There will be medical bills, hospital bills, funeral costs. There may also be bills and loans to pay as well as your final tax remittance. Based on the experience of others, these costs will range from $1,000 to a half-year's income.

2. *Family Period Income.* Your second essential need is to provide a minimum monthly income for your dependents, if you have any. If there are two or three young children, it will be difficult, if not impossible, for your spouse to go off to work to support them. To stay home and take care of them, a minimum monthly income is needed. It's been estimated that the surviving family can live three fourths as well as before on half the income. You won't be able to duplicate your present income, but you won't need to, because part of your present budget involves your own expenses. If you are covered under social security, then your spouse and children will receive monthly survivors benefit payments until the youngest child is 18—or 22 if still in school. Payments to the spouse

will cease when the youngest child reaches 18, but they will continue directly to the student until the end of the term in which the 22nd birthday is reached. Social security payments to the widow or widower will resume at age 60. In estimating the need for minimum monthly income until the little ones grow up, figure from one third to one half of your present monthly income.

3. *Pay Off the Mortgage.* If you live in a house which you "own," but on which the bank has made a substantial mortgage loan, this is your next need to be taken care of by insurance. There is no need for estimating here. You know the exact monthly cost of interest and principal repayment on your mortgage. And there's a special insurance policy designed to handle just this situation. If your spouse wants to keep the house and continue to live in it, you can buy a policy—reducing term insurance—which will pay off the mortgage. On the other hand, if the house is to be sold, then all you need is enough insurance to meet the mortgage payments for six months or a year so that there is no need to sell the house under pressure.

4. *An Emergency Fund.* Savings may provide this, but if not, you'll have to use insurance to set it up, provided, of course, that you can afford the cost. Every family needs an emergency fund in case of major illness, an accident, sudden hospitalization, and other misfortunes. It's a sort of "reserve for contingencies," and for young families something between $500 and $1,000 is about right.

5. *Income for a Spouse's Middle Age.* Remember that social security survivors benefits payments to your family cease when the youngest child reaches 18 or 22. They don't resume again until your spouse reaches 60. This gap is known as the "blackout period" in the insurance agent's jargon. Perhaps you can provide a monthly income for your spouse during this blackout period until social security payments resume at 60.

6. *Income for a Spouse's Old Age.* When your spouse's social security payments resume, they will range from approximately $83.20 to $335.40 per month for life, depending on what your average earnings were. You may be able to supplement this by monthly insurance payments, but if your

FIGURE 6–2

The Varying Needs for Insurance upon Death

cleanup expenses			cash available		
medical care	$		savings	$	
funeral			social security death benefit		
debts & bills			group insurance		
taxes			other		
insurance loans			other		
estate settlement					**needed from life insurance** ▶
extra family expense					
total needed	$	less	total available	$	= $

mortgage			cash available		
			savings	$	**needed from life insurance** ▼
balance outstanding, or payments pending sale	$	less	other		
			total available	$	= $

family's monthly expenses			monthly income available		
housing	$		social security	$	
utilities & household operation			investments		
food			earnings		
clothing			other		
medical care			other		
incidentals (car, personal, recreation)					**needed monthly from life insurance** ▼
total needed	$	less	total available	$	= $

emergency fund			cash available		
			savings	$	
			investments		
			group insurance		**needed from life insurance** ▼
			other		
estimated need	$	less	total available	$	= $

wife's monthly expenses to age 62			monthly income available		
			investments	$	**needed monthly from life insurance** ▼
			earnings		
estimated budget (follow family-period headings)	$		other		
		less	total available	$	= $

wife's monthly expenses after age 62			monthly income available		
			investments	$	**needed monthly from life insurance** ▼
			social security		
estimated budget (follow family-period headings)	$		other		
		less	total available	$	= $

special funds			cash available		
for	$		investments	$	**wanted from life insurance** ▼
for			other		
total wanted	$	less	total available	$	= $

Source: Adapted from *Changing Times, the Kiplinger Magazine.*

family is young, it isn't likely that you'll be able to afford the cost of reaching this far into the future.

7. *A College Fund for the Children.* This is your next goal, and we use the term *goal* advisedly. Paying for your child's college education is a goal; buying groceries for the family when the youngster is in first grade is a need. If your income permits the extra insurance cost involved, by all means buy the special kinds of policies that have been devised to cover the cost of four years at college.

8. *Retirement Income.* Almost all the insurance you buy to cover the previous expenses can be converted, as you will see, to provide retirement income if you are lucky enough to live long enough to retire. You may find that you want a higher monthly retirement income even after you take social security benefits into account. If so, insurance, using endowment policies or annuities, can provide it. As your income rises and your children grow older, you'll want to look into this possibility, but right now it's probably the most expendable goal on the list.

People at every income level find life insurance about equally important for financial security, but for differing reasons. Those making under $10,000 are more concerned about funeral expenses and leaving a debt-free estate. Those with an income of over $10,000 place greater emphasis on savings, education for children, and retirement.

What Kind of Policy Shall I Buy?

You have only a limited amount of money to spend on life insurance, and you find that for one type of policy you have to pay $4.30 per $1,000 of insurance protection and that for another type you have to pay $41.60 per $1,000. Or, for a given expenditure of $100, one policy you can buy provides $19,000 worth of protection while another provides only $2,100. You will begin to think about the kinds of policies available and about the differences among them (see Table 6–2). Naturally you may wonder at these large differences and at the reasons for them. Various kinds of policies offer differing advantages and limitations. To be able to buy insurance intelligently, you'll need to examine and understand the basic differences.

KINDS OF LIFE INSURANCE

Life insurance may conveniently be grouped as follows:

1. Ordinary
   a. Term
   b. Straight or whole life
   c. Limited payment (20 or 30 years) life
   d. Endowment
   e. Combination plans
2. Group
3. Industrial
4. Credit life insurance

When you buy life insurance, you receive a policy which is the contract between the company and you. The money you send to the company at regular intervals to pay for your life insurance is known as the premium. The person you name to receive the money from the policy if you should die is the beneficiary. A contingent beneficiary may also be named to receive the money if the beneficiary dies before you do. The face value of the policy is the amount stated on the first page of the contract that will be paid in case of death, or in the case of an endowment policy, at maturity. As you pay premiums on your policy, a certain amount of reserve accumulates to its credit. This is called its cash value. The loan value is the amount you may borrow on your policy while it is still in force. Usually, this is close to the cash value.

Ordinary Life Insurance

Ordinary insurance is sold on an individual basis for larger amounts than industrial insurance, and premiums are usually paid by check or at the insurance company office on a quarterly, semiannual, or annual basis. Nearly half of the total number of policies issued are ordinary policies, and account for more than half of the total value of life insurance in force in the United States today. Generally, the smallest amount for which an ordinary policy is written is $1,000; the average size of such policies in force today is $18,010, and is continually increasing. The more usual policy is $25,000 and over. Today straight life or whole life is the more typical, but there is a rising proportion of term insurance both as to the number of policies and their amount. Straight life policies are usually written with level premiums (annual premiums fixed in amount and continuing at the fixed amount throughout the life of the policy), and in most cases they provide both living and death benefits.

By "living benefits" we mean the values in most life insurance policies which enable you to benefit from them while you are still alive. These living benefits include the ability to convert an ordinary policy to retirement income at 65, the ability to surrender the policy for cash, the ability to borrow against it, matured endowments, disability benefits, dividends, and "nonforfeiture" provisions, which will be explained subsequently. The various ways in which the death benefits can be paid are known as "settlement options." They too will be explained later.

Term Insurance

When you buy term insurance, you buy pure insurance protection and nothing else. Everyone seems to know that if a policy is bought from a fire insurance company, nothing will be collected from the company unless there is a fire and the policy will be worthless when the time for which it has been written has expired. Exactly the same sort of situation exists for a person who buys term insurance from a life insurance company. If death comes within the term of the policy, the company will pay the beneficiary the face value of the policy; but if the insured is still living at the expiration of the time for which the policy was written, then the policy is of no value. Term policies are usually issued at level premiums for terms of 1, 5, 10, or 15 years; sometimes they are written to expire at age 65. Some companies write one-year term policies which are renewable one year at a time for a given number of year—perhaps five or ten—with-

out further medical examination. The insured pays the lowest premium the first year and a higher premium at each succeeding renewal. Such a policy has the lowest possible premium in the first year, because the premium is not averaged for the later years, when the age of the insured and the risk of dying will be greater. A five-year policy with a level premium would tend to have a premium equivalent to what would be paid in the third year of renewal of a one-year term policy. **It is usually advisable to purchase a term policy which is renewable without another medical examination for a fairly large number of years, if such a policy can be obtained, since you may later want the protection longer than you had originally planned.** Many term policies are convertible into permanent types of life insurance policies, but the premiums you must pay on the policies to which you convert are based on your age at the time of conversion. Naturally, this will make the premiums higher than they would have been if these policies had been taken earlier. The chief advantage of the conversion feature is that you know you can have the policy if you want it— you need take no medical examination at the time of conversion. Since term policies have no savings or investment feature, they are the least expensive form of insurance to buy in the short run and at young ages. Another way to express it is that a given amount of money will buy a larger face amount of term insurance than of straight life or endowment. For example, as Table 6–2 shows, if you can spend (at age 22) only $100 annually for insurance, this amount will provide $19,000 of term insurance protection as against only $8,000 of straight life, $7,200 of limited payment life, or $5,700 of endowment (at age 65) insurance.

Advantages of Term Insurance

It should be clear, therefore, that term insurance may be, temporarily, the most convenient insurance for a young family to buy when it needs a maximum amount of protection but cannot afford to pay the larger annual premiums which other forms of insurance require. To generalize: at the

TABLE 6–2

What a $100 a Year Premium Will Buy in Life Insurance (male age 22)

	Type of Policy	Annual Rate per $1,000 Insurance	Amount of Insurance $100 a Year Will Buy	Cash Value at Age 65 per $100 Annual Premium	Monthly Life Income at Age 65, Men (10 years certain)
1.	Term (5-year renewable and convertible)	$ 4.30	$19,000	None	None
2.	Term (10-year convertible, nonrenewable)	4.04	22,000	None	None
3.	Straight life	11.22	8,000	$4,660	$30.75
4.	Life—paid up at 65	12.46	7,200	4,986	31.10
5.	Modified life (5 years)*	13.92	6,800	4,683	28.00
6.	Family income (20 years) $10 monthly	14.65	7,700	4,504	28.19
7.	Endowment at 65	15.73	5,700	5,700	35.68
8.	Twenty-payment life	19.69	4,400	3,036	19.00
9.	Retirement income at 65	22.60	4,000	6,250	38.50
10.	Twenty-year endowment	41.60	2,100	Matured (age 42)	

* The cost of the first five-year term insurance is $5.60. Then the cost rises to $13.92 at age 27 for whole life.
Source: American Council of Life Insurance.

younger ages, term insurance costs only about a third of the cost of straight life insurance and about one tenth of what 20-year endowment insurance costs. But remember that term insurance provides no "living benefits" to the policyholder. Since most younger men with families simply can't afford as much protection as they need, their choice narrows down to the lower premium forms of policies which provide the greatest protection for what they can afford to spend. Older men, whose family responsibilities may be less, may wish to place less emphasis on protection and more on an income at retirement.

Another typical use of term insurance is to protect your family against mortgage foreclosure in the event of your death. You can buy a decreasing term policy where the amount and premium on the insurance will decline at exactly the same rate as the amount of the mortgage which you are paying off month after month. If you should die at any time during the mortgage term, the amount of insurance payable under the policy will cover the remaining amount of the mortgage. Frequently, the family income or family maintenance policy is used not only to protect the spouse and children from loss of the home but to provide additional protection as well.

Several life insurance companies offer whole life or term policies whose face value increases automatically in line with the Consumer Price Index, until they are doubled. Naturally an indexed policy has a much higher premium cost than a regular policy.

Term insurance does not help in an investment or savings program, nor is it the best kind of insurance to carry as one grows older, because the premiums become so large as to be prohibitive for most people. The cost at age 40 doubles at age 50 and triples at age 55. Since the premium for a term policy pays only the cost of protection during the term of the policy, the policy seldom has any nonforfeiture values, which permanent policies have. Thus, if unemployment or sickness makes it impossible to keep up the premiums, since there is no reserve available, the policy will terminate at the end of the grace period, usually 30 days, from the premium due date.

Term policies are not emphasized in sales to college students, while whole life policies are, even though the latter are less appropriate to the students' needs. Agents usually earn 40 percent of the first year's premium for selling term as against 55 percent for whole life. Moreover, the general agents who employ the selling agents earn an additional 5 percent on whole life policies.

One life insurance company pushing sales to college students allows the use of promissory notes to pay the student's first-year premium. The student is persuaded to designate his school the beneficiary. What the insurance company labels "a goodwill gesture" is regarded by critics of this policy as an attempt both to get a college endorsement and to make it difficult for the student to drop the policy.[1]

Straight or Whole Life Insurance

Such a life policy is a plan of insurance for the whole of life, with premiums payable until death. It has the lowest premium rate of any permanent policy on the level premium plan. It is the most widely used type of life insurance policy, and it is a good all-purpose policy, which meets many different needs and family situations. The face value of the policy is payable to the beneficiary upon the death of the insured. Because the level premiums in the early years of the policy are in excess of mortality and other costs, they are reserved, and in effect they act as savings combined with protection. In the later years these reserves or savings make it possible to keep the premium level even though mortality and other costs are greater than the premium.

This type of policy combines protection with saving; but since the premium, and therefore the saving, is moderate, the cash surrender or loan value also grows at a moderate rate. The straight or whole life policy fits the needs of those who wish to secure protection for beneficiaries and to do some saving in addition. It provides both "living" and "death" benefits. If the death of the insured occurs, the beneficiary is paid the face value of the insurance policy. On the other hand, if the insured lives, the straight life policy can be borrowed against or cashed in. The loan value is the amount which may be borrowed with the policy as sole collateral. But you cannot eat your cake and have it too: if you surrender the policy for its cash value, the protection will be gone; if you borrow on the policy, your beneficiary will receive at your death the face value of the policy reduced by the amount of the loan and any unpaid interest thereon.

If someday, say upon retirement, the holder of a straight life policy wishes to discontinue premium payments, any one or, if the policy is large enough, a combination of the following alternatives can be selected:

1. Continue the protection at a reduced amount for the balance of his lifetime.
2. Continue the full amount of protection for a definite period of time.
3. Cancel the policy entirely in return for a cash settlement of guaranteed amount, plus dividends, if any.
4. Discontinue life insurance protection and elect to receive an income from the policy for a certain limited period of time for life.

In the next chapter it will be shown that social security provides something for the old age of many people but that in many cases it must be supplemented to provide reasonable retirement comforts. Savings built up through life insurance can help in supplementing social security benefits, and indeed, modern insurance programming builds from the social security base to meet family needs more adequately.

The straight life policy averages the increasing risk of death over the years at a level premium. If you buy $10,000 worth of whole life insurance at age 20, you will pay $115.50 per an-

---

[1] *Wall Street Journal,* January 5, 1978, quoting Professor Joseph Belth of Indiana University—a well-known critic of life insurance company practices.

num for the rest of your life. A renewable five-year term policy for the same amount would cost you $52.80. But if you kept renewing the term policy every five years, at age 50 you would pay $144 per annum, more than the whole life policyholder, and when you renewed at age 60 (the last time you would be permitted to renew), you would pay $330.30 a year for the next five years. At age 65, your term policy would expire. You would have no accumulation to show for your 45 years of payments, although, of course, you had protection over this period. However, the holder of the straight life policy who wished to stop paying premiums at age 65—and any whole life policyholder can exercise this privilege—could give up the policy and receive $5,190 (the cash surrender value) in cash or as income over a period.

Most important, Figure 6–3 shows you what each type of policy offers in approximate cash value. As discussed later in this chapter, cash value has many important uses—as savings, as a basis for loans and as an opportunity to obtain investment funds. In choosing among life insurance policies, you should consider the cash value buildup in relation to the best premium rate. Although the primary purpose of insurance is protection against death, an advantage of buying insurance while young, is that the cash value is likely to increase and become a desirable investment, since the death rate is low among the young.

If you buy straight life or endowment insurance, you not only buy protection, but in addition you pay enough so that for all practical purposes you have a savings account with the insurance company. This is the reason that your policy has a cash surrender value or loan value.

Limited Payment Life Policies

The one difference between limited payment life policies and straight life policies is that the premium payments of the former are not made for life but a limited term, such as 20 or 30 years. Limited payment life policies have been called "hurried-up" ordinary life policies. Since the insured contracts to make fewer premium payments, naturally those that he does make will have to be larger, for the insurance company is obligated to insure him for his lifetime. Since the insured makes larger payments and makes them during the first 20 or 30 years that the policy is in force, the cash (and loan) value accumulates faster than it does in the straight life policy.

The limited payment life policy is attractive to those who for one reason or another want to cut short the burden of paying premiums. Often the insured wishes to complete premium payments before earnings start to decline. Or he may have a "life-begins-at-40" philosophy and may aim to have many of his obligations squared away by middle age so that he will have less to encumber a free and easy existence from his 40s or 50s to the end of his days. Of course, this puts a larger burden on his most active working years than if he spread the loan payments over a longer span. Sometimes, fear that work will not be available later leads to the decision to strike while the iron is hot and pay while earnings are at their peak. This is particularly true for professional athletes and movie stars.

For a young person, especially one with family responsibilities, limited payment life is not the best plan. You get less protection for your premium dollar than you would if you bought ordinary life. A 22-year-old with $100 a year to spend on insurance would get about $8,000 of straight life protection and only $4,400 for 20-payment life. Of course, if you can afford it and if you outlive the premium-paying period, there is a big advantage. Your insurance is paid up. You are insured for life, but you need make no more premium payments. A life paid-up-at-65 policy makes a good deal more sense than a 20-payment life if you are under 30 and insist on a limited payment plan. It's less costly for one thing. At age 22, life paid up at 65 will cost only $12.46 per $1,000 compared to $19.69 for 20-payment life and $11.22 for straight life. Since your highest earning period may be from 40 to 65, there is no need to try and pay off your insurance by 40, although there is a good deal more sense in trying to get it paid up by 65. (See Table 6–2.)

170

FIGURE 6–3
Approximate Cash Values of the Four Kinds of Life Insurance ($10,000)

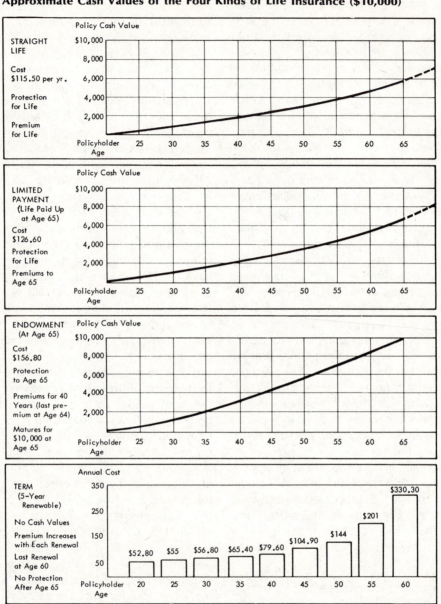

Source: American Council of Life Insurance.

Here are four $10,000 life insurance policies bought by people who are 20 years old. Approximate cash values and costs are shown in this chart. The limited payment policy becomes "paid up" at age 65, and the endowment "matures" at age 65.

Endowment and Retirement Income Policies

Both of these types of policies place the emphasis on savings rather than on protection. Both cost more than any other type of policy. An endowment policy is one that is written for a given period of time and for a stated face value. Endowment at 65 and 20-year endowments are the most common types. If you die before the stated period is up, your beneficiary receives the full face value. If you live until the maturity of the policy, you receive the full face value. Once you have received the full face value on maturity, however, you are no longer insured. The company has paid off under the contract, and the policy terminates.

Naturally, since the cash value must build up to the face value by the time the contract period is up, an endowment premium is much costlier than any other type of policy. As you can see from Table 6–2 a 20-year endowment would cost $41.60 per $1,000 face value for a 22-year-old as compared with $11.22 for straight life and $19.69 for 20-payment life.

There is a great difference, of course, between a limited payment life policy and an endowment policy. When you have finished paying on a limited payment life policy, you are insured for life but you collect nothing, although your cash value has built up to about three fifths of the face value. On the other hand, in the case of the endowment policy, once you have finished paying (a) you are no longer insured, (b) you collect the face amount of the policy, and (c) the policy terminates.

Endowments

For young people, endowments are not very sensible. As insurance protection they are very expensive, and as savings they are costly. You can see from the figures in Table 6–2 that $1,000 of protection at age 22 costs $30.38 more if you buy it as an endowment than if you buy it as straight life. Ah, yes, you say, but I'm saving the difference. Perhaps you are, perhaps you're not.

Suppose you have a 20-year endowment and you die in the 19th year. What your beneficiary receives is 95 percent of your savings and almost no insurance. Had you bought straight life or a family income policy, and saved the difference in premiums, your beneficiary would have gotten the full face amount of the insurance and your savings as well. Every young family needs life insurance, but it doesn't need the most expensive kind. If you buy an endowment policy at age 22, the endowment at 65 is much less costly—$15.73 per $1,-000—than the 20-year endowment (see Table 6–2), and it makes more sense for a younger person.

The Retirement Income Policy

The retirement income policy differs from the endowment in that it pays a monthly income from the date of its maturity rather than a lump-sum cash amount. It is, of course, an insurance policy, and therefore has a stated face value and pays a death benefit of this amount to your beneficiary if you should die before the maturity date. However, to build cash value to pay the retirement income, the reserve behind the policy builds up very rapidly, and in time it exceeds the face value. If you die after that has happened, your beneficiary will receive more than the face value of the policy. He or she will receive the full cash value, which is now greater than the face value. This is no windfall. It's your accumulated savings. A retirement income policy is expensive—less expensive than a 20-year endowment, more expensive than an endowment at 65.

Sometimes parents take out endowment policies, maturing at ages 15 or 18, on children, to provide funds for a college education. Generally speaking, however, in families of moderate income, practically all life insurance should be placed on the wage earners, without whose income the family finances would be sadly crippled.

Money for a college education can be accumulated, if the parent lives, by saving in a savings bank or a savings and loan association. If it is desired to combine protection with saving for a college education through life insurance, the policy should be taken out on the life of the parent, the child being thus assured of cash for an education if the parent dies, whereas if the insurance were on the life of the child, the parent's death might result in the policy's lapsing before a sufficient sum had accumulated for the desired education. (For a small extra premium, however, a clause can usually be added to a child's policy waiving further premiums should the head of the family die or become disabled before the child reaches a certain age.) If the parent lives, the cash surrender or loan value of the policy can be used, if necessary, to meet part of the child's college costs. Thus, in insuring to cover the costs of a college education, as well as in other general life insurance situations, the best principle to follow is to have the insurance placed on the life of the breadwinner rather than on that of a dependent.

Some Comparisons

The many different kinds of policies described thus far may be a bit puzzling. Stop, then, and try to put all of this together, to compare and contrast. Study Table 6–2. The range of policies is from those with maximum protection and minimum (or no) savings to those with less protection (per premium dollar) and more savings. The term policy provides maximum protection and no savings for your premium money. The 20-year endowment provides the least protection and the maximum savings for your premium dollar. Generally speaking, the more costly the insurance, the faster it is building a cash value and, therefore, the more it is emphasizing savings. This may be all right for the established person of 40–45 with married children, but for the young person of 20–25 the emphasis should be placed on protection.

Group Insurance

Would $5,000 of life insurance offered to you for an annual premium of $25 interest you? It should. It's quite a bargain, and it may well be your introduction to life insurance. It's group insurance, of course, the kind a firm might make available to you when you start your first career job.

Increasingly, responsible firms are providing employees with group life insurance, on which the employer pays at least half, sometimes all, of the premium cost. Usually, the amount of group insurance that you can buy is equal to at least one year's salary.

Group insurance is usually term insurance written under a blanket (master) policy issued to an employer or sponsoring association on all or some of the members of the group. Group insurance usually costs less per $1,000 of protection than ordinary insurance. Since the groups are frequently large—often running into the thousands—with all being covered by one sale, the selling cost is low per thousand dollars face value of insurance, even though considerable effort may be expended in arranging the details so that the needs of the group will be satisfied. Another factor making for lower costs is that the employer does much of the bookkeeping, since he makes collection through payroll deductions of the employees' share of the premium and pays the insurance company one sum covering the premium for the whole group. In many ways group insurance resembles a wholesale operation rather than a retailing of insurance. Costs of group insurance are so low that eligible employees who can use the added insurance protection should think twice before passing up the opportunity to obtain it. Group insurance is generally written for one year, renewable.

Special Features of Group Insurance

One of the chief advantages of group insurance is that no medical examination is required of the members of the group. Risk is spread sufficiently by the very size of the group—which varies from a low of perhaps five persons to a high of thousands in some of the larger organizations. By means of group insurance, some persons obtain life insurance protection who, because of their health status, might be unable to obtain it otherwise. One disadvantage of group insurance is that you cannot borrow against the policy.

The employer pays some part of the premium cost and often all of it. His contribution may be reduced if because of favorable experience a dividend on the master policy is returned to him. Each member of the group is given an individual certificate indicating his rights in the group contract. Generally, each employee pays the same amount per $1,000 of protection, regardless of age.

In some cases, group insurance is now being written as a combination of term and straight life. Therefore, it may carry no cash surrender or loan provisions. Group insurance customarily terminates when the employee leaves the job, whether before or at retirement age. It is, however, a common provision to allow employees covered by group insurance to convert it into the standard forms of straight life or endowment within 30 days after severing their employment. Group insurance usually does not cover retired employees—or at least it covers them to a smaller extent than it did when they were actively employed; this cuts down claims against the insurance company and is a further reason for the low cost of this type of insurance.

An increasing number of employers are making group life insurance available to their retiring employees, in lesser value after 65, and at minimum or no cost to them. Otherwise employees would face a gap in financial planning that would require a decision on whether to convert at high premiums to straight life or adjust either to less insurance as the group policy ends—or to none at all. This affects all levels of incomes, with those at the lowest levels relying almost completely on social security. Even those who can afford conversion might well hesitate when they find that the $10,000 straight life no-dividend policy that at age 30 would have cost $150 a year, now at age 65 will cost $670 a year.

A recent development in group life insurance offers, instead of the usual lump-sum payment, survivor benefits designed to meet family needs by providing a continuing monthly payment to the surviving spouse in an amount related to the employee's years of service. Payments may extend for life or to the age at which social security retirement payments begin.

If your first job offers group insurance, don't turn it down. It protects a new family, the cost is very low, the employer pays all or part of the premium, you won't need to take a medical examination, and in most cases you can convert to ordinary insurance if and when you leave the company.

So rapidly is group protection growing in the United States that it represents 43 percent of all life insurance in force today. Low-cost term group life insurance can now be bought through Master Charge, brokerage firms, and mutual funds, in addition to the traditional sources of corporations, unions, and professional associations. The term *group* can now be stretched to include any combination of people together for any purpose except buying insurance. The insurance lasts as long as you belong to the group.

For example, a shareholder in a mutual fund can buy this low-cost insurance. If the shares are sold, the insurance ends unless it is converted to an individual policy at a higher rate. This might strengthen shareholder loyalty and also sell more mutual fund shares.

The group rate is so low that it undercuts savings bank life insurance. For example, Master Charge, which acts as a sales and collection agency for insurance companies, offers $25,000 of term life for a 34-year-old at $57.60, whereas the savings bank policy would cost about $84 a year.

Industrial Insurance

Industrial insurance policies, which are sold in sums of less than $1,000, involve weekly premiums collected at the home by the insurance agent. The name of this insurance is derived from the fact that it is usually sold to industrial workers who are paid weekly, and, therefore, find it convenient to pay for insurance weekly. The little protection that these policies afford means that all of them together amount to but a small fraction of the total life insurance protection in force. These policies were particularly useful for paying funeral expenses, and it was not unusual to find a half dozen of them, covering both parents and children, in force in a single family.

There is a 20 percent higher mortality experience for the holders of industrial policies than for the holders of other types of life insurance policies—one factor making for the high cost of industrial insurance.

Industrial policy lapses are large in number, sometimes amounting to as many as the new policies written, in spite of the fact that the agent is penalized for allowing these policies (technically, "in his debit") to lapse. Thus the life of industrial policies is short. The expense of writing the policies and the need for the agent's commissions to be absorbed quickly are primarily responsible for their relatively high cost. The decline in industrial insurance is due to the growing awareness of its limitations, the economic gains of the worker, and the wider prevalence of group policies, making it possible for workers to be more easily covered at their place of employment.

Only 2 percent of all legal reserve life insurance in force is industrial insurance.

Credit Life Insurance

Over the last decade a phenomenal growth in credit life insurance has paralleled the growth of consumer credit. Credit life insurance is written through lenders (banks, finance companies, credit unions, and retailers) on the lives of borrowers and installment purchasers. It assures the full payment of loans in the event of death, thus leaving survivors in the debtor's family free of his indebtedness. More than 79 million credit life insurance policies are outstanding, for a total of $139 billion. The average amount covered per policy or certificate under credit life insurance is $1,410. Most credit life insurance is written on a group basis, and it is therefore relatively inexpensive.

Credit life insurance is term insurance that generally decreases in amount as a loan is repaid. It protects the borrower's family as well as the lender. It covers loans of ten years' duration or less, and so it can also include mortgage protection for that time. You are not required to take credit life insurance in order to obtain a loan, although some creditors give the impression that it is necessary. Truth in lending regulations are very specific on that point.

Savings Bank Life Insurance

Savings bank life insurance has many advantages. Among them are the lower cost—because you must buy it directly from the bank (in person or by mail), there is no commission—and the variety of plans available. Beginning with the first year, all of these plans pay dividends which may then be used to reduce premium payments or to buy additional amounts. The major disadvantage of this type of insurance is that it is available in only three states—New York, Connecticut, and Massachusetts—and you must either live or work in the state where you purchase it. Once you own savings bank life insurance, you may keep it no matter where you live or work. If *you* are eligible you may also apply on members of your immediate family.

All savings bank life insurance policies pay dividends as earned, starting the very first year. Those dividends may be (1) taken in cash, (2) used to reduce premium payments, (3) used to purchase more insurance, (4) left to accumulate at interest, or (5) used to buy one-year term insurance.

All such policies (except term) have guaranteed cash and loan values at the end of the first year.

All can have additional low-cost premium disability waivers that waive all premiums if you are totally disabled before you are 60 for as long as you are disabled. Table 6–3 indicates the low rates on savings bank life insurance at ages 21 and 23.

Combination Policies

The straight life policy has many variants—in fact, the insurance companies are constantly trying to devise new contracts which meet the needs of certain people better than do the older forms. Thus we hear of family income and family maintenance policies, of family policies and of modified life. These are combinations of whole life and term policies. A 20-year family income policy is a combination of decreasing term insurance and a straight life insurance policy. If the insured lives on beyond the 20-year term, the whole life portion of the policy can be continued at the rate for straight life that was in effect when the policy was bought. The premiums on these combination policies run

TABLE 6–3
Example of Rates for Savings Bank Life Insurance

SAVINGS BANK **SBLI** LIFE INSURANCE

RATES NEAREST BIRTHDAY **AGE 21**
(see reverse side for age 22)

Dividends payable, as earned, on all policies beginning the first year. Liberal cash and loan values, except Term policies. Premiums are also payable semi-annually and quarterly.
Waiver of premium benefits available.

LOW COST **21-22** PROTECTION

PREMIUM RATES

KIND OF POLICY	$2,000		$5,000		$10,000		$20,000	
	Annual	Monthly	Annual	Monthly	Annual	Monthly	Annual	Monthly
Straight Life..............	$ 27.44	$ 2.46	$ 58.60	$ 5.25	$112.20	$10.10	$219.40	$ 19.80
Life Paid Up at Age 65....	29.20	2.62	63.00	5.65	121.00	10.90	237.00	21.40
Endowment at Age 65......	34.28	3.08	75.70	6.80	146.40	13.20	287.80	26.00
20-Payment Life...........	42.02	3.78	95.05	8.55	185.10	16.70	365.20	32.80
20-Year Endowment........	84.18	7.58	200.45	18.05	395.90	35.60	786.80	70.80
5-Year Renewable Term.....	—	—	17.90	1.60	30.80	2.80	56.60	5.00
20-Yr. Decreasing Term.....	—	—	13.45	1.20	21.90	2.00	38.80	3.40
25-Yr. Decreasing Term.....	—	—	14.25	1.30	23.50	2.10	42.00	3.80
30-Yr. Decreasing Term.....	—	—	15.40	1.40	25.80	2.30	46.60	4.20

Policy limit $30,000. For other rates, plans, and policy benefits, ask at our Life Insurance Department.

SAVINGS BANK **SBLI** LIFE INSURANCE

RATES NEAREST BIRTHDAY **AGE 23**
(see reverse side for age 24)

Dividends payable, as earned, on all policies beginning the first year. Liberal cash and loan values, except Term policies. Premiums are also payable semi-annually and quarterly.
Waiver of premium benefits available.

LOW COST **23-24** PROTECTION

PREMIUM RATES

KIND OF POLICY	$2,000		$5,000		$10,000		$20,000	
	Annual	Monthly	Annual	Monthly	Annual	Monthly	Annual	Monthly
Straight Life..............	$ 28.88	$ 2.60	$ 62.20	$ 5.60	$119.40	$10.70	$233.80	$ 21.00
Life Paid Up at Age 65....	30.92	2.78	67.30	6.05	129.60	11.70	254.20	22.80
Endowment at Age 65......	36.48	3.28	81.20	7.30	157.40	14.20	309.80	27.80
20-Payment Life...........	43.84	3.94	99.60	8.95	194.20	17.50	383.40	34.60
20-Year Endowment........	84.32	7.58	200.80	18.05	396.60	35.70	788.20	71.00
5-Year Renewable Term.....	—	—	18.20	1.65	31.40	2.80	57.80	5.20
20-Yr. Decreasing Term.....	—	—	13.90	1.25	22.80	2.10	40.60	3.60
25-Yr. Decreasing Term.....	—	—	14.95	1.35	24.90	2.20	44.80	4.00
30-Yr. Decreasing Term.....	—	—	16.35	1.45	27.70	2.50	50.40	4.60

Policy limit $30,000. For other rates, plans, and policy benefits, ask at our Life Insurance Department.

only a little higher than those for ordinary life policies, and these policies are often excellent for families with young children.

For example, if a man who has a wife and a one-year-old baby takes out a 20-year, $10,000 family income policy and dies three years later, the policy will assure the widow and child of $100 a month income until the child is age 21. Then the face of the policy will become due and payable to the widow, either as a lump sum or as income. If the man had lived, he could have continued paying on the policy as an ordinary whole life policy after the 20-year period was up.

Family maintenance policies are similar, except that a 20-year policy of this kind would pay its monthly income for 20 years *after the death of the insured* should death occur within 20 years after the purchase of the policy. To illustrate the difference: suppose that two women buy policies of the two types in 1975 and that both die in 1985: the beneficiaries under the family income policy will receive a monthly income until 1995 and will then receive the face value of the policy, whereas the beneficiaries under the family maintenance policy will receive a monthly income until 2005 and will then receive the face value of the policy. Naturally, therefore, family maintenance policies cost more, since the company faces the possibility of having to extend the monthly income payment over a longer period. Both kinds of insurance are available in 10-year and 15-year policies as well as 20-year policies.

Modified life is a type of policy which starts as term insurance and then after a stated period, usually five years, automatically changes to whole life at a higher premium. During the first five years the low term premium rate prevails. The basic purpose of modified life, of course, is to provide permanent insurance for young people who aren't yet in a position to pay for it. It is therefore a very useful policy for newlyweds or for the young family.

The family policy (not to be confused with the family income policy) is one of the insurance industry's combinations of term and straight life. It provides a "package" of insurance coverage for the whole family—husband, wife, and children. The policy is issued in $5,000 units, with each unit providing $5,000 of whole life insurance for the husband, $1,250 of term insurance for the wife (if she is the same age as her husband), and $1,000 of term insurance for each covered child. The wife's insurance coverage is more than $1,250 if she is younger than the husband and less if she is older. The premium is not affected by the number of children covered. Children born after the plan is issued are automatically eligible for children's coverage when they are 15 days old, at no extra premium.

Extra protection policies also combine term and ordinary life. There are "double," "triple," and even "quadruple" protection policies. **The double protection policy,** for example, may be $1,000 of straight life with $1,000 of term tacked on; triple protection adds $2,000 of term to the $1,000 of whole life; and so on. The term portion usually runs until age 60 or 65 and then expires, leaving the straight life protection only. These policies give less "extra" protection in the early years than does a comparable premium expenditure on a family income policy, but the "extra" protection lasts longer—to 60 or 65.

Preferred risk policies are regular policies issued at specially reduced rates to those who are in very good health and in safe occupations and who will buy a large minimum amount of insurance, usually $25,000 or $50,000. The rate is significantly less than that for the regular types of policies. If you are going into the professions and enjoy excellent health, inquire about the preferred risk policy. For those who qualify, it means buying regular insurance at very favorable rates.

The Adjustable Life Policy

Planned as a "life cycle" policy to adjust to a family's changing needs, this new form of life insurance has gained instant popularity. You determine the amount of coverage you need and the amount of premium that you can afford at any given time. The minimum term is ten years, but unlike conventional term insurance, the adjustable life policy builds a cash value. A policyholder can increase the insurance coverage by as much as 20 percent every three years without a medical examination. Naturally this policy is more expensive than any traditional type of policy.

The Contingent Life Policy

This is another new type of coverage. It is the same as whole life insurance—with all its advantages—and in addition it covers two or more people. The more persons covered, the lower the premium, because the risk is spread. The contingent life policy has advantages for a family if each member desires coverage. There has been a growing awareness of the advantages of coverage on a wife—especially a working wife. There is a useful guaranteed future in that the policy can be converted to cover changing needs.

What's in Your Life Insurance Policy?

"The big print gives it to you, the fine print takes it away," a lawyer once remarked in reading a contract. In the case of your insurance policy, however, the fine print confers many more benefits than it takes away. Most likely your policy came to you carefully folded. On its back you will notice your name, your policy number, the amount of the policy, and the date it was issued. The amount of your premiums and the type of policy are also written here.

Open your policy. On the first page you will find the main part of the contract. Your policy states that the XYZ Life Insurance Company insures your life. You are called the insured. The company agrees to pay $_____, the face amount, to the person you have named, called the beneficiary. In return, you promise to make a periodic payment, called a premium, to the company. If you fail to make the premium payment within the grace period (usually 31 days after a premium is due), your policy lapses, which means that the policy comes to an end unless it can be kept in force on a different basis by nonforfeiture provisions, such as cash value, reduced paid-up insurance, or extended term insurance. Sometimes, after your policy has lapsed, you may put it into full effect again (reinstate it), provided (a) that you have not turned it in for cash, (b) that you again qualify as a good risk (are insurable), and (c) that, of course, you pay the overdue premiums plus interest. Your policy will be incontestable after either one or two years, usually two. During this initial period the company has the opportunity to check the information you gave in your application. After the period of contestability, the company cannot withdraw from the contract or contest it.

Special Clauses

Your policy will probably have a number of special clauses. Life insurance policies will not pay off for death by suicide if it occurs during a stated period, usually the first year or two of the contract. The **suicide** clause states that the company will return the premiums paid in case of suicide during this period. There are occasionally other limitations of coverage, which may exclude payment when death results from abnormal risks, such as travel in dangerous places or by dangerous means of conveyance, or is due to war.

In some states, the law permits you to include in the settlement arrangements a so-called **spendthrift clause,** which protects your beneficiaries from the claims of their own creditors. In most states, your life insurance, if payable to named beneficiaries rather than to your estate, is protected from the claims of your own creditors, unless it can be shown that funds were purposely diverted to it in order to bypass the creditors.

Your policy may contain **waiver of premium** and **double indemnity** riders. Under the former, any premiums which fall due after the beginning of total and permanent disability will be waived. In effect, the company will pay them. Disability must occur before you reach a certain age, usually 60, and before the policy matures, if it is an endowment. The disability must last for at least six months before premiums will be waived.

The accidental death benefit, or **double indemnity,** provides that an additional sum, equal to the face of the policy, will be paid if death occurs by accidental means. Accidental death must occur within a certain time after the injury, usually 90 days, and before a certain age, usually 60 or 65. The double indemnity rider usually says that certain causes of death are not covered. Although this rider enjoys much publicity, accidental deaths are relatively infrequent.

Both riders require small additions to the premium to cover the extra cost to the company, but both enjoy wide favor, especially the waiver of premium rider, without which many incapacitated insured persons would be forced to drop their policies. Life insurance thus protects against "economic death," whether casket or disability. The latter, however, must be total and permanent. Partial or temporary disability comes under health insurance.

One rider that can be added to a regular insurance policy is designed primarily for young people who can purchase only a limited amount of insurance at first. It gives you the right to purchase additional insurance later at standard premiums, within certain limits, even if your health should become impaired, making you uninsurable under ordinary circumstances.

The rider, which can generally be purchased up to age 37, gives you the right to buy more insurance at specified intervals, without a medical examination, in amounts equal to the face value of the basic policy. The number of option dates depends on your age when you buy the basic policy. For example, on a policy purchased at age 22, you can buy up to $10,000 more (if the face value of your basic policy is $10,000 or more) at ages 25, 28, 31, 34, 37, and 40. Thus you could buy an additional $60,000 of insurance, until age 40, regardless of the condition of your health or the type of job you hold. At age 23, for example, the rider would cost approximately $1.52 a year for each $1,000 of insurance you add at any option date. The rider doesn't buy the insurance for you. It simply gives you the right to buy the insurance regardless of health. You pay the standard premium for your age each time you buy an extra policy. The rider is an option to buy insurance tomorrow. It doesn't add to your insurance today.

Beneficiaries

When you take out a policy, you have the right to name a beneficiary to whom the policy is payable in case of your death. You may also retain the right to change the beneficiary later, if you deem it wise to do so.

If a beneficiary is not named, the proceeds will be paid to the insured's estate, where they will be subject to creditors' claims and inheritance taxes. In some states, the proceeds are subject to inheritance taxes even when there is a named beneficiary; but sometimes amounts of less than about $10,000 escape this tax if they are left to immediate relatives.

At times it is sensible to name a contingent beneficiary to receive the proceeds if the primary beneficiary should predecease the insured. Frequently, children are named contingent beneficiaries. If the children are young, money for them may perhaps be better left to a trustee, to be administered for their benefit. Possible future children should be included in the wording. In the event that one child dies, his share may be left to his children or be divided among his brothers and sisters.

How Life Insurance Policies Pay Off

Should a lump-sum cash settlement ever be considered? Is it always wiser to favor a set monthly payment for life? Is the choice a matter of personality—adventure versus security—or is there any economic reasoning involved? The advantages of the lump-sum choice would be felt most in an era of high interest rates and capital gains, when investment opportunities are more plentiful. Additional considerations are age, other income, the background of knowledge needed for investment decisions, and the resultant taxes.

The Settlement Options

Apart from a lump-sum cash settlement, there are four settlement options, as Table 6–4 shows. All four are explained in your life insurance policy. If the interest option is chosen, the company holds and invests the money until the beneficiary needs it; in the meantime, it sends out regular checks for the interest which this money has earned. If the amount option is chosen, a regular income of as much money as you want per month will be paid until the money and interest are gone; for example, if you have a $10,000 policy and want $100 a month, the company will be able to pay you this amount for nine years and five months. If you choose the time option, the company will pay, for the period you specify, a monthly amount fixed to last for the period selected; for example, if you wish some income for at least 20 years, the company will pay $54 a month for the 20 years. If the lifetime income option is chosen, a regular income is paid as long as the person named to receive it lives; the monthly amount will be less for a younger person, more for an older person.

If the insurance company has contracted to pay monthly installments for a certain number of years and the beneficiary dies before payments are completed, the remaining payments will be made to the estate of the insured in the absence of a second, named beneficiary. You, as the insured, may either choose the plan by which settlement is to be made or leave the choice of settlement options to your

TABLE 6–4
The Four Optional Settlements for $10,000 (as income rather than a single cash payment)

The interest option:
Money left at interest until the family asks for it

$275 a year at 2¾ percent interest, until the money is withdrawn*

The amount option:
A regular income of as much money as you want, paid until money and interest are gone

$100 a month for 9 years and 5 months,
or
$200 a month for 4 years and 4 months

The time option:
A monthly income to last as many years as you want, paid until money and interest are gone

10 years income of $95 a month,
or
20 years income of $54 a month

The lifetime income option:
A regular income guaranteed for the person's lifetime

$57.60 a month for life (for a woman 65 years old)
$67.25 a month for life (for a man 65 years old)

* This is the legally guaranteed rate in a typical contract. Companies actually pay about 5 percent and higher now.
Source: American Council of Life Insurance.

beneficiary. Some people have their insurance payable to a bank as trustee and indicate in a trust agreement how the money is to be used. The method you select should take into consideration the financial capacity of your beneficiary and his or her needs.

The interest payment option is the most widely used, providing safety for the principal and flexibility in interest payments. Both the amount option and the time option are forms of installment payments that are most advantageously used in advanced age or during a period when children are growing up.

The lifetime income option is used mainly to provide for a widowed spouse, children, or independent parents. There are several options within this choice:

1. You can provide the largest life income for the beneficiary under a life only annuity, which then forfeits the remainder of the principal if the beneficiary has an early death.

2. Another possibility provides a refund to a second beneficiary, either in lump-sum or installment payments of the difference between the principal and the amount paid to the first beneficiary.

3. A variation helpful to a widow with small children provides set payments for a fixed period after the original beneficiary dies.

Lately some insurance companies have been offering a 6 percent and higher interest return to those who will leave their matured endowment policy money or life insurance benefits on deposit for five more years. Doing this could doubly benefit a widowed spouse. It gives a good return during a planning period, and it also provides a lump sum five years later, at which time, as an older person, he or she can purchase higher annuity income with the insurance proceeds.

Don't count on the untouched cash value in your policy to increase the face payment of your policy to your beneficiary. It belongs to the reserves set aside to enable the company to pay the policy's face value.

Premium Rates

In the level premium policies (the premium remains constant as long as the policy is in force), one pays more than the current cost of insurance in the early years but less in the later years. The company collects a larger premium than is necessary to meet death claims during the early policy years. Consequently, a reserve fund accumulates to one's credit. The policyholder can borrow against his pro rata share of the reserve fund; or if he wishes, he can surrender the policy and collect it as cash value. Thus, level premium insurance provides a savings or investment feature along with your protection or insurance. Collecting more funds than are needed in the earlier years of life creates definite obligations on the part of the company to its policyholders. These obligations are called "policyholders' reserves" or "legal reserves" and are carefully supervised by the state, for the company's solvency depends on the ownership of assets equal to these reserves (which are really liabilities). The reserves are separate from profits and are not available for distribution as dividends.

When basic premium rates are set, something must be added to cover the cost of running the insurance company. This charge is known as the "loading." Efficient companies hold expenses low. Thus the premium charged you for life insurance depends on three factors: (a) the real cost of insurance based on mortality experience, (b) the return earned on the reserves accumulated under level premium policies, and (c) the costs of running the insurance company.

Premiums do vary from company to company. When comparing rates, use the interest-adjusted index of comparing the costs of similar policies. Here at least is a source that enables the consumer to measure value in an industry whose product is complex, which lacks uniform federal regulation, and over which 50 states exercise varying degrees of supervision.

Basically this method takes into account the pos-

sible investments that a policyholder might make with the excess funds used to pay the excess premiums of the earlier years of a life insurance policy. Based on actuarial risk, premiums are higher than they need be in the early years to keep the costs down in the later, higher risk years. Furthermore, if dividends are paid by one company regularly and by another in a lump sum after many years, although the total amounts may be the same, the policyholder of the second company has suffered by not having the use of the money during that time.

Comparison Shopping

The "interest-adjusted cost" is equal to that sum of money (premiums, dividends paid, and the cash surrender value of the policy) which if placed in a conservative (5 percent) interest-bearing account, would equal the buyer's net dollar cost of the policy after 10 or 20 years. This method takes into account the "time value of money." What is being measured is the use of your money. It shows you the return you would have if that money were invested over the same period of time it is tied into your insurance policy. An index using these same factors in rating all insurance companies enables you to determine which of seemingly similar policies would give you the best value.

Many state insurance commissions publish cost comparison tables on companies doing business in their area.[2] Many insurance companies now provide interest-adjusted cost figures for their policies.

This method assumes the policy will be surrendered for its cash value on either its 10th or 20th anniversary, and therefore according to critics of this method it is not really measuring lifetime protection. This index does not measure the value of such features as conversion privileges, the availability of loans, and other options. Nor, unless the entire time span is reviewed, does it rank ade-

[2] One of the most complete is the free 92-page *Consumers Shopping Guide for Life Insurance* published by the New York State Insurance Department. Write Publications Unit, New York State Insurance Department, Agency Building I, Empire State Plaza, Albany, N.Y. 12223.

quately the dividend policies of two companies if one of them pays small dividends over nine years and a large one in the tenth year and the other pays equal dividends each year. Lower indexes mean lower costs, and higher indexes mean higher costs. But a company may have a low index, and yet your plan, depending on age, sex, and amount involved, may not have a low index in that company. It is therefore important to make valid comparisons. Identical life insurance policies may vary by as much as 300 percent. For example, a $25,000 whole life policy sold by the most costly of 72 insurance companies would, if surrendered after 20 years, have cost $2,337 more than that sold by the least costly.[3] A 20-year average gross premium $25,000 nonparticipating, term insurance policy for a 20-year-old male could vary $75 in premiums, depending on which company sold the policy.

Now that both companies and consumers have become interest-adjusted-cost conscious, a new development may weaken its usefulness. It has been customary in the insurance field for all policyholders to receive dividends based on the same rate of return on the company's investments. It is reported that some companies are now paying higher rates of interest to new policyholders, using an "investment year" formula based on the year the policy was sold. If the company pays a higher rate to some policyholders on the rationale that the new money invested now is bringing in a higher dividend return, the projected 20-year interest-adjusted cost drops for that company and the competitive companies' policies look costlier. They in turn will adopt the same policy. Cost illustrations will look steadily better, but the comparisons are made unreal by 20-year projections based on today's money rates instead of on the relatively low generally accepted industry-wide rate that was used previously. Those who have had policies over a long period will suffer because investment income

"It says, 'If you can read this the contract will have to be renegotiated.'"

Reprinted by permission *The Wall Street Journal*

will not be averaged. If you are shopping for life insurance, all of these factors must be considered.

The Payment of Premiums

It is preferable, if possible, to pay premiums on an annual basis. However, arrangements can usually be made to pay semiannually, quarterly, or even monthly. In the last two cases, the company does not have the use of the total premium as soon, and it must therefore be paid interest for the delay. In addition, having several payments made each year rather than a single premium payment increases the cost of sending out notices and keeping records, so that it may cost you 8 to 10 percent extra to avail yourself of the privilege of making partial payments. Of course, the average person is paid weekly or monthly; and it is somewhat of a hardship to pay a large insurance premium at one time, just as it is to pay a large real estate or income tax bill. One way out of the diffi-

---

[3] Ernest P. Welker (ed.), *Life Insurance from the Buyers' Point of View* (Great Barrington, Mass.: American Institute for Economic Research, 1977). See also Richard B. Corbett, "Analyzing Cost Differences in Life Insurance." *The Journal of Consumer Affairs,* Winter 1978.

culty is to take out several smaller policies, instead of one larger one, and having each payable in a different month, provided, of course, that you stay with ordinary insurance and do not resort to industrial insurance. Each of the smaller policies can be paid on an annual basis, with staggered due dates, thus achieving the economies of annual payment for the policyholder. Only one policyholder in five pays annually—reaping savings that many others could achieve by doing some financial planning. Another method is a plan whereby your bank automatically places in a special account during the year preceding the annual premium date an appropriate amount from your regular account and then pays the premium when due. The bank makes no extra charge for this service.

What Happens if You Can't Pay Your Premiums?

In a permanent policy, where a cash value has been built up, you don't usually lose the policy. The nonforfeiture provisions come into play. If you are temporarily unable to meet your premium payments, you can borrow against the cash value of your policy and thus continue payments through the loan. If it looks as though you will be unable to resume payments again, or if you become 65 and you don't want to continue to pay premiums, you can choose one of the various nonforfeiture options.

Every type of permanent policy, of which the whole or straight life type is the most popular, has built-in "nonforfeiture values." There are three kinds of nonforfeiture or guaranteed values:

1. *Cash Value.* This is the money you will get if you give up your permanent life insurance policy. A policyholder who has purchased life insurance on the level premium plan has paid premiums which were more than needed to pay claims in the earlier years, thus building up a fund of assets with which to meet claims in later years. It follows that if you withdraw, there is an accumulation of assets out of the premiums paid by you to which you are entitled.

The cash value is your share of this accumula-

tion. It will be paid to you as guaranteed in the insurance contract and as required by law. It may be taken in a lump sum or in a series of regularly recurring payments over a period of years, providing it amounts to $1,000 or more. The longer you have your policy, the more your cash value will be. Today, many people reaching retirement arrange to take their cash value in the form of income that will be paid for life over the retirement period. Some requests for cash reflect an upset in family finances as a result of unexpected illnesses or loss of a job. Though life insurance is not designed as a way of preparing to meet such financial difficulties, in some cases it may help more in this way, than it would if kept in force as regular life insurance coverage.

You can borrow against your cash value at any time; if you die before the loan is repaid, the payments to your beneficiaries will be reduced by the amount of the loan and any interest owed. In an emergency, then, the loan provision of your life insurance policy can be used to secure money or to pay premiums due. Some policies have a special provision for the latter, called the "automatic premium loan." If this provision is in your policy, your company will automatically pay any premium that is not paid when due. The company will charge such premiums as loans against your policy to the extent of the available loan values. The policy continues in force until such time as the total loan against the policy equals the cash value. At that time the policy terminates without further values.

2. *Reduced Paid-up Life Insurance.* This is a nonforfeiture or guaranteed value that you can use if you want to keep some protection but are not in a position to or do not wish to pay any more premiums. The amount of your insurance will be reduced. For example, if you bought a $1,000 policy at age 20, and then at age 65, you were unable to continue paying premiums because of illness, you could arrange to have $857 of paid-up insurance as long as you lived without any further payments of premiums. That is, if you have a permanent life policy, the paid-up insurance feature will protect you for life without further premium payments, but the insurance is reduced in amount to

what your net cash value will buy as a single payment at your attained age.

3. *Extended Term Insurance.* Suppose you can no longer pay premiums on your policy but want to continue the maximum amount of protection as long as possible. Extended term insurance gives you continued protection for the full face value of your policy (less any loan outstanding) for a limited length of time. If, at age 65, you were unable to continue to pay premiums on the $1,000 policy you bought at age 20, you could continue to enjoy the protection of the full face value of your policy, without paying any more premiums, for an additional 15 years and 348 days. The time is determined by what your net cash value will purchase when it is used as a single payment to buy the extended term protection at your attained age.

Loans

Let us assume you have found just the house you want for a home. You need a $20,000 loan and the best mortgage rate available is 9½ percent. You have a life insurance policy that has built up cash value. The interest rate for loans from the insurance company against the cash value may be only 5 percent. Think of the interest charges you can save. In the majority of states, the insurance companies have persuaded the state legislatures to permit them to raise the interest rates charged against the cash value because loan volume has soared. The old rate remains for the life of the policy. The higher rate applies to new policies. Rates vary in the 50 states, from a low of 5 percent to a high of 8 percent.

Loan opportunities are most desirable in a period of light money and high interest rates, since you can borrow freely against your own policy and at a fixed rate—usually lower than the going rate. If the loan is repaid, the borrower has had the use of his money at a lower cost than the current market rate, the interest on the loan is tax deductible, and the face value of the policy is unimpaired. You do not need to repay a loan. If the loan is not repaid, the only penalty is the decreased value of the policy, which may seem justified if the purpose of the loan was, for example, to provide a college education for the future beneficiary.

Some policyholders borrow on their cash value to make promising investments or to use the money in long-term savings accounts to get a higher return and profit despite the cost of repaying the interest charges on the loan. A six–seven-year savings account paying 7½–7¾ percent interest against a 5 percent cost for the loan is an attractive possibility—with no risk. Interest payments can be arranged monthly, quarterly, or annually, and this flexibility allows you to make interest payments when you can most easily do so.

Dividends

"Why do some companies pay 'dividends' on policies, while others do not?" First of all, the term *dividends* as used in insurance parlance does not mean the same thing as it does in finance and investments. In insurance *a dividend is a partial return of your own money;* it is a *refund* of part of the premium you paid. To make this clear, a number of other things need to be explained first.

Insurance companies are of two kinds: stock and mutual. Policies are of two kinds: participating and nonparticipating. A stock company is similar in its corporate organization to any other corporation. The stockholders own the capital and surplus. They take the risk of loss and are entitled to any profits. The stock company sells life insurance at guaranteed rates—guaranteed neither to increase nor decrease. Because of competition, the premium rates are kept as low as possible. If they are too low, the stockholders take a loss; if they are more than is exactly sufficient, there is a profit. Most stock companies issue only nonparticipating policies.

A mutual company, on the other hand, is "a cooperative association of persons established for the purpose of insuring their own lives." There are no stockholders to receive any profits or to absorb losses. Nearly all mutual companies issue only participating policies. Hence, the gross premium rates in mutual companies are higher than the rates in stock companies in order to cover all contingencies. Mutual company rates are set high enough so that there is usually a refund, which the insurance company calls a dividend, to the policyholder after the policy has been in force for a certain time.

The more options you have in the use of your dividend, the better. Companies usually give you the following choices:

1. Cash—a check each year for the amount of the dividend.
2. Use of the dividend to reduce the premium.
3. Leaving the dividend with the company in an interest-bearing account. You would probably receive a higher interest rate in a bank.
4. Buying a paid-up addition to the basic policy. This option is most useful to the policyholder who is no longer insurable or is insurable only at a high rate.

Pointers for Policyholders

1. *Keep Your Company Informed of Your Address.* Each year a number of policyholders move without either leaving a forwarding address or notifying their insurance companies. There may be dividend checks to be mailed to you; or if you let your policy lapse, the company will want to mail you a form on which to indicate your choice of nonforfeiture options.

2. *Discuss Your Insurance Program with Your Family or Other Beneficiaries.* It is usually advisable to have them share in the planning from the outset and to discuss with them each addition to or change in the program. It is also a good idea to leave a letter outlining your insurance policies and indicating any choices that the beneficiary may have in the settlement of the policies. It may be well to point out *(a)* that no outside assistance is needed in order to collect the insurance money and *(b)* that your life insurance agent will help your beneficiary fill out the "proof of claim" papers and assist in selecting a settlement option if the choice is left to the beneficiary.

If there is a question as to whether a deceased relative was covered by a life insurance policy, you can contact the American Council of Life Insurance, 1850 K Street, N.W., Washington, D.C.

20006. It will send you a questionnaire to get the pertinent details and will circulate the query among more than 600 companies.

3. *Review Your Insurance Program Periodically.* We live in a changing world. A program for insurance which is sensible for any of us when we are 20 years old may no longer fit our needs when we are 40 and may be ridiculous when we are 60. Inflation is diminishing the value of your coverage, which should be increased an equal amount to offset the loss. Consequently, the wise person will review his insurance periodically, perhaps every five or ten years, and consider its adequacy, not only alone but in connection with his other assets and with the needs of the persons who look to him for protection.

Such a review is especially important just before retirement. Will the retirement income be sufficient to continue the same premium payments? Even more important, will the choices made at retirement time be sufficient to provide for the remainder of life?

4. *Beware of Swapping Policies.* If you do this, you may not only lose the cash loan values you have built up, but you will have to pay a higher premium because you are older. It pays to research before you buy your policy or to switch in the early years rather than later. If you still think that there are more advantages in the other policy, remember that you again face the two-year period of contestability over any health or age statements you make. You also pay again. There is again the initial cost of writing the insurance policy and the agent's fee. If you want to go ahead anyway, be sure you ask for a Disclosure Statement from the seller, giving comparisons between the existing policy and the proposed policy.

Checking Your Insurance Company

Make sure your company is licensed to do business in your state. This is especially important if you are buying insurance by mail. It is difficult to file suit against an out-of-state company. *Best's Insurance Reports* publishes ratings for insurance companies. It is probably available in your library and comes in two volumes. One volume lists life and health insurance companies as either "most substantial" or "very substantial." The other volume lists the best property and liability insurers as "A" or "A+." Ask the agent whether the company offers similar policies in New York or Pennsylvania. These states have strict regulations for the advertisement and sale of insurance.

Life Insurance and Inflation

Life insurance is particularly vulnerable to inflation due to both its fixed dollar value and its lengthy contracts. This has tended to more than double the purchase of term policies and to motivate the idea of variable life insurance policies.

Variable Life Insurance—A Gamble with Your Life

If your have faith that stock market prices will be rising over your lifetime, you will be interested in the purchase of a variable life insurance policy (minimum $25,000) that ties the death benefit payment to your heirs to the market performance of the special account portfolio over the life of the policy. If the market drops, the death benefit will also drop, but not below its face amount for a given year.

A policy for a man aged 40 whose annual premium was $1,000 would have an initial face amount of $30,747. This same annual premium would buy this man $49,500 of ordinary life insurance. However, if the market rose, the owner of the variable life insurance policy would have gained.

Based on the performance of the stock market during last five years, there would have been no gain. During the ten-year period 1966–75 the Standard & Poor's index of 500 common stocks rose 3.3 percent.

Over the past 50 years common stocks have shown a 9 percent compound annual rate of return, including dividends and capital growth. The variable insurance policy may be your hedge against inflation—if your life span starts when the market is low and ends when it is high. That's the gamble.

The policy is nonparticipating (no dividends), and so it costs less than the usual fixed-benefit policies—but more than is usual for a policy that pays no dividends. The SEC now regulates this type of policy because it regards the policy as a security rather than as an insurance policy. Other insurance policies are state regulated.

The policy can be surrendered for its cash value—but there isn't any guaranteed minimum cash value.

The policy can be exchanged for a regular cash value policy within 18 months, without your having to meet medical standards—or you can get a refund if your change your mind within 45 days.

Government Insurance

Insurance sold by the government to soldiers who served during World War II and those who served thereafter up until April 25, 1951, is known as National Service Life Insurance. NSLI was issued to eligible persons in any amount from $1,000 to $10,000 in multiples of $500. Originally, five-year level premium participating term insurance was sold. By an act of Congress in 1945, all five-year term policies applied for and issued before January 1, 1946, were automatically extended to an additional period of three years at the same premium rates. At present, the term insurance may be renewed every five years, prior to the expiration of the term, for new terms, without a physical examination, at the premium rate for the then attained age. It may also be converted into any one of six permanent plans: ordinary life, 30-payment life, 20-payment life, 20-year endowment, endowment at age 60, or endowment at age 65.

NSLI insurance was one of the best insurance buys ever offered, and those who have it should retain it. The cost was and is very low, for a variety of reasons. There was no loading charge, that is, the government paid the costs of the insurance operation out of budgetary funds, with no premium charge. Veterans who died in service or as a result of service-connected disabilities had death benefits paid from government appropriations rather than from insurance reserves. The dividends have been very generous. It has been reported that 67 cents has been paid out in dividends for every dollar collected in National Service Life Insurance premiums. The dividend windfall resulted primarily because fewer World War II veterans died than experience had indicated. There are many favorable clauses and features, such as settlement option no. 4—refund life income—which no commercial insurance company can match at the low NSLI rate. The advantage of refund life income is that the beneficiary may not only choose to receive the proceeds of the policy in monthly installments as long as he or she lives but that if, upon his or her death, the amount paid out in these monthly installments has not equaled the face amount of the policy, the remainder is paid to the contingent beneficiary.

Veterans of the Korean conflict, that is, all those called to active duty for 31 days or more on and after June 27, 1950, as well as those who served after the war, until January 1, 1957, were treated differently under the Servicemen's Indemnity and Insurance Acts of 1951, which became effective April 25, 1951. They were automatically covered by a free indemnity against death in active service for $10,000, less any NSLI or USGLI in force at the time of death. This free indemnity protection, at no charge to the servicemen, continued for 120 days after separation from service. The insurance was payable only to a surviving spouse or surviving children, parents, brothers, or sisters; and the insured could name one or more beneficiaries within this permitted class. The $10,000 indemnity was payable in 120 equal installments of $92.90 per month.

Within 120 days after they were released from active service, but before January 1, 1957, veterans who were *not disabled* could apply for a five-year level premium term policy that could be renewed every five years at the premium rate for the then attained age. This insurance was at first not convertible to any other form of government life insurance, and it did not pay dividends. No physical examination was needed to obtain it—only payment of the first premium. A veteran was allowed to take out

from $1,000 to $10,000 of this term insurance, less any other government life insurance in force at the time of application. In 1958 the law was changed to permit conversion to any of a variety of permanent plans.

Servicemen's Group Life Insurance (SGLI), first offered in 1965, is group life insurance that was originally intended to cover servicemen going into a combat zone who would otherwise have been limited to commercial policies with war exclusion clauses. It is term insurance with no cash surrender values.

The SGLI program is supervised by the Veterans Administration, but it is operated under an arrangement with nearly 600 commercial insurance companies. Unless refusal to join is submitted in writing, all members of the armed services are automatically insured for $20,000, for which $3.40 a month is deducted from their pay. While still on active duty and up to within 120 days after separation a member of the armed forces had the right to convert to an individual commercial policy without regard to physical condition. The advantage of conversion is especially desirable for the service-disabled veteran who might otherwise have difficulty in getting commercial insurance at standard rates.

A veteran separated after August 1, 1974, is automatically covered by SGLI, but he must make application for it and pay the first premium before 120 days have passed. SGLI is the "insurance company" for the next five years, after which the group policy can be converted into an individual policy with any company then participating in the SGLI program.[4]

Conclusion

Although you now understand the basic differences in kinds of life policies, you have found not only that there are variations within variations in

---

[4] For further information, write Office of Servicemen's Group Life Insurance, 212 Washington St., Newark, N.J. 07102. See also *Federal Benefits for Veterans and Dependents* (Washington, D.C.: Veterans Administration Information Service, latest edition).

different companies but that there are many methods of evaluating costs.

In addition to cost comparisons, other factors to consider are: premiums vis a vis your budget, estimated dividends in participating policies, and settlement options that suit your individual needs.

Life insurance, with its triple purpose of replacing income, meeting emergencies, or supplementing income on retirement serves best when a particular plan fits your particular needs and goals and offers some protection for an uncertain future.

SUGGESTED READINGS

American Council of Life Insurance. *Life Insurance Fact Book.* A free copy may be obtained by writing to the council at 1850 K St., N.W., Washington, D.C. 20006; latest annual number.

Belth, Joseph M. *Life Insurance: A Consumer's Handbook.* Bloomington: Indiana University Press, 1973.

National Better Business Bureau. *Facts You Should Know about Life Insurance.* Write to the bureau's Educational Division, 1107 17th St., N.W., Washington, D.C. 20006; latest edition.

New York State Insurance Department. *Consumers Shopping Guide for Life Insurance, 1977.* For a free copy, write to the Publications Unit at Agency Building I, Empire State Plaza, Albany, N.Y. 12223.

Pennsylvania Insurance Department. *A Shopper's Guide to Term Life Insurance* and *A Shopper's Guide to Straight Life Insurance.* Write to the department at Harrisburg, PA, 17120 for a free copy; postage required.

CASE PROBLEMS

1 Martin Skoler is 25 years old. He lives with his widowed mother and is just about to set up a law practice. Martin's mother is self-supporting, and her home is fully paid. Now he is thinking of buying some life insurance and is trying to decide which kind would be best for him. What would you suggest?

2 Mildred Becker is a 40-year-old accountant with an income of $25,000 a year. She is married and has four children ranging from three to ten years old. She already carries a $10,000 straight life insurance policy and would now like to take out enough insurance to protect her family until the youngest child reaches 21. What insurance program would you suggest for her?

3 Grace Robinson (age 26) is a kindergarten teacher. She is single; her father, mother, and two older brothers are living. An agent tries to sell her $10,000 of five-year term insurance. Should she buy it? Explain.

4 John Sullivan (wife and two children, ages six and nine) has a $20,000 term policy which is expiring. It is convertible into straight life (cost, $18 per $1,000) or endowment (cost, $40 per $1,000). The family has been able to save little. They have had difficulty paying the premium on the term policy. What should John do?

5 Ronald Smithers (two children, ages nine and three) works for the Jonas Corporation. He and his wife think that, with $20,000 of straight life insurance, they have enough insurance. What they have costs $224 a year, which seems to be large in relation to what he earns ($180 a week). The Jonas Company offers Smithers a group participation of $4,000 of insurance for 60 cents per month per $1,000. Smithers is 50 years old, and his health is beginning to fail. Should he take the group insurance?

APPENDIX: COMPUTATION OF PRESENT VALUES

Source: From Joseph M. Belth, *Life Insurance: A Consumer's Handbook* (Bloomington: Indiana University Press, 1973), pp. 191–193. Copyright © by Joseph M. Belth. Reprinted with permission.

The purpose of this appendix is to explain how to calculate the present value of your income needs and the present value of your estimated social security survivors' benefits. The phrase "present value" means the amount of funds which, if available at the beginning of a time period and invested consistently at the assumed interest rate, would be precisely sufficient to produce the given yearly payments. For example, Table 6A–1 shows tht $10,899 would be the present value of $1,000 per year for 15 years at 5 percent interest. In other words, $10,899 would be precisely sufficient to produce

TABLE 6A–1
Present Value of $1,000 per Year (payable at beginning of each year)

Number of Years	0%	1%	2%	Interest Rate 3%	4%	5%	6%
1	$ 1,000	$ 1,000	$ 1,000	$ 1,000	$ 1,000	$ 1,000	$ 1,000
2	2,000	1,990	1,980	1,971	1,962	1,952	1,943
3	3,000	2,970	2,942	2,913	2,886	2,859	2,833
4	4,000	3,941	3,884	3,829	3,775	3,723	3,673
5	5,000	4,902	4,808	4,717	4,630	4,546	4,465
6	6,000	5,853	5,713	5,580	5,452	5,329	5,212
7	7,000	6,795	6,601	6,417	6,242	6,076	5,917
8	8,000	7,728	7,472	7,230	7,002	6,786	6,582
9	9,000	8,652	8,325	8,020	7,733	7,463	7,210
10	10,000	9,566	9,162	8,786	8,435	8,108	7,802
11	11,000	10,471	9,983	9,530	9,111	8,722	8,360
12	12,000	11,368	10,787	10,253	9,760	9,306	8,837
13	13,000	12,255	11,575	10,954	10,385	9,863	9,384
14	14,000	13,134	12,348	11,635	10,986	10,394	9,853
15	15,000	14,004	13,106	12,296	11,563	10,899	10,295
16	16,000	14,865	13,849	12,938	12,118	11,380	10,712
17	17,000	15,718	14,578	13,561	12,652	11,838	11,106
18	18,000	16,562	15,292	14,166	13,166	12,274	11,477
19	19,000	17,398	15,992	14,754	13,659	12,690	11,828
20	20,000	18,226	16,678	15,324	14,134	13,085	12,158
25	25,000	22,243	19,914	17,936	16,247	14,799	13,550
30	30,000	26,066	22,844	20,188	17,984	16,141	14,591
35	35,000	29,703	25,499	22,132	19,411	17,193	15,368
40	40,000	33,163	27,903	23,808	20,584	18,017	15,949
45	45,000	36,455	30,080	25,254	21,549	18,663	16,383
50	50,000	39,588	32,052	26,502	22,341	19,169	16,708
55	55,000	42,569	33,838	27,578	22,993	19,565	16,950
60	60,000	45,405	35,456	28,506	23,528	19,876	17,131
65	65,000	48,103	36,921	29,306	23,969	20,119	17,266
70	70,000	50,670	38,249	29,997	24,330	20,310	17,368

payments of $1,000 per year for 15 years (with the payments at the beginning of each year), if the remaining funds were consistently invested at 5 percent interest.

Table 6A–1 shows the present value of $1,000 per year (with the payments at the beginning of each year) for various numbers of years at various interest rates. The table can be used to calculate not only the present value of a series of equal payments but also the present value of a series of unequal payments. Some of the uses of the table are illustrated by the following four examples.

Example 1—Equal Payments

Suppose the objective is to determine the present value of an income of $8,000 per year for 15 years at 5 percent interest. Table 6A–1 shows that the present value of $1,000 per year for 15 years at 5 percent is $10,899. The present value of $8,000 would be eight times that, or $87,192. In other words, the present value of the desired yearly income is determined by multiplying the appropriate figure from Table 6A–1 by the number of thousands of dollars of desired yearly income.

Example 2—Decreasing Payments

Suppose the objective is to determine the present value of an income of $12,000 per year for 10 years, followed by an income of $9,000 per year for the subsequent 20 years, at an interest rate of 4 percent. The overall income pattern may be viewed as $9,000 per year for the entire 30 years, plus an additional $3,000 per year for the first 10 years. The present value of $9,000 per year for 30 years at 4 percent interest is $161,856 ($17,984 multiplied by 9). The present value of $3,000 per year for ten years at 4 percent interest is $25,305 ($8,435 multiplied by 3). The sum of these two results is $187,161 ($161,856 plus $25,305), which is the present value of an income of $12,000 per year for 10 years, followed by an income of $9,000 per year for the subsequent 20 years, at 4 percent interest.

Example 3—Increasing Payments

Suppose the objective is to determine the present value of an income of $9,000 per year for 10 years, followed by an income of $12,000 per year for the subsequent 20 years, at an interest rate of 4 percent. The overall income pattern may be viewed as $12,000 per year for the entire 30 years, minus $3,000 per year for the first 10 years.

The present value of $12,000 per year for 30 years at 4 percent interest is $215,808 ($17,984 multiplied by 12). The present value of $3,000 per year for ten years at 4 percent interest is $25,305 ($8,435 multiplied by 3). The difference between these two results is $190,503 ($215,808 minus $25,305), which is the present value of an income of $9,000 per year for 10 years, followed by an income of $12,000 per year for the subsequent 20 years, at 4 percent interest.

Example 4—Delayed Equal Payments

Suppose the objective is to determine the present value of an income of $7,000 per year for 15 years, with the income to start 20 years from now, at an interest rate of 4 percent. The overall income pattern may be viewed as $7,000 per year for the entire 35 years, minus $7,000 per year for the first 20 years. The present value of $7,000 per year for 35 years at 4 percent interest is $135,877 ($19,411 multiplied by 7). The present value of $7,000 per year for 20 years at 4 percent interest is $98,938 ($14,134 multiplied by 7). The difference between these two results is $36,939 ($135,877 minus $98,938), which is the present value of an income of $7,000 per year for 15 years, with the income to start 20 years from now, at 4 percent interest.

Social Security, Annuities, and Pensions

The essence of social insurance is bringing the magic of averages to the rescue of the millions.
WINSTON CHURCHILL

SOCIAL SECURITY

Your little white-and-blue social security card represents a combination of retirement pension, life insurance, and disability protection which may be worth more than $500,000 to you and your dependents.

If you were told that you had inherited that amount—free from income and estate taxes—you would be interested, wouldn't you? You would want to know more about it. Well, social security can yield this amount and more. How?

If the 29-year-old father of two small children, both under five, is killed in an accident, and he had maximum covered earnings each year, social security would provide that sum for his family.

1. His widow would receive a lump-sum death payment of $255.
2. His two children and their mother would receive $1,160 each month, about $13,920 each year, until the older child is 18. The family has now received $180,000.[1] But still to come

[1] *Social Security Information for Young Families,* HEW Publication SSA–78–10033.

"My ultimate goal? Retirement."
Reprinted by permission *The Wall Street Journal*

are the monthly payments for the mother and the younger child until that child is 18. Both children can also receive payments until the age of 22 as long as they stay in school.

3. The widow receives no more funds until she is 60. She then draws a benefit of $260 a month for the rest of her life.

The total sum will probably be even higher, because these figures do not include recent across-the-board increases or the automatic benefit increases made annually under the current law to keep pace with the rise in the cost of living.

Johnnie Wilson, 25, of Okmulgee, Oklahoma, was an operator of heavy equipment with a highway construction crew. Recently, the young father of two children was paralyzed when he injured his back in an automobile accident.

While Johnnie is undergoing a program of therapy at the Okmulgee Rehabilitation Center—a treatment that will last at least two years—he and his family will receive over $400 a month in social security payments as part of the social security disability insurance benefits program. Most people believe that social security is something that only "old" people need think about, but that is not true for 25-year-old Johnnie Wilson, who said, "With-

out social security, I don't know what I would have done."[2]

Richard A. Harder of Bay Port, Michigan, has the rare distinction of having received at 17 a monthly check for $64 as a disability payment based on his own work credit. He had worked on construction in 1967, 1968, and 1969 and had earned the six quarters of coverage required while at school, so that when his routine high school TB checkup disclosed that he needed medical care, he was hospitalized, continued his schooling in the hospital, and graduated with his class, all the while receiving his monthly check until he recovered.

Captain Riley Leroy Pitts, the first black American officer to receive the Medal of Honor, left a young widow with two small children. Social security could not bring back the husband and father lost in Vietnam, but it could make living easier for the survivors. The $425 a month that will come until the youngest child finishes college will amount to over $80,000.

You are mistaken if you think of social security only as retirement insurance for the far distant future. Today 95 out of 100 children under 18 and their mothers can count on monthly cash benefits if the working father dies. The families of the disabled worker are also covered—and the unmarried children of such workers can collect benefits based on a parent's (in some cases a grandparent's) earnings up to age 22. Medicare now goes to people who have been getting social security disability benefits for two years, regardless of age. The wife, husband, or children of an insured person of whatever age, as well as the insured person, are eligible for dialysis treatment or kidney transplant.

Student Benefits

If you are between 18 and 22, unmarried, and a full-time student at an educational institution, you are eligible for social security payments if one of your parents gets social security disability or retire-

_____
[2] Social Security Administration, Office of Public Affairs, Press Office, Baltimore, Md. (Although social security records are confidential, persons mentioned gave permission to be quoted.)

ment benefits. You are also eligible if you are disabled. If you were over 18 when a parent died and you fulfill the previously stated requirements, you can receive benefits as a student until you are 22.

If you attend college but have not completed the requirements for a bachelor's degree, your checks can continue until the end of the semester or quarter in which you become 22. If you attend a trade or vocational school, your checks can continue until you complete your course or for two months after the month you reach 22, whichever comes first.

Your checks will stop earlier if you marry, stop attending school, or reduce your attendance to less than full time.

Who Is a Full-Time Student?   Under the social security law, you're a full-time student if you attend a university, college, or junior college in the United States and the college considers you to be in full-time attendance according to its standards for day students.

If you attend high school or trade or vocational school, you're a full-time student if: *(a)* the school considers you to be in full-time attendance; *(b)* you're enrolled in a course of study lasting at least 13 weeks; and *(c)* you're enrolled for at least 20 hours a week.

You're not eligible for student benefits if you are paid by an employer to attend school because he asked or required you to do so.

Benefits are payable to the student or to the parent or a legal representative if the student agrees. Benefit payments are made during a vacation period of not more than four months, provided that you are a full-time student at the end of that time. If you are working as well as studying, your annual earnings must not exceed $3,240. If they do, you lose $1 for every $2 you earn above that amount. If your benefit payments depend on your parent, his or her earnings above $3,240 will affect you.

If you are a student who became eligible after you were 18, you must apply. Benefits do not come automatically. Even if you apply late, you can receive payments retroactively for as many as 12 months.

About 600,000 young Americans are receiving in excess of $500 million annually from social security—more than is received from all the scholarship funds made available by colleges and universities.

The Social Security Act

Congress first passed the Social Security Act in 1935, but it has been amended a number of times, adding categories of people covered and increasing the amounts of individual benefits and the amounts paid in taxes.

Only about 22,000 people were entitled to benefit payments for the month of January 1940, when monthly benefits started; about 400 of them, now 95 years or older, have each received more than 380 benefit checks. The first social security check ever issued went to Mrs. Ida M. Fuller, of Brattleboro, Vermont, who died in 1974 at the age of 98. Her total contribution was less than $22, but counting the check she received in January 1974, her payments totaled $19,685.[3]

Although the Social Security Act covers a wide variety of social insurance, employment insurance, public assistance, and health and welfare services, our discussion will be confined to the old-age and survivors insurance and disability insurance programs.

Under the act, persons who work in employment or self-employment covered by the law make social security tax contributions during their working years to provide, as a matter of right and not as a matter of need, an income for themselves and their families when their earnings cease in old age or for their families in the event of their death.

One out of seven Americans is now receiving social security checks, and nine out of ten workers in the United States are covered. Some 116 million living persons in the United States are fully insured, and over 34 million are already receiving monthly benefits. Of those who are receiving benefits, 21 million are retired workers and their dependents, 7½ million are survivors of insured workers, and over 4 million are disabled workers.

[3] *American Association of Retired Persons Bulletin,* January 1974.

TABLE 7–1

Summary of Annual Budgets for a Retired Couple at Three Levels of Living, Urban United States, Autumn 1977

Component	Lower Budget	Intermediate Budget	Higher Budget
Total budget*	$5,031	$7,198	$10,711
Total family consumption	4,815	6,765	9,898
Food	1,535	2,035	2,554
Housing	1,745	2,518	3,936
Transportation	337	658	1,215
Clothing	214	360	555
Personal care	146	214	313
Medical care	628†	632†	637†
Other family consumption	209	347	687
Other items	217	433	813

* Beginning with the autumn 1973 updating of the budgets for a retired couple, the total budget has been defined as the sum of "total family consumption" and "other items." Income taxes are not included in the total budgets

† The autumn 1977 cost estimates for medical care contain a preliminary estimate for "out-of-pocket" costs for medicare.

Note: Because of rounding, the sums of individual items may not equal totals.

Monthly benefit checks are now deposited directly into the accounts of social security recipients at commercial banks, savings and loan associations, and credit unions. It is the obligation of the financial institutions to notify their customers that the checks have been deposited. No longer need social security recipients fear theft or loss from their mailboxes or stand on long lines at the banks. The government has been sending checks to be delivered on Friday if the third day of the month is Saturday—so that retirees might not be without funds over a weekend.

Many of the amendments to the basic law since 1937 have been three-part: (a) an increase of benefits and coverage, (b) an escalation of the wage base to match rising wage levels, and (c) an increase in the tax rate.

Currently, if the Consumer Price Index (CPI) increases 3 percent or more during the year it will trigger an automatic increase in social security benefits equal to the rise in the cost of living. A CPI which measures price increases for urban workers would not seem to be the best instrument for measuring the costs of retirees. The needs differ. A retiree spends proportionately more income on food, housing, and medical care, including drugs, while an urban worker spends proportionately more income on transportation, clothing, and education. In 1950 a retired couple found that the average social security benefit met half of their budget, but today it meets less than one third.

Although senior citizens are technically living in the "golden years," the members of this age group run the gamut from poverty to wealth—as do those of all other age groups. The only element that makes their budget problems different is that for most of them the age of retirement has come and they must think in terms of saving funds or cannibalizing capital because their days of increasing capital are disappearing.

Supportive programs for medical services, food and nutrition, and income supplements are available through both government and private agencies to supplement tight budgets.[4]

---

[4] The state agency on aging can supply information on social security, supplemental social security, food stamps, meals, medicare, medicaid, housing, transportation, counseling, homemaker-health aides, and other services. There is also the Senior Community Service Employment Program with regional offices of the U.S. Department of Labor, Washington, D.C. 20210. The Nu-

"Now that I've retired, I have time for all the things I dreamed of doing, but I forget what they were!"

Reprinted by permission *The Wall Street Journal*

At the other end of the scale are the retirees from the major U.S. corporations who were high level managers and professionals. Their median family income is $20,600 a year (after taxes) compared with $7000 (before taxes) for the country's over 65 population. Investments and company pensions are the major source of their income.

Early Retirement—Pro and Con

More than half of recent retirees stopped work before 65. Reports from business and unions indicate that many would like to retire early, but fear of inflation keeps them working another year or two to add to the pension. Nonetheless, a recent

Conference Board study[5] found that "only 29 percent of all men between 65–69 were in the labor force in 1976, down from 57 percent in 1955." On the other hand, a growing proportion of women work until age 60 to 64. Another survey[6] would indicate that retirement attitudes vary according to income and type of work. Upper-income and white-collar workers are opposed to mandatory retirement. Blue-collar workers and large numbers of those in low-income brackets who are doing physically demanding work with less job satisfaction favor early retirement.

Government and military personnel tend to favor early retirement with attractive pensions. They then accept private industry jobs for a second career and a later second pension as well as social security.

Even those who do not want to keep working object to the idea of being forced out by compulsory retirement laws. The new Retirement Age law extends mandatory retirement from age 65 to 70, with some few exceptions. The government hopes that this will lead to significant social security savings. By 1987, the 1977 amendments to the Social Security Act will triple the amount of taxes that an employee and an employer have to pay for an employee earning the taxable maximum. Congress, sensitive to the resultant uproar, is rethinking the financing. One school of thought favors the use of income taxes from the general fund instead of the increased contribution from payroll taxes. This approach is opposed by those who fear that social security would then change from an insurance program to a need-based welfare program. It has been suggested that disability and medicare coverage be divorced from social security coverage, that the age of retirement with full benefits be raised, and that the disability insurance requirements be tightened—all of which would ease the financial strain on the social security system.

As you can see in Table 7–2 the amount of pay

trition Program for Older Americans, Community Food and Nutrition, and Senior Opportunities and Services are administered nationally by the Community Services Administration (HEW) and locally through the community action agency.

[5] Shirley H. Rhine, "Older Workers and Retirement," Conference Board, New York, April 14, 1978.

[6] National Family Opinion Inc. of Toledo, Ohio, for the Conference Board, October 19, 1977.

TABLE 7–2
Social Security Taxes (social security tax rates and income ceilings scheduled to take effect under current law)

Year	Income Subject to Tax	Employees		Self-Employed	
		Tax Rates	Maximum Contributions	Tax Rates	Maximum Contributions
1978	$17,700	6.05%	$1,071	8.10%	$1,434
1979	22,900	6.13	1,404	8.10	1,855
1980	25,900	6.13	1,588	8.10	2,098
1981	29,700	6.65	1,975	9.30	2,762
1982	32,100*	6.70	2,151	9.35	3,001
1983	34,500*	6.70	2,312	9.35	3,226
1984	39,600*	6.70	2,653	9.35	3,703
1985	39,600*	7.05	2,792	9.90	3,920
1986–1989 .	42,000*	7.15	3,003	10.00	4,200

* The income subject to tax for years after 1981 is determined under an escalator formula. These amounts are based on assumptions in the 1978 Annual Report of the Board of Trustees of the Social Security Funds and may differ from the actual limits.
Source: Ernst and Ernst.

to be covered by social security rises rapidly—but so does the tax on it to pay for social security.

How Social Security Taxes Are Paid

Federal old-age and survivors insurance is paid for by a contribution (or tax) on the employee's wages and on the self-employed's earnings from trade or business. If you are employed, you and your employer will share equally in the tax. If you are self-employed, you pay two thirds as much as the total payment of the employee and the employer would be on the same amount of earnings.

If you are employed, your contribution is deducted from your wages each payday. The employer sends your contribution and a matching contribution to the Internal Revenue Service. Employers of household workers may use a special envelope report. If you are self-employed, you must report your earnings and pay your contribution each year when you file your individual tax return. As long as you have earnings that are covered by the law, you continue to pay the social security tax, regardless of your age.

What Doesn't Count As Earnings? Generally, only income from a job or self-employment counts as earnings for social security purposes. The following types of income don't count as earnings:

Investment income in the form of dividends from stock you own.

Interest on savings accounts.

Income from social security benefits, pensions, or other retirement pay, or Veterans Administration benefits.

Income from annuities.

Gain (or loss) from the sale of capital assets.

Gifts or inheritances.

Other types of payments don't count under certain conditions. These include sick pay received under a plan or a system, payments from certain trust funds, payments from certain annuity plans, sick pay received more than six months after employment was terminated, loans from employers (unless repaid by work), moving expenses, travel expenses, and pay for jury duty.

Over eight out of ten workers are not affected by increases in the taxable earnings base, as they earn less than the base limits. It will be years before a worker can retire at age 65 with average annual earnings of $25,900 (the new maximum taxable base earnings, effective 1980). He would then receive a monthly benefit of about $552. All the previous years of much lower covered yearly earnings, ranged from $3,000–$6,600 which were the maximum taxable base earnings effective from 1937 to 1967. The average social security base of $7,600, with a maximum monthly retirement benefit of $437 is what today's retiree can expect.

The middle-income worker who is now only in the early stages of a working career will receive more generous maximum benefits. But for those who have already been in the labor force a long time, the maximum benefits cannot apply, since their earlier contributions were at a lower tax rate and on a lower base. The average earnings on which the computation of benefits is based for current retirees under recent legislation will therefore be lower than maximum monthly benefits shown in the tables.

People who don't get benefit checks because their earnings from work are too high sometimes wonder why others, with good incomes from stocks, bonds, or real estate, are nevertheless paid benefits. The reason is that the purpose of the program is to insure against the loss of earnings from work because of age.

Self-Employment Contributions   You pay the social security self-employment contributions for each year in which you have self-employment income of $400 up to the same maximum amount which the law sets for earnings (see Table 7–2). In 1951 the maximum self-employment social security tax was $81. By 1980 it will rise to $2,097.90. After 1980, as you can see in Table 7–2, the figure is scheduled to rise.

Earnings from employment or self-employment up to a total of $25,900 (1980) a year are subject to the social security tax. From the social security tax report, your wages and self-employment income are posted to your individual record by the Social Security Administration. This record of your earnings is used to determine your eligibility for benefits and the amount of social security pension you will receive.

Special Refunds   Your social security taxes apply only to the defined earning ceiling in that calendar year. If you have more than one employer, each employer must deduct the tax from that ceiling. You should keep a record of your employers' names and addresses and of the wages paid by each. If the total tax withheld in a given year is more than that required you may claim the excess tax as credit on your income tax return for that year.

Becoming Insured

For you to become eligible for monthly payments for yourself and your family, or for your survivors to get payments in case of your death, you must first have credit for a certain amount of work under social security. Social security credits are called "quarters of coverage." You can get social security credit for up to four quarters in a year. You may have earned social security credit (quarters of coverage) by working in employment covered by the law at any time after 1936 and in self-employment covered by the law after 1950. Today coverage is no longer figured in *calendar* quarters. One quarter of coverage is now $260 of covered earnings in a year. Four quarters will be credited for annual earnings of $1,040 or more. There will be future increases in the amount of earnings required for a "quarter of coverage" based on increases in average wage levels.

There is no age limit. You get social security credit for work covered by the social security law no matter how young or how old you are. Most jobs, businesses, and professions are now covered by social security. Active duty in the armed forces is also under social security. Your base pay is credited to your social security record. If you should stop working under social security before you have earned sufficient credit to become insured, no benefits will be payable to you. If you should later return to work covered by social security, regardless of your age both your past earnings and any additional earnings will be combined in determining whether you qualify for benefits.

Just how much credit you must have in order to be fully insured depends upon the year in which you reach 62, or upon the date of your death or disability if you die or become disabled before reaching that age.

The amount of work that a person needs in order to be covered varies from 1½ years to 10 years, depending on his or her age. Any worker who dies before his 28th birthday is insured with as little as 1½ years of work under social security, and death benefits to qualified survivors will be paid.

Work Credit

A new method is used to figure out work credit for coverage. You used to need $50 or more in a three-month calendar quarter. Now, you have a quarter of coverage for each $260 of earnings in a year. Only four quarters can be credited in a year. The $260 will increase automatically in the future as average wages increase. The self-employed used to receive four quarters if they had a net profit of $400 or more. Now the $260 requirement applies to them as well. Table 7–3 shows the years of credit that will be needed in the near future.

Kinds of Benefits

Broadly speaking, there are three different kinds of benefits, namely, "retirement" benefits, "survivors" (or "death") benefits, and "disability payments." When you become age 62 and retire, you and certain members of your family can become eligible for monthly insurance payments if you are fully insured. After you reach age 72 (70 in 1982), the payments may be made even if you have not retired.

In the event of your death at any age, certain members of your family may receive insurance payments if you were insured at the time of death.

If you become totally disabled and are unable to work, you may become eligible for monthly payments if you have social security credit for at least five years in the ten-year period ending when you

TABLE 7–3
Work Credit for Retirement and Survivors Benefits

Work Credit for Retirement Benefits

If You Reach 62 in	Years You Need
1975	6
1976	6¼
1977	6½
1978	6¾
1979	7
1981	7½
1983	8
1987	9
1991 or later	10

Work Credit for Survivors Benefits

Born after 1929, Die at	Born before 1930, Die before Age 62	Years You Need
28 or younger		1½
30		2
32		2½
34		3
36		3½
38		4
40		4½
42		5
44		5½
46	1975	6
47	1976	6¼
48	1977	6½
50	1979	7
52	1981	7½
54	1983	8
56	1985	8½
58	1987	9
60	1989	9½
62 or older	1991 or later	10

Source: HEW Publication SSA-78-10035, February 1978.

become disabled. The types of payments are shown in Table 7–4.

The Benefit Formula

The benefit formula has been changed. Formerly social security payments were based on your *aver-*

TABLE 7–4
Types of Payments

Retirement Benefits

Retired worker, 62 or over.
Wife, or divorced wife, 62 or over.
Wife, any age, if caring for child (except student age 18 or over) entitled to benefits
Child, or grandchild, under 18, 18–21 if student, or any age if disabled.
Husband, 62 or over.

Survivors Benefits

*Widow, widower, or divorced wife,** 60 or over, or 50–59 and disabled.
Widow, surviving divorced mother, or widower, any age, caring for child (except student age 18 or over) entitled to benefits.
Child, or grandchild, under 18, 18–21 if student, or any age if disabled.
Dependent parent, 62 or over.

Disability Benefits

Disabled worker.
Unmarried children, 15 or over, disabled before 22.
Widow or widower, 50 or older, who becomes disabled not later than seven years after worker's death.

Lump-Sum Payments (death)

Widow or widower, or others

* If married for ten years.

Source: U.S. Department of Health, Education, and Welfare. Social Security Administration.

age earnings over the years, using the actual dollar amount. This method will continue to be used for workers who reach 62, become disabled, or die before 1979, as shown in Table 7–5. Those who reach 62 after 1978 and before 1984 will have the benefit of whichever calculation is higher—the old or the new. Those who become disabled after 1978 and the survivors of workers who die after 1978 will receive benefits figured only under the method starting in 1979.

Under the new formula a worker retiring after 1979 will receive benefits amounting to about 42 percent of his final preretirement earnings. The computation will be structured as follows:

Annual earnings to $2,160—90 percent credited.

Annual earnings of $2,160 to $13,020—32 percent credited.

Annual earnings of $13,020 to the maximum—15 percent credited.

Today's 25-year-old earning $10,000 a year and retiring in 40 years (in the year 2018) can expect social security benefits to equal 40 percent of his average yearly pay before retirement.[7] This is much less than he would have received under the old law. This assumes an inflation of 4 percent a year in the cost of living and of 5 percent a year in pay.

A worker's earnings (and the benefit formula) will be indexed to reflect the change in wage levels during his working lifetime. For example, if a worker earned $3,000 in 1956 and retired at age 62 in 1979, the $3,000 would be multiplied by the ratio of annual wages in 1977 ($10,002) to average annual wages in 1956 ($3,514), as follows:

$$\$3,000 \times \frac{\$10,002}{\$3,514} = \$8,539$$

In this manner the worker's actual earnings for 1956, which were $3,000, would become his relative or indexed earnings of $8,539. The earnings for each year would be adjusted in the same fashion to keep changing wage levels in the same proportion.[8] After retirement, the automatic cost-of-living protection against inflation will go into effect. The new law seeks to stabilize pensions as a percentage of the final earnings of covered workers. Through this complicated formula, it is increasing

---

[7] A study made by Kwasha Lipton, an actuarial firm in Englewood Cliffs, New Jersey, and reported in the *Wall Street Journal,* February 6, 1978, and the *New York Times,* January 28, 1978.

[8] Legislative Report #17, Office of Program Evaluation and Planning, Social Security Administration, December 16, 1977. For a detailed indication of how HEW estimates benefits under the new law see the Appendix to this chapter.

TABLE 7–5

Examples of monthly payments**

Benefit Category	Current Payment*	6.5 Percent Increase
I. *Maximum and minimum social security benefits*		
Maximum benefit, worker retiring in 1978 at age 65	$459.80	$489.70
Minimum benefit, worker retiring in 1978 at age 65	114.30	121.80
II. *Average social security benefits*		
Retired worker alone	239.00	254.00
Aged couple, both receiving benefits	407.00	433.00
Mother and two children	562.00	598.00
Aged widow	225.00	240.00
Disabled worker, wife, and children	532.00	567.00
All disabled workers	268.00	285.00
III. *Maximum federal SSI payments†*		
Individual	177.80	189.40
Couple	266.70	284.10

  * As of June 1978. Provided by the Social Security Administration for their information booklet (see footnote**).

  † Most states provide payments supplementing the federal SSI payment levels for some or all categories of recipients.

  ** Using the new calculations makes this table, which is the average model in terms of current benefits, now more realistic and less of an understatement than before in view of the lesser benefits under the new law. Also the C.P.I. increases should be factored into it. As of January 1979 this table will be affected by the new method of calculating benefits. See Appendix.

reserves, and at the same time, offering more benefits in dollars but less in proportion to one's contribution. The same goal is expected by the yearly raising of the earnings base at steadily increasing tax rates.

Early Retirement?

If you decide to start receiving benefits before you are 65, the amount of your monthly benefit will be reduced according to the number of months you are under 65. For example, if you retire at 60 you will receive $247 a month, but if you wait until 65 you will receive $316 a month. A widow of an insured worker may start receiving benefits as early as age 60 if she decides to accept a reduced monthly amount. The closer you are to 65 when you start receiving payments, the larger the payments will be. If you elect to retire at age 62 you will receive roughly 80 percent of what would be yours if you had waited until age 65 to retire.

A retiree at 62 will also receive only 80 percent of each year's future cost-of-living increase. Assuming current inflation, the benefit will show this kind of difference:

	62	65
1978	$355	$460
1980	399	542
1982	462	554

Are you better off financially retiring at 62 or 65? That depends, among other things, on how long you expect to live! If you die before 75, you come out ahead if you had retired at 62. If you die after 75, you'd probably have been better off waiting until 65 to retire because it catches up in seven years.

Retiring Later?

If you delay in retiring past 65 you earn a special credit of 1 percent for each year until 72 that you did not collect benefits. For workers who reach 65 after 1981, this special credit increases to 3 percent. Beginning in June 1978, a surviving spouse will also be eligible for larger pensions by delaying payments.

Special Minimum Benefit

The law provides an extra for those persons with very low earnings who have been covered under social security for 30 years. After January 1979, their payment will be $230 plus the automatic cost-of-living benefit.

Special payments are made under the social security program to certain people 72 and over who do not qualify for full social security benefits. These payments are intended to assure some regular income for older people who had little or no opportunity to earn social security protection during their working years.

Military Service

Since January 1, 1957, under the Servicemen's and Veterans' Survivor Benefits Act of 1956, members of the armed forces have been covered by social security in the same way as people in civilian employment. They receive social security credit for their base pay for active duty, and their share of the social security tax is deducted from their base pay, just as the social security tax is deducted from the wages of civilian workers. Also, they receive additional earnings credits of $300 for each quarter. The credits do not appear on their earnings statement but are counted automatically when a claim for benefits is made. From September 16, 1940, to December 31, 1956, Congress enacted laws giving *free* social security wage credits of $160 for each month of active military service. Military service since January 1, 1957, can be counted toward both military retirement pay and social security benefits.[9]

---

[9] See *Social Security for Servicemen and Veterans,* SSA-10031, Social Security Administration, U.S. Department of Health, Education, and Welfare, Washington, D.C.

Inequities in Coverage

If you qualify for benefit payments on the record of more than one worker, you will only receive one, whichever is larger. For example, either a husband or wife can choose whichever is larger—his or her benefit based on personal earnings as a worker or the benefit derived as a husband or wife from the earnings of the other.

If a working wife elects benefits on her own earnings record at age 62, before her husband retires, she has reduced her pension for life. However, she may later qualify as a wife, on her husband's earnings—if she desires. If she has never worked, she qualifies on her husband's earnings. The working wife who has contributed to social security during her working life has gained no advantage for that contribution over the nonworking wife who will receive exactly the same benefit from a husband's earnings. A working husband and working wife each paying social security taxes pay more than a man making the same income would pay and receive less.

The provisions of the disability pension operate against the working wife since payments are made only if the worker has coverage for five out of the ten years preceding the disability. Since the working wife may have quit for a while to care for a family, she is handicapped in meeting that requirement.

Housewives are now seeking recognition in dollar terms for their services as housekeeper, cook, baby-sitter, and nurse, both for social security retirement and disability insurance.[10] The costs of replacing these varied functions in case of disability can be ill afforded in most households. The homemaker's real economic contribution is not now part of the GNP unless someone is hired as a replacement while she works at something else. Although the value of housework is difficult to measure, various studies have done so. A Chase Manhattan survey found that housewives worked 99.6 hours a week at tasks that would cost $235.40 to purchase.

---

[10] The Commerce Department plans the study of the value in dollars and cents of a housewife's work as a basis for inclusion in the GNP.

Changing Times concluded that in a typical family a housewife not employed outside the home does work worth $5,600 a year, which dips to $3,600 if she works outside the house. If a housewife is considered a home economist, her value as a professional would increase. If she joins the work force after her children are older, she faces still another disadvantage, as her late start at the lower salary base will prevent her from qualifying for a significant social security benefit.[11]

Recent Supreme Court rulings grant husbands and widowers the right to collect social security based on a wife's work record without having to prove dependency. The court ruled that they constituted sex discrimination.

If you qualify as a dependent or a survivor under social security and in addition receive a pension based on public employment not covered by social security, your social security benefit will be reduced by the amount of that pension unless you become eligible for that pension before December 1982.

If, however, you are entitled to both a social security pension and a governmental pension based on your own work, there will be no reduction of any sort.

Claiming Benefits

Benefit payments, whether retirement, disability, or survivors, monthly or lump sum, are not made automatically. *An application for benefits must be filed before monthly payments or the lump sum can be paid.* The application should be filed promptly. Only 12 months of back payments can be made when an application is filed late; years of payments may be lost by a failure to file in time. The lump sum may be paid only if an application is filed within two years after the death of an insured person. Benefits payable to a child or to an incompetent adult are usually paid for his use to a parent

_____
[11] Recognition of the problem has been made public in the report of the HEW Task Force on the Treatment of Women under Social Security *HEW News,* March 6, 1978. A six-month HEW study of proposals to eliminate dependency and sex discrimination under social security, was published February 16, 1979.

or near relative. The place to file a claim is the nearest Social Security Administration field office. There you and your family will receive, free of charge, any help you need to make out the claim papers. If, because of sickness or distance, you cannot go to the social security office, you may write or telephone. The local post office or a phone book will furnish the address of the nearest social security office.

Lump-Sum Death Payment

After your death, in addition to regular monthly survivor payments to your spouse and your children under age 18, a lump sum of three times the amount of your monthly benefit may be paid to your widow or widower if you were living together. If there is no widow or widower, the person who paid the burial expenses can be repaid up to the amount of the lump sum. The payment may be three times the primary monthly insurance benefit, but not more than $255.

Five Times for Action

There are five times when it is especially important to consult the social security office:

If a Worker in Your Family Dies Some member of the family should inquire promptly at the social security office to learn whether survivors insurance benefits are payable.

If You Become Disabled If you become disabled after you have been in work covered by social security, you should get in touch with your social security office. You and your dependents may be eligible for monthly payments.

When You Are Near Retirement Age When you approach 65 (62 if you are not working or are working for low earnings), get in touch with your social security district office. Application for benefits may be filed three months in advance of retirement age, but even if you do not plan immediate retirement you should get information about your social security benefits.

When You Are 72 At age 72 (70 in 1982) benefits are paid no matter how much is earned.

If you work after you start receiving benefits, your wages are subject to social security and medicare taxes, regardless of your age. A worker who delays retirement until 72 receives a 7 percent increase in benefits (1 percent for each year) but only he benefits–and not his dependents or survivors.

Every Three or Four Years Check with the Social Security Administration periodically for a record of your earnings. If you wait too long, you lose the chance to correct any error, since there is a 3 years + 3 months + 15 days time limit for any such change. The statement does not show the amount of contributions you or your employer paid except indirectly.

Checking Your Account

Each employer is required by law to give you receipts for the social security taxes deducted from your pay. This must be done at the end of each year and also when you stop working. These receipts will help you check on your social security account because they show not only the amount deducted from your pay but also the wages paid you.

You may check your own record as often as once a year by writing to the Social Security Administration, P.O. Box 57, Baltimore, Maryland 21203, and asking for a statement of your account. You can get an addressed postcard form at any field office for use in requesting wage information (see Figure 7–1). It costs ten cents a page for a copy of your record. The minimum fee is $1, so if your record is less than ten pages it will be free.

If an error has been made in your account, the field office will help you get it corrected. Even though the statement of earnings does not show your contributions or your employers', it will show whether your earnings have been reported. If reported, contributions would have to have been made. Your receipts will reveal any error. It's the earnings on which benefits are paid, not the contributions.

Account Number Cards

If you are employed or self-employed in any kind of work covered by the Social Security Act, you must have a social security card. Your card shows your account number, which is used to keep a record of your earnings. You should use the same account number all your life, for the number on

Source: Social Security Administration

How Many People Have the Same Last Name as Yours?

Smith	2,400,000	White	636,000
Johnson	1,800,000	Thompson	635,000
Williams and		Jackson	630,000
Williamson	1,600,000	Clark	549,000
Brown	1,400,000	Roberts and	
Jones	1,300,000	Robertson	525,000
Miller	1,100,000	Lewis	495,000
Davis	1,000,000	Walker	486,000
Anderson	826,000	Hall	471,000
Wilson	788,000	Allen	458,000

This sample can show the possibilities of confusion.

your social security card distinguishes your account from the social security accounts of other people who have names similar to or exactly the same as yours. Both your name and account number are needed to make sure you get full credit for your earnings. Show your card to each employer so that when reporting your wages he can use your name and account number exactly as they appear on the card.

Your nearest social security office used to issue a social security card or a duplicate card to replace one that had been lost. Now all cards and numbers are issued from the Baltimore headquarters because of the increasing importance of the number. Applicants are prescreened against central files for error or the issuance of more than one number to the same individual. If you have no number and are going to look for your first job, apply early, as there may be delay of about four to six weeks. If your name has been changed, ask your social security office for a new card showing the same account number and your new name.

Native-born applicants under 18 need to submit a public or religious record of birth. If you have neither you can use another document, if it is at least one year old and shows such information as your name, address, age, signature, or photograph. A second record, such as a vaccination record, a school record, or a driver's license, must also be submitted. This can be done by mail, and the documents will be returned by mail. Applicants 18 and over must apply in person and bring both the birth certificate and another document proving identity.

Parents applying for a number for their preschool child need furnish only a birth record.

For the replacement of a lost card, you must show proof of your identity. The proof you furnish will be checked against the information already in your file. Each year 7 million new numbers and 4½ million replacement cards are issued.

Your card is a symbol of your social security account not to be treated casually. The benefits payable to you or your family over a lifetime are figured from the earnings recorded in your social security account.

There is an ever-increasing use of the social security number as identification for other purposes, such as income tax, civil service records, as a veterans hospital admission number, and as a military service number. The Social Security Administration repeatedly assures the public this use will not affect the confidential nature of social security records. Programs exist to provide a social security number to children entering school or to those now at the ninth-grade level.

The need for careful identification has intensified because more than 900 employers and the armed forces now make social security reports on reels of magnetic tapes prepared by electronic computers. The Social Security Administration's computers then read and record the information directly at tremendous savings and without the possibility of human transcribing errors. Of course, the original input by humans could have errors—so the use

"First, give me your Social Security number so the computer can check whether you've wished on another lamp."

Reprinted by permission *The Wall Street Journal*

of computers has not eliminated the need for checking. There is no escape if you feel overwhelmed by being just a number; the Social Security Administration reports that even the 2,141 Micronesian islands along the equator in the Pacific have started a social security system.

Proof of age is needed to receive the first payment of medicare and social security. The identification number is not sufficient. If you have neither a birth certificate nor a baptismal certificate, one of the following could be a substitute:

A school record.

A federal census record (from the U.S. Census Bureau).

A marriage record.

An employment or union record.

A hospital record.

The birth certificate of a child showing the age of a parent.

You must send the actual document, which will be returned. No photocopy is acceptable unless it is certified by the custodian of the record.

For those born abroad, usable documents are a foreign passport, an immigration record, or a naturalization certificate (all of which are illegal to photocopy).

However, even a dated baptism cup has been accepted as proof.

When Payments Stop

When you become entitled to monthly old-age or survivors insurance payments, you will receive a check each month unless certain events occur. The law lists some events that will stop the payment of monthly checks for one or two months or for some longer period, and some that will end your right to receive payments. These events are listed below. You must report promptly to the Social Security Administration if any of them happen to you.

If You Work after Payments Start If you are 62–65, there is a lower earnings ceiling than if you are 65 or older. If you are 65 or older but not 72 (70 in 1982) and are receiving monthly social security payments as a retired worker but you earn more than $5,000 (in 1980; $5,500 in 1981; $6,000 in 1982) during a *year,* your benefits will be reduced by one half of the amount over the limit. Your social security benefits will come in a lump sum after the end of the year. This is an important change in the law because the old law only deducted in those *months* that you earned more than the allowed amount. A retiree used to be able to earn without limit in those months and also receive social security in the remaining months of the year. If as a self-employed retiree you perform substantial services you risk the reduction of benefits under the same regulations governing a retired worker. The decision as to whether you are performing substantial services in self-employment depends on the amount of time you devote to your business, the kind of services you perform, how your services compare with the services you performed in past years, and other circumstances of your particular case.

These rules do not apply the year you retire, no matter how much you made in the months previous to retirement. Starting in 1982, after you reach 70 you can earn any amount and still receive your full social security benefit.

If There are Family Changes   When a child reaches 18, or 22 if at school, payments are stopped unless the child is disabled.

A widow or widower or a divorcée under 60 will not receive payments if the child for whom he or she was caring is 18 or 22.

When a person receiving monthly benefits dies, payments end. The last payment in such cases is for the month immediately before the month of death. All of these changes affect the payments received by younger members of a family dependent for their benefits upon the status of the recipient of social security.

Payments no longer end if a widow or widower remarries after age 60.

Supplemental Security Income System

This program, which began in January 1974, helps single persons whose income does not exceed $1,500 or couples whose assets are not more than $2,250 if they are 65 or older, or blind or disabled. The program provides $189.40 a month to meet the basic living expenses of a single person and $284.10 for a couple.

The SSI payments are increased automatically when the cost of living for the first quarter of the year is at least 3 percent higher than it was during the first quarter of the previous year. Adjustments, effective June 1, are reflected in the checks received in July.

The SSI payments replace the joint state-federal programs of public assistance for the aged, blind, and disabled. The state must pass along the higher federal payment to SSI recipients. The state may

also supplement the federal payments by providing medicaid, food stamps, and other services.

A person is not disqualified for SSI payments by owning a home, or a car valued at not over $1,200, or over that figure if it is used for transportation to a job or medical treatment. Having an insurance policy with a face value of not over $1,500 also will not disqualify, but other assets, such as a savings account, will. One can earn a total of $85 a month and still receive payments. Unlike Social Security payments, SSI payments come from the general fund of the U.S. Treasury. A person may receive both social security and Supplemental Security Income if eligible. Application for SSI is made at the nearest social security office because the Social Security Administration runs the program.

If You Become Disabled

If you become disabled before age 65, you may qualify for monthly disability benefits, and your spouse and children are also paid monthly benefits. The time element is very important in applying for disability benefits—too long a delay in making an application may result in your losing these benefits. However, disability benefits are payable retroactively up to 12 months.

How Disabled Must You Be?   To be found disabled under the social security law, you must have a condition so severe that, in the words of the law, it makes you unable to "engage in any substantial gainful activity." If you can't do your regular work, but you can do other substantial gainful work, you will not be considered disabled.

Your disability must be expected to last for at least 12 months or be expected to continue for a long and indefinite time. Payments start with the month following the five-month waiting period.

How Much Work Credit Is Required?   In general, if you have social security credit for at least five years in the ten-year period ending when you become disabled, you have enough work credit to qualify for disability insurance benefits— if the disability begins at age 31 or later.

If you become disabled before you are 24, you

need credit for having worked half of the time before you become disabled, subject to a six-quarter minimum. Unmarried disabled persons under the age of 22 can get payments based on the earnings of a parent or, in some cases, a grandparent.

Disabled widows or widowers or the surviving disabled divorced wives of workers who were insured at death may receive payment as early as age 50. A person whose eyesight is so poor that the law considers him blind can, if "fully insured," not only collect disability benefits but will also be allowed to earn income to the highest limits for the elderly without loss of benefits.

Proof of Your Disability   When you apply for disability insurance benefits, your social security office will give you a medical report form to have filled in by your doctor or by a hospital or clinic where you have had treatment. If your earnings from work are in excess of $230 per month, this will ordinarily be deemed to demonstrate your ability to perform substantial gainful activity and therefore to indicate that you are not disabled.

If a person receiving disability benefits recovers or returns to work, payments (and any payments to dependents) will stop, but not right away. The person will first be given a chance to test his ability to work and to adjust.

If a person goes to work despite a severe handicap, disability benefits will continue to be paid for as long as 12 months. If a beneficiary recovers from a disability, the benefits will continue to be paid for three months.

The Amount of Your Disability Benefit   The amount of your monthly disability insurance payment depends on your earnings level just prior to the advent of the disability. Unfortunately many disabled persons are further handicapped if they have the private disability insurance which has an offset clause. A disabled worker granted a fixed monthly benefit from this policy which is in addition to his social security, loses a dollar from his private insurance benefits for every dollar increase in social security benefits. Those receiving government pensions may face offset provisions. Offset provisions are prohibited in several states. If you are a disabled worker under 62 and are entitled to both social security disability benefits and workmen's compensation, the total payments may not exceed 80 percent of your earnings before you became disabled.

Insurance and Social Security

Modern insurance programming builds on a social security base and adds insurance to meet felt needs—within the limits of financial capacity.

Even those insurance agents who were originally opposed to social security now recognize that it was one of the best things that could have happened to their industry. Why? Simply because without social security the average middle-income family could not afford sufficient insurance to provide for essential needs in case of either premature death or retirement. Now, with part of the burden met by social security, it is easier to show the average family that the amount of insurance it requires for meeting minimum needs is, coupled with social security benefits, financially attainable. As a result, insurance is sold more easily—and more intelligently; and, what is most important, the average family is somewhat closer to financial security than it was previously.

Each situation is different, and a program prepared for one family will hardly fit the needs or resources of any other. A plan tailored to your situation can be developed by the agent of any good insurance company, who will figure out your social security payments in the event of death and show you how to make the best use of your government life insurance (if you have it), and then will point out the gaps and indicate how much it would cost to fill them, in whole or part. You can build a program gradually, as your resources and earning power grow. If you have a program, you will be able to see where you are going and to plan wisely instead of either ignoring your responsibilities or trying to meet them in a hit-or-miss, illogical way.

The Dawsons

The Dawsons live in California, where Mr. Dawson is a mechanic. They have two children—Jack, eight, and Margaret, four. Mr. Dawson is now 32 years old, and his wife is 28. Their annual income amounts to $14,500, but this will probably increase. They own their own home, on which there is a $15,000 mortgage at present.

Mr. Dawson has taken particular care in planning his life insurance program. The company he works for does not offer any group life or retirement insurance plan, but he is covered by federal social security.

An inventory of the Dawsons' life insurance shows that they own a total of $47,000 of insurance, all on Mr. Dawson's life, as shown in Table 7–6.

If Mr. Dawson Dies Now   The diagram (Figure 7–2) shows what Mr. Dawson's life insurance will do should he die now. There will be a monthly income of $80 from the life insurance policies left at interest until Margaret is age 18. Added to that will be an income from Mr. Dawson's social security ($602.10 until Jack is age 18 and then dropping to $508.40 until Margaret is 18). If Margaret is a full-time student her own benefit will be $254.20 per month to age 22.

Because social security income stops when Margaret is 18, Mr. Dawson has arranged to have the bulk of his life insurance provide $84 a month income for Mrs. Dawson for the rest of her life. Unless Mrs. Dawson can provide for herself, this will be a difficult period. When Mrs. Dawson is age 60, the social security income will start again and pay her $242.40 a month as long as she lives. Added to that will be $84 a month from Mr. Dawson's insurance, thus increasing her monthly income to $326.40.

Policy 5 is a $15,000 reducing term policy purchased to pay off the mortgage at his death. Policy 1 plus a $255 lump sum from social security will be used to pay Mr. Dawson's final expenses.

At Retirement Time   The chances are that Mr. Dawson will live to see his children grown and with families of their own. As Mr. Dawson's income increases, he can convert the $10,000 term to 65 to an ordinary policy, adding to his permanent life insurance program. This will give him a total of $32,000 in permanent life insurance. Then this program will provide a retirement income for him and his wife. At age 65 his policies will have a total cash value of about $16,840. Mr. Dawson will continue about $2,000 of his insurance. The cash values of the balance will be used to purchase an immediate joint and survivors annuity for retirement. This will be sufficient to pay the Dawsons a monthly income of $90 for as long as they both are living. Mr. Dawson's social security will provide a monthly income of $338.90. When both Mr. and Mrs. Dawson are 65, their income from social security will be $508.40 a month. Thus, for the first three years of Mr. Dawson's retirement, he will have a combined (insurance plus social security) montly income of $428.90, and thereafter it will rise to $598.40.

ANNUITIES (FIXED AND VARIABLE)

An annuity is a contract that provides an income for a specified period of time, such as a number of years or life. A life annuity is a way of taking a certain sum of money, or building up a fund, and then using it up month by month, year by

TABLE 7–6
John Dawson's Life Insurance Policies

Policy Number	Taken at Age	Amount and Kind	Annual Premium
1	20	$ 2,000 straight life	$ 31.10
2	22	15,000 straight life	168.30
3	26	5,000 straight life	70.80
4	28	10,000 term to 65	85.90
5	29	15,000 reducing term	52.10

FIGURE 7–2

Income Distribution—The Dawsons' Life Insurance Program

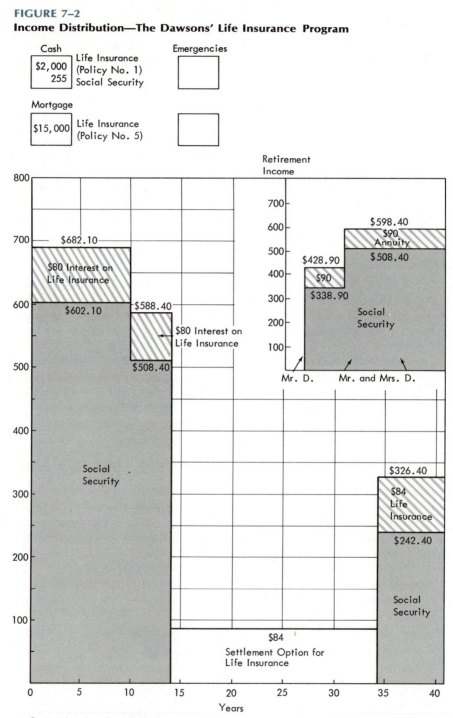

Source: American Council of Life Insurance.

year, principal as well as the interest thereon, and yet being absolutely sure that you will not run out of money as long as you live. That is the reason why anyone who is planning to retire someday, whether soon or in the distant future, ought to know something about annuities.

Insurance provides protection against dying too soon. An annuity, strange as it sounds, provides protection against living too long. Annuities may be bought by the payment of a lump sum or by installment payments. The same companies that sell life insurance also sell annuities; the same care in choosing a company from which to buy insurance should be used in choosing a company from which to buy an annuity.

The Annuity Principle

Annuities are based on the principle of having a group of people get together and share risks. Individually, these people could not spend their savings without fear of outliving their principal. Some would die before their principal was exhausted, but others would live long after their money had disappeared. As members of a group of annuitants, however, each of these people can turn all or part of his savings over to a life insurance company and secure in exchange a promise that the company will pay him a regular income for life. Although the life insurance company does not know how long any individual member of the group will live, it does know approximately how many in the group will be alive at the end of each successive year. A company can thus calculate the amount of annuity payments for each member of the group. The annuitant receives a certain income each year. Moreover, if he is over 50 years of age, he would have a greater assured income for life than he could safely obtain by investing the same amount otherwise. For example, a man of age 65 can obtain an income equal to 8 percent of his investment in a straight life annuity. In general, no medical examination is required for any annuity unless the annuity includes insurance features.

Payments for Annuities

Suppose a person of age 40 has $50,000. It would be possible to give the $50,000 to an insurance company in return for the promise of the company to make a small monthly payment for life, to begin immediately. Or, if the person needed no immediate income from the money, there would be a much larger monthly payment if the $50,000 were allowed to grow at interest with the company and the monthly payments to begin at 60, 65, or 70 years of age. The later the payments begin, the greater each one will be. If the person had no such lump sum to give the company, an equivalent accumulation could be built through regular installments over a period of years and in return obtain monthly payments later on.

Who Is Protected?

The ordinary life insurance policy gives protection primarily to beneficiaries in the event that the insured dies and secondarily builds up cash surrender (and loan) values for the insured; the annuity policy is primarily for the benefit of the insured (the annuitant) and only secondarily of benefit to others. Since life insurance gives protection to others in the event the insured dies and annuity policies are primarily for the benefit of the insured (the annuitant), the purposes and use are very different. To put it briefly, life insurance is primarily to protect others; annuities are basically to protect oneself. It should be remembered, however, that the proceeds of life insurance policies are often paid out to beneficiaries in the form of annuities. Or the insured may take the cash value of a policy—or, in the case of an endowment, the maturity value—and elect to receive the money in the form of an annuity.

Annuities Assure a Maximum Income

If you turn your money over to an insurance company in return for an annuity policy that guarantees you a given monthly income for life, you can be sure that you cannot possibly outlive your money, unless you make a poor choice of an insurance company which fails. Of course, you may also worry lest you give the insurance company $100,000 today and die after receiving only a few monthly payments. In that case the insurance company would retain the balance of what you paid (plus earnings thereon) so that it could pay other annuitants who lived beyond expectation. We shall see later that there are ways, at a price, to avoid such a worry. In fact, annuities remove so much worry that this is often said to be the reason that annuitants live longer than others.

Kinds of Annuities

Annuities are sold both to individuals and on a group basis. Group annuities are used largely to fund pension plans. Group or individual, the same kinds of contracts are available.

Every annuity has three variables: how you pay for it, when you collect, and how you collect. In the same fashion, every annuity contract has a three-part name. One part specifies when you collect; one, how you pay; and one, how you collect. For example, a single-premium, deferred, straight life annuity is one (*a*) for which you pay a lump sum in a single premium; (*b*) on which the company starts paying you a periodic income at a future date, for example, when you become age 65; (*c*) with an income for as long as you live, but all payments stop at your death. Figure 7–3 sets out these three classification points for quick reference and shows you the various types of annuities available.

Immediate Annuities

When a person pays the insurance company a lump sum and wants annuity payments to begin

FIGURE 7–3

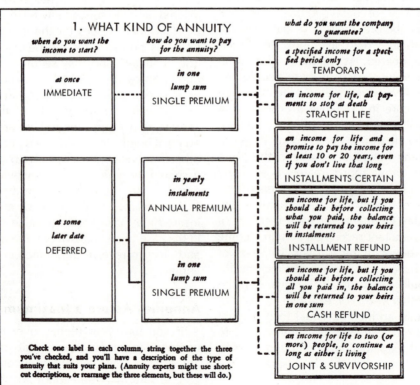

Source: *Changing Times, the Kiplinger Magazine.*

without delay, we have an immediate annuity. We also have smaller periodic payments than if payments were to begin later. To obtain such an annuity of $100 a month at age 40, you would have to spend over $30,000. By the time you are 65 you could probably buy it for about half that amount. Ordinarily, people buy immediate annuities just about the time they want to have payments to them begin, that is, when they are older and approaching retirement. They want this income to begin almost at once and to continue as long as they live.

Deferred Annuities

Payments on deferred annuities begin at some time in the future, whether they are paid for in a lump sum or in a series of installments. When a deferred annuity is paid for in installments, the company assumes the burden of investing the money as received and of paying the annuitant beginning with the arrival of the contracted date for payments to start. Naturally, more people can undertake to buy annuities on the installment plan than can produce a lump sum with which to buy them. The younger person is likely to prefer the annual (or installment) payment deferred annuity. The older person is more likely to prefer the single-premium, immediate annuity. If you think about it, you'll realize why this is so.

Annuity Payments

Annuitants have various options as to how they will receive annuity payments. The following are usual:

A. Types of immediate annuities.
   1. The straight life annuity.
   2. The life annuity with installments certain.
   3. The installment refund annuity.
   4. The cash refund annuity.
B. Variations of the deferred annuity.
   1. The retirement income annuity.
   2. The retirement income policy.
C. Joint and survivorship annuities.

The Straight Life Annuity

The straight life annuity is the original and basic type of annuity. It is purchased for a lump-sum premium, and the annuity payments are immediate. It does not have a cash value. Payments cease, and there is no value left in the policy, upon the annuitant's death, no matter how soon he dies. This type of annuity (returning both principal and interest to the annuitant) provides the annuitant with the largest possible payments, but there is no value left in his policy, should he die even a month or two after buying the policy. Notice that this type of annuity protects the annuitant only and provides nothing for his dependents beyond what they obtain out of the payments made to the annuitant. It is something like a pension for life: when the pensioner dies, the pension ceases, regardless of how many dependents the pensioner leaves.

The Life Annuity with Installments Certain

The straight life annuity is not favored by some people, who dislike the idea of a contract that might pay them an income for only a few months and then stop if they died at that time. These people feel that they would like some close relative to get something out of their purchase money besides the few payments they received. Actually, of course, the company does not get the apparently unused part of the purchase money. This money, according to the risk-sharing principle, goes to other annuitants who live a long time and receive much more than their purchase money.

To meet the objection to the straight life annuity, however, the life annuity with installments certain was developed. This not only pays the annuitant an income for life, but if death occurs within the guaranty period, the income payments for the balance of the guaranty period are paid to a beneficiary selected by the annuitant. The guaranty period is usually 10–20 years, and it is often expressed as 120 or 240 months. The company is obligated to pay income benefits, in any case, for 10 or 20 years.

The Installment Refund Annuity

The installment refund annuity also pays an income to the annuitant for life. But if the annuitant dies before he has received as much money as he paid for the annuity, income payments are continued, in installments, to his beneficiary until the total benefit payments equal the amount paid by the deceased annuitant.

The Cash Refund Annuity

The cash refund annuity is also a life annuity, but the company guarantees to pay out (all told) a sum equivalent to the cost of the annuity policy, either to the annuitant if alive or to the annuitant and the beneficiaries in the event that the annuitant does not live long enough to collect it all. If $10,000 is paid for such a policy and the annuitant dies after receiving $2,000 in payments, $8,000 would still be due the beneficiaries, making a total of $10,000 to be paid out by the company. A policy of this type assures the annuitant that none of the principal (but not interest) will be lost. For this guaranty the annuitant must pay by accepting smaller annuity payments (sometimes as much as 20 percent smaller) than could be received without it. In contrast to the installment certain annuity, in which the beneficiary is paid for the remainder of the guaranteed installment period, under the cash refund annuity the beneficiary is paid the remainder of the total amount of the annuity in one lump sum.

A straight life annuity is advisable for the person who wishes to receive the largest possible income for the money paid. A life annuity with installments certain or a cash refund annuity is advisable for the person who not only wants a lifetime income but also wishes to provide some payment to a beneficiary in the event of the annuitant's early death. The income to the annuitant is less, it should be remembered, under the installment refund and cash refund than under the straight life annuity, since additional benefits are provided.

Variations of the Deferred Annuity

The Retirement Income Annuity The companies give various names to this plan, which is issued to meet the needs of people who want to save regularly for a life income but who need no insurance protection. This contract is really an accumulation at interest of premiums paid, less expenses. The amount accumulated by the end of the deferred period is used to buy a life annuity of the straight life or, more often, the refund type.

Added to each unit of retirement income is a very small amount of life insurance protection—just enough during the early years of the policy to provide a death benefit equal to all premiums paid. After that time, the savings accumulation exceeds the total of premiums paid and becomes the death benefit, the insurance element ceasing. As the savings accumulation builds up, the death benefit likewise increases.

Prior to the maturity date, the policy has a cash surrender value and also a loan privilege equal to the savings accumulations. During the early years of the policy, due to sales expenses and insurance costs, the cash and loan values will be less than the total of premiums paid.

A retirement income annuity enables you to set aside funds for retirement regularly. Your beneficiary will receive at least the amount of the premiums you paid if you die before the retirement age. You can borrow on the accumulated fund in case of need. You can cash the policy in if your situation changes, and, except for the early years, you will get back at least what you paid in.

The Retirement Income Policy This is a variation of the retirement income annuity. It includes a substantial insurance element coupled with units of income at the retirement age selected. The insurance element ranges from $1,000 to $1,500. In all other respects this contract is identical in principal to the retirement income annuity.

The retirement income policy fits the needs of many types of people. Single persons often find that the insurance furnishes them all the protection they need, while the policy directs their premium dollars principally toward filling retirement needs.

People with dependents who have purchased nearly all the insurance protection that they want and now wish to strengthen their retirement program find this policy helpful. It adds to their insurance protection, which is an advantage, while it lays the principal stress on building a retirement income.

Joint and Survivorship Annuities

Joint and survivorship annuities are especially useful where it is desired to have a retirement income for both a husband and wife. They receive the annuity jointly during the life of both of them, and then payments of like (or lesser—often two thirds) amounts are made to the survivor as long as he or she lives. This type of annuity may meet the needs of an elderly couple with no dependents. Deferred joint and survivorship annuities are similar to immediate joint and survivorship annuities, except that the annuity payments do not begin immediately.

One of the principal advantages of an immediate joint life and survivorship annuity is that it eliminates much of the need for life insurance. For example, if a husband and a wife have such an annuity, providing sufficient income for their needs, the husband would have to carry insurance sufficient only to cover cash for final expenses and one year's readjustment income, because the wife will be supported by the annuity income after his death.

The Cost of Annuities

The price of an annuity is based on the amount of income it will pay. You can look at price in two ways: you can take the amount you can pay and see what income it will buy, or you can take the income you want and see what it will cost. The amount you will pay for a given income— say, $100 a month—depends on what income plan you select, how old you are when payments begin, and whether you are a man or a woman.

Things to remember about annuity costs are:

1. The older you are when the income is to start, the less you will pay. In the case of an immediate annuity, the older you are when you buy, the less your cost will be.
2. With a deferred annuity, the younger you are when you sign up, the less your annual premium cost will be. The lower premiums result from spreading payments over a longer period and from the interest your payments can earn.
3. The total of the annual premiums paid for an annuity of so much a month will be less than the single premium you will pay for an immediate annuity of the same amount beginning at the same age. All of the latter comes out of your pocket, whereas the annual premiums are built up with the aid of compound interest.
4. At the same age, a woman pays more than a man for the same income, because women, on the average, live longer and collect more.
5. For each dollar of income, you pay least if you take a straight life plan, most if you take a cash refund joint and survivorship plan.

Life insurance premiums are based on an "integral" age, which is usually the insured's age as of his last birthday. Annuity premiums, however, change with each month. Life insurance premiums increase as one gets older; premiums for immediate annuities decrease the older one is and the shorter the time for which the company contracts to make payments. It is sensible to buy life insurance just before your age changes and to buy a life annuity just after attaining a higher age.

Fixed Annuities and Investments

The major limitation of fixed annuities is that the fixed dollar income which they provide is not protected from shrinkage in purchasing power due to inflation. On the other hand, putting all of one's retirement funds into investments might be too risky; or if safety is desired and a more conservative investment policy is therefore pursued, the resultant income might not be sufficient to meet needs.

People choose fixed annuities for all sorts of

reasons, ranging from taxes to timidity. The tax advantage is that money put into annuities during your working years earns interest, but you do not need to pay income taxes on the interest until you actually collect it late in life when your income and your tax bracket will presumably be lower. Timidity enters because people mistrust their ability to invest wisely, especially their ability to handle the somewhat complicated operation of continuing to invest while using up capital gradually over the retirement period. They cannot live on earnings alone because their capital fund is not large enough; they must, therefore, gradually draw on principal, but there is the danger that they may use it up too rapidly, live longer than they anticipated, and thus face destitution. The annuity relieves them of such worries.

Variable Annuities

To combine the safety advantages of fixed annuities with the alleged long-run inflation-hedging protection of common stock investment, the "variable" annuity has been developed. It is an annuity providing a life income, not of a fixed number of dollars, but of variable amounts keyed to an underlying common stock investment portfolio. Under a variable annuity your premiums are invested primarily in common stocks and provide a retirement income that increases as stock prices and dividends increase, and decreases as they decline. A fixed annuity, on the other hand, invests your premiums primarily in bonds and mortgages and provides a guaranteed fixed dollar annuity income that does not change in amount from year to year, except as extra dividends are added.

How the Variable Annuity Developed It was fear of inflation and its debilitating impact on retirement income which gave rise to the variable annuity. The modern variable annuity was first developed by the Teachers Insurance and Annuity Association of America. The association established the College Retirement Equities Fund (CREF) in 1952 to enable college teachers who were contributing to the TIAA retirement system (buying an individual fixed dollar annuity) to have up to one half[12] of their contribution (including the college's contribution) go toward the purchase of a CREF variable annuity, with the balance going to TIAA to purchase the fixed dollar annuity.

Based on careful studies of investment and price trends, over a previous 70-year period, the TIAA concluded that investing retirement plan contributions partly in fixed dollar obligations, such as bonds and mortgages, and partly in common stocks offers promise of providing retirement income which is at once reasonably free from extreme fluctuations in amount and from serious depreciation through changes in the price level.[13]

Some 375,000 college teachers are now contributing to the College Retirement Equities Fund,[14] and today some major insurance companies are offering variable or balanced annuities in addition to fixed annuities. In addition, a growing number of companies have provided for either the variable or the balanced annuity in their pension plans. A *balanced annuity* is a combination of a variable annuity and a fixed dollar annuity.

The variable annuity balanced by the fixed dollar annuity was thought to provide offsetting protection. The fixed dollar annuity would provide a base income and protect against falling stock prices, while the variable annuity would provide a hedge against inflation—theoretically. The TIAA–CREF combination is a *balanced annuity*. TIAA is the *fixed dollar* component; CREF is the *variable* annuity segment.

How the Variable Annuity Works Suppose you decide to set aside $50 a month over a period of years for a variable annuity.

1. The funds you pay in would be placed in the insurance company's variable contract account

---

[12] It may now be up to 75 percent of their contribution or as little as 25 percent.

[13] Adapted from William C. Greenough, *A New Approach to Retirement Income,* Teachers Insurance and Annuity Association of America, 730 Third Ave., New York, N.Y. 10017; latest edition.

[14] A prospectus of this fund may be obtained by writing to the TIAA.

FIGURE 7–4
CREF Annuity Unit Values since 1952 (annuity year, May through April)

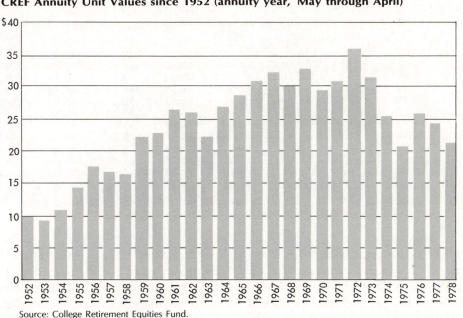

Source: College Retirement Equities Fund.

and invested separately, primarily in common stocks, from the company's regular insurance or annuity funds.

2. Each $50 monthly payment, after deduction of a specified allowance for expenses, would be applied to credit you with a number of Variable Contract Account Units, determined by the current dollar value of an accumulation unit. The dollar value of an accumulation unit would go up and down, depending on changes in the value of the assets in the account. Each $50 that you paid might buy a different number of units. The dollar value of the units credited to you would change each month. The company makes no dollar guarantees. Its liabilities for the variable annuity are always in terms of the current value of its assets.

3. When you retire, all of your Variable Contract Account Units are be converted, on a basis set forth in your contract, into a fixed number of annuity units. As in a straight life annuity, you are guaranteed a payment each month for as long as you live. But instead of providing for the payment of a fixed number of dollars each month, your variable annuity contract will provide for the payment each month of the current value of the fixed number of annuity units credited to you.

You may find of interest the trend in CREF annuity unit values since the CREF was established in 1952. The CREF's performance is shown in Figure 7–4 and in Table 7–7.[15]

Why Not Invest in Common Stock Directly? Why not buy common stock directly and provide this variable income in retirement by a systematic liquidation of your investments over your retirement period? There is one big reason why you can't. You can set up an investment program, but you can't predict how long you will live. Therefore, after retirement you can't know how much of your principal it is safe to spend each

---

[15] For further detail on variable annuities, see "Variable Annuities," *Barron's,* January 17, 1977.

TABLE 7–7
CREF Accumulation Unit Values at Month-End

	1970	1971	1972	1973	1974	1975	1976	1977	1978
January	$37.90	$41.37	$48.27	$50.36	$40.75	$30.67	$40.31	$40.27	$35.72
February	40.01	41.57	50.49	47.11	40.83	32.80	39.76	39.30	34.96
March	39.95	43.14	51.36	46.44	39.32	33.77	40.75	38.73	36.15
April	36.04	45.23	51.80	43.69	37.58	36.12	40.10	38.73	39.28
May	32.93	43.81	53.74	42.06	35.11	38.07	36.69	37.96	39.52
June	30.76	43.58	51.80	41.40	34.29	39.88	41.60	39.91	38.94
July	32.73	41.24	51.15	44.80	31.71	36.81	41.21	39.34	41.03
August	34.36	44.01	51.95	44.06	29.51	35.86	40.94	38.56	42.17
September ...	35.76	43.85	50.98	46.63	25.09	34.31	41.59	38.65	41.86
October	35.27	41.84	50.80	47.06	30.29	35.89	40.62	36.91	38.18
November ...	36.88	42.38	52.53	41.30	29.23	36.61	40.40	38.01	38.80
December ...	39.19	46.21	53.25	42.61	28.35	36.34	42.66	38.21	39.44

year. You might figure on drawing down your money over, say, 15 years—and then live only half as long. Or you might still be hale and hearty after 20 years—but with all your money gone.

Only an insurance company spreading the mortality risk on a sound actuarial basis over a large group of people can guarantee you a distribution of your savings over your full retirement lifetime no matter how long you may live. The insurance company can do this because dealing with a large number of annuitants enables the company to offset its "losses" on those who live longer than the "average" by "gains" on those who do not live as long as the average.

YOUR COMPANY PENSION PLAN

When you graduate and are deciding which job to take, check the pension plan of each of the companies that have made you an offer. Today many medium and large corporations provide attractive retirement plans. A generous plan will enable you to use funds that you might otherwise have to husband for retirement.

Will you contribute to the plan, or does the company pay the entire cost? Practice varies. When you contribute, by payroll deduction, your benefits

may be larger. At any event all the income that the money earns during your working years is tax-free until your retirement. In some companies there is no payroll deduction on the first $5,000 or $10,000 of income but a significant contribution from higher compensation. Plans vary widely in this respect.

How much will you get? Here, too, it is hard to generalize. Some plans are tied to profit sharing; others use formulas and pay benefits without any formal relationship to profit. Pensions may be based on length of service or on level of salary, or on both. The company, for example, may pay 1 percent for each year's service. The 1 percent may be on your average salary or it may be on your salary for the five years prior to retirement. The latter would probably be more advantageous, since your last five years' salary is likely to be higher than your average salary with the firm. Almost all corporate pensions are in addition to social security benefits.

The company's pension fund may be invested by a bank or a trust company, in which case when you retire, your pension benefits are paid directly from a trust fund. Or the pension fund may be handled by an insurance company, in which case the fund is in effect used to purchase annuities payable to you upon your retirement.

The Pension Reform Act of 1974

This act, technically called the Employee Retirement Income Security Act, and also known as ERISA, was passed to correct abuses which had developed in private pension plans over the years. It's a very complicated statute, but several provisions may be of interest to you. Any employee who is at least age 25 and has one year on the company payroll must be taken into the pension plan—assuming that the firm has one—and must be given credit for past service up to three years.

Companies are not required, under the new law, to set up retirement plans, nor are they told precisely how benefits are to be computed; but where plans are operating—new or existing ones—employees must be permitted to accumulate pension credits in some fair and orderly way. For example, vesting is now required, with a choice of several options, but under any of the options an employee must become at least 50 percent vested after 10 years of service and 100 percent vested after 15 years, regardless of the employee's age.

In the past, even full vesting has not always guaranteed a worker the pension earned. Thousands of employees lost out when their companies failed, merged with other companies, or simply dropped pension plans. Now companies with pension plans must meet new standards of financing or funding. Formal pension funds have to be managed and administered under trust arrangements or invested through an insurance company. Pension plan assets have to be made independent of the future fortunes of the employer. Companies are now required to "fund" currently the normal costs of pension rights as they accrue.

Extending the protection concept to pensions, a Pension Benefit Guaranty Corporation has been set up to insure all of a worker's vested benefits up to certain limits.

Evaluating ERISA   ERISA has not been all that was expected. Revisions are in process. The number of plans ended exceeded the number begun, partly because the law limited the types of investments that were acceptable under the "prudent man" rule for the pension funds. The pension fund manager was not only required to preserve the body of the fund, but if he did not increase it sufficiently to pay benefits when due the corporation had to make up the difference from earnings or face a suit.

Lengthy and complex regulations and complicated paperwork have made it more attractive to drop the plans rather than cope with the provisions of ERISA.

The headache of dealing with three administering agencies—not only the Pension Benefit Guaranty Corporation, but also the Labor Department and the Internal Revenue Service—needs a sweetener to reverse the decline and increase the growth of private pension plans.

What is being offered is a tax credit to employers who establish new plans and to employers who make significant improvements in existing plans. A tax credit is also to be offered to employees whose contribution will increase low benefit levels by supplementing employer contributions.

A master plan is being considered—so that the many small companies need not be overwhelmed trying to do the paperwork or investing on their own. They would contribute money and data on their employees to a master plan run by a financial institution.

One of the benefits of ERISA was supposed to be the opportunity it gave a worker to take a pension from employer to employer (vesting) and not lose benefits. The Pension Benefits Guaranty Corporation was supposed to set up reserves to insure these multiemployer pension plans. Those reserves did not do so sufficiently and therefore the multiemployer part of ERISA becomes effective July 1, 1979—five years after the law itself went into effect.

More Equal

Although women live longer than men, on the average, an employer who charges women more than men to participate in a pension plan is guilty of sex discrimination according to a Supreme Court decision of April 25, 1978. This decision applies to all contributory plans, whether the employer is private or governmental.

The ruling *may* also cast doubt on pension plans that deduct equally from both sexes but pay women lower monthly benefits after retirement because women live longer. This procedure was not specifically barred by the Supreme Court decision, but a question remains as to whether the court might reject such plans.

Private Pension Plans and Social Security

The pension plan of the auto industry, which typifies a growing number of similar industry plans, has a "30 and out option." It offers generous monthly payments for those who have worked 30 years, and grants pension supplements to employees who quit before social security payments begin. At Chrysler, for example, the worker will have a $700 monthly pension until he becomes eligible for social security. At that point his company pension drops to $330 a month, but with the combined social security benefit for himself and his wife he would probably have $900–950 per month.

Other industries cannot afford equal generosity. After 30 years an Amalgamated Clothing worker can expect to add $157 to his social security benefits.

Many corporate pension plans are "integrated" with social security. An "offset" integration formula might set a retirement pay goal, counting on social security to provide part of the retirement income and on the corporation to provide the remainder. As social security benefits lessen under the 1977 amendments to the Social Security Act, corporation contributions might have to increase to reach the previously set goals. One formula uses "a step-up" meant to increase the corporation's contributions for employees as the employees' earnings exceed the social security wage base. Under the 1977 amendments, that formula may mean a lesser corporation contribution because the act now mandates an increased wage base every year. On the other hand, some corporations are also considering employee-contributory pension plans because higher payroll taxes and higher pension fund financing have increased their costs.

IRA—Individual Retirement Account

The 40 million private industry employees who are not covered by any pension plan other than social security are now allowed to set up their own tax-free retirement plans. Under the new law, these workers may create Individual Retirement Accounts, or IRAs, and eligible employees may place as much as 15 percent of their pay in an IRA, up to a maximum of $1,500 a year, and take a tax deduction for the amount. This deduction is available even for those who do not itemize deductions on their income tax forms.

Funds put into IRAs can be invested in one of several ways: *(a)* they can be used to buy special annuities that will not begin to pay off until age 59½; *(b)* they can be invested in a special type of Treasury bond that currently pays 6 percent; or *(c)* the money can be put into a trust to be administered by a bank or other approved institution, *(d)* in a savings account in any thrift institution, or *(e)* in a mutual fund.

The annual earnings from the invested funds, as well as the income put aside each year, is tax-free. Withdrawals of funds from IRAs, at age 59½ or later, will be fully taxable income, though usually at lower rates than people pay in their working years.

Beginning January 1, 1977, housewives who have no paying job can build up a tax-sheltered individual retirement account in their own names. A husband opening an IRA for a nonworking wife is entitled to a $1,750 tax deduction—an extra $250 tax deduction for him, in a sense, but the pension and its interest are irrevocably hers.

IRAs are not subject to estate taxes if payments from the plan are spread over a three-year period.

You need not keep your money in only one IRA. Every three years you can "roll over" your money—without penalty—into another IRA to change your investment strategy. The 1978 Tax Act now permits the roll-over of a portion of a

TABLE 7–8

Examining the Impact of Tax-Deferred Retirement Savings

Annual Deposit for 40 Years*	Amount Deposited over Life of Plan	Net Interest	Total Accumulated Amount under IRA/Keogh	Total Accumulated Amount Assuming 35 Percent Marginal Tax Rate	Total Accumulated Amount Assuming 45 Percent Marginal Tax Rate	Annual Payout for 15 Years under IRA/Keogh
$1,500	$ 60,000	$ 414,544.61	$ 474,544.61	$ 308,454.00	$ 260,999.54	$ 56,970.50
2,500†	100,000	690,907.68	790,907.68	514,089.99	434,999.23	94,950.84
3,500†	140,000	967,270.75	1,107,270.75	719,725.99	608,998.92	132,931.17
4,500†	180,000	1,243,633.83	1,423,633.83	925,361.99	782,998.61	170,911.51
5,500†	220,000	1,519,996.90	1,739,996.90	1,130,997.99	956,998.30	208,891.84
6,500†	260,000	1,796,359.97	2,056,359.97	1,336,633.98	1,130,997.99	246,872.18
7,500†	300,000	2,072,723.05	2,372,723.05	1,542,269.98	1,304,997.68	284,852.51

* Annual deposits into 8 percent, eight-year time deposits; effective annual yield of 8.45 percent.
† Annual contributions to IRA plans are limited to $1,500 at present. The table assumes the allowable annual contribution will be raised.
Source: The Bowery Savings Bank, November 1978.

lump sum pension payment—as well as the formerly allowed total lump sum—into an IRA to continue its tax deferred status.

What's Wrong with IRA?

A recent Federal Trade Commission report charged that some investments sold as IRAs do not carry out the intent of the law.[16] For example, they mention a life insurance company plan which requires fixed payments over the lifetime of the contract. The holder could become ineligible as a result of enrollment in an employer pension plan or if personal income for the year dropped, which by law would make a payment of $1,500 excessive. The resultant cancellation penalties imposed by the insurance company for not meeting the scheduled payment would cause the IRA holder to lose money.

Suppose that you are 27, working in an area where private pension plans are nonexistent and that you buy a fixed-payment insurance plan in order to get a tax break now, some insurance coverage, and some income when you retire. After all—as Table 7–8 shows—a yearly contribution grows into a goodly sum at retirement. When, for any of the reasons discussed earlier, you can't meet your payments, it's a shock to discover that you are not only saddled with a penalty for missing a payment but that you have probably lost everything because in the early years of insurance coverage payments go to cover sales commissions and administrative costs and are usually not refundable. Even though you saw a computer printout showing the cash value of your policy after each of 20 years and at age 65—you may not have realized its significance. Since you probably also signed a disclosure statement (that you saw the printout), you can't claim deception.

You would not be alone in such an experience. Many have fallen victim to such a situation, through lack of knowledge of the legalese of insurance. Sell-

ers of any commodity are not known for alerting buyers to possible problems.

The F.T.C. report offered several recommendations to the IRS:

1. It should revise its Publication no. 590, *Tax Information on Individual Retirement Savings Programs,* so as to make it more understandable to the average consumer.
2. The booklet should be given to consumers before they purchase IRAs.
3. New regulations standardizing the methods for computing the rates of return should be developed.
4. All disclosures by sellers should be in a language that the average consumer can understand.

To reduce the inequities and complexities will require considerable revision of an already difficult law. According to a newspaper report, "It is so complicated that the FTC is rejecting overtures that it assume authority over the consumer aspects of the program. 'It's a maze,' one commission staffer says"![17]

Pensions for the Self-Employed[18]

If instead of going to work for a company you set up your own small business or enter one of the professions, you will be interested in the provisions of the Self-Employed Individuals Tax Retirement Acts of 1962, popularly known as the Keogh Act and amended by the Pension Reform Act of 1974 and 1978. The act permits self-employed persons to establish tax-favored retirement plans for themselves.

If you are self-employed as an accountant, architect, author, decorator, dentist, doctor, farmer, or lawyer, or you are an owner or partner in an unin-

---

[16] *Consumer News,* Department of Health, Education, and Welfare, Office of Consumer Affairs, July 1, 1978. For more detail, see the revised edition of *Frank Talk about IRA's*—free. Write Federal Trade Commission, Room 1300, Washington, D.C. 20850.

[17] *Wall Street Journal,* May 5, 1978.

[18] See Internal Revenue Service Publication no. 560, *Retirement Plans for Self-Employed Individuals,* which may be obtained free of charge by sending a postcard to your local IRS office. See also IRS Publication no. 566, *Questions and Answers on Retirement Plans for the Self-Employed.* This too may be obtained free of charge from your local IRS office.

corporated business and receive self-employment income from personal services rendered, you can set up a retirement plan and be eligible for tax benefits under the Keogh Act.

The self-employed person can determine what the annual contribution to the retirement fund will be up to the maximum set by law—which for most persons is up to 15 percent of earnings, with a top limit of $7,500. For beginning, low-earning self-employed, $750 can be set aside tax-free, no matter how small the earnings are.

A 1978 change allows an individual who qualified and earned $50,000 a year to deduct up to $15,000 annually if that person is an owner of a partnership or a small partnership corporation or the owner of a sole proprietorship. A defined benefit plan, which allows you to set aside as much cash as is necessary to provide a specified pension at retirement, is possible if—you are earning at least $50,000 a year or proportionately less if you are over 59.

The tax advantage you receive is that you can deduct your annual contribution to your retirement plan from your taxable income. Furthermore, the income or capital gains from your invested fund are free from taxes until withdrawn. You will not be taxed until you actually receive distributions upon retirement. By that time your tax rate may be lower than it was in your active earning period.

There are some limitations, of course. You cannot withdraw funds until you reach age 59½ without incurring tax penalties. However, earlier distribution is permitted in case of permanent disability. Also, your beneficiaries can receive benefits upon your death, even though that occurs before you reach age 59½. If you set up a plan for yourself, you must also set up a plan for all your employees who have completed three years of continuous service at the date of the plan's adoption. Full tax deduction is permitted, however, for contributions made on behalf of "regular" employees. Also, you are restricted as to how you can invest the money. You have five main choices:

1. You may put the money into a trust.
2. You may open a time deposit savings account.
3. You may purchase annuity contracts from an insurance company.
4. You may open a special "custodial" account which can be invested wholly in mutual fund shares or wholly in annuity, endowment, or life insurance contracts issued by an insurance company.
5. You may purchase special U.S. government "retirement" bonds. Those bonds can't be cashed until you are 59½, unless you die or become disabled earlier.

The self-employed retirement plan must be approved by the Internal Revenue Service, which also provides a plan number. Most large banks, brokerage houses, mutual funds, and insurance companies have already approved master and model plans. Also, many trade and professional associations have developed group plans involving, for example, group annuity contracts or mutual fund plans.

Setting up a self-employed retirement plan isn't simple. The act is more complicated than has been indicated above. If and when you decide to take advantage of it, consult a lawyer, or an accountant, or your insurance agent, or your local banker.

THE ADEQUACY OF SOCIAL SECURITY AND RETIREMENT INCOME

The foregoing discussion of social security, annuities, and pensions does not pretend to be an exhaustive treatment of all ramifications of these subjects. It should, however, give you a fairly good indication of your future stake in the programs. A family may receive benefits from social security which could otherwise be obtained only by having saved thousands of dollars or by having insurance policies upon which thousands of dollars of premiums have been paid.

In view of the fact that high living costs and high taxes are making it difficult for many families to save adequately in order to have reasonable income for survivors if the wage earner dies or for the wage earner if he retires, pension plans and the forced saving of social security make the future more secure.

SUGGESTED READINGS

Ball, Robert M. *Social Security Today and Tomorrow*. New York: Columbia University Press, 1978.

Boroson, Warren. "A Check on Your Social Security Savvy," *Money*, July 1977.

Clark, Robert; Kreps, Juanita; and Spengler, Joseph. "Economics of Aging: A Survey," *Journal of Economic Literature*, vol. 16, no. 3 (September 1978).

Srodes, James L. "The Drive to Revise ERISA," *Institutional Investor*, August 1977.

Unthank, L. L., and Behrendt, Harry M. *What You Should Know about Individual Retirement Accounts*. Homewood, Ill.: Dow Jones-Irwin, 1978.

Year-end Tax Planning for Individuals, annual. New York: Ernst & Ernst, 1978.

Social Security Administration bulletins. For the latest editions, write to U.S. Department of Health, Education, and Welfare, Washington, D.C., 20203.

Apply for a Social Security Number, SSA-10064.

How Recent Changes in Social Security Affect You, SSA-10328.

If You Become Disabled, SSA-10029, 10153, 10068, 10108, 11000, 10012, 10002.

Social Security Benefits—How to Estimate the Amount, SSA-10032.

Social Security Benefits for People Disabled since Childhood, SSA-10012.

Social Security Benefits for Students 18–22, SSA-10048.

Social Security Credits—How You Earn Them, SSA-10072.

Social Security Information for Young Families, SSA-10033.

Special Information for Self-Employed People, SSA-10022.

A Woman's Guide to Social Security, SSA-10127.

You Can Work and Still Get Social Security Checks, SSA-10092, 10071, 10069.

Your Rights and Responsibilities—Special Payments, SSA-10080.

Your Social Security, SSA-10035.

Your Social Security Earnings Record, SSA-10044.

Your Social Security Rights and Responsibilities, SSA-10077.

CASE PROBLEMS

1 When George McNair (annual earnings, $14,000) received his monthly salary, he found that $70 had been deducted as his social security payment. He figured that this was too much because at that rate he would be paying $840 a year. What mistake had been made? He began to worry about the record of his past earnings. When the statement came from the Social Security Administration, in response to his request, he found a mistake had been made by his second employer five years ago. What can he do about this?

2 Rita Ramirez is 19, and she has been living alone with her father, a disabled World War II veteran, since her mother died when she was six years old. She is a business major at college and is afraid she may have to drop out because her father can no longer afford the college expense and she does not want to get a loan. Someone told her that social security would help, since her mother had worked in a department store before she died. But Rita says that was too long ago. What are facts in this situation?

3 Mrs. Stephens, a court stenographer, left four children, all under 18, when she died in an auto accident last year. Her husband is working, and they had a modest savings account. For what social security benefits are they eligible?

4 John Peters has joined the college as a tenured instructor and been offered a choice of a retirement program that includes fixed or variable or balanced annuities. How should he decide what proportion to select. If he were an older man making a decision on settlement options, what factors should influence his decision?

5 Maria Jethro is an assistant sales manager in a large suburban discount house which has no company pension plan. She resents deductions from her salary for social security and thinks her friends who are establishing IRA plans are foolish in looking so far ahead. How do you convince her that she is being nearsighted?

APPENDIX

Projection of Social Security Benefits Based on Average Indexed Earnings to the Year 2000

The number of years used in the computation are determined by counting the number of years elapsing after 1950 or after the attainment of age 21 if this is after 1950, up to but not including the year of attainment of age 62 and reducing this number by five.

Before the selection of the earnings to be used can be made, the earnings after 1950 through the year of attainment of age 60 must be indexed to express them in terms of their dollar value as of that year, in accordance with the following formula:

$$\frac{\begin{array}{c}\text{Average total}\\\text{wages for all}\\\text{persons in the}\\\text{year the indi-}\\\text{vidual attains}\\\text{age 60}\end{array} \times \begin{array}{c}\text{Individual's}\\\text{earnings for}\\\text{the year to be}\\\text{indexed}\end{array}}{\begin{array}{c}\text{Average total wages for all}\\\text{persons in the year being indexed}\end{array}} = \begin{array}{c}\text{Indexed}\\\text{earnings}\end{array}$$

The average total wages for all persons in given years are contained in Table 1. Average annual total wages after 1977 are estimated on the basis of an average wage increase of 5.5 percent per year.

After indexing, the highest indexed and nonindexed earnings after 1950 up to but not including the year of entitlement are selected. The number of years selected is equal to the number of computation years. The earnings are added and their sum is divided by the number of computation years to derive the average indexed monthly earnings.

TABLE 1

Year	Amount	Year	Amount
1951	$2,799.16	1975	8,630.92
1952	2,973.32	1976	9,226.48
1953	3,139.44	1977	9,779.44
1954	3,155.64	1978	10,317.31
1955	3,301.44	1979	10,884.76
1956	3,532.36	1980	11,483.42
1957	3,641.72	1981	12,115.01
1958	3,673.80	1982	12,781.34
1959	3,855.80	1983	13,484.31
1960	4,007.12	1984	14,225.95
1961	4,086.76	1985	15,008.38
1962	4,291.40	1986	15,833.84
1963	4,396.64	1987	16,704.70
1964	4,576.32	1988	17,623.46
1965	4,658.72	1989	18,592.75
1966	4,938.36	1990	19,615.35
1967	5,213.44	1991	20,694.19
1968	5,571.76	1992	21,832.37
1969	5,893.76	1993	23,033.15
1970	6,186.24	1994	24,299.97
1971	6,497.08	1995	25,636.47
1972	7,133.80	1996	27,046.48
1973	7,580.16	1997	28,534.04
1974	8,030.76	1998	30,103.41

The benefit payable at age 65 is determined by applying the following table to the average indexed monthly earnings.

Average Indexed Monthly Earnings	Benefit Determination
up to $180	90% of average indexed monthly earnings
$181 − $1,085	$162.00 + 32% of the amount in excess of $180.00
$1,086 or more	$451.60 + 15% of the amount in excess of $1,085.00

The money amounts in the left column of Table 2 are contained in the law. They are subject to change in future years as average total wages rise or decline.

Example:

A person born in 1936 attains age 21 in 1957 and age 62 in 1998. The number of computation years to be used is 35. (The 40 years elapsing after 1957 minus 5.) The number of months in 35 years is 420. Filing for benefits occurs in 2001 at age 65. The earnings record is credited as follows:

TABLE 2

Year	Actual Earnings	Indexed Earnings
1961	$ 4,800	$31,766.76
1962	4,800	30,251.92
1963	4,800	29,527.80
1964	4,800	28,368.45
1965	4,800	27,866.69
1966	6,600	36,146.97
1967	6,600	34,239.73
1968	7,800	37,862.82
1969	7,800	35,794.22
1970	7,800	34,101.90
1971	7,800	32,470.36
1972	9,000	34,121.81
1973	10,800	38,535.07
1974	13,200	44,455.76
1975	14,100	44,184.79
1976	15,300	44,850.38
1977	16,500	45,633.18
1978	17,700	46,399.95
1979	22,900	56,901.97
1980	25,900	61,001.32
1981	29,700	66,304.56
1982	30,900	65,387.22
1983	31,700	63,583.04
1984	32,900	62,549.72
1985	33,700	60,730.50
1986	34,900	59,614.23
1987	35,700	57,801.66
1988	36,900	56,629.92
1989	37,700	54,841.39
1990	38,900	53,636.97
1991	40,700	53,193.27
1992	41,900	51,906.76
1993	42,000	49,318.14
1994	43,000	47,860.09
1995	44,000	46,420.01
1996	45,000	45,000.00
1997	46,000	46,000.00
1998	47,000	47,000.00
1999	48,000	48,000.00
2000	49,000	49,000.00

Low years excluded: 1961, 1962, 1963, 1964, 1965
Total indexed earnings: $1,711,477.71
Average indexed monthly earnings: $4,074
Benefit amount: $900.00
Source: Social Security Administration, HEW, 1979.

The Social Security Act of 1972 included an automatic adjustment to the benefit as the cost of living increased. The current law, amended in 1977, decouples that double benefit an individual would receive from an increase in earnings and from that increase gained because of the rise in the C.P.I. The goal of indexing is to stabilize the retirement benefit so that with financial planning from other sources, a retiree can hopefully maintain a desired income level.

If the average yearly earnings in 1979 are $10,500, it is projected that the yearly retirement benefit for 1979 will be $4,900—a 46 percent replacement rate. If, in the year 2000, the average yearly earnings are $35,000 then the benefit is expected to be $14,000 or a 42 percent replacement rate.

There can be only a reasonable estimate because the indexing factor must be revised yearly to meet the changing inflation rate.

Increases in the wage base raise benefits, but indexing will slow that increase. Survivor's benefits and disability benefits must now be figured on the new calculation which averages about $100 a month *less* for families. The effect of this fundamental change in the basis of payment has been masked.

Meeting Medical Bills

*With health—everything is a source of
pleasure; without it nothing else, whatever it
may be, is enjoyable.*
SCHOPENHAUER

You are playing softball. You run and fall on
your thumb, which aches horribly and seems out
of shape. Off you go to the emergency room of
the nearest hospital, where you have X rays taken,
the thumb is put in a splint, and you are told to
exercise it—or the tendon will be damaged permanently. Several days later, you get a call from the
hospital. Someone checked your X rays. You have
a fracture that now needs an operation. Mistake?
Carelessness? Malpractice? Consultant needed?
You check into the hospital, to be told "$200 in
advance"—even though you are covered by insurance 100 percent for the first $1,000 minus a de-
ductible of $100 and 80 percent for all above
$1,000. Your expected three-day hospital bill was
estimated at approximately $1,400. If you think
that hospital costs are high, you can see why you
have a strong interest in the need to cut medical
costs—especially hospital costs.

Not even mentioned are doctors' bills, pain, the
upsetting of personal plans, or future related problems.

Medical needs for the individual are unpredict-
able, almost impossible to budget. One severe illness, or a number of minor ones in a short period,
can wreck the family budget and bring on indebted-

225

ness. A hospitalized illness "involves a severe physical shock, a high emotional crisis, and a large economic expenditure." In one year illness cost U.S. families $200 billion. The average hospitalized illness costs in the neighborhood of $625, apart from loss of income, and in some cases the cost rises to several thousand dollars. Last year one out of every seven persons in the United States was hospitalized.

Hospital Costs

Ten years ago the national average cost for a semiprivate hospital room per day was $34. Today it is $105. Hospital costs have been rising at the rate of 15 percent a year in recent years—twice the rate of prices generally. A federal proposal to limit the price rise to 9 percent by setting a maximum fixed cost above which there can be no expenditure has been opposed by hospital administrations. The hospitals want no outside interference and prefer to try to cut costs by 2 percent yearly, for a given period, claiming that their selective cuts will be better for good health care than an across-the-board clamp at the top.

Claims and counterclaims blame higher hospital costs on:

1. The increased wages and salaries of previously underpaid hospital workers.
2. The competitive purchase by every hospital of expensive technological equipment to attract both doctors and patients. There is also the use of intensive care units—highly expensive but highly successful in saving lives.
3. An oversupply of hospital beds—which studies show exist—even though you have to wait for a bed before admission to a hospital.
4. Excessive and unnecessary treatment—hospital stays that are longer than needed, defensive medical tests (not against illness—but against possible malpractice suits), and increased diagnostic testing.
5. The reimbursement policies of the federal government and Blue Cross and other private insurers, which automatically repays a hospital

"Don't worry, we'll have you on your feet and out of here in no time. Your hospital insurance doesn't cover much."

Reprinted by permission *The Wall Street Journal*

on an average per diem cost calculated for all its patients on any given day, whether the patient is undergoing complicated surgery or is just about to go home.
6. Medicare and medicaid payments amount to 40 percent of the nation's total hospital bill and are increasing, while at the same time increased costs are making the elderly and poor pay more of the costs they really can't afford.

You may approve having a larger percentage of GNP go for medical care than for defense.[1] If you have not yet had to pay any part of a hospital bill, you may feel relaxed knowing that 90 percent of the bill will be covered by government or insurance—if you don't stop to think that your taxes are paying it. But maybe you will be jolted by the HEW secretary's statement at a congressional hearing that the cost of health insurance added $119 to the cost of each Ford car sold in 1975. "General Motors," according to a consultant on employee

[1] Professor Uwe E. Reinhardt, "a widely respected health economist at Princeton University," said, "I personally am not burned up about the percent of GNP going to health care. I'd let it go higher. After all we rejoice when the automobile industry grows. The health care industry, doesn't cause as much pollution" (quoted in *New York Times*, May 7, 1978).

benefit programs "says that the cost of health care adds more to the price of a car than does the cost of steel. The Blue Shield–Blue Cross program has now surpassed the steel industry as its largest supplier."[2] Health insurance for its workers costs GM more than steel for its cars and trucks.

Suggested Cures

The real question is whether costs can be contained without reducing the quality of patient care. Also of concern are the figures of the National Center for Health Statistics showing that 24 million Americans are still not covered by any kind of health insurance and that an additional 20 million are not adequately covered.

1. It has been suggested that rising hospital costs could be curbed if hospitals had a system for determining what it costs to provide care for each particular type of case or diagnosis. The hospitals have claimed that each case is different even though the same procedure is used. Concern has been voiced that it might become routine to use certain procedures in order to get higher reimbursement.

2. The social security system has contributed funds to a series of experiments that would make a lump yearly advance payment to hospitals for the actual kinds of cases they would handle. Every ailment would be placed in one of 383 diagnosis-related groups (DRGs) and be given a tentative estimated cost figure based on the medical data associated with it (as well as the drugs, surgery, linen, and food involved). A hospital's lump-sum reimbursement would depend on the volume and mix of its cases.

3. Some states are developing programs of reimbursement by diagnosis, case by case. Hospitals would be paid for what they did, not for the time spent doing it.

4. Nine states now regulate hospital costs, reviewing rates in similar hospitals, all using the same accounting system.

5. Some hospitals limit themselves to providing basic care and avoiding money-losing services, such as maternity care, or sophisticated procedures, such as open-heart surgery and lung operations.

6. Rural satellite hospitals are associating themselves with modern medical centers, which will do the testing, provide food and linen, handle the billing—and be more cost efficient.

7. A plan known as PAT (preadmission testing) has been tried in various areas. Almost 50 Blue Cross groups repay in full all presurgical testing provided that it is completed seven days before a scheduled surgery and that it is done in the same member hospital in which the surgery takes place. The Harvard University Community Health Plan in New England, some suburban Los Angeles communities, and some larger private insurance companies are using PAT. This plan is being adopted in an increasing area.

8. Surgery without hospitalization—sometimes known as verticare or ambulatory surgery—is practiced now in one out of seven hospitals in the American Hospital Association. By eliminating overnight stays for minor surgery, it frees beds for the more seriously ill; cuts hospital medical expenses for room service charges, nursing care, and laundry

"Yes, this is the doctor. My answering service is busy at the moment."

Reprinted by permission *The Wall Street Journal*

---

[2] *Wall Street Journal,* February 17, 1977.

bills; allows the operating room to be utilized more fully; and saves money and time for the patient. Variations of the plan provide for having the patient check in for breakfast and get home in time for dinner or for allowing patients to come for surgery between 4:00 and 9:00 P.M. after having had presurgical tests early in the day, thus freeing the patients to spend the time in between at home or at work. George Washington University Hospital in Washington, D.C., which has used this system since 1966, has had to hospitalize only 1 percent of its 14,000 patients. A 20-minute cataract operation allowed a patient to leave a New York hospital shortly afterward, check into a nearby hotel, and visit his surgeon daily instead of spending days in the hospital. Almost all of the 74 U.S. Blue Cross plans pay the full cost of outpatient care.

Cost Cutting by Blue Cross

1. The amount Blue Cross will pay per day for a bed patient is determined in advance. The hospital is then responsible for keeping within this limit or itself bearing the cost of the difference.
2. Most hospitals now have a utilization committee which reviews every admission and checks lengthy stays.
3. A home care posthospital program has been initiated which, with the doctor's approval, is covered by Blue Cross.
4. A recently completed detailed study of hospital costs and uses has been made through a new Blue Cross computer program.

If through fear of rising hospital costs, you are considering a supplementary insurance policy offering extra cash when you are hospitalized, study carefully what the large advertised sums amount to when they are broken down by day payments and remember that the usual hospital stay for those under 65 is about a week. Will that extra premium cost give an adequate return? Equally important: look at the small print. Do you get coverage from the first day of hospitalization? Do you get immediate coverage for all possibilities as of the time you sign, as the big print seems to say—or is there a subtly worded exemption requiring a long wait, such as a year or two, before benefits will be paid on a physical condition you had before the policy went into effect?

Physicians' Fees

Health has become a transaction—it is no longer a personal relationship with the family doctor. Nevertheless, for most patients the doctor is still a father figure—rather impersonal and remote, but someone to whom the patient, although also a consumer, has surrendered almost all decisions about treatment tests and costs. The doctor doesn't think about the costs either. The insurers, not the patient, pay most of the doctor's fee which is usually based on the highest prevailing rate in the area, and also most of the patient's expenses, so neither the doctor nor the patient is limited by any economic standards or cost restraint.

Doctors' fees, according to the Council on Wage and Price Stability, have risen 50 percent more than other consumer prices. Doctors are paid on a service for fee basis. A doctor sets his fees according to the fees of his peers with comparable skills in a comparable area. Blue Shield–Blue Cross keeps a profile on each doctor on the basis of which it pays the "usual, customary, and reasonable fees." An older physician's fees can't change much—his fee schedule is in the profile—but the new doctor can set his sights at the top of his peers. The supply of doctors in proportion to the population has been increasing, without any effect on fees. Physicians' fees are highest where the supply of physicians is greatest—a violation of economic law but a tribute to the procedure by which new doctors set fees at a level that will provide adequate insurance repayment for them. The new doctor sets his fee based on the highest prevailing rate in his area. His fee profile will be high. His reimbursement rate from the insurance payer will be high, because that fee has become his customary fee.

Physicians' and surgeons' fees vary widely within an area and from region to region, even allowing for regional cost-of-living differences. A study by the Health Research Group (a branch of

Ralph Nader's Public Citizen Organization) of 39 localities, including the nation's 25 largest metropolitan areas, found New York and Los Angeles to be the two costliest areas. A study by the staff of the Senate Finance Committee came to the same conclusion. Social security data for medicare payments provided such contrasts as this: a gall bladder operation in a New York City hospital would reimburse the surgeon $1,000, whereas the same operation done in Finlay, Ohio, would pay a maximum fee of $290. Although the cost of living at that time was 37 percent higher in New York City than in Finlay, Ohio, it was the differential in surgeons' fees that resulted in 245 percent higher cost for the patient.

Filling a Need

The National Health Service Corporation has attempted to redistribute medical professionals so that communities with fewer than one doctor for 4,000 residents will benefit. In return for two years of service, young doctors who join are paid about $12,000 a year in salary and are forgiven 60 percent of their personal medical education loans. In exchange for three years of service, 85 percent forgiveness is offered. A similar idea, adopted by the University of New Mexico Medical School seniors to fill a health care gap, is now being funded by a grant from the Bureau of Health Manpower Education of the Department of Health, Education, and Welfare. The students needed practical clinical experience, and isolated areas needed medical care. Another program offers "supernurses," of whom there are now 10,000, to fill the gap. Usually they practice in association with physicians, jointly providing more effective health care.

North Carolina has established 21 primary care clinics in rural areas throughout the state. Except for four run by physicians, these are headed by physician's assistants or family nurse practitioners who have had a year or more of university special training leading toward such degrees.

There are several hundred primary care clinics around the country, eligible for reimbursement under medicare and medicaid, whose patient load is rising. Each clinic is run by a local board and is partly financed by contributions from at least 500 families in the community.

Complaints

A special Harris opinion poll on doctors reported that large sections of the public feel that doctors jam too many patients into office hours, have raised their fees to take advantage of medicare and medicaid, and are reluctant to make house calls. People complain that general practitioners are mainly a referral source, and they say that doctors should concentrate more on preventive medicine. In a recent year, more than four out of five physicians described themselves as specialists.

The medical profession is also unhappy about the public. The number of malpratice suits has increased. Premium costs in most states have tripled. Since malpratice suits have become more common, doctors have been engaging in "defensive medicine"—more tests, X rays, and consultants than in the past—which raises costs to the patient. A recent Rand Corporation report, *Doctors, Damages, and Deterrence: An Economic View of Medical Malpractice,* coauthored by Dr. William Schwartz, professor of medicine at Tufts University, and Neil Komesar, professor of law at the University of Wisconsin, stated, "Many more incidents of malpractice occur, it appears, than result in a claim for damages. At most only one out of every six or seven incidents can be expected to result in a claim."

Insurance companies trying to reduce malpractice claims have been conducting loss-control programs that educate nurses in record keeping, patient monitoring, and the avoidance of medication errors. Insurance companies have also been requiring hospitals to use peer review boards more strictly than in the past. "A doctor who might do something careless without thinking stops to think when he knows that the peer review board will be tough rather than understanding," says one hospital industry specialist.[3]

---

[3] *Business Week,* October 3, 1977, p. 110.

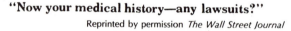

"Now your medical history—any lawsuits?"

Reprinted by permission *The Wall Street Journal*

However, a recent study showed 12 percent of the population, or 24 million Americans, had neither a physician nor access to a service providing regular care, such as a clinic.[4] Low-income groups and minorities were unlikely to have their own doctor, but according to this study, access to medical care had increased greatly, partly because of medicare and medicaid, with the result that 74 percent of blacks and 76 percent of whites saw a physician in 1976, compared to 49 percent of blacks and 68 percent of whites who saw one in 1963. Once-a-year visits to dentists were made

by less than 40 percent of low-income groups, compared to more than 60 percent of higher income groups. Although it is low, that 40 percent is testimony to the useful part that insurance plays in access to health care, because without the insurance the percentage would have been much lower.

Prepaid Voluntary Medical Care Insurance

Accident and sickness can (1) cut off family income, (2) quickly wipe out savings slowly accumulated over a long period, (3) leave a hopeless muddle of debt, or (4) be so costly that a family cannot afford all the medical services it needs. For these reasons, increasing millions have turned to prepayment insurance plans to ease the monetary pains of heavy hospital, surgical, and medical bills. And public funds now bear a larger share of medical care costs.

Surveys indicate that most Americans are not really sure of what their health insurance policies cover. When they discover the omissions, it is too late. It has been said that "buying adequate health insurance may be the single most difficult purchase a consumer may ever make." The legalese and the hidden booby traps in the small print make evaluating a policy difficult. The following pages should help clarify some aspects.

Health insurance can be considered in five categories: *(a)* disability insurance *(b)* hospital expense insurance, *(c)* surgical expense insurance, *(d)* regular medical care insurance, and *(e)* major medical expense insurance. When a health insurance plan covers hospital, surgical, and nonsurgical medical insurance, it is often referred to as a "base" or "basic" plan. When the basic plan is combined with a major medical plan, it is called a comprehensive plan.

Loss of Income, or Disability, Insurance

Protection against loss of income resulting from sickness or accident pays benefits when you are

---

[4] Study financed by the Robert Wood Johnson Foundation and the National Center for Health Service Research and prepared by researchers under Dr. Ronald Andersen at the University of Chicago's Center for Health Administration Studies—1978. For a free copy of the summary, write Special Report—Access, Robert Wood Johnson Foundation, P.O. Box 2316, Princeton, N.J. 08540.

unable to work. Policies of this type provide as much as 50 to 65 percent of wage earners' normal earnings for a specified period of disability. Usually a company will not pay more than three quarters of the wage earner's regular weekly or monthly income for a very good reason: if a person were able to buy a policy which paid as much or more than what was earned while working, there would be a strong incentive toward feigned illnesses and delay in returning to work.

Disability can be interpreted in many ways in your contract. If you can do any kind of gainful work—not necessarily your usual job—the company may say that you are not disabled. It may not recognize partial disability as coming within the coverage—or it may be generous, which, of course, costs higher premiums.

The possibility that disability is caused by illness increases as you get older. The noncancelable policy that covers both accident and illness offers effective protection and value for your money. The longer the payments covered, the higher the premium cost. If you try to balance the longer period by a smaller amount of disability payment so as to reduce expenses, you are working against yourself statistically. Most disabilities last for a relatively short period. Based on averages, you give yourself better protection by buying higher coverage for a shorter period.

Disability payments under social security have been liberalized and should be taken into consideration in planning your disability insurance. Previously, benefits were paid only to those whose disability was expected to continue indefinitely or to result in death. Now short-term disability is covered, with payments beginning 5 months after incapacitation and lasting 12 months or more.

The longer the waiting period, the more inexpensive the insurance. To avoid small claims, costly in paperwork and overhead, the insurance companies will pass the benefit to the insured person in either larger monthly income or longer coverage. In determining the length of the waiting period, the insured should consider the amount of personal savings and other disability payments that can be used for living expenses during this period. For the long term, the best policy, then, is the one with a moderately long waiting period, noncancelable, and guaranteed renewable until the day the policyholder reaches a certain age.

The number of persons protected by group loss of income plans through private industry and government is greater than the number covered by individual policies. This is also true of other forms of health insurance, since most of the people who have health insurance today obtain it as members of employed groups.

Women, who account for over half of the American work force, have trouble getting disability insurance. A woman who is alone or supporting children or whose income is needed for the family would be in financial difficulties if she were disabled and her earnings were lost. Her disability insurance would cost twice the amount that a man would pay. A free-lance male artist, working at home if he were disabled, would have no problem. In contrast, a female artist in the same situation would find her indemnity automatically reduced 50 percent. Although insurance companies claim that women have much more illness than men, social security disability claims granted in 1976 amounted to 713 per 100,000 for men and 545 per 100,000 for women. The insurance industry supports its unequal treatment of women needing disability insurance by insisting that they are only part-time workers, despite Department of Labor statistics that prove otherwise.

Hospital Expense Protection

Hospital expense protection provides benefits toward the payment of hospital charges for room, board, and miscellaneous services. Benefits have been steadily liberalized and expanded since this form of coverage began its major growth some two decades ago. Present-day coverage usually includes payment for use of an operating room, for laboratory fees, X-ray examinations, medicines, and all other services incidental to medical care and treatment which are furnished by the hospital.

You are allowed so much per day up to a maximum number of days, usually 120 to 365.

Blue Cross

Rates More than 40 percent of those who hold some form of insurance against the costs of hospital care are insured through 69 nonprofit, tax-free, autonomous Blue Cross plans. A majority of these plans contract with hospitals to provide most or all of their services in semiprivate accommodations with a minimum of additional charges. If you are a member of Blue Cross, the rate you pay depends on the type of plan you select and where you live and work. There are contracts for individuals or for families (including all unmarried children under 19), enrolled either through a group or separately. Group enrollment costs you less. Rates differ from plan to plan, largely because of the variation in hospital costs in different areas and the different benefits offered. In general, hospital protection in semiprivate accommodations for 120 days will cost an individual from $150 to $254 a year in premiums and from $250 to $400 for a family.

Benefits Benefits vary somewhat, but they follow a general pattern. Some provide more care than others, and some allow more special services. Most of the standard contracts provide full hospitalization 120 or more days in a year, or for each admission. In most areas it is customary to provide bed, board, general nursing care, customary drugs, special diets, the use of the operating room, anesthesia, laboratory tests, and special equipment, suh as oxygen and X-ray examinations, as part of the semiprivate service.

Room and board coverage provided by the plans varies from coverage in full in semiprivate accommodations to per diem allowances. All of the participants are entitled to full coverage in semiprivate accommodations, regardless of the cost. The plans provide an allowance, equal to the hospital's average semiprivate charge, toward the cost of a private room. With rare exceptions, dependents are entitled to the same benefits as the subscriber. Since 1969, Blue Cross plans have been paying more outpatient than in-hospital claims.

Typical Limitations Contracts usually exclude admissions for diagnostic care, rest cures, and blood, blood plasma, or blood donor services. Mental care in a general hospital is covered within limitations. Only a few of the plans exclude all dental care, with most allowing benefits when such care is necessitated by an accident. Maternity hospital costs are usually covered if conception took place while the subscriber was covered under a Blue Cross contract that provides maternity benefits. In states that have no-fault automobile insurance, contracts are being revised to avoid duplication of payment for injury, from both Blue Shield–Blue Cross and no-fault automobile insurance.

Organization The plans coordinate enrollment, public relations, and statistical research through the Blue Cross Association, but each plan exercises complete local independence over the benefits and rates included in its contracts. The plans arrange with local member hospitals to furnish care to subscribers, and they pay for the hospitalization according to the contract agreement. Almost all Blue Cross plans have a working agreement which allows for the transfer of a subscriber from one plan to another when the subscriber moves to another community. A second agreement gives benefits to a subscriber hospitalized in any community serviced by Blue Cross, whether or not it is in the home area. Although most of the emphasis is on group enrollment, all of the plans enroll individual subscribers. Approximately one out of every three persons in the United States now belongs to Blue Cross.

Pioneered by Blue Cross, hospital expense insurance is now sold by all the major insurance companies as part of their total health insurance package. Over a period of a year, the actuarial risk involved in a possible serious illness requiring hospitalization is about 7 percent for a 30-year-old male, 12 percent for a female in the same age bracket, and 5 percent for a child.

Surgical Expense Protection

The next largest form of protection is surgical expense protection. A later development than coverage for hospital care, surgical expense protection has shown a rapid growth over recent years because of the high fees paid for the services of a surgeon. The protection provides payments in accordance with a schedule of fees fixing the maximum reimbursement for each type of operation, which is usually much lower than what you pay.

The policy you buy prescribes the maximum that the insurance company will pay according to the schedule. If an operation costs more than the sum that the company will pay under the schedule, you pay the difference. The cost of the policy bears a direct relationship to the maximum that the company contracts to pay. Naturally, the higher the maximum, the higher the cost; the lower the maximum, the lower the cost.

Regular Medical Expense Protection

This type of coverage pays for visits to a doctor's office or for his visits to you at your home or in a hospital, as well as diagnostic, X-ray, and laboratory expenses. The maximum number of calls for each sickness or injury is usually specified in the policy. Some companies will not write this type of policy, because they feel that these costs should be budgeted rather than insured. They will, however, cover them in combination policies, either surgical-medical or comprehensive. The Blue Shield organization sells different kinds of general medical policies, depending upon your income.

Blue Shield

While Blue Cross is entirely a hospitalization insurance plan, mostly on a service basis, its 69 allied Blue Shield plans cover the costs of physicians' services, mostly on a cash indemnity basis. The former emphasis on service programs for Blue Shield subscribers is being phased out. There are plans for various and income benefit levels.

The Blue Shield plans contract with participating physicians to accept payment according to a standard fee schedule. Claims are paid according to two distinct methods. The "usual, customary, and reasonable charge" program provides payment in full to physicians for covered services based on prevailing fees in the locality in which they practice. Since most physicians are reluctant to accept this low return, new plans for a six-month review and adjustment on the scheduled payments in line with the CPI are now offered.

"Indemnity," the second payment method, represents the allowance of a fixed dollar amount toward payment for medical care. You will be charged the difference between the participating physicians' regular fee and the amount set in the Blue Shield fee schedule. If you select a nonparticipating physician, you are allowed a cash indemnity up to the amount set in the Blue Shield fee schedule, and you make your own financial arrangements with the physician. Blue Shield plans are either sponsored directly by a medical society or are officially approved by it. Blue Shield surgical-medical coverage is usually added to a Blue Cross hospitalization enrollment. Like Blue Cross plans, Blue Shield plans provide for transfer from plan to plan without a waiting period. Each Blue Shield plan designs its own local program.

Blue Shield generally offers two kinds of coverage: (a) surgical-medical and (b) general medical. No new surgical only contracts are being written—although the old ones still exist. The surgical-medical coverage includes allowances toward the doctor's fees for surgery performed in the hospital, or in the doctor's office, or in your home, and maternity allowances under family enrollment *plus* medical care in the hospital when no surgery is involved. The general medical care coverage provides all of the benefits given in the surgical-medical plan *plus* home and office medical care and specialists' consultation. Supplemental major medical is also offered in a majority of the plans.

The Million Dollar Master Medical plan has $1 million coverage for hospital, doctor, and major medical for each member. There are minimal claim forms, as each member's personal file is computerized. This maximum coverage is sold to groups as small as three, so that even a family or a small group of friends can have the advantage of group coverage.

What You Pay The cost of Blue Shield coverage varies with the scope of the covered services, local medical economics, and local patterns of utilization. As an indication of the range involved, quarterly rates for most widely held group service benefit medical-surgical programs ranged from $25 for individual coverage to $77 for family coverage. You will want to check your local organization to determine the current rates in your area.

In tune with the times, Blue Shield is trying to cut costs by refusing to pay doctors for 28 procedures deemed obsolete or ineffective unless the doctors justify the need for their use in writing. Blue Shield has also established a network of qualified HMOs under joint Blue Cross–Blue Shield sponsorship, and offers programs for a second opinion in surgery. It has joined the chorus of voices that has been advocating preventive medicine and reminding the individual of a personal responsibility for good health.

Major Medical Expense Coverage

Major medical expense coverage is designed to help meet the catastrophic costs resulting from very

"Doctor, that medication you prescribed for my husband did have a side effect. He fainted when I told him what it cost."

Reprinted by permission *The Wall Street Journal*

serious illnesses and from prolonged disability. Broadly speaking, the financial benefits under this form of coverage are paid toward virtually all kinds of health care prescribed by a physician. Major medical has had a very rapid growth.

For those who may be hospitalized for long periods, or those who require extensive treatment by medical specialists, major medical is a form of protection against large medical bills not covered by the usual types of hospital and surgical plans. As one authority put it: "Major medical takes up where the basic health plans stop." Major medical expense insurance ordinarily pays benefits whether hospitalization is involved or not. Major medical policies, furthermore, insure against expense arising from almost any conceivable medical cause, not just such rarities as polio, spinal meningitis, or a selected list of diseases. A few major medical policies exclude mental illness, but most group insurance doesn't.

There are three distinguishing features of major medical insurance: (1) There are high maximum limits—to $100,000 or more. The maximum may apply to any one illness, to a policy year, or to a lifetime. (2) A deductible provision, similar to that found in most automobile collision policies, is used. This is to eliminate what would otherwise be an undue burden of many small claims, costly to handle and process. The deductible is the beginning amount of medical expense which the policyholder himself must pay before insurance coverage takes effect. The deductible amounts commonly range from $100 to $1,000, with $250 or $500 the most usual. The higher the deductible, the lower the premium. (3) There is a "coinsurance" clause. This requires the policyholder to pay part of the total bill over and above the deductible. The purpose is to prevent demands for excessive medical service. How does the deductible apply? Per person? Per family? Per time? Are there exceptions in the expenses that apply to the deductible?

What does major medical cost? Most major medical policies are sold under group plans. Don Thomas, an accountant with General Sales, purchased a major medical policy through his company. It had a $30,000 maximum benefit, a $250 deductible clause, and a 20 percent coinsurance provision. It cost $150 per annum. If he had had an individual policy, the premium would have been $310 a year.

Let's see how major medical works. Don Thomas developed a severe case of hepatitis which necessitated an extended period of hospitalization followed by a convalescence at home. He is covered by a basic plan and by major medical insurance. His expenses are shown in Table 8–1.

As you can see, he paid only $860 of a total bill of $6,375; major medical paid $2,440 and the base plan paid the difference. Usually, major medical pays the larger amount, but in this illness, where the hospital stay was unusually long, it was the base plan that covered the greater cost.

Comprehensive Medical Insurance

Now popular is the combination type of health insurance that ties together the basic plans of hospi-talization, surgical expense, and regular medical expense protection with major medical insurance into one big package policy called "comprehensive."

The Federal Employees Health Program, offered by a consortium of health insurance organizations, is one of the largest group comprehensive major medical plans in force. Table 8–2 illustrates the benefits, exceptions, and costs that the many different groups offer in their comprehensive major medical plans. The program consists of a high and a low option, with about three fourths of the perons included selecting the high option. The high option described here has a $50,000 maximum a year for each enrollee and each member of his family, with exhausted benefits automatically restored in the amount of $2,000 per person a year until the top limit is again reached. If family expenses exceed $10,000 in any given year, they are paid in full.

Prepaid medical plans and health maintenance organizations (HMOs) usually provide comprehensive medical care. See page 241 for detail.

TABLE 8–1
How Insurance Covered a Hospital Stay

	Total Charges	Covered by Base Plan*	Covered by Major Medical
Hospital room and board 25 days @ $100 per day	$2,500	$1,875	$ 625
Other hospital charges X rays, blood tests, medicines, etc.	1,350	550	800
Registered nurses $55 per day for 15 days	825		825
Physicians' fees	1,700	650	1,050
Totals	$6,375	$3,075	$3,300
Less: Deductible of $250			−250
Balance subject to coinsurance			3,050
Less: Coinsurance at 20 percent			−610
Amount paid by major medical			$2,440

Summary	
Paid by base plan*	$3,075
Paid by major medical	2,440
Paid by patient	860
Total	$6,375

* Hospital room and board and general medical expense.
Source: Health Insurance Institute.

TABLE 8-2

FEDERAL EMPLOYEES HEALTH BENEFITS PROGRAM

Monthly Individual and Family Premiums and Examples of Extra Charges and Limitations
on Selected Benefits for Federal Enrollees of the Forty-Eight Comprehensive
Group Practice Plan Carriers and the Two Government-Wide Plans; January 1, 1978

Plan	Monthly Individual	Premiums[1] Family[2]	Extra Charges		Physicians' Care		
			Hospitalization	Maternity	Office or Clinic Visits	Home Calls	Prescription Drugs[5]
ABC-HMO Phoenix, Arizona	$36.70	$97.67	No limit	$2 per visit	$2 per visit	......	$2 each prescription
Anchor HMO Chicago, Illinois	$39.80	$115.38	No limit	......	......	......	no coverage
Arizona Health Plan Phoenix, Arizona	$36.53	$108.03	No limit	$2 per visit	$2 per visit	$4 per call	covered only in hospital or out-of-area emergencies
Capital Area Community Health Plan Latham, New York	$31.42	$84.63	No limit	......	......	$10 per call	......
Central Medical Health Services Pittsburgh, Pennsylvania	$36.70	$89.96	No limit	......	......	......	......
Columbia Medical Plan Columbia, Maryland	$40.97	$127.79	No limit	$2 per visit	$2 per visit	$5 per call	$2 each prescription
Compcare Milwaukee, Wisconsin	$49.94	$125.02	No limit	......	......	......	no coverage
Community Health Care Center Plan New Haven, Connecticut	$42.32	$118.11	No limit	......	......	......	40% of prescription cost
Community Health Plan of Greater New York	$50.48	$114.83	No limit	......	......	......	$2 maximum each prescription
Family Health Program, Inc. Long Beach, California	$39.39	$115.66	$300,000 per confinement	......	......	......	$1.50 each prescription
General Medical Centers Health Plan Pomona, California	$43.70	$111.30	No limit	$2 for initial visit; $2 for specialty referral	$2 per visit; $2 for specialty referral	$2 per call	$2 each prescription
Genesee Valley Group Health Association, Rochester, New York	$35.08	$90.13	No limit	......	......	$5 per call	$2 each prescription at a participating pharmacy; 75% after a $2 copayment at a non-participating pharmacy
Georgetown University Community Health Plan, Washington, D.C.	$47.54	$119.90	No limit	......	......	......	$1 each prescription or refill
George Washington University Health Plan, Washington, D.C.	$49.83	$120.03	No limit	......	......	......	$1 each prescription
*Group Health Association, Inc. Washington, D.C.	$48.32	$122.16	No limit	......	......	......	20% after first $50 each enrollee
Group Health Association of Northeastern Minnesota Virginia, Minnesota	$41.58	$98.06	365 days per confinement	......	......	......	$1 each prescription at a participating pharmacy; $2 each prescription at a non-participating pharmacy
Group Health Cooperative of Puget Sound Seattle, Washington	$38.52	$96.72	No limit	......	......	......	......

TABLE 8–2 (*continued*)

Plan	Monthly Individual	Premiums[1] Family[2]	Extra Charges			Physicians' Care		
			Hospitalization	Maternity	Office or Clinic Visits	Home Calls	Prescription Drugs[5]
Group Health Plan, Inc. St. Paul, Minnesota	$35.30	$99.52	365 days per confinement	......	......	$3 day; $5 night	$2 each prescription
Harvard Community Health Plan Boston, Massachusetts	$41.95	$108.75	No limit	$1 day; $3 night	$1 day; $3 night	$5 per call	no coverage
Health Alliance Health Plan San Jose, California	$33.63	$94.55	No limit	......	$2 per visit	$5 per call	$2 each prescription
Health Care of Louisville, Inc. Louisville, Kentucky	$38.13	$108.68	No limit	......	......	$15 per call	$1.50 each prescription
Health Insurance Plan of Greater New York (HIP)-Blue Cross[3]	$25.03	$80.88	365 days per confinement	......	......	$2 night	no charge from designated pharmacy; 20% in excess of $25 if obtained elsewhere
Health Maintenance Plan Cincinnati, Ohio	$44.46	$121.29	No limit	......	......	$10 per call	$2 maximum each prescription
Health Service Plan of Pennsylvania Philadelphia, Pennsylvania	$34.60	$83.31	No limit	......	......	......	no coverage
Hunter Foundation for Health Care, Inc. Louisville, Kentucky	$40.45	$95.83	No limit	......	......	......	...... if prescribed by a plan physician and obtained at the plan pharmacy or a plan-approved pharmacy
Kaiser Community Health Foundation, Ohio Region	$39.76	$108.42	No limit	......	$1 per visit	$5 first 2 calls each illness	$1 not in excess of smallest therapeutic package or 34-day supply, whichever is greater
Kaiser Foundation Health Plan Northern California Region	$33.71	$86.15	No limit	......	$1 per visit	$3.50 per day; $5 night	$1 for each prescription of specified quantities
Kaiser Foundation Health Plan Southern California Region	$39.13	$101.03	No limit	......	Reasonable charge for injections	$5 per call	$1 for each prescription not to exceed 100-day supply
Kaiser Foundation Health Plan Colorado Region	$36.29	$96.63	No limit	$2 per visit	$2 per visit	no coverage	$1 for each prescription not to exceed 60-day supply
Kaiser Foundation Health Plan Hawaii Region	$31.20	$86.36	No limit	......	$1 per visit	$5 per call	$1 not in excess of smallest therapeutic package or 34-day supply, whichever is greater
Kaiser Foundation Health Plan Oregon Region	$33.61	$89.01	No limit	$1 per visit	$1 per visit	$2 per call	$1 not in excess of smallest therapeutic package or 30-day supply, whichever is greater
Maxi-Care Health Plan Los Angeles, California	$51.11	$134.40	No limit	......	......	$10 per call	$1 each prescription
Medical Care Group St. Louis, Missouri	$35.84	$107.08	365 days per confinement	......	......	......	$1 each prescription
Metro Health Plan Indianapolis, Indiana	$35.40	$95.27	No limit	......	......	......	$2 each prescription or refill
Metro Health Plan Detroit, Michigan	$55.88	$132.49	No limit	$3 per visit	$3 per visit	$4 day; $6 night; first call each illness	$2 (or retail price if less) each prescription per 5-week supply
Michael Reese Health Plan Chicago, Illinois	$46.35	$123.78	No limit	......	......	$15 per call	no coverage

TABLE 8–2 (*concluded*)

Plan	Monthly Individual	Premiums[1] Family[2]	Extra Charges			Physicians[1] Care	
			Hospitalization	Maternity	Office or Clinic Visits	Home Calls	Prescription Drugs[5]
NorthCare Evanston, Illinois	$42.27	$101.49	No limit	....	......	$10 per call	no coverage
Penn Group Health Plan Pittsburgh, Pennsylvania	$45.39	$101.88	No limit	......	......	......	...... when provided in hospital or at PGHP Center
Philadelphia Health Plan Philadelphia, Pennsylvania	$35.47	$97.37	No limit	......	......	......	no coverage
PimaCare Tucson, Arizona	$43.51	$104.89	365 days per calendar year	$2 per visit	$2 per visit	$5 per call	$2 each prescription not to exceed 30-day supply
Prime Health Kansas City, Missouri	$39.52	$96.89	No limit	......	......	......	$2 each prescription
Prucare Health Plan Houston, Texas	$35.86	$104.56	No limit	$2 per visit	$2 per visit	$15 per call	no coverage
Rhode Island Group Health Assn. Providence, Rhode Island	$46.43	$112.60	No limit	......	......	......	......
Ross-Loos HMO Los Angeles, California	$46.41	$108.27	No limit	......	......	no coverage	no coverage
Share St. Paul, Minnesota	$34.39	$98.11	365 days per confinement	......	......	$10 per call	$2.50 each prescription
Sound Health Association Tacoma, Washington	$46.61	$125.47	No limit	......	......	$5 per call	prescription drugs prescribed by a plan physician and obtained at a plan-approved pharmacy
Union Health Service Chicago, Illinois	$36.05	$106.38	365 days per confinement	......	......	$2 first call each illness	cost to plan plus $.50 dispensing fee
Westchester Community Health Plan, White Plains, New York	$31.09	$87.30	No limit	$2 per visit	$2 per visit	$5 per call	$2 each prescription
*Blue Cross-Blue Shield (Government-Wide Service)	$47.99	$111.69	365 days per confinement	......	First $100 of physician's bills beyond Basic Benefits + 20% thereafter[4]		Covered under Supplemental Benefits, subject to deductible and coinsurance
*Aetna (Government-Wide Indemnity)	$40.02	$87.56	Rm. & Bd.; first $2,000 plus 80% thereafter for other expenses; Hospital Outpatient and Surgical and Medical Expenses; 80% after first $75. After $10,000 of personal expense is incurred by a family in one calendar year, 100% of the remainder is paid.		First $75 of medical + 20% thereafter		Covered under Other Hospital and Surgical and Medical Expenses, subject to deductible and coinsurance

*"High Option" or "Premium" Benefits of these plans.

.......Full coverage provided.

1. Government pays $23.80 for individual coverage and $57.82 for family coverage except in four cases. Government contribution cannot exceed 75% of premium. Exceptions for individual coverage are Kaiser Foundation Health Plan, Hawaii Region ($23.40); Westchester CHP ($23.32); Capital Area CHP ($23.57); and HIP ($18.77).

2. Family is two or more.

3. HIP secures hospitalization through Blue Cross; other plans provide or self-insure for hospitalization.

4. Basic Benefits cover essentially all physician care in hospital, including intensive care and physician anesthetist, and specified non-hospital physician services without deductible or coinsurance.

5. If drugs are prescribed by a plan physician and obtained from the plan or plan-affiliated pharmacy with the exception of prescription coverage under Group Health Association, Inc., Blue Cross-Blue Shield, and Aetna where drugs may be obtained where so desired.

Compiled by GROUP HEALTH ASSOCIATION OF AMERICA, INC., 1717 Massachusetts Ave. N.W., Washington, D.C. 20036 (202) 483-4012

Dental Insurance

With emphasis on total health care today, one of the fast-growing areas of coverage is prepaid dental insurance. It is estimated that more than one fourth of all Americans have never been to a dentist or have not seen one for at least five years.

Dental coverage is provided primarily on a group basis, although a few policies are issued on a non-group basis. The principal suppliers are Blue Cross–Blue Shield associations, state dental societies, insurance companies, and local group dental practice plans.

A typical dental prepayment plan would pay 75 to 100 percent of the cost of treatment after a $25, $50, or $100 deductible. There is also a maximum amount payable of between $600 and $1,000. Covered expenses include diagnostic services, such as examinations, consultations, and X rays; preventive procedures, including cleaning, polishing, and the application of fluorides; oral surgery for extractions and surgery; restorative treatment with amalgam, porcelain, or plastic restorations, and gold restorations, crowns, and jackets; endodontic and periodontal procedures for the treatment of diseases of the teeth and gums; and prosthodontic procedures, which include the construction, placement, and repair of bridges and dentures. Orthodontic treatment that is done purely for appearance' sake is often not covered. The dental plans can be designed in various ways to pay for the above services after the necessary deductibles and coinsurance provisions have been met. There are scheduled plans that place dollar limits on the covered dental procedures, with the excess being paid by the patient.

Sometimes dental coverage is incorporated into comprehensive medical coverage or into other plans. When this is done, the dental bills may be either on a scheduled basis or on a reasonable and customary fee basis. If combined with major medical, the dental expenses are tied to the deductible in the major or comprehensive medical contract. The costs for dental coverage vary, but for a family the premium could range from $9 to $20 per month.

Other Special Health Insurance Coverages

Four other types of health coverages are available in addition to the more traditional ones discussed previously. They are prescription drug coverage, eye care insurance, special nursing home care, and rehabilitation coverage. Many of these plans are tied to the other, more common forms of health insurance where there are specific exclusions for these items. Prescription drug coverage may include all drugs ordered by a doctor on an outpatient basis. Eye care coverage would include examinations, treatments, and the cost of eyeglasses. Nursing home insurance benefits would be paid when an individual is not a patient in a regular hospital but receives nursing care in an extended care facility. Rehabilitation coverage is often made a part of disability income plans. Here payments are made to help restore the disabled worker to a productive life following a serious accident or illness.

Mail-Order Health Insurance

Practitioners of the big promise and little return may be found among the mail-order insurance companies. Small by comparison with the giants of the health insurance industry, is the mail-order share, but its growth in new business is leaping. Promises of $1,000 a month cash free when you go to the hospital sound great, until you realize that most hospital stays average five days and that the benefits usually start after the sixth day. Also, although everyone is accepted without an examination, the insurance company doesn't pay claims if they result from ailments that you had two years before the claim. It's the insurance company that decides whether you had the ailment when the policy was issued—even if you didn't know about it. Some ads promise $50,000 hospital payments, giving hope of coverage in a catastrophic illness. Usually a patient with a long-term illness is shifted to a nursing home, rarely staying in the hospital long enough to benefit from such a claim, and nursing homes are not covered.

Although state regulatory agencies, the Senate

Antitrust and Monopoly Subcommittee, and the Federal Trade Commission are continuing to expose the deceptive language and statistics, the small print exclusions, and to control the misleading or deceptive advertising, it is really your own obligation to read the offers carefully to see if the supplementary coverage fits your needs and covers probable possibilities. A famous person's endorsement does not prove that you will be getting your money's worth.

Types of Organizations Which Provide Voluntary Medical Care Insurance Protection

At present, medical care insurance is provided by three large groups of organizations: (a) the nonprofit Blue Cross and Blue Shield plans; (b) the casualty, life, and other commercial insurance companies; (c) a number of organizations independent of the first two groups, including industrial and labor union plans, consumer cooperatives, private medical groups, some medical societies, and community organizations. Blue Cross is concerned primarily with hospital insurance; Blue Shield, with surgical, limited, and general medical service insurance; the independent organizations provide hospital, surgical, or comprehensive medical care. None of the Blue Shield plans provide for the group practice of medicine, although many of the independent plans do.

Prepaid Medical Plans

Although they cover only about 5 percent of all persons in private health insurance organizations, nonaffiliated health insurance plans that provide health care benefits on a prepayment or insurance basis make a significant contribution to the health insurance field. The plans consist of community group or individual practice plans, employer-employee union plans, private medical group clinic plans, and private dental group or dental service plans. Some of the plans contract with hospitals; some own their own hospitals. Each membership

has been able to obtain the type of plan which meets its own needs, generally providing comprehensive medical care in the home, the doctor's office, the group clinic, or the hospital, as required.

The community health plans are usually group practice plans, under which full health benefits are usually provided. Of these the largest is the Kaiser Permanente Medical Care Program, with its 2.5 million members. It operates in California, Oregon, Hawaii, Colorado, and Ohio, and it includes 2,100 doctors in nearly every specialty. Exact coverage varies by region and contract. For example, in northern California $86.15 a month covers a family for surgery and hospital care, but each visit to a doctor costs $1; maternity benefits are an extra $60; home calls are $3.50 during the day, $5 at night; and drugs are low cost. There are no personal doctors, and whatever can be routinized is; dental care is excluded, as is psychiatric care or hospital treatment for alcoholism or drug abuse.

Nonetheless, the National Advisory Commission Report on Health Manpower found that the quality of the plan's medical services was "equivalent, if not superior to, that available in most communities." In addition, the average member's medical care cost was "20 to 30 percent less than it would be if he obtained it outside." The plan's cost control is "due almost entirely to the elimination of unnecessary health care, particularly hospitalization." While the general population averaged 137.9 hospital admissions a year per 1,000, Kaiser cut its admissions to only 80 per 1,000. Kaiser's patients stayed only 6.65 days, compared to a national average of 7.8 days, according to the commission.

Another reason for Kaiser's successful cost control is the year-end bonus given partner doctors (after three years on a straight salary), which is dependent on how successfully the group has been in living under its budget for the year.

The automated screening program to detect and thereby prevent illness which was started by the Kaiser group has become the model for the Health Insurance Plan of New York's computerized testing center, which will check for more than 50 possible medical ills and take a medical history in either English or Spanish before the patient sees a doctor.

The testing center is intended to make preventive medicine available to large numbers at low cost and with a limited use of medical manpower. Comprehensive medical care and preventive medicine seem to have a natural affinity, which is further enhanced by the possibility of cutting costs and improving medical care.

The community individual practice plans provide benefits with a choice of physician from a local panel. Although most of these plans are small, one of the largest is the Health Insurance Plan, which serves the metropolitan area of New York and has almost 800,000 subscribers. This plan offers benefits providing surgery, obstetric care, and in-hospital physician visits, as well as comprehensive physician services. Also available at an additional charge are dental care benefits.

Other Group Health Plans

In addition to the Kaiser Permanente plan, the 27-year-old Group Health Corporation of Puget Sound in Seattle, the 44-year-old Ross-Loos Medical Group in Los Angeles, the 30-year-old Health Insurance Plan of New York, the 40-year-old Group Health Association, Inc., of Washington, D.C., and the 30-year-old St. Louis Labor Health Institute are successful versions of the prepaid comprehensive health plans (see Table 8–2).

The employer-employee union plans operating under jointly managed welfare funds, employers, and employee benefit associations or unions, are somewhat different from the community plans in that more of the participants are covered for physicians' office care, dental care, drugs, appliances, and nursing home care, while fewer are covered for hospital care, surgery, or in-hospital visits. The two largest plans are those of the United Mine Workers of America and the National Association of Letter Carriers. Both of the plans offer services to about 1.0 million enrollees.

Although there are many private medical groups operating in the United States, mostly small, the largest is the Ross-Loos Medical Group in Los Angeles, California, with an enrollment of over 150,000. This is a prepayment plan with relatively compre-

hensive hospital and physicians services available to participants.

The majority of the independent groups are cooperative organizations whose members control their financial, economic, and general policies. However, in the medical sphere and in the relationship between the doctor and the patient, the professional medical staff has complete control. Most of the member plans provide direct service to covered individuals, while others offer cash indemnity payments. Some plans provide hospitalization to their members through Blue Cross; others have made their own arrangements with hospitals.

The Health Maintenance Organizations (HMOs)

Ever since the enactment of the 1973 law that required employers of more than 25 persons who offered health insurance plans to their employees to include a qualified HMO as an alternative, these one-stop health care centers have been increasing in number. There are about 200 of them now, but they still represent only a small percentage of the population and of the nation's health expenditures. They are subsidized by federal loans and grants until they have enough members to become self-supporting.

Advantages

1. One reason for their growth has been the difficulties a person has in finding and keeping a family physician, as well as resentment over the referrals from one specialist to another, as is so common today. At least in the HMO it's all under one roof.
2. A young family is entitled to unlimited pediatric care.
3. Employers find the premiums less costly, and because there is less hospitalization, there is also less absenteeism.
4. Those physicians who want to practice medicine without the headache of running a business and who desire more leisure time prefer being well salaried.

5. During one month each year, prepaid plans must accept any person who applies, regardless of medical history.

Disadvantages

1. Most HMO membership is through a corporation or a union group—membership is rarely individual.
2. In the interest of efficiency, doctor-patient relationships are often impersonal and short (which doesn't differ too much from the private doctor-patient relationship).
3. Usually you are limited to the doctors and hospitals in a plan. This is also true in many parts of the United States, especially rural areas.
4. Benefits for care outside the HMO area—on a trip, for example—are limited.
5. In an effort to be cost effective, an HMO may go to the extreme of limiting diagnostic tests, lab work, and other procedures that it may not favor.

In the beginning the fixed monthly fee for a family's entire health care seemed high, especially as most people, especially the young, were willing to gamble on not needing care. Now, according to HEW's Office of Health Maintenance Organizations, the average monthly premium in most HMOs has fallen below the cost of being insured just for hospitalization by Blue Cross, and though both HMO and Blue Cross premiums are rising, HMO premiums are rising much more slowly than those of Blue Cross, so that the gap between the two has widened, to the advantage of the HMO.[5]

The law permits enrollees to pay medicare premiums and deductibles directly to an HMO and to receive medicare services from the doctors and from hospitals operated by the HMO. Thirteen states permit medicaid recipients to join.

The goal is preventive medicine—providing comprehensive care from checkups to surgery.[6] Each plan operates from a fixed revenue pool ob-

---

[5] New York Times, May 21, 1978.
[6] For information on an HMO near you, write the Group Health Association of America, 1717 Massachusetts Ave, N.W., Washington, D.C. 20036, or the HMO Program, Room 7–39, Parklawn Bldg., 5600 Fishers Lane, Rockville, MD 20852.

"Do you have any 'I hope you're insured' get well cards?"

Reprinted by permission *The Wall Street Journal*

tained from monthly prepayments. Each doctor has an incentive to pare expenses because not only salaries but year-end bonuses are paid from the surplus that the organization earns. If the HMO shifts the emphasis of care to the doctor's office and reduces the use of hospitals, the patient benefits at less cost.

Commercial Insurance Company Plans

There are so many varieties, shapes, and sizes of policies that for the most part generalization is useless. Two policies with a face value of $10,000 which purport to pay this amount if you or some member of your family contracts one of a number of dread diseases may be as different as day and night. The list of diseases may differ. One list may contain many diseases that are no longer widespread in the United States. One policy may have a specific exclusion for travel abroad and may pay only if you contract the disease in the United States.

Commercial policies will pay all or nearly all hospital charges for a cancer patient's stay of more than 90 days. Government statistics show that fewer than 10 percent of cancer patients stay in the hospital for as long as 35 days. The benefits for stays of shorter than 90 days are skimpy. Some commercial policies cover doctors' bills only when the patient is in the hospital. One commercial policy may cover members of the family from the ages of 21 through 65 only. Another may cover children and older members as well. It is essential to read the policy you contemplate buying very carefully. Generally, the lower the cost, the greater are the policy's limitations, exclusions, and exceptions and therefore the less potentially useful it is.

The cost of any commercial health insurance policy depends upon the extent of benefits provided. You may pay $20 a year for very limited benefits or larger sums for contracts that offer much more. Those which pay many claims on small illnesses are expensive. Others which pay large benefits on types of claims which rarely occur cost the company less. You can buy a program which covers only the extremes of loss of limb or accidental death; and since these are rare occurrences, the cost is little, and the odds are small that you will ever use the policy. At the other end of the scale, you can, for a substantial premium, buy a comprehensive policy providing $100,000 or more in various medical benefits, guaranteed renewable for life. Today's trend is away from the guaranteed renewable. Although life time policies are no longer being issued, if you have such a policy, it will be honored.

Several of the large private insurance companies have taken direct roles in forming plans, and many others have been influential in support of new HMOs. Ten major insurance companies have joined with Massachusetts Blue Cross and Harvard Medical School and some of its teaching hospitals to provide comprehensive care through such plans as the Harvard Community Health Plan—a university-sponsored prepaid medical care plan for a metropolitan community.

Privacy of Medical Records

Most life insurance companies belong to the nonprofit trade association known as the Medical Information Bureau, which has a computerized centralized file of health data on insurance applicants which it keeps in coded form for seven years and makes available with certain safeguards to its members. In tune with these consumer-oriented times, all companies belonging to this clearing house must now notify applicants for insurance, in writing, that significant medical history or conditions may be provided to the Medical Information Bureau.

Upon receipt of a request from you, the bureau will arrange for the disclosure of any information it may have in your file. (Medical information will be disclosed only to your attending physician.) If you question the accuracy of information in the bureau's file, you may contact the bureau and seek a correction in accordance with the procedures set forth in the Federal Fair Credit Reporting Act.[7]

There is a National Commission on the Confidentiality of Health Records[8] which has expressed alarm over the ease with which seemingly confidential records can be obtained and sold under false pretenses. A study sponsored by the National Bureau of Standards[9] found that the observance of strict confidentiality of medical records had been lessened by the need for health data in making social decisions and by the desire of insurance companies for this valuable information.

Health Insurance for Older People

Naturally this section does not now relate to you, and so it will be brief. Perhaps, however, through your awareness and knowledge of available services you may be of help to an older member of your family. Since your taxes will be paying the bill and the issues of costs and the extension of benefits have become controversial, you may

---

[7] The address of the bureau's Information Office is P.O. Box 105, Essex Station, Boston, MA 02112; the bureau's telephone number is (617) 426-3660.

[8] Suite 1205, 1701 K St., N.W. Washington, D.C. 20006.

[9] Prepared by Professor Alan F. Westin of Columbia University, the 381-page National Bureau of Standards Monograph 157, entitled *Computers, Health Records, and Citizen Rights,* can be purchased for $4.55 from the Superintendent of Documents, U.S. Government Printing Office, Washington, D.C. 20402.

be interested in knowing something about health insurance for older people.

With the advent of medicare, health insurance for those 65 and over changed drastically. Many older persons had been without funds to provide adequate health services for themselves, and traditionally had found health insurance difficult to buy and, if available, very costly. When policies they already held lapsed, the policies were frequently not renewable. Prior to the passage of medicare, suppliers of health insurance provided some private health coverage for the aged. Blue Cross, Blue Shield, and commercial insurance companies extended coverage to provide nongroup policies for persons over 65 years of age, including a limited right to conversion when an employee retired. Group-type health plans were also offered through a mass enrollment program for a specified period on a state, regional, or nationwide basis. However, when the government-sponsored medicare became effective, many private plans could not compete, and as a result private coverage showed a substantial decline.

Financing the Medicare Program

Part A, the basic hospital insurance, is paid for by payroll deductions from employees and their employers and by self-employed persons. Both the employee and the employer pay the same rate.

The rate as of 1980 is 1.05 percent of the first $25,900 earnings in a year. The contribution for hospital insurance (medicare, Part A) is included in the 6.13 percent social security rate paid by both the employer and the employee. These rates are subject to change—usually upward—as the social security law is frequently amended.

For the self-employed the social security rate is 8.10 percent of the earnings base, of which 1.05 percent is for medicare.

Medicare Benefits

Medicare, an important addition to the Social Security Act, became law on July 30, 1965, took effect one year later, and was subsequently amended. If you receive social security payments

you are entitled to Part A, hospital insurance, but you must pay extra for Part B, medical insurance.

You should apply for social security about three months before you turn 65 in order to receive medicare without delay. When your social security comes through, you are automatically enrolled in medicare—Parts A and B. If you do not want Part B you tell social security; otherwise they will deduct the premium from your social security checks. Even if you plan to continue working, you must apply or you won't get medicare.

Disabled persons who have been receiving disability benefits for 24 consecutive months are eligible. People under 65 or their dependents who need kidney transplants or dialysis for kidney treatment are eligible for medicare if they worked as little as 1½ years. Those not eligible when reaching 65 will need a certain number of quarters of social security coverage to get hospital insurance.

There is no charge for hospital insurance for those now 65 or older. Medicare provides two different kinds of health coverage for people 65 and older.[10]

Part A—*Hospital Insurance* (Basic Plan)—will pay most of the cost of services in a hospital or extended care facility or as a home care patient receiving services from a participating home health agency. Included are the cost of rooms, meals, regular nursing services, and the inpatient cost of drugs, supplies, and other necessary equipment.

Part B—*Medical Insurance* (Supplementary Plan)—will help pay for part of the cost of doctors' services as well as certain medical costs and services not covered by a the basic plan.

Hospital Insurance Program— Medicare Part A

The law requires an annual review of hospital costs under medicare and an adjustment of that

---

[10] For information on medicare, see U.S Department of Health, Education, and Welfare, Social Security Administration, *Your Medicare Handbook,* SSA 10050, issued annually; *A Brief Explanation of Medicare,* SSA 10043; *Basic Facts about Medicare,* SSA 10014; and *How Medicare Helps during a Hospital Stay,* SSA 10039.

portion of the bills for which the medicare beneficiary is responsible, according to a set formula. Therefore, all coverage is subject to yearly changes.

Currently, the hospital insurance program, Part A of medicare, will pay the cost of covered services for the following hospital and posthospital care:

1. Up to 90 days in any participating general care, tuberculosis, or psychiatric hospital in each benefit period, with all covered costs paid for the first 60 days except for the first $160. For the next 30 days, all covered costs above $40 per day are met. A "benefit period" starts on the first day you enter as a patient. It ends after you have been out of a hospital or an extended care facility for 60 consecutive days.

2. If more benefit days are needed, the lifetime limit of an additional 60 days can be used, but any additional days used reduce this lifetime limit. The program pays for all covered expenses for these additional days beyond $80 a day. It should be noted that treatment in a mental hospital has a lifetime limit of 190 days. Outpatient services for diagnosis such as X rays, blood tests, and other tests within a 20-day period are paid 80 percent by hospital insurance after you pay the first $60 deductible.

3. Up to 20 days of semiprivate accommodations in an extended care facility (defined as a qualified facility furnishing skilled nursing care and related services) are completely covered. Also covered are an additional 80 days in an extended care facility for each benefit period, if needed after a hospital stay of at least three days. For such additional days you pay $20 per day, with medicare covering the costs above this amount.

4. This program also covers 100 home health visits and may be used for this purpose for as long as one year after your most recent discharge from a hospital or from an extended care facility where you received covered services.

5. Some services are not covered. No payment will be made under hospital insurance for the services of a physician, but those services are covered under Part B, medicare insurance. Payment will not be made for private nurses, cost of the first three pints of blood, or for items furnished for the patient's convenience, such as telephone, television, and personal services.

Medical Insurance Coverage— Medicare Part B

Part B, medical insurance (supplementary plan), will help pay for part of the cost of doctors' services as well as certain medical costs and services not covered by the basic plan.

For medical insurance, however, there is a charge of $8.70, which is deducted from social security benefit checks each month. This charge has been increased every July, subject to the announcement made the previous December. Persons not on social security must pay the premium to the Social Security Administration every three months, in advance. If the insured does not like the program or the increase in the premium rate, there is the opportunity to drop out of the program. Even if one does drop out, there is a chance to get back in, but only one chance. Those eligible are permitted to sign up again in one of the "general enrollment periods" between January 1 and March 31 within three years after they cancel their medical insurance. Then they will pay a premium that is 10 percent higher for each full year that enrollment was possible, if they later want it.

The medical insurance program will help pay for the following:

1. Physicians' and surgeons' services in a hospital, doctor's office, home, or elsewhere, including the services of medical doctors and osteopaths, and podiatrists and certain services of dentists involving surgery or the setting of fractures of the jaw.

2. Up to 100 home health visits under an approved plan by a health home agency each year with no need for prior hospitalization. This is in addition to the 100 visits provided under the hospital insurance program. If home health services by a physical therapist, a home health aide, or other health workers are ordered by a doctor and are furnished by a home health agency that take part

in medicare, they can be provided. A visit is counted each time a health care worker calls. If both a visiting nurse and physical therapist come at the same time, this is counted as two visits.

3. Diagnostic services, X-ray or other radiation treatments, surgical dressings and splints, casts and the rental or purchase of medical equipment, such as wheelchairs, hospital beds, oxygen equipment, and crutches, when the doctor prescribes these.

4. Medical supplies furnished by a doctor in his office, the services of the office nurse, and the cost of administering drugs, if these are part of the services. Outpatient physical therapy services performed in a participating facility and certain ambulance services are all covered.

5. Physicians' charges for clinical laboratory, X-ray, and radiological services when you are in a hospital.

Medical insurance does *not* pay for the full cost of these services. The insured patient pays the first $60 in each calendar year for these services and then pays 20 percent of the remaining costs. Medical insurance pays 80 percent of the reasonable charges for additional services, beyond the $60 deductible. For example, if covered medical bills were $500 in a given year, the medical insurance program would pay $352; the patient would pay $148, the first $60 plus 20 percent of the remaining $440. It is important to note that there is only *one* $60 deductible each year and not a separate deductible for each kind of service. Doctors treating medicare patients can also accept assignment and receive the prevailing fee directly from medicare. They may also refuse assignment and charge what they wish. Medicare pays 80 percent of *reasonable* charges—which may not be the doctor's idea of reasonable. You pay the remainder. If Senior Care or one of the other "Blue" medigap supplemental insurances pays the 20 percent difference—it means 20 percent of medicare's "reasonable," not necessarily the doctor's "reasonable."

The medical insurance program does not cover such services as the cost of routine physical checkups, drug prescriptions and patient medicines, eyeglasses, hearing aids, ordinary dental treatment, orthopedic shoes, personal comfort items, and the first three pints of blood.

Supplementary Policies

A number of separate private policies offered to the aged build on medicare and seek to fill in the gaps and add to the coverage of government plan.

Medicare covers less of medical costs each year. Today over 52 percent of medicare cardholders buy increasing amounts of private insurance to fill the medigap.

A Federal Trade Commission staff report described medicare coverage as paying for only 38 percent of the health care costs of the elderly but pointed out that one out of four purchasers of so-called medigap insurance have bought unnecessary, expensive duplication of coverage.[11] Representative Claude Pepper who heads the House Select Committee on Aging said, "We have found that many unscrupulous insurance agents have been preying on the fears of the elderly and selling them three, four, five, and sometimes as many as thirty different health insurance policies, although they generally contain a clause saying that only one policy will pay." He cited, as an extreme example, "the case of a 76 year-old Illinois woman who has 42 policies in effect and whose premiums cost her $15,000 a year." This is because there is no standardization of private insurance policies and because there is a lack of consumer information in the medicare supplemental market, so that buyers cannot comparison-shop.

The report notes, "Even if they could compare policies, the present supplemental policies often do not compete on price and return only a small percentage of premiums to policyholders in the form of benefits." The authors of the report suggest a joint project by HEW and the National Association of Insurance Commissioners to evaluate the effectiveness of existing state regulation of medicare supplemental insurance.

Senior Care

Senior Care, developed by Blue Shield and Blue Cross, is one of the more widely used supplemental

---

[11] Report delivered before the U.S. Senate Special Committee on Aging, Washington, D.C., August 18, 1978.

policies. It pays a large part of the first deductible under hospital insurance and a large part of the deductible in the charges from the 61st through the 90th day and provides full coverage for semiprivate room, board, and services from the 91st day through the 120th day in any Blue Cross hospital. It pays part of the per diem cost not carried by medicare in an extended care facility, and the 20 percent balance not covered by medicare for surgical-medical services. It pays slightly less in non-Blue Cross hospitals. Senior Care benefits are automatically paid after your medicare benefit, so that there is no need to submit a separate claim. Senior Care premiums have been rising to cover the higher cost of deductibles.

Two private insurance policies that extend medicare coverage to 365 days are the Aetna Life Senior Major Medical Expense policy and Guardian Life's Guardian 65 Health Insurance policy. Since the average hospital stay for a medicare patient is 11½ days, which is usually more than covered by medicare's 60-day period, these policies are mainly useful, for catastrophic illnesses. The premiums are high and rising, and there is a reluctance to sell new policies to everyone, regardless of medical history.

In addition to covering copayments, as does Senior Care, these commercial policies also provide somewhat for the two important areas of nursing and drugs, which are not covered by Senior Care.

Nursing Homes

Faced with the problem of a sick, elderly parent, you will not find a happy solution in a nursing home. Highly expensive, physically condemned by almost every investigation, relatively scarce, overcrowded, cheerless, and with underpaid, inefficient staffs, a large number of the homes cannot be used for medicare patients, since they do not meet the standards set.

Today there are over 16,000 nursing homes in the United States, of which 73 percent are operated for profit and 27 percent nonprofit. They provide care for over 1 million residents, or around 5.2 percent of the U.S. population aged 65 or over. The homes can be divided into the following categories: those certified as extended care facilities by medicare and those certified as skilled nursing homes or intermediate care facilities by medicaid.

An experimental substitute for nursing homes has been attempted by a federally funded program under the guidance of Johns Hopkins Hospital in Baltimore and Massachusetts General Hospital in Boston. Volunteers willing to take older persons into their homes will receive compensation and will learn basic nursing skills in classes taught by a physician, nurse, physical therapist, nutritionist, and social worker. According to a study by the National Center for Health Services, at least one in every four nursing home residents doesn't really need to be institutionalized.

Medicaid

In addition to medicare, there was also enacted into law in 1965 Title XIX of the Social Security Act, which established a federal-state medical public assistance program called medicaid. Each state, at its option, makes payments to providers of medical services for those receiving cash maintenance payments from the state (public aid) and for others who are medically indigent and need help in meeting medical expenses. The individual states control the expenditures under medicaid, and the federal government will pay up to 50 percent of the cost in high-income states and up to 83 percent of the cost in low-income states. For the state to qualify

"Now this is an interesting case."
Reprinted by permission *The Wall Street Journal*

for federal reimbursement, it must provide hospital care, outpatient care, doctors' services, nursing home care, and laboratory and X-ray services.

Preventive Medicine

The University of California School of Public Health checked hospital and medical records to see whether patients in two established HMOs in Southern California received more preventive services than other health care systems. On a preventive service index that the school constructed—zero (means no service) to 1.0 (maximum provision),—the records showed that commercial insurance subscribers had 0.384, Blue Cross–Blue Shield members 0.404, and HMO patients 0.452.

Another study found that 58 percent of the men and 63 percent of the women enrolled in a Kaiser-Permanente plan had physical examinations in a year, compared to 43–46 percent of the men and 49–57 percent of the women who had conventional insurance policies. Taken together these two studies would indicate a greater interest in preventive medicine in the HMOs.

The Business-Union Interest in Preventive Medicine

Speaking before senior executives from 322 of the 800 largest U.S. corporations and 200 labor leaders, the Secretary of Health, Education, and Welfare estimated that big business could have saved up to $150 million last year if just 5 percent of the employees of Fortune's 500 companies had belonged to HMOs.[12]

Business corporations whose health premiums for employees have doubled in the last few years are interested in preventive medicine.

From supervised exercise facilities and jogging on company time, to bonuses for employees with below-average medical expense, to financing tough hospital admission programs, to the soliciting of second surgical opinions, to community involvement for the control of unneeded hospital building

expansion, American corporations are involved in preventive medicine. An increasing number of corporations have shown great interest in employee participation in HMOs—because of the cost savings that HMOs effect.

There is also tremendous labor union interest in HMOs because when companies' medical costs rise, less money is available for wage increases. There are increases in the premiums that union members must now contribute, in contrast to the time when the employer paid for it all.

An 18-month FTC study[13] found that Blue Cross maintains its lowest bed utilization rates in the state in which HMOs have the greatest share of the market—California. The study also noted that doctors or hospitals organized similar groups of their own where HMOs had made a community aware of costs. There was a similar "spillover effect" on traditional health care insurance, in that benefit coverage and peer review of hospital care was broadened.

Professional Standards Review Organizations (PSROs)

The quality of the medical care given to patients whose costs are paid in whole or in part by taxpayer money is reviewed by 182 local doctors' groups under a national program. This program, with its two-pronged goal for medical care of the highest quality and lowest cost, is highly controversial. Peer review is not new. Several large comprehensive medical prepayment plans have used it for a long time to monitor costs and complaints. Hospital bed utilization review has been a practice for some time. Now there is the first national mandated program to function in hospitals and HMOs, and naturally personalities and policies have problems in conforming.

Medicare and medicaid now refuse to pay for hospital care unless the PSRO certifies that it is acceptable. More than 20 Blue Cross plans use a

---

[12] *Wall Street Journal,* May 10, 1978.

[13] *The Health Maintenance Agency and Its Effects on the Corporation,* August 1977. Copy free from the Bureau of Economics, Federal Trade Commission, Washington, D.C. 20580.

similar system to keep costs down. Peer review has been used increasingly because it is a control procedure that medical specialists will accept—if unhappily. Under congressionally mandated peer review, the American College of Surgeons has developed guidelines for 20 surgical procedures, which describe how an operation should be done.

HEW conducted a study of 8 million federal employees who had a choice between an available HMO and conventional health insurance to determine the number of days that each group of 1,000 persons spent in the hospital per year. Those who had Blue Cross–Blue Shield coverage averaged 924 days; those employees with other insurance, 987 days; those who were HMO members, 422 days. Federal employees in the "Blue" plans underwent twice as much surgery of all types as did federal employees in HMOs—including three times as many tonsillectomies and twice as many gynecological operations.[14]

"To doctors, prevention is intellectually dull, emotionally unrewarding, and financially unremunerative," according to Dr. John H. Knowles, president of the Rockefeller Foundation. "Both private and government insurers pay doctors and hospitals for diagnosis and treatment but not for prevention."[15]

Despite themselves, however, doctors have become preventive medicine–minded—if only to halt the skyrocketing costs. One major effort that they support is the "second-opinion program."

Do You Need This Operation?

The overall rate of surgery in the United States jumped by 23 percent between 1970 and 1975. Under insurance programs in which the surgeon was paid for each operation, twice as many operations were performed as under the prepaid plans. Under second-opinion programs, the insurer will pay a second doctor to check whether a patient really needs an elective (nonemergency) operation. Some states have mandated that insurance companies provide this opportunity at no expense to the patient, but it is the patient's decision whether or not he wants a second opinion. In New York a medicaid patient must have a second opinion for elective surgery.

A Cornell University Medical College study found that 11 percent of the subjects in their study who had been told by a physician to have an operation might not need the surgery after all. These results projected nationally meant that perhaps more than 2 million operations performed each year were unnecessary. Naturally insurance companies favor programs that will cut surgical payments.

Preventive medicine can save money, and there is also preventive medicine as a way of life.

A Working Model

The Midpeninsula Health Service[16] (California) is similar to an HMO because of its emphasis on preventive medicine and its comprehensive medical care program, but it does not qualify as an HMO since it charges a fee for service and is not prepaid.

It offers a home care service with interrelated physicians' coverage, house calls, skilled nursing care, a referral service to community and social resources, health education for the patient and the patient's family, volunteer help, and many other valuable support services on a fee-for-service basis.

Since it is a nonprofit organization owned by its members, its services are likely to be coordinated and used. Its emphasis on self-care, the use of members as nonphysician health personnel, and emphasis on telephone reassurance and information makes its program viable and weakens dependence on insurance to cover costs. Young and idealistic, with tax-exempt status, operating in a

[14] "Health Maintenance Organizations: Are HMOs the Answer to Your Medical Needs?" *Consumer Reports,* October 1974, Consumers Union, Mount Vernon, N.Y.

[15] Jane E. Brady, "The Rising Cost of Health," *New York Times,* May 30, 1978.

[16] Louis E. Crown, ACSW, and Jeanne Ewy, MPH, "The MHS Approach to a Solution," Midpeninsula Health Service, July 20, 1977, Palo Alto, CA 94301.

community setting, and stressing both cost cutting and joint individual-professional participation in health care, the Service is a small-scale challenge to traditional medicine.

Home Health Care

Many studies document the considerable savings home care has over hospital care. Cashwise, the insurance companies or the government benefits, but unless your insurance policy covers home care (and few do), you pay more if you use it. Half of the Blue Cross plans pay for home visits (usually 90), but most require hospitalization first. Very few commercial insurers include home care in their policies, although these policies may include nursing. Part A of medicare pays for 100 home visits, but only after hospitalization and only if the patient has skilled nursing care or speech therapy under a doctor's direction.

If you have no hospital insurance, then home care is cheaper. There are around 5,000 agencies that send health workers of varying abilities and skills to homes. Most of these are nonprofit home health agencies or nursing registries.[17] There are a few proprietary chains. The largest is Homemakers Upjohn—a subsidiary of the drug company— which has 220 offices in most states. The proprietary firms are not yet eligible for reimbursement under medicare and medicaid. There are no national standards for home care and no regulations to ensure quality home care.

Home care has advantages beyond the money it saves. People are happier among familiar possessions. Home food may be more to their liking. The family is around in normal fashion—not regulated by visiting hours. At home there may be a greater sense of well-being—a psychological advantage, some doctors say, in learning to take responsibility for self-care. Wounds seem to heal faster; fewer sleeping pills are needed; and patients move around more.

Self-Care

Strange as it may seem, self-care—learning to by your own doctor—has become a facet of preventive medicine. Habit control is basic to your day-to-day life style. A lengthy study of 7,000 adults in Alameda County, California found that those practicing one or more of seven good health habits increased their life expectancy by many years. These seven habits are not smoking, moderate drinking, seven–eight hours of sleep a night, regular meals, a daily breakfast, keeping normal weight, and exercising.

Self-care believers informed through radio, TV, more than 600 recently published books, and courses taught by doctors are practicing varying degrees of medical care, which they believe holds promise of increased disease prevention.[18]

Drugs

If you purchase a medication by its generic name, you can save perhaps 50 percent or more. The doctor has to write the prescription using the generic name before you can benefit and save money, unless you live in a state whose laws allow the druggist at either his discretion or yours to fill the prescription generically—if the doctor has not specified otherwise. The doctor can add "a generic equivalent" on the prescription—if he feels that it does not matter medically and if he wants to save you money. Most people don't know a medicine by its generic name and don't know what to ask for, in order to save money. Advertising has popularized the brand name. The FTC has found that the first firm to offer and promote a new product has a substantial advantage. It also notes that "when other things are equal, physicians appear to prefer the brands of existing sellers to those of new sellers."[19] The now required listing

---

[17] For details on home care, write the National League for Nursing, 10 Columbus Circle, New York, N.Y. 10019.

[18] For information on self-care, write National Self-Help Clearinghouse, 184 Fifth Ave., New York, N.Y. 10010; and Health Activation Network, P.O. Box 7268, Arlington, VA 22207.

[19] *FTC News Summary,* April 22, 1977.

of drug prices makes comparison shopping possible and saving more likely, especially if you know the generic name.

Toward National Health Insurance?

There is such widespread dissatisfaction with many aspects of our present health care delivery system that groups as disparate as the American Medical Association, private insurance companies, the Health, Education, and Welfare Department, labor organizations, and various senators and congressmen are all offering plans for some form of national health insurance.

Fears of policy cancellation, difficulties in conversion from group to individual coverage on change of job or other status, doctor shortages, overcrowded hospitals, nonexistent or understaffed neighborhood clinics, the limitations of nursing homes—these are some of the inadequacies of existing medical services.

It is generally agreed that savings would occur if (a) hospitals within an area specialized in particular fields instead of providing duplicate expensive equipment; (b) less expensive outpatient facilities were made available as a substitute for longer stays in hospital beds; (c) more paraprofessionals were trained to relieve doctors in routine matters, making the doctor's expertise more readily available when it was needed; and (d) some incentive were offered to reduce costs. These suggestions receive support from people of every shade of opinion. Endorsement of some form of national action is also widespread.

The Louis Harris Survey reports that 54 percent of the American people favor a comprehensive federal health insurance program that "would combine government, employer, and employee contributions into one federal health insurance system that would cover all medical and health expenses." Until there are compromises on the issues of how workers and employers should contribute to premiums, how much federal money should be contributed, and whether federal, state, or private agencies should administer the system, there can be no agreement on how much coverage there should be.

In such a climate of readiness, proposals for national health insurance abound, varying greatly as to breadth of benefit and cost. There have been more than 20 such bills introduced in Congress lately, with more than 400 representatives and senators either introducing or cosponsoring them. Some favor only catastrophic coverage—others are "cradle to grave advocates." The important question for any coverage is how to deliver quality care, at reasonable cost.

The face of national health insurance is not yet recognizable, but that it has a foreseeable future is certain.

Conclusions on Health Insurance

It is the general consensus that a large sector of the population is not receiving adequate health care and that change and action to expand the capacity of the health services to meet the demands are necessary. It is also felt that currently health care costs are excessive.

An increase in health care personnel, more emphasis on prepaid health maintenance organizations, extensive development of preventive medicine, more availability and use of extended care facilities, and neighborhood health centers are all agreed-upon needs.

The method and amounts for funding these accepted goals are the controversial heart of the current debate on the rising costs, delivery, and effectiveness of health care.

SUGGESTED READINGS

Dun's Review. "The Race to Cut Medical Costs," May 1977.

Galton, Lawrence. *The Patient's Guide to Surgery.* New York: Avon Books, 1977.

Karp, Richard. "Physician, Heal Thyself—Blue Cross, Blue Shield Are Taking Their Medicine." *Barron's,* September 11, 1978.

Money. "Getting Well at Home," October 1977.

Rosett, Richard N. (ed.). *The Role of Health Insurance in the Health Services Sector.* Washington, D.C.: National Bureau of Economic Research, 1976.

"Getting Yours: A Consumer's Guide to Obtaining Your Medical Records," 1978. Health Research Group, Department MR, 2000 P. St. N.W., Suite 708, Washington D.C. 20036.

"How to Shop for Health Insurance." HEW Publication 1979. For free copy write Consumer Information Center, Department 582 G, Pueblo, Co. 81009.

CASE PROBLEMS

1   Brooks Elliott is a young lawyer, aged 27. He is still a bachelor. He earns $21,000 a year. His small law firm does not provide any fringe benefits—no hospitalization or health insurance of any sort. He recognizes a need for some sort of medical insurance protection. What kind of coverage should he have?

2   Rogers had formerly worked for a company which provided Blue Cross and Blue Shield for its employees. When he left the company, he paid for his family certificate individually ($300 a year). On his new job he is offered the opportunity to take $10,000 of group life insurance in combination with hospital and surgical benefits similar to those provided by Blue Cross and Blue Shield, at a cost to him of $360 a year. Rogers is married, has two children (ages eight and ten), and earns $18,000 a year. He wonders whether he should drop Blue Cross and Blue Shield. What advice would you give him?

3   Your father has just become 65. He knows you are taking a course in personal finance, and he writes to you for advice and information on medicare. He wants to know how he is covered. He asks what the hospitalization portion covers and what he must pay for it. He asks what the medical portion covers and whether he should purchase coverage. Finally he inquires about Senior Care, what it is, what it covers, and what it will cost. Write an appropriate answer to each of his questions.

4   At this writing a great national debate is under way about the future nature of the nation's health care system, its costs and benefits, and its financing, public or private. Write to your congressman and ask for copies of the various bills which have been submitted in the House and in the Senate on health care in the last two years. Also write to the Secretary of the U.S. Department of Health, Education, and Welfare in Washington, D.C., for information on the various proposals. After you have read and studied the material received, outline the different proposals and explain which one you would favor.

5   Tests show that Mariam Snorton, 33, needs a mastectomy. She works as a secretary at the University, has Blue Cross and Blue Shield coverage. She wonders whether she is eligible for coverage for this operation and if not what alternative sources of financing there are. She is also uncertain about the cost of such an operation. Can you advise her?

9

The Roof over Your Head

I never saw an oft-removed tree nor yet an oft-removed family that throve so well as those that settled be.

POOR RICHARD'S ALMANACK

Six million families that bought homes in 1977 stretched their incomes beyond traditional safe standards, according to a report of the U.S. League of Savings Associations. The old rule of thumb about committing 25 percent of family income to housing is being exceeded by two out of every five home buyers. In a survey of families that purchased new homes between July 1976 and June 1977 the National Association of Home Builders found that households with a median income of $22,247 bought homes at a median price of $45,000 with median mortgage and utility costs running $455 monthly.

These housing vignettes are intended to illustrate the unusual situation in housing today. The following pages examine the reasons for it.

To Buy or to Rent?

The heart of the decision whether to rent or to buy lies in your choice of investing in your own house and seeing its equity increase or of collecting rent receipts and investing the money which would have been spent to purchase a house in other opportunities with a possibility of even greater returns.

Money placed even conservatively in a six-year certificate of deposit savings account returns 7¾ percent. Let us assume a 9½ percent rate over 25 years on a $40,000 mortgage for a $50,000 home. The interest owed is $64,844, and the tax-deductible saving (in a 30 percent bracket) would be $19,453. That leaves $45,391 to be paid by you (without any help from Uncle Sam)—a sum larger than the original mortgage. The real advantage in owning a house lies in the increasingly inflated value of the house—*when you sell it.* The sale price of a one-family house went up 57 percent over the last five years. Meanwhile, for example, over the same period the national average increase in maintenance repairs went up 50 percent, property taxes, 63 percent; fuel utilities, 65 percent; and mortgage payments, 74 percent—all while you (or the bank) owned the house. On the consumer price index, where 1967 = 100, home ownership costs have risen to 202.3, whereas rents on that same scale are 152.2.

Rentals tend to cost less than a house in the same range. The higher the renter's income and the more income taxes he has to pay, the less money he will have to invest. When that level is reached, the homeowner has the decided financial benefit because he has the greater tax deduction.

The decision to buy or to rent is usually made on the basis of needs and wants. A recently married young couple may prefer to rent for a variety of reasons. They may both work, and they want to be within easy transportation range of their jobs. In a city this may mean rental housing. His career isn't set yet. He may change jobs several times, or be transferred by the company. Her career opportunities face the same possibilities.

There are so many variables to consider. Renters have more flexibility in meeting changing personal situations and in the uses to which they can put their money.

Other factors of importance enter into the rent-or-buy decision. The convenience of having the landlord make repairs, provide maintenance, service, and sometimes utilities, at his expense, are advantages in renting. Adding to the problems of homeowning are the costs of garbage and trash collection, heating fuel, and water, as well as the difficulty of finding skilled repairmen. On the other hand, renters may have problems in keeping pets, playing musical instruments, or turning the volume on their stereo too high. A more serious problem for renters is that at the time they sign the lease, they don't know what the rent will be when it's time to renew the lease several years later. The choice can be an emotional one—the freedom from responsibility compared to the joy of roots attract different personalities. Status goals play a part. In second- or third-generation immigrant families, or mobility-conscious upward-bound working-class families, home ownership symbolizes having arrived. The desire for privacy or for socializing, independence, or security, a concern and love for the land, and the need for proximity to transportation and convenient shopping all motivate the decision.

The American Dream?

The last census statistics show that the North Central region of the United States had the highest rate of owner occupancy and that the Northeast had the lowest. Homeowners outnumbered renters in every state but Hawaii and New York and the District of Columbia. California had the largest number of owner-occupied units, New York the largest number of rented units. Nationally 37 percent of all households lived in rental housing.

Home ownership is directly related to the age of the head of the household: from the age of 35 to 54 almost three out of four own their homes; over 70 percent of those over 65 are homeowners. Income obviously affects home ownership: of those with income under $7,500 a year, about half are homeowners. As income rises, so does the proportion of homeowners, becoming over 85 percent beginning at the $15,000 income bracket. The percentage of homeowning blacks increased to 41.6 percent—or nearly 2.6 million persons. The census also reported that 4.6 percent of all American households own second homes.

Young families with limited income face larger cash down payments, difficulty in getting mortgage loans, and high interest rates on mortgages and thus often have no choice but to rent. For families headed by women, whose income is lower than that of the average family, this is even more probable.

The moving costs of homeowning must be included in evaluating renting versus owning. It is estimated that the average homeowner moves every eight years. It is also estimated that the average house increases in value by about 7 percent a year, and in desirable suburbs by as much as 10 percent. Your investment improves the longer you stay. Little equity is accumulated in the first seven–ten years of home ownership, as most of the payments cover interest charges and allowance must be made for depreciation. If we add points and the brokerage fee, which are also paid at this time, the transfer of ownership can cost about 10 percent of the selling price. The profits of real estate ownership shrink somewhat when you sell and then must purchase another home whose value has risen under similar condition, even though you benefit from a tax advantage in the sale.

In the final analysis, renting offers more flexibility—less maintenance responsibility.

Inflation and Home Ownership Costs

Inflation seems to be putting the goal of owning your own home out of reach. During the period of your lifetime alone, the average cost of a new home has gone up 191 percent and the total cost of operating that home has increased 303 percent. During the same period, average take-home pay has increased only 183 percent. The home buyer who paid $24,600 for a house in 1967 must now pay $46,700 for a comparable house. This house could be worth more than $70,000 in seven years—based on recent experience. As fears of inflation spread, many people think that no matter how high a price now, it's cheaper than it will be a year from now.

A newspaper article[1] describes a simple cottage in Greenwich, Connecticut, that sold for $5,000 in 1950, passed through six owners, each of whom

made improvements and then sold it at a substantial profit; and is now the $112,000 home of a banker. Inflation plus desirable location is the story of that house, but the story is duplicated in a national pattern because of municipal growth restrictions (fear of water scarcity, pollution, and higher taxes); higher prices for land, construction materials, and labor; scarcity of land close to urban and suburban areas; rising property taxes; and even new government regulations for environmental protection, the tightening of building codes, and improved sewer and utility installation in land development.

A study by *Professional Builder,* an important trade journal, finds that $41,000 is about all most families are willing and able to spend for a house and that 42 percent of home buyers are looking for something under $35,000.

One highly regarded financial source with a different viewpoint finds that rising incomes have kept pace with rising home prices. "The ratio of the median sales price of a new home ($48,700) to estimated median family income ($16,300) at 3.0 was essentially unchanged from the ratio maintained throughout the post-war period."[2] Talking about the "median" house is less startling than using the term *average,* which would send the national price of a new house up to $57,600.

The prices of new and used houses fluctuate widely. In 20 metropolitan areas, the average high for new houses was New York at $80,600 and the average low was Tampa/St. Petersburg at $45,700. For used houses, prices range from an average high of $75,700 in San Francisco/Oakland to an average low of $36,500 in St. Louis.[3]

Facts to Prove Your Point of View

Two differing studies have examined the "affordability" of home ownership. Discounting the "want" aspect of affordability, which can't be discounted, a Harvard-MIT Joint Center for Urban Studies concluded that fewer than three out of ten

[1] *New York Times,* August 15, 1976, sec. D, pp. 1–2.

[2] Morgan Guaranty Survey, April 1978, published by Morgan Guaranty Trust Company of New York.

[3] *American Council on Consumer Interests Newsletter,* April 1978.

families in the nation can afford a median-priced new house. American Standard, Inc., leading manufacturer of building products, naturally disagreed, on the basis of government census and income data as well as data supplied by the National Association of Home Builders. Both studies used as a gauge of affordability the rule of thumb commonly used by the mortgage lender that the costs of owning a home shouldn't exceed 25 percent of a family's total yearly income. But each study used a different base year, which accounts for the differing conclusions.

To prove that home ownership was a good investment, American Standard chose 1965 as its base year. At that time the average buyer of a new median-priced home would have spent 29 percent for home ownership costs in the first year. The base year used by the Harvard-MIT study was 1970, when median house prices were unusually low. To afford the average $23,400 house in 1970, a family needed a yearly income of around $11,450. The proportion of families with that income was then 46.2 percent. Currently, only an estimated 27 percent of American families can afford today's median-priced house. Both studies agree that lower-income families are having greater difficulties in today's housing market, but they disagree on the extent to which middle-income families are being squeezed out or must downgrade their expectations. Both studies agree that the purchase of a home is a good investment decision. The equity in a house rose an average of 7 percent a year from 1965 to 1975, bettering the rise in the consumer price index over the same period by almost 2 percent.

Costs of house purchasing are basically two-part. Mortgage payments, which consist of interest and amortization, usually remain fixed. Maintenance and operation costs rise. The Harvard-MIT study emphasizes the difficulties of the first-year crunch. Recognition of this problem has led to the development of the graduated payments mortgage, to be discussed in detail later in the chapter. This type of mortgage is gaining acceptance as a way of lowering traditional fixed costs in the early years and thus easing the burden of rising maintenance and operation costs. A study by Citibank of New York notes that middle-class families in the Northeast have faced an average annual 19 percent increase since 1972 for all home-related costs. American Standard' response is that the young family's income rises over the years and can therefore meet these costs. The Savings and Loan Association study quoted earlier supports this view. But the study also shows that one third of the families buying new homes had two incomes.

The Harvard–M.I.T. study, quoted earlier, concluded that poor and middle-income families are increasingly unable to keep up with rising housing costs. "If the trends for 1971–1976 continue for another five years, typical new homes in 1981 would sell for $78,000 and only the most affluent groups would be able to afford them."[4] An increasing number of families are "housing deprived" and in a "high rent burden category." These are defined in the study as two or more people, with the household head less than 65 years old, who are paying more than 25 percent of their income for rent, or two or more people, with the household head 65 or over, who are paying more than 35 percent of their income for rent.

One of the authors is quoted as saying, "Women's lib may be the salvation of the housing industry"—working wives are providing that needed money to make up the difference. It requires a two income family to buy a house these days. The current credit regulation that requires banks to count the wife's income on the same basis as the husband's income, without restrictions as to age or child-bearing intentions, has made home buying easier for young couples.

There is no doubt that rising prices have put increasing limitations on who can buy homes. A recent survey by the National Association of Home Builders found that the typical home buyer is older—about 33 years of age—and that more than half had owned homes before. Most such buyers used the proceeds of the sale on their former home

---

[4] Arthur P. Solomon and Bernard J. Frieden, Joint Center for Urban Studies of the Massachusetts Institute of Technology and Harvard University, (Cambridge, Mass.: MIT Press, 1977), p. 141.

to cover a 20 percent down payment on a new home.

Escalating resale prices provide the means by which present homeowners can trade up into more expensive housing. This pattern contributes to a further upward price spiral. The Federal Reserve Board noted that "the average down payment on conventional mortgages—the major financing instrument used—exceeded $13,000 in early 1977. This was more than 10 percent above a year earlier and three-fifths higher than levels prevailing in 1973."

It's the first-time buyer who suffers the most. Without a house to "trade in," the higher down payment is difficult—if not impossible. These days a mere 35 percent of new home buyers can afford to be first-time buyers. For these buyers, the Congressional Budget Office reported that during the recent five-year period the cost of a new home increased twice as fast as family income and the cost of existing homes 1½ times as fast. Nevertheless, if the money can be found, the thinking is that a house will be a hedge against inflation.

How Much Can You Afford for a House?

One bank loan officer uses two basic rules: first, the amount of a loan should not exceed 2½ times the gross yearly income; second, the monthly payments for borrowing, including mortgage payments, should not exceed one fourth of the gross monthly income. Since the mortgage affects how much house you can afford, these rules offer a useful basis for judgment.

One method for figuring out how much of your income you can devote to either renting or buying a home is to list your expenses and income—either on a monthly or a yearly basis—as shown in Figure 9–1. Now subtract "Your total expenses" from "Your total take-home pay." You get the figure, $_____, which is the amount of money you can afford to pay for a roof over your head. This figure is referred to as your income for housing.

Now that you have your income for housing, either on a yearly or a monthly basis, consult Table 9–1. Find your housing income in the table to learn the amount of the loan you can afford. The figures in this table include not only principal and interest charges on a mortgage but also an estimate for taxes, maintenance, and insurance. Suppose you have found that your income for housing is $100 a month. According to Table 9–1, this would, for example, permit you to afford a home loan of $11,940 at 8 percent for 20 years. This figure represents what you should be able to finance from your current income. Assume you can't get a mortgage for less than 10 percent. As you can see from

FIGURE 9–1

What is your total income? . . . . . $_____	Monthly savings budget . . $_____
What are your total current assets $_____	Food and clothing . . . . . . $_____
What are your withholdings for income taxes, retirement, social security benefits, hospitalization insurance, and any other deductions from your wage or salary . . . . $_____	Medical care . . . . $_____
	Life insurance . . . . $_____
	Educational costs . . . . $_____
	Recreation . . . . $_____
	Utilities and fuel . . . . $_____
Substract the second figure from the first. Your total take-home pay is . . . . $_____	Automobile expenses . . . . $_____
	All other expenses . . . . (membership dues, contributions, charge accounts, installment purchases, etc.) . . . . $_____
	Add these up. Your total expenses are . . . . $_____

TABLE 9–1

Income Available for Housing: How Much Mortgage Can You Afford?

For (years)	$100 per Month Available ($1,200 per year) for Loan of:	$200 per Month Available ($2,400 per year) for Loan of:	$300 per Month Available ($3,600 per year) for Loan of:	$400 per Month Available ($4,800 per year) for Loan of:	$500 per Month Available ($6,000 per year) for Loan of:
At 6%					
20 years . . .	$13,940	$27,890	$41,840	$55,780	$69,730
25 years . . .	15,500	31,000	46,510	62,010	77,510
30 years . . .	16,660	33,330	50,000	66,660	83,330
At 7%					
20 years . . .	12,880	25,770	38,650	51,540	64,430
25 years . . .	14,140	28,280	42,430	56,570	70,720
30 years . . .	15,010	30,030	45,040	60,060	75,070
At 8%					
20 years . . .	11,940	23,890	35,840	47,780	59,730
25 years . . .	12,950	25,900	38,860	51,810	64,760
30 years . . .	13,620	27,240	40,870	54,490	68,110
At 9%					
20 years . . .	11,110	22,220	33,330	44,440	55,550
25 years . . .	11,904	23,800	35,710	47,610	59,520
30 years . . .	12,420	24,840	37,260	49,680	62,110
At 10%					
20 years . . .	10,350	20,700	31,050	41,400	51,750
25 years . . .	11,000	22,000	33,000	44,000	55,000
30 years . . .	11,380	22,770	34,160	45,550	56,940

Source: United States Savings and Loan League.

the table, it would take you 30 years to pay off that mortgage of $11,000.

A Limit to Cost

If a family is going to buy a home, it is most important to buy one which can be paid for comfortably. The usual rule is that the family should buy a house at a price not exceeding 2½ times the family's annual income. This means that a family with annual earnings of $13,000 should try to be content with a home costing about $32,500. Since in many parts of the country $16,000 is a fairly typical family income today, and since it is not easy to find suitable new housing costing $40,000 or less, it is obvious that many families will be tempted to pay more in order to become homeowners. Yet they cannot do so without mak-

ing substantial sacrifices of other things that they would like to have.

Another useful rule is that rent or housing costs per month should not exceed more than one week's take-home pay. Since the monthly housing cost is usually roughly 1 percent of the total purchase price of the house, a $26,000 house is likely to cost $260 a month to carry (this will vary somewhat, depending on the terms of your mortgage, the size of your cash down payment, and your consumption of fuel). Obviously, if your take-home pay is $240 a week, this is too expensive a house for you. Another measure would be annual carrying costs of approximately 25 percent of annual income. You probably could carry the house using this rule. There are probably as many yardsticks as there are experts, but you must notice that they all express some form of caution.

FIGURE 9–2
Credit Analysis for a Mortgage Loan

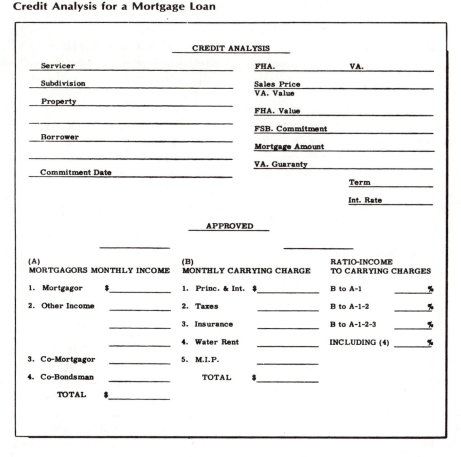

CREDIT ANALYSIS

Servicer	FHA.	VA.

Subdivision	Sales Price
Property	VA. Value
	FHA. Value
	FSB. Commitment
Borrower	Mortgage Amount
	VA. Guaranty
Commitment Date	
	Term
	Int. Rate

APPROVED

(A) MORTGAGORS MONTHLY INCOME	(B) MONTHLY CARRYING CHARGE	RATIO-INCOME TO CARRYING CHARGES
1. Mortgagor $	1. Princ. & Int. $	B to A-1 _____ %
2. Other Income	2. Taxes	B to A-1-2 _____ %
	3. Insurance	B to A-1-2-3 _____ %
	4. Water Rent	INCLUDING (4) _____ %
3. Co-Mortgagor	5. M.I.P.	
4. Co-Bondsman	TOTAL $	
TOTAL $		

One bank has developed a very simple form for quickly estimating whether or not to grant a proposed mortgage loan. Look at the bottom half of Figure 9–2. If the ratio of income to carrying charges is about 20 percent, the loan will be granted. If that ratio exceeds 25 percent, the proposed loan will be studied carefully by the mortgage loan officer and becomes a matter for his critical judgment. In a period of tight money, the loan would probably be rejected. In a period of easier money, it might well be granted.

The Equal Credit Opportunity Act forbids discriminatory conditions or terms imposed on a woman that are not required of a man in the same economic circumstances. Many states now apply similar regulations to the lending institutions under their jurisdiction.

A House Built to Specifications

Naturally, if a family has a home built to its specifications, it should expect to be able to get a house meeting those specifications. However, it is common for persons not used to reading blueprints to get quite a surprise when they see the house which was built from them. Sometimes it is far different from what they imagined it would be. As they see the house going up, it is not unusual for them to discover things that they want changed to make the house what they had visualized. Making these changes may involve much more expense than can be comfortably financed. In a great many cases, it is wise to secure the services of a competent architect, who may charge from 12 to 15 percent of the total construction cost for drawing plans that will suit the family's needs and wants and for seeing that the contractor is building according to specifications. Honest and able architects and builders can do much to smooth the path of the unwary person who is having a house built for the first time, for mistakes can be very expensive.

The fair price for having a house built can be obtained by having a few contractors bid independently for the privilege of building it. The contractors base their bids on their study of plans and specifications drawn by the architect. But far too often contractors are mere carpenters who have decided to go into business for themselves, so that it is only common sense to make sure that the contractor can and will perform the work competently for the agreed price.

The National Established Repair, Service, and Improvement Contractors Association suggests that you check the contractor's bank references, contact at least two wholesale suppliers who sell materials to the contractor, and talk with at least three homeowners whose houses the contractor has finished within the last year. It is also wise to be sure that the contractor has public liability insurance— a protection to you in case of property damage or injury to third persons.

A detailed written contract covering the brands and the quality grades of materials, room by room, is vital for your protection. The contract should also include a provision for sketches (subject to your approval) and a starting and finishing date.

Detailed door and window hardware, better bathroom tiling, finer lighting fixtures, an extra-large garage, or a fireplace add to value and cost. Sometimes it is cheaper in the long run to consider a more expensive house per unit cost than to plan to add on the extras to an inexpensive one at what will be a higher future cost. For example, the cost of finishing a dormered attic ranges from $2,000 to as high as $5,000, depending on the materials used and the layout.

Building your own home is usually a long, costly, and often a bitter process. If your funds are limited and your patience short, it is not a good idea. Much study and time are needed to acquire enough information to talk intelligently with your architect and contractor.[5] If you do decide to build, a construction loan can be obtained.

In most cases it is better to buy a house already built. At least you can see what you are getting. An older house will probably give you more space for your dollars, although you may also need large sums for repairs and perhaps modernization. Where you are merely adding modern equipment, such as rewiring, plumbing, or a heating-cooling system, or you are doing inside alteration, such as installing a bathroom or a kitchen, a contractor may be adequate. But if you want to create new space or to alter the old, an architect is needed to save money and prevent mistakes.

Remodeling

If you are going to buy an older house which requires extensive remodeling to make it suit your needs, it may ultimately cost more than a new house. Things which have already cost money have to be removed and scrapped, and substitutes have to be installed at further expense. Then, again, there is always the danger that the remodeled home will be a hodgepodge, inferior to one built from scratch to a carefully drawn plan. Some houses built in former days, have materials and workmanship that today can be duplicated only with difficulty. They are apt to be large, with big rooms, and, in some climates, high heating expense. Help in reducing that expense can come from banks and utilities which offer financing on easy terms and from the federal government, which is offering tax credits to insulate. The resulting savings in fuel average three times the cost of the insulation. Of course, any house that is more than five or ten years old

---

[5] For a useful checklist, see "Business Dealings with Architect and Contractor," Small Homes Council–Building Research Council, the University of Illinois, One E. St. Mary's Rd., Champaign, IL 61820.

requires more in the line of repairs than do most of those which have just been built. Older houses, however, may be cheaper—perhaps 8 percent to 38 percent lower in price than new ones, depending on the area—but cost more in mortgage money. They are better buys for those who are content to live in them as they are and not undertake extensive remodeling.[6]

The new house has the advantages of the latest in kitchen equipment, new types of construction that require less maintenance, modern bathroom fixtures, built-in air conditioning, fewer bedrooms, and more entertainment space (for smaller families). But it probably also has smaller rooms, lower ceilings, and sparse landscaping.

Examining the House

You have never bought a house before, and when the real estate agent ushers you into the gleaming new house, aside from your wife's noting with approval the colorful ceramic tile and flocked wallpaper of the bathroom and the mechanical wonders of the modern kitchen, with its dishwasher, garbage disposal unit, refrigerator, trash compactor, washing machine, dryer, and microwave oven, all of which will probably require periodic visits from a host of mechanics to service, how do you tell whether or not the house is soundly constructed? What do you look for, and how will you know what is right and what is not right?[7]

A checklist for your guidance is presented in Figure 9–3. Merely glancing at it will indicate what a complicated job you face. You cannot possibly know whether the strip flooring is good or bad; whether the doors will warp; whether good or bad ''dry wall,'' Sheetrock, fiberboard, or plastered wall

has been used and finished properly; whether the windows will continue to open and close a month hence or after a heavy rain; whether the heating system is adequate; or whether, if there is a basement, it is going to drain properly if it leaks a little or a lot; whether the insulation thickness in the attic is adequate; or whether the plumbing is designed to hold up for 12 months or 12 years. Since you know little or nothing about such things, and it is costly to learn the hard way by buying, moving in, and waiting to find out, the best suggestion we can offer is to get expert advice before you buy.

Hire an expert to look the house over for you if you think you are interested in it; go out to the house with him when he examines it; have him explain his observations to you. Charges for such inspections vary according to the size or value of the house. Armed with the expert's findings, you may be reassured, or avoid a terrible mistake. If serious defects have been uncovered and you still want to buy, you have leverage for bargaining. And if the expert notes a number of things that need to be corrected and you do want to buy the house, insist that the builder or seller agree in writing to make the necessary changes or corrections.

In some areas, local real estate brokers act as appraisers as a sideline. In other areas, professional engineers estimate the condition of a home. The Society of Real Estate Appraisers has members who are qualified to tell what a house is worth and what is wrong with it. These professionals charge $50 to $200, depending on the value or size of the house. Another source, with branches in major cities, is the Nationwide Real Estate Inspectors Service, Inc.

A third is the National Home Inspection Service, with offices in 30 metropolitan areas. This firm will examine the condition of the major structural, mechanical, and electrical elements of the house you want to buy and give a detailed report. If the roof, walls, ceiling, basement, plumbing, and heating are sound, the company will guarantee its inspection against unforeseen defects for one year. These inspectors are not appraisers.

A National Association of Home Builders survey on the problems that 10,000 new homeowners

---

[6] If you do want to remodel, see *The Old House Journal Buyer's Guide,* $5.50 from Universe Books, 381 Park Ave. S., New York, N.Y. 10016; and *The Old House Catalog,* Lawrence Grow, $14.95, hardcover, $7.95 paperback. Both give advice and list buying sources, craftsmen, and products.

[7] *Old House Journal* (Clem Labine, editor), 199 Berkeley Place, Brooklyn, N.Y. 11217, has a free four-page checklist for homeowners who want to inspect on their own.

FIGURE 9–3

Checklist for Use in Buying or Building a Home

This checklist is offered to aid you in selecting your home. The list does not cover everything but does include the principal items which you should consider.

CHARACTERISTICS OF PROPERTY (Proposed or existing construction)

Neighborhood

Consider each of the following to determine whether the location of the property will satisfy your personal needs and preferences:

Remarks

Convenience of public transportation ☐
Stores conveniently located ☐
Elementary school conveniently located ☐
Absence of excessive traffic noise ☐
Absence of smoke and unpleasant odors ☐
Play area available for children ☐
Fire and police protection provided ☐
Residential usage safeguarded by adequate zoning ☐

Lot

Consider each of the following to determine whether the lot is sufficiently large and properly improved:

Size of front yard satisfactory ☐
Size of rear and side yards satisfactory ☐
Walks provide access to front and service entrances ☐
Drive provides easy access to garage ☐
Lot appears to drain satisfactorily ☐
Lawn and planting satisfactory ☐
Septic tank (if any) in good operating condition ☐

Exterior Detail

Observe the exterior detail of neighboring houses and determine whether the house being considered is as good or better in respect to each of the following features:

Porches ☐
Terraces ☐
Garage ☐
Gutters ☐
Storm sash ☐
Weather stripping ☐
Screens ☐

Interior Detail

Consider each of the following to determine whether the house will afford living accomodations which are sufficient to the needs and comfort of your family:

Rooms will accommodate desired furniture ☐
Dining space sufficiently large ☐
At least one closet in each bedroom ☐
At least one coat closet and one linen closet ☐

FIGURE 9–3 *(continued)*

		Remarks

Convenient access to bathroom ☐
Sufficient and convenient storage space (screens, trunks, boxes, off-season clothes, luggage, baby carriage, bicycle, wheel toys, etc.) ☐
Kitchen well arranged and equipped ☐
Laundry space ample and well located ☐
Windows provide sufficient light and air ☐
Sufficient number of electrical outlets ☐

CONDITION OF EXISTING CONSTRUCTION

Exterior Construction

The following appear to be in acceptable condition:

Wood porch floors and steps ☐
Windows, doors, and screens ☐
Gutters and wood cornice ☐
Wood siding ☐
Mortar joints ☐
Roofing ☐
Chimneys ☐
Paint on exterior woodwork ☐

Interior Construction

Plaster is free of excessive cracks ☐
Plaster is free of stains caused by leaking roof or sidewalls ☐
Door locks in operating condition ☐
Windows move freely ☐
Fireplace works properly ☐
Basement is dry and will resist moisture penetration ☐
Mechanical equipment and electrical wiring and switches adequate and in operating condition ☐
Type of heating equipment suitable ☐
Adequate insulation in walls, floor, ceiling or roof ☐

The following appear to be in acceptable condition:

Wood floor finish ☐
Linoleum floors ☐
Sink top ☐
Kitchen range ☐
Bathroom fixtures ☐
Painting and papering ☐
Exposed joists and beams ☐

Are You Sure . . .

That the basement will stay dry after heavy rains?

That the foundations are sound?

That there has been no TERMITE damage?

You'd better get EXPERT ADVICE on the condition of existing construction, if you want to *be sure* the house is a good buy.

Source: Veterans Administration.

had shortly after moving in, revealed that 29 percent had to make minor repairs, that 27 percent had difficulties with the plumbing, and that 20 percent complained about defective doors and windows. If you are buying an older house or having a new one built under VA or FHA financing, the construction will have to meet certain standards. An FHA appraisal costs less than the usual appraiser's fee, and it includes a report on needed repairs or changes.

Many small towns and some large cities have presale inspection laws of various types to see that a house meets local livability standards. The inspections made under such laws are not as detailed as a building code inspection. The cost is borne by the seller.

Warranties

A warranty program for new houses has been started by the National Association of Home Builders. Known as HOW (Home Owners Warranty Program), it includes a ten-year warranty against major construction defects; a two-year warranty on defects of plumbing, heating, electrical, and cooling systems; and one-year's protection against faulty workmanship and defective materials. The plan is to be administered by local building groups which will pay the cost ($2 for each $1,000 of a home's sale price). The warranty becomes effective only when the buyer takes title. It goes with the home, so subsequent buyers are automatically protected.

Some Basics in Choosing a House

Land cost is a variable factor which is closely related to both location and convenience. It has been found that the cost of land declines to the extent that people must pay higher transportation costs to get to and from it.

If there are children in the family, it becomes necessary to consider whether a house is conveniently situated to schools. Investigate the present school tax and the prospects for the future. If a new school is badly needed and the community

quite properly authorizes it, you may find your school tax suddenly doubled. If you are considering a new development populated by young families, this is especially likely.

A home which is convenient to a local or even a major shopping center, so that daily shopping can be accomplished with a minimum of time and effort, will merit serious attention.

Proximity to community facilities is also to be borne in mind when you are choosing a homesite. If busy thoroughfares are too close, you may be bothered by noise.

It is worth noting whether the neighborhood is populated with families that would probably prove to be congenial. There are young people's neighborhoods in which older persons feel out of place; and there are neighborhoods filled with older persons in which growing children find it hard to meet suitable playmates. Studies of consumer preferences are made by industry associations and land developers that segment the housing market into particular lifestyles. One company has 40 different plans to meet the needs of specific groups—such as young singles, adult singles, young marrieds with and without children, family "move-ups" and "move-downs," and "empty nesters."[8] Are there local building codes that determine zoning, lot size, sidewalks and curbs, that would keep property values more stable? The house you buy should conform in price and size to the houses around it. A $90,000 house in a $30,000 neighborhood has less resale value. The checklist in Figure 9–3 shows the more important points that you should consider before buying.

For most purposes, a level, rectangular lot of reasonable size is preferred by most people. Getting automobiles out of sunken garages on icy pavements can be expensive. Corner lots may seem attractive from some points of view, but to some of us they mean extra sidewalks from which to remove snow. More land than the family can reasonably use and service involves a useless financial burden. The presence of sheltering trees and the direction that the lot faces has a bearing on the

---

[8] Irvine Company, California.

placing of the house. Unusual design may be very interesting and attractive, but it may also narrow your market for resale at a later date. Has the lot been graded away from the house to permit proper drainage of surface water? Is there shrubbery along the perimeter of the property to provide privacy?

Are you so far out in exurbia that sewerage, water and garbage disposal create continuing headaches and expenses because you must arrange for private services? Are there adequate streetlights? Have the streets been surfaced and deeded to the municipality so that they are a community responsibility? The absence of such utilities or community services is likely to involve future assessments or higher taxes to provide for their installation and upkeep. Check on zoning, taxes, and extra assessments.

Appraising the Lot

If you plan to build you must first select a lot which will suit your needs. How are you to know that a fair price is being asked for the lot? You can use the comparison or market data method commonly used by real estate appraisers. This consists of comparing the price asked for the particular lot with the prices at which comparable lots are being offered. Such a procedure takes time and effort; but it will save you from paying a price that is far out of line from what other people are paying for similar properties.

Appraising the House

Generally, it will be found helpful to try to obtain a value figure by two or three methods (comparison, cost less depreciation, and capitalization of income).

1. The comparison or market data approach that worked in appraising a lot is also valid for appraising a house. However, several cautions must be observed because few houses are precisely alike. Is it possible to compare two houses that seem alike if each was bought at a different time? Market values go up and down. Property locations vary—one may be better than another. Neighborhoods change—do they all change equally?

2. Banks and dealers in builders' supplies can give information as to present building costs per cubic foot and per square foot of living space for houses of various sorts (frame, or brick, or stone). A typical family of four requires a house with 1,-300–1,600 square feet of living area. Climate and area cause the price per square foot to vary considerably. Costs are lower in the South—about 5 percent less in suburban Atlanta than in a Northern city suburb.

With such information it is possible to approximate how much a house would cost to build new. If we deduct from this cost an allowance for the fact that a building is partially worn out, we can get a figure (cost less depreciation) for its value which may prove of some help in knowing whether the price being asked for it is reasonable.

The Hartford Insurance Company offers *Dwelling Replacement Costimeter,* a free publication which tells you how much it would cost to rebuild your home, depending upon *(a)* type of construction, *(b)* construction materials, and *(c)* the number of units in your home. Using a base cost table, you find the appropriate cost figure, multiply it by the Current Locality Multiplier (materials and labor costs vary across the country) to find the current replacement cost of your home.

3. Another useful method (usually applied to commercial or business property) is to find the valuation of a property by capitalizing its net income. A simple way to approximate the method is to determine how much a property should rent for by finding out what rentals similar properties are commanding. If you think that the property should rent for $100 a month, application of the 1 percent rule will tell you that the property in question should be worth something like $10,000. This is not the best method for assessing the value of a single-family home, because such homes are most usually owner occupied.

A professional real estate appraiser uses these methods in arriving at his educated judgment when a value figure is needed for an insurance estimate, for mortgage financing, for a potential house buyer, or for the homeowner who wants to sell and is in doubt about his asking price.

Most families have to borrow from some financial institution a large part (sometimes 70 to 80 percent) of what they pay for a home. The financial institution will, through its investment or mortgage committee, which is usually composed of persons with long experience in the real estate field, assure itself of the value of the property that is to serve as security for the loan. The prospective homeowner can profit from the advice obtained from such an institution as to the value of the lot (and the buildings, if any). Experienced bank mortgage loan officers know more about the value of a lot than the average person can learn in a reasonable time. Financial institutions which make a business of lending on home mortgages often charge a modest fee for appraising property. Some careful persons submit applications to two or more such institutions, and pay the required fees, simply to obtain the assurance that the price to be paid is not excessive.

The family, therefore, which independently does a reasonably competent job of deciding whether the price at which a lot and house is offered is fair, and then gets support for its decision by obtaining the opinion of impartial experts, is not likely to pay an unduly high price. It should be remembered that sellers who ask a certain price for a given property are frequently ready to do business at a lower price; bargaining over real estate prices is rather common.

Financing the House

Once you have selected the house you think you want to buy, your next step is to arrange for financing. If you are like most people, you will be able to make only a modest down payment, 25 percent or less, and you will need to get the rest of the purchase price by mortgage from a financial institution. No family should thoughtlessly decide to part with all of its cash resources to make a down payment. Some savings should be kept for emergencies.

Where to Go for a Mortgage Loan

Today most home loans on mortgages are made by savings and loan associations, savings banks, commercial banks, insurance companies, and credit unions. Of these, only the savings and loan associations specialize exclusively in lending on mortgages. They (including cooperative banks in Massachusetts, homestead associations in Louisiana, and building and loan associations generally) make a business of obtaining savings from the public and putting this money to work earning interest by lending it out on mortgages, largely on residences. They have from 80 to 95 percent of their funds invested in mortgages and hold more than half of the mortgages outstanding. Savings banks have a relatively small share of the mortgage volume; commercial banks, as their name implies, endeavor to put most of their money to work in commercial loans and place only a relatively small proportion of their assets in mortgages.

The Old-Type Straight Mortgage

When a loan is made on the security of a mortgage, the mortgagee—the lender—makes the loan to the mortgagor—the homeowner or borrower—in return for a promissory note secured by the mortgage of the property and adequate insurance thereon. The promissory note can be payable in any number of years, depending on the agreement. These "straight mortgages" had no provision for the partial payment of the principal of the loan during the period for which the note was written. Customarily, only the interest was paid periodically—every quarter, every half year, or every year. At the end of the note's term, it really became a demand instrument, full payment of which could be demanded immediately. Many borrowers would forget about the principal until the full amount of the note was due and payable, and then they would attempt to renew the loan for another term of years. If the note came due in a period of prosperity, there might not by any difficulty in renewing it; but if it came due in a recession, the borrower could lose the property. For these reasons the straight mortgage is now thought to be disadvantageous.

The Amortized or Direct Reduction Mortgage

Both government and private mortgage financing agencies now insist on the amortized mortgage. They want the loans paid off in the foreseeable future—during the economic life of the building. The direct reduction or amortized mortgage is thus named because the borrower makes a fixed monthly payment which not only includes interest (and perhaps taxes and insurance) but also reduces the principal of the mortgage debt.

The earlier monthly installments include primarily interest and only small amounts of principal repayment. Gradually a larger percentage of the monthly payment is applied to repayment of principal, until the loan is entirely repaid. Under this plan, interest at the stipulated rate is figured on the declining unpaid balance of your loan. As the regular payments of the monthly amount are made, that part of the payment used to pay interest becomes smaller, and the part applied to reducing the loan becomes larger.

As compared with the old-type straight mortgage, the amortized mortgage requires a higher monthly payment but results in a very large saving in interest costs. For example:

Under the old-type straight mortgage:

You make a mortgage loan of $20,000.

You do not make payments to reduce the principal of the mortgage.

You make 240 monthly payments of $133.33.

You pay in interest, over 20 years at 8 percent per annum, $32,000.

You still owe the original mortgage amount of $20,000.

Under the amortized mortgage:

You make monthly payments of $167.29 both to pay interest and to reduce the principal.

You pay in interest, in 20 years at 8 percent per annum, $20,149.60

Thus you save $11,850.40 in interest costs, and the principal is entirely paid off at the end of the 20th year.

The rate of interest that you pay affects the total cost of your home. A variation of one half of 1 percent may amount to a savings of $2,450 over the period of the loan, as shown in the following example. On a $40,000 house, you made a down payment of 20 percent or $8,000, requiring a mortgage loan of $32,000.

Interest Rate	Monthly Payment (principal and interest)	Total Interest (over 20 years)
if 8.5%	$277.71	$34,650
9.0	287.92	37,100

The amount of interest you pay may exceed the original loan if you spread the payments over a very long period (note the 20-year payment). From the creditor's viewpoint, this seems reasonable. You have borrowed and had the use of the money for a longer term, so naturally, you must pay more interest. Using the same house purchased above at 9 percent:

Payment Period	Monthly Payment	Total Interest
20 years	$287.92	$37,100
15 years	324.57	26,422
10 years	405.00	16,644

The chief justification for the longer payment period is that it makes the monthly payments small enough so that the borrower can meet his obligations. It can be difficult for the average person to make monthly payments of $405.00, whereas more persons could pay $287.92 monthly without spending more than a reasonable portion of their income for payments on a house.

Thus you can see why, with the trend to the amortized mortgage and the sharp increase in the prices of houses, the tendency has been to write mortgages with longer maturities so as to bring the required monthly payment within the financial

"You might as well have told them my age, after bragging that we have a 5¼% mortgage on our house."

Reprinted by permission *The Wall Street Journal*

reach of the average family. Formerly, the straight mortgage ran for 5 years on the average, and mortgages for more than 15 years were virtually unknown. Today, however, savings banks and savings and loan associations are making 25- and 35-year loans. With today's high real estate prices, few persons can afford the huge monthly payments necessary to pay off a large mortgage in as short a period of time as five or ten years.

The Down Payment

The larger the down payment, the lower the interest cost will be. As you can see, over 20 years that $40,000 house at 9 percent benefits from the increase of the down payment from $8,000 to $15,000 by a saving in interest charges of $8,115.

Down Payment	Loan Amount	Monthly Payment	Total Interest
$ 8,000	$32,000	$287.92	$37,100
10,000	30,000	269.92	34,780
15,000	25,000	224.94	28,985

If you can manage the monthly payments, and are eligible for a GI loan but lack the savings for a down payment, you can buy that house if the VA approves the loan because then no down payment is required. The VA guarantees repayment of the first $25,000 you borrow.

The FHA down payment requirements are 3 percent on the first $25,000 of the purchase price and 5 percent on the rest up to $60,000, which would amount to only $1,750 on a $45,000 house. If you can qualify, you have a real advantage.

But it is foolish to make so large a down payment in cash that there is little or nothing left in the bank with which to meet emergencies. Temporary unemployment, sickness, the need to replace a leaking roof, a sudden breakdown of the heating system, and other possibilities too numerous to mention make it very desirable to have an emergency fund in the bank. If your mortgage payments are not met on time, the loan is in default; after a few months of default (generally about three or four), the lending institution, under the terms of the mortgage contract, has the right to begin foreclosure proceedings to sell the property and apply the cash received from the sale to the debt. Unless you have the wherewithal to keep up your mortgage payments, you may lose your home.

The opposite approach suggests that since inflation reduces the real cost of repayment, it would be wise to borrow as much as possible and make a minimum down payment. The bigger mortgage can be paid off with dollars that will have less purchasing power than they do now. Then, too, it may be easier to sell your home if you have a mortgage that can be transferred to another buyer at a lower rate than the rate at which the prospective buyer can obtain new mortgage money.

Private Mortgage Insurance Companies

For those who need to reduce the down payment, there is a relatively unknown but growing source in the private mortgage insurance companies. Suppose that you can get a mortgage of $37,500 on a $50,000 home and that you have $5,000, but not the $12,500 that you need for the down payment. One of the 15 private mortgage insurance companies which can be found in all 50 states could write a policy for the remaining $7,500. Coverage is arranged by the mortgage lender and paid for by the buyer. The first year's

decreasing
...aid balance
...g the down
...he purchase
...s.

...lan is partic-
...ers because
... than would
...ge. Monthly
... more years
...ne period as
...A regulations
...ns offer five
...payments in-
...creases. De-
...d, mostly in-
...e principle is
... On the other
...would prefer
...at they have
lower payments to make during retirement time when income decreases.

In the long run a graduated payment plan costs more in interest payments than the conventional loan. After the first five or ten years, the monthly payments are also higher. Those expected salary increases had better keep coming. Down payments are generally higher. But as time and inflation move on, the home buyer's income and equity in the house grow, making it easier to meet the later payments.

FHA data show that GPM (graduated payment mortgage) buyers have 14 percent lower incomes than regular FHA borrowers and choose bigger, more expensive homes than is normal for their income group. The chances of being "house poor" are real. A bigger house triggers higher costs for fuel, electricity, taxes, and upkeep.

Variable Rate Plans Savings and loan associations and a number of savings banks in 17 states, especially California and New England, have pushed these controversial plans. The interest rate is not fixed in the variable-rate mortgage, but is tied to an index of money market rates. In a typical plan, rate changes are at six-month intervals, and rate rises and reductions are usually limited to not more than 2.5 percent during the life of the mortgage. Labor, housing, and consumer groups argue that increases are more likely than decreases.

Four types of variable rate plans have been developed: (1) variable monthly payment contracts in which the payment changes but the maturity term remains constant; (2) VRMs in which the payment is fixed but the maturity term can be extended or reduced; (3) a combination of the first two; and (4) a five-year renewable note.

Pegging variable rate mortgages to an index of money market rates sweetens the idea for lenders and makes more mortgage money available.

Rollover Mortgages In some cases lenders will write long-term mortgages as a series of five-year fixed-rate, guaranteed renewable notes, but at the then existing market rate. The customer can accept the new rate or pay off the loan without penalty. If a rate increase is necessary, the monthly payment can be kept the same by extending the maturity of the loan from 30 years to a maximum of 40 years.

Such loans are favored by people who plan to own their home only a few years before selling it. VRMs are usually assumable at the same rate by a new buyer and can be paid off in advance of maturity without penalty.

Reverse Mortgages The retired with a debt-free home can purchase a reverse annuity mortgage of up to 80 percent of the value of the home which will pay cash monthly over five to ten years. Part of the cash pays the interest on the loan. If the elderly homeowner survives the term of the annuity, he must repay the entire loan. For those able to manage the repayment, a monthly income gained in this way is useful. There is the frightening possibility that this "balloon" payment might necessitate the sale of the home unless automatic refinancing is possible. It would seem as dangerous as Russian roulette for an older person to risk a home for a relatively short-term use of funds. A lifetime annuity however, that would repay the loan by the sale of the house after the death of the borrower could be advantageous to a single older person.

The Fixed-Payment Variable Yield Mortgage This mortgage benefits from inflation. It has two parts. The first part consists of a fixed-level amortization and an interest payment rate at or below the market. The second part is paid when the property is sold. The amount paid the lender at this time is equal to the yield promised in the contract. Interest rates may have risen during the life of the mortgage, but the lender's return is delayed until the property is sold. If the final payment is tied to appreciation, and there is none, then no payment is required.

Second Mortgages

Homeowners are raising cash by borrowing against the appreciation in the market value of their homes. This borrowing on future capital gains is replacing consumer loans to finance education, a car, or home improvements. Only recently acceptable to banks, the second mortgage is becoming one of the fastest-growing forms of consumer financing. It is attractive to the homeowner because the interest cost is not only usually lower than installment loans (12–15 percent), but can also be stretched over a longer period—ten years—and for larger amounts. To the homeowner, it is less expensive than refinancing the first mortgage, which would entail charges for reappraisal, lawyers' fees, title insurance, and points. Some states do not allow second mortgages—a legacy of the losses that occurred during the Great Depression.

Taking Over a Mortgage

A real bargain would be to find the perfect house with an old VA loan of 6.5 percent on which the present owner had made a very small down payment and for which he wants the repayment of his down payment and his mortgage payments to date plus a fair profit. Since the VA will allow the loan to be transferred to you as the new owner if your credit is good, you will have managed a big saving. You and the seller will also be able to avoid several closing costs, for example, a placement fee of 1 percent, survey costs, and document fees for you and a prepayment penalty and points for the seller.

An owner who has an FHA insured mortgage on a home can sell the home or trade it without paying off the insured mortgage in either of two ways. The FHA and the lender who holds the mortgage can agree to substitute the new owner's name on the mortgage, thereby releasing the old owner from any personal liability. The original owner can sell without the consent of the FHA and the lender, but if he does he will still be liable for the mortgage. An FHA-mortgaged house usually has a low down payment, and so if it has a lower mortgage rate, it too is a good buy—but like the similar VA example, it is harder to find than property that is covered by a conventional mortgage (neither FHA nor VA).

A conventional mortgage can be assumed without obtaining the lender's consent, but it leaves the seller of the house still liable to the original lender if the buyer fails to meet the mortgage payments. Under these circumstances, the seller must take careful precautions to be sure that the buyer who assumes the mortgage is financially responsible.

FHA Insurance

Your lender may ask you if you wish to have FHA insurance on your loan or, for protection, may insist that you apply for it. Under an FHA-insured mortgage, you borrow from your lending agency and then the U.S. government, through the Federal Housing Administration, insures the lending agency against any loss of principal if you fail to meet the terms and conditions of your mortgage. The FHA will not insure loans of more than $60,000 on one family dwelling. Under the FHA plan, you pay—for the full term of your loan—an "insurance fee" of 0.5 percent, computed monthly, on the outstanding amount of the principal. This is in addition to the normal interest on your loan. You also pay an FHA "processing or application fee" when you apply for the loan. The FHA insurance fee, to which you and millions of other home buyers contribute, is used to build up a fund to take care of the losses that are incurred when homeowners default on their mortgages and foreclosures become necessary. The fee protects the lender, not you; but you do derive some benefits from FHA insurance.

An advantage of an FHA-insured loan is that the property is inspected carefully by an FHA appraiser; and if it is judged to be worth less than what you expect to pay for it, you will learn this in time to avoid an unwise commitment. If you are building your own house on an FHA loan, or if the builder from whom you expect to buy has an FHA construction loan, the FHA will supervise each step in the building of the house, and the builder or contractor will have to comply with the exacting standards of the FHA. The FHA staff will check the construction several times while it is under way to see that specifications and conditions are met. It may be worth the extra 0.5 percent to be reassured that your house is being constructed properly and checked by an impartial outside agency. FHA insurance also provides a negative sort of benefit, in that if you did not have it, your lender might be forced to charge you a higher rate of interest because of the greater risk that he assumes.

Prepayment

If it can be arranged, the prepayment privilege—or the right to pay off your mortgage ahead of time—should be included in the mortgage agreement, instead of the usual prepayment penalty. This privilege enables you to take advantage of favorable circumstances when they exist and so possibly lighten your debt burden. In Inflationary times, the banks give discounts to homeowners who make partial or full prepayment on their mortgages, especially if the interest rate is low. The banks can make more profit lending out these funds at the current higher interest rate.

Points

Frequently, in periods of tight money, the lending institution may require you, the borrower, to pay "points." A point is 0.125 percent of interest or 1 percent of the face value of the mortgage loan. For example, if you have an 8 percent mortgage of $20,000 for 20 years, and are required to pay four points, the payment amounts to 4 percent × $20,000, or $800. The $800 is deducted immediately from the face value of the loan; therefore, you receive the use of only $19,200 in credit—not the full $20,000. Furthermore, your mortgage payments are actually something more than the 8 percent stated rate, since your interest costs are based on a loan of $20,000, or $800 more than the amount you actually receive. The four points are equal to 0.5 percent. The interest charged is therefore 8.5 percent. The shorter the maturity of the mortgage, the greater is the true rate of interest if points are paid. The more cash you put up, the less likely you are to pay heavily in points, which can go as high as 10 or 12. The number of points you may have to pay depends not only on the liquidity of money in general, but also on the lender who is involved, and the house you are buying. In some states points are forbidden on conventional loans, and although both the VA and the FHA frown on points, builders or sellers have been known to merely add the cost of points to the selling price of homes with VA or FHA-insured mortgages, and so indirectly pass the points on to the buyer. In fact, since VA and FHA mortgages are usually at lower rates than the conventional mortgage, such mortgages have been known to require more points. The VA and the FHA insure repayment, but they can't make a lending institution give you a loan.

Usury laws, which vary from state to state, have ironically hurt the mortgage borrower, the very person the laws are supposed to protect. The idea behind these laws was to ensure borrowers against paying very high interest rates, but when free market interest rates climb to 8 percent and a state law prohibits interest rates above 7 percent, lending institutions may choose to stop granting mortgages, since the law restricts them from charging the current competitive rate. In this case, the prospective borrower would be unable to obtain a mortgage, since no money is available, even if he were willing to pay 8 percent, because the state limited his right to do so.

Points paid by a buyer can be deducted from income tax as an interest expense. The seller cannot deduct the points, but can include them in the costs when computing the profit or loss on the sale of the house. The Truth in Lending law requires that points be disclosed.

Renegotiation

When interest rates vary dramatically in a short time, it is possible to renegotiate the terms of your loan, but certain caveats must be borne in mind. It is possible to refinance the mortgage at another bank or your own, but if the new expense equals the difference—or comes close—doing so may not be worthwhile. For example, getting a 7.5 percent mortgage instead of an 8.5 percent mortgage on your 25-year $25,000 loan may look attractive. But if you are charged a prepayment penalty of 2 percent, or $500, on the old loan (since the rate was computed on 25 years, and you are paying sooner), to which is added a service fee of 1 percent, or $250, to the new lender plus $500 for a new title search and title insurance and other costs for paperwork, it adds up to a grand total of about $1,400. You want to be sure that you are really saving and not just appearing to save. Unless you have at least eight years more of mortgage time left, you will not have saved much, since only then will you have reduced your monthly payment from $201 to $185, a savings of $192 a year, or $1,536 in eight years.

Death, Mortgages, and Insurance

Will you live to pay off the 20-year mortgage on your home? One out of four homeowners aged 40 will not. One out of six aged 35 will not. One out of ten aged 25 will not. But statistics do not really matter when you are the one. What will happen to your family if you die prematurely and there is an unpaid mortgage? In a way, a mortgage is a one-sided contract. It protects the lender and the investment in every possible way. For this protection the lender has:

1. A mortgage on your home.
2. A bond signed by you and your wife.
3. A fire insurance policy.
4. A title insurance policy.
5. Monthly payments from your income.

But unless you tie your insurance program to your mortgage, you have no protection against death or adversity, such as unemployment or financial reverses. The leading insurance companies have all developed plans which, by the use of decreasing term insurance (on top of ordinary life) that matches the decreasing principal owed over the life of the mortgage, guarantee your family the home free and clear of debt if you should die. In addition, these companies provide a reserve fund that you can draw upon if financial reverses hit during your lifetime and threaten your ownership of the house. Any good insurance agent will explain what one company calls its "assured home ownership plan." It is a sound idea and well worth investigating when you buy a home and obtain a mortgage loan. Mortgage redemption insurance protects the widow.

The Purchase Contract

When you have selected the house, given some thought to the financing, and decided to buy, the builder or seller will usually require a cash deposit as evidence that you really intend to go through with the deal. When you hand over the deposit, make certain that you get a signed agreement from the seller providing for a refund of your deposit if you are unable to obtain financing or if the builder or seller fails to carry out his part of the agreement. You may also expect to be asked to agree that if you fail to comply with your pledges, you will forfeit your deposit. Such clauses are customary in sales agreements. Try to be sure that the person to whom you are giving the deposit is reliable. Some prospective purchasers have lost their deposits to persons who were dishonest or went bankrupt.

The seller will also expect you to sign a contract of purchase. This sales contract is a legal agreement containing legal terms with which the average person is unfamiliar. Each term has specialized meaning based on tradition, court decisions, and precedents that vary from state to state and are not translatable by commonsense interpretation. The contract of purchase may be called a binder, a bid, a deposit receipt, an earnest money agreement, a memo, an offer to buy—but it is a contract and therefore binding in all the details of the agreement that you are signing. Consequently, you must be sure that your interests are protected, because the other party to the transaction is under no obligation to advise you as to the meaning and effect of the clauses contained therein. Since you will need a lawyer at some point in the proceedings, this is the time to consult one to be sure you are not signing future problems for yourself. If the agreement is drawn by the other side to the deal, have it carefully studied by your own attorney before you sign. Once you bind yourself to the agreement, you must abide by its consequences. Before you sign anything, be sure that you know what you are agreeing to and that you are able to comply with the financial arrangements. Neither party need do anything not specified in the contract, which is subject to negotiation.

The sales contract should cover the following points:

1. The sales price should be specified. For your protection, it is usually best if the contract states that the sales price is not subject to change. Some builders' contracts contain a so-called escalator clause which permits them to increase the price because of future cost increases. Such a clause should be avoided, but some builders may insist upon it. If they do, and you agree, in order to protect yourself you should insist upon a maximum beyond which you will not go.

2. The sales contract will state the amount of cash payment that will be required from you and the method of financing the balance. It must state the annual percentage rate, but under the Consumer Credit Protection Act, mortgage credit for the purchase of a home need not show the total amount of the finance charge in dollars and cents. Nor are charges for credit reports and appraisal fees included in the annual percentage rate for this type of mortgage loan. However, if "points" are to be paid, this must be shown. If the loan is for home improvements, not for the purchase of a home, then all charges must be shown in dollars and cents. If the contract requires that you arrange to obtain a loan for the balance due, it should provide that any cash deposit you make will be refunded to you if you cannot obtain appropriate financing.

3. The contract should require the seller to deliver the property to you on or before an agreed date, often 30 days after closing, and should set forth your right to withdraw and get your deposit back if the property is not delivered on time.

4. If you are buying a new house, it is desirable to have indicated in the contract (or by separate written agreement) what responsibility the builder will assume after you move in. You will want him to agree in writing to correct any defects due to poor material or workmanship within a limited period after you move in, without any cost to you. If the landscaping and seeding is not completed before you take possession, you may find that you will have to do it yourself unless there is an obligation in writing to complete the work.

5. In the case of new construction, the contract should provide that the builder will complete the home in accordance with definite plans and specifications, which you should either review or have an expert review for you for a small fee. Furthermore, you should be given a copy of the plans and specifications for your retention.

6. You should not sign any contract containing a so-called safety or escape clause which would enable the builder or seller to back out of the contract any time he wants to, unless you have similar rights. If you do sign such a contract, be sure it specifies that the builder or seller must advise you in writing on or before a definite date that he will accept your offer or that it will expire and you will be free to get your money back.

7. Be sure you have protection against mechanics' liens. The seller should agree to indemnify you

for any losses due to unpaid bills for labor or materials. Unlike other purchases, the buying of a home often carries with it a liability for the unpaid claims by those who supplied labor or materials for the house. If the bills for labor or materials are unpaid when you take title, craftsmen or tradesmen holding the unsatisfied bills can under certain circumstances file liens (mechanics' liens) against the house and collect from you—the purchaser.

8. There should be a clause protecting you against a defective title and providing for the return of the down payment or for clearing the title in case the title search should prove the title to be defective.

These are just a few of the items to check. Legal documents are complicated, and your best bet will be to retain a lawyer. The small fee may save you a large loss or an unhappy experience.

Deeds and Titles

Do you know the difference between a dower and curtesy? Between abstract and deed? Probably not! But you ought to before you buy a house!

A *deed* is a written instrument which is used for the purpose of transferring the title to real estate from one party to another.

Naturally, when you make as large a purchase as a house (and the land on which it stands), you will want to be as sure as you can that you really own it, that no one with a prior, unsettled claim will come along and dispute your title. But to try and make sure, prudent and cautious people have devised four techniques for checking the safety of their titles.

1. The first method used is the *abstract*. This involves having someone, usually a lawyer or a title guarantee company, trace and write up the history of the ownership of the property. The resulting legal document, the abstract, indicates whether there are any liens or claims outstanding, and if so, it states just what they are. An abstract does *not* evidence or guarantee title, but if the search has been careful and thorough and no unsettled claims appear, it provides reassurance.

2. A *certificate of title* may be used in some

areas in place of the abstract. It is merely a certification by an attorney that he has examined all records affecting the property and that in his opinion there appear to be no unsettled or prior liens or claims. But he is not guaranteeing this, and if his search has been made with due care, he cannot be held liable if in fact some obscure claim does arise to impair title.

3. The *Torrens certificate* is one issued by an official recorder or registrar stating ownership after all those who could possibly have a claim or lien have been notified and invited to sue. If no suit develops, as is usually the case, then a court orders the registrar to record the title in the new owner's name and to issue a certificate to this effect.

4. Finally, there is *title insurance*. A title guarantee company searches the records, and having established to its own satisfaction that a clear title is being transferred writes a policy in favor of the new owner, for a fee, insuring him against any loss from defects in the title other than those which may be stated in the policy. If a lawsuit should arise, the title company will defend for the owner and pay the expenses and costs involved. Although title insurance is now found mainly in the larger cities, its use is growing. Title insurance is nontransferable. Each new owner must buy a new policy.

Even though a married man or woman owns real estate in his or her own right, in some states good title cannot be passed to another person without having wife or husband join in the deed to release *dower* or *curtesy*. By common law, dower is the wife's right to a life interest in one third of her husband's real property in the event of his death. Dower and curtesy (the husband's right in his deceased wife's property, providing the couple had a child, even though the child may have predeceased the mother) still exist unimpaired in some states. In most states, these rights have been much modified by statute, so that if you are acquiring real property, it would be worthwhile to find out about the law in your state.

In many states a *homestead status* can be placed upon the house you buy. Under these statutes, the property is declared to be the home of the parties and is then protected from seizure for liability for debts. The amount of property exempted under the right of homestead differs from state to state; and in the same state, more property is exempted in the country than in a city. Some states fix the amount by area, some by value, and some by both. The statutes usually provide that a husband cannot transfer a homestead estate without his wife's consent. In many states, the widow or minor children succeed to the homestead right on the death of the husband.

The Final Settlement, or Closing the Loan

After financing has been arranged, the lender will set a date for "settlement" or "closing." On settlement day the property officially becomes yours. You will also remember it as the "paper signing" day. Among the papers that you will sign is the *note* or *bond* or other evidence of debt which is used in your area. This document is your promise to repay the loan with interest within a specified period of time, and it will show the repayment terms by means of an amortization schedule. Another paper that you will sign is the *mortgage* or *deed of trust,* which is a conditional lien and serves as security for the note or other evidence of the debt. Most of this document is devoted to outlining the rights of the lender in enforcing payment on the debt, including the right to "foreclose the mortgage" (take over the property) should you fail to make prompt payment of interest, principal, taxes, and insurance or should you neglect the property so that it is not in a good state of repair. The mortgage is recorded with the county clerk (or other proper official) in the county, town, or city in which your property is located. It remains on record there as a lien or claim against your property until the loan has been paid off.

A *title search* will have been made, and you will probably have purchased a *title insurance policy* to protect you from any loss that might result from defect in the title. You will receive a copy of this policy. A *survey* showing the exact boundaries of your property will perhaps have been made, and you will receive a copy of this. You

should also receive a copy of the bond, the mortgage, and the deed—the legal document conveying title to you. The original will probably have been sent to the proper local official for recording. Thus you should receive five documents: the *bond,* the *mortgage,* the *deed,* the *survey,* and the *title insurance policy,* as well as receipts for all of the payments you make. Ask for copies of all papers. Ordinarily they will be provided. Obviously, closing is a complicated business involving a number of legal documents which you have probably never seen before. Do not be afraid to ask questions about any or all of them; but even if you do ask many questions, you will probably not know or cover all the angles, and therefore it is a very good idea to have your lawyer along with you. The fee for this service will be well worth the reassurance and peace of mind that come from knowing that everything is being arranged properly.

Closing costs will probably run higher than you anticipated. These are the fees which you will have to pay at the settlement for all of the various documents that have been drawn and all of the services that have been rendered in connection with your buying the house, borrowing, and taking title.

Approximate closing costs on the purchase of a house ranging in price from $20,000 to $40,000 may run approximately as follows:

Credit report fee	$25–50
Survey	$75–250
Title fee	$100–400
Mortgage fee	$110–300
Recording fees	$10–20
Title insurance	$145–300
Bank's lawyer	$150–200
Buyer's lawyer	$100–500
Engineer's appaisal	$35–200
Advance real estate taxes ⎱ The amount required for
Advance insurance ⎰ the next due payment date

Closing costs as revealed in a national survey by the Department of Housing and Urban Development and the Veterans Administration average about $558.

Lenders are required to send you at this time a special booklet prepared by the U.S. Department of Housing and Urban Development (HUD).[9] This free booklet outlines settlement procedures and suggests ways of comparing costs. The lender must clearly identify firms you will be required to use for insurance and title examination. You must be given a Truth in Lending statement showing the APR on the mortgage loan—including possible points. On the day before the closing, you have the right to inspect the settlement statement to check out the more detailed and exact charges that should now be available.

To prevent borrowers from failing to keep up their tax and insurance payments, 1/12 of the estimated yearly tax and insurance payments is added to the monthly payments for principal and interest. The lending institution keeps this in a special "escrow" account and uses it to pay the taxes and insurance when these fall due. Taxes in arrears for one or more years would seriously shrink the security (the value of the property pledged for the loan), since the government has a first lien for property taxes. The lender cannot afford to take a chance on the borrower letting the insurance lapse.

The federal Real Estate Settlement Procedure Act limits escrow accounts to 1/12 of the amount projected for a year's taxes and insurance. Most regulation is on a state level and some states insist that interest payments be made to mortgage borrowers, but not necessarily at the same rate as interest payments on bank accounts. Consumer groups are focusing on two goals—a national law requiring interest on escrow accounts to be at passbook levels and mortgage borrowers to have the option of paying their own tax and insurance bills.

Tax Savings for the Homeowner

The homeowner, has a definite tax advantage over the renter. The homeowner may deduct from adjusted gross income (a) interest paid on a mortgage loan, (b) points paid in the year that the mortgage was taken, (c) real estate property taxes, (d) any casualty losses in excess of those compensated for by insurance, and (e) interest paid on loans for repairs and improvements.

Assume that A rents an apartment, that B owns a house, and that both have the same adjusted income after all other deductions. In addition, however, B pays $370 in real estate taxes and $530 interest on a mortgage. Now assume that both A and B are in the same income tax bracket of 30 percent. B can claim another $900 in deductions ($370 + $530) that will save him $270 in income taxes (0.30 × $900), which A cannot do.

Ordinarily, if you sell your house at a higher price than you paid for it, you will be taxed (at capital gains rates) on the profit. However, if you buy another house within 18 months of your sale of the old one, and the new house costs as much as or more than you received for the old one, you do not pay a capital gains tax on the profit from the old house. This was explained in more detail in Chapter 5. If you sell your old house and build a new one, you have 24 months following the sale to build and move in. Furthermore, you can start construction 12 months before you sell. The 18- and 24-month rules apply only to your "principal residence" and not to a vacation house. The 1978 tax law allows more than one tax-free "rollover" within 18 months to a homeowner, if the homeowner moves for employment reasons. They apply in similar fashion when you sell and then buy a co-op apartment or a condominium apartment. If instead of realizing a profit on the sale, you take a loss, you cannot deduct the loss either from other capital gains or from regular income.

If you sell your home at a profit and don't buy another, you can minimize your capital gains tax by adding to the original cost of the house all of the capital improvements that you put into it during your ownership. You can also add your initial buying costs, such as attorney's fees and title search charges. Finally, you can subtract from the price you received all sales costs, such as attorney's fees, broker's commission, the cost of advertising, and "fix up" costs prior to sale.

An individual who is 55 years of age or older

---

[9] Complaints about RESPA (Real Estate Settlement Procedure Act) violations should be sent to the governmental agency supervising that particular type of lender from whom you obtained your loan, with a copy to the Assistant Secretary for Consumer Affairs and Regulatory Functions, Real Estate Practices Division, Department of Housing and Urban Development, Room 4100, Washington, D.C. 20410.

may exclude $100,000 of capital gains in a once-in-a-lifetime sale of a personal residence occupied for at least three of the previous five years.

According to the Tax Foundation, Inc., every state has adopted some form of tax relief for homeowners who are 65 years or older and have a minimum income. Similar federal legislation is pending. The relief takes different forms. In Connecticut, where the income ceiling is $7,500, a rebate is given, depending upon the income. In New York it takes the form of a 50 percent reduction in assessed valuation. In New Jersey it is a flat $160 reduction in the homeowner's property tax bill. The Bureau of the Census reports that persons 65 years or older paid more than 8 percent of their incomes for real estate taxes. All other age groups paid about 4 percent.

Home Improvement Loans

Want to borrow to install air conditioning, wall-to-wall carpeting, or a swimming pool in the back-yard? The FHA won't help you do this. But it will help if you want to add a room or bath, or redo the porch or roof, or put in a new heating system or a septic tank. The FHA has a program for *insuring*, not making, loans for home improvements.

The purpose of the loan must be for a permanent, structural improvement. FHA home improvement loans, unlike FHA mortgage loans, do not guarantee the approval of any product or installation.

The FHA insures your lender. For this the FHA collects a premium of 0.5 percent of the net proceeds of the loan. By protecting the lender, the insurance helps you get the loan, because the lender is encouraged to make what is a virtually riskless loan. You can, of course, obtain a non-FHA-insured home improvement loan from various commercial lenders, but such a loan will cost you more, because the lender is taking the whole risk. FHA Title I loans are for a maximum of $10,000, with a maximum APR of 12 percent. If the amount of the loan is above $7,500, a lien is required. Maximum maturity is 15 years.

Section 203K loans are for a maximum of 20 years, and may be for normal rehabilitation if the house is at least ten years old. If the house is not that old, a Section 203K loan may be used to correct a major structural fault or to repair damage caused by a disaster, such as a fire. Loans can range from $12,000 up to $17,400 per family unit, depending on the cost levels in the area. Interest rates are those current in the area, plus the 0.5 percent FHA insurance premium.

The FHA regional office has on file—available for inspection—a list of companies and individuals that are thought to have done unsatisfactory work on home improvement jobs financed by the FHA. However, the FHA will not spell out the details.

The Veterans Administration guarantees repayment of 60 percent of a home improvement loan or $17,500, whichever is less, and it allows the borrower up to 30 years to repay. However, the interest rate of 8½ percent may be below the market rate, and a lender may not be interested in making such a loan. To get a VA guarantee you must naturally be a veteran and you must either own your own home or be buying it with GI financing.

Other sources for home improvement loans are credit unions, banks, savings and loan associations, and finance companies, all of which charge varying rates that are naturally lower for secured loans than for unsecured loans.

The home improvement business is booming—20 percent more was spent this year than last year to modernize or expand the family home. A trade publication, *Building Supply News,* estimates that there are two modernization projects every year for each of the country's 40 million single-family homes. The most expensive projects can be the remodeling of the kitchen and the adding of a room. Significant savings result when the do-it-yourselfer contributes what has become known as "sweat equity". The National Home Improvement Council estimates that 50 percent of home improvement work is being done this way. Sometimes, it's because it's easier to learn to do the work oneself than finding a professional who will do a fairly small job. A survey based on written responses to a questionnaire conducted by National Family Opinion, Inc., of Toledo and the Bureau of Building Marketing Research found that more than 900,000 families add rooms to their homes each year. Converting basement space to rooms was about $500 cheaper per room than conversion of attic space, and so five times as many basements were converted.

Why the boom? In a time of scarce and costly mortgages, rising home prices, and hesitancy over what to do, home remodeling becomes a solution. Lenders are willing to make remodeling loans because such loans yield more than mortgage loans. You can borrow up to 90 percent of your equity for a home improvement loan. Experts suggest plans with an eye directed toward adding to the future sales value of your house. "Your remodeling dollar comes back 100 percent on resale if it is spent on adding new space to the house, 75 percent if you modernize existing rooms, and 50 percent if you add fancy luxuries such as patios and pools."

A decision on the financing method for home improvements depends on a number of factors, some of the most important being the kind and amount of indebtedness that already exists on the property, the borrower's financial condition, and the type and extent of the improvements that are to be made. Sometimes, depending on the circumstances, it might be more advantageous to refinance and to include the cost of the improvements in a new long-term mortgage, which carries a lower interest charge than a short-term loan.

When you use your home as security in financing a home improvement job, the lender must provide you with the proper forms and with notice of your right to cancel without obligation within three business days. If payment is allowed in more than four installments, the contractor must wait until three days have passed before beginning work unless you, by letter or wire (no telephone call), waive your right because of an emergency. The purpose of this section of the Truth in Lending law is to protect your home against high-pressure or unscrupulous dealers who trick you into agreements that, after some thought, you would like to void.

Through banks and credit unions, state programs are offering homeowners home improvement loans

for energy saving at an average 8–11 percent, fully two percentage points below the usual rates.

Potential problems abound, whether you deal with reputable contractors or unknowingly become involved with the phony repair gyp artists. The latter are more likely to canvass a neighborhood looking for work. They use scare tactics to get jobs. Your roof, seen while they were doing work at a neighboring home, needs quick repair. They would do it—at a bargain price for all cash. The danger signals here are obvious. If a contractor is licensed, you feel that he's legitimate. The license number on a business card or an estimate form can be checked by a call to the Consumer Affairs Department in your area, to see whether the license is still valid. But even a licensed contractor can do shoddy work. Consumerists suggest that you get competitive written bids from at least three licensed contractors and that each furnish a number of addresses of prior customers. These should be called to verify that they were really customers and not friends and that the contractor did the work in the time specified, and in a satisfactory manner.

After you select the most competent contractor, who should also be checked for credit references and liability insurance coverage, it is advisable to spell out in writing how and when payments are to be made. If the payment schedule calls for payment as the work progresses, it is prudent for the homeowner to arrange never to pay more than the proportion of the work that has been done and to still have money due to the contractor at the completion of the job. You should specifically detail in writing the fixtures, sizes, colors, and brands that are to be supplied and the guarantees and responsibilities of everyone involved. One bank even suggests that the check for the final payment of the loan be issued on a joint basis to you and your contractor. You can protect yourself by not endorsing and releasing the funds until you are satisfied with the project.

The Co-op

The purchaser of a cooperative apartment buys an interest in a nonprofit corporation which will own and run the building. In this sense the owner of a co-op apartment is a landlord, but also a tenant in responsibility to the board of directors of the co-op.

A member of the cooperative does not directly own the apartment. You own a membership certificate which carries the right to occupy your apartment and to participate in the management as a member of the board or as a voter. Mortgage charges, real estate taxes, maintenance costs, repairs, replacements, and administration are budgeted annually, and the overall costs are divided among the members of the cooperative in proportion to the number of shares they hold. That number is based on the value of the apartment. The sale of an apartment is done by the transfer of shares in the cooperative, and must be approved by the co-op board. The cooperative has a blanket mortgage. Before purchasing an apartment it is vital to see if a reputable institution holds the mortgage, check its rate of amortization and its time for refinancing. If the latter comes too soon, and in a period of rising interest rates, it would mean higher maintenance costs for you.

The Co-op versus Leasing

Carrying charges for a co-op may be lower than the rental price for a similar apartment. Also, as a co-op member, you have income tax benefits because of your share in the ownership of real estate. You may deduct your share of the interest on the co-op's mortgage and your share of the real estate taxes that the co-op pays. The amount you can deduct will vary according to your tax bracket.

As a tenant you have the advantage of using your capital in any investment venture, since it is not frozen into the cost of your apartment. You need not worry about the sale of your apartment in the future, nor about whether you can recoup your investment. Although you know that your rent may go up, you do not have to share increased maintenance costs with other co-op owners if there is a high vacancy rate or unexpected repair expense.

The co-op buyer should check to determine whether the maintenance budget includes adequate reserves for major repairs or replacements. The total cost and valuation of the prospective co-op building should be compared with those of similar buildings in the same or comparable neighborhoods.

Even after you carefully and deliberately buy into a co-op in which the major part of your maintenance fee is included in mortgage interest and amortization charges, you will soon find, if current trends continue, that your cost will grow. As fixed expenses rise sharply through increased fuel costs, payroll pacts, inflation-affected repair costs—and even an increased assessed valuation of property for rising real estate taxes. Today's higher costs and interest rates increasingly necessitate financing for the purchase of units in co-ops. New banking laws in some states, for example, now permit both savings and commercial banks to offer housing-type loans that use co-op shares as security, instead of the short-term, high-interest personal loans which were the only possibility before. Some states allow financing of up to 75 percent of the purchase price for a maximum term of 20 years to be repaid in equal installments of principal and interest.

Co-op or Condominium?

You are closer to true ownership when you buy a condominium. The purchaser actually gets a deed to his own apartment, plus an undivided share in the halls, elevators, heating equipment, and other common facilities.

1. In condominiums, an individual takes title to a unit; in cooperatives, an individual owns stock in the cooperative and has the right of occupancy to a specific unit.

2. In condominiums, individuals vote proportionately according to the value of their units; in cooperatives, each individual has one vote, regardless of the size of the unit.

3. In condominiums, individuals are taxed separately; in cooperatives, individuals pay their share of the taxes on the project in their monthly carrying charges.

4. In condominiums, individuals are responsible only for mortgage indebtedness and taxes involving their own property and for their proportionate share of the expenses of operating the common property. They have no mortgage indebtedness, tax, or other liability for the other properties; in cooperatives, each individual is dependent upon the solvency of the entire project.

5. The condominium owner is free to sell his apartment to anyone, but the co-op owner is bound by the need to have the purchaser approved by the board of directors. A co-op purchaser must assume the seller's pro rata share of the unpaid indebtedness under the blanket mortgage. Therefore, a co-op seller must find a buyer with enough cash to make such a purchase. The purchaser of the condominium, on the other hand, can mortgage his unit to finance his purchase—like any other home buyer. The FHA has been authorized to provide mortgage insurance—under the National Housing Act of 1961—for condominiums which provide ownership of apartments in multiple dwellings.

6. The condominium apartment is treated like a separate parcel of real estate—even assessed and taxed separately. On the other hand, if the owner of a cooperative apartment does not pay his share of the maintenance charges, that share must eventually be distributed among the other owners.

7. If the stockholder-tenant of a cooperative violates the terms of agreement (lease), he may be dispossessed in the same manner as a defaulting tenant (renter). However, in the absence of special statutory authorization, the condominium owner cannot be ousted from possession for infraction of the bylaws or regulations.

One experienced condominium owner notes that although it is true that the owner of a condominium unit is legally free to sell his apartment to whomever he chooses, actually he is apt to accept a stipulation in the articles of the condominium that any new owner must be acceptable to the board and that the condominium association will have the prior right to purchase at the market price. "Most owners," he says, "are willing to accept this because it means that the characteristics which made the complex suitable for them in the first place will not be drastically changed."

If you are a typical condo buyer, you probably rented before buying and you probably belong to one of two distinct age groups. Those in the first group are between 45 and 64 years old, have grown families, and are seeking a smaller dwelling. Those in the second group are 25 to 34 years old, are likely to be professionals, and live in either single-person or two-person households.

Both condominiums and co-ops run the gamut from luxury to low-cost facilities. Speculation and high profits create special dangers for prospective purchasers of both types of unit. In the co-op area, profit-hungry owners of rental property may push co-opting upon tenants and unload property at self-serving sales prices and under management contracts which prove to be expensive to a new co-op association. For the individual purchaser this may mean higher maintenance costs to pay the resultant high mortgage debt that the association faces. It may also mean long delay in occupying an apartment that has been paid for, if a reluctant tenant occupant won't move without court action. In many states, new regulations increase the percentage of the tenants whose approval is required before a co-op can be created. This provides protection for both current tenants and future owners.

The future condominium owner faces a different risk. During a seemingly booming market, overexpansion in building and speculative buying and selling of units under construction may not only increase prices but also lead to foreclosure. The investor who puts down 10 percent on a condominium unit under construction can lose the deposit if the project folds.

Other special risks to the prospective condominium buyer result from the fact that in large areas consumer protection provisions are nonexistent. The expectation is that half of the population will live in condominiums within 20 years. In Milwaukee, 45 percent of new housing is condominium housing; in Cleveland, 57 percent; in Bridgeport, Connecticut, 83 percent. This rush to condominium living has revealed many problems, including lack of state regulation and possible conflicting regulation among federal agencies.[10]

Sometimes title to the land is kept and leased back to the buyers for 99 years. In other instances, builders warranties, usually a year in length, often run out before the last owner moves in.

Condominium boards may discover that they have to cope with a costly long-term management built into the agreement by the developer. The ads promise "Carefree Condominium Living." But as someone said, "It's true. The developer doesn't care, and nobody else cares either."

In 1974, after two years of public hearings and commission study, however, the state of Florida, long a condo mecca, passed a comprehensive condominium regulation law tightening the reins on developers in an effort to eliminate the various abuses which had been observed. For example, the developer's control of common parking areas and recreational facilities was made much more difficult to achieve and the developer's ability to dominate the condominium association was curbed. Condominium buyers were given 15 days in which they might cancel a contract for the purchase of a unit.

Some insurance companies provide insurance tailored especially for condominium owners. If fire or an accident occurs on the common property of the condominium, each unit owner is liable for the damage and assessed accordingly. The common practice of renting out a condominium unit during the owner's absence requires a special type of coverage against loss or damage.

When You Buy—A Baker's Dozen

1. Check on the reputation of the builder.
2. Make sure you know what you are buying and what you are responsible for.

[10] In an effort to guide buyers, the booklet *Questions about a Condominium—What to Ask before you Buy* has been published by HUD. It may be obtained by writing the Office of Public Affairs; Department of Housing and Urban Development, Washington, D.C. 20410. See also "Condominium Crack Down," *Barron's,* April 14, 1975.

3. Read all the legal documents—with the aid of a lawyer.
4. Find out whether the developer is retaining the right to manage the project and whether residents can fire him.
5. Make sure that the management fee includes everything, so that you don't face unexpected assessments for the use of common and recreational facilities.
6. If the developer promises "maintenance-free living," is this exterior or interior maintenance?
7. What kind of warranty do you have on all equipment?
8. Don't allow your deposit to be commingled with the developer's funds. Your deposit should be held in escrow.
9. Read the operating budget. It should clearly spell out assessments and services.
10. Check the estimated real estate taxes.
11. What are the restrictions on the resale of your unit? Or on the leasing of your unit?
12. Has the developer provided reserve funds to correct construction flaws after the buyer moves in?
13. Who pays the maintenance costs for unsold units? You don't want to.

Mobile Homes

The most common type of mobile home is the single unit 12 feet wide by 65 feet long. There are "expandables" which telescope inside the home during highway movement and can add 60 to 100 square feet to a room at the homesite. There are double-width units with 28-foot living rooms. The current average price is $8.50 per square foot, including furnishings and appliances. The average mobile home costs from $7,800 to $11,000 nationally, and the average resale value of a mobile home is $5,000. There are extremes, though, especially in California, Florida, and Arizona, where you can find five-star-rated mobile parks and mobile homes whose facades, landscaping, and furnishings cost as much as $78,125. Four out of five mobiles have

282

become "immobile mobiles" and are being treated as permanent housing. Space in mobile parks can be rented or purchased. Rents in luxury Western parks run from $95 to $225 a month, as compared to Eastern rentals of $80 to $120 a month. When you examine the average price for a mobile home, the growth of the industry from 103,700 in 1960 to almost 600,000 today is understandable. Mobile homes cater to both ends of the housing market—95 percent are in the below-$5,000 sector, and the remainder are superluxury. Many mobile home manufacturers have gone into mobile park development to ensure a place for their products.

Extras to Buy Although furniture, drapes, and carpeting are included in the purchase price, extras are frequently required by mobile home communities. These may include steps with handrails for the outside door, skirting to conceal the wheels, and supports or piers to provide a foundation.

Standards and Improvements More than 65 percent of the mobile homes produced today are built to established national standards. These were developed by the American National Standards Institute (ANSI).[11] However, the high fire risk of mobile homes and the lack of state and federal supervision have been criticized.

Financing The VA may guarantee or make direct loans to finance mobile home purchases of up to $10,000 for a mobile home and of up to $17,000 if a lot is purchased together with the home. Once the mobile home loan is paid off, the GI can use the VA loan benefits to purchase a conventional home. The purchase price for a mobile home is much lower than that for a house, but the additional cost of renting ground in one of the 22,000 mobile parks must be considered.

The FHA also insures mobile home loans of up to $10,000 and for as long as 12 years. If the mobile home is made up of two or more modules, the loan limit rises to $15,000 and can last for 15 years. The minimum down payment is 5 percent of the first $6,000. The maximum annual percentage rate ranges from 7.97 percent to 10.57 percent, de-

pending on the amount and the term of the loan. The payments must be in equal monthly installments. An FHA Title I loan is applicable on a mobile home only if the mobile home is the borrower's principal residence, not a summer home, on a site that meets FHA requirements.

The buyer of a mobile home can expect lower charges for insurance, utilities, taxes, and maintenance, and he also has the opportunity to change his location. An experienced owner warns, however, that if you try to move a mobile home off the original site, you may have a difficult time finding another place to park it. People have often had to buy a new mobile home to gain entry into a desirable mobile home park. Resale values of mobile homes are low. Mobile homes values usually go down like car values, 20 percent depreciation in the first year, 10 percent in the second and third years, and 5 percent in each of the next few years.

The Town House

The very opposite of mobile homes has also found a new appeal. The town house (called the brownstone in New York)—available in the older areas of most big U.S. cities—has had a revival through renovation for those who want space, prefer city living, and seek a bargain. In areas whose town houses have already been successfully converted, there are few bargains left, as prices have escalated. Taxes are usually lower than in the suburbs. Most town houses are so built that it is possible to convert them into separate apartments and thus pay off the mortgage, and perhaps even live rent-free, by renting to tenants. Renovation is possible by either of two extremes. An architect and a contractor supported by a goodly sum of thousands can do a beautiful job. Or there is "sweat equity."

Town houses are no longer purely urban, as their name would imply. The term now refers to houses with shared party walls, wherever they may be. In a recent Urban Land Institute survey of residents in 49 town house projects on the East and West coasts, two out of five owners replied that they

---

[11] *Buying and Financing a Mobile Home,* HUD Publication no. 243 (Washington, D.C.: U.S. Government Printing Office, September 1973).

planned to stay five or more years. But 75 percent declared that they would not move to another town house. The reasons offered were lack of privacy, noise, and monotonous development views.

Cluster Housing

Home ownership has become identified with other types of units than the single-family home. In order to cope with the rising cost of the limited amount of land that is within commuting distance from city jobs, there has been an increasing use of suburban residential units in "cluster zoning." The trend toward multifamily, garden apartment house communities developed quickly—especially when such communities were planned with recreational and environmental "amenities" that compensated for the loss of the privacy of individual lots. Clustering residential units makes land areas available for tennis courts, swimming pools, and golf courses. Changing lifestyles have shifted emphasis to human ecology—to new planned communities with elements of "togetherness" around the community swimming pool or the neighborhood village shopping center.

The Zero Lot Line

A new housing concept is the "zero lot line" which either separates single-family homes by a very narrow space or connects them by means of a garage or a storage room. Builders figure that by eliminating large side yards they save so much on land costs that they can offer three- and four-bedroom houses for less than $45,000.

Prefab Housing

Prefabricated houses used to be temporary summer homes or inexpensive, unsubstantial shelters that were hedged in by zoning laws and building codes. Today they are available in choice designs, range up to $40,000 in price (not including the lot), and are now acceptable in many localities. Restrictions on their use are being removed. Financing prefabs is easier today than it was in the past.

There are still problems. To get the home erected, you must frequently employ the one local firm that specializes in this type of housing, regardless of its reputation for quality and regardless of which company sold you the prefab. It is also often necessary to adapt the plumbing and electrical equipment of prefabs to fit existing codes. But since the construction costs of prefabs are lower and construction time is halved, prefab housing has become an acceptable choice for a growing number.

INSURANCE

The Homeowner's Policy

Homeowner's policies have been rewritten in simple English. Called the Homeowner's 76, the new homeowner's policies have been accepted in a number of states, but they must still get approval from state insurance regulators in some states and legislative approval in others. As discussed in Chapter 4, simple English clarifies coverage and limitations in understandable fashion, but in the process raises problems of translating legalese into acceptable judicial interpretation.

Aside from the change in language, the homeowner's policy offers the same advantages it has in the past. You have only one policy and one premium to worry about, and by packaging a number of perils in one policy, the insurance companies are able to offer the policy at 30 to 40 percent less than that of separately purchased coverages.

The homeowner's policy provides both property and liability coverage. The property coverage includes your house or dwelling and your garage. Your personal property is insured, including household contents and personal belongings used, owned, worn, or carried by you or your family. Even away from home you are covered up to 10 percent of the amount of your policy. If you wish, this coverage may also apply to the personal belongings of your friends while they are on your premises. Certain limits are set on the amount of coverage on money, stamps, jewelry, and furs. If you want to recover full value for loss of or damage to such items, you should have them covered under separate policies. You are also insured for additional living expense when damage to your home requires you to live elsewhere—in a hotel, for example—while a house damaged by fire is being repaired. Automobiles, although personal property, are not protected under a homeowner's policy. The standard policies explicitly cover students if they have been in residence at school 45 days. If not permanently installed in a car, stereo equipment is covered without limit.

Against what perils is your property insured under the homeowner's policy? That depends on the form of the policy (see Figure 9–4). The *Basic Form* insures against 11 named perils. The *Broad Form,* which is the most popular, covers 18 perils. The *Comprehensive Form* is a so-called all-risks contract. Actually, no policy gives you protection against every possible peril. Generally speaking, an all-risks contract is one that covers you for everything except—and then it lists the exceptions. In the Comprehensive Form, the perils excluded are earthquake, flood, war, and nuclear attack. The major difference between the Comprehensive Form and the other forms is that the Comprehensive Form lists the perils that you are *not* insured

against, and the other forms list the perils that you *are* insured against. The former names the exclusions; the latter name the perils.

Liability coverage in all forms of the homeowner's policy includes comprehensive personal liability, medical payments, and physical damage to the property of others. *Comprehensive personal liability* protects you against claims arising from bodily injury to others or damage to their property. For example, suppose your neighbor slips and falls on your icy steps, suffers a head injury which impairs vision, and then files suit for damages. Your insurance company will represent you in court, and if the court verdict goes against you, damages will be paid by your insurance company up to the limit of your policy. A note of caution: in states where workmen's compensation insurance is required by law, the personal liability coverages under the homeowner's policy do not provide coverage if a cook, housekeeper, maid, or other employee is injured.

Medical payments coverage protects you when persons are accidentally injured on or away from your premises if the injury is caused by you, by members of your family, or by your animals. The

FIGURE 9–4
Perils against Which Properties Are Insured by a Homeowner's Policy

Forms	Perils
BASIC (HO-1)	1. fire or lightning 2. loss of property removed from premises endangered by fire or other perils 3. windstorm or hail 4. explosion 5. riot or civil commotion	6. aircraft 7. vehicles 8. smoke 9. vandalism and malicious mischief 10. theft 11. breakage of glass constituting a part of the building (not included in HO-3 & HO-4)
BROAD (HO-2)	12. falling objects 13. weight of ice, snow, sleet 14. collapse of building(s) or any part thereof 15. sudden and accidental tearing asunder, cracking, burning, or bulging of a steam or hot water heating system or of appliances for heating water 16. accidental discharge, leakage or overflow of water or steam from	within a plumbing, heating or air-conditioning system or domestic appliance 17. freezing of plumbing, heating and air-conditioning systems and domestic appliances 18. sudden and accidental injury from artificially generated currents to electrical appliances, devices, fixtures and wiring (TV and radio tubes not included)
COMPREHENSIVE (HO-5)	All perils **EXCEPT:** flood, earthquake, war, nuclear attack and others specified in your policy. Check your policy for a complete listing of perils excluded.	

Source: Insurance Information Institute, "A Family Guide to Property and Liability Insurance.

insurance company reimburses the injured party, regardless of who is at fault, for medical and surgical services incurred within one year of the accident. The basic amount of this protection under the homeowner's policy is $500 for each person. Unlike medical payments in the case of automobile insurance, the coverage in the homeowner's policy applies only to outsiders—not to you or to members of your family. *Physical damage to the property of others* is easy to understand. If your child kicks a football through the neighbor's picture window, under your homeowner's policy the insurance company will pay the damages up to the limit of the policy.

If you live in an apartment, a rented house, or a co-op, you will find that the same sort of insurance package that is offered to homeowners is now widely available. It's called the Residence Contents Broad Form, or Tenant's Form HO-4. It protects your furniture and your personal belongings against loss or damage from the 18 perils as seen in figure 9–4. It also provides the three liability coverages. For insurance on $25,000 worth of personal property in a city apartment, the cost will range from $200 to $600 for three years, depending on the city, the neighborhood, the type of construction and the available fire protection.

How Much Property and Liability Insurance Do You Need?

It is difficult to estimate insurance needs because you cannot know ahead of time how large the claim or suit against you may be. Even against persons of average means, jury awards may be very high. Therefore, most people, especially those who have assets and salaries or other income to protect, should carry at least $25,000 of liability insurance. As to property insurance, the amount you need depends on the replacement value of your house and personal property. If your home burned to the ground, how much would it cost, at today's prices, to replace it? Do you know the value of the contents of your house? Replacement cost is the basis for determining how much property insurance is enough. It is figured by multiplying the original cost of your house by a factor that is determined both by the year in which the house was built and by the material used. Your insurance company can provide that factor.

Assume that your house would cost $40,000 to rebuild and that your household contents are valued at $20,000. To receive full payment (replacement cost) for partial loss or damage to your house under the homeowner's policy, you need to insure it for at least 80 percent of the replacement value. Otherwise, the company will pay only actual cash value, which is replacement cost minus depreciation. Replacement cost is paid only on structures, while the contents of a house are covered for no more than depreciated cash value.

Inflation and Insurance[12]

In many states you can obtain homeowner's inflation protection. This provides for an automatic increase in the amount of insurance protection provided by your policy whenever the cost of living and of building construction rises because of inflation. The automatic adjustment can work in several ways. Many policies provide for an increase in protection every three months at the rate of 1 percent of the face of the policy. At least one policy increases the protection monthly, based on changes in the Composite Construction Cost Index computed by the Department of Commerce and on changes in the consumer price index computed by the Department of Labor. Under either plan there is no charge for the additional coverage during the policy period. However, when the policy is renewed, the premium is adjusted, based on the new amount of insurance. Insurance experts say that many homes are underinsured, as construction costs have increased more than 50 percent since 1967. Therefore, an automatic annual increase in coverage of only 4 percent may not be adequate in light of the inflated replacement costs. Some insurance companies automatically increase coverage 8–10 percent at each annual renewal. Some insurance companies have developed tables that estimate what those costs might be. Such factors as the number of room units and the type and

---

[12] "Pacing Insurance to Inflation." Supplement. *Business Week,* March 5, 1979, pp. 102–104.

materials of construction provide the primary expense estimate. To figure the replacement costs fairly accurately, this must then be multiplied by an area cost modifier that takes the varying local material and labor costs into consideration.

Fire Insurance Policies

Fire insurance reimburses the homeowner for the replacement value (less depreciation) of property destroyed, not for its original cost.

When you buy fire insurance, a "form" or "endorsement" is attached to the standard contract by the company. It contains all the personal details of the contract, for example, the amount of insurance, a description of the property covered, its location, and the owner. The form, or endorsement, becomes part of the contract. In fact, without it the standard policy insures nothing. Basically all fire insurance provisions fall into two categories:

1. The provisions that explain the risks covered and the risks excluded.
2. The provisions that should be considered before a loss occurs and those that should be considered after a fire.

Annual Fire Premiums Annual premiums for fire insurance vary widely, depending on such factors as the property's construction, use, location, and nearness to a hydrant; the adequacy of the water supply; and the fire-fighting facilities. Fire insurance rates are customarily expressed as the number of dollars or cents which would be charged for $100 of insurance for one year. Thus a rate of 20 cents means that you pay 20 cents for each $100 of fire insurance protection. An $8,000 policy would thus cost $16. Under the best conditions an annual rate approaching $1 per $1,000 of insurance may be expected, whereas the rate can be a much as $8 per $1,000 under extremely unfavorable conditions. A rate in the neighborhood of $3.20 per $1,000 has been fairly typical for an ordinary frame house, but, like everything else, fire insurance rates have tended to go up. Some companies will reduce the rate if a smoke detection system is installed. As a contribution to safety—and perhaps health—the Hanover Insurance Company is offering a 5 percent discount to families of nonsmokers.

Extended Coverage on Fire Policies Since fire insurance is designed only to reimburse the loss resulting from fire or lightning, it is sensible to consider whether additional insurance should be carried to obtain protection against other hazards. Fire policies often add *extended coverage* offering protection against damage by cyclones, tornados, hurricanes, hailstorms, windstorms, and such unrelated things as damage caused by motor vehicles, airplanes, explosions, riots, or smoke damage. The fee for extended coverage is small, ranging from 4 to 20 cents per $100 of protection for one year. The fire insurance companies have also developed another "endorsement" or "clause" which may be added to your fire policy. This is called *additional extended coverage,* and it provides protection against water damage from plumbing and heating systems; vandalism and malicious mischief; glass breakage; ice, snow, and freezing; the fall of trees; and building collapse. The rate for additional extended coverage is six cents per $100 of protection for one year. Most extended coverage policies and all additional extended coverage policies are sold with $50 deductible clauses.

Many buyers of homeowner's policies are not aware that price competition exists. A combination of state laws and industry-sponsored proposals began in 1970 to phase out standard set rates and to substitute "open rating." Insurers had historically been exempt from antitrust laws because they had used standard rates based on a broad sampling of losses that was not available to any one company. The Insurance Services Office, the industry-owned rating service, is now supplying insurers with raw data on prospective losses and expenses in order to allow insurers to formulate their own rates. The "open rating" now used in many states allows insurance companies to change rates before notifying the insurance regulatory authorities, a practice previously forbidden. Rates have been cut over widespread geographic areas, increasing competition. For example, among some 180 insurance companies doing business in New York State, there is as much as 50 percent divergence in the prices they offered for identical coverage.

Cancellation   There is a commonly misunderstood fact that deserves mention. If a person buys a fire policy and wants to cancel it, he will probably not receive a pro rata refund of his premium but will receive a refund based on a short-rate table contained in or on the policy. This refund is considerably smaller than the pro rata amount. If the company wishes to cancel, it must give you written notice five days (in some states ten days) before the insurance is to be terminated. The purpose is to give you a few days to seek protection from some other company.

Coinsurance   Many people underinsure their properties either because they expect a fire loss, if it occurs, to be only a small percentage of the total value of the property or because, having bought the property and originally taken out the fire insurance some years back, they have not taken into consideration the property's subsequent appreciation in value due to inflation.

In states having a "coinsurance" clause in the standard fire insurance contract, the underinsurer is often surprised and shocked to find that only part of the amount of a fire loss can be recovered from the insurance company, even though the face amount of the policy actually exceeds the amount of the fire loss. If you fail to carry insurance amounting to 80 percent of the value of your property, in the event of a loss you must share the loss with the insurance company and you may collect only that proportion of the loss which the amount of insurance that you actually have bears to the amount of insurance that you should have under the coinsurance clause. For example, if you own a property valued at $20,000, you should, under a typical coinsurance provision, carry $16,000 worth of fire insurance. Suppose that you carry only $8,000 in fire insurance and that a fire causes an $8,000 loss. You will be surprised to find that you cannot collect the whole $8,000 from the insurance company. You are a coinsurer with the company for one half of the loss, since you were carrying only one half ($8,000) of the insurance

that you should have been carrying ($16,000). You will therefore collect only $8,000/$16,000, or one half of the loss, namely, $4,000.

Some people, on the other hand, believe that in the event of any loss, either partial or total, the property owner is entitled to collect only that percentage of his loss which is stated in the coinsurance clause. For example, they think that if a man owns a building worth $20,000 and carries $16,000 of insurance with an 80 percent coinsurance clause, he will collect only 80 percent of any loss. Thus, if he has a $2,000 loss, they believe that he would collect only $1,600. This impression is incorrect. He would collect $2,000. He will collect in full any loss up to $16,000, since he has purchased the full protection required, namely, 80 percent of the property's value.

Things to Watch in Fire Policies   A fire policy may be unknowingly voided for various reasons stated in the policy. You will not know about these unless you read your policy carefully. For example, if you leave your house unoccupied for more than 60 consecutive days, you may void your policy. If you add a room, you may need more insurance. Does your policy cover your household furnishings as well as the house itself? If so, do you have an inventory of the furnishings, so that you can prove your loss in the event of fire? Your insurance broker can give you a room-by-room form which makes inventory taking easier. Put the completed inventory in your safe deposit box. Some homeowners take their inventories with a camera, photographing each room and then putting the pictures in a safe deposit box. If household furnishings are covered, you may also have a 10 percent off-premises clause in the policy, protecting your personal property away from your home. You may not know about this, suffer a fire loss while traveling, and fail to collect. Policies cover the losses due to damage by water used to extinguish the fire. They also cover the cost of removing debris.

The 10 percent provision is important in three instances.

1. Ten percent of the insurance on your dwelling can be applied to cover losses on other buildings on your premises. Suppose your house is in-

sured for $12,000. Your garage burns down. The company will pay up to 10 percent of $12,000, or $1,200, on the loss of the garage. If the garage was worth $1,200, the 10 percent clause would pay for it in full. If it was worth $1,000, that is the amount the insurance company would pay. If the garage was worth $1,500, you could collect only $1,200.

2. Up to 10 percent of the household contents coverage can be applied to any additions, alterations, or improvements you may make should they be destroyed by fire. For example, let us say that you live in a rented apartment. Since the landlord won't paint it, you do. If fire should break out and ruin the apartment, you can collect not only for your household contents but for the cost of your paint job as well.

3. Finally, the 10 percent protection on household contents covers your personal property even though you are away from home. You are traveling. Fire breaks out in the hotel where you are staying. You flee to the street. Your luggage is destroyed. You can collect up to a maximum of 10 percent of your fire insurance coverage.

If you are forced to rent a hotel room or an apartment temporarily because your dwelling was destroyed by fire, the insurance company will cover the cost of your actual expense for rental of temporary quarters up to a maximum of 20 percent of the insurance on the dwelling.

When You Have a Fire Loss There are four things to do:

1. Report the loss to the company at once.
2. Safeguard the remaining property.
3. Prepare an inventory of lost or damaged property.
4. Submit the "proof of loss," supported wherever possible by bills, vouchers, and canceled checks that show how much you paid for the things lost.

It is an excellent idea to call your insurance agent right away and to sign nothing until you have discussed your loss with him. A loss is payable, as a rule, 60 days after the property owner's sworn statement, called the "proof of loss," is received

by the company. Most companies pay claims in much less time, however. The company will probably send its adjuster to inspect your lost.

If you and the company adjuster cannot agree on the value of what was lost, take the matter to your agent. If the agent agrees with you, he can ask the insurance company for a special investigation. You may get a better settlement. If, however, you still cannot reach an agreement, your policy provides that the dispute may be settled by two appraisers, one selected by you and the other by the company. These two should select a competent and disinterested umpire, and the dispute is then arbitrated. But you pay half the costs of appraisal and arbitration. Although you may not want to go this far because of the expense, do not settle for an unsatisfactory amount simply because you are in a hurry to get your check. The adjuster, though normally fair, may perceive this or count on it, and you may get less than you would have received if you had been more determined.

In large cities there are licensed "public adjusters" who persuade the harassed and excited homeowner who has just suffered a fire loss to sign a paper authorizing the "public adjuster" to represent the homeowner in dealing with the insurance company. Initially the homeowner may be glad to have someone else handle the problem for him; until he finds out that the public adjuster gets 10 percent or more of everything that the insurance company pays. On the other hand, there may be times when the difficulties of determining value and depreciation may make the public adjuster useful to you.

Other Separate Policies on the Home

1. A *comprehensive personal liability policy* covers your legal liability. Such a policy is well worth its small cost. It is a must not only for the homeowner but for the apartment tenant as well. If you are a tenant living ten stories up and your air conditioner falls out of the window and kills someone, or if your bathtub or washing machine overflows due to your negligence and ruins the apartment below, comprehensive personal liability

is a very useful policy to have. As a homeowner, you may want a separate policy for your added protection. If someone visiting you slips on the porch steps and falls and breaks his back, you may find yourself facing a costly lawsuit for damages, even though you had nothing to do with the accident. It was on your property, and you may thus be liable.

2. A *personal articles floater* is very useful. It is in addition to the limited coverage for the loss of securities, jewelry, furs, precious stones, rugs, and art objects. Under the Homeowner's 76 policy, jewelry is treated like money and platinum, with loss coverage limited to $100. The personal articles floats insures specifically listed items, such as furniture, clothing, sporting goods, cameras, linens, rugs, silverware, luggage, furs, and books, both in the home and away from it, against almost all risks of loss or damage, with a few minor exceptions, such as moths, vermin, and dampness. A personal property articles policy is a good idea for valuables costing $500 or more—with each article appraised and listed separately. There's no geographic limitation—the property is covered no matter where you take it. The rates vary, depending on where you live and on the items insured. Fine arts insurance rates vary widely, but a typical premium is $10 per $1,000 of value, or $100 a year for your $10,000 Dufy. The rates are on a sliding scale downward above $25,000. It's wise to keep all bills of sale in a safe place, such as your safe deposit box. Ironically, it is difficult to buy floater coverage in a high-crime area—where it is most needed. Walter Hoving of Tiffany advises going without insurance: "If you're rich enough, you can stand a good robbery."[13] In case of a robbery, the loss can be taken as an income tax deduction. You can get a lower insurance rate for jewelry normally kept in a bank vault; however, this doesn't apply to furs kept in storage. Some states will not permit a company to cancel a jewelry coverage after a theft until the policy lapses. After that it is up to the company. Jewelry thefts of more than $100 are tax deductible, minus the insurance paid.

For the wealthy, a tax deduction has more use than jewelry. You may be surprised to learn that the insurance on men's jewelry is about double the premium on comparable jewelry belonging to women. In answer to a discrimination charge, an Aetna Life and Casualty Company assistant vice president said, "Men damage and lose more jewelry than women."

3. *Theft* insurance covers burglary, robbery, and larceny. You will want residential theft insurance that covers both the stealing of property from your home and damage to your home and property by thieves. This will cost from $25 to $35 per $1,000 of protection for one year. You'll want your theft insurance to cover not only burglary, robbery, and larceny but also "mysterious disappearance" (its just gone, but you don't know how!) and "theft damage." The last is important. Often burglars will twist, shatter, and break far more than they steal. A "broad form" theft policy will cover all of this whereas the "limited form" is more restricted.

It is no longer regarded as "mysterious disappearance," but as theft, when you leave a ring on a washstand in a restaurant and return shortly afterward to find it gone. But if something disappears and you have no idea what happened, that can only be covered by a special policy. Such a policy will cover all circumstances which in themselves do not necessarily suggest theft.

4. *Low-cost flood insurance* has recently become available to homeowners under a program subsidized by the federal government. Otherwise, the rates for flood insurance would be very high, as the only persons who would want it would be those who are almost certain to have flood losses. This insurance is available through the Federal Insurance Administration of the U.S. Department of Housing and Urban Development and is administered by the National Flood Insurance Association, which consists of about 100 private insurance companies. Protection is provided against losses caused by the overflow of inland or tidal water or by the unusual and rapid accumulation or runoff of surface waters from any source. It can be purchased through local agents in about 3,000 communities in the United States at an annual premium cost

---

[13] *New York Times,* December 3, 1973.

of 25 cents for each $100 on the building up to $35,000 on a one-family house and up to $30,-000–$100,000 on two-to-four-family structures. The coverage for personal belongings may be up to $10,000 at an annual cost of 35 cents for each $100.

Why You Might Not Get Insurance

Getting and keeping insurance on homes, cars and property has become more difficult, as the risks mount and companies become less eager to meet the demands for such insurance. Since the basis for writing insurance has always been actuarial tables which, until recently, reflected the normal trend over the years, the companies have just not been prepared for the rise in auto thefts and home burglaries or for the inflation in medical and legal costs and in car repairs on accident claims. The exclusion policy of selling only to arbitrarily selected good risks has been the companies' way of staying solvent, but this leaves many unprotected. If you have made too many claims—even legitimate ones—you run the risk of a canceled policy or one not renewed. Your probable answer would be to increase the deductible (since under those circumstances you hesitate to make small claims anyway). This indirectly lowers your premium rate and in that way, perhaps balances the costs of higher premium charges.

Government-Assisted Programs

The underlying principle of insurance—the spreading of risks among many—has been converted into the principle of insuring only those least likely to make claims. Those who are desperate for protection, and most in need of it, cannot get it. The federal government and some states have moved into the void. There are laws that provide for pools into which all the bad risks are placed. Some states have also mandated coverage on fire insurance. Fire insurance is based on full metropolitan areas—not on sections or individual buildings within a metropolitan area. In 26 states, Puerto Rico, and the District of Columbia, the pool called

FAIR (Fair Access to Insurance Requirements) provides limited maximum coverage. In some states, premiums have become so high that properties just go uninsured.

Conclusion

Inflation would seem to be both housing's blessing and headache. If you already own a home, you have the advantage of increasing equity. If you are a first-time buyer you must deal with higher prices and rising interest rates.

Women's earning power has also had a double impact on today's housing problems. In two-income families women have provided that additional source of income needed to pay rising prices, and also because of the antidiscrimination laws, their income is now an asset when the bank's mortgage officer considers a loan. On the other hand, the ability of two-income families to pay the higher prices has raised prices for everyone else.

SUGGESTED READINGS

Bordewich, Fergus. "Real Estate: How High the Boom?" *New-York Magazine,* December 11, 1978, pp 82–87.

Case, Fred E. *The Investment Guide to Home and Land Purchase.* Englewood Cliffs, N.J.: Prentice-Hall, 1977.

Consumer Information Center. Pueblo, CO 81001
Home Buying Veteran. No. 596-F; 1976; 34 pp.; free.
Homeowner's Glossary of Building Terms. No. 690-F; 1977; free.
House Construction: How to Reduce Costs. No. 057-F; 1977; 16 pp.; 50 cents.
How to Save Money by Insulating Your Home. No. 603-F; 1977; 22 pp.; free.
Selecting and Financing a Home. No. 091-F; 1977; 23 pp.; $1.10.
Settlement Costs. No. 060-F; 40 pp.; 45 cents.
Tips for Consumers Insulating Their Homes. No. 665-F; 1977; 5 pp.; free.
Understanding Your Utility Bills. No. 600-F; 1977; 11 pp.; free.

Consumer Reports. "Are Those New Low-Payment Mortgages Worthwhile?" Vol. 44, no. 1, January 1979.

Financing for Home Purchases and Home Improvements—A Guide to Financing Costs and Home Buying Ability, Federal Housing Administration, Washington, D.C., latest edition. A free copy may be obtained by writing to the Office of Public Information of the FHA.

Forbes. "Let the Mortgager Beware," March 20, 1978.

Gettel, Ronald E. *You Can Get Your Real Estate Taxes Reduced.* New York: McGraw-Hill, 1977.

Hubin, Vincent J. *Warning: Condominiums May Be Dangerous to Your Health, Wealth, and Peace of Mind.* Homewood, Ill.: Dow Jones-Irwin, 1976.

Insurance Company of North America. *The Underinsured Home.* Philadelphia, 1977. Write to the company at 1600 Arch St., Philadelphia, PA 19101 for this booklet on how to estimate replacement costs; 12 pp.; free.

Money. "Buy Now—Sell Now," April 1977.

———. "Shoring Up Your Homeowner's Insurance," May 1977.

———. "Mortgages Cut to Fit Your Finances," October 1977.

———. "Cashing In on the Equity in Your House," March 1978.

Real Estate Review. "A Promising Future for the Mobile Home," Spring 1976. Davidson, Harald, A.

———. "A New Twist to the Variable Payment Mortgage," Summer 1977. Lusht, Kenneth M.

CASE PROBLEMS

1   Ralph and Ethel Gould are 28 and 26 years of age. They live in Minnesota. A ten-room house, 30 years old, which they like, comes to their attention. It is common knowledge that houses cost $3,000 a room to build in their town, and ordinary rooms are nowhere near as large as the rooms in the house in question. They feel that they have an opportunity to make a very attractive purchase for $28,000. Since the price is reasonable, why do they hesitate?

2   Raymond and Ruth Wilkes have two children (ages two and five). Raymond is a young lawyer earning $18,000 net a year. They have been living in an old house which was rented to them for $275 a month, but this house has been sold and they must move. In their town, properties for sale are hard to find. One that is available has four bedrooms, is 30 years old, and is being offered for $25,000. A new house large enough for the family would cost at least $37,000. No rental property is vacant. Outside of $50,000 of straight life insurance which Raymond has carried, the family has been able to do little saving. What should they do?

3   Ellen and John are both graduating college in June. They are to be married the day after commencement. They have both been offered positions in Chicago. Their joint earnings are $425 a week. They have surveyed housing possibilities and have narrowed down their choices to two alternatives. They can rent a three-room apartment in the heart of town for $350 a month. They can buy a new five-room house in a suburban development for $35,000 ($10,000 down, 9.5 percent, 30-year mortgage for the balance). Which would you choose? Why?

4   Rollins insured his $28,000 home for $20,000 against the threat of fire. A fire caused $2,000 damage to the property. Rollins wants to repair the property, but he did not get enough money to do so. What two reasons would make the money he received insufficient for his need?

5   Jane and William Carleton have been married three years. The birth of their daughter, Linda (now seven months), made them decide to give up living in an apartment in town and instead buy a house in the suburbs. They have decided on a $40,000 house. In shopping for financing, they have received the following offers:

a. $8,000 down, $32,000 mortgage at 9.5 percent for 30 years.

b. $5,000 down, $35,000 mortgage at 9 plus 0.5 percent FHA insurance fee, for 25 years.

c. $23,000, $17,000 mortgage at 9.0 percent for 20 years.

Which should they choose? Why?

part three

MANAGING YOUR MONEY

10

Meeting Saving and Banking Needs

Money makes money
And the money
That money makes
Makes more money.

POOR RICHARD'S ALMANACK

A bankbook makes good reading—better than
most novels.

SIR HARRY LAUDER

Most American families, especially young families, report that almost all their income goes for living expenses, leaving little margin for emergencies or savings. There is also a question of whether today's NOW generation wants to save. For which of the reasons listed below would you save—if you recognize the advantages of saving? Priorities will naturally vary, depending on age, income, and personal lifestyle.

Reasons for Saving

Emergencies	Medical expenses
Education	Down payment on a house
Travel/Education	Future investment
Inner security	Retirement
Start a business	Family estate

A Savings Plan

One can save haphazardly, putting aside any surplus that seems to be left over after the essential

295

expenditures of the moment have been made, or one can draw up and try to stay with a savings plan (long term or short term, or both). The latter method usually results in more systematic, consistent, and therefore larger savings, just as spending is made more efficient by the use of a plan. But there is no perfect savings plan, and there is no plan that will fit every family. A good savings plan will involve at least five elements. In order of priority, these are:

1. A decision, and it should be a realistic one, as to how much of annual, monthly, or weekly income may really be considered surplus and thus available for savings. It should be remembered that the average family is probably engaged in a considerable amount of contractual saving—paying premiums on life insurance, contributing to a pension fund each month via payroll deduction—and that this may leave less room for voluntary saving.

2. How large a cash reserve can you and should you maintain? No matter how well ordered one's life may be, there are always emergencies that strain one's finances; and when they come, it is better to be able to fall back on a cash reserve in the bank—or in other forms of savings that can be readily liquidated—than to have to borrow. By consensus of financial experts an adequate emergency fund is thought to be the equivalent of three months' salary.

3. How much life insurance (not just a policy,

but an insurance plan) will provide reasonable security for your dependents? Can you afford this insurance? Will you have any surplus left over after you provide for it?

4. Is your surplus large enough to permit you to meet 2 and 3 and, in addition, buy a home—assuming that you want to own your own home?

5. After meeting 2, 3, and 4, do you have any money left over for other forms of savings, such as investments? If so, what are your objectives?

You can look in vain for a place to put savings that will be safe, liquid, inflation resistant. and will yield a large return as well. There is no such place. One or more of these elements must be sacrificed in whole or in part to achieve the others; and in formulating a savings plan, considered judgments must be made. Table 10–1 illustrates the decision and the reason given for their decision by the persons who were questioned.

The Louis Harris & Associates survey referred to in Figure 10–1 indicates that the higher the income, the larger the proportion of people who have savings plans and the more confident they are that they will achieve their goals.

Forms of Savings

Savings can take many forms, can be held and used in many different ways. From simple to complex, the range includes keeping cash under the

TABLE 10–1
Choices

Preferred Vehicle	High Return on Investment Most Important	Forced Savings Most Important
Life insurance	6.6%	30.3%
Stocks	42.7	4.7
Savings accounts	14.2	37.0
Government bonds	21.1	31.5
Real estate	29.8	9.1
Mutual funds	11.3	6.3
Pension funds	4.3	22.4

Note: Percentages add to more than 100 because of multiple responses.
Source: American Council of Life Insurance, *MAP—Monitoring Attitudes of the Public,* annual public attitude survey.

FIGURE 10–1
How Important to You Is Saving Money?

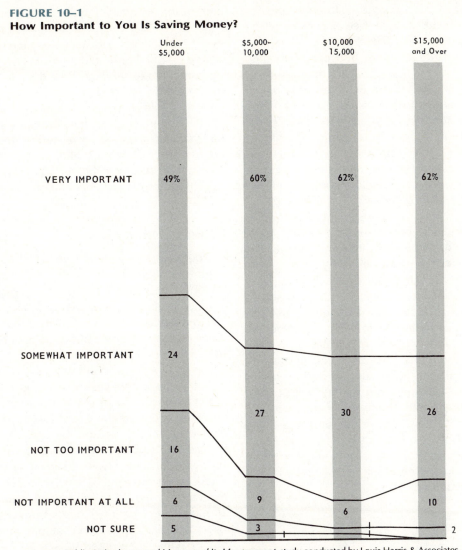

Source: *Public Attitudes toward Money and Its Management,* study conducted by Louis Harris & Associates for *Newsweek* magazine.

mattress; accumulating cash balances in bank demand deposits; holding savings deposits, accounts in credit unions, or shares in savings and loan associations; building equities in pension funds, annuities, or life insurance; buying saving bonds or other government securities; or buying capital assets, such as homes, personal small business enterprises, or corporate stocks or bonds. Although this chapter deals primarily with "liquid" forms of savings (deposits, savings accounts, savings bonds), it is worth noting that an individual who pays for a home in monthly installments on a mortgage is saving just as effectively as one who puts comparable sums in a savings bank. Most life insurance policies involve not only the purchase of protection but a large element of savings as well, and such policies are regarded as a fast way to build an estate. The policyholder builds up a tax-free cash reserve from year to year.

There are various savings instruments to meet different objectives. If you want a high return on your savings, you cannot expect safety of principal. If you want safety of principal, you cannot expect the same instrument to provide a good hedge against inflation. Under most conditions, if you want liquidity, you cannot hope for long-term growth. If you want certainty of continued income, you cannot expect a high yield. People at different income levels favor different forms of saving.

Quite clearly, no one instrument or institution combines all savings objectives successfully. Those instruments which combine safety and liquidity sacrifice return and the possibility of growth. For a number of instruments the reverse is true. Your income level and your savings objectives should determine your choice. If you need a reserve against financial trouble or loss of a job, you will want a very different type of savings instrument than if you are trying to protect yourself against long-run (secular) inflation and loss of purchasing power. If you can spare the money for a period of years, you will want a different medium of savings than if you expect to use the fund as a down payment on a house a year or two from now. Many families have several objectives and therefore spread their funds, choosing several rather than one form of savings.

Savings Patterns

Who saves and how much depends on how savings are measured and who does the measuring. If savings are defined as liquid assets, the younger the family head, the smaller the asset accumulation, and as is to be expected, the older the family head, the larger. In education, similar expectations are realized. The less the education of the family head, the smaller the liquid assets holdings on the average, and the more advanced the education of the family head, the larger they are.

Different stages of of a family's life cycle bring significant variations in savings and dissavings. Sav-ings, or the accumulation of liquid assets, by young single persons, though frequent, are generally limited by insufficiency of income. Marriage and the setting up of a household are usually accompanied by numerous expenditures for durable goods, and thus some degree of dissavings. Several years after children are born, positive saving rises again, particularly as purchases of life insurance and houses tend, at this stage, to increase the importance of contractual, though not liquid, savings. Savings tend to reach a peak after the children have left home, but then there is less incentive to save, and with retirement there is less income.

Savings Institutions

The American people have accumulated a great volume of savings, and they have chosen a variety of forms and institutions in which to place those savings, as shown in Figure 10–2.

Personal savings, as calculated by the Department of Commerce, subtracts estimated expenditures for goods and services from the aftertax income of families and individuals. The calculation is not really complete because the expansion of credit as well as income can be used for the purchase of goods, services and assets and is not included in the calculation, nor is cash, which can be used to reduce debt as well as for personal outlays. Whichever way financial saving is measured, it will move into whatever source maximizes the return. In a process known as disintermediation, an individual withdraws funds from a savings account and places them in a money market instrument paying higher interest such as Treasury bills, federal agency notes, or bank certificates of deposit. Savings depositors also move their money from lower paying accounts to higher interest four–six-year certificates, frequently in the same bank. The reverse cycle—back to the savings accounts, as rates elsewhere fall—also occurs.

Cash

The disadvantages of cash as a form of savings are quite apparent. The money is lost or stolen

FIGURE 10–2
Where People Save: Savings Accounts in Major Financial Institutions ($ millions)

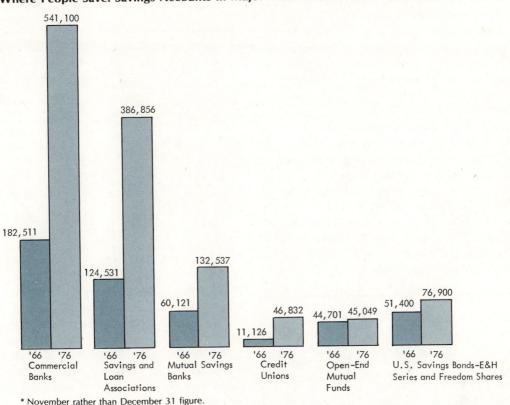

* November rather than December 31 figure.

Courtesy Credit Union National Association, Inc., January 1979

much too easily, and it earns no income. One is reminded of the eccentric old lady who confided to her neighbor that she kept her money at home, hidden in a coffee can. "But," reminded the neigh-

bor, "you're losing interest." "Oh, no, I'm not," the old lady insisted serenely. "I'm putting away a little extra, just for that." With deposit insurance covering commercial banks, savings banks, and savings and loan associations, credit unions, and with government savings bonds available, there is no longer need to "put away a little extra" to achieve safety.

Do You Know How Interest Is Computed on Your Savings Deposit? Which Gives You the "Highest" Interest on Your Savings?

Banks vary not only in the basic rate of interest that they pay but also in the methods and timing

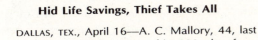

Hid Life Savings, Thief Takes All

DALLAS, TEX., April 16—A. C. Mallory, 44, last night reported his life savings of $7,800 taken from its hiding place under his house. Mallory said the money was in two pint fruit jars suspended in a pillowcase under a hallway trapdoor. He said he had been saving the money since he was 12 and never kept it in a bank.

Associated Press.

that they use in computing interest on savings accounts. You will be amazed to know that the American Bankers Association found that at least 54 different methods were used.

The power of compound interest alone will double your capital at 4 percent in 17 1/2 years, at 5 percent in 14 1/2 years, and at 6 percent in just 12 years. The "rule of 72" is an easy way to estimate how long it will take to double your money. Just divide the interest rate into 72. If, for example, your money is earning 6 percent, it will double in 12 years. If it is earning 9 percent, it will double in 8 years. And the power of compounding interest daily instead of quarterly, as some banks are doing, affects the nominal rate, as shown in Table 10–2. The more often interest is compounded, the higher the return. Note in Table 10–2 how daily (365 times) compounding increases the rate of return in your money.

TABLE 10–2
Compounded Rates of Return

Nominal Rate	Quarterly	Compounded Daily 365 Days $\left(\frac{365}{360}\right)$
4.0%	4.06%	4.14%
4.5	4.58	4.67
5.0	5.09	5.19
5.5	5.61	5.73
6.0	6.13	6.27
6.5	6.66	6.81
7.0	7.18	7.35
7.5	7.61	7.90
8.0	8.24	8.45

Maximum Allowable Savings Rates

	Commercial Banks	Thrift Institutions*
Regular account	5 %	5.25%
90-day	5.5	5.75
1 to 2½ years	6	6.5
2½ to 4 years	6.5	6.75
4 to 6 years	7.25	7.5
6 years or more	7.50	7.75
8 years	7.75	8.00

* The thrift institutions are offering money market certificates of 6 month maturity whose interest rate is tied to the rate set at the prior week's auction of 6 month U.S. Treasury bills. Rates have been as high as 10 percent.

In a survey of California savings institutions, a consumer group called Consumer Action found that there are at least 84 ways to compute interest on accounts that have the same annual interest rate. The top-ranked savings and loan association paid 45 percent more interest than the lowest-rated commercial bank. Or, phrased differently, the identical account with the same activity over the same period earned $51.56 in interest at one bank and $35.19 at another. The difference is determined by whether the institution pays on a 360-day year

(higher) or on a 365-day year, whether interest is paid from the day of deposit to the day of withdrawal, the existence of "grace periods," and by the frequency of compounding.

There are four principal methods of calculating interest based on activity in the account.

Method 1: Fifo Under Fifo (first in, first out) withdrawals are deducted first from the starting balance of the interest period and then, if the starting balance isn't large enough, from subsequent deposits. In effect, this means that you lose interest on withdrawals from the start of the interest period or the earliest deposit date rather than from the date you actually take the money out. Some banks charge withdrawals against the beginning balance of the interest period; others against the first deposits of the interest period. The latter method provides more interest for the saver, though both calculations are relatively unfavorable, as we shall see.

Method 2: Low Balance Under this method, interest is computed on the *minimum* balance on deposit in a savings account for the entire interest period, which may be a half year or a quarter. No interest is paid on deposits made in the midst of the interest period.

Method 3: Lifo. The last in, first out method computing interest is one in which funds withdrawn are deducted from the funds that were most recently deposited within the stated interest period, such as a quarter or a half year, whatever the crediting period may be. Accrued interest lost as a result of a withdrawal against deposits under this method is less than under Fifo, since the withdrawn dollars here had less time to earn interest.

Method 4: Day of Deposit to Day of Withdrawal (DD–DW). Under the daily interest method, all funds earn interest for the actual number of days that they remain on deposit. The highest cost to the bank and the highest yield to the saver result from the day of deposit to day of withdrawal method. The use of this method has spread rapidly in recent years, principally in large banks in metropolitan areas around the country.

The method of treating withdrawals is extremely important. You, as a saver, are favored by a method which charges withdrawals against the most recent deposit, and you are hurt by one which charges them against the beginning balance of the period or first deposits. Let's assume that your bank charges withdrawals against the first deposit and that you make your first deposit of $100 on January 20. You deposit another $100 on August 10, a third $100 on October 1, and then you withdraw $100 on December 1. Assuming that the bank is paying interest from the first day of the semiannual period and that it charges the $100 withdrawal against the January 20 deposit, as in Fifo, you lose all interest on that deposit even though it has been in the bank for over 10 months. If, on the other hand, the withdrawal is charged against the last deposit, as in Lifo, the one made on October 1, you lose nothing, since interest on that deposit would not start until the following January 1.

Date	Withdrawals	Deposits	Balance
January 20		$100	$100
August 10		100	200
October 1		100	300
December 1 . .	$100		200

Now what does all of this mean? It may seem confusing at first, but it's important to you as a saver to understand it clearly. You ought to avoid banks that use Methods 1, 2, and 3 and to favor those that use Method 4. One aspect ought to be quite clear. Method 1 tends to discourage withdrawals, and also customers, since the yield is less. In Method 4, the bank starts paying interest on

the day of deposit. Suppose you deposited $100 on January 20 of any given year. Under Method 4, your deposit on January 20 would start earning interest beginning January 20. Thus under Method 4, you would earn interest for the exact number of days of deposit.

A comparison of the interest computation in Table 10–3 for Method 1 (Fifo), which benefits the saver least, and Method 4 (DD–DW), which benefits him most, will illustrate how this works. The calculation is done by using a nominal 1 percent which can be multiplied by the current interest rate to arrive at the actual interest.

Obviously, therefore, several different banks could state that they pay interest at the rate of 5 percent per annum, but, depending on how they compute your minimum balance or the amount to be used for crediting interest, the variations in what you actually get might be as extreme as $3.78 to $7.59 for a half year, as shown in Table 10–4. It would pay, therefore, to deposit savings funds in a bank which uses Method 4.

An examination of the methods now in use reveals that most of them penalize the overactive or in-and-out saver. Indirectly, this benefits the true saver, as the benefits derived from semiannual or quarterly compounding, even over a fairly long period of time, do not make as much appreciable difference in the amount of interest earned as does the activity of the account and the method of interest calculation.

The rate of interest and the method of calculating interest are most important in determining the return, but other factors, such as the length of the interest period and of the grace period, affect the return too. The longer the grace period (usually at the beginning of the interest period and at the end of the quarter) and the shorter the interest period, the more the saver has freedom to make withdrawals and deposits without losing interest.

Is Your Deposit Safe?

Over 98 percent of commercial banks and two thirds of mutual savings banks operating in the United States are members of the Federal Deposit Insurance Corporation. Savings and Loans associa-

TABLE 10–3

Comparison of Interest Computation of the Fifo and DD–DW Methods

Date	Withdrawal	Deposit	Interest	Balance	Interest Memo
Fifo method:					
January 1				$1,000.00*	$4.96†
April 1		$1,000.00		2,000.00	7.45‡
May 15		1,000.00		3,000.00	8.74§
May 20	$1,000.00‖			2,000.00	3.78#
July 1			$3.78	2,003.78	
DD–DW method:					
January 1				1,000.00*	4.96†
April 1		1,000.00		2,000.00	7.45‡
May 15		1,000.00		3,000.00	8.74§
May 20	1,000.00**			2,000.00	7.59††
July 1			7.59	2,007.59	

* Operating balance.

† Calculation of anticipated interest as if no additional deposits or withdrawals are to be made:

$$\$1,000 \times 1\% \times \frac{181 \text{ days}}{365 \text{ days}} = \$4.96.$$

‡ Calculation to cover additional deposit:

$$\$1,000 \times 1\% \times \frac{91 \text{ days}}{365 \text{ days}} = \$2.49$$
$$\$4.95 + 2.49 = \$7.45.$$

§ Calculation including $1,000 additional deposit:

$$\$1,000 \times 1\% \times \frac{47 \text{ days}}{365 \text{ days}} = \$1.29$$
$$\$7.45 + 1.29 = \$8.74.$$

‖ $1,000 withdrawal on May 20 calculated against balance of $1,000 on January 1.

Anticipated interest of:

$$\$8.74 - \$1,000 \times 1\% \times \frac{181 \text{ days}}{365 \text{ days}} = \$4.96$$
$$\$8.74 - 4.96 = \$3.78 \text{ (interest for the six months).}$$

** Deposit of $1,000 on May 15 earned interest for five days—equal sum withdrawn on May 20.

†† Anticipated interest of $8.74—interest loss calculated:

$$\$1,000 \times 1\% \times \frac{42 \text{ days}}{365 \text{ days}} = \$1.15$$
$$8.74 - 1.15 = \$7.59.$$

tions are insured in the same fashion by the FSLIC (the Federal Savings and Loan Insurance Corporation). Savings in credit unions are protected by the National Credit Union Administration (NCUA) under the same terms. Each depositor is protected to an upper limit of $40,000 if the institution should fail. For this insurance, each bank contributes semiannually to the deposit insurance fund, based on its total deposits. When a failing insured bank is closed, the insurance fund either pays the depositor in cash or opens another account in his or her name for the same amount in a solvent, going bank. The money in this new account may be withdrawn at once.

The $40,000 protection limit applies to a single depositor in a given bank, regardless of the number

TABLE 10–4

Summary of Interest Earned, Using the Four Methods (same activity patterns as in Table 10–3)

Method	Amount of Interest for Period
Low balance	$4.96
Fifo	3.78
Lifo	7.45
DD–DW	7.59

of accounts that he may have. A person who has a $2,000 balance in a checking account in a given bank and a savings account with a $39,000 balance in the same bank would be insured for $40,000 (not $41,000); if he had only the savings account, he would be fully insured for the $39,000. If his savings account balance were $42,000, he would be insured for only $40,000. The insurance coverage is based upon all deposits maintained by a person at a single insured bank, not upon his total deposits throughout the banking system.

The law limits insurance basically to $40,000 for any one depositor in any one bank, but it does not prohibit you from splitting your funds among a number of banks. Moreover, if you are married, your own deposit account, your spouse's separate deposit account, as well as your joint deposit account, *with right of survivorship,* are each separately insured to the maximum of $40,000, even though they are all in the same bank. If you have accounts in the main office and a branch or in several branches of one insured bank, the accounts will be added together in determining your insurance, since the FDIC considers the main office and all branches as one bank.[1]

The deposits of a partnership are insured separately from the individual deposits of each partner if the individual partners and the partnership are engaged in an independent activity. If you act as

a trustee, guardian, administrator, executor agent, or in some other fiduciary capacity, deposit accounts which you open and maintain in any or all of these capacities are insured separately from the deposits in your individual account. In fact, you can maintain deposits in an insured bank in each of the following rights and capacities and be separately insured to the maximum of $40,000 on each of the accounts shown. It is possible for ten accounts to be insurable up to $400,000 in the same bank. Some possibilities are:

John Doe	$40,000
Mary Doe	40,000
John Doe and Mary Doe, joint account with right of survivorship	40,000
John Doe and Richard Doe, joint account with right of survivorship	40,000
Mary Doe and Richard Doe, joint account with right of survivorship	40,000
John Doe, executor of estate of [name] deceased	40,000
John Doe, trustee of [name] irrevocable estate	40,000

All trust interests created by the same person in the same bank for the same beneficiary must be counted toward one insurance of $40,000. If the account is a revocable trust and there is another account at the same bank in the name of the grantor of the trust, then the two accounts are counted as one account under the insurance. If a deceased person's estate is divided into separate accounts at the same bank, as held by an executor and by an administrator, those accounts are regarded as one account.

Save at a Commercial Bank?

The commercial bank has frequently been called a "department store of finance" because it performs so many financial functions. It grants commercial, personal, mortgage, and other types of loans. It receives demand and time deposits (that is, it has both checking and savings accounts). It rents safe deposit boxes, performs investment services and gives investment advice, handles collections, issues letters of credit and traveler's checks, sells and redeems U.S. savings bonds, performs

---

[1] *Your Insured Deposit,* issued by the Federal Deposit Insurance Corporation, gives all essential facts about insurance coverage. A copy may be obtained by writing to the Information Office, Federal Deposit Insurance Corporation, 550 17th St. N.W., Washington, D.C. 20429.

304

executor and trust functions, and provides Christmas Club and other systematic savings schemes.

At one time, commercial banks paid interest on demand deposits. Then for a time, the law no longer allowed it. Since November 1978, the Federal Reserve Board regulations allow you to authorize your bank to automatically transfer funds from your interest bearing savings account to cover your checks as written. There are still limitations to be considered. Unless you leave a considerable balance in your checking account (varying from bank to bank) there are service charges on your checking account that might well offset your interest gain. Some banks figure the charges on a minimum balance. Some use the average monthly balance to determine if your check writing is free or must pay a service charge. If you keep a minimum balance and write a lot of checks, your interest bearing transfer arrangement might cost you more than a regular account. The banks are using the new rules to adjust fees on already charged items and institute fees for services where no charge had previously existed. Funds kept in a checking account materially in excess of the required minimum balance earn no income for the owner, nor, of course, does the minimum balance, but you would have free checking. The bank keeps the income from the minimum balance to cover the cost of the checking service rendered and to yield a reasonable profit.

The "savings," "thrift," "special interest," or "compound interest" accounts, as these are variously called which are maintained by the 14,000 commercial banks throughout the U.S. were once very separate, but can now be considered practically integrated with demand deposits, if the customer so desires. More than 90 million depositors have entrusted more than $462 billion in these time deposits. In some communities the commercial bank is the only institution in which an individual may deposit savings and receive interest. On these time deposits, commercial banks pay interest rates which have been about 0.5 percent lower than those paid by savings and loan associations or savings banks. Rates vary with changes in economic activity, but in the past few years or so, commercial banks have paid savers 5 percent annually.

Although seemingly attractive, you must weigh your checking activity, versus the required balance—as well as alternative savings opportunities for that money used as a balance—to decide if this combined account is best for you. If you find it is, you can get it to work for you as a valuable personal money management tool, because you now have the opportunity to time payments in a way that will earn interest to the last moment. It is almost as if you are earning interest on your checking account.

Perhaps the first service that everyone uses at a bank is the checking account. According to a Louis Harris poll, more than 68 percent of adult Americans now use a regular checking account. Roughly 450 million checks are written weekly, and the number has been growing by 10 percent a year. In recent years there has been much talk about electronic money—a checkless, cashless society with computer-governed, punch button, credit card finance—but the flood of checks continues.

Check Processing

Suppose you sent your parents who live in Los Angeles a check to buy themselves a gift. You are working in New York. Let's assume that they cannot immediately decide what they want to buy, and so they deposit the check in their local bank in Los Angeles, which, in turn, deposits the check to its credit at the Federal Reserve bank in San Francisco, since the Los Angeles bank is part of Federal Reserve District 12, of which San Francisco is the headquarters. The Federal Reserve bank of San Francisco sends the check to the Federal Reserve bank of New York for collection. The Federal Reserve bank of New York sends the check to your bank, which deducts the amount of the check from your account. Your bank then authorizes the Federal Reserve bank of New York to deduct that amount from its reserve on deposit with the Federal Reserve bank. The Federal Reserve bank of New York then pays the Federal Reserve bank of San Francisco from its share in the Interdistrict Settlement Fund. Finally, the Federal Reserve bank of

San Francisco credits the Los Angeles bank where your parents deposited your check with the amount of the check, and the Los Angeles bank credits your parents' account. This transaction is multiplied on the order of 450 million times each week.

Automation, Computers, and MICR

To clear, collect, and process the billions of checks we write each year, banks resort to automation. Computers and MICR are the answer. The odd-looking numbers at the bottom of checks serve a very useful purpose. They allow checks to be read and sorted automatically by new electronic machines, and they enable computers to post accounts and print statements.

Checks carry two sets of figures at the bottom: the first, at the left, is the American Bankers Association routing symbol, the number of the bank on which the check is drawn, and the city and the Federal Reserve district in which the bank is located. This is equivalent to the printed number in the upper right-hand corner of the check. Thus, for example,

$$\frac{1-12}{210,}$$

where the 1 stands for New York, N.Y., the 12 for the Chemical Bank, and the 210 for the New York Federal Reserve bank (2 for 2d district; 1 for head office, not branch; and 0 for immediate availability), becomes in MICR (Magnetic Ink Character Recognition):

⑆0210⑉0012⑆

This is followed by the branch identification number and then the number of your account at the bank. Thus the check can be automatically sorted and sent back to the right bank and the right account. When the check is presented for collection, figures may be added by the use of a machine which inscribes MICR characters on de-posit slips or checks. For example, it is now customary to inscribe the amount of the check in MICR. This permits processing by a computer which can then adjust accounts and issue daily statements. In large banks there are delivered each morning, before the bank opens for business, computer-compiled sheets showing the closing balance in each account at a given branch as of the close of the most recent clearing the night before. Thus the teller knows how much is in every account and does not need to call the head office to find out. The computer also puts together the monthly bank statement.

In this age of intercontinental ballistic missiles, the larger urban banks now each have a depository in more remote locations, where duplicate sets of account records, statements, deposit slips, are available in case of atomic attack. Daily computer tabulations are sent to these depositories to keep accounts up to date, and officials of one such bank estimate that the bank could open for banking transactions at the remote location with a complete, up-to-date set of records within 48 hours after an atomic attack. Whether anyone would or could show up to make a deposit or a withdrawal is another question.

Checkless Banking

Obviously MICR is transitional to the checkless society, still not yet around the corner. Inexorably, EFT (electronic fund transfer—the use of computers and transmission wires to speed the flow of currency) is spreading throughout the nation, but with deliberate speed.

Consumer resistance, as much as technical limitation, is slowing electronic banking. Banks benefit through reduction of paperwork and its cost. A check goes through ten hands before returning to its writer. The customer, however, wants a canceled check as a record. Today's world demands legal records of everything, even though electronic services show transactions on statements. The Federal Reserve bank of Atlanta commissioned a study which showed that people in its area did not react favorably toward preauthorized bill payments or checkless payment systems. A worker's comment typified the feelings of others, "I like looking at the weekly paycheck even though the money goes quickly."

There has been opposition by those who fear invasion of privacy and by those who fear electronic fraud, which one consumer representative has labeled "remote mugging." Retailers are reluctant to let the credit card of a big bank come between them and their customers, and small-town bankers fear the invasion of big banks which can afford the expense of computerized centers. A new law has been passed requiring the Federal Reserve System to write regulations that would give consumers protection against the fraudulent use of electronic bank accounts, limit the liability of the depositor for the unauthorized use of bank cards if these were lost or stolen, and make financial institutions liable for mistakes in the handling of consumers' electronic fund accounts. Until these regulations are approved, a stolen card can empty an account through a money machine, and the bank is not liable. Or a depositor can receive a money machine receipt for cash placed in an envelope in an automated teller machine, and if the deposit is not credited, even though there is a receipt, the bank may not be legally liable if it claims that there was no cash in the envelope.

But EFT has begun. California has SCOPE (Special Committee on Paperless Entries) and Georgia has COPE (Committee on Paperless Entries) as functioning electronic fund transfer systems, cooperating with the regional Federal Reserve bank. A company delivers its payroll to its bank on computer tape. The bank then electronically transfers an employee's pay, through the Federal Reserve bank, to the individual's bank, where it is credited to each employee's account before the bank opens on payday. The system works in Hempstead, N.Y. Hempstead Bank's customers have Instant Transaction (IT) cards which they insert in a terminal. The merchant punches keys that identify the buyer and record the value of the item sold. On a smaller terminal, the buyer punches out a secret identification. The computer at the bank verifies that the customer has enough money to pay for the goods,

and automatically sends a credit for the required amount to the store. The whole transaction takes 20 seconds, and the customer receives a receipt.

National concerns that have large mailings of interest payments, dividend checks, or paychecks and government agencies such as the VA, which sends pension checks and dividend checks, and HEW, which sends social security checks, expect large savings from direct deposit. Any institution or company can hook into the ACH (Automated Clearing House) whose 31 regional associations are being linked electronically through the Federal Reserve's automated communications system.

The VISA cards being pushed by the big banks can be fed into the increasing number of ATMs (automated teller machines), which in turn become EFT links into the ACH. To make the ATMs attractive to people who like people tellers—not ATMs—the banks have been personalizing their robot tellers in campaigns that call them "Buttons," "Tillie," or "Miss X." These machines accept deposits, move funds from one account to another, and tell you your balance. To compensate for the ATMs, some banks have been designating specific bank employees to handle all the banking needs of individual customers. For many customers the idea of having a "personal banker"—someone whom you know and who will know you—is a truly welcome development.

Interest-Bearing Checking Accounts

The differences between commercial and "thrift" banks are lessening now that checking accounts that earn interest or savings accounts that have check-writing privileges are becoming widespread.

The "thrifts" in New England, New York, and Pennsylvania issue "negotiable orders of withdrawal," under a variety of names, on their savings accounts—now known as NOW accounts. Their share of the checking account market has been growing at the expense of the commercial banks, which formerly had a monopoly.

Competition caused the thrifts (mutual savings banks, savings and loan associations, and credit unions) to offer the NOW accounts free of all banking charges or minimum balance requirements. As their share of the checking market has increased, service charges have begun to appear, making these accounts more similar to commercial bank checking accounts. The latter, however, are limited to paying a quarter of a percentage point less than the thrift banks on interest accounts.

Both types of banks offer automatic payment of bills, the withdrawal of funds by means of banking terminals in retail stores, and the transfer of funds between a savings account and a checking account by telephone.

Writing checks through commercial checking accounts or through NOW accounts costs more than using EFT to transfer funds. EFT supporters therefore feel that more and more users will be attracted to EFT. Until that time comes, traditional checking is "in," for all of the following reasons.

It's a most convenient way to pay. There is a vast saving in time and effort. You write out your checks at your desk and then mail them, and do not have to run from store to store or office to office and possibly stand in line to pay bills. A check allows you to pay the exact amount due. It represents safety because you don't have to carry large sums of cash around. Furthermore, it provides an automatic receipt. Your canceled check, which is returned to you after it has been cashed, is a receipt. You can keep your accounts straight through checkbook stubs, the bank's monthly statement to you, and the returned canceled checks.

A check is simply an order to your bank to pay someone you name an amount of money that you have on deposit. Sooner or later you will need to write a check, and once you open a checking account and try it, you'll never be without one. It's a tremendous convenience. You may frequently be asked to name your bank in connection with transactions involving credit, such as opening a charge account or renting a house or an apartment.

At the same time that checking account advantages are being increasingly recognized, it has become increasingly difficult to cash a check, especially where you are unknown. This has become true even if you have a handful of identification cards—all of which might have been stolen. For this reason, the "line of credit" or "reserve checking" accounts have gained an added value. Stores regard these as "guaranteed accounts" and willingly accept checks drawn on them, because the I.D. given by the bank with each account indicates that the credit is good. It may even be difficult to cash your own check in your own bank. Some big-city banks provide all account holders with personal check-cashing cards that can be read by a computer terminal to see whether there are sufficient funds. Other banks provide "convenience" cards for cashing limited amounts if you have a bank credit card. There are probably some banks that trust their customers!

Over most of the country, the charges on special checking accounts appear to be small and reasonable. If there are a number of banks in your community, shop to see which has the most reasonable service charge consistent with your financial position and requirements. The fees in Table 10–5 are not necessarily the same as the fees of the banks in your community, but they are fairly typical.

Usually an account is opened in the name of one depositor alone. A husband and wife, however,

"All I ever get is checks!"

Reprinted by permission *The Wall Street Journal*

TABLE 10–5
Your Choice of Check Plans

The check system offers you two ways of paying for your account. Both are clear and easy to understand. You choose the plan that suits you best, the one that's least expensive for you. All the benefits and extra services available are the same for both plans. Only the fee structure is different.

The Special Check Plan. With this plan, there is no minimum balance requirement. You pay a monthly fee of 75¢, plus 10¢ for each check drawn.

The Regular Check Plan. If you use this plan, there is no charge per check—no matter how many checks you write. The monthly fee is based on the lowest balance in your account during the month. And if you keep a balance of $500 or more, your account is free. Here's the complete story:

Lowest Balance during Month	Monthly Fee
$500 and over	Free
$400 to $499	$1
$300 to $399	$2
$200 to $299	$3
$0 to $199	$4

Which plan is best for you? That's easy to decide. Just estimate the number of checks you write each month and the lowest balance in your checking account. The table below will show you whether you should have a regular (R) or special (S) plan.

Checks Written	Lowest Balance				
	Below $200	$200s	$300s	$400s	$500+
0	S	S	S	S	R
5	S	S	S	R	R
15	S	S	R	R	R
25	S	R	R	R	R
35	R	R	R	R	R

often open a joint account, with right of survivorship. Then each of them can draw checks on the same account. In case of the death of a person who has an account in one name alone, no one except the legally appointed executor or administrator of the estate can draw on the account. Sometimes this may tie the account up for months before the court takes action.

Usually the survivor or survivors of a joint account can arrange with little difficulty to continue drawing checks on the account; they must merely give the tax authorities assurance that all taxes due will be paid. When two or more persons use the same account, they must exercise care to avoid confusion and not draw checks for more money than is in the account. Each person should keep a full and clear record of every check drawn, and frequently the complete record should be brought together so that everyone will know just what has been deposited and withdrawn.

In some states, the law does not automatically assume that the balance in a joint account goes to the survivor. It has been held that the survivor's right may be lost by proof that before his death the decedent did not intend to make any gift of his contribution to the account. This may apply to checking or commercial accounts as well as to savings accounts.

How to Endorse Checks

Before you can cash or deposit a check made out to you, you must sign it on the back, preferably, custom dictates, at the extreme left end. This is known as endorsement. If you want to take a check which has been made out to you and give it to another person in payment for something, you must first endorse it and then the other party must also endorse it before it can be cashed or deposited. If your name is misspelled or incomplete, write your first endorsement in the same way—and then write your correct signature.

You should never endorse a check until you get to a bank. If you endorse a check beforehand and then lose it, the finder may cash it. By endorsement the person to whom the check is made out passes title to the check to someone else. If you lose a check made out to you, you may be able to arrange to have payment on it stopped, *provided that you haven't endorsed it.*

A check, of course, is a negotiable instrument. When you receive a check and endorse it, giving it to someone in payment, you are responsible if it turns out to be bad, even though you passed it along in good faith. You, in turn, can try to get your money back from the person who gave it to you in the first place. If your checkbook should be lost or stolen, and your name forged for fantastic sums, you are not responsible; but notify the bank immediately.

Certified Checks

There are occasions when a certified check is required in payment. In a real estate transaction, for example, when the parties meet at the registry of deeds to "pass papers," the seller should deliver a deed to real estate only in exchange for cash or for a check which is certified by a bank. The prospective buyer can make out a check payable to himself, present it at the bank for certification, and then endorse the check to the real estate seller when it is found that everything is in order and that the deal is to be consummated. If the deal falls through, it is a simple matter for the disappointed buyer to deposit this check, payable to himself, to his own account again. If the check is made payable to the real estate seller in the first place and is then not used, it is sometimes a bit more troublesome to have it canceled and to have the amount of the certified check credited back to the buyer's account.

When the check is first presented to the bank for certification, the bank ascertains immediately whether there is enough money in the account to cover the check. The check is then stamped "certified" across its face, the stamp also bearing the name of the bank and a space for a proper officer to append his signature. By its certification the bank guarantees that sufficient funds have been set aside to pay the check when presented. In other words, the bank guarantees payment on the check. The amount of the check is immediately subtracted from the depositor's balance, and an offsetting credit is made to the bank's "Certified Checks" account, which thereby records the liability of the bank. A small charge is sometimes made for certification, but usually banks will certify without charge for regular customers. When the certified check is cashed, the bank retains the check for its records; and it includes a slip, stating the amount of its charge for certification, when it returns the other canceled checks to the depositor. The recipient of an ordinary check can also present it to a bank for certification if, for one reason or another, the check is not to be cashed immediately; the effect is that the bank is responsible for payment later rather than relying on what may or may not be in the depositor's account when the check is cashed.

How Long Can You Hold a Check before Cashing It?

Theoretically, you can hold a check for a long time, but it isn't a good idea. Legally, a check is good as long as the statute of limitations allows—usually six years. The real answer depends more on facts and circumstances, on bank rules and practices. As a practical matter, a check becomes stale after a reasonable length of time has elapsed. In general, banks usually refuse to honor checks that are more than six months old. "Reasonable time" is as long as the bank feels it can collect the funds. The staleness of a check does not make it bad or void. It merely puts the bank on notice that irregularities may exist—that something may be wrong and therefore the check shouldn't be paid. Under such circumstances, the bank will not pay the check without obtaining the maker's consent.

Unless a check is presented to the bank for payment within a reasonable time after it is issued, the maker of the check will be relieved of liability on it if the payee suffers a loss by reason of the delay. What constitutes a reasonable time depends on the circumstances in each case. Ordinarily, a reasonable time is the length of time that it would take an ordinarily prudent person to present the check for payment under similar circumstances. Williams gives Stone a check for $100 drawn on the Bankers Bank. Although the bank is only a few blocks away, Stone, being busy, does not deposit the check. He remembers it and presents it for payment five weeks later. Meanwhile, Williams died. At worst, the check may not be honored at all; at best, payment will be delayed until Williams' estate is settled.

Stopping Payment

If you write a check and later for some reason you do not want the bank to pay it, you may ask the bank to stop payment. Commonly, you will be asked to fill out a form, giving the number and amount of the check, its date, and the name of the person to whose order it is payable. This is good procedure when a check is lost. It is also useful if after giving someone a check you cannot obtain what you were supposed to receive for it, or if what is received is not of the agreed quality or quantity.

After the bank receives a stop notice from the depositor, it puts a tab or colored flag on the record of the depositor's account and notifies all tellers who might possibly cash the check. If the check should be presented, it will ordinarily be refused. Most banks insert a clause in the stop payment form, which must be signed by the person who wishes to stop his check, relieving the bank of any liability if by oversight or error one of its employees pays a check after it has been stopped. With a

computerized operation, however, it is practically certain that the check will be stopped.

An oral stop payment order is binding on the bank for 14 days, and a written stop payment order is good for six months—subject to renewal. Sometimes the stop payment order can create a problem for the bank. A news article reported that a wife ordered a stop payment on a check drawn by her husband on their joint account. The bank honored the check, and a court upheld the bank's position.

Why the Bank May Not Honor a Check

Figure 10–3 indicates 19 reasons why a bank may not honor a check that has been drawn upon it. Of these, the following seven are the most important:

1. The depositor's account may lack sufficient funds to cover the check. Normally, depositors are immediately notified when such checks are presented at the paying teller's window, and the checks are turned back to persons who present them. The person writing a bad check is usually given, by law, a certain number of days to make the check good. If the check is not made good, the act becomes an offense under the bad-check law, and its maker becomes subject to prosecution.

2. The check may have been altered. If you make a mistake in writing a check, you cannot erase or cross out. The check will not be honored. It is best to tear up the check on which you made

FIGURE 10–3

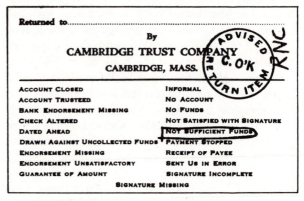

the mistake and to write another if you are using a regular checking account. If you have a special checking account and you spoil a check for which you have already paid, the bank will exchange it for a new check without extra charge.

3. The signature may not be genuine. Every bank keeps a file of signatures of all depositors. The signature card you signed when you opened your account is consulted in case of doubt. The bank must know its depositors' signatures so that if a forged check is cashed it cannot be charged against a depositor's account. If a bank pays out money on a forged check, it is paying out its own money and not that of the depositor. Banks protect themselves against such losses by carrying forgery insurance.

4. The check may have been postdated, or the words and the figures on the check may not agree. A postdated check cannot be paid until the date specified, though at times a busy bank teller may accidentally pay a check which is dated ahead.

If the words and figures on a check do not agree, many banks will refuse to cash it and will return it unpaid. Some, however, will pay the written amount, because by law the written amount has precedence over the figure. Upon proper authorization, bank employees sometimes make corrections on such checks.

5. There may be a stop order on the check.

6. A check may not be cashed by a bank after it has received notice of the death of the person who wrote it.

7. Even if the check has been drawn on the bank and the signature of the person who wrote the check has been verified, a stranger may not be able to get the check cashed, even if adequate identification is shown. Many large banks now issue identification cards to *depositors* so that checks can be cashed at any branch.

Your Check Stub

Every deposit you make and every check you write should be entered on your stub record. This is your only means of keeping an accurate record of your bank account and of reconciling your figures with the bank statement you receive at the end of the month. In fact, your stub is so important that it is advisable to fill out the stub *before* you write the check so that you won't forget to do so. Enter the check number, the date, the amount of the check, the name of the person or company to whose order the check is payable, and what you are paying for, all in the space on the stub. Then, if a month later you are asked whether you paid that particular bill, you can look over your stubs and see exactly when you did. One example of the proper way to fill out a check stub is in Figure 10–4.

Monthly Statements

Customarily, banks prepare monthly statements of each account and submit them, with canceled checks, to the depositors, in person or by mail. Banks do not necessarily prepare the statements

> If a man's after money, he's money-mad; if he keeps it, he's a capitalist; if he spends it, he's a playboy; if he doesn't get it, he's a ne'er-do-well; if he doesn't try to get it, he lacks ambition. If he gets it without working for it, he's a parasite; and if he accumulates it after a lifetime of hard work, people call him a fool who never got anything out of life.
>
> *Victor Oliver*

FIGURE 10–4

No. _123_ $ _26.52_		
Date _Jan. 18_ 19 _79_		
To _the Star Store_		
For _Sweater_		
	Dollars	Cents
Bal. Bro't For'd	74	02
Amt. Deposited	40	00
" "		
Total	114	02
Amt. this Check	26	52
Bal. Car'd For'd	87	50

as of the end of the month; to spread the work, a bank may have one third ready as of the 10th, one third as of the 20th, and the remaining third as of the end of the month. In order to get statements out promptly, banks that operate on a monthly basis may record transactions up to the 25th of the month only, with later transactions appearing on the next month's statements.

How to Reconcile Your Balance

Usually the depositor receives a bank statement and canceled checks once a month. The statement shows the balance at the beginning of the month or on the previous closing date, all individual charges for checks and notes paid, all service charges, and the balance at the end of the month or on the new closing date. For several reasons, the ending balance on the bank's statement probably will not be in agreement with the depositor's checkbook stub balance as of the same date. Therefore, it is necessary to reconcile the two balances. If the depositor has been keeping his record correctly, all checks drawn have been deducted by the depositor from the balance at the bank. Some of these checks have, however, probably not yet been presented to the depositor's bank for payment; they are therefore said to be "outstanding." Since these checks, nevertheless, were given by the depositor in payment for something, the proper procedure is to deduct them from the bank's balance on the reconciliation statement. Sometimes a bank statement provides space for this purpose.

Therefore, if deposits in transit are added to the bank's final balance and outstanding checks are deducted from it, you should usually be able to ascertain the true cash balance.

The depositor has two objectives: (1) to prove that the story told by the checkbook stubs is in agreement (reconciles) with the same story as told by the bank statement and (2) to ensure that the checkbook stubs reveal the true cash balance for the ensuing period. It is important to you to keep your checkbook in agreement with the balance in your account at the bank. Be sure to enter each check on the check stub and to substract that amount from the balance in your checkbook. In

this way you can avoid overdrawing your account and having your checks returned unpaid.

As soon as you receive your canceled checks and a statement of your account from the bank, look them over carefully. If no errors are reported, the bank will consider the account correct. The following procedure is recommended to balance your record with the bank's statement of your account:

1. Sort checks numerically or by the dates they were issued.
2. Reduce your checkbook balance by the amount of any service charges not previously recorded.
3. Enter statement balance here .... $ _____
4. Check back each paid check to your checkbook stubs and make a list of all checks that were issued but have not yet been paid by the bank. Enter and subtract the total of these unpaid checks here ..... $ _____
5. Enter and add any deposit made later in transit than the date of this statement .... $ _____
6. This balance should be the same as your checkbook balance ...... $ _____

Perhaps a simple illustration will clarify the procedure. Let us suppose that your bank statement reveals a final balance of $1,732.49, whereas your checkbook stubs show that you ended the month with $1,536.29. When you compare the canceled checks returned by the bank with the record of checks drawn according to the stubs, you find that check no. 62 for $88.29 and check no. 67 for $109.45 are still outstanding. Inspection of the bank statement shows service charges of $1.54 that have not yet been recorded on the checkbook stubs. You can arrive at the true cash balance by two independent methods.

One method is to start with the bank's balance of $1,732.49 and to reconcile it with the checkbook stub balance of $1,536.29:

Balance on bank statement		$1,732.49
Less: Outstanding		
checks: No. 62	$ 88.29	
No. 67	109.45	197.74
Total		$1,534.75
Plus: Service charges		1.54
Balance shown on check-		
book stubs		$1,536.29

Or you can begin with the checkbook stub balance of $1,536.29 and reconcile it with the balance of $1,732.49 on the bank statement:

Balance on checkbook stubs		$1,536.29
Add: Outstanding		
checks: No. 62	$ 88.29	
No. 67	$109.45	197.74
Total		$1,734.03
Less: Service charges		1.54
Balance as shown by bank		
statement		$1,732.49

Now that you have reconciled the two stories, you must remember to deduct the service charge of $1.54 from your checkbook stub balance so that you may begin the next month with your true cash balance of $1,534.75. Canceled checks, bank statements, and checkbook stubs should be retained for a reasonable number of years. The ordinary statute of limitations provides that creditors must bring action for the recovery of debts within six years or lose the right to sue for them. In case of a dispute as to whether a bill has been paid, a canceled check may prove to be an effective receipt.

Other Ways to Transfer Funds through Banks

If you want to transfer funds to someone at a distance who does not know you very well and who will therefore not accept your personal check, there are several alternative possibilities.

The Cashier's Check   This is a check which the bank draws on itself. It can be used by nondepositors. If you do not have a checking account at a bank, you can nevertheless ask for a cashier's check made out payable to the order of the distant party that you want to pay. You give the bank the appropriate amount. The bank gives you a check that it has drawn on itself, payable to the order of the party you name. As with the certified check, you have no personal receipt in the form of a canceled check, since the bank keeps it. In contrast to the certified check, however, the cashier's check is used mainly by those who do not have checking accounts.

The Bank Money Order or Register Check   In recent years the use of these instruments has grown rapidly for domestic transfers of sums up to $500. The bank money order contains a space for the sender's name and has a detachable stub or record copy which serves as a receipt and bears (for identification) the same serial number as the main part of the money order itself.

Sending Money Abroad   For this purpose you can use either international postal money orders or American Express or bank drafts. For small amounts the postal money order is less expensive. For transmitting larger sums than $100, the bank draft is much more convenient. A remittance abroad can be sent by cable, airmail, or regular mail, depending on the speed with which you wish to effect the transfer. You, of course, pay the cable or airmail costs. The American Express charge is more than the bank charge.

The Traveler's Letter of Credit   In order to have large sums available when you are traveling, you use a traveler's letter of credit. This is issued by a bank to a customer who is preparing for an extended trip. The customer pays for the letter of credit, and the bank issues it for a specified period of time in the amount purchased. The bank furnishes a list of its foreign offices and its correspondent banks, where drafts drawn against the letter of credit will be honored. The bank also identifies the customer by exhibiting a specimen signature of the purchaser on the folder enclosing the list of correspondent banks. The purchaser may go to any bank listed, draw a draft against the letter of credit, and receive payment. The letter of credit then operates like a mobile checking account, letting you cash checks or drafts as you travel. Each bank that honors a draft endorses on the letter of credit: the date a payment was made, the bank's name, and the amount that the bank paid out against the letter of credit. These drafts may also be purchased in foreign currencies.

Traveler's Checks

If you are going on a trip, you will find many opportunities to make use of traveler's checks. It is, of course, hazardous to carry large amounts

"You approved my loan? No wonder you're on the list of potential trouble banks!"

Reprinted by permission *The Wall Street Journal*

of money with you, and your personal checks are generally unacceptable. Traveler's checks usually cost 1 percent of the face amount of the checks purchased and are issued in denominations of $10, $20, $50, $100, and $500, and even $1,000.

The banks are glad to issue these checks, not so much because American Express gives two thirds of the fee to them as because of "the large float": the use of the money which they have for the period that elapses between the time the checks are sold and the date they are cashed. When the checks are purchased, the buyer signs each check with his usual signature at the upper left. Later, for identification, he signs the same signature at the lower left in the presence of the person cashing the check for him.

The checks are generally sold to the buyer in a folder, which contains a form on which to record the serial numbers and the places and dates where each check was cashed. Uncashed checks can be replaced if they are lost or stolen, provided that records of the purchase and of the serial numbers have been kept. Perhaps needless to say, the records should not be kept in the same place as the checks. American Express Company, Bank of

America, Cook's, First National City Bank of Chicago, Citibank, Republic National Bank of Dallas, and Barclays among others, all issue traveler's checks. You will find that hotels, motels, restaurants, gas stations, and large stores are universally acquainted with traveler's checks and accept them readily. They are a real convenience in traveling, you may keep them as long as you like. They are good until used, and there is no time limit on their use.

Bank Loans

There are personal loans to meet emergencies, or for a vacation and travel, and loans to consolidate debts and thereby reduce interest costs. There are many educational loans available—varying from bank to bank and from state to state—which finance education at all levels and may even include a life insurance coverage equal to the outstanding balance of the loan at no extra cost.

You can borrow not only to meet large-scale medical or dental expenses but also to buy a boat, or you can make a low-cost property improvement loan, financed in advance (before you select your contractor or the boat)—and "on the spot" as some banks say—for which all you need do to qualify is to show that you have a steady job or income and are of legal age. Most of these loans do not even require a checking account in the bank where you are applying for the loan. Auto loans are available on the same basis. Some banks offer to take your loan application by mail, and a large New York bank is even willing to do this on a Dial-a-Loan service 24 hours a day, seven days a week.

Check Credit or Line of Credit

Your line of credit is the amount of funds which a bank will allow you to draw over and above the actual amount of money you have in your account. You can spend up to this maximum amount, and as you repay monthly or in a lump sum, the credit replenishes itself. The larger banks are encouraging this use of line credit instead of installment loans as an easier method for making consumer loans. It eliminates the need for a borrower, as long as his credit is good, to process separate loans. Interest charges are set in advance, generally at 1–1½ percent a month.

Several large metropolitan banks offer a service called "No-Bounce Checking." This provides a line of credit to an agreed amount at no advance cost—and a low bank rate when the service is used. Simply stated, this means that the bank will cover your check up to a limited maximum at a small cost. The method is also known as "writing your own loan."

Overdrafts

When an individual writes a check in excess of the amount in his account and the bank honors it, it is an overdraft. When the bank and the customer agree on this as a procedure up to a certain amount, it is a line of credit. When a depositor overdraws his account on his own, the bank charges a fee—less than $10—regardless of the amount. It is up to the bank whether it will honor an overdrawn check. Frequent overdrafts or checks that bounce are reported to credit rating agencies. You cannot cover insufficient funds by postdating a check, because a bank is not supposed to accept such a check. If it does, accidentally, it is supposed to make payment on the check within 24 hours after it has been received. The Federal Reserve Board and the FDIC recently gave most of the nation's commercial banks the right to transfer money automatically from customers' savings accounts into overdrawn checking accounts, if customers request the service.

The once common expression "bankers' hours," denoting late morning opening and early afternoon closing, bears no relationship to today's extended banking hours. Citibank now advertises "the Citi never sleeps," referring to the Citicard Banking Center—an example of the new electronic customer service concept that large urban banks are introducing. At any hour, day or night, these machines, activated by a bank card and personal identification code, enable you to withdraw cash, make deposits, make payments (on personal loans, credit cards, mortgages, line of credit), transfer funds between savings and checking accounts, and get receipts for all of the above, as well as information about the status of your accounts.

The Bank Secrecy Act

Based on a Supreme Court decision of 1974, banks must keep a record of all depositors' identities, copies of all personal checks for five years, and copies of all loans over $5,000 except mortgage loans. A bank must report any transaction in which at least $5,000 (including traveler's checks) passes in or out of the country and in which at least $10,000 is withdrawn or deposited within the country. Since 1973, when the law went into effect, the banks have been photocopying checks at the rate of 30 billion a year. None of this information is supposed to be divulged to anyone—except under proper legal authority. An amendment has been proposed that would make it illegal for the banks to furnish any information without notifying the customer first.

Safe Deposit Boxes

Safe deposit boxes are metal containers that are kept under lock and key in a section of a bank's vault. The boxes are kept in small compartments, each with a separate lock. They are rented with the compartment to depositors and other customers for a rental that varies with the size of the box, ranging from $8 per annum for the smallest box to $600 for the largest. A typical small box is 2 × 5 × 22, that is, 2 inches deep, 5 inches wide, and 22 inches long. A very large box is 45 × 47 × 22. Each customer has an individual key to the safe deposit box that is rented. The bank also has a separate key to each box. The box cannot be opened unless both keys are used—the customer's key opening one set of tumblers and the bank's key opening another set.

A safe deposit box is an excellent place in which to keep a variety of valuable papers, such as insurance policies, stock certificates, bonds, real estate deeds, car titles, valuable receipts, and even jewelry. If the renter of a box dies and the key is not found, the box is opened, either by drilling or by a factory man, in the presence of authorized legal officers and the executors. If the box is in the joint names of husband and wife, the survivor will not have access to the box until certain formalities are observed. The box is immediately and temporarily sealed when the bank receives a notice of death, and it may not be reopened until a tax officer is present to take an inventory of the contents of the box for estate and inheritance tax purposes. Therefore, for obvious reasons, wills or savings bank passbooks that are needed for ready cash should not be in safe deposit boxes.

Something that is expensive or is difficult to replace (for example, discharge papers from the Army) belongs in a safe deposit box. If a stock certificate is lost or stolen, you can replace it only by furnishing an unlimited liability indemnity bond. This costs 3 percent of the market value of the stock.

Every precaution is taken by a bank to safeguard the contents of a safe deposit box. Carefully constructed steel vaults are guarded by alarms and police protection. Every entrant to a safe deposit department is carefully identified. In addition, insurance policies are carried to protect boxholders against possible loss because of fire, flood, and other hazards. Bank employees cannot get into your box when the box is rented because you have possession of one of the two keys necessary to open the box, and the bank has no master key which will open every box. If you lose your key, it is usually necessary to destroy the lock by drilling into it.

It is wise to have an accurate current list of the contents of safe deposit boxes in order to estimate values in case of loss. Banks do not insure the contents, though they do insure themselves against negligence. Even in cases where a bank employee has stolen the contents of a safe deposit box—a highly unlikely situation because of the security surrounding the area—a bank is not liable. There is no way for a bank to know what a customer has placed in a box unless he tells it, and then there is no way for a bank to know whether it should

believe him. Several insurance companies are marketing a group rate insurance to allow banks to cover the contents of safe deposit boxes automatically. If not covered by insurance, a customer would have to sue the bank and prove negilgence. Thus you deposit in a safe deposit box at your own risk!

After four days of complex argument in Federal Court in Newark, John Jacob Astor 3d accepted a $350,000 out-of-court settlement from the First Jersey National Bank, which, he charged, had misplaced or lost $465,000 worth of diamonds he had left 20 years ago in a safe deposit box. The 62-year-old Miami Beach social figure and financier said he had put the diamonds, including a 25.84-karat oval that once belonged to Eugenie, wife of Emperor Napoleon III of France—in the box in 1954 while involved in divorce proceedings with his second wife, Gertrude. During remodeling of the bank in 1963, he was asked in writing to move his treasures to another box. But he ignored the letter and the bank transferred the diamonds. Mr. Astor contended they were missing when he tried to claim them two years ago. The bank in court admitted that, after the box switch, as many as 41 persons might have had access to the contents of the box.

New York Times, April 5, 1974.

Savings Banks

Your deposit in a savings bank is usually evidenced by a passbook which you keep in your possession. In it the bank enters all of your deposits and withdrawals. The passbook is a duplicate of the bank's own record of your account. More and more savings banks have been offering "statement" accounts, with an indentification card taking the place of the passbook. Under such plans, the depositor receives periodic statements showing deposits, withdrawals, interest credits, and the savings balance.

Opening a savings account is a very simple procedure. The prospective depositor fills out a signature card, which also contains space for address and for other information which will help in identification, such as the names of mother and father;

makes an initial deposit, which often need not be more than $1; and receives a passbook or entry of deposits, withdrawals, and interest credits. The passbook must be presented along with a deposit slip or withdrawal slip, duly filled out, every time that a deposit or a withdrawal is made. Forms are available which may be sent to the bank with the passbook if the depositor wishes to do business by mail in free postage-paid envelopes supplied by the bank.

Which Type of Account Is Best for You?

Individual Accounts Owned by only one person, adult or minor. You are the sole owner, and the money is payable only to your order. Such an account can be opened with a small amount, usually as little as $1, and can be increased to the limit prescribed by the law in your state.

Joint Accounts May be opened by two persons, most frequently by a husband and wife. Either may deposit or withdraw. In case one of them dies, the balance is payable to the survivor. Such an account is opened "Richard Doe or Jane Doe—payable to either or the survivor."

Voluntary Trust Accounts Can be opened by you in trust for a child or other person. The account is controlled by you during your life-time; after your death, it is payable to the person named as beneficiary. The trust is revocable in the sense that you have the right to change the beneficiary at any time. Such an account is opened "Richard Doe in trust for Mary Doe."

Custodial Accounts If you open such an account for a minor in New York State, for example, the account is under the New York Uniform Gifts to Minors regulations. The account is irrevocable, and it becomes the property of the minor when the legal age is reached. It can be expended in whole or in part *for the minor's benefit* up to this age.

Lease Security Account or Landlord Trust Account An interest-bearing account for the benefit of tenants whose lease security deposits must be placed in such an account.

Fiduciary Accounts If you are appointed as executor or administrator of an estate or as guardian for a minor or an "incompetent" person, you may open such an account for the funds entrusted to you.

Organization Accounts These are accounts in the names of nonprofit organizations, such as religious groups, lodges, clubs, and fraternal organizations.

School Savings Accounts Over 2 million savings bank accounts are owned by students, who deposit and withdrew in schools that are cooperating with savings banks. Thus habits of thrift are learned at an early age.

Payroll Deduction Accounts May be opened by any business firm for the convenience of its employees. The employee authorizes his company to deduct a stated amount from his wage each payday and to deposit that amount directly into his savings bank account.

Special Accounts If you wish to accumulate funds for a special purpose—such as insurance, taxes, travel, or U.S. savings bonds—the bankbook can be marked accordingly. These are regular accounts on which dividends are paid. Funds may be withdrawn at any time, but the bank may ask that a small balance be left if you intend to save for the same purpose the next year. This avoids the expense and inconvenience of having to open a new account each year.

Christmas, Hanukkah, and Vacation Club Accounts You accumulate extra money by depositing a fixed amount—$2 to $20 a week—and in 50 weeks you receive a check by mail for the total that you have deposited plus dividends at the current rate compounded daily from the dates of deposit.

Other Savings Plans The Tax Saving Retirement Plan for self-employed individuals—known as the Keogh Plan—can be met by deposits in a savings bank, subject to approval by the Internal Revenue Service. The deposits increase by having dividends compounded quarterly until at least retirement at age 59½, but not later than age 70½, at which time they are subject to income tax.

The Bill-Me-Monthly Club uses the softest sell

of all in its effort to encourage regular monthly savings. The bank sends you a postage-paid envelope with a deposit slip monthly at the time you say you usually pay your bills.

Time Deposit Savings Certificates are offered to provide a range of guaranteed rates of interest higher than the rates on regular accounts, but a minimum deposit of $1,000 may be required and there is usually a two-to-seven-year maturity. Before you buy a higher rate certificate, it is essential that you balance the pleasure of the higher rate against the disadvantage of losing the use of your money for a fairly long period, and in addition the possibility of a penalty if you withdraw your money before the agreed time. On $10,000 deposited at 7.5 percent, the interest for one year is $750. If the deposit is withdrawn during the year, the interest could drop to the passbook rate of

5.25 percent, or ..	$525.00
plus a penalty loss	
of one quarter...	(−131.25)
Total interest	$393.75 = 3.94% annual interest

On the other hand, some banks have offered a new plan to pay the interest from these accounts monthly, free from any withdrawal penalties. Recent rulings by the federal agencies that supervise the financial institutions issuing certificates of deposit (CDs) permit, but do not require, full payment without an interest penalty if a depositor or a co-depositor dies before the time requirement has been met.

Retirement Savings Accounts or Automatic Payout Plans Under this arrangement, the bank will mail you checks in the amount you specify—monthly, quarterly, semiannually, or annually, as you instruct. A minimum balance and a minimum payment are usually required. As an example: a deposit of $1,000 will with interest (not guaranteed in advance) provide payments of $25 a month for three years and eight months.

Abandoned Savings Accounts

Although it is hard to believe people sometimes forget a savings account. If a passbook has not

been presented for a specified number of years, an account is legally deemed abandoned. If the bank is then unable to locate the depositor by advertising, banking law usually requires that the balance be turned over to the state comptroller. Even then, the balance may be reclaimed by the depositor from the comptroller. To guard against this, it is best to have dividends entered at least once a year and to keep the bank informed of all changes of address.

Other Savings Bank Services

In addition to these services, savings banks perform a variety of others, such as making mortgage loans, student loans, passbook or personal savings loans, home improvement loans, and co-op apartment loans; and providing safe deposit facilities, money orders, traveler's checks, low-cost savings bank life insurance, financial counseling, and bill-paying services. Just as the commercial bank is offering a comprehensive package of financial services, so, too, the mutual savings banks are becoming family financial centers that satisfy all aspects of consumer financial needs.

Savings and Loan Associations

In recent years, savings and loan associations have grown more rapidly than mutual savings banks. Perhaps the major reason for their more rapid growth is that savings and loan associations are found in all 50 states and in Puerto Rico, Guam, and Washington, D.C. Mutual savings banks are located in only 18 states and Puerto Rico. Savings and loan associations are second to commercial banks in the size of their total assets. Credit unions have about 1 percent of the assets of savings and loan associations, but currently are growing at a faster pace. A savings and loan association is a locally owned and privately managed thrift and home-financing institution. There is a growing trend toward the conversion of mutual savings and loan associations into corporations which gather together the savings of individuals and uses these savings to make long-term amortized loans to purchasers of homes. The loans are made for purposes of construction, repair, purchase, or refinancing of houses, and their repayment is secured by first mortgages. Such loans total 85 percent of the assets of savings and loan associations. Although about equally divided between federal and state charters, almost all savings and loan associations are FSLIC insured. As members of the Home Loan Bank System, they may borrow from the Home Loan Bank on the security of mortgages which they pledge. Most of the 4,800 associations are medium-sized, but 854 associations hold about 70 percent of all association assets.

Supermarkets and S&Ls team up in a new consumer-discount plan.

The participating store gives discounts of from 1 percent to 3 percent, but instead of deducting it from the customer's bill, the cash is deposited in the customer's account at the local savings and loan association. To take advantage of the plan, the customer opens a new account with a minimum deposit of $10; the supermarket transfers his accumulated discounts directly into the account.

Called Savings-Plus by John Wilson, the Missouri lawyer who devised it, the plan had its initial success in southeast Missouri, where it was tested. It recently moved into supermarkets in St. Louis and soon will be in Baton Rouge, La.; Cincinnati, Ohio; Kansas City, Mo.; Little Rock, Ark., and Miami, Fla. Both the supermarkets and the S&Ls pay Savings-Plus to use the franchised plan. James M. Beaird, president of Security Federal Savings & Loan in Sikeston, Mo., says "a consumer can build himself up a nice little nest egg."

Carondelet S&L in St. Louis figures it'll double the number of customers it has within 12 to 18 months under the plan.

The Wall Street Journal, August 10, 1978.

Types of Savings Accounts

Although losing in popularity because of their lower rate of interest, passbook accounts are still one of the two major types of savings instruments at savings and loan associations. The interest rate is 5.25 percent. Any amount may be added or withdrawn at any time. Accounts that require a 90-day notice of withdrawal carry a 5.75 percent interest rate.

The certificate accounts, the second major type of savings instrument, are issued in fixed amounts with fixed maturities at higher interest rates, ranging from 6.5 to 8 percent. They represent more than half of the total savings held by the associations. It is possible for an association to issue more than ten different types of accounts. The accounts differ in the maximum interest rate that can be paid, the time over which the account must be held, and the minimum balance required.

Normally the associations will pay out savings and repurchase shares on demand. Furthermore, the safety of the savings and loan association is ultimately assured by *(a)* its ability to borrow from the Home Loan Bank in time of need; *(b)* its reserves, *(c)* its holdings of cash and government bonds; *(d)* the amortized nature of its mortgages, which usually insures an adequate margin of safety should it have to foreclose properties and sell them; *(e)* the regular monthly repayments of principal which flow in on amortized mortgages; and *(f)* the VA and FHA guarantees on a considerable share of its mortgage holdings.

Credit Unions

A credit union is a cooperative association that has been organized to promote thrift among its members and to accumulate savings out of which loans are made at reasonable rates of interest, to members only, for useful purposes. Today state and federally chartered credit unions number about 23,000 and have more than 34 million members. With assets of $47 billion, credit unions rank seventh among financial institutions today, but they are the fastest growing and are viewed as a serious competitive threat by the others. The latest regulations (1978) permitting members of federal credit unions to write drafts on new share draft accounts will make the credit unions even more competitive. This will increase their earnings, which will improve

320

dividend rates or lead to a reduction in loan interest rates. It will encourage more people to join and place money in a federal credit union. It will save the cost of money orders.

The federally chartered credit unions now have new banking functions, such as making long-term mortgage loans and issuing savings certificates and credit cards with unsecured lines of credit. Congress created a new Central Liquidity Facility which would act as the Federal Reserve does for the banks, as a lender of last resort for credit unions facing financial difficulties. Most state-chartered credit unions have been using these privileges made possible by their network of 38 state or regionally organized banks, called "corporate centrals."

In the past most credit unions paid an average of 6 percent on savings. New-type accounts which individual credit unions can now make available are:

1. *Notice accounts:* require a minimum of 90 days' written notice of intent to withdraw funds. This notice may be waived at the end of a dividend period if the funds have been kept in the account at least a minimum time.

2. *Minimum balance accounts:* have a specified minimum, at least $500, in the account throughout a dividend period to get a special interest rate.

3. *Split-rate accounts:* pay varying interest rates on different portions of the savings. For example, 5 percent might be paid on savings of up to $500, 5½ percent on savings between $500 and $1,000, and 6¼ percent on savings of more than $1,000.

4. *Share certificate accounts:* are similar to the certificates of deposit available at banks. They have a qualifying period of from 90 days to six years.

As with the similar bank accounts, there is a penalty for early withdrawal. The maximum interest rate allowed for the share certificate accounts is 7¾ percent. On the other accounts, the maximum allowed is 7 percent.

Savings by credit union members are made in the form of share purchases, each share being valued at $5. Amounts as small as 25 cents per month can be purchased, and may be withdrawn at will. Although the credit union's board of directors may

require two months' notice for withdrawal of funds, as in a savings bank, this provision is seldom invoked. The regular saving of small sums by members is encouraged; the cultivation of the habit of systematic thrift is a basic purpose of credit unions. Average shareholdings (savings) per credit union member amount to slightly over $1,000. In order to borrow, credit union members must maintain a minimal balance of $5–$10. Credit union members have the dual advantage of a low borrowing rate and a high interest payment on their accounts. Three fourths of all credit unions in the United States have assets of under $1 million. There are however a number of units with assets in the hundred millions, such as Navy Federal ($498 million), which serves sailors and marines on duty all over the world; Pentagon Federal Union ($223 million); United Airlines Employees in Illinois ($175 million); and the Los Angeles Teachers' Credit Union ($122 million).

Membership in a federal credit union is limited to persons having a common bond of occupation or association and to groups within a well-defined neighborhood, community, or rural district. For this reason, most credit unions remain small. There is a movement now to stretch the meaning of "common bond." For example, to join the Wisconsin State Central Credit Union, you only need to live in the state. The first credit union organized to meet the financial needs of women—gender being the common bond—was chartered in Detroit and now has over 900 members.

With college financing aid and student loans diminishing, students have begun to adopt the credit union idea. The first two campus credit unions were formed at the University of Massachusetts and the University of Florida.

Joining a credit union is easy. Not much money is needed. In fact, credit unions are intended primarily for people who do not have much money. The membership entrance fee is generally only 25 cents. A minimum investment of at least one share is required. A credit union is run by its members, and each member is entitled to only one vote, regardless of the number of shares held. Once you are a member, two kinds of service are available:

(1) savings facilities and (2) loan service. Money is deposited in a credit union very much as it is in a savings bank. Savings may be used to buy shares on which dividends are paid. These are usually 7 percent a year, paid by the federal credit unions, and 8.75 percent, from state-regulated credit unions. As in savings and loan associations, savers are owners, not creditors. Sums due members comprise over 85 percent of the liabilities of federal credit unions. Credit union earnings come largely from loans to members.

U.S. Government Savings Bonds

As a no-risk, competitive 6 percent return, redeemable without loss, and never-callable investment, U.S. savings bonds are an increasingly desirable investment. All they lack is to be inflation proof. Professor Milton Friedman, the economist, has the answer to that. He proposes "purchasing power securities" redeemable at prices that provide holders with returns offsetting inflationary price increases.

Series E These were appreciation rather than current income bonds. They were purchased at 75 percent of the maturity value, and they increased in value by the periodic accretion of interest, so that they gradually rose to full par value at maturity. In contrast, the current income bond (Series H) required full initial payment and the bond-holder received interest by check every six months. At maturity the bondholder received back the amount he paid originally.

The present Series E bonds were issued in denominations of $25, $50, $75, $100, $200, $500, $1,000, and $10,000 (maturity value). For these you paid $18.75, $37.50, $56.25, $75, $150, $375, $750, and $7,500, respectively.

It should be noted that no interest as such is paid on appreciation bonds. The return comes to the saver in the form of the difference between what was paid for the bond originally ($37.50, for example) and the $50 that was received when the bond was cashed at maturity.

Series H This is a current income, not an appreciation, bond that bears an investment yield approximately equal to that of the E bond. It is issued in denominations of $500, $1,000, $5,000, and $10,000, and these are the amounts that the saver pays when he buys the bond. The original purchase price and the amount payable at maturity are the same. The government paid the return (interest) by check semiannually, beginning six months after the issue date. The yield was 5 percent the first year, 5.80 percent for the next four years, and 6.50 percent for the second five years. The yield over the entire life of the bond, however, averaged out to 6 percent.

New Series EE and HH Bonds

In the first major change since 1941, the government will issue two new series of savings bonds EE and HH, end the sale of E & H bonds, and eliminate the $25 bond, all beginning January 1, 1980.

The new EE bond will differ from the old E by doubling in value between its purchase and maturity date because it will be sold at 50 percent of its face value instead of the previous 75 percent and will mature in 11 years, 9 months compared to the 5 year plus 10 year allowable extension of the E bond. EE will be redeemable after 6 months, instead of the 2 month period of the E bond. An individual cannot buy more than $15,000 annually.

The HH bond, if redeemed before the 10 year maturity period, will lose the redemption at par before maturity advantage that the old E & H bonds had, and will be subject to an interest penalty. There is no 10 year extension of maturity for the HH bonds. It will have an advantage over the old H bond of a steady 6 percent interest payment rather than a graduated one. The minimum denomination will remain $500. An individual cannot buy more than $20,000 annually. After January 2, 1980 holders of E and EE series can exchange them for HH bonds in multiples of $500.

How Savings Bonds Are Registered

EE and HH bonds may be purchased by individuals and registered in one of three ways: *(a)* in the name of one person, e.g., "Richard Roe, 418 Main Street, Sunrise, Iowa"; *(b)* in the name of two persons as co-owners, e.g., "Richard Roe *or* Mrs. Mary L. Roe, 418 Main Street, Sunrise, Iowa"; or *(c)* in the name of one person, with one beneficiary, e.g., "Richard Roe, 418 Main Street, Sunrise, Iowa; payable on death to Carla Lee Roe." In the case of co-ownership, whichever co-owner has possession of the bond can cash it by endorsement without the consent of the other. If one of the co-owners dies, the advantage to the other co-owner lies in becoming sole owner of the bond, without having to establish proof of death. All savings bond buyers must now provide their social security number at the time of purchase.

Advantages and Disadvantages of Savings Bonds

The savings bond offers investors and savers some very valuable features. There is an advantageous combination of safety and yield. The 6 percent paid compares favorably with the yield from other savings media, and the safety is unequaled elsewhere. The option to redeem before maturity is a unique privilege in a bond. You get compound interest, and the income from your bond is exempt from state and local income taxes and personal property taxes.

In addition, the Series EE bonds offer the holder the alternative of deferring federal income taxes on the increase in redemption value—which is itself considered as interest—until the holder actually redeems the bonds, presumably at an advantageous time. In contrast to all other government and corporate securities, which are paid off by the issuers in cash only at maturity, U.S. savings bonds may be redeemed without advance notice, at any financial institution which is an authorized paying agent.

A tax-free savings plan for education is possible through the purchase of EE bonds. If they are bought in the child's name with the parent as beneficiary, *not* co-owner, they can be reported on the child's income tax return, listing the increase in value for the first year. Unless the child's income exceeds $3,300, no tax will be due. Thus, when the bonds are cashed to meet college costs, all of the accrued interest is free from federal income tax.

There is probably no security available to savers or investors that is as safe as a U.S. savings bond. It is actually safer than cash. Your dollars can be lost or stolen, but if your savings bond is lost, stolen, or destroyed, you may obtain a substitute bond, upon filing proper proof of loss or theft or destruction. For such a contingency, it is a good idea to keep a record of the bonds you own, by serial number, amount, and issue date. Keep the list separate from the bonds, so that you will have one if the other is lost. Then, if your bonds disappear, write to the Bureau of the Public Debt, Division of Loans and Currency, 200 Third St., Parkersburg, W. Va. 26101, stating the serial number (with prefix and suffix letters), the issue dates (month and year), and your name and address. The division will then send you a special form to fill out in order to obtain substitute bonds. The division keeps records of savings bonds by names of owners, by serial numbers, and now by social security numbers; so even if you do not have the serial numbers or the issue dates of your bonds, the division can probably still help you.

Unlike other stocks and bonds, U.S. savings bonds are purchasable without the payment of any commission. Banks sell or redeem them free of charge, and you can buy or redeem them at any time. There is no problem of marketability, no pricing problem, no unfortunate experience of buying high and selling low. You can always get your money back at any time you want it—not only the amount you put in, but interest on your money to the date of redemption in EE but not in HH bonds.

Systematic Savings Plans

Different financial institutions have developed a variety of systematic savings plans. One of the country's largest savings banks has come up with an ingenious "Packaged Savings" plan. Under it, one deposit a week brings you a three-way package: *(a)* a constantly increasing bank balance, *(b)* a steadily growing number of U.S. savings bonds, and *(c)* savings bank life insurance. You can arrange to pay in $3, or $5, or $10 a week for 5 years, or 10 years, or 20 years. The bank publishes tables to show what each amount will accumulate over a stated period in each of the three resource categories. Table 10–6 shows one page from the bank's descriptive booklet, which contains a whole range of other tables for varying amounts over varying periods.

Your own retirement plan to supplement social security or other pension begins small if you start at age 25. Fifty dollars a month saved until you reach 65 will add up to $24,000. Based on an average interest rate of 5.25 percent being earned and compounded daily and credited quarterly, the power of money at work will increase your own savings to a cumulative principal amount of $83,678. In each of the 15 years after your retirement you will be able to withdraw from the bank $673 a month of combined principal and interest,

as shown in Table 10–7. If you don't touch the principal, the dividends alone will give you $366 a month for the rest of your life. Combining the principal and interest over a 15-year period will give you a total of $121,140, or a $97,140 gain over what you paid in, due to interest accumulated over the 40 years.

If you are one of those who find it difficult to save, there are a number of ways to help make it easier. Your firm, if you so request, will probably deduct a specified sum from your paycheck and send it directly to your bank. Social security and corporate dividend checks can be deposited directly. You can have your firm deduct for savings bonds, too, or you can have your bank buy one a month for you from your account. You can open a Vacation Club or Christmas Club account at a savings bank, or start the bonus savings plan at a savings and loan association. Or you can resort

TABLE 10–6

The Packaged Savings Plan with Straight Life Insurance (plans available for ages 1 month to 70 years)

Starting Age	Cash* in Bank	Savings Bank Life Insurance†	U.S. Savings Bonds (face value)
$5 a week for ten years brings you all three			
20	$1,650	$5,000	$500
25	1,560	5,000	500
30	1,440	5,000	500
35	1,290	5,000	500
40	1,090	5,000	500
45	1,330	3,000	500
50	1,130	3,000	500
55	860	3,000	500
$10 a week for ten years brings you all three			
20	$3,730	$10,000	$500
25	3,550	10,000	500
30	3,310	10,000	500
35	3,010	10,000	500
40	2,620	10,000	500
45	2,100	10,000	500
50	3,100	5,000	500
55	2,650	5,000	500

* The cash in bank figure does not include cash dividends which will be paid to you.
† In addition, you will receive yearly cash dividends, as earned, on your policy. Your straight life insurance policy, of course, may be kept in force after ten years with no increase in premium. Or you may convert your insurance into its cash value, or accept a reduced amount of paid-up insurance.
Source: Bowery Savings Bank.

TABLE 10–7
Typical Monthly Withdrawal Amounts

Amount of Principal at Age 65	Monthly Withdrawal for 10 Years (dividends plus principal)	Total Principal and Dividends Received	Monthly Withdrawal for 15 Years (dividends plus principal)	Total Principal and Dividends Received
$122,972	$1,318	$158,160	$989	$178,020
83,678	897	107,640	673	121,140
62,893	674	80,880	506	91,080
31,446	337	40,440	253	45,540

When you reach retirement age, you may prefer to use part of your principal each month as part of your income. Whatever you leave in the bank, of course, continues to earn dividends. If you use both dividends and principal, here are typical examples of the approximate amount you could withdraw each month over a period of 10 or 15 years.

All figures are calculated at the Dime's latest dividend rate of 5.25%, a year compounded daily from the day of deposit, which will yield 5.47% when deposits remain in your account for a year. The rate of dividends depends on earnings, and therefore no specific rate can be guaranteed. Also, these figures are gross and make no allowance for income taxes, to which savings dividends, like all other taxable sources of income, are subject. The tables assume therefore that any taxes due will be paid from other income sources.

Source: Dime Savings Bank of New York.

to the very familiar device of saving one kind of coin—a dime, a quarter, or a half-dollar. Every time you get one in change, you put it apart from the rest of your change, and then, when you get home, you drop it in a coffee tin that you have set aside for savings. Or you can automatically deposit a paycheck every quarter, or half a paycheck every other month. When you find the method that suits you best, if you put it on an automatic basis, you will see your savings grow.

It helps to save if you have some definite purpose or goal in mind, preferably one which is realizable.

Saving for Retirement

The farther away your investment goal is, the more you should consider the power of compound interest as an integral part of your plan. This is especially true for IRAs (Investment Retirement Accounts) and Keogh Plans, where the interest accumulates tax-free. Over a ten-year span, interest on interest amounts to 33 percent of the total return. Over 30 years it will mean 75 percent of the total return.

It will seem odd to think of retirement now, but if you consider Table 10–8 and think of what it may mean to you later, the advantage is obvious.

All of the savings media discussed in this chapter are characterized by safety rather than risk; steady, moderate return rather than high, erratic return; an insured, dependable return of principal; and easy liquidity.

Investments that offer a high return and uncertainty will be studied in later chapters.

Conclusion

Sooner or later, at one time or another, every family or individual sets out to save. It may be the result of a New Year's resolution, and it may last but two days, or, because of the nature of one's personality, it may take hold and last a lifetime. Some people can save and some people can't. It takes willpower, self-denial, patience, and perseverance to save, and not everyone has these qualities. Level of income is not of overriding importance. There are some who can set aside something from an income of $10,000 a year, while others find it difficult to make ends meet on $50,000 a year. If you can save, it makes life

TABLE 10–8

EXAMPLES of monthly retirement payments you can receive at age 65, in addition to your Social Security, if you start saving at age 35.

Annual Income	Maximum Annual Contribution*	Total Contributions	Total You Will Have at 65	Monthly Payouts For 10 Years
$10,000 and up	$1,500	$45,000	$189,638	$2,278
9,000	1,350	40,500	170,675	2,050
8,000	1,200	36,000	151,710	1,822
7,000	1,050	31,500	132,747	1,594

*Note: If both husband and wife qualify the maximum combined contribution can be $3,000 a year.

An example where only one spouse is working, and contributions are made for both. Starting at age 35 to retirement at age 65.

$12,000 and up	$1,750	$52,500	$221,245	$2,658

Figures are based on annual rate of 7.75% a year available on our 3 to 7 year Retirement Account Savings Certificates with a minimum deposit of $500. Available future rates may be more or less than current rates, depending on economic conditions and government regulations. Premature withdrawals on Savings Certificate funds can be made only with the consent of the Bank. Then, FDIC regulations provide that the rate of interest on the amount withdrawn be reduced to the passbook rate at the time of withdrawal from the date of deposit and 90 days interest be forfeited. There is also a tax liability and penalty imposed by the IRS if withdrawals are made from the plan before age 59½.

Source: The Dime Savings Bank of New York.

smoother. If you lose your job, you have a cushion to fall back on and can take longer to look around and perhaps get a better job than if you have to take the first thing that comes along. If there is sudden illness or surgery, financial tragedy does not accompany the physical distress. Vacations, automobiles, better furnishings, a home—all are more easily within your reach. You may be able to accumulate a modest financial beginning for a small business which in time may develop into a bigger one. You may be able to provide security and self-support for your old age instead of having to depend on the charity of others. It is surprising how small sums set aside regularly accumulate rapidly into substantial and usable surpluses.

SUGGESTED READINGS

Bankers Magazine. "EFTS '78," March–April 1978.

Kidwell, David S., and Peterson, Richard L. "A Close Look at Credit Unions," Bankers Magazine, January–February 1978.

Mayer, Martin. The Bankers. New York: Weybright & Talley, 1975.

Martin, Jackie. Understanding Savings Accounts. June 1978. Free from Cooperative Extension Service, Box 3AE, New Mexico State University, Las Cruces, NM 88003.

National Commission on Electronic Fund Transfers. EFT in the U.S.: Policy Recommendations and the Public Interest. Washington, D.C.: U.S. Government Printing Office, 1977; 389 pages; $6.

CASE PROBLEMS

1 John and Sally Yates are a young couple who believe they should have a checking account. Should the account be opened in either name or in the names of both jointly? What are the advan-

tages or disadvantages of either possibility? Should the account be a regular or checking account? What considerations are involved in that choice?

2   Grace Smithers, a student in college in New York City who banks at Chase Manhattan, suddenly found herself with a number of financial problems, just before vacation time. Short of funds, she had called her father in San Francisco, who sent her a check for $500. She deposited the check, but forgot to endorse it. She made several purchases against it. What will happen? She is also puzzled about her bank statement, which showed a balance of $283.17, but her checkbook showed a balance of $222.16. She deposited a check for $50 and cashed one for $22. The canceled checks returned by the bank did not include three of the checks she had drawn during the month (for $20, $27, and $43.44). From the statement, she learned that the bank had made a service charge for the month of $1.43. She reconciles her statement and is upset by the discrepancy. How do you account for it?

3   Discuss how a certified check can be helpful in each of the following situations to either party:

a. You are selling your house.
b. You have bought a table made to your order.
c. You are temporarily out of town and have bought ten shares of IBM over the phone through your regular brokerage firm.

4   You have just inherited $10,000, and you want to use it in the near future for a down payment on a house. Meanwhile you are interested in keeping it safe and watching it grow. Which type of savings do you think will do the most for you, and why: day-to-day savings account; a government EE or HH bond; a certificate of deposit account?

5   You are 22 years old and are weighing the practical advantages and disadvantages of a savings plan over a long period. Philosophically you agree that it's a good idea. Practically you wonder whether there *is* an advantage in saving even a small sum monthly toward buying a home or travel or future investment or even further away—retirement. Inflation seems to you an added reason for spending now. Any decision?

11

Credit and Borrowing

So far as my coin would stretch; and where it would not I have used my credit.

SHAKESPEARE

If you want the time to pass quickly, just give your note for 90 days.

FARMER'S ALMANAC

If you use your credit wisely, you are a good risk for a loan. Do young people constitute the greatest credit risk? "A record club reports that classical record buyers are 'very good customers' while those who order pop records are 'the greatest risk.' " A book club has found that "ads in publications such as *Playboy* produce a much higher percentage of nonpayers than one in such as *Smithsonian.*"[1]

Your credit history determines whether you can borrow. Credit is a form of borrowing—of using purchasing power—only technically yours. The more you use your credit and repay, the more desirable you are as a borrowing risk. If you have never used credit and you have always paid cash for what you bought, ironically, you are a poor risk for a loan. On the other side of the coin, as we will see, if you have overused credit—you are in trouble.

The credit bureau has a complete file on all your transactions. The minute you apply for credit or a loan, the machinery swings into action. The fol-

---
[1] *New York Times,* September 23, 1977.

lowing pages give you a complete picture of a full credit report and an explanation of its symbols so that you know what's being said about you.

The Credit Bureau and the Credit Investigation

A credit bureau contacts the references, usually by telephone or by sending forms to be completed and returned. In most of the larger cities the credit bureau can furnish all needed information about local applicants. The local credit bureau is a clearinghouse for the exchange of information among the merchants on the credit experience which each has had with the purchaser. Each firm supplies the bureau with all the details about its dealings with the credit applicant. The bureau is usually maintained by the joint contributions of all its members. A person with a good credit record may find that while waiting in the store's credit office, a phone call to the credit bureau may be sufficient to establish identity and past good record and permit the credit manager to approve the application without further delay.

If the credit applicant is unknown to the credit bureau, it will, at the store's request, make a detailed investigation of the applicant. Just what it looks for may be seen in Figure 11–1. The explanation and the procedure are shown in Figures 11–2 and 11–3. If you have just moved from one city to another, the credit bureau in the city in which you are now applying for credit will get in touch with the credit bureau in the city in which you formerly resided via the national organization of credit bureaus, the Associated Credit Bureaus, Inc., or TRW, another credit system. In this way a person with a bad credit record may find it difficult to obtain credit anywhere in the country. Sometimes persons who fail to pay in one city and then establish themselves in another are located by the credit bureau network. The usual credit investigation is made by phoning the applicant's landlord, employer, bank, and trade references.

A credit bureau furnishes the data about the paying habits of individuals to firms which are permitted by law (Fair Credit Reporting Act) to receive

"Our credit check indicates that you're a solid citizen, Mr. Whitley. You've been married ten years, held the same job for eight years and had the same CB handle for two years."

Reprinted by permission *The Wall Street Journal*

this information, and it charges fees for the service. Credit bureaus do not comment on the information they furnish. The acceptance or rejection of an applicant is solely the responsibility of the credit granter.

Credit information may be transmitted to the credit granter by telephone, by mail, or by computer terminal. The sequence is determined by the standard written form ACB Form 2000. The trade name Crediscope was devised by Associated Credit Bureaus, Inc., to indicate a concept of reporting only factual, objective information. Crediscope attempts to insure against ambiguous, confusing, or misleading terminology and to include only "objective" information. As a result of all the new consumer credit legislation, credit bureau procedures have changed.

The Fair Credit Reporting Act

Formerly a credit report was a secret document that might contain fact, error, fiction, hearsay, or invalid information unavailable to you but not necessarily to others whom you might not want to

FIGURE 11–1

NAME AND ADDRESS OF CREDIT BUREAU MAKING REPORT		

Credit Bureau of Anytown
1234 Main
Anytown, Anywhere 22222

☐ SINGLE REFERENCE ☐ IN FILE REPORT ☐ TRADE REPORT
☒ FULL REPORT ☐ EMPLOY & TRADE REPORT ☐ PREVIOUS RESIDENCE REPORT
☐ OTHER _____

FOR Second National Bank First & P Sts. Anytown, Anywhere 22222	Date Received **10/1/79** Date Mailed **10/2/79** In File Since **8/70** Inquired As: **2**

CONFIDENTIAL
crediscope® REPORT
☐ Member
Associated Credit Bureaus, Inc.

REPORT ON: LAST NAME	FIRST NAME	INITIAL	SOCIAL SECURITY NUMBER	SPOUSE'S NAME
Consumer,	Daniel	R	123-45-6789	Annette

ADDRESS: CITY	STATE:	ZIP CODE	SINCE:	SPOUSE'S SOCIAL SECURITY NO.
9547 Oak St., Anytown,	Anystate	12345	1975	987-65-4321

COMPLETE TO HERE FOR TRADE REPORT AND SKIP TO CREDIT HISTORY

PRESENT EMPLOYER:	POSITION HELD:	SINCE:	DATE EMPLOY VERIFIED	EST. MONTHLY INCOME
Osborn Motors	Sr. Mechanic	5/76	10/2/79	$ 950

COMPLETE TO HERE FOR EMPLOYMENT AND TRADE REPORT AND SKIP TO CREDIT HISTORY

DATE OF BIRTH	NUMBER OF DEPENDENTS INCLUDING SELF:			OTHER: (EXPLAIN)
4/40	3	☐ OWNS OR BUYING HOME	☒ RENTS HOME	☐

FORMER ADDRESS:	CITY:	STATE:	FROM:	TO:
Rt. 1 Box 82	Thattown	Anystate	1971	1975

FORMER EMPLOYER:	POSITION HELD:	FROM:	TO:	EST. MONTHLY INCOME
Ace Auto Repair	Mechanic	12/72	5/76	$ 800

SPOUSE'S EMPLOYER:	POSITION HELD:	SINCE:	DATE EMPLOY VERIFIED	EST. MONTHLY INCOME
Independent Tel. Co.	Supervisor	5/78	10/2/79	$ 700

CREDIT HISTORY (Complete this section for all reports)

WHOSE	KIND OF BUSINESS AND ID CODE	DATE REPORTED AND METHOD OF REPORTING	DATE OPENED	DATE OF LAST PAYMENT	HIGHEST CREDIT OR LAST CONTRACT	BALANCE OWING	PRESENT STATUS PAST DUE AMOUNT	NO. OF PAYMENTS	NO. MONTHS HISTORY REVIEWED	HISTORICAL STATUS TIMES PAST DUE 30-59 DAYS ONLY	60-89 DAYS ONLY	90 DAYS AND OVER	TYPE & TERMS (MANNER OF PAYMENT)	REMARKS
3	D-10	9/79 A	2/71	7/79	212	85	34	2	12	1	1		R-$17	
1	B-16	9/79 A	1973	9/79	2500	500			12				I-$150	
2	N-91	8/79 A	6/77	6/79	650	225	--	-	12				O	DRP

This information is furnished in response to an inquiry for the purpose of evaluating credit risks. It has been obtained from sources deemed reliable, the accuracy of which this organization does not guarantee. The inquirer has agreed to indemnify the reporting bureau for any damage arising from misuse of this information, and this report is furnished in reliance upon that indemnity. It must be held in strict confidence, and must not be revealed to the subject reported on, except by reporting agency in accordance with the Fair Credit Reporting Act.
FORM 2000-1/77

With the exception of one major credit reporting firm, Form 2000 is used generally by most other credit bureaus. The exception is TRW Credit Data Corporation of Anaheim, California.

The following narrative explains the illustrated typed credit report.

This is a fictitious Full Report, consisting of all the current information available. It has been prepared for the Second National Bank, which has a contractual agreement with the Credit Bureau of Anytown.

The factual data about Mr. & Mrs. Consumer fills the spaces down to Credit History. Line by line, these are interpreted as follows:

1st Column—Digit "3" means this account is probably in the name of "Daniel Consumer" and his wife Annette is authorized to use its credit privileges. It could just as well mean the reverse, with the account in her name. The Equal Credit Opportunity Act requires that all accounts be so identified when reported by the credit granter.

FIGURE 11–1 *(continued)*

2nd, 3rd, 4th, 5th & 6th Columns—Using the explanations on the reverse of Form 2000, these columns say: "A department store (D-10) furnished current data (9/79) through computer tape (A) that the Consumers opened their account 8 years ago (2/71), made their last payment 2 months ago (7/79) and that the most they ever owed the store was $212.

7th, 8th & 9th Columns—The Consumer family owes $85 now and have missed their last 2 payments, totaling $34.

10th Column—The department store's computer is programmed to report data only for the past 12 months.

11th, 12th & 13th Columns—Prior to the past-due status of this account, the Consumers were past due before. At one time during the past 12 months, they were over 30 days in arrears before they paid, and another time, they reached a 60-day past due status. They have not been over 90 days in the past 12 months.

14th Column—The "R" stands for Revolving Account, with monthly payments of $17.

Let's review the second trade line. The "1" in "Whose" column means this Bank account is in Daniel's name and is his responsibility alone. It is not past due, although $500 was owed at one time. The I-$150 means an Installment Account with monthly payments of $150.

Third Trade Line—The "2" indicates that Daniel and Annette are jointly responsible. The account (N) is for credit extended by a National Credit Card Company or an Airline. Note that no payment has been made since June 1979. This would usually show up in the Past Due columns, but the absence of any indication there and the letters "DRP" in the Remarks Column mean that the consumers have exercised their rights under the Fair Billing Act. When a credit granter has not yet resolved the dispute of a customer who has complained about its billing, that credit granter may not report the account as past due. DRP means Dispute—Resolution Pending. (The "O" refers to an Open Account, requiring a single payment or 30-60-90 day terms.)

In the upper right-hand corner under "In File Since" the digit "2" has been filled in under "Inquired as" This means that the Second National Bank has a credit application from *both* Daniel and Annette, so the credit bureau may reveal information they have on both individuals. If it had a credit application from, say, Annette Consumer, who wanted her own account, then the Bank trade line (B-16) would have been suppressed because the firm ordering the report would not then be entitled to information on the spouse. All this is contained in the Equal Credit Opportunity Act.

Source: Associated Credit Bureaus, Inc.

see it. Since April 25, 1971, the federal Fair Credit Reporting Act has closed your file to snoopers and opened it to you. Unless you permit opening records or a court order compels it, your records are restricted to those—including government agencies—who must evaluate you for credit, insurance, or employment. Information may not be reported after it has become obsolete, that is, 14 years after bankruptcies, or 7 years for unfavorable matters, such as suits, judgments, liens, or records of arrest, indictment, or conviction of a crime, except when the transaction involves credit on life insurance of $50,000 or more, or a job paying at least $20,000 annually.

If the consumer thinks that a bank or credit file may contain unfair remarks, the information and the source may be requested in writing or by providing proper identification in person or by telephone. The law provides stiff penalties against per-

sons who obtain a consumer credit report under false pretenses. If the consumer questions the information, the agency must reinvestigate, and then, at no cost to the consumer, it must inform those who have received employment reports within the preceding two years or credit reports within the preceding six months concerning the results of the new investigation.

The consumer must be given written notice if personal interviews (of friends and others) are to be used in a credit investigation, and the consumer has the right to request disclosure of the nature and scope of the interviews.

When making a consumer report, a consumer-reporting agency must reverify all information which is not a matter of public information if it has been more than three months since the adverse information was received.

Any person who, based on a consumer's credit

FIGURE 11–2

Three-letter abbreviations used in the "Remarks" column:

ACC—Account closed by consumer.
AJP—Adjustment pending.
*BKL—Account included in bankruptcy.
CCA—Consumer counseling account. Consumer has retained the services of an organization which is directing payment of his accounts.
CLA—Placed for collection.
DIS—Dispute following resolution.
DRP—Dispute resolution pending.
†JUD—Judgment obtained for balance shown.
MOV—Moved. Left no forwarding address.
PRL—Profit and loss write-off.
RLD—Repossession. Paid by dealer.
RLP—Repossession. Proceeds applied to debt.
RPO—Repossession.
RRE—Repossession redeemed.
RVD—Returned voluntarily. Paid by dealer.
RVN—Returned voluntarily.
RVP—Returned voluntarily, proceeds applied to debt.
RVR—Returned voluntarily, redeemed.
STL—Plate stolen or lost.
*WEP—Wage Earner Plan Account (Chapter XIII of the Bankruptcy Act).

* The creditor should not report any balance owing on any such accounts which have been legally discharged in bankruptcy or have been included in a Wage Earner Plan.

† Credit bureau will avoid listing such accounts twice. If the account is included in the Public Record paragraph, it will be deleted from the Credit History.

Kind of Business Classification

Code		Kind of Business
A	—	Automotive
B	—	Banks
C	—	Clothing
D	—	Department and variety
F	—	Finance
G	—	Groceries
H	—	Home furnishings
I	—	Insurance
J	—	Jewelry and cameras
K	—	Contractors
L	—	Lumber, building material, hardware
M	—	Medical and related health
N	—	National credit card companies and airlines
O	—	Oil companies
P	—	Personal services other than medical
Q	—	Mail-order houses
R	—	Real estate and public accommodations
S	—	Sporting goods
T	—	Farm and garden supplies
U	—	Utilities and fuel
V	—	Government
W	—	Wholesale
X	—	Advertising
Y	—	Collection services
Z	—	Miscellaneous

Source: Associated Credit Bureaus, Inc.

FIGURE 11–3

Illustration of payment record:

Month	Current	30/59 p.d.	60/89 p.d.	Over 90
March 1978	X			
April		X		
May	X			
June	X			
July		X		
Aug.			X	
Sept.		X		
Oct.	X			
Nov.	X			

Shown above is an illustration of how a creditor might review a ledger record to arrive at the Crediscope method of reporting credit history.

In December 1978 the creditor reports to the bureau on his experience. The first charge on the account was in February 1978. The first payment, due in March, was on time. There was no payment in April, but in May the account was current again (which means that two payments were made that month). The June payment was on time, but the July payment was not made—thus the account was 30/59 days past due. The absence of a payment in August brought the account to 60/89 days past due. In September two payments were made (for July and August), which left the account 30/59 days past due. Then two payments were made in October, bringing the account current again. The November payment was on time. In December, the creditor reviews nine months' history. No history of over 36 months is reported. No words are used so as not to color the report and in order to maintain uniformity.

Source: Associated Credit Bureaus, Inc.

report, increases the charge for or denies credit or insurance must inform the consumer of this action and provide the name and address of the agency that furnished the report. The user of the report must also inform the consumer that if a written request is made within 60 days, the user will disclose the nature of the information to the consumer.

A consumer can bring a civil damage suit against the reporting agency or the information user for willfully or negligently violating the Fair Credit Reporting Act.

The act is enforced by the Bureau of Consumer Protection in the Federal Trade Commission. Violations are subject to "cease and desist orders."[2] Each violation of such an order is punishable by a $5,000 fine. The law also authorizes consumers to sue violators for damages. Punitive damages, as well as actual damages, without specified limits may be imposed for willful violations.

**First Charges Filed under Act
Covering Credit Data Abuse**

WASHINGTON—A Kansas City, Mo., television retailer and North Kansas City, Mo., collection agency became the first concerns to be accused of violating the Fair-Credit Reporting Act of 1970.

The Justice Department charged that Vesto Inc., the TV outlet, and its vice president, Malcolm Magers, gave the confidential number that the store used as a member of the Credit Bureau of Greater Kansas City to Lawrence Wager, doing business as Law & Credit Co., the collection agency.

According to a 10-count criminal information filed in a Federal Court in Kansas City, Mr. Wager, who wasn't a member of the credit bureau, used the TV store's number to get information on consumers between Nov. 17, 1976, and the following Jan. 24. Law prohibits anyone from obtaining information about consumers' credit under false pretenses.

If convicted, the individual defendants could receive a maximum $5,000 fine and one year in prison on each count. The concern could be fined a maximum $5,000 on each count.

The Wall Street Journal, May 15, 1978.

The Fair Credit Reporting Act provides that you cannot be charged for an interview with a credit bureau if within 30 days you have either been denied credit because of a credit report from the credit bureau or you have received a notice from a collection department affiliated with the credit

---

[2] In June 1978 one of the largest credit reporting agencies in the country, The American Service Bureau of Chicago, agreed to a consent order of the FTC to stop collecting "impermissible" types of information that it had been asking consumers to give as identification before revealing data in the consumers' files. The agency, which specializes in preparing investigative reports for insurance companies, had misrepresented the law by telling consumers that they had to give such facts about themselves.

bureau. Under the same conditions, you cannot be charged for notification to previous recipients that information is being deleted from your file or for the addition of an explanatory statement.

Under certain circumstances, a credit bureau may make a reasonable charge for a consumer interview, but it must advise the applicant in advance of any charges. It has been alleged that credit bureau personnel do not fully disclose the information to which consumers are entitled unless the consumers are able to interrogate, to ask the right questions. You have to take the interviewer's word that all information had been disclosed. Files are not always updated. Name mix-ups can be a problem.

If you are denied credit, find out why. There may have been an error or a confusion of names. Computer billing, its many errors and slow, frustrating delay in correction, compounded by human mistakes in input and machine stubbornness, has created endless credit tangles. Despite the incredible complications in straightening out mistakes, it is essential to persevere lest your credit rating be hurt.

Credit Scoring Systems

Credit scoring systems are a means of more readily discriminating between good and poor credit risks. Weighted values—points—are assigned to various credit characteristics. For example, a homeowner may receive 25 points; a renter who has lived in the same place for five years or more, 15 points; a new renter, 0 points; and a boarder, −10 points. A person may receive 25 points for having held a position as a supervisor for the past five years; a clerk on the job one year, 5 points; a construction worker on a temporary job, 0 points; and an unemployed person, −20 points. Elaborate studies have been made to develop point scores for identifiable credit characteristics of good borrowers and to detect signs indicative of possible or probable default.

Credit scoring systems may use as few as 5 or as many as 350 characteristics. Locally based systems reflect the conditions of the area. The ownership of industrial life insurance was included as a

TABLE 11–1
Credit Risk Probability Table

Credit Score (points)	Number Bad	Number Good	Total	Probability of Going Bad	
200–300	5	1	6	83%	(5 ÷ 6)
301–400	10	10	20	50	(10 ÷ 20)
401–500	13	25	38	34	(13 ÷ 38)
501–600	24	115	139	17	(24 ÷ 139)
601–700	19	140	159	12	(19 ÷ 159)
701–800	19	260	279	7	(19 ÷ 279)
801–900	6	200	206	3	(6 ÷ 206)
Over 900	4	240	244	2	(4 ÷ 244)

factor in one scoring system in a low-income area when those who owned industrial life insurance were found to be much better credit risks than those who did not.

Preventing Discrimination

Federal laws such as the Equal Credit Opportunity Act (ECOA) prohibit discrimination based on race, color, religion, national origin, sex, mental status, age, or the receipt of public assistance, so you can see why the computer is programmed so that it should be impersonal. No longer can a loan officer regard a divorce as a negative item. Nor can a person over 62 receive a different score from one under 62 even though experience shows that the over-70 age group has the best credit record. A creditor can only ask for this information about a spouse: whether the spouse will be using or be liable for the account or whether the applicant is relying on the spouse's income or property in order to be eligible for credit. Stability counts. The longer you hold a job and live in one place—the higher your score. A home telephone shows more stability than a high income—since the latter could indicate an appetite for expensive items and cause difficulties in payment.

Sometimes the use of seemingly innocent data may have hidden significance. A credit card applicant's postal zip code compared with census tract information may "result in a disproportionately larger number of rejections for black than for white applicants." The FTC will investigate "indirect, unintentional discrimination such as the use of telephone listings to determine credit worthiness—which could discriminate against married women whose telephones have usually been listed in their husband's names.[3] The Fed defines discrimination as 'to treat less favorably' rather than 'to treat differently.' "

Credit scoring systems usually predict a borrower's behavior fairly accurately: the selected questions allow for the needs of the company, the type of customer it attracts and the geographic area. National companies such as Sears or Bank America, with 4½ million credit card holders and a half-million new applicants yearly, rely on the computer's judgment rather than on that of the loan officer.

One scoring system developed a probability table, such as is shown in Table 11–1. A lender using a scoring system associated with this table might decide to reject all prospective borrowers with scores of 400 or less, thereby sharply increasing the probability that the loans granted (to those with scores of 401 or better) would be repaid.

An effective scoring system enables risk to be determined more from a lending organization's accumulated experience than from the "human element" based on the judgment of an individual

---

[3] *Wall Street Journal,* August 8, 1977—statement by Commissioner Elizabeth Hanford Dole of the FTC.

credit specialist, which may influence the lender to refuse credit unfairly. Such a point score can be shown to an applicant and be an objective explanation for a refusal of a loan. The opposite is also true—the low-risk applicant is more easily recognized, and could be given the opportunity of a larger loan.

If you are rejected for credit, you have a right to know not only that you scored too low, but more specifically, why.

Cash versus Credit

Before discussing charge accounts and credit cards of all descriptions, let us examine another option—cash—and its advantages.

An old-fashioned idea has returned—cut-rate prices for cash payments. As a result of an out-of-court settlement recently, American Express advised the retailers who honor its credit cards that it is permissible to allow a discount, "if such discount is clearly and conspicuously offered to all cash customers." Consumers Union had charged that American Express and Carte Blanche were illegally forbidding cut-rate prices to cash customers at their client stores and were therefore forcing the cash customers to help finance the cost of credit. The retailer who has to pay the credit company a service charge ranging from 2 to 8 percent on each transaction, but keeps all the profit from a cash sale, may be understandably reluctant to publicize the opportunity for a discount.

Asking discounts for cash works—sometimes. Some merchants even volunteer the cash amount. There is even a cash credit card (UNIC) which advertises itself as an un-credit card. Its members, mostly on the West Coast, obtain discounts for cash.

Want to save? Use cash—it inhibits impulse buying. A recent analysis of department store activity discovered that shopper purchases averaged $8.25 when the shoppers used "real" money, $15.93 when the purchases were charged to the stores' own charge plates, and $20.47 when the purchases were made with bank credit cards.

The Federal Reserve Board recently issued guidelines for a two-price system—one for cash and one for credit—if a retailer desires to offer a discount of up to 5 percent for cash purchases.

The average one-car American family buys eight cars over a life span. Including trade-in value and additional dollar expenditure for the new cars, it has been estimated that if they had been bought for cash, the savings on interest alone would have bought eight other "big-ticket" items for cash during the family's life span.

THE CHARGE ACCOUNT—OPEN-END CREDIT—REVOLVING CREDIT

Over half of all retail sales are done on a charge basis. Charge or "open account" purchases differ in a number of ways from installment purchases. Charge accounts do not call for a down payment; most installment transactions do. To installment prices are added carrying charges. Charge purchasers do not pay this extra cost for the use of credit; it is merged in the price of the article itself, which is paid by cash customers too. For very slow payment of end-of-month bills, a few stores sometimes add on a small carrying charge. On the other hand, many stores allowed charges to run up to 90 days without penalty. The average "30 day" account, a retail credit survey revealed, averaged 60–74 days, varying with the line of business. Now all charges are governed by the Consumer Credit Protection Act, known as the Truth in Lending law. For the customer who buys on a charge account, there is usually no contract to be signed and hence no right of repossession by the dealer should the customer fail to pay. When you purchase on a charge account, you get title to the goods purchased. In most installment sales, title does not pass until the final installment is paid.

In recent years a flexible or revolving charge account has developed. When merchants perceived that many customers were slow in paying at the end of 30 days, they decided to capitalize on this situation by imposing a finance charge. Customers were urged to make additional purchases which would increase the balance due the store and could be paid in installments. As the balance due was reduced by payments, additional purchases could be made. As long as the required minimum was paid at the stated time, further credit was continually advanced to cover new purchases. This was, in a way, the adaptation of the "line of credit" concept which commercial bankers applied to business customers. It is also called open-end credit.

Approximately three quarters of the sales of goods by furniture stores, appliance stores, and jewelry stores are financed with consumer credit and more than half of the sales made by men's clothing stores, women's apparel stores, department stores, and mail-order houses are also financed.

Credit granting has changed completely within one generation. In the past, neighborhood food stores and company stores "locked in" customers by carrying accounts until payday, and nonfood retail chains insisted on cash purchases. Today the supermarket is almost completely cash, but such stores as Sears, Montgomery Ward, and J. C. Penney have revised their former cash-only policy and now rely heavily on credit. These stores have carefully refined their credit scoring systems so that they suffer few credit losses.

They prefer credit cards (preferably their own) because credit purchasers—unlike cash customers, who are anonymous—leave a record that indicates customer preferences. They also regard their credit cards as "guaranteed money," unlike checks that might "bounce." Although checks are accepted with adequate identification.

The Cost of Charge Accounts

The Consumer Credit Protection Act of 1968 requires that you be told how the finance charge is determined. This includes a statement of what is defined as an unpaid balance and what percentage is used to compute the finance charge.

Let's use the example of 1.5 percent per month. This seems to be an 18 percent (1.5 × 12) annual rate, but it and your dollar charge will vary, depending on the interpretation of unpaid balance. If a store does not credit partial repayments made during a billing period, but calculates the charge on the total, the cost to you will be drastically different from what it would be if the partial payment had been taken into account.

Rates cannot be higher than allowed under the state usury laws. Table 11–2 shows how your un-

TABLE 11–2
State Variations in Finance Charge Regulations

If You Reside in the State of	Amount Subject to Finance Charge	Monthly Rate (%)	Annual Rate (%)
Arizona California	$1,000 or less Over $1,000	1.5 1	18 12
Connecticut	Entire	1	12
Florida Georgia Illinois Maryland Massachusetts Michigan New Jersey New York Texas	$500 or less Over $500	1.5 1	18 12
Missouri	$500 or less Over $500	1.5 .75	18 9
Pennsylvania	Entire	1.25	15

paid balance faces varying finance charges in different states.

To save the most when using revolving credit, pay within the 25 or 30 days allowed without finance charges. This gives you convenience at no extra cost. To have four months interest-free use of money, use the cards just after the billing date.

However, if you wait until almost the last day to pay in order to get an additional "free ride" you may end up with a finance charge, because the payment might be late if you have not allowed enough time for postal handling and company processing. It helps to mark the due date for charge account bills on the calendar.

Methods of Computing Finance Charges

1. *The previous balance method* is the most common and most expensive for the consumer. No matter how small a balance is left outstanding at the end of the current period, the interest charged is figured on the amount outstanding at the beginning of the period. For example, you owe $200 at the beginning of February, and the finance charge is 1.5 percent per month, or 18 percent per year. During February you paid $100. However, when the new balance is figured at the end of February, the 1.5 percent finance charge is figured on the $200 beginning balance (not the $100 ending balance), for a charge of $3.

2. *The average daily balance method* is less expensive for the consumer than the previous balance method. The finance charge is based on the average amount per day which you owe during the previous month. For example, suppose that you owe $200 on February 1 and that on February 14 you pay off $100. For the first 14 days of the month your balance was therefore $200, and for the last 14 days your balance was $100. Thus the average daily balance for February was $150. The 1.5 percent finance charge is then taken on the $150 average daily balance, for a charge of $2.25.

3. *The adjusted balance method* is clearly the least expensive of the three major methods, since the finance charge is based upon the remaining balance at the end of the month. Thus, the 1.5 percent finance charge would be figured on the $100 balance at the end of the month of February, for a charge of $1.50. Retailers obviously are not too eager to use the adjusted balance method because it keeps the finance charges relatively low.

Many stores are switching to the average daily balance method because of mounting criticism of the previous balance method, which had formerly been favored. If you don't understand your billing statement, and don't actually know what you are paying, it can be costly. The adjusted balance method is obviously better for the customer, as you can see in Table 11–3.

FAIR CREDIT BILLING ACT

Whichever the method, if the bill arrives within a day or so of the payment date, it is almost inevitable that a late payment will result and that angry, confused consumers will complain of unfair service charges. The Fair Credit Billing Act of 1974 requires that bills be mailed at least 14 days before payments are due. Checking your bill to note how long it

TABLE 11–3

Comparison of Computing Charges

Method	Opening Balance Owed	Payments	Monthly Rate of Finance Charge	Actual Charge	Annual Rate of Finance Charge
Previous balance.........	$200	$100	1.5%	0.015 × $200 = 3.00	36%
Average daily balance	200	100	1.5	0.015 × 150 = 2.25	27
Adjusted balance	200	100	1.5	0.015 × 100 = 1.50	18

takes the company to post your payment from the day you sent it will help avoid late payments.

The store's bills must show the following information: the previous balance owed, the date of transactions, the closing or billing date, payments made, the new balance, the finance charge with an explanation, the required minimum payment, and the time deadline to avoid additional finance charges.

You must also receive, along with the monthly bill, a statement of your rights in questioning the bill as well as the address to which your inquiries must be sent.

Billing error caused by humans or computers also receives attention under another section of the Fair Credit Billing Act. Within 30 days from the time that a creditor mails his statement, a consumer who thinks there is an error must send a written, detailed notice of his complaint by registered or certified mail. The creditor can neither take legal action nor communicate unfavorable credit information within the next 60-day period—subject to penalties—but must by that time either make the appropriate correction or show in writing why the original bill is correct.

If you still feel there is an error you can repeat the process. Undoubtedly the creditor will report to the credit bureau that you are delinquent. It will also have to say that the delinquency was caused by an item in dispute. The creditor must notify the credit bureau when the dispute is settled. This procedure only applies to billing errors. It cannot be used if the disagreement is over merchandise.

There are six accepted categories of billing error: (1) amounts charged because of unauthorized use of the credit card; (2) a finance charge for late payment when the customer was not billed at his current address, if the creditor was notified of the address change ten days before the end of the billing period; (3) charges for goods not accepted or for goods delivered to the wrong party; (4) a failure to credit payments; (5) accounting errors, including errors in computing finance charges; (6) amounts questioned by the customer. The law does not exempt you from paying the undisputed part of the bill during this waiting period.

"I'm sorry to say, Mr. Wilcox—our computer seems to have taken a personal dislike to you."

Reprinted by permission *The Wall Street Journal*

The customer should also be careful to make sure that any credits for overpayment or returns which may be unused for a while do not disappear from the monthly statement and then from the account if it lies dormant and the statements cease to be sent for a while. If you have a file for all your purchase slips, and paid bills for easy reference this can't happen. Furthermore, if you want it, you have the right to receive a check for your credits within five days, when you request it.

CREDIT CARDS

You may aspire to the fascinating world of credit cards and expense accounts. The *New York Times* reported on a man who did—in a large and fraudulent way: "A 29 year old Alabamian landed at Kennedy Airport and was taken into custody after a $27,278 tour of Europe that he was accused of financing with a Diners' Club card, which he had obtained with a check that bounced." He had spent eight months in Europe running up bills at some of the finest hotels in Rome, Paris, Vienna, and Zurich, where he was arrested while trying to rent a car and buy a watch.

Go now and pay later. Eat and charge it. It's

the new way of life, and if you become a professional or an organization man, you will probably join the ranks of the millions who currently carry general-purpose credit cards.

Half of all American families use at least one credit card. The average family has three, but mostly uses the ones good only at a particular store or chain of stores. Use is above average among families with higher income, more education, young families with children, and families living in the suburbs. The use of credit cards is directly related to the level of family income.

A survey found that 75 percent of all persons interviewed said that credit cards made it too easy to buy things they might not really want or could not afford. Half of all credit card holders used the debt feature of their credit cards. Lower- and middle-income families tended to value the credit feature of the cards more than the service benefits.

To some people a credit card is considered a service, not a source of debt. You can rent a car, stay at a hotel or motel, dine at expense account restaurants, hire an African safari, put your horse up at a Las Vegas horse motel where oats are free, buy anything from a mink coat to a salami, arrange bail, take a plane trip, make a long-distance phone call to Tokyo or Teheran or Tallahassee, buy gasoline, obtain an advance of cash, or pay your income tax up to $500 or medical, dental, or hospital bills—all on credit cards. You can even play luncheon Russian roulette. Credit cards are laid face down on the table, and the waiter picks one to pay the bill. Culture comes via the credit card, thanks to an arrangement between the American Ballet Theatre and Diners' Club, and your credit card enables you to phone a reservation for the Metropolitan Opera!

In addition to the general-purpose credit cards, there are retail credit cards, telephone credit cards from AT&T; air travel cards of the Universal Air Travel Plan; car rental credit cards; and railroad travel cards good on almost all U.S. railroads—a total of almost 600 million credit cards. Table 11–4 shows the percentage breakdown on credit cards, illustrating the small number that are T&E (travel and entertainment) cards, usually regarded as "ex-

TABLE 11–4
Credit Cards in the United States—1977

Retail store	298,000,000	50.82%
Oil company	133,000,000	22.68
Financial (bank)	92,972,000	15.85
Check-cashing	14,000,000	2.38
Debit (EFT)	14,000,000	2.38
T&E	10,250,000	1.74
Auto rental	6,100,000	1.03
Airline	4,800,000	0.81
Motel	4,100,000	0.69
Restaurant	3,600,000	0.60
Hotel	3,100,000	0.52
All other	3,000,000	0.50
Total	586,322,000	100.00%

Source: H. Spencer Nilson, *The Nilson Report,* Issue no. 185, April 1978.

pense account" cards. Total card credit in the United States according to the card companies, is only 6 percent of all installment credit, and the average unpaid balance is about $400. Delinquency on payments is a low 3 percent.[4] Paying cash has almost become passé.

As has been said, "Debt is sinful, but charging is chic."

The credit card companies cover costs and earn profits by charging members an annual fee and by making deductions on the restaurant and other bills that the companies pay on behalf of cardholders. Approximately three fourths of all general-purpose credit charges are made in restaurants, and this costs the restaurants from 5 to 7 percent of the amounts billed. The credit card organizations deduct this when making payment. The restaurant which honors credit cards, therefore, probably takes this charge into account in setting its prices. It is likely to be what one might term an "expense account" restaurant, more costly than restaurants which do not honor credit cards.

American Express now issues to the established cardholder a supplementary card, for an added small fee, for wife or child. It also issues an execu-

---

[4] Robert Levy, "The Clash of the Credit Cards," *Dun's Review,* June 1978.

tive credit card (gold) if there is a participating bank in your area—which then enables you to draw on a line of credit amounting to $2,000 or more, permits deferred payment on all charges over $100 at your request, and is an open sesame to emergency funds in traveler's checks, up to $500 in the United States and up to $1,000 in areas where a passport is needed.

Credit Card Loss

No credit card holder can be held responsible for more than $50 of unauthorized purchases made by someone who uses a lost or stolen card. Even that liability does not exist if the company issuing the credit card has not notified the cardholder of his possible liability and provided him with a self-addressed, prestamped notice to be returned when the card is lost or stolen or a toll-free number to call as soon as the loss is noted. If you report the loss before an illegal purchase is made, you don't have to pay a penny.

If you have many credit cards and no system, for an annual fee of $9–$12 you can use a credit card service bureau that, after one phone call (800-336–0220) from you, will notify all of your credit card companies if you have lost your cards. Some suspicious people would hesitate to give such a credit card service bureau the numbers of their credit cards even though credit card companies, such as Master Charge and VISA presumably endorse it.

Certain elementary precautions should be taken. A list of credit cards should be kept in a place separate from the wallet in which they may be carried. Credit billings should be carefully checked against receipts, as charges could be doctored to boost the amount. A dishonest clerk could use the charge card to imprint blank slips, to be used later for unauthorized purchases, and you would receive the bill much later—too late.

American Express has been gradually reissuing its 4 million cards with a magnetic stripe that has two tracks, one for the numeric code approved by the American Bankers Association and one sponsored by the International Air Transport Asso-

ciation (IATA) which has standard data and includes the cardholder's name and number. With the combination of coded data and computer terminals, the credit card companies count on instant validation and telltale patterns of use to discourage fraud.

Truth in Lending has made it harder for someone to use a stolen credit card. All cards newly issued are required to bear some type of identification, usually a picture or a signature.

New rules also set new maximum penalties of a $10,000 fine or five years in prison, or both, for making unauthorized purchases totaling more than $5,000 on a credit card.

The illegal use of credit cards has been called a $20 million racket by the Better Business Bureau, which estimates that about one fifth of the 1.5 million cards annually reported lost are actually stolen. Hot credit cards sell for as much as $250 in some big cities, the bureau says, "where travelers' credit cards are accepted as readily as cash and no questions asked."

Bank Credit Cards

Bank credit cards have flourished in the last few years. Two dominant networks have emerged: VISA (formerly Bank Americard), operated by the Bank of America and over 5,000 banks, and Interbank Card Association, a nonprofit cooperative that serves as a clearinghouse in most states to interchange the cards of its members, which range from individual banks to its biggest customer, *Master Charge*—which has almost 6,000 banks. The Interbank National Authorization System (INAS) is headquartered in St. Louis, Missouri, with a 24-hour, seven-day-a-week network system. It polls all nationwide on-line computers and terminals twice a second, picks up each authorization inquiry and authorization response, and matches the messages. This instant communication capability is also useful for broadcasting "hot card" information to Interbank centers in a constant fight against fraud and theft.

Both systems operate their own networks for the authorization of credit at the point of sale. Both bank cards are issued free. By prudent and reliable use of the bank credit card, a credit history can easily be established.

Banks are currently offering both credit cards. Some banks offer customers two lines of credit of equal amount. Other banks have started the second credit card at a lower line of credit and then raised it as experience justified the increase. Still another procedure has been to give the two credit cards a single line of credit. Both cards are also being offered to new "bank" institutions. This aggressive competition can result in a real saving for the customer, especially when the bank combines the balances of both cards to compute interest. It may cost you more to use several credit cards, spreading your purchases, instead of lumping as much as possible on one card. Some credit cards charge lower interest on amounts over $500.

To fight fraud, just as we have seen American Express has done, the ABA after long testing has approved a magnetic stripe with numeric coded data on bank credit cards readable by computer terminals and providing instant credit checks. Because it was feared that the new bank credit cards with the magnetic stripe were easy to duplicate or alter, a contest was sponsored by the chairman of a subsidiary of Citibank who offered prize money to 22 teams of students at the California Institute of Technology—to prove it was fraudproof. Instead the Cal Tech students found 22 ways to beat the system. It has not been regarded as the final answer, especially after the Cal Tech students went to work on it. Some banks are still experimenting with other technologies—for example, optical scanning, pinhole coding by laser, or combinations of several methods—to provide more security.

A network of banks, restaurants, and stores can drop either bank credit card into an automatic reader, dial the bank's computer via a telephone line terminal, and have an instant authorization. As more terminals are installed and while equipment makers test for new technology to reduce losses by fraud, banks are, of course, still distributing the credit cards.

Bank credit cards were formerly, for the most part, of a regional nature, primarily because of the legal restrictions on branch banking and the consequent limited market for consumer lending. As interchange systems developed, cardholders of any bank in the system could use their cards to make purchases from any of the merchants signed up by other banks participating in the system. The bank credit card has extended the boundaries of banking geographically. Participating merchants find advantages in immediate credit received for all deposited slips, reduction in credit losses, fewer accounting and bookkeeping costs, and a decrease in their own credit needs.

The furor raised by the indiscriminate and unsolicited distribution of bank credit cards during the early expansion days resulted in the enactment of an amendment to the Truth in Lending Act in October 1970 which forbade unsolicited mailing of credit cards. By that time, however, the banks had suffered loss through fraud, thieving, and poor-risk accounts, and had therefore mostly discontinued the practice. Now they are again sending mailed offers of credit lines—but not the cards this time.

Bank credit cards are used primarily at retail stores in place of charge accounts or installment plans, although both VISA and Master Charge have also been expanding into the travel and entertainment field. The general-purpose (T&E) card plans, such as American Express, Diners', and Carte Blanche, expect bills to be paid promptly. The banks, on the contrary, want cardholders to take their time about paying, because the outstanding balances are, in effect, installment loans at a maximum 18 percent annual rate of interest. Interest rates and methods of computation vary from bank to bank. They also vary among the states, depending upon the state usury laws. In some states where the maximum rate is low, banks are considering an annual fee for new members similar to that levied by the T&E cards.

Paying finance charges on a credit card will cost you more than paying cash or borrowing the same amount from the bank, or even getting a cash advance on your bank credit card, as you can see from the following example:

The Chase Manhattan Bank's VISA, for example, costs 1 percent a month—a maximum of 12 percent for 12 months—for a cash advance, while charges for purchases are 1.5 percent a month, with a maximum of 18 percent a year. That means paying back a cash advance of $500 in one year will cost you $32.48, but paying off purchase charges of $500 in equal installments for 12 months will cost you $48.71. There is also the personal loan from a bank. If Chase Manhattan approves you as a risk, you can get $500 at a cost of $27.72, or 10.07 percent, over 12 months.

"And if your loan payment is in the mail, please disregard these insults."

Reprinted by permission *The Wall Street Journal.*

Banks like credit cards—they provide additional income from interest on accounts and a percentage from the stores where the purchases are made. A number of banks also offer a credit card checking plan under which the customer writes a check which is charged to a credit card account. This is useful where credit cards are unacceptable to the store and personal checks are risky, because these checks against credit cards are viewed as bank guaranteed. Banks have settled delinquent credit card accounts by using the funds in a depositor's account even without authorization.

THE INSTALLMENT PLAN

The Installment Contract

Unfortunately the average buyer fails to gain the protection that is available by reading carefully and understanding thoroughly all of the papers signed in many transactions, including installment sales. For no good reason at all, a person feels embarrassed to take the necessary time to read a lengthy document in which a lot of important stipulations may appear in very fine print.

Some aspects of installment contracts to watch out for are:

The Add-on Clause   Add-on, or open-end, contracts should be avoided by the consumer. This type of contract is drawn to cover a succession of installment purchases, and it provides that the seller retains title or mortgage on each article until the very last one is paid for. A thousand dollars' worth of house furnishings, bought over several years, might be seized because the customer failed to meet a $20 payment on a recently purchased $100 item.

The Acceleration Clause   This provides that a default in one payment makes all other payments immediately due and payable. If the buyer is dishonest, this drastic safeguard is necessary. But an honest buyer may miss a payment date because of an emergency, perhaps sickness in the family or a temporary layoff from the job. Unscrupulous dealers take advantage of the acceleration clause to swoop down and immediately repossess the car, or refrigerator, or television set, and cart it off for resale.

The Wage Assignment   The most drastic form of security in the installment contract may be the wage assignment. An obscure clause may give the dealer power of attorney to collect all or part of the buyer's paycheck or pay envelope if the buyer misses a payment. Most wage assignments are probably signed because the buyer does not know what he is signing. Long contracts in legal verbiage and fine type make it difficult for the buyer to read or understand the contract.

Originally the installment contract was used to sell only products for which there was a definite resale market. If an individual lagged behind in payments on a piano or a car, the dealer could repossess the item and probably make up the unpaid balance by reselling it. The merchandise itself was adequate security until the installment dealers, trying to conquer new markets, made their terms so "easy" that often the unpaid balance exceeded the resale value of the article. Resale of a repossessed pair of pants brings little return. Wage assignments provide the security for soft goods sold on the installment plan.

The legal process of attaching the debtor's wage is known as "garnishment" or "garnisheeing wages." By court order, the employer of the debtor (buyer) is obliged to pay all or a certain percentage of the wages of the debtor to the creditor (installment seller) until the debt is paid in full. Some states limit by law the percentage of a wage earner's salary which may thus be taken by a creditor at any given pay period or prohibit assignment entirely under certain conditions. Some employers dislike being bothered with legal forms and with the added bookkeeping routine involved in turning wages over to a creditor. They therefore fire employees whose wages are garnisheed.

One of the cruelest causes of default judgments, ruined credit, and garnisheed salaries is the "sewer service," or the practice of filling out false affidavits that the process has been served. Thousands of such judgments are issued yearly when the purchaser stops payment on faulty merchandise and a store or loan company sues for nonpayment on an installment contract. Its lawyer issues a summons on the person being sued, who usually has ten days to appear in court to answer the suit. If he does not appear, and the process server swears in an affidavit that he delivered the process in person or tried to, then the court can declare the defendant in default. The next step is the marshal's attempt to collect—and the purchaser may have been completely unaware of the entire proceeding.

Garnishment   The 1968 Consumer Credit Protection Act has a section on garnishment that became effective July 1, 1970. It provides that the amount of an individual's disposable earnings for any workweek which may be subjected to garnishment may not exceed the lesser of the following:

1.   Twenty-five percent of his disposable earnings for that week.
2.   The amount by which his disposable earnings for the week exceed 30 times the federal minimum hourly wage prescribed under the Wages and Hour law at the time such earnings are payable.

There is also a prohibition against discharging an employee for garnishment of earnings for any one indebtedness. The act also provides that where a state law is more restrictive than federal laws, the provisions of the state law shall govern.

The Balloon Contract   A contract which has as its final installment a payment substantially in excess of the preceding installments is known as a "balloon contract." For example, the contract may call for 11 monthly installments of $25 each and one (the 12th payment) of $300. This is a highly undesirable type of payment arrangement because the necessity of refinancing at least once and sometimes two or three times makes for higher total charges to the purchaser. It should be noted that the balloon contract is usually found in the financing of automobiles as this example from *Business Week* shows:

Advertised price of a used car	$1,795.00
But a heater is necessary	60.00
So that the cost now stands at	1,855.00
Add state tax on $1,855	56.65
Add cost of title transfer, etc.	6.36
So the total cost is	1,918.00
The buyer is talked into paying	118.00
Leaving a balance to be financed of	1,800.00
Two years' insurance	194.00
Which brings the price back to	1,994.00
Add interest at 6% and carrying charges for two years	269.00
And, as the owner drives away, he owes .	2,263.00
The buyer makes 23 monthly payments at $40 each	$ 920.00
And the balloon note amounts to	1,343.00

Meanwhile, the car has depreciated to perhaps $1,450 at the end of the first year, and perhaps in the same proportion during the second. At any rate, the owner can't afford to pay out $1,343 in a lump sum. So he refinances the 24th note for another two years. It works this way:

Amount of the balloon note	$1,343.00
Add another two years' insurance	181.00
Add interest and carrying charges for another two years	200.00
And the buyer starts paying again on	1,724.00
And so he makes 23 more payments at $40 each	$ 920.00
And he runs smack up against another balloon note this time for	804.00
(The car is now four years older)	
So he adds another two years' insurance	120.30
And another two years' interest and carrying charges	146.90
And he starts the fifth year paying on	1,071.60
So he makes 23 more payments of $40 each	920.00

Obviously, a balloon contract is to be avoided. Now, under Truth in Lending, the payment must be clearly labeled *"balloon,"* which hopefully will be a warning signal to the buyer.

The Cost of Installment Financing

In one way or another a seller must be paid for financing the buyer who acquires goods on credit. The various expenses of investigation, collecting, bookkeeping, repossession, reconditioning, reselling, bad debts, and insurance must be covered, either by an inflated price for the article sold, by separate fees and charges, or by inclusion in the interest charge. In the past, though a nominal rate of 5 or 6 percent may have been quoted, analysis of the charges usually revealed that the real rate was often far in excess—and it had to be in order to cover the cost of the service rendered.

Suppose an article selling for $75 is sold with a 20 percent down payment, the balance to be paid in installments over a period of nine months. If a charge of 6 percent of $75 is made for the service rendered, it amounts to $4.50.

But the 1st month the buyer has the use of $60.00
the 2d month the buyer has the use of $53.33

the 3d month the buyer has the use of $46.67
the 4th month the buyer has the use of $40.00
the 5th month the buyer has the use of $33.33
the 6th month the buyer has the use of $26.67
the 7th month the buyer has the use of $20.00
the 8th month the buyer has the use of $13.33
and the 9th month the buyer has the use of $6.67

One way to look at these figures intelligently is that if the buyer had the use of $60 the first month and only $6.666 during the ninth, he had the use of

$$\frac{\$60 + \$6.66}{2} = \frac{\$66.66}{2} = \$33.33$$

on the average for the nine-month period. Since $4.50 was paid for this accommodation (for nine months), this amounted to paying $6.00 for a year's use of an average amount of $33.33.

Now,

$$\frac{\$6}{\$33.33} \times 100 = \frac{\$600.00}{\$33.33} = 18 \text{ percent.}$$

The Time-Honored 6 Percent

Interest rates were often not given in installment contracts. When they were given, they were seldom what they seemed. Usually they were disguised as forms of the time-honored 6 percent. In the course of the years, 6 percent had come for many people to be synonymous with a "fair return." As one merchandiser put it, "Six percent has sex appeal for the customer."

When installment sellers who were to be repaid in equal installments over the year stated their charge as a percentage of the total unpaid balance at the start, the true rate, in the absence of other manipulations and distortions, was roughly twice the stated rate.

"One percent a month" appears to be a reasonable charge; but depending on the way it's calculated, it is much more than it seems to be. It is 12 percent a year if it is levied on the new reduced unpaid balance each month; but if it is levied as a percentage of the total unpaid balance at the beginning of the contract, it is about 24 percent, since over a year the average balance outstanding is only half the original unpaid balance.

Notice how much you are paying each month. Total all the finance charges from your bills for a typical month. Multiply by 12 for the yearly cost. Is the credit worth it?

Can you do better by arranging a closed-end credit deal? Credit unions may offer an APR lower than 18 percent—as do some banks on their check credit plans (see Chapter 10).

The Federal Consumer Credit Protection Act (Truth in Lending Act)

After some years of debate, Congress passed and the president signed the Consumer Credit Protection Act in 1968, already discussed in part in connection with the cost of charge accounts (see pages 334–37). The act does not limit any charge for credit that may be made, but it does require disclosure of credit terms, including clear disclosure of the finance charge.

Under Title I of the Truth in Lending Act, creditors had to make clear to consumers the exact amount of the finance charge to be paid for the extension of credit (see Figure 11–4). The rules and regulations for truth in lending were spelled out by the Federal Reserve in Regulation Z. Disclosure of credit terms is expected to help consumers by allowing them to decide whether the charges are reasonable and to help them compare the cost of credit by shopping for the best credit terms.

The *finance charge* and the *annual percentage rate* are the two most important concepts embodied in Regulation Z. They are designed to tell you at a glance how much you are paying for credit and the relative cost of that credit in percentage terms. In general, *the finance charge,* which must be stated in dollars and cents, is the total of all costs imposed by the creditor and paid either directly or indirectly by the consumer or another party in connection with the extension of credit. It includes such costs as interest and time price differential, that is, any difference between the price of an item sold for cash and an item sold on credit. It also includes amounts paid as a discount; service, transaction, activity, or carrying charges; loan fees; "points"—extra sums figured as a percentage of the loan amount and charged in a lump sum; finder's fees or similar charges; fees for an appraisal, investigation, or credit report (except in real property transactions); and premiums for credit life insurance if it is required by the creditor as a condition for obtaining credit.

The *annual percentage rate* represents the relationship of the total finance charge to the total amount financed. It must be computed to the nearest one quarter of 1 percent. The method of computation depends on whether the credit is open end or of the installment type. For credit other than open end, the annual percentage rate must be computed by the "actuarial method," or the "U.S. rule." In fact, companies are likely to use government-prepared tables or similar commercially produced schedules from which the relevant figures can be taken. See Table 11–5 for the way it is done.

The law requires that if any lender advertises the rate of the finance charge, it must be expressed as an "annual percentage rate." Also, if the amount of any down payment or that no down payment is required is advertised, or the amount of any installment payment, or the dollar amount of any finance charge, or the number of installments, or the period of repayment, all of these items must be stated.

In the case of installment sales and loans, the information given to you must include the total amount being financed; an itemized account of the charges being made; the total finance charge in dollars; the finance charge as an annual percentage rate; the number, amount, and due dates of the payments to be made; any charges that will be added for late payment of installments; a description of any security that the creditor will hold; the

FIGURE 11–4

Truth in Lending—Consumer Credit Cost Disclosure

Seller's Name: _____   Contract #_____

RETAIL INSTALLMENT CONTRACT AND SECURITY AGREEMENT

The undersigned (herein called Purchaser, whether one or more) purchases from _____(seller) and grants to _____ a security interest in, subject to the terms and conditions hereof, the following described property.

QUANTITY	DESCRIPTION	AMOUNT

Description of Trade-in:

	Sales Tax	
	Total	

Insurance Agreement

The purchase of insurance coverage is voluntary and not required for credit. ____ (Type of Ins.) Insurance coverage is available at a cost of $_____ for the term of credit.

I desire insurance coverage

Signed_____ Date_____

I do not desire insurance coverage

Signed_____ Date_____

PURCHASER'S NAME_____
PURCHASER'S ADDRESS_____
CITY_____STATE____ZIP____

1. CASH PRICE $____
2. LESS: CASH DOWN PAYMENT $____
3.   TRADE-IN   ____
4.   TOTAL DOWN PAYMENT ____$____
5. UNPAID BALANCE OF CASH PRICE $____
6. OTHER CHARGES:
                                                  $____
                                                  $____
7. AMOUNT FINANCED $____
8. FINANCE CHARGE $____
9. TOTAL OF PAYMENTS $____
10. DEFERRED PAYMENT PRICE (1+6+8) $____
11. ANNUAL PERCENTAGE RATE   ____%

Purchaser hereby agrees to pay to_____ _____ at their offices shown above the "TOTAL OF PAYMENTS" shown above in _____ monthly installments of $_____(final payment to be $_____) the first installment being payable _____ 19____, and all subsequent installments on the same day of each consecutive month until paid in full. The finance charge applies from ____ (Date)

Signed_____

Notice to Buyer: You are entitled to a copy of the contract you sign. You have the right to pay in advance the unpaid balance of this contract and obtain a partial refund of the finance charge based on the "Actuarial Method." [Any other method of computation may be so identified, for example, "Rule of 78's," "Sum of the Digits," etc.]

This form, when properly completed, will show how a creditor may comply with the disclosure requirements of the provisions of paragraphs (b) and (c) of §226.8 of Regulation Z for the type of credit extended in this example. This form is intended solely for purposes of demonstration and it is not the only format which will permit a creditor to comply with disclosure requirements of Regulation Z.

Source: Board of Governors, Federal Reserve System, Exhibit C—"Consumer Credit Cost Disclosure."

penalties, if any, for prepayment; and whether the installments include any "balloon" payments—which is defined as a payment that is more than twice the amount of a regular installment.

Keep in mind that the act requires facts about the credit charge to be stated. It does *not,* however, fix or specify in any way maximum or minimum charges for credit. Nor does it cover credit transactions within states that request and obtain exemption because their laws have the same requirements

TABLE 11–5

Sample Page from Table for Computing Annual Percentage Rate for Level Monthly Payment Plans

EXAMPLE

Finance charge = $35.00; Total amount financed = $200; Number of monthly payments = 24.

SOLUTION

Step 1—Divide the finance charge by the total amount financed and multiply by $100. This gives the finance charge per $100 of amount financed. That is, $35.00 ÷ $200 = .1750 x $100 = $17.50.

Step 2—Follow down the left-hand column of the table to the line for 24 months. Follow across this line until you find the nearest number to $17.50. In this example $17.51 is closest to $17.50. Reading up the column of figures shows an annual percentage rate of 16%.

NUMBER OF PAYMENTS	14.00%	14.25%	14.50%	14.75%	15.00%	15.25%	15.50%	15.75%	16.00%	16.25%	16.50%	16.75%	17.00%	17.25%	17.50%	17.75%
	(FINANCE CHARGE PER $100 OF AMOUNT FINANCED)															
1	1.17	1.19	1.21	1.23	1.25	1.27	1.29	1.31	1.33	1.35	1.37	1.40	1.42	1.44	1.46	1.48
2	1.75	1.78	1.82	1.85	1.88	1.91	1.94	1.97	2.00	2.04	2.07	2.10	2.13	2.16	2.19	2.22
3	2.34	2.38	2.43	2.47	2.51	2.55	2.59	2.64	2.68	2.72	2.76	2.80	2.85	2.89	2.93	2.97
4	2.93	2.99	3.04	3.09	3.14	3.20	3.25	3.30	3.36	3.41	3.46	3.51	3.57	3.62	3.67	3.73
5	3.53	3.59	3.65	3.72	3.78	3.84	3.91	3.97	4.04	4.10	4.16	4.23	4.29	4.35	4.42	4.48
6	4.12	4.20	4.27	4.35	4.42	4.49	4.57	4.64	4.72	4.79	4.87	4.94	5.02	5.09	5.17	5.24
7	4.72	4.81	4.89	4.98	5.06	5.15	5.23	5.32	5.40	5.49	5.58	5.66	5.75	5.83	5.92	6.00
8	5.32	5.42	5.51	5.61	5.71	5.80	5.90	6.00	6.09	6.19	6.29	6.38	6.48	6.58	6.67	6.77
9	5.92	6.03	6.14	6.25	6.35	6.46	6.57	6.68	6.78	6.89	7.00	7.11	7.22	7.32	7.43	7.54
10	6.53	6.65	6.77	6.88	7.00	7.12	7.24	7.36	7.48	7.60	7.72	7.84	7.96	8.08	8.19	8.31
11	7.14	7.27	7.40	7.53	7.66	7.79	7.92	8.05	8.18	8.31	8.44	8.57	8.70	8.83	8.96	9.09
12	7.74	7.89	8.03	8.17	8.31	8.45	8.59	8.74	8.88	9.02	9.16	9.30	9.45	9.59	9.73	9.87
13	8.36	8.51	8.66	8.81	8.97	9.12	9.27	9.43	9.58	9.73	9.89	10.04	10.20	10.35	10.50	10.66
14	8.97	9.13	9.30	9.46	9.63	9.79	9.96	10.12	10.29	10.45	10.62	10.78	10.95	11.11	11.28	11.45
15	9.59	9.76	9.94	10.11	10.29	10.47	10.64	10.82	11.00	11.17	11.35	11.53	11.71	11.88	12.06	12.24
16	10.20	10.39	10.58	10.77	10.95	11.14	11.33	11.52	11.71	11.90	12.09	12.28	12.46	12.65	12.84	13.03
17	10.82	11.02	11.22	11.42	11.62	11.82	12.02	12.22	12.42	12.62	12.83	13.03	13.23	13.43	13.63	13.83
18	11.45	11.66	11.87	12.08	12.29	12.50	12.72	12.93	13.14	13.35	13.57	13.78	13.99	14.21	14.42	14.64
19	12.07	12.30	12.52	12.74	12.97	13.19	13.41	13.64	13.86	14.09	14.31	14.54	14.76	14.99	15.22	15.44
20	12.70	12.93	13.17	13.41	13.64	13.88	14.11	14.35	14.59	14.82	15.06	15.30	15.54	15.77	16.01	16.25
21	13.33	13.58	13.82	14.07	14.32	14.57	14.82	15.06	15.31	15.56	15.81	16.06	16.31	16.56	16.81	17.07
22	13.96	14.22	14.48	14.74	15.00	15.26	15.52	15.78	16.04	16.30	16.57	16.83	17.09	17.36	17.62	17.88
23	14.59	14.87	15.14	15.41	15.68	15.96	16.23	16.50	16.78	17.05	17.32	17.60	17.88	18.15	18.43	18.71
24	15.23	15.51	15.80	16.08	16.37	16.65	16.94	17.22	17.51	17.80	18.09	18.37	18.66	18.95	19.24	19.53
25	15.87	16.17	16.46	16.76	17.06	17.35	17.65	17.95	18.25	18.55	18.85	19.15	19.45	19.75	20.05	20.36
26	16.51	16.82	17.13	17.44	17.75	18.06	18.37	18.68	18.99	19.30	19.62	19.93	20.24	20.56	20.87	21.19
27	17.15	17.47	17.80	18.12	18.44	18.76	19.09	19.41	19.74	20.06	20.39	20.71	21.04	21.37	21.69	22.02
28	17.80	18.13	18.47	18.80	19.14	19.47	19.81	20.15	20.48	20.82	21.16	21.50	21.84	22.18	22.52	22.86
29	18.45	18.79	19.14	19.49	19.83	20.18	20.53	20.88	21.23	21.58	21.94	22.29	22.64	22.99	23.35	23.70
30	19.10	19.45	19.81	20.17	20.54	20.90	21.26	21.62	21.99	22.35	22.72	23.08	23.45	23.81	24.18	24.55
31	19.75	20.12	20.49	20.87	21.24	21.61	21.99	22.37	22.74	23.12	23.50	23.88	24.26	24.64	25.02	25.40
32	20.40	20.79	21.17	21.56	21.95	22.33	22.72	23.11	23.50	23.89	24.28	24.68	25.07	25.46	25.86	26.25
33	21.06	21.46	21.85	22.25	22.65	23.06	23.46	23.86	24.26	24.67	25.07	25.48	25.88	26.29	26.70	27.11
34	21.72	22.13	22.54	22.95	23.37	23.78	24.19	24.61	25.03	25.44	25.86	26.28	26.70	27.12	27.54	27.97
35	22.38	22.80	23.23	23.65	24.08	24.51	24.94	25.36	25.79	26.23	26.66	27.09	27.52	27.96	28.39	28.83
36	23.04	23.48	23.92	24.35	24.80	25.24	25.68	26.12	26.57	27.01	27.46	27.90	28.35	28.80	29.25	29.70
37	23.70	24.16	24.61	25.06	25.51	25.97	26.42	26.88	27.34	27.80	28.26	28.72	29.18	29.64	30.10	30.57
38	24.37	24.84	25.30	25.77	26.24	26.70	27.17	27.64	28.11	28.59	29.06	29.53	30.01	30.49	30.96	31.44
39	25.04	25.52	26.00	26.48	26.96	27.44	27.92	28.41	28.89	29.38	29.87	30.36	30.85	31.34	31.83	32.32
40	25.71	26.20	26.70	27.19	27.69	28.18	28.68	29.18	29.68	30.18	30.68	31.18	31.68	32.19	32.69	33.20
41	26.39	26.89	27.40	27.91	28.41	28.92	29.44	29.95	30.46	30.97	31.49	32.00	32.52	33.04	33.56	34.08
42	27.06	27.58	28.10	28.62	29.15	29.67	30.19	30.72	31.25	31.78	32.31	32.84	33.37	33.90	34.44	34.97
43	27.74	28.27	28.81	29.34	29.88	30.42	30.96	31.50	32.04	32.58	33.13	33.67	34.22	34.76	35.31	35.86
44	28.42	28.97	29.52	30.07	30.62	31.17	31.72	32.28	32.83	33.39	33.95	34.51	35.07	35.63	36.19	36.76
45	29.11	29.67	30.23	30.79	31.36	31.92	32.49	33.06	33.63	34.20	34.77	35.35	35.92	36.50	37.08	37.66
46	29.79	30.36	30.94	31.52	32.10	32.68	33.26	33.84	34.43	35.01	35.60	36.19	36.78	37.37	37.96	38.56
47	30.48	31.07	31.66	32.25	32.84	33.44	34.03	34.63	35.23	35.83	36.43	37.04	37.64	38.25	38.86	39.46
48	31.17	31.77	32.37	32.98	33.59	34.20	34.81	35.42	36.03	36.65	37.27	37.88	38.50	39.13	39.75	40.37
49	31.86	32.48	33.09	33.71	34.34	34.96	35.59	36.21	36.84	37.47	38.10	38.74	39.37	40.01	40.65	41.29
50	32.55	33.18	33.82	34.45	35.09	35.73	36.37	37.01	37.65	38.30	38.94	39.59	40.24	40.89	41.55	42.20
51	33.25	33.89	34.54	35.19	35.84	36.49	37.15	37.81	38.46	39.12	39.79	40.45	41.11	41.78	42.45	43.12
52	33.95	34.61	35.27	35.93	36.60	37.27	37.94	38.61	39.28	39.96	40.63	41.31	41.99	42.67	43.36	44.06
53	34.65	35.32	36.00	36.68	37.36	38.04	38.72	39.41	40.10	40.79	41.48	42.17	42.87	43.57	44.27	44.97
54	35.35	36.04	36.73	37.42	38.12	38.82	39.52	40.22	40.92	41.63	42.33	43.04	43.75	44.47	45.18	45.90
55	36.05	36.76	37.46	38.17	38.88	39.60	40.31	41.03	41.74	42.47	43.19	43.91	44.64	45.37	46.10	46.83
56	36.76	37.48	38.20	38.92	39.65	40.38	41.11	41.84	42.57	43.31	44.05	44.79	45.53	46.27	47.02	47.77
57	37.47	38.20	38.94	39.68	40.42	41.16	41.91	42.65	43.40	44.15	44.91	45.66	46.42	47.18	47.94	48.70
58	38.18	38.93	39.68	40.43	41.19	41.95	42.71	43.47	44.23	45.00	45.77	46.54	47.32	48.09	48.87	49.65
59	38.89	39.66	40.42	41.19	41.96	42.74	43.51	44.29	45.07	45.85	46.64	47.42	48.21	49.01	49.80	50.60
60	39.61	40.39	41.17	41.95	42.74	43.53	44.32	45.11	45.91	46.71	47.51	48.31	49.12	49.92	50.73	51.55

Source: Board of Governors of the Federal Reserve System, Exhibit G—"Truth in Lending—Consumer Credit Cost Disclosure."

as the federal law and adequate provision for enforcement.

The annual FTC reports to Congress indicate that Truth in Lending has contributed significantly to increased consumer awareness of credit costs, including the annual percentage rates charged on various types of consumer credit. The 1969 and 1970 annual reports of the FTC indicated that awareness of rates increased sharply in the first 15 months after Truth in Lending went into effect,

TABLE 11–6
All Types of Installment Credit: Changes in Awareness of Annual Percentage Rates

Type of Credit	Level of Awareness (percent)			Change in Awareness (percent)		
	1969	1970	1977	1969–1970	1970–1977	1969–1977
Closed-end credit	14.5	38.3	54.6	23.8	16.3	40.1
Retail revolving credit.....	35.2	55.5	64.7	20.5	9.2	29.5
Bank credit cards	26.6	63.4	71.0	36.8	7.6	44.4

Source: Robert P. Shay and Milton W. Schober, *Consumer Awareness of Annual Percentage Rates of Charge in Consumer Instalment Credit: Before and After Truth in Lending Became Effective,* Technical Studies of the National Commission on Consumer Finance (Washington, D.C.: U.S. Government Printing Office, 1978), vol. 1, no. 1, table 1: 1977 Survey of Consumer Credit.

TABLE 11–7
Types of Closed-End Credit: Changes in Awareness of Annual Percentage Rates

Type of Credit	Level of Awareness (percent)			Change in Awareness (percent)		
	1969	1970	1977	1969–1970	1970–1977	1969–77
New automobiles	17.5	43.3	70.5	25.8	27.2	53.0
Used automobiles	7.2	17.3	37.8	10.1	20.5	30.6
Appliances and furniture*	11.7	35.0	44.7	23.3	9.7	33.0
Home improvement........	15.3	43.3	67.2	28.0	23.9	51.9
Personal loans	20.2	49.2	54.8	29.0	5.6	34.6
All types	14.5	38.3	54.6	23.8	16.3	40.1

* Figures for 1977 are for durable goods and recreation goods.

Source: Robert P. Shay and Milton W. Schober, *Consumer Awareness of Annual Percentage Rates of Charge in Consumer Instalment Credit: Before and After Truth in Lending Became Effective,* Technical Studies of the National Commission on Consumer Finance (Washington, D.C.: U.S. Government Printing Office, 1978), vol. 1, no. 1, table 2; 1977 Survey of Consumer Credit.

but the 1977 report showed that there had been significant further increases in consumer awareness over the last eight years, as Table 11–6 shows. Table 11–7 indicates that purchasers of new automobiles and users of credit for home improvements had the highest rate of awareness, with the lowest level shown by users of credit for the purchase of used automobiles. Table 11–8 indicates that there was a much greater growth of awareness of APR in persons who used banks, credit unions, and finance companies as contrasted with those whose credit was furnished by retail dealers.[5]

Truth in Lending has been amended four times in the ten years since it became law, and a fifth amendment is now under consideration. To be known as the Truth in Lending Simplification Act, it aims to make compliance with the act easier and to enlarge administrative enforcement powers, but at the same time its proposed reduction of the number of currently required disclosures will not be advantageous to the consumer. As an example, consumers would be told only the "amount financed" without the creditor having to itemize the "cost price," or the "down payment."

[5] *Annual Report to Congress on Truth in Lending for the Year 1977,* Board of Governors of the Federal Reserve System, January 3, 1978. In October 1978 the Federal Reserve Board of Governors agreed by a vote of 3–2 that it had the legal authority to require reimbursement of customers to correct violations of Truth in Lending resulting from incorrect finance charge disclosures.

TABLE 11–8
Closed-End Credit: Changes in Awareness of Annual Percentage Rates by Source of Credit

Source	Level of Awareness (percent)			Change in Awareness (percent)		
	1969	1970	1977	1969–1970	1970–1977	1969–77
Banks	12.8	42.0	52.1	29.2	10.1	39.3
Credit unions	27.8	36.1	66.1	8.3	30.0	38.3
Finance companies	16.7	38.7	57.6	22.0	18.9	40.9
Retail dealers	9.4	32.8	42.1	23.4	9.3	32.7

Source: Robert P. Shay and Milton W. Schober, *Consumer Awareness of Annual Percentage Rates of Charge in Consumer Instalment Credit: Before and After Truth in Lending Became Effective,* Technical Studies of the National Commission on Consumer Finance (Washington, D.C.: U.S. Government Printing Office, 1978), vol. 1, no. 1, table 5; 1977 Survey of Consumer Credit.

The Office of Consumer Affairs feels that Truth in Lending disclosures are now too complex for many consumers. There are, for example, no plain English explanations of prepayment terms. There is a need for clarification of disclosure requirements for "acceleration clauses" and for full disclosure of all charges included in default penalties. Truth in Lending disclosures are now given to consumers only when they sign a credit contract, instead of prior to the point of sale "to encourage comparison shopping and give consumers a real opportunity to reject undesired credit transactions."[6]

The Role of the Sales Finance Company

You may sign an installment agreement to purchase an automobile from a dealer only to find that you must make your payments to a finance company. Often you are told of the arrangement immediately; sometimes you are not. The dealer may utilize a finance company because he does not have sufficient capital of his own to finance the volume of business he can do if he sells on time. A finance company pays him at the time the car is sold, thus replenishing his capital and at the same time financing the extension of credit to the purchaser.

---

[6] *Consumer News,* U.S. Office of Consumer Affairs, August 15, 1978, and October 1, 1978.

There are nearly 4,000 sales finance companies and offices operating throughout the country. These hold about one fifth of all consumer installment paper outstanding. They account for about 18 percent of the total automobile paper, while commercial banks have 58 percent. The giants in the field are General Motors Acceptance Corporation, which finances General Motors cars; CIT Financial, which finances Ford cars, grants home modernization loans, and finances other consumer durable sales; Commercial Credit Corporation, which finances Chrysler cars; and Associates Investment Company, which finances miscellaneous auto paper. Sears, Roebuck has established the Sears, Roebuck Acceptance Corporation.

Sales finance companies have increased the absolute amount of their loans on automobiles over the last decade, but the relative importance of this type of lending—traditionally their specialty—has declined as the companies have stepped up activity in other areas, such as financing other retail consumer goods.

In shopping for auto credit, several surveys found that banks charged the lowest rates, that national sales finance companies were a close second, and that local finance companies charged the highest rates.

Finance companies are anxious to have a promise to pay from the purchaser which cannot be impaired by any disputes or claims between the dealer and the purchaser. Far too often, the purchaser will not find servicing or repairs satisfactory, or will claim that an inferior or damaged product was received and will, therefore, refuse to pay. To guard against this, the finance companies employed a variety of devices. One has been to provide in the contract that the purchaser will settle all claims with the dealer directly and will not set up any such claim in an action involving the finance company. Known as "a waiver of defense" clause, this provision once furnished complete protection for the finance company. The seller who sold the original agreement to the finance company was also in a position to ignore all complaints.

The Holder in Due Course

The "holder in due course" doctrine has been the legal reason for the consumer credit tangle that results when the car or appliance bought from the dealer on credit is found unsatisfactory. You complain to the dealer, but the credit contract has been sold to a bank or a finance company or a loan company which is the "holder in due course." If the lender refuses responsibility for the defective item, you can sue the original dealer. If you stop payment to bring pressure on the dealer, the company that holds your financial agreement can take action against you. You must continue to pay for the worthless item. Or you can go to court.

The Federal Trade Commission by regulation

"Sorry, but a mantra isn't sufficient collateral."

Reprinted by permission *The Wall Street Journal*

now limits such separation of responsibility by the seller to the buyer. The seller is now forbidden to include a waiver of defense clause in a contract. The FTC rule states that anyone who purchases an installment contract is equally responsible with the seller for any deception or any faulty goods or services. Sellers cannot sell a contract to a lender that does not recognize the consumer's right to "claims and defenses" against the lender.

The burden of redress is still on the consumer—either by negotiation with the holders of the contract or through the courts. The consumer cannot appeal to the FTC for help in forcing a seller to correct a faulty purchase. Nor does the FTC ruling apply in cases in which Master Charge or VISA credit is used to pay for merchandise about which the buyer and the seller are disputing. In that situation the Fair Credit Billing Act invalidates waivers of defense if a purchase of more than $50 is made within a hundred miles of where the card was issued or in the state where the cardholder lives. The role of the FTC is to ensure proper language in the credit agreements using either federal court injunctions or fines against violators. Forty states now have laws affecting the holder-in-due-course doctrine to some degree.

Protection for the Seller

Merchandise sold on the installment plan is usually paid for, with interest, in monthly installments which may range over a period of a year or more. Commonly the seller protects himself until he has received the total payment due. If the buyer has paid any substantial sum on the price at the time of his default, he is entitled to get that sum back, less the depreciation on the goods caused by wear and tear. The amount of depreciation will ordinarily be estimated by selling the goods a second time, frequently at auction, and seeing what they bring. Depreciation is the difference between what the installment seller sold the goods for originally and what the second, auction sale brings in. For example, Smith bought a suite of furniture from a dealer on the installment plan for $600. He paid $100 down, got possession of the furniture, and agreed to pay the balance in 20 installments of $25 each. Title to the furniture was to remain with the seller until Smith paid the entire purchase price. After paying $200, Smith took sick, lost his position, and failed to make a payment that was due. The dealer took the furniture back. If the dealer sold it again at auction for $400, he would have to pay Smith $100, since the $300 he had received from Smith plus the $400 at the auction sale added up to $700, or $100 in excess of the original selling price of $600. Smith would lose $200 of his $300 paid because the furniture, as evidenced by the second sale, had depreciated $200.

Repossession

In the hands of a sharp seller, an uninformed buyer may not be able to discover what the furniture brings at the second sale; or the second sale may be rigged to establish a low price so that there need be no repayment. Only rarely does the defaulter recover what has already been paid. The following example may be a portent of new enforcement.

Ford Motor Company and its credit subsidiary agreed to an FTC order for the prompt refund to consumers of an estimated $1 million a year in surpluses from the sale of repossessed cars. The Seattle regional office survey showed that in a recent one-year period approximately 15 percent of the vehicles repossessed by Ford Credit and resold by Ford dealers resulted in an average surplus of more than $200. The order will affect some 3,500 dealers and as many as 40,000 vehicles a year. The consent order requires refunds to consumers of all surpluses realized since May 1, 1974, by approximately 200 dealerships in which Ford owns all or part of the voting stock. According to the commission's February 1976 complaint which began the case, surpluses have generally been kept by the selling dealer.[7]

When the goods or property that have been sold under the installment plan have been repossessed and resold, the proceeds of resale applied to payment of the debt may not be sufficient to cover the total amount. To satisfy this deficiency, a judgment may be secured against the debtor through court action. Thus the installment buyer may lose not only the cash paid and the article purchased, but additional amounts as well.

From his thorough study of events leading up to default, Professor Caplowitz makes this observation:

> One might suppose that the better educated debtors in default would be more likely than the poorly educated to understand the conditions embodied in their contracts and would know that their obligations do not automatically end with the repossession. But oddly enough, this is not at all the case. In fact, the better educated seem to be more confused than the poorly educated in this matter. Thus, 49 percent of those who never graduated from high school understand that the repossession did not end their obligation, compared with 45 percent of those who did graduate from high school. (Among the relatively small number who attended college, only 45 percent understood the meaning of repossession.) Not only did formal education fail to differentiate those who did and did not understand their obligations following repossession, but education based on experience also makes no difference. Thus we expected that those debtors who had experienced debt problems in the past, especially those who had experienced prior repossessions, would be more likely than those in debt trouble for the first time to know that their obligations did not end with repossession. But this turns out not to be the case. There is no relationship whatsoever between the index of prior debt trouble and understanding of repossession. In fact, not even those who had experienced repossessions before had greater awareness of their obligations in the present instance.[8]

Sales of repossessed merchandise, especially automobiles, offer much opportunity for abuse. Fre-

[7] *FTC News Summary,* October 20, 1978.

[8] David Caplowitz with the assistance of Eric Single, *Debtors in Default* (New York: Bureau of Applied Social Research, Columbia University, 1970), vol. 1, chap. 10, p. 34.

quently there is no requirement for public sale. Repossession when only one or two payments remain may wipe out the entire equity that the purchaser has established. Ethical dealers find ways of avoiding such repossessions, but some firms, particularly in the used car field, appear to specialize in repossession. They draw up contracts, such as those with "balloon clauses," which encourage delinquency and then, when a payment cannot be met, seize the car without notice and either sell it at a rigged sale or collect excessive fees for its return to the customer. In larger cities, in a number of states, dozens of cars are reported to the police as stolen, though in fact they have been repossessed without notice to the installment purchaser.

Legal Interpretation

In many jurisdictions, collateral can be retaken without notice to the purchaser if there is no breach of the peace. Breaching the peace, in this connection, is generally interpreted as breaking into a garage, removing a car from a private driveway, or taking a car from a resisting installment buyer. When a purchaser in default will not surrender a car peacefully, a writ of replevin is served on him by the sheriff. In some states, if the collateral is retaken without notice to the purchaser, he may redeem the collateral within ten days after the retaking by tendering the amount due under the contract, together with any expenses incurred by the seller; but he frequently does not know about this legal right, or he may not have or be able to obtain the funds needed to take advantage of it.

In the historic Fuentes case (1972) the Supreme Court in a four-to-three decision seemed to have made invalid laws that did not allow notice and under which repossession took place before any hearing was held. The Court did not question the power of a state to seize goods "before a final judgment to protect creditors as long as these creditors have tested their claim through the process of a prior hearing." The Court also exempted situations in which seizures were required by public interest, such as to collect taxes or to protect the

public from misbranded drugs or contaminated food. But two years later, in May 1974, the Court upheld a Louisiana statute (*Mitchell* v. *W. T. Grant*) that permitted an installment seller to obtain a writ to seize property when payments were overdue, without notice to the purchaser—or a hearing.

This would seem to have whittled down the Fuentes case. To sum up in nonlegal terms: the Court seems to recognize repossession if a state official participates in the seizure of property and due process of some sort is involved.

Credit Life Insurance

A purchaser on the installment plan is often required to buy *(a)* credit life insurance and *(b)* credit disability insurance. The purpose is to protect the seller or the finance company in case the buyer dies or becomes disabled and cannot continue to pay off installments due. Truth in Lending requires that the consumer know that the purchase of credit life insurance is optional. But even when told that he will be denied credit if he doesn't get insurance, he is rarely told that credit insurance can be bought from someone other than the creditor.

If the dealer wants to sell you credit life insurance, you must be told the cost and asked to sign a statement saying that you want the insurance. If the dealer won't sell the car without the insurance, and you agree to buy it, the full amount for the insurance must be included in the finance charge and in the annual percentage rate. A recent study asserts that most purchasers regard the insurance protection favorably.

If the goods are damaged, lost, or destroyed while the buyer is holding them and making payments, the loss falls upon the buyer, under most security agreements, and he must complete the payments. Since under these circumstances the buyer may have no financial means of meeting this obligation, the seller is customarily protected through insurance, which is paid for by the buyer.

What Does the Agreement Say?

All over the country thousands of legal forms are being redrafted and put into simple English so that you and I can understand them when we read them. This was discussed in Chapter 4, and an example appropriate to this subject can be seen in Figure 4–1 on page 102 showing a Citibank simplified loan form.

The Uniform Commercial Code

The Uniform Commercial Code, in effect in every state except Louisiana, deliberately changed all the terminology for past personal property security devices that had been used to protect the interest of the creditor as security for the payment of a debt. Article 9 of the Code abolished all formal distinctions between chattel mortgages, conditional sales, trust receipts, and all other instruments based on passage of title but did not abolish their use. The new language instead refers to a *security interest,* which is synonymous with the older terms, and includes all the protective requirements needed to safeguard the secured party (the seller or creditor) until the buyer has completed payment for property which remains in his possession.

The seller, wishing protection against the buyer's creditors and against innocent purchasers from the buyer, is obliged to file a contract in a public office, such as the county clerk's, in certain states. For example, Simpson, a radio dealer, sold Thompson a television set on installment but did not have the notice of his security interest recorded in a public office, as required by statute. Thompson used the television set for a month and then sold it to Hillman. Hillman received good title to the set because Simpson, through his failure to record the security interest, lost his rights in the television set when it came into the hands of an innocent third party. Suppose you bought a washing machine from a neighbor who was moving away. It might have an outstanding lien or security interest against it. Unless you check, you may have no clear right to your purchase.

Cosign?

Frequently, as a substitute protection, a cosigner to the loan agreement is required, a situation that can change a personal relationship with a friend or relative into a business relationship with a company that you had not quite planned. If you are a cosigner on a loan, you are as responsible as the borrower—in case of default. You are just as liable to have a salary garnisheed or a judgment entered against you, and perhaps as a result, your credit rating may even be affected.

If you're asked to cosign a note—don't!

THE AGE OF CONSUMER DEBT

In recent years it has become possible to buy anything from a baby carriage to a tombstone on the installment plan. As one sprightly author declared:

> The ordinary life cycle in the United States starts with a lay-away plan in the baby department of a convenient store, wends its way past the diamond counter of a credit jeweler, finds shelter beneath an FHA mortgage and is eventually laid to rest in a time-payment cemetery plot. After that, presumably, the terms are strictly cash.

In some stores all sales are on installments, and sometimes sellers try to hide the fact that they are engaging in the practice by giving the installment plan some such name as "Budget Plan" or "Thrift Plan."

"Sail Now—Pay Later" was the eye-catching headline in a newspaper, indicative of the wide-ranging appeal of installment selling. "Own this boat today . . . ten years sooner than you think."

In recent years consumer credit has become easier and easier to obtain. Indeed, the consumer's problem is more how to resist it than how to get it. Merchants have found that it increases their volume. Customers buy more; and if they are tied to a store by a charge account or an installment contract, they tend to come back to that particular store because their credit is now known—has been established—and the initial red tape involved in opening an account need not be repeated.

In 1947 combined consumer debt was 22.5 percent of disposable personal income. Thirty years later consumer debt is more than three times what it was then, showing a consumer trend that can be "viewed with alarm" when the concern is about the individual's current involvement in debt and credit—or viewed with satisfaction if the consumer is regarded as the prime stimulant of the economy.

It is the young marrieds who are responsible for most of the consumer debt. The *Survey of Consumer Finances* of the Survey Research Center, University of Michigan, found: "Young people are apparently willing to incur debt regardless of their income level. Furthermore, at each income level the incidence of installment debt declines with increasing age." "A large proportion of credit users in the younger age brackets apparently remain in debt most of the time," the Federal Reserve noted.

The most favorable attitudes toward installment buying were, as expected found among the younger age groups. The most frequent argument advanced in favor of borrowing was that it was the only way that many families could buy certain things they needed. On the other hand, a sizable percentage held that credit encourages overspending and is expensive. The extensive use of credit coupled with the increasing rate of inflation has caused 3 in every 100 families to overextend themselves, with the expectation that the numbers will rise to as many as 10 of every 100 families. Credit is used in the purchase of 66 percent of new cars and 49 percent of used cars. Almost half of purchasing families with incomes under $10,000 used credit to buy consumer durables such as appliances and furniture, while only one third of the purchasers with incomes exceeding $10,000 made use of installment credit.

How Much Debt Can You Afford?

It's been so easy to get into debt over the past decade that many people have overdone it. If you are in debt, or contemplating the plunge, there are a number of yardsticks that you can use to judge your position. First, your total debts should not exceed 20 percent of your annual (take-home) salary. Second, your total debt should not exceed the amount that you can pay off with 10 percent of

your income over 12 to 24 months. Third, what you owe should not exceed one third of your "discretionary" spending (or saving) for the year. By discretionary spending we mean what you have left to spend from your income after you have made essential expenditures, such as those for food, shelter, and clothing. Naturally these are flexible rules, but applying them in your own case will give you a range within which to operate.

Changes in family needs are reflected in the changing ratio of debt to income—declining from 81 percent in the young family (head under 35 years), to 78 percent for the growing family (head 35–54 years), to 41 percent for the contracting family (head 55–64 years), to 38 percent for the retired family (head 65 years and over).

Financial Vulnerability—Can You Afford It?

A simple checklist has been devised to test the financial vulnerability of installment debtors.[9] There are three questions to answer:

1. How much cash do you have available to meet emergencies? Add what you have in savings accounts, in government savings bonds, and in your checking account. (You should consider the usual balance just before payday rather than just after payday.) This sum represents your liquid assets. Place a check in the A or F box.

2. How long are you committed to your present installment debt? To figure this, add your outstanding installment debts, and divide the total by the sum of the installment debt payments that you make each month. Even if some debts can be repaid in a few months and others run for a longer period, you divide by your current monthly payment be-

---

[9] See Gwen J. Bymers, *A Financial Checkup on the Use of Credit*, rev. ed. (Ithaca, N.Y.: Cooperative Extensions Service, New York State College of Human Ecology, Cornell University).

cause you are trying to estimate how long it will take you to complete repayment at your current rate. The result will be the number of months it will take to clear up your outstanding debt. Example:

Balance due on car	=	$1,230
Balance due on washing machine	=	110
Total debt	=	$1,340
Car payments per month	=	$78
Washing machine payments per month	=	12
Total per month	=	$90

$$\$1,340 \div \$90 = 14.8+ \text{ months}$$

If the result is 12 months or less, you can be out of debt in less than one year. Check the A box. If the result is more than 12 months, as in the above example, it will take more than one year to liquidate your present installment debts. Check the F box.

	A		F
12 months or less	☐	More than 12 months	☐

3. How much of your monthly income is committed to installment debt payments? To obtain this figure, divide your monthly income after taxes by the total monthly installment debt payment estimated in 2. Example:

$$\text{Monthly income (after taxes)} = \$575$$
$$\text{Estimated monthly installment payments} = \$90$$
$$\$90 \div \$575 = 15.6\%$$

If installment debt payments take less than 20 percent, check the A box; if they take 20 percent or more, check the F box.

	A		F
Less than 20 percent	☐	20 percent or more	☐

Three F checks mean "very vulnerable." Two F checks indicate vulnerability; either liquid assets are too small, or to large a portion of income is committed to debt repayment, or debt is likely to run too long. One F check may not be serious, and three A checks probably indicate that the

"Getting back to those interest rates, could you be a little more specific than 'it's going to cost a pretty penny?' "

Reprinted by permission *The Wall Street Journal*

household can manage its installment debt without difficulty.

Consumer Attitudes Toward Borrowing

More people would rather save than borrow for something they "need," according to a survey by Louis Harris & Associates for *Newsweek*. Yet, except among the lower-income group sampled, there is no longer any stigma attached to borrowing. The affluent exhibit the least fear of being in debt. Fewer than one in three feel that borrowing is a reflection on their ability to live within their income. When asked what the main disadvantages of borrowing were, the answers "too costly" and "burden of repayment" were cited most frequently. As income increases, borrowers become more concerned over interest costs and less over payment size. Many indicated a willingness to borrow for "education"; few, for "travel/vacation" or "investment in stocks" (see Figure 11–5).

The Overextended American

Today almost 250,000 Americans each year seek refuge from excessive debt in personal bankruptcy. In our affluent society, personal bankrupt-

Four Major National Credit Bureau Chains

Credit Bureau Services	2819 North Fitzhugh Avenue	Dallas, Texas 75221	(214) 828-6111
Credit Bureaus Inc.	3 Executive Park Drive	Atlanta, Georgia 30347	(404) 325-5235
Trans Union Credit Information Co.	444 North Michigan Avenue	Chicago, Illinois 60611	(312) 645-6000
TRW Credit Data Division	1761 West Katella Avenue	Anaheim, California 92804	(714) 776-6580

For information about the credit bureau nearest you, contact: Associated Credit Bureaus Inc., Member Services Dept., 6767 Southwest Freeway, Houston, Texas 77074. Phone (713) 774-8701.

cies have been rising sharply, resulting in millions of dollars of losses to creditors and personal hardship to the unfortunate debtors. Families with a fairly high level of income, accustomed to ample credit, are in debt as inflation has cut into their discretionary income, creating hopefully temporary problems. Blue-collar workers, the purchasing power of whose weekly spendable income has declined, according to government statistics, have been squeezed by installment payments and face more long-term difficulty.

Most people tend to live up to their income. A sudden crisis—a job loss, an illness—upsets that steady flow of income, and if there has been no saving—debts and loans grow. Some people are compulsive spenders, use the easy availability of credit cards as supplementary income, and suddenly find themselves paying 18 percent interest on every credit card. A Brookings Institute Study found that the majority of bankrupts were not from the poorest or most poorly educated groups: 75 percent had been to high school; 18 percent to college. The study reported that most people gave more than one reason for their troubles, and most named poor debt management, unwise refinancing, and too many debts.[10]

A different type of personal bankrupt (perhaps the largest on record—$59 million of liabilities and $25.6 million of assets), Lammot du Pont Copeland, Jr., agreed to pay creditors between 10 cents and 20 cents on the dollar over the next ten years.

For those who cannot cope with their personal debts and seek the protection of the bankruptcy

procedure, there are usually two courses to follow: the insolvent can either file a "straight" or ordinary petition or he can seek shelter under chapter XIII of the Federal Bankruptcy Act. Once a person has his debts discharged he cannot file again for six years, but he need not worry about paying any of his unsecured debts. However, property such as a house or car may be repossessed if it is pledged as collateral and payments have not been made.

Straight Bankruptcy

In straight bankruptcy a debtor turns over all his nonexempt property to the court so that it can be sold and the proceeds distributed among his creditors. Frequently these are "no asset" cases in which the lenders emerge with nothing. Sometimes a secured item—if it is not exempt in that state—may be lost even after bankruptcy, unless the debtor works out repayment arrangements with creditors holding secured loans on furniture or a car.

In California married debtors can keep $30,000 worth of equity in a homestead from creditors. In New York State the exemption is $10,000 and color TV sets. Vermont exempts one car; Texas—a "homestead." Usually the car that a debtor drives to work, the tools of his trade, home furnishings, clothing, and life insurance policies are exempt from seizure.

Until the addition to the bankruptcy law passed in 1970, a consumer who had been freed from debts in federal proceedings could be sued again in state courts for the same debts.

Previously a debtor who did not appear in state court to defend himself in a suit (either because he did not know he was being sued or because

[10] *Consumer Views,* May 1978, published by Citibank.

FIGURE 11-5
Why People Borrow

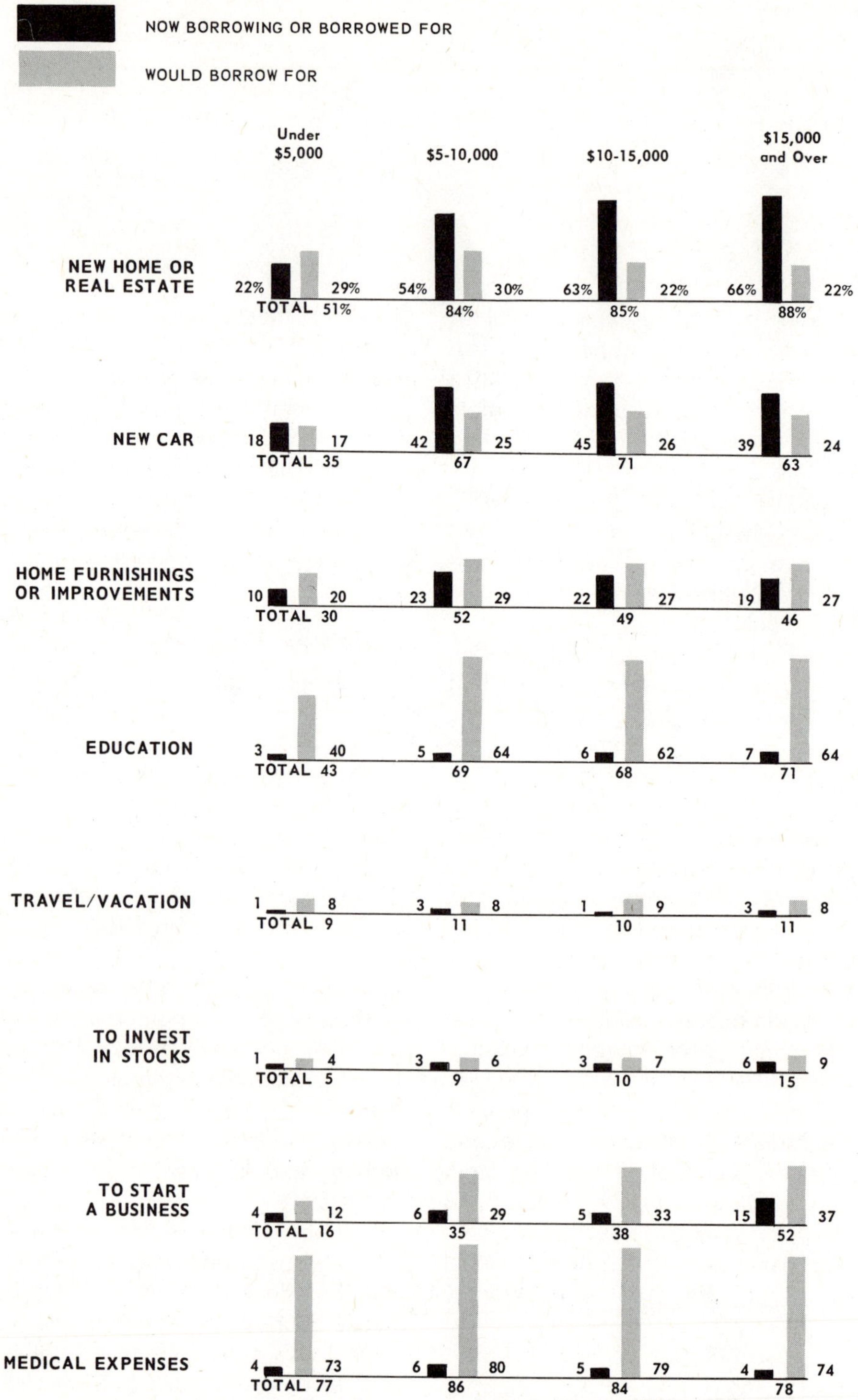

▮ NOW BORROWING OR BORROWED FOR

▮ WOULD BORROW FOR

	Under $5,000	$5-10,000	$10-15,000	$15,000 and Over
NEW HOME OR REAL ESTATE	22% — 29% TOTAL 51%	54% — 30% 84%	63% — 22% 85%	66% — 22% 88%
NEW CAR	18 — 17 TOTAL 35	42 — 25 67	45 — 26 71	39 — 24 63
HOME FURNISHINGS OR IMPROVEMENTS	10 — 20 TOTAL 30	23 — 29 52	22 — 27 49	19 — 27 46
EDUCATION	3 — 40 TOTAL 43	5 — 64 69	6 — 62 68	7 — 64 71
TRAVEL/VACATION	1 — 8 TOTAL 9	3 — 8 11	1 — 9 10	3 — 8 11
TO INVEST IN STOCKS	1 — 4 TOTAL 5	3 — 6 9	3 — 7 10	6 — 9 15
TO START A BUSINESS	4 — 12 TOTAL 16	6 — 29 35	5 — 33 38	15 — 37 52
MEDICAL EXPENSES	4 — 73 TOTAL 77	6 — 80 86	5 — 79 84	4 — 74 78

Source: "Public Attitudes toward Money and Its Management," study conducted by Louis Harris & Associates for *Newsweek* magazine.

he thought the federal bankruptcy proceedings under Chapter XIII had ended the matter) was faced with a state court judgment. Now such state actions are brought under the jurisdiction of federal bankruptcy referees, who make the final decision on these debts—usually on the issue of whether there has been "material misrepresentation." If a debtor who earns $5,000 a year concealed other debts amounting to $2,000 when the loan application form was made out, this would be regarded as "material misrepresentation" and the referee would require the debtor to pay.

The 1970 law offers some relief in that the creditors must see that the debtor's lawyer is advised of any new action—presumably while he still has a lawyer during the bankruptcy proceedings.

Is Bankruptcy Necessary?

A poorly publicized alternative, appropriate if a debtor has some regular income, is the "wage earner plan" under Chapter XIII of the Bankruptcy Act. Under it, a person files a petition in U.S. district court for approval of a budget for basic monthly living expenses plus a specified amount to be paid to creditors. Such plans are administered by court-appointed trustees and usually last about three years. Expenses are paid by the debtor and amount to about 7.5 percent of the money that the court pays the creditors. The advantages are protection from dunning or from garnishment of wages.

This is the answer for the debtor who really needs just time and freedom from pressure to get on his feet. In general, the essential living expenses should not take more than 75 percent of the take-home pay, so that 25 percent can be turned over to the trustee for repayment to creditors. This plan is better than straight bankruptcy for the debtor whose obligations are for secured loans on vehicles, furniture, or appliances. A debtor could lose these after a straight bankruptcy, but he can keep them after successfully paying off the debt under the wage earner plan.

When debts become overwhelming, the *Consumer Credit Counseling Service* offers an alternative to bankruptcy. The National Foundation for Consumer Credit, which has over 209 service cen-

ters around the country, provides two types of services, budget counseling and debt management, for which it charges $10 a month.

The *Consumer Credit Counseling Service* is supported by banks, business, and community groups, which have as much to gain from it as the bewildered debtors. If repayments are made—even on a reduced scale—that's better than bankruptcy for all concerned. Debtors come from all income groups, but increasingly the service centers see middle-income individuals and families. One outgrowth has been the formation of a self-help organization called Debtors Anonymous, whose members function for mutual support and aid just like the members of Weight Watchers and Alcoholics Anonymous.

After Bankruptcy?

Most of those who have been legally released from debt through bankruptcy proceedings use credit again. According to David R. Earl, chairman of the state board that supervises collection agencies in Oregon and author of the book *The Bankruptians,* about 80 percent of those who do use credit again are in debt trouble within five years "to the point of repossession and collection procedures. Within 7 years, 10 percent of bankrupts file for bankruptcy again and within 10 years, the figure reaches 20 percent."[11]

"The federal bankruptcy laws are a form of consumer protection," said Gerald Mann, head of legal services for District Council 37 of the American Federation of State, County, and Municipal Workers. "I think individuals are beginning to realize that it's no more dishonorable for them to go into bankruptcy than it was for Penn Central or W. T. Grant." As you can see from this statement, there is new thinking about bankruptcy. At present both straight bankruptcy and Chapter XIII remain on a consumer's credit record for 14 years.

After bankruptcy—strangely enough—a debtor may find that his credit chances are better than

---

[11] Write for fact sheets on both bankruptcy and the wage earner plan to Administrating Office of the U.S. Courts, Bankruptcy Division, Supreme Court Building, Washington, D.C. 20544.

"We find it difficult to meet payment on our
one big loan, so we'd like to change
back to lots of little bills."

Reprinted by permission *The Wall Street Journal*

they were before bankruptcy. Creditors may be more willing to lend funds, because bankruptcy has eliminated debts and this means more cash on hand. In addition, there can be no repetition of bankruptcy for another six years—which makes a creditor feel safer.[12]

No two consumers are alike in handling credit, but in general the formula worked out by the Consumer Credit Counseling Service is a guide on how much debt is safe. Based on monthly take-home pay, not including a mortgage, and after taxes and other deductions:

—10 percent is comfortable.
—15 percent is manageable.
—20 percent is credit overload.

[12] The federal bankruptcy law is in process of revision, mainly of technical procedures and organization. A major exception is the expected abolition of the device of "reaffirmation"—a method by which the debtor reaffirms the old loan (after the Bankruptcy Court has cleared the debt) in exchange for additional credit.

Shopping for a Loan

The emergency that induces us to borrow may leave us disturbed and troubled and so distracted by the intense need to obtain the money that straight thinking goes by the board.

It would be well, therefore, to become acquainted with the various sources of loans, the services offered, the requirements, the different rates charged, and the different methods of computation before the emergency or crisis occurs which induces the borrowing. Few want to get into debt; but sooner or later many of us do, and for some this proves to be a very painful lesson which could have been made somewhat less painful if the emergency had been faced coolly because the borrower had previously determined which lenders were reliable, how much could be borrowed, and what the terms would be.

The borrower with such knowledge may then calmly apply for the loan as a business transaction, without fear or apology or emotion. Since a wide variety of financial institutions want to make loans, there is no need to approach the lending institution as if you were seeking a favor. Thus, if you need a loan, you should go out and shop for it. If your credit standing warrants it, most financial institutions will want to lend to you. Ironically, your credit standing improves if you have already borrowed and repaid. If you have never borrowed you have no credit rating. If reliable lenders refuse—unreliable ones (loan sharks) only spell trouble.

When you shop for a loan, there are a variety of things to look for; but the two most important are the reliability of the lender and the real total cost of the loan. Any national or state commercial bank with a personal loan department, any insurance company or mutual savings bank, may be considered a reliable lender. An easy test to use for any other type of lender is whether or not it is licensed by the state in which it operates. If there is no state license, then beware! The large personal loan companies which operate on a national scale are reputable and sound business enterprises, but some of the very small, local companies, even though licensed by the state, may charge concealed and exorbitant rates. The lender who has no office—who just lends at the corner drugstore or barbershop, or who comes around to your home or office or factory gate—is almost invariably a loan shark and someone you should stay away from.

How Much Will the Loan Cost?

If, when you were shopping for a loan of $100, repayable in equal monthly installments over a 12-month period, one lender required you to repay $10.07 per month, a second $9.75, a third $8.87, and a fourth $8.67, and all other factors were equal, you would probably be inclined to borrow from the lender who quoted the lowest rate, namely $8.67. Over the year you would save $16.80 by borrowing from the last rather than the first lender. These are actual rates. The first lender was a small personal loan company; the second was a large national consumer finance company; the third was a credit union; and the last was the personal loan department of a very large commercial bank.

Before Truth in Lending, rates were often not quoted on a simple, comparable basis, and it was frequently difficult to know exactly what comparable costs were. There were different ways of measuring costs. Lenders used varying methods of

charging for loans, and in some cases there might be several scattered charges instead of a single one. Interest can be discounted, added on, or figured on the declining balance. The last is the least expensive of the three methods, as you only are paying for the money you are still using.

Dollar Cost   If you look at Table 11–9, you will see that there is no way of knowing how much is payment of principal and how much finance charge. You therefore do not know the interest rate you are paying and you can not compare it with other loan sources to see whether you are getting the best buy. If the loan is $100 and you repay $9.75 per month for 12 months, 12 × $9.75 × 117 − $100 = $17, which is the true dollar cost of the loan.

This "true dollar cost" is one of two basic methods of measuring and comparing costs. You add up all the money that you pay the lender from the time you apply for the loan until it is repaid, including all fees, and then you subtract the amount of cash that you get from the lender. The difference is the true dollar cost. It is the real figure you are looking for, but it affords an accurate comparison only when two loans have the same length and the same method of repayment. When they do not, then it is better to use the second basic method, the annual percentage rate, which is the method

TABLE 11–9

Illustration of Incomplete Borrowing Information before Truth in Lending

Amount of Loan	Number and Amount of Monthly Payments			
	6 Payments	12 Payments	15 Payments	20 Payments
$ 50	$ 9.08			
75	13.62	$ 7.31	$ 6.06	
100	18.15	9.75	8.08	$ 6.41
200	36.13	19.33	15.98	12.65
300	54.02	28.82	23.80	18.80
400	71.53	38.00	31.31	24.64
500	88.83	46.94	38.57	30.22

The company's charge is 2.5 percent per month on balances of $100 or less, 2 percent per month on that part of the balance in excess of $100 and not in excess of $300, and 0.5 percent per month on that part of the balance in excess of $300, up to a maximum of $500.

required in Truth in Lending. This will enable you to compare costs when loans differ in length and payment plans.

In the dollar cost illustration just given, you might imagine at first glance that the true annual rate was 17 percent. You paid $17 for a loan of $100 over a period of a year. Offhand, that looks like 17 percent, but it is not. Why? Because you did not have the use of the whole $100 for a complete year. During the second month you would have the use of only $^{11}\!/_{12}$ of the loan, during the third month only $^{10}\!/_{12}$ loan, and so on, and during the final month only $^1\!/_{12}$, so that, for the whole year, you would have had, on the average, the use of only about $50.

APR To approximate the annual percentage rate, you apply the following constant ratio formula:

$$r = \frac{2ml}{p(n+1)},$$

where

r = the annual rate percentage charged,
m = the number of payment periods in one year (12 if you are repaying monthly, regardless of the number of months you actually take, and 52 if you are repaying weekly, regardless of the number of weeks you take),
l = true dollar cost of the loan,
p = the net amount of the loan, and
n = the number of repayments that you will actually make.

Applying this formula to the illustration above, of the $100 loan repayable over a year, which cost $17, we find

$$r = \frac{2 \times 12 \times 17}{100(12+1)} = 31+ \text{ percent.}$$

Thus, it is apparent that the annual rate of interest is about 31 percent under the constant ratio method.

In the past one had to apply this formula to each case as one shopped for a loan before comparative costs became clear and evident. Now all you need do is compare the annual percentage

rates which must be disclosed as required under the Consumer Credit Protection Act.

DIFFERENCES AMONG LENDERS

Prospective borrowers will find that lenders differ not only in their charges but in the security or collateral required, in the extent of the credit risks taken, in size of loans, and in length of time allowed for repayment. Some lenders require co-makers, or cosigners; others require a specific pledge of collateral, such as the signing of a chattel mortgage on household furniture or an automobile; still others will grant loans merely on the borrower's signature if the credit investigation indicates that there is a reasonable probability that the loan will be repaid. Some lenders will not extend credit to unemployed persons or to those whose income is below a certain level. Most lenders will want to know why you need the money or for what you propose to use it. Some banks will not grant loans if the proceeds are to be used to repay old debts, while, on the other hand, a leading personal finance company reports that 30 percent of its loans are to pay family debts already contracted.

The length of time for which loans are made varies from a few months to as much as three years. Some lenders will not bother with loans of only a month or two. Others will not lend for as long a period as three years even when repayment is on a monthly basis. Personal loans run in size anywhere from $10 to $32,500. Some lenders are limited by law to a maximum amount of $500; others will not wish to bother with a loan of $50 or less. To obtain the kind of loan you want, on the most favorable terms available, it is useful to shop around before you make your commitment.

Borrowing on Life Insurance Policies

One of the least expensive ways of obtaining a personal loan is to borrow on your life insurance policy. After the first two or three years, most life policies, except term insurance, accumulate a "cash" or "loan" value, which increases each additional year that the policy is in force. This cash or loan value for each year of the policy's life is shown in a table in your contract. This table also tells you at what rate the company will lend you the cash you need against the loan value of the policy. You will pay from 5 to 8 percent, depending on the company and your contract, which is better than you can do elsewhere.

Because both loan volume and interest rates soared elsewhere, state legislatures have permitted insurance companies to raise their rates. If you have an old policy, the old rate still applies. However, even the new interest charges are advantageous to a borrower, compared to the charges made on loans from other sources.

On veterans' U.S. government insurance the rate is 5 percent. This is the true annual rate, so that the real dollar cost for a loan of $100, borrowed for a whole year and repaid, not in monthly installments, but all at the end of the year, is only $5.

The insurance company cannot turn you down when you ask for a loan within the limit of the cash value of your policy. Cash value builds up gradually, so that in 12 to 13 years it roughly equals the total of premiums paid in. Your right to obtain the loan is part of the contract, and your credit standing, good or bad, has nothing to do with your right to the loan, provided that premiums have been paid and the policy is in force.

Usually, you can get your loan at any time merely by requesting it. There is no credit investigation and no extra fee, and the company does not ask, nor has it any control over, what you do with the proceeds of the loan. You can take as long or as short a period as you want to repay, and indeed you do not need to repay at all if you so choose. If the interest charge is not paid, it is usually added to the loan. Whenever the policy becomes payable, whether due to death or maturity, any outstanding loan is deducted from the amount of the claim that the insurance company pays. This unique feature of a policy loan has both advantages and disadvantages. The loan reduces your insurance protection, and there is a constant temptation to postpone repayment because there is an absence of pressure. On the other hand, if you just cannot repay the loan, your salary is not garnisheed, nor

is your car or your household furniture taken from you.

Savings Bank Passbook Loans

You can obtain a personal loan from $100 up to the available balance in your savings account at relatively low rates for as long as three years by using your savings account as collateral.

The reason savings bank passbook loans carry a relatively low rate is that the loan is fully protected by your savings account. The bank takes no risk. Why would you in effect want to borrow your own money? Why not draw out the savings and use the funds instead of borrowing?

There are several answers. Many people after making numerous small deposits slowly over a considerable time do not want to withdraw their savings suddenly. If they borrow, they continue to earn interest. Thus the loan costs little. If they earn 5.25 percent and pay 8 percent, the net cost is 2¾ percent, and when they repay the loan they still have the savings account paying 5.25 percent. In addition, psychologically there is more pressure on the average person to repay a loan than to rebuild a savings account. Furthermore, when interest is credited quarterly if it is left in the savings account until the end of the quarter, you may lose interest for two thirds of a quarter if you withdraw your savings during the last month of that quarter. The loss is even greater when interest is credited semiannually if funds are on deposit for the half year and you withdraw them in the fifth or sixth month.

Personal Loan Departments of Commercial Banks

At one time, commercial banks looked down upon loans and would have little to do with them. Today, commercial banks are a large source of such funds, sharing the field with the small loan or consumer finance companies. They are able to make consumer loans at rates considerably lower than those charged by consumer finance companies. Yet they have found the business quite profitable, and they have, therefore gone after it vigorously, through advertising.

In recent years, commercial banks have developed several new plans to give them a greater share of the consumer loan market. The two most popular have been charge account banking and revolving personal credit. The basic tool of the charge account system is the credit card, issued to those who meet the bank's credit requirements. With this card the consumer can charge purchases at any store belonging to the bank's plan. When a purchase is made, the customer signs a sales slip which, in effect, is a note to the bank. At the end of the month the customer gets a single bill from the bank, covering all purchases. He then has the choice of either paying in a lump sum or of spreading payments over a number of months and paying a fee—1 percent or 1.5 percent a month—on the unpaid balance. The credit is revolving. As the account is paid down, new purchases may be made up to the credit limit.

Revolving Personal Loans

Revolving personal loans, on the other hand, sometimes called Check-Credit, or Readi-Credit, do not involve a credit card. The customer simply applies for a "line of credit" based on ability to make monthly repayments. If the bank allows 24 months for repayment and the borrower can afford to repay $50 per month, then he can apply for a $1,200 "line of credit." Upon approval, after a credit investigation, the borrower gets a special book of checks to use in drawing on the $1,200 account that the bank sets up for him. This is popularly known as a "guaranteed checking account" because the borrower will receive an identification card issued by the bank, which provides check-cashing privileges where the customer is unknown and a regular personal check might be refused. The borrower is charged only for the amount actually used. The usual charge is 1 percent a month on the outstanding balance. As in all revolving plans, the credit is rebuilt, up to the designated ceiling, as the account is repaid. The main advantage of the revolving personal loan plan is that you can buy what you want where you want.

A variation is the Checking Plus account. This is an overdraft system which permits you to write checks in excess of the balance in your account. You fill out an application for such an account, and the bank sets up a credit reserve for you of from $400 to $5,000, depending on your needs and your ability to repay.

Once the reserve is set up, you don't need to use it unless you want to do so. It doesn't cost anything if it isn't used. But you can write a check for more than you have in your checking account. Money sufficient to cover the check is transferred automatically into your checking account from your credit reserve. The reserve is available when you need it. You can draw on it up to the limit of your approved credit. And as you repay, you rebuild your credit reserve so that you can use it again.

Each month you receive a credit reserve statement showing the amount, if any, which has been transferred to your checking account and the amount you have to repay. Once your credit reserve is established, no advance notice to the bank is necessary to use it. You just write your usual check. No one knows that you are using credit. And under this plan, unlike other revolving check plans, your canceled checks are returned to you.

Discount Rates versus Simple Interest

Banks found that they could handle personal loans at the traditional discount rates charged on commercial loans, since the installment method of repayment for the personal loan made the annual percentage rate of return on the loan roughly double the stated discount rate. For commercial banks, stated discount rates on the full amount of the loan ranged from 4.75 to 13 percent. Since loans are repaid in equal monthly installments and only about half of the full amount of a loan is outstanding for the entire repayment period, the annual percentage rates range from 9 to 27 percent, with 12 or 13 percent as a common average.

Increasingly, banks throughout the country are changing from discount rates to rates calculated on a simple interest basis. As a result of full disclosure of interest rates, borrowers had found that a discounted loan is not to their advantage, since they pay the interest in advance and have to borrow more to get the amount they need. Especially if some installments are paid ahead of time or if the remaining balance is paid in a lump sum ahead of schedule, a discounted loan costs more than a loan calculated under the simple interest method, even though both methods are figured at the same rate. This is because the simple interest method charges on a declining balance; you pay only on what you still owe. Truth in Lending disclosure has also raised questions about an old banking practice of figuring interest on a year of 360 days. Exact simple interest requires using the number of days in a calendar year—365. Otherwise, the bank is increasing the real rate of interest.

Commercial banks are able to make personal loans at lower costs to borrowers than most other lenders because they obtain their loan funds from bank depositors at very low cost, whereas consumer finance companies frequently borrow their funds from the banks. Most of the overhead of a bank's operation is paid for out of earnings on commercial loans, and very little needs to be charged to the personal loan department. Rent is a good example. In the small loan company, the borrowers carry the entire burden; in the commercial bank, they bear only a very small share.

Are You a Good Risk?

The American Bankers Association *Bank Manual on Personal Loans* sheds interesting light on what banks look for in granting or refusing personal loans. The first question the bank asks itself is, "Does the applicant have adequate borrowing capacity?" People frequently want to borrow to "consolidate other debts," and in this case the bank wants to know about *all* the other debts; then it will seek to determine whether the borrower's income is sufficient to meet living expenses as well as cover the monthly payments on the consolidated debt.

If you want a home improvement loan, the bank will want to be sure that your income is sufficient to meet living expenses, to pay interest and principal on your mortgage, to pay taxes, and to meet the monthly installments on your improvement loan as well. If you are applying for a car loan, the bank will want to be sure that you can make repayments on the debt even when your pocketbook is under the added strain of paying for gasoline, tires, repairs, and the other expenses which a car involves. The most common reason for rejecting a loan is lack of income from which repayment can be made. Personal loans are, in a great majority of cases, loans against future income; and if, after careful calculation, it becomes apparent that future income will not be adequate, the loan application is likely to be rejected. As a rule of thumb, banks tend to limit advances to an amount which will require monthly payments that are no greater than 10 percent of the borrower's income.

The banker is concerned with three important factors: the character of the borrower; ability to repay, not out of present capital, but from future income; and, finally, the borrower's capacity for using the money beneficially. In a credit investigation the bank asks itself three more questions about the borrower in addition to the income estimate. "Does he work where he says he works?" "Does he live where he says he lives?" and "Does he pay his bills?" The bank uses various means to check each. The prospective borrower will be asked to fill out an application, and this form is then checked by phone or spot investigation. One side of such an application form is shown in Figure 11–6. When he returns to the bank to obtain the funds, he will be asked to supply additional information. The ABA *Manual* declares:

> With the check in his hand, made payable to the borrower, the banker should ask for information regarding close relatives not living with the borrower, the names of two or three friends, and the names and ages of any of the borrower's children and whether they are in school. The purpose in getting this addi-

FIGURE 11–6

APPLICATION FOR PERSONAL LOAN
(INCLUDING DIRECT INSTALMENT SALES FINANCING)

FORM DESIGNED AND APPROVED BY CONSUMER CREDIT DEPT.
AND BANK MANAGEMENT COMMISSION
AMERICAN BANKERS ASSOCIATION

NAME _____

(DATE)

TO _____

(BANK)

(FILL ALL BLANKS, WRITING "NO" OR "NONE" WHERE NECESSARY TO COMPLETE INFORMATION)

AMOUNT OF LOAN APPLIED FOR _____ DOLLARS $ _____

PURPOSE: PROCEEDS OF THIS LOAN, IF GRANTED, ARE TO BE USED AS FOLLOWS: _____

THE _____ DAY OF EACH MONTH IS MOST CONVENIENT FOR MAKING PAYMENTS.

FOR THE PURPOSE OF OBTAINING THE AFOREMENTIONED LOAN, THE UNDERSIGNED MAKES THE FOLLOWING STATEMENT OF _____ FINANCIAL CONDITION AS OF THE _____ DAY OF _____, 19___, AND CERTIFIES TO THE ABOVE-NAMED BANK THAT THE INFORMATION HEREINAFTER SET FORTH IS IN ALL RESPECTS TRUE, ACCURATE AND COMPLETE AND CORRECTLY REFLECTS THE FINANCIAL CONDITION OF THE UNDERSIGNED ON THE DATE AFOREMENTIONED.

PERSONAL

HOME ADDRESS _____ CITY _____ STATE _____ PHONE _____

NUMBER OF YEARS AT THIS ADDRESS _____ NUMBER OF YEARS IN THIS COMMUNITY _____ PREVIOUS ADDRESS (IF AT PRESENT ADDRESS LESS THAN TWO YEARS) _____

AGE _____ MARRIED—YES ☐ NO ☐ IF YES, NAME OF SPOUSE _____ NUMBER OF DEPENDENTS INCLUDING WIFE _____

NAME OF NEAREST LOCAL RELATIVE _____ ADDRESS _____

EMPLOYMENT | **IF IN BUSINESS FOR SELF, PLEASE STATE**

FIRM _____ | FIRM OR TRADE NAME _____

ADDRESS _____ PHONE _____ | ADDRESS _____ PHONE _____

KIND OF BUSINESS _____ | KIND OF BUSINESS _____

YOUR POSITION _____ | YOUR INTEREST IN THE BUSINESS _____ HOW LONG _____

NAME AND TITLE OF SUPERIOR _____ HOW LONG WITH THIS EMPLOYER _____ | TRADE REFERENCES _____

PREVIOUS EMPLOYER _____ HOW LONG _____ | PREVIOUS EMPLOYER _____ HOW LONG _____

IF SPOUSE IS EMPLOYED, WHERE? _____

MONTHLY INCOME

SALARY, WAGES AND COMMISSIONS _____ $ _____

SALARY OF SPOUSE (IF EMPLOYED) _____ $ _____

OTHER INCOME (STATE SOURCE) _____ $ _____

TOTAL MONTHLY INCOME _____ $ _____

MONTHLY EXPENSE

RENTAL OR MORTGAGE PAYMENTS _____ $ _____

ESTIMATED LIVING EXPENSE (FOOD, UTILITIES, INSURANCE, ETC.) _____ $ _____

PRESENT CONTRACT OBLIGATIONS _____ $ _____

TOTAL FIXED EXPENSES _____ $ _____ $ _____

BALANCE, INCOME OVER EXPENSE

BANKING

CHECKING ACCOUNT $ _____ BANK _____ | SAVINGS ACCOUNT $ _____ BANK _____

HAVE YOU HAD A PREVIOUS LOAN WITH US? YES ☐ NO ☐ TYPE OF LOAN _____ YEAR? _____

LIFE INSURANCE

AMOUNT $ _____ CASH VALUE $ _____ AMOUNT BORROWED ON INSURANCE $ _____

COMPANY _____ BENEFICIARY _____

SECURITIES

FACE VALUE (BONDS) NUMBER OF SHARES (STOCKS)	DESCRIPTION OF SECURITY	MARKET VALUE	INCOME RECEIVED LAST YEAR
		$	$

tional information . . . is that such information is necessary in the event of a "skip."
Experience will show that a skip can usually
be traced if the collector has information regarding two or three friends, two or three
relatives or a child or two in school.[13]

Credit Unions

A credit union is a cooperative association
whose members accumulate and pool savings and
make loans at reasonable rates to one another from
the accumulated funds. Credit unions will make
very small loans, at times for as little as $5 or $10—
loans of a size which other lending institutions tend
to avoid. The board of directors of each federal
credit union has authority to fix maximum limits
for loans and to revise them as the credit union
grows. Repayments may be made weekly, semi-
monthly, monthly, or according to any agreed
schedule. Occasionally charges are as low as 0.5
percent per month and may not exceed a maximum
of 1 percent per month on unpaid balances, inclu-
sive of all charges and fees. This is a maximum
true annual rate of 12 percent a year. Each credit
union fixes its own rate within this limit. Losses
on loans are quite low.

Rates can be low because, as cooperatives,
credit unions usually have little or no expense for
rent, salaries, investigations, collections, or federal
income taxes. Because the members are usually
known to the credit committee, credit investigation
is reduced to a minimum.

Even if the prospective borrower is not known
to the committee, the credit union (since it is
formed by people who work together, or have a
common church or union or fraternal society, or
live in the same housing project) seldom has difficulty in securing reliable information quickly, with
little or no expense.

[13] *A Bank Manual on Personal Loans* (New York:
Consumer Credit Department. American Bankers Association), pp. 12–13. See also *Analyzing the Cost Factors
of Installment Lending* (New York: American Bankers
Association).

Frequently, the employer will regularly deduct
the payment due to the credit union from the employee's paycheck or salary envelope, thus reducing collection costs for the credit union to zero.
If an employee leaves the firm, his final paycheck
may be held back until he permits the deduction
to pay the credit union advance in full. In this way,
the firm becomes a collector for the credit union.
In some cases, the service is free of charge, in
others, the credit unions pay a fee for payroll deductions. Credit unions can now offer revolving
credit, eliminating the need for approval of each
separate loan. For reasons such as these, credit
unions costs are relatively low, and credit unions
can afford to lend at rates which only large commercial banks can match.

Consumer Finance Companies

One out of every five American families is going
to borrow some money from a finance company
this year. Such companies range in size from the
nationally known Beneficial Loan Corporation and
Household Finance Corporation to the small local
company which does a strictly neighborhood business.

A study comparing the personal loans of consumer finance companies with those made by a
group of banks found that about half of the bank
borrowers were white-collar workers and half blue-
collar, whereas only about one quarter of the consumer finance company borrowers were white-collar and three quarters were manual workers. Consumer finance company borrowers, in the main,
came from somewhat lower income brackets than
did bank borrowers. Fewer bank borrowers than
consumer finance company borrowers were under
30 years of age, and more over 40 years.

The small loan company is largely designed for
people without established credit, and its charges
are set to cover the costs of extensive investigations
and more elaborate collection procedures, even
on the very small loans. The average size of consumer finance loans has been rising, and it is now
around $1,300, carrying an average APR of 20.5

percent. Most loans are made to families in the $9,000 to $12,000 income bracket.

A little more than half of the loans made are on the borrower's signature alone. Most of the remainder are protected by a security interest on the borrower's household possessions, by pledges of automobiles or insurance, or by the added security of a cosigner.

The Maximum Loan Size Formerly $500 was the maximum size permitted by the small loan law—now more than 43 states permit over $2,000, and the ceilings are steadily rising. In Oklahoma and other states where the Uniform Consumer Credit Code is in effect, the loan ceiling is $25,000 (or more, when adjustment is made on the CPI). In California the loan ceiling is $10,000, and in New York it is $2,500. Some states which have low loan ceilings have other laws known as industrial loan laws or consumer discount acts, which permit loans to a much higher ceiling.

The Maximum Rate The charges of consumer finance companies and credit unions are customarily stated as a monthly percentage of the balance of the unpaid principal. Consequently, the effective annual cost to the borrower is 12 times the monthly rate. The principal methods of setting rates are the "percent per month on the unpaid balance," or the "add-on" in dollars decreasing as the amount of the loan increases.[14] In New York the rate is 2.5 percent per month on the first $100, 2 percent on the next $200, 1.5 percent on the amount from $300 to $900, and 1.25 percent on the amount from $900 to $2,500.

Ohio's small loan law provides the following maximum charges: $16 per year per $100 on the original amount of the loan to $500; $9 per year per $100 on the original amount between $500 and $1,000; and $7 per year per $100 on the original amount between $1,000 and $2,000. Under "stepped" rates (a usual procedure) your repayments will first be applied to the lowest interest part of the loan, leaving the highest interest rate part to last the longest. The lower rates do not apply to the entire loan but only to the part above a certain amount. Taking into account the lower rates on larger amounts of loan balances, true annual rates range from 13 percent to 36 percent. The larger the loan, the lower will be the cost per $100, since a sliding scale of rates is often used. The interest cost can vary for an identical loan in different states because of the differing legal loan rate provisions. It should be noted that under most small loan laws the stated rate *must* be calculated on the decreasing periodic balance, not on the entire original credit. Banks are not subject to this regulation, and neither are installment sellers. Small loan companies and credit unions are, however.

Usury Laws Usury laws, limiting the rates to be charged for loans, are intended for the protection of the poor. According to some experts, they hurt those they are meant to protect since by decreasing the possible credit available at high rates, they cause a greater share of such credit to go to lower-risk applicants who would have been easily able to get credit anywhere. The poor risk whose need is great is caught between the high cost of repayment or no loan.

Consumer Credit Code

Considering the variety and complexity of the small loan laws in the United States, it would seem desirable to have some uniformity. The Uniform Consumer Credit Code was completed in 1974, and as of now, seven states have adopted it. Its purpose is to replace the hundreds of overlapping and conflicting state laws governing consumer credit transactions, including usury statutes and small loan laws, with one overall regulatory law.

Consumer organizations, while agreeing that the Uniform Consumer Credit Code is an improvement over many state laws, are afraid that it will weaken consumer protection in states that have strong consumer legislation. Although there are advantages in uniformity, some consumer groups oppose the code because they don't feel it is the best law obtainable.

---

[14] See *Consumer Finance Rate and Regulation Chart* (Washington, D.C.: National Consumer Finance Association, latest edition).

Remedial Loan Societies

Out of the need to help a poverty-stricken borrower using his last possessions to get cash before resorting to charity or public relief, and out of the desire of philanthropic citizens to prevent persons in such desperate straits from being subjected to excess charges, grew the remedial loan societies. These are semiphilanthropic pawnshops, the most famous of which is the Provident Loan Society of New York. It has made loans for as little as 25 cents and for as much as several thousand dollars; currently the society makes 100,000 loans a year.

Its interest rates are the lowest known for pledge loans. It no longer regards itself as a remedial loan society. Its rates are 1.5 percent per month (18 percent per annum), computed for the exact number of days on any loan not exceeding the sum of $100, and 1.5 percent per month for the first six months, and after that 1 percent for each succeeding month (15 percent per annum), computed for the exact number of days on the part of any loan in excess of $100.

Provident loans involve no investigation of credit, income, or employment. This assures absolute privacy. Ordinarily a Provident loan requires only a few minutes; loans on elaborate jewelry may require slightly longer. Once the appraisal is made, the borrower receives the full amount of the loan and is not required to repay either the principal or the interest for a full year. Loans can be made by mail on the same day that collateral, such as jewelry, silverware, stamps, or coins is received, provided that the shipment includes a signed statement that the articles are owned free and clear.

The loan may be outstanding for a year before the pledge is sold. Interest is not deducted in advance, and loans may be repaid fully or partially at any time during the year, at the convenience of the borrower. At any time during the life of the loan, the payment of interest due plus a small reduction of principal will extend the loan for another year. The society advises the borrower never to destroy an expired loan ticket without first inquiring whether a surplus is due. Any surplus realized above the loan amount when the pledge is sold

at public auction is paid to the borrower on presentation of the loan ticket. If the sale results in a loss, it is borne by the society.

The Repayment of Loans

Most lending institutions permit the early repayment of consumer loans without penalty (usually not mortgages). But the mathematics is not what you might expect. The "rule of 78" applies. This is the formula used for computing a refund on a consumer loan if the loan is repaid before the time agreed. You might assume that if a loan for $1,200 for a year at 6 percent discounted (11.58 percent APR) were returned after six months, you would get a refund of half your interest payment. It isn't so! Since the loan is discounted, you only received $1,128 ($72, equal to 11.58 percent, is deducted). You sign a note to pay $100 a month for 12 months. There are 12 units of principal outstanding the first month (12/78), 11 units the second (11/78), 10 units the third (10/78), for 12 months—which add up to 78. At the end of six months you will have repaid 57/78ths (12 + 11 + 10 + 9 + 8 + 7 = 57), or 73 percent, of the interest. This leaves 21/78ths (6 + 5 + 4 + 3 + 2 + 1 = 21), or 27 percent of the interest still outstanding. One half of $72 is $36, while 21/78ths of $72 = $19.38 which is much less than you expected. You would receive a refund of $19.38 if you repaid the loan of $1,200 in six months instead of one year.

Mail-Order Loans

State regulation will be of little help if you succumb to the lure of an attractive mail solicitation offering you a loan of $600—no collateral, no cosigners, no security required. According to a news, story a finance company from Kentucky could charge you a total of $866.75 for the use of that $600 over a 27-month period. The parent company of that same company would be able to collect only $161.60 for a similar loan if you made it not by mail but in a state where there is regulation. All this was done with full compliance with Truth in Lending, which only requires disclosure. Disclosure would show that you paid at a rate of 34.75 percent if the mail advertisement of "only $31.57 a month" caught your eye.

If you need speed and secrecy, if you don't care about the interest rates, and if you are in a prosperous occupational group, such as the executives of large companies, doctors, or airline pilots, you can tap a different kind of loan-by-mail company. There are about 20 companies making $2,000 to $20,000 sight-unseen loans with repayment in one to five years that will send your loan by return mail if you have a good credit record. Mail solicitations go only to the well-heeled, and the credit check, although fast and discreet, is thorough. Without collateral the APR would be 18 percent, compared to a banks' 10 percent or 11 percent. A basic problem of regulation involves whether you should be charged according to the maximum permitted in the state where you live or according to the maximum allowed in the state where the loan company is located. Many mail loan agreements contain a provision in which you waive your right to the ceiling interest rate in your state.

Pawnbrokers

You will probably never need to resort to a pawnbroker, but for thousands of families he is still a possible source of emergency credit. The role of the pawnbroker has diminished greatly since the advent of the small loan company, but there is still no other lender who will let you have $5 for a few days at legal rates of interest, or who will lend you $100 on five minutes' notice, without any investigation of your credit standing or your lack of it.

A pawnbroker lends money on the security of personal effects, household or sporting goods, jewelry, and furs left by the borrower. The contract by which loans of this description are effected is called a "pawn" or "pledge," and the same terms are also applied to articles deposited. The pawn or pledge must have resale value, and the pawnbroker, who through long experience has become an expert judge of values, appraises it in terms of the price he can get for it on resale. He will probably lend 60 to 90 percent of the estimated resale value to allow a margin of safety in case he is forced to sell the pledged article to recover his loan.

If his offer is accepted, he gives the borrower the money and a ticket which identifies the merchandise and gives the borrower the right to redeem it at any time within a given period by repaying the amount loaned plus interest. The article is left at the pawnshop as security for the loan. If the loan is not repaid within the specified time, or if no time is specified, then within a reasonable time as defined by state law, the pawnbroker may sell the pledged article and retain the proceeds if this sum does not exceed the amount of the loan plus accumulated interest. If there is, by chance, a surplus, it is supposed to be turned over to the borrower. If you repay the loan, you do it in a lump sum, not in installments; and you can pay it back at any time within the overall period. Interest charges range from 2 percent a month all the way to 10 percent a month, depending upon the state. A common rate is 3 percent per month. Thus you would pay from 20 cents to $1 a month (30 cents in the case of a 3 percent rate) on each $10 borrowed.

The Federal Trade Commission insists that pawnshops, since they are lenders, comply with the provisions of Truth in Lending. They must tell their customers how much they charge at an annual rate and how much the loan costs in dollars and cents.

As an idea of how complicated this can get, in New York loans of more than $100 are levied at an annual rate of 24 percent a year for the first six months and at a rate of 12 percent a year for the second six months, or at a rate of 18 percent a year for one year. For loans under $100, the rate is 36 percent a year for the first six months and 24 percent a year for the second six months, or 30 percent a year if the loan is kept for a year. In St. Louis the rate is 24 percent a year; in Chicago it is 36 percent; and in Los Angeles it works out to 30 percent a year.

Loan Sharks

Loan sharks are lenders of money who operate outside the pale of the law. In the field of credit, they are the bootleggers. Although unethical *licensed* lenders will occasionally take advantage of an unwary borrower and overcharge, the term *loan shark* is reserved for those who operate without license or supervision and who violate the letter of the law as well as its social purpose. Loan sharks flourish in states which do not have effective small loan laws.

If someone offers to lend you $5 today if you promise to repay $6 a week later, on payday, beware! He is a loan shark. The "five for six" racket is an old and lucrative one, and it still mulcts many an unsuspecting borrower. If you pay one dollar for the use of five for one week, you are being charged interest at the rate of 20 percent a week, or an incredible 1,040 percent per year. Borrow $10 until payday two weeks later, and you will usually pay back $12. A $2 charge on $10 for two weeks is 520 percent a year.

Even worse than the exorbitant interest charge is the loan shark's practice of making it difficult, often impossible, for the borrower to repay the principal. The loan shark is glad to have the borrower fall behind in payments of principal, as long as interest is paid; and, indeed, in order to mire the borrower still deeper, the loan shark may grant another loan to enable the borrower to keep up the interest payments on the first loan.

The schemes and devices whereby the loan sharks sidestep the law and ensnare victims are myriad. A common device is salary buying. The victim does not borrow; he "sells" the loan shark part or all of his salary. In the middle of the month, for example, the borrower sells $20 of his salary, due at the end of the month, for $18 cash. The loan shark appoints the borrower his agent to collect the salary at the end of the month and deliver it. The borrower is threatened with prosecution for embezzlement if delivery is not made. Frequently, no attempts is made to collect the full amount which was "sold," but only the charges are collected and the loan is renewed for another two weeks. This goes on and on. Many states now have statutes which prohibit salary buying, but a number do not, and it is still widespread.

Another illegal procedure used is to have the borrower sign a note for an amount in excess of the sum actually loaned and then charge interest on the fictitious amount of the signed note. A borrower will frequently submit to this because of desperation for a loan.

The borrower usually does not want anyone to know about this debt, and the illegal lender is well pleased to have the loan kept secret. Everything is done quietly—at first. There is no red tape. No one knows—only the borrower and the lender. No credit investigation, no cosigners, no calls to employer or landlord to verify job and residence claims. But this initial secrecy boomerangs, for should the borrower fail to pay an installment, the loan shark threatens to tell the borrower's family, his employer, or the neighbors. In more extreme cases, borrowers who are late in payments or who try to pay off the principal entirely are beaten up.

Under the Consumer Credit Protection Act it is now a federal offense to engage in "an extortionate extension of credit." This is defined as the use, or the threat of violence to obtain repayment of a loan. Thus the FBI is involved in investigating loan shark activities. If certain factors are present in connection with an extension of credit, there is prima facie evidence that the extension of credit is extortionate. One of these is a rate of interest in excess of 45 percent per annum.

The Fair Debt Collection Practices Act

Professional bill collectors can no longer harass a debtor by telephoning at all hours, calling at work, pretending to be a lawyer or to represent the government, threatening violence, or threatening the garnishment of salary unless the collector intends to take legal action. The Federal Trade Commission enforces the act,[15] and it keeps a record of all

---

[15] For a free pamphlet explaining consumer rights under the law, write FTC Debt Collection Practices, Washington, D.C. 20580.

complaints. A debt collector who violates the act can be sued for damages and is required to pay the debtor's legal costs.

This act only applies to debt collection agencies, not to anyone else trying to collect a due debt.

Giving Credit to Women

Everyone has benefited from the consumer credit reforms. But since women have had a peculiar handicap based on a tradition of noninvolvement in financial matters, their entry into the world of credit and borrowing requires some special orientation. All that has been said in this chapter naturally applies to women, but there have to be some special elements if until recently you were regarded as a financial nonperson.

Many women have had no credit history, so how do they start? Whether you are single, married, widowed, or divorced, the problem is the same. There are basic steps. You have to establish a financial identity. Here are some possible ways:

1. Open a checking and savings account in your own name. Your legal name is your personal first name and whatever last name you prefer— your maiden name or your married name, or any combination of the two.
2. Step 1 will be only background for Step 2—if you want a credit history. Open a charge account in your own name in a retail store, stating only your income. No one can get credit who hasn't income.
3. Bank credit cards and checking accounts with a line of credit will give you a chance to show that you can pay your bills responsibly.
4. A small loan promptly repaid.

Special Problems How can a homemaker get credit? Under the law, part-time income as well as such assets as stocks and bonds or a car can be borrowed against.

Since 1977, charge accounts formerly considered in your husband's credit history could be used by you to have credit information also reported in your name.

Many women are not taking advantage of their rights. Between June 1977 and October 1977, banks, department stores, oil companies, and other credit institutions sent out 310 million notices, as required by law, to inform women of their rights to have jointly used accounts listed in their own name in order to develop their own credit history. This huge mailing brought an average 9 percent response rate.

All new joint loans and accounts must now be recorded in both names. The mailing was a chance to change old accounts which recorded the account in the name of the husband. Even though the account was used jointly and the wife was legally responsible for debts, but it gave her no credit history.

Getting married, separated, or divorced? Lenders can't force you to reapply for credit unless they have reason to believe that your ability to pay will be affected by your new status.

If you and your husband are separated—close your joint accounts and open new ones.

Alimony and child support payments are regarded as income if they are paid consistently.

Getting a Mortgage? No longer can a woman of child-bearing age have her income count as half or not at all by a loan officer determining whether a couple are eligible for a mortgage loan.

Nor can a single woman be denied a mortgage merely because she is single or a woman.

Violations can be reported to the Federal Home Loan Bank in your region.

The Equal Credit Opportunity Act The experience of the Equal Credit Opportunity Act is correcting some previously accepted stereotypes and is making women more acceptable credit risks. Statistics confirm that:

1. Women workers are not just part-time temporaries.
2. Alimony and child support can be counted on, since 46 percent and 47 percent, respectively, are paid regularly.[16]

---

[16] *Credit,* National Consumer Finance Association, September 1977.

FIGURE 11–7

TO FIND OUT MORE

If you have any questions about Truth in Lending, you can get information from the federal agency which enforces the law for a particular business. The nine agencies involved, and the businesses they cover, are listed at the end of this leaflet. The law provides criminal penalties for willful violators.

You as an individual may sue if a businessman fails to make the required disclosures. You may sue for twice the amount of the finance charge—for a minimum of $100, up to a maximum of $1,000—plus court costs and reasonable attorney's fees.

FEDERAL AGENCIES

From the list that follows, you will be able to tell which Federal agency covers a particular business. Any questions you have should be directed to that agency.

Retail, Department Stores, Consumer Finance Companies, and all other creditors not listed below

1. Division of Consumer Credit
   Federal Trade Commission
   Washington, D.C. 20580

National Banks

2. Comptroller of the Currency
   United States Treasury Department
   Washington, D.C. 20220

State-Chartered Banks that are members of the Federal Reserve System

3. Federal Reserve Bank serving the area in which the State member bank is located.

State-Chartered Nonmember Banks that are insured by the Federal Deposit Insurance Corporation

4. Federal Deposit Insurance Corporation Regional Director for the Region in which the nonmember insured bank is located.

Savings Institutions insured by the Federal Savings and Loan Insurance Corporation and members of the Federal Home Loan Bank System (except for savings banks insured by Federal Deposit Insurance Corporation)

5. The FHLB's Supervising Agent in the Federal Home Loan Bank District in which the institution is located.

Federal Credit Unions

6. Regional Office of the Bureau of Federal Credit Unions, serving the area in which the Federal Credit Union is located.

Airlines and other creditors subject to Civil Aeronautics Board

7. Director, Bureau of Enforcement
   Civil Aeronautics Board
   1825 Connecticut Avenue, N.W.
   Washington, D.C. 20428

Meat Packers, Poultry Processors and other creditors subject to Packers and Stockyards Act

8. Nearest Packers and Stockyards Administration area supervisor.

Creditors subject to Interstate Commerce Commission

9. Office of Proceedings
   Interstate Commerce Commission
   Washington, D.C. 20523

Source: Board of Governors of the Federal Reserve System, Washington, D.C. 20551.

3. Married women under 45 don't quit work to raise a child, since figures show that 37 percent of working women have preschool children.

The Equal Credit Opportunity Act is on your side. But it does not guarantee you credit. If discrimination in any form, subtle or otherwise, prevents your actually getting credit, you can sue. Sometimes knowing your rights and sounding as if you are ready to invoke them may provide the credit and eliminate the need for a suit.

> "A study of 500 banks" reported by the Associate Deputy Comptroller of the Currency before the Senate Banking Committee showed that 26 percent had violated the equal credit opportunity laws as then enacted. He said that in some cases, banks might ask for a husband's signature when, under the law, only the wife's was needed. A bank might ask for information on alimony or child support, he added, but fail to disclose (as required) that the applicant did not have to answer unless she wanted to answer." [17]

Enforcement The Justice Department has announced the establishment of a special unit to enforce the Equal Credit Opportunity Act. The unit, consisting of 12 lawyers, will investigate complaints and take legal action. The attorney general is authorized to bring suit when he believes that creditors are violating the law. Citizen complaints are the key basis for investigations.[18] The Federal Trade Commission also pursues those who are guilty of other unfair trade practices, of false advertising, and of violations of Truth in Lending, and it enforces Federal Reserve Board regulations on consumer credit.[19]

---

[17] *New York Times,* March 24, 1977.

[18] If you have a complaint, contact the Housing and Credit Section, Civil Rights Division, Justice Department, Washington, D.C. 20530; telephone 202-739-4123. See *Federal Reserve Bulletin,* May 1978, for the results of a survey of selected creditors to determine to what extent consumers were exercising their rights under the Equal Credit Opportunity and Fair Credit Billing acts.

[19] Federal Trade Commission, Consumer Protection Bureau, Pennsylvania Ave. and Sixth St., N.W., Washington, D.C. 20580.

Conclusion

Shopping for a loan is a complicated business, but it obviously pays to shop, since it may mean the difference between paying 5, 40, or 520 percent for your money. Generally speaking, an insurance company, a commercial bank, or a credit union will be your least expensive source of personal credit; personal loan and consumer finance companies are somewhat more costly; and illegal and unlicensed lenders are simply extortionate. Where you borrow is likely to depend on your credit standing, because if it is good—if your prospective future income is adequate and regular—you will need to go no further than the commercial band or the credit union. If these institutions are reluctant to help you, a consumer finance or personal loan company may. If you cannot get a loan, however, it means that persons skilled at analyzing people's finances have decided that you should not borrow, since you have little or no prospect of paying back. If they could with reasonable safety lend to you, they would.

Federal and state regulations have made credit reporting more open, have made it easier to compare interest charges, and have provided more equal opportunities and some protection for borrowers.

SUGGESTED READINGS

Board of Governors, Federal Reserve System. *What Truth in Lending Means to You.* Free pamphlet may be obtianed from the board at Washington, D.C. 20551.

Commercial Credit Corporation. *Women: To Your Credit.* Write to the corporation at Baltimore, MD 21202.

Denenberg, Herbert S. *A Consumer's Guide to Bankruptcy.* Harrisburg, Pa.: Pennsylvania Insurance Department, 1975.

Federal Wage Garnishment Law. Rev. Washington, D.C.: U.S. Government Printing Office, 1976; 3 pages; 35 cents.

First National City Bank. *Borrowing Basics for Women,* 1975. Write to the bank's Public Affairs Department, P.O. Box 939, Church St., New York, NY 10008.

Forbes. "A Pound of Flesh," June 15, 1977.

Money, "Struggling Back from Debt," January 1975. Donnelly, Caroline.

_____, "A New Way to Score with Lenders," February 1977. Main, Jeremy.

Subcommittee on Consumer Affairs, U.S. House of Representatives, *Give Yourself Credit (Guide to Consumer Credit Laws),* 1977. For free copy, write to the subcommittee at House Annex I, Room 212, Washington, D.C. 20515.

Tabor, Joan S., and Bowers, Jean S. "Factors Determining the Credit Worthiness of Low-Income Consumers," *Journal of Consumer Affairs,* Winter 1977.

CASE PROBLEMS

1   If there is a small loan company in your town, arrange an interview with the manager and discuss:

a.   The general economic status of the loan company's borrowers. Does the manager think they differ as a group from those who go to a commercial bank for small loans?

b.   The credit tests the company applies to loan applicants.

c.   The cost of granting small loans, both absolute and annual percentage rate.

d.   The loss expenditure of the company.

e.   The collection procedure the company follows if installments are not paid when due.

State whether you would do business with this institution, and explain your reasons.

2   If there is a commercial bank with a small loan department in your town, arrange an interview with the manager and collect information on:

a.   How an applicant's credit status is investigated and checked.

b.   What the loss experience of the bank has been on small loans.

c.   What fees, if any, the bank charges on a small loan in addition to the stated interest.

d.   What security or collateral the bank requires.

e.   What collection procedure the bank follows if the borrower is late in his payments.

What are the advantages or disadvantages of having a small loan from this bank?

3   If there is a credit union in your locality, interview the chairman of the loan committee and discuss:

a.   The general economic status of those who borrow from the credit union.

b.   The credit tests the union uses for loan applicants.

c.   The costs of granting loans.

d.   The loss experience of the union.

e.   The collection procedure followed in case a borrower is late in paying installments.

In your opinion, why might this be a good place to obtain a loan?

4   Visit your local Chevrolet or Ford dealer. Select any standard four-door sedan model and find out what the finance charge and the annual percentage rate would be if you made the minimum down payment permitted and paid the balance in equal monthly installments over a three-year period. Then visit your local bank and find out what the finance charge and the annual percentage rate would be if you borrowed an amount equal to the balance you would owe on the car to be repaid over the same period of time. Compare the rates, and give your conclusion as to which would be preferable for you.

5   *The Poor Pay More* is the title of a provocative book. To ascertain whether this is so in your area, visit a TV and radio appliance store located in a "poverty" or "ghetto" section. Select a store that advertises and sells primarily for credit. Select any standard RCA or Zenith color TV set and find out what it would cost if you paid for it on installments over 18 months. Ascertain the total cost, including the finance charge. Then ask what it would cost if you paid cash. Next visit a department store in a central shopping area, and, using the same model color TV set, ascertain the prices for the same two methods of purchase. Finally, visit a discount appliance store in a central shopping area and find out the cash price. If the discount store also sells on the installment plan, find out the total cost if you pay for the set over 18 months. What conclusions do you reach from this experience? Do the "poor pay more"?

APPENDIX: THE LANGUAGE OF CREDIT*

Acceleration Clause. A provision allowing the creditor to ask that all future installments be paid at once if one or more installments have not been paid when due.

Add-on Clause. A provision for adding new purchases to an existing installment contract.

Add-on Charge. The finance charge calculated on the amount financed for the term of the contract and added to the amount financed to determine the total of payments.

Annual Percentage Rate. The ratio of the finance charge to the average amount of credit in use during the life of the contract, expressed as a percentage rate per year.

Bank Credit Card. A credit card issued by a bank offering a line of credit and enabling the borrower to make purchases or obtain a cash loan.

Bankruptcy. A proceeding in the federal or provincial court whereby a person who is unable to pay his debts in full may be discharged from the legal obligation to do so.

Chattel Mortgage. An instrument which transfers title to personal property to another as security for the payment of a debt. If the indebtedness is not paid according to the terms of the agreement, the holder of the mortgage has the right to obtain possession of the mortgaged property.

Collateral Note. An instrument by the terms of which the credit user delivers possession of real or personal property to the creditor as security for payment of the debt. If the credit user fails to make the payments according to the terms of the note, the creditor has a right to sell the collateral and apply the proceeds to the payment of the debt.

Composition. A settlement under the Wage Earner Plan by which a potential bankrupt pays off his obligations by paying only a part of the total amount owed to each creditor.

Conditional Sales. Sales made under a payment contract where security interest remains with the seller until all payments are made.

---

* This information taken from the Money Management Institute booklet titled *Managing Your Credit,* printed by the Money Management Institute of Household Finance Corporation, Prospect Heights, Illinois.

Consolidation Loan. Combining several debts into one loan for the purpose of reducing payments into a single lower payment plan over a longer period of time.

Cosigner. One who agrees to pay a debt if the credit user does not.

Credit Bureau. A firm which collects, stores, and distributes consumer credit history information to credit grantors under the requirements of the Fair Credit Reporting Act.

Credit History. A record of an individual's past performance with credit.

Creditor. A person or firm that extends credit services and to whom credit users are indebted.

Credit Rating. An appraisal made by an individual credit grantor of an individual's credit worthiness—the ability and willingness to pay credit obligations. These appraisals are based upon the credit grantor's own, privately developed criteria for granting credit.

Credit Risk. The chance of a loss through noncollection of a credit obligation.

Credit Worthiness. The ability and willingness to repay a debt; having a good credit history.

Default Charge. Also called *penalty charge.* An additional charge generally calculated upon an installment payment which is not paid when due.

Defer. To put off until a future time; postpone or delay. Charges made to defer payments on credit contracts are called deferral, deferment, or extension charges.

Disclosure. Statement by the creditor to the debtor of all terms relevant to a contract.

Discount Charge. The finance charge calculated on the total of payments for the term of the contract and deducted in advance to determine the amount financed.

Down Payment. The initial payment on a credit purchase made before the amount to be financed and charges for credit are figured.

Durable Goods. Products which provide long-lasting and continuing services.

Extension. A provision under the Wage Earner Plan which permits a potential bankrupt to pay off his credit obligations by making smaller payments extended over a longer period of time. In Canada, similar provisions are provided by Part X, Orderly Payment of Debts.

Face-of-note. Also called *total of payments.* The

total amount which the credit user promises to repay, including the finance charge and all additional charges in connection with a credit transaction.

Finance Charge. Also called *cost of credit*. The dollar amount of charges for credit, excluding taxes, filing and recording fees, license fees, registration, title, and certain other legal fees when authorized; formerly called interest, carrying charge, service charge, or time price differential.

Instrument. A legal document, contract, note, or any other type of written agreement.

Interest. The cost of borrowing money; included in the finance charge.

Investment. Anything in which money is or may be invested to earn a return thereon.

Line of Credit. The amount of credit a lender will extend to a borrower over a period of time.

Maturity Date. The date on which final payment is due.

Note. A written promise to pay a certain sum of money at a certain time.

Obligation. A debt, promise, or moral responsibility; a duty imposed legally or socially.

Open-End Credit. A credit agreement which provides a line of credit up to a set limit, with the choice of paying in full at the end of each billing period, or paying over several billing periods with a finance charge applied on the unpaid balance.

Outstanding. Still owing.

Principal. The amount of a loan or the unpaid price of a purchase before finance charges of any kind are either added or deducted; also known as *amount financed*.

Proceeds. Also called the *amount financed*. In borrowing, the actual amount of money given or credited to the credit user; on a time purchase transaction, the balance financed.

Promissory Note. See **Note**.

Refinance. The rescheduling of payments on an installment contract; generally smaller payments extending over a longer period of time.

Refund. Unearned portion of a finance charge which is returned or credited to the credit user because of prepayment of the contract.

Repossession. Forced or voluntary surrender of merchandise as a result of inability to pay as promised.

Reserve. A sum of money or assets set aside.

Retail Installment Contract and Security Agreement. Also called a *conditional sales contract*. A written agreement between creditor and credit user which permits the credit user to receive goods and services at the time of the purchase but allows the creditor to retain title to the merchandise until payment is completed.

Revolving Credit. See **Open-End Credit**.

Right of Rescission. The right of a consumer to cancel, within three business days, a credit contract in which his or her principal place of residence is used as security. This right does not apply to first-mortgage loans.

Sales Finance Agency. A financial institution which purchases contracts from retailers, after which the credit user whose contract is purchased usually makes payments to the sales finance company.

Scheduled Payment. Payment due at a particular time (or times); each of the installments in a credit agreement specified as to amount and date due.

Secured Note. A note which provides that, upon default, certain pledged or mortgaged property may be applied in payment of the debt.

Security Interest. The right granted under stated law that allows the creditor to obtain possession of the property covered in the event you do not pay on time or fulfill other contract obligations. Generally the creditor can sell the property, apply the amount received (less expenses) to the balance owed, and sue the customer for any remaining amount due. State laws vary regarding creditors' rights and obligations in this area.

Share Drafts. Similar to checking accounts and offered by some credit unions, they allow members to withdraw funds, pay bills, etc., from their credit union share accounts.

Simple Interest. The finance charge computed on the principal balances outstanding as long as any portion remains unpaid.

Term. The period of time between the date a credit agreement is signed and the date final payment is due.

Terms. The conditions written into a note or contract, such as the amount of the loan or purchase, balance financed, charges, size, number, and dates of payments, which set forth the rights and responsibilities of either the credit user or the creditor.

Title. Proof of ownership.

Unsecured Note. A credit agreement in which the lender's only security is the credit user's signature and personal financial situation as demonstrated through the credit application.

Wage Assignment. A signed agreement which permits a creditor to collect a certain protion of a credit user's wages from his employer if payment of the contract is not made according to terms. (Prohibited by law in some states and provinces.)

Wage Earner Plan. A petition filed under Chapter XIII of the Bankruptcy Act which allows a credit user in serious financial difficulty to pay off credit obligations without declaring Bankruptcy. A trustee of the court enforces the plan. The law requires that a majority of creditors, not all, have to agree to the plan; in Canada, similar provisions are provided by Part X, Orderly Payment of Debt.

Wage Garnishment. A court order requiring that a certain amount of the credit user's wages be paid by the employer directly to the creditor; legal action taken only after a credit user has defaulted. The Consumer Credit Protection Act limits the amount of disposable income subject to garnishment and prohibits the dismissal of an employee for garnishment of any one indebtedness. In Canada, most provinces have a similar law.

Investment Alternatives

*October. This is one of the peculiarly
dangerous months to speculate in stocks. The
others are July, January, September, April,
November, May, March, June, December,
August, and February.*

MARK TWAIN

"Thrift is a wonderful virtue, especially in an ancestor," someone said. If your father or grandfather had bought 100 shares of International Business Machines (IBM) in 1913 at a cost of $4,450, by 1979 as a result of stock splits and stock dividends, this would have amounted to thousands of shares with a market value of millions.[1]

Nor are investment opportunities of this type a matter only of the early 1900s. Such opportunities have been available in the more recent past as well. To cite several examples: *(a)* A $1,000 investment in Food Machinery stock in 1932 was worth $100,000 by 1946; *(b)* the old Homestake Mining gold stock rose from 81 in 1931 to 544 in 1936; *(c)* Control Data rose from 37½ cents a share (adjusted for a stock split) in 1958 to a high of $165½ in 1967; *(d)* Burroughs Corporation rose from 22⅛ in 1965 to a high of 252¾ in 1973; *(e)* Houston Oil and Minerals stock rose from the equivalent of 75 cents a share following its listing in late 1972 to a high of 42⅜ in 1977, after splitting several times. This meant that the stock increased approxi-

---

[1] Find the closing price of IBM today and calculate the value of those shares now.

THE BAWL STREET JOURNAL.

Annual Lampoon of the Financial Community

"What do you mean exactly when you say I can expect 'frequent advances'?"

1978 Limited Edition　　　**Published: June 2, 1978**

Source: *The Bawl Street Journal.*

mately 80 times in value in less than five years. An investment of $100 in the stock at its listing in 1972 would have been worth around $8,000 by early 1977.

In the market, however, what goes up often comes down. LTV, a conglomerate which traded as high as 169½ in August 1967, fell to 6¼ in 1977, a decline of 98 percent. Some of the so-called performance stocks took a terrific beating. Four Seasons Nursing Centers dropped from $90 to $1 in a year. Minnie Pearl, subsequently renamed Performance Systems, went down from $23 to 50 cents. Avon Products fell from 140 in 1973 to 18⅝ in 1974.

Investment has many facets. It may involve putting money into bonds, or Treasury bills, or notes, or common stock, or paintings, or real estate, or mortgages, or oil ventures, or cattle, or the theater.

Investment could mean buying new land or new homes. For example, new homes in southern California have become a speculative commodity, with investment syndicates buying them when completed and selling them a year or so later in a sizzling market that often doubles or triples their money, according to the *New York Times*. When done on the leverage of mortgage debt, this may mean a return of from 50 to 250 percent of the money invested. It may involve speculating in bull markets or selling short in bear markets. It may involve choosing growth stocks, or blue chips, or defensive stocks, or income stocks, or even penny cats and dogs. It may involve options, straddles, rights, warrants, convertibles, margin, gold, silver, mutual funds, money market funds, index funds, and tax-exempt bond funds, and it may result in the accumulation of wealth or the dissipation of resources. Diversity and challenge characterize the field. For the able or the lucky, the rewards may be substantial. For the uninformed, the results can be disastrous.

Investment Objectives

Investment objectives vary with each stage in the life cycle. The young family looks for income, but more often for growth, and it has time to wait out a developing situation. However, it should not be so preoccupied with growth as to risk losing its initial nest egg. Investors at midstream (age 35–55) know more, have higher earnings, and can afford more risk, but like their younger counterparts they have to weigh risk against a relatively uncertain return and they are thought to be basically risk-averters. The third stage—the later years of the life cycle—brings a need for considerable caution and conservatism in investments. Older investors are retired or on the verge of retirement and cannot afford to lose much, if any, capital because they have limited ability to replace it. Moreover, they may no longer have the drive and concentration which are necessary for venturesome investing.

To the extent that it is possible—and, as we shall see, it is difficult—older investors usually seek to combine safety and income. While it is not easy to combine even these two goals, it is almost impossible to achieve the avowed goals of most inves-

tors—high income, safety of principal, and capital gain.

All investment is a balancing of objectives and purposes. A very safe investment may not provide protection against inflation. An inflation-resistant investment may not provide liquidity. And there is and has been an ongoing debate over the risk-return trade-off. It has been widely assumed that the higher the risk undertaken, the more ample the return and, conversely, the lower the risk, the more modest the return. But recent research has shown that this is often not the case.

The average investor seeks a safe, inflation-resistant investment which provides a good return, with capital gains opportunities, but which can be liquidated quickly if necessary, and is not excessively volatile. As the following pages make clear, there is probably no such investment.

Public Views of Investing

A very important study was just concluded under the auspices of the New York Stock Exchange.[2] Based on a nationwide survey, it was prompted largely by a desire to understand why millions of Americans with investable funds have continued to turn their backs on corporate share ownership during a period of relative national prosperity. The Exchange's 1975 "Census of Shareowners" showed a net decline of some 5½ million individual owners of corporate stock or mutual fund shares between 1970 and 1975, and there is no indication that the trend has been reversed.

Summary of Findings   Based on in-depth interviews with 2,740 households with annual incomes of $10,000 or more:

1. The American public, shaken by inflation and fearing more to come, is deeply cautious about managing its money.
2. The primary financial goals are defensive: to avoid loss of both principal and purchasing power.

---

[2] Conducted by the Opinion Research Corporation, Princeton, N.J., 1978.

"I'm getting worried. Everything I own is tied up in dollars!"

Reprinted by permission *The Wall Street Journal*

did nontraders. Other people think that stock investments will become more attractive if inflation is brought under control.

7. Misunderstanding and lack of knowledge about most types of securities investments critically influence public attitudes toward, and participation in, the market.

8. Barely one fourth of all financial decision-makers consider themselves knowledgeable about listed common stocks.

9. Households with incomes of above $25,000 put above-average emphasis on obtaining capital appreciation, minimizing taxes, minimizing downside risk, maximizing leverage, and diversifying investments.

10. A majority of financial decision-makers regard three investment vehicles as most appropriate for meeting their own financial goals—life insurance, cash savings (both of which are widely considered to be necessities), and real estate other than one's own home.

11. Treasury bills and municipal bonds are rated low-risk but are not widely held—possibly because most financial decision-makers are not very familiar with them.

12. Common stock, considered moderate in risk, is ranked the sixth riskiest of 20 vehicles.

13. Nearly all holders of listed stock, have life insurance and a passbook savings account, and own their own home or apartment.

14. Smaller, but significant, numbers have U.S. savings bonds and savings certificates, participate in an employee savings plan, and own other real estate or such tangibles as gems or art.

15. Twenty-five percent of those queried also hold unlisted common stock, preferred stock, or stock in mutual funds.

3. Seventy percent are unwilling to take more than the barest minimum risk or small risk, and the most widely held investment vehicles are those which are perceived as involving the smallest element of risk.

4. Despite the prevailing mood of caution, the public clearly believes in investment and expects to invest more during the next few years.

5. The suggestion that it makes more sense to spend than save is *strongly rejected.*

6. People who traded stock in the past year viewed common stocks more favorably than

The essence of the study is summarized also in the following four tables. Note that the tables emphasize the close connection between investment goals and investment vehicles. They also underline the relationship between familiarity, knowledge, or lack of experience and the choice of investment vehicles.

TABLE 12–1
Ranking of Financial Goals by Degree of Importance

	Total	Stock Owners
"Very" or "fairly" important to majority of households		
Income/normal expenses	91%	85%
Keeping up with inflation	88	85
Protection for family	87	86
Income/retirement	87	85
Personal control of assets	82	84
Improved standard of living . .	78	70
Estate for spouse/children	74	70
Tax minimization	67	67
Purchase of home	65	55
Guaranteed fixed return	62	61
Children's college expenses . .	59	55
Liquidity—cash or equivalent	54	59
"Very" or "fairly" important to minority of households		
Long-term capital appreciation	47%	61%
Fun/challenge	45	41
Minimal downside risk	42	45
Maximum leverage from available funds	40	49
Quick profits	31	28
Savings/investing for "big ticket" expenditure	27	30
Diversification	24	39
Action—frequent trading	12	10

Source: *Public Attitudes toward Investing,* New York Stock Exchange, June 1978.

INVESTMENT OBJECTIVES AND COMMON STOCKS

You would not think of going into a drugstore and asking for a dollar's worth of medicine. You would want a certain kind of medicine to treat a particular condition or illness. In just the same fashion, you do not buy $1,000 worth of securities. You want a certain type of security in order to meet an investment aim or objective. Generally four major objectives are discernible in investments:

1. Growth (or capital gains or appreciation).
2. The best possible income for the risk undertaken.
3. Safety (no dollar loss of capital invested) and liquidity.
4. Stability—which to an individual investor means the absence of excessive volatility and a continuing source of steady income.

Common stocks are, on the average, better for growth than other types of securities, because they reflect the earning power and the prospects of a company. Common stocks are called "equities"

TABLE 12–2
Investment Vehicles Viewed as Best Meeting Most Important Financial Goals

Goal	Vehicle (percent of households)
Protection for family	Life insurance (57%)
Income/normal expenses	Real estate other than home (22%), savings certificate (19%)
Income/retirement	Life insurance (25%), savings certificate (22%), real estate other than home (19%)
Keeping up with inflation	Real estate other than home (32%)
Personal control of assets	Savings certificate (25%), real estate other than home (24%)
Purchase of home	Savings certificate (21%), real estate other than home (20%)
Estate for spouse/children	Life insurance (47%), real estate other than home (26%)
Improved standard of living	Real estate other than home (30%)
Children's college expenses	Savings certificate (34%), life insurance (26%)
Tax minimization	Real estate other than home (24%)
Guaranteed fixed return	Savings certificate (21%), life insurance (20%)

Source: *Public Attitudes toward Investing,* New York Stock Exchange, June 1978.

TABLE 12–3
Ownership of Investment Vehicles

	Percent of Households	
	Own Now	Once Owned
Life insurance	92	4
Passbook savings account	86	4
Own home	83	3
U.S. savings bonds	47	22
Employee savings plan	34	12
Savings certificate	34	8
Real estate other than home	30	9
Tangible investments	29	2
Listed common stock	**27**	**11**
Employee profit-sharing plan	25	10
Ownership in private company	19	10
Investment retirement account	16	1
Stock mutual funds	11	9
Annuity	10	2
Unlisted common stock	9	8
Preferred stock	9	5
Long-term U.S. bonds	6	5
Municipal bonds	5	5
Convertible securities	5	5
U.S. Treasury bills	5	4
Corporate bonds	5	3
Tax-free mutual funds	3	1
Tax shelters	2	2
Money market mutual funds	2	1
Options	1	2
Warrants	1	2
Commodity contracts	1	1

Source: *Public Attitudes toward Investing*, New York Stock Exchange, June 1978.

income than many of the railroad bonds which went into default over the first half of the century. Many common stocks are not only good, sound investments; they have survived more business setbacks than many bonds, which, though originally considered safe, subsequently went into default. The common stock of the Bank of New York, which has paid dividends uninterruptedly for more than 195 years, has been a much safer investment than were the bonds of the Missouri-Kansas-Texas Railroad.

Generally speaking, though, common stocks vary more in price than either preferred stocks or bonds. If by "safety" is meant the assured return of the same number of dollars that one put into an investment, then there is no certainty that a given common stock will, if sold next year, bring in the same number of dollars that were paid for

TABLE 12–4
Knowledge of Different "Investment Vehicles"

Vehicle	Households Considering Themselves Knowledgeable
Life insurance	68%
Savings certificate	56
Real estate other than home	54
Long-term U.S. government bonds	37
Listed common stock	**26**
Investment Retirement Account or Keogh plan	25
Municipal bonds	25
Stock mutual funds	22
Annuity	22
U.S. Treasury bills	20
Preferred stock	19
Unlisted common stock	16
Corporate bonds	16
Tax-free mutual funds	14
Tax shelters	13
Convertible securities	10
Warrants	10
Money market mutual funds	10
Put or call stock options	9
Commodity contracts	8

Source: *Public Attitudes toward Investing*, New York Stock Exchange, June 1978.

because they receive what is left of earnings after a company's fixed charges are paid. Since what is left over may go largely to common stock holders, when a company prospers and its earnings rise, much of the increase benefits the holders of common stock.

Although income is characterized as variable, some common stocks have paid regular dividends for decades and have been a steadier source of it today. If you must sell in a recession, then common stocks may not return the same number of dollars. However, fixed-value securities (bonds) face an interest rate hazard.

Common stocks may preserve purchasing power in *the long run under inflation,* while the worth of the fixed-value security, even though it may continue to return the same number of dollars, shrinks in purchasing power. Therefore, one must conclude that, in investments, safety is a relative term; that in seeking safety or protection against certain hazards, such as price decline, you necessarily expose yourself to other hazards, such as loss of purchasing power due to inflation. There is, then, in investments, never absolute safety.

Total return is an important concept which must be understood for common stock investing. The total return on common stock is what you earn by combining dividend return and price appreciation (capital gains). Current yield, or the purchase price divided into the annual dividend, is only part of the picture. Assume that you paid $60 for a share of common stock and receive an annual dividend of $3. The current yield is 5 percent ($3 ÷ $60 = 5 percent). Compared to the 8 percent yield on a high-grade bond, the return on stock may not seem particularly attractive. But if the price of the stock were 7 percent higher at the end of the year, then the total return on the common stock would be 12 percent, better than the 8 percent return on a bond.

Common Stock Returns: Past and Prospective   A basic study by Fisher and Lorie, covering all common stocks listed on the New York Stock Exchange, found that over the entire period 1926–76 the average annual rate of return compounded annually was 9.0 percent.[3] The rate of return on long-term Governments during the same period was 3.4 percent. Both of these calculations were in current dollars. Such a return on your investments would have provided a fair hedge against inflation; the average annual increase in the cost of living over this period was 4.1 percent.

Another basic study, by Ibbotson & Sinquefield, showed that common stocks over the period 1926–76 returned 9.2 percent per year compounded annually. One dollar invested at year-end 1925 grew to $90.57 by the end of the 51-year period. The inflation-adjusted return over the entire 51-year period was 6.7 percent for common stock. Although stocks outperformed other types of assets, their returns were far more volatile.

The compound total return on common stock for the period 1977–2000 is expected to be 12.5 percent per year. Thus the forecast of the returns for common stocks is substantially higher than were the historical returns. This results directly from the high forecast inflation rates, which are compounded into all asset returns. The compounded inflation rate is expected to be 5.4 percent over the period 1977–2000, compared to the historical average annual rate of 2.3 percent over the period 1926–76. Because some stocks are risky, realized returns may differ substantially from expectations.

"Ed, you're the only person I know who *always* makes money in the stock market. What's your secret?"

Reprinted by permission *The Wall Street Journal*

---

[3] Lawrence Fisher and James H. Lorie, *A Half Century of Returns on Stocks and Bonds* (Chicago: University of Chicago Graduate School of Business, 1977), p. 1.

FIGURE 12–1

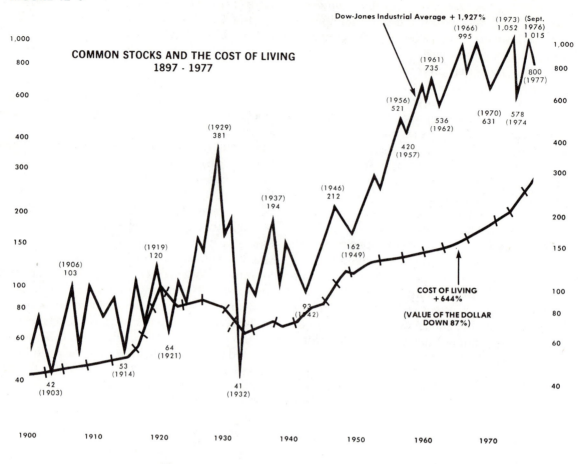

COMMON STOCKS AND THE COST OF LIVING
1897 - 1977

Dow-Jones Industrial Average + 1,927%

(1973) (Sept.
1,052 1976)
(1966)   1,015
995

(1961)
735

(1956)   536   800
521   (1962)   (1977)

420   (1970) 578
(1957)   631   (1974)

(1929)
381

(1946)
212

(1937)
194

(1919)
120

(1949)
162

(1906)
103

COST OF LIVING
+ 644%

(VALUE OF THE DOLLAR
DOWN 87%)

64
(1921)

53
(1914)

93
(1942)

42
(1903)

41
(1932)

1900   1910   1920   1930   1940   1950   1960   1970

COMMON STOCKS AND THE COST OF LIVING 1897 - 1977

During this period of 81 years, common stocks as measured by the history of the Dow-Jones Industrial Average increased 1,927%, while the Cost of Living, as measured by the Consumers' Price Index of the Bureau of Labor Statistics, was up 644%. Over the very long term, common stocks provided an effective hedge against inflation, but there were shorter periods, during sharp declines in the market, where the opposite was true (1906-1914, 1937-1942, 1946-1949, 1966-1974, 1977-1978).

Subsequent market recovery, however, has always made up this difference in the past, as can be seen on the above chart.

Over the past 5 years, the Cost of Living increased at a compound rate of 7.9% per year. Although it dropped in 1976 to 4.8% from 7.0% in 1975 and 12.2% in 1974, it increased to 6.8% in 1977. Over the past 10 years the compound rate of inflation was 6.2%. At a rate of only 5% in the future, inflation would cause the following results:

	Cost of Living	Value of the Dollar	Loss of Purchasing Power
10 Years	+ 63%	$ .61	−39%
15 Years	+108	.48	−52
20 Years	+165	.38	−62
25 Years	+239	.29	−71

Source: *Johnson's Charts,* 1978 edition.

The study's comparison of returns from other forms of investment makes interesting reading.

Long-term government bonds did well in 38 out of the 51 years (1926–77), returning 3.4 percent per year compounded annually. Inflation-adjusted, the return became 1.0 percent.

Long-term corporate bonds returned 4.1 percent over the same period, but inflation-adjusted this became 1.7 percent.

U.S. Treasury bills returned 2.4 percent, approximately equal to the inflation rate of 2.3 percent over the 51-year period.

Thus Ibbotson and Sinquefield found that the return on common stock, over the long run (51 years), was higher than the return for any other financial instrument. They also showed that *over that same long period common stocks were an effective hedge against inflation.*[4]

Just how effectively common stocks serve as a long-term hedge against inflation may be seen in Figure 12–1. Over the 81 years 1897–1977 the common stocks in the Dow-Jones Industrial Average rose 1,927 percent, the cost of living went up 644 percent. Over the very long term, common stocks provided an effective hedge against inflation, but there were shorter periods, during sharp declines in the market, when the opposite was true (1906–14, 1937–42, 1946–49, 1966–74, and 1977–78). Subsequent market recovery, however, has always made up this difference in the past.

The Anchor Corporation asked two questions about common stocks and the cost of living. The interesting questions and the relevant answers are found in Figure 12–2.

The Nature of Investment Risks

Most individual investors are risk-averters. They seek a maximum return for the level of risk that they are willing to assume. It has been generally believed, though never proved, that the greater the risk undertaken, the greater the return. It may be

[4] See Roger C. Ibbotson and Rex A. Sinquefield, *Stocks, Bonds, Bills, and Inflation: The Past (1926–1976) and the Future (1977–2000)* (Charlottesville, Va.: Financial Analysts Research Foundation, 1977).

that the greater the risk undertaken, the greater the loss. Risk can be expressed in either qualitative or quantitative terms. Major types of investment risks to which investors are vulnerable are:

1. Business risk (i.e., a decline in earning power), which reduces a company's ability to pay interest or dividends.
2. Market risk (i.e., a change in "market psychology"), which causes a security's price to decline apart from any fundamental change in a company's earning power.
3. Purchasing power risk (i.e., a rise in prices or a decline in the value of the dollar), which reduces the buying power of income and principal.
4. Interest rate risk (i.e., a rise in interest rates), which depresses the price of fixed-income-type securities.
5. Political risk (i.e., price-wage controls, tax increases, changes in tariff and subsidy policies.

Common stocks are most vulnerable to 1, 2, and 5. Bonds are subject to 1, 3, 4, and 5. No securities are free of all risks. Even U.S. government bonds are subject to 3 and 4.

The effort to quantify risk has centered on the use of the beta coefficient. This is a method of measuring risk which relates the volatility of a stock or a portfolio to the volatility of the market as a whole.

Beta seeks to anticipate what will happen to a stock or to a portfolio of stocks given a change, up or down, in the total market. A high-risk stock, a volatile stock, has a high beta; a low-risk stock has a low beta. If a stock moved exactly as the market moved, it would have a beta of 1. General Motors has a beta of about 1. It tends to move with the market. If a stock were more volatile than the market, its beta would be above 1. For example, a stock with a beta of 2 should move up twice as fast as the market moves up. If a stock were less volatile than the market, its beta would be below 1. AT&T is an example. But stocks seldom behave precisely as they are supposed to, which is where another measure, alpha, comes in. It is used to account for changes in a stock's price that are *not* attributable to its beta.

Suppose, for example, that the market advances by 5 percent over a year's time. If a stock has a beta of 1, it should go up by 5 percent. If, instead, it went up 15 percent, the 10 percent difference between the anticipated and the actual performance would be the stock's alpha. If a stock had a beta of 2—a more volatile or riskier stock—and it went up by 15 percent in the same year that the market advanced by 5 percent, it would have an alpha of 5 because, based on its beta, it should have gone up 10 percent, twice as much as the market.

According to beta theory, there are two possible ways of achieving superior portfolio performance. One is to forecast the market more accurately (an impossible task) and adjust the beta of your portfolio accordingly. If you foresee a substantial market rally, you might buy some high-beta stocks and sell some low-beta stocks in order to raise your portfolio to a beta level of, say, 2. If you are wrong and the market drops, your portfolio will, of course, decline twice as much as the market.

The second way of obtaining above-average performance is to achieve a positive alpha, or "excess return." When one stock has a higher or lower rate of return than another stock with the same beta—when it does better or worse against the market than its beta would have predicted—this is said to be due to its alpha factor, or the various residual nonmarket influences unique to each stock. If you can select enough stocks with positive alphas, your portfolio will perform better than its beta would have indicated for a given market movement.

But as you add more stocks to a portfolio, you tend to diversify away both the chance of obtaining a positive alpha and the risk of getting a negative alpha. Your portfolio's volatility will also become very much like that of the market as a whole. A fully diversified portfolio, if there is such, would have a beta of 1 and an alpha of 1.

Types of Common Stocks

There is a diversity in common stocks. In the loose and flexible language of the Street, it is customary to speak of blue-chip stocks, of growth

FIGURE 12–2
Common Stocks and the Cost of Living, 1871–1977

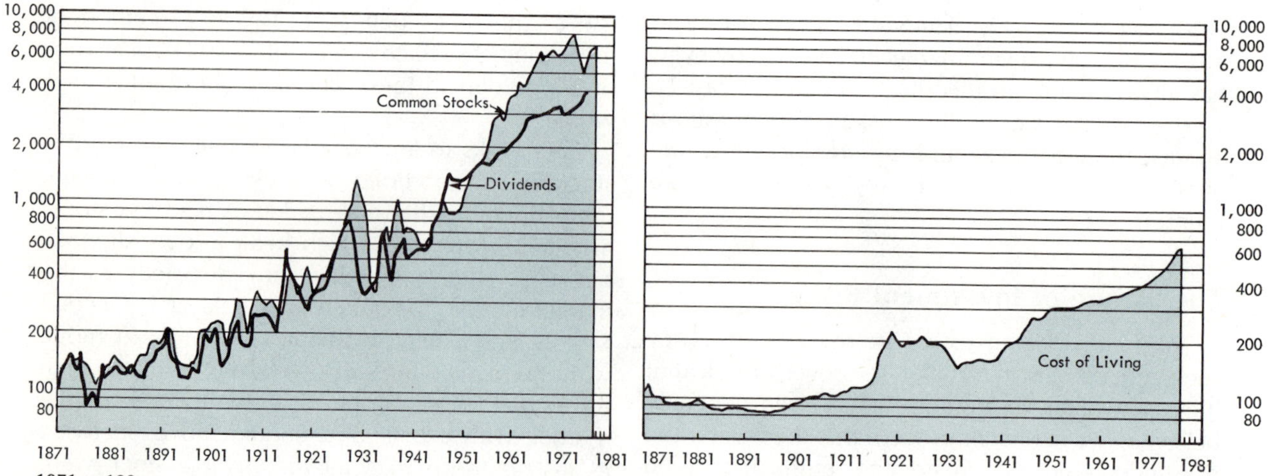

1871 = 100.
Stock prices (January 1): Standard & Poor's Index of Industrial Stock Prices.
Dividends (annual total): For the years 1925–77 Standard & Poor's index of dividends of industrial stocks was employed. For prior years, the Cowles Commission index of dividends on industrial stocks was adjusted to the Standard & Poor's index.
Cost of living (annual average): The U.S. Bureau of Labor Statistics index of living costs (annual average) was used throughout.
Source: © Anchor Corporation, March 1977.

FIGURE 12–2 *(continued)*

Q A RISING LIVING COSTS — HOW OFTEN HAVE THEY OCCURRED?

How often have investors faced inflation in the past? This tabulation is concerned only with the direction and not the extent of changes in living costs.

TABLE 1 — PERIODS OF INFLATION 1871 TO 1977

A Length of Periods	B Total No. of Periods	C Number of Deflationary Periods	D Number of Inflationary Periods	E Number of Periods Unchanged	F Inflationary Periods as % of Total
1 Year	105	24	66	15	63%
10 Years	96	32	64	0	67
15 Years	91	23	67	1	74
20 Years	86	16	69	1	80
30 Years	76	2	72	2	95

Living costs rose in 63% of the one year periods since 1871 and in 67% of the ten year periods. When longer periods were tabulated, it was found that living costs increased in 74% of the fifteen year periods, 80% of the twenty year periods and in 95% of the thirty year spans.

Whether they have invested for one year or longer — investors have had inflation in store for them more than half the time since 1871. Over twenty year spans they have experienced inflation three-quarters of the time; over thirty year spans nearly all the time.

Q A HOW HAVE COMMON STOCK PRICES BEHAVED DURING INFLATION?

Next, our attention is turned only to the periods of inflation shown in Table 1, Column D. How did stock prices behave when living costs rose?

TABLE 2 — STOCK PRICES AND INFLATION

A Length of Periods	B Total Number of Inflationary Periods	C No. of These Periods in Which Stock Prices Also Increased	D % of Inflationary Periods in Which Stock Prices Increased
1 Year	66	44	67%
10 Years	64	62	97
15 Years	67	61	91
20 Years	69	66	96
30 Years	72	72	100

Table 2 shows that stock prices rose in 67% of the one year inflationary periods and in 9 out of 10 of the longer periods of rising prices (Column D, Table 2).

Since 1871 common stocks have increased in value in 96% of the **twenty** year periods and in all thirty year periods of rising living costs.

Source: © Anchor Corporation, March 1977.

stocks, of cyclical (or smokestack) stocks, of income stocks, of defensive stocks, and of speculative stocks—both highfliers and low-priced issues. Lines of demarcation between types are not precise and clear, but investors have a general notion of what is meant by each of these imprecise categories.

Blue-Chip Stocks Blue-chip stocks are high-grade investment-quality issues of major companies which have long and unbroken records of earnings and dividend payments. Stocks such as American Telephone & Telegraph, General Motors, Du Pont, Exxon (Standard Oil of New Jersey), and Sears, Roebuck are generally considered "blue chip." The term is generally used to describe the common stock of large, well-established, stable, and mature companies of great financial strength. The term was undoubtedly derived from poker, where blue chips (in contrast to white and red chips) had the greatest money value.

What constitutes a blue chip does not change over time, but the stocks that qualify as blue chips do. The railroad issues, once the bluest of the blue chips, no longer qualify. On the other hand, Minnesota Mining & Manufacturing and Johnson & Johnson, which were not considered blue chips in the 1950s, do qualify today. Blue chips, or high-quality companies, hold important, if not leading, positions in their industries, where they are sometimes pacesetters and where they frequently determine the standards by which other companies in their fields are measured. The companies have foresighted managements that have taken steps to ensure future growth without jeopardizing current earnings. Such companies have the advantage of size—in a recession they should be able to hold their own and then they should record strong earnings gains during the subsequent economic upswing because they have the resources to capitalize on a recovery. By and large, investors who seek safety and stability and are conservative in their approach to the market turn to the blue chips.

Growth Stocks Many of the blue chips may also be considered growth stocks. A growth stock is that of a company whose sales and earnings are expanding faster than the general economy and faster than the average of the industry. The company is usually aggressive and research minded, plowing back earnings to facilitate expansion. For this reason, growth companies, intent on financing their own expansion from retained earnings, pay relatively small dividends and have a generally low yield. Over time, however, substantial capital gains may accrue from the appreciation of the value of their common stocks as a result of the plowback and expansion.

Growth stocks are usually quite volatile. They go up faster and farther than other stocks, but at the first hint that their high rate of earnings is either leveling off or not being sustained, prices can come tumbling down. For example, Texas Instruments, a high-flying growth company of the late 1950s saw earnings fall from some $15 million in 1960 to about $9 million in 1961. The common price fell from $256 a share in 1960 to $95 a share in 1961. From a high of 172½ Itek Corporation fell to a low of 4⅞ in 1974. Over the 1960–70 decade IBM ranged from a high of 387 to a low of 72½, and in 1971–75 from a high of 426¾ to a low of 150½, returning to 316¼ in 1979.

Declines in the prices of leading growth stocks are usually due more to a collapse in the price-earnings ratio than to major actual decrease in the earnings themselves. For example, from its 1973 high of 91⅝, Minnesota Mining & Manufacturing, which was then selling at 35.1 times earnings, fell to 48.50 in early 1977, when its price-earnings ratio dropped to 14. Johnson & Johnson fell from a 1972 high of 133, with a price-earnings ratio of 61.9, to a price of 63 and a price-earnings ratio of 15.1 in April 1977. Eastman Kodak fell from a 1973 high of 152, at a time when its P/E ratio was 37.5, to 62 in early '77, when its price-earnings ratio had dropped to 14.18. The leading growth stocks suffered a sharp deflation of price-earnings ratios between 1973 and 1977. Perhaps the best example is Polaroid, whose P/E ratio dropped from 114 in 1972 to 12 in early 1977.

The larger brokerage houses publish lists of growth stocks from time to time. These houses do not always, however, explicitly indicate the statistical basis for their selection. Merrill Lynch, Pierce,

Fenner & Smith once issued an elaborate study of "101 Growth Stocks," and from time to time it publishes select lists of growth stocks. An example may be seen in Table 12–5. By and large, the Merrill Lynch growth stock selections are of the larger, more mature, and more conservative growth companies.

Two leading, large no-load growth stock funds present an interesting contrast in growth stock investing. T. Rowe Price Growth Stock Fund, the larger, more mature fund, listed its ten largest growth stock holdings as shown in Table 12–6.

On the other hand, the ten largest growth stock investments of the newer, more volatile T. Rowe Price New Horizons Fund are shown in Table 12–7.

Thus growth stocks can mean different things to different investors, and it makes a big difference whether, psychologically, you take a conservative or an adventurous view of the market.

Income Stocks Some people, particularly the elderly and retired, buy stock for current income. Although in recent years current dividends on stocks have yielded less, on the average, than the interest on bonds or the returns on savings accounts, there are some stocks which may be classed as income stocks because they pay a higher than average return. Income stocks are those that yield generous current returns. Such stocks are often sought by trust funds, pension funds, university and college endowment funds, and charitable educational and health foundations. Selecting income stocks can be a very tricky business. A stock may be paying a high return because its price has fallen due to considerable uncertainty as to whether the dividend can be maintained in the light of declining earnings. Or it may be the stock of a company located in a foreign area where there is a large risk due to political instability. On the other hand, perfectly good overlooked stocks may be paying

TABLE 12–5
How Growth Stocks Grow*

	Mid-1953	Mid-1963	End 1966	End 1971	Mid-1976	March 31, 1977	October 14, 1978
American Cyanamid ..	$1,000	$ 2,610	$ 2,726	$ 3,038.82	$ 2,279	$ 2,279	$ 2,592
Bristol-Myers	1,000	15,671	34,727	36,857.96	50,196	39,226	44,040
Caterpillar Tractor	1,000	5,356	8,694	11,736.89	22,682	20,353	22,356
Corning Glass Works ..	1,000	5,548	10,033	6,023.04	6,089	5,084	4,992
General Electric	1,000	3,320	3,720	10,529.49	9,605	8,260	8,199
Grumman Aircraft	1,000	2,540	5,619	2,504.12	2,956	3,180	3,404
Gulf United	1,000	4,336	2,695	5,067.23	3,263	4,059	4,656
Honeywell Inc........	1,000	3,500	4,658	9,359.86	3,483	3,281	4,877
International Business Machines	1,000	14,557	23,256	86,366.37	88,790	88,709	91,757
Minnesota Mining & Manufacturing	1,000	7,235	9,879	34,196.53	28,181	25,394	31,347
Pacific Gas & Electric .	1,000	2,601	2,929	2,652.49	1,669	1,905	1,956
Pitney Bowes	1,000	7,557	7,442	15,154.61	10,361	11,211	16,469
Polaroid	1,000	33,777	137,700	308,795.00	140,953	117,967	182,154
Procter & Gamble	1,000	5,071	4,887	21,020.79	25,406	21,155	24,066
RCA	1,000	3,106	6,478	5,625.63	4,394	4,319	4,526
Safeway Stores	1,000	4,857	4,070	6,021.08	6,839	7,573	7,342
Texaco	1,000	5,646	6,012	11,561.53	9,460	8,913	8,534

* The table shows how a $1,000 cash investment in any of the above stocks regarded as growth stocks in 1953 would have grown since mid-1953. Full adjustment has been made in this tabulation for splits and stock dividends. But no account has been taken of cash dividends or rights offerings, and no allowance has been made for brokerage fees.
   Source: Merrill Lynch, Pierce, Fenner & Smith, Inc.

TABLE 12–6
Ten Largest Holdings, March 31, 1978

	Year of First Purchase	Market Value	Percent of Fund
IBM	1950	$ 55,599,666	6.1%
Coca-Cola	1961	36,049,425	3.9
Johnson & Johnson	1973	35,332,800	3.9
3M	1962	27,912,500	3.0
Avon Products	1955	27,587,175	3.0
Texas Instruments	1958	24,491,950	2.7
K mart	1970	23,017,888	2.5
American Hospital Supply	1973	21,075,750	2.3
Merck	1973	20,996,275	2.3
Hewlett-Packard	1974	20,022,375	2.2
		$292,085,804	31.9%

Source: T. Rowe Price Growth Stock Fund.

high yields because the public has not bid them up due to lack of knowledge.

Utility companies, which frequently seek additional funds, tend, on the average, to have higher yields than industrial stocks because they have to bid for new capital more often than companies in other industries.

Cyclical Stocks Cyclical shares, or "smokestack" stocks in Wall Street terminology, refer to stocks of companies in basic industries whose earnings fluctuate with the business cycle and are accentuated by it. When business conditions improve, the profitability of such a company is restored and enhanced. The price of its common

TABLE 12–7
Ten Largest Holdings, March 31, 1978: Common Stock and Convertible Securities

	Year of First Purchase	Market Value	Percent of Fund
Tropicana Products	1970	$11,751,025	3.0%
Leaseway Transportation	1969	10,455,552	2.6
American International Reinsurance	1972	10,148,275	2.6
Wal-Mart Stores	1970	10,096,875	2.6
W. W. Grainger	1974	10,087,450	2.6
Denny's	1976	9,661,438	2.4
Mervyn's	1976	9,564,750	2.4
Millipore	1965	9,564,325	2.4
American Television & Communications	1971	7,885,000	2.0
Helmerich & Payne	1976	7,875,000	2.0
		$97,089,690	24.6%

Source: T. Rowe Price New Horizons Fund.

stock rises. When business conditions deteriorate, the activity of the cyclical company falls off sharply, and its profits are greatly diminished.

Industries which may be regarded as cyclical include steel, cement, aluminum, chemicals, paper, machinery and machine tools, airlines, railroads and railroad equipment, and automobiles. Commenting on the so-called two-tiered market, which for a time placed growth stocks on one level and cyclical or smokestack shares on a lower level, *Forbes* stated:

> Probably never before in history has Wall Street had such a split personality. Call a stock a Growth stock and it sells for 40, 50, or even 60 times earnings. Call it Cyclical . . . and it sells for 10 times earnings or less. The market is saying that if General Motors earns $1, that $1 should be capitalized at only $10.90, but if, say, Johnson and Johnson earns $1, it is worth $64. This kind of disparity can go on for a long time, of course, but it can't go on forever.

In the 1973–74 bear market the two-tiered market came apart as former favorites plunged. Avon Products fell from 140 to 18⅝, Xerox from 171⅞ to 49, Walt Disney Productions from 119 to 17. But cyclical issues moved up as the economic recovery unfolded: U.S. Steel rose from 25 to 89; International Paper, from 28½ to 78¾; Du Pont, from 84 to 161; General Motors, from 28 to 70¼. Cyclicals surge in the early stages of recovery and tend to top out prior to the peak of the business cycle, yielding market leadership to the newly anointed "concept" stocks or "performance" issues of the period. Basic industry stocks led the market in its sharp recovery in 1975–76.

Defensive Stocks   At the opposite pole from cyclical stocks are the so-called defensive stocks. By defensive stocks are meant shares of companies which are likely to do better than average, from an earnings and dividends point of view, in a period of deteriorating business. If a recession is anticipated, a growing interest tends to develop in certain recession-resistant companies. Although such stocks lack the glamour of the fallen market leaders, they are characterized by a degree of stability that

is desirable when the economy faces a period of uncertainty and decline.

Utility stocks are generally regarded as defensive issues, since their slow but steady growth rate (5 to 7 percent) tends to hold up in recession years as well as in boom years. They are, however, very sensitive to interest rate changes, falling in price if interest rates rise sharply and increasing in price if interest rates decline. In addition to the shares of the electric and gas utilities, the shares of gold mining companies have tended to be effective defensive issues. The price of gold either rises or remains stable during recessions, while the cost of mining may decrease due to lower costs. Other defensive issues are found among companies whose products suffer relatively little during recession periods. These include shares in companies producing tobacco, snuff, soft drinks, gum, and candy bars. The shares of companies that provide the essentials of life, particularly foods and drugs, tend to be stable during economic downturns. Packaged foods and grocery chain companies are examples.

Speculative Stocks   Webster's defines *speculation* as a "transaction or venture the profits of which are conjectural." In this sense all common stock investment is speculative. When you buy shares you have no promise, no certainty, that the money you receive when you ultimately sell your stock will be more, or less than, or the same as the number of dollars you paid originally. Since they provide a variable rather than a fixed dollar outcome, common shares are speculative in Webster's sense. Yet in the accepted parlance of the Street, speculative shares or speculative stocks have a more limited meaning. High-flying glamour stocks are speculative. Likewise, hot new issues and penny mining stocks are speculative. Other types of speculative stocks can be identified as they come and go from time to time. Some speculative stocks are easy to identify; others are more difficult. The high-flying glamour stocks can usually be recognized by their very high price-earnings ratios. Speculative buying of these shares would appear to be discounting the future quite far ahead.

There usually comes a point in a bull market

when small, hitherto unknown companies go public or little new companies are formed, and the offerings of the low-priced shares of these companies find a fierce speculative demand. Prices double, triple, or even quadruple within a few days after the shares are issued. Dynatronics, issued at 7½, went to 25 overnight. Cove Vitamin soared from 3⅛ to 60. Simulmatics, a two-year-old company with a net worth of minus $21,000, offered stock to the public at 2, and within a few hours it was quoted at 9. While stocks in companies and names ending in "tron" or "ics" were particularly coveted, even prosaically named issues such as Leaseway Transportation and Mother's Cookie Company leaped 50 percent or more in price. Many of these companies usually have meteoric rises, shooting across the investment horizon and then disappearing.

Playboy Enterprises came out at 23½, but in a matter of weeks, like an aging "bunny," it sagged

TABLE 12–8
Klinker Index

	Recent Price	High	Percent Decline	Former Business
Acme Missiles & Constr.	0.06	25	−100.0	Missile launching sites
AITS	0	93	−100.0	Travel agency
Airlift Int.	0.19	12	−98.4	Airfreight carrier
Alphanumeric	0.10	84	−100.0	Computer peripheral equipment
Astrodata	0.25	36	−99.3	Electronic data equipment
Beck Indust.	0.01	42	−100.0	Leased shoe departments
Bermec*	0.05	31	−100.0	Truck leasing
Borne Chem.	1.12	27	−96.0	Textile oils
Cognitronics	1.12	39	−97.1	Optical scanning
Commonwealth United†	0.25	25	−99.0	Conglomerate/theaters
Corporation S	0.38	64	−99.4	Data services
Dolly Madison*	0.13	47	−100.0	Ice cream, furniture
Elcor Chem.	3.38	80	−96.0	New sulfur process
Energy Conver. Devices	4.25	155	−97.2	Electronic breakthrough
FAS Int.	0.38	63	−99.4	Famous artist schools
Farrington*	0	66	−100.0	Optical scanning
Fotochrome	0.06	25	−100.0	Film processing
Four Seasons Equity	0	49	−100.0	Financing nursing homes
Four Seasons Nursing‡	3.38	91	−96.3	Nursing homes
Gale Indust.	0.50	26	−98.1	Heat-conductive windowpanes
R. Hoe	0.06	60	−100.0	Printing presses
King Resources	0.08	34	−100.0	Computerized oil development
Liquidonics	0.06	155	−100.0	Magnetic door locks
Management Assistance	0.50	46	−99.0	Leasing data equipment
Nat'l Student Marketing	0.30	36	−99.1	Still trying to determine
Omega Equities	0.05	36	−100.0	Questionable ventures
Panacolor	0.06	40	−100.0	Color film processing
Performance Systems (i.e., Minnie Pearl)	0.05	24	−100.0	Greasy chicken franchisor
Transitron	0.50	60	−99.0	Semiconductors
Viatron*	0.10	62	−100.0	Computer systems

* In bankruptcy or receivership.
† Name change 1/73—Iota Industries.
‡ Name change 11/72—Anta Corp.
Source: Spencer Trask & Co., Incorporated.

to 15½. National Video was issued at 3¾, soared to 120, and then went into bankruptcy. Four Seasons Nursing Homes was a hot new issue when it went public at $11 a share in 1968. It soared to more than $100 a share the same year. After a two-for-one split, it shot up again—to 90¾—in 1969, went into receivership in 1970, and in 1972 a number of those who had been associated with the stock were indicted for alleged fraud. Other examples of speculative issues which have had a sad demise are shown in Table 12–8, which is entitled the Klinker Index.

Styles in Stocks

Fads and enthusiasms can be either very costly or very profitable to investors, or both, depending on investor's footwork. Or, as one Wall Street pundit put it: "If you want to make your pile, you got to be in style." Reviewing past enthusiasms (which in due course faded), one can go back as far as World War I, during the course of which Bethlehem Steel was in high fashion. It jumped from $10 a share in 1914 to $200 in 1915. In the 1920s talking pictures and radio swept the country. Warner Brothers Pictures soared from 9¾ in 1927 to 138 in 1928. RCA skyrocketed from 12½ in 1922 to 573 in 1929. Bank stocks took off in the mid-1920s. The ordinarily conservative First National City Bank of New York (now Citibank), for example, jumped from the equivalent of 131 in 1926 to 580 in 1929. In the ensuing collapse the bluest of blue chips fell dismally (see Table 12–9). With the repeal of Prohibition, in 1933, National Distillers became a magic word, and the stock jumped from 13 in 1932 to a peak of 124⅞ one year later, and then is too went out of style.

Aluminum stocks were very much in style in the early 1950s. Alcoa went from 46 in 1949 to the equivalent of 352 in 1955. Reynolds Metals rose from 19 to the equivalent 300 over the same period. The advent of the computers helped push IBM from 40 to over 600 and Control Data from 2 to over 100. The ephemeral popularity of Metre-

TABLE 12–9

A Dozen Good Common Stocks, 1929–1932

Company	1929	1932
Anaconda Copper	174⅞	3
AT&T	310¼	70¼
Chrysler Corporation	87	5
Du Pont	503	22
General Motors	224	7⅝
Montgomery Ward	156⅞	3½
New York Central	256½	8¾
Standard Oil of New Jersey	83	19⅞
Standard Oil of California	81⅞	15⅛
Sears, Roebuck	197½	9⅞
U.S. Steel	261¾	21¼
Western Union	272¼	12⅜

cal as a dieting fad sent Mead Johnson shares up by 230 percent, but then the style changed and sales fell 31 percent in 1962, net fell 90 percent, to just three cents a share, and Mead Johnson stock went down to its 1958 pre-Metrecal level.

Electronics shares boomed in the late 1950s. Fairchild Camera, which had risen from 13¾ (adjusted) to 144½ per share, fell to 64½, though if investors held on during the deep gloom, they might have had the satisfaction of seeing the stock rise again during 1967, from 73 to 134. Then Fairchild ran into rough weather, and by 1970 its stock reached a low of 18.

Conglomerates were all the rage in the late 1960s. Litton peaked in 1967, selling at 120. By 1972 it was down to 10.

Pollution control stocks waxed and waned. The advent of computers pushed IBM from 40 to over 600. Technology stocks rose and fell spectacularly. Control Data went to 163½ and then fell to 28¾, but has since come back partway. Memorex reached a bull market high of 173⅞ and then fell to 14⅞. Telex ranged from a high of 159½ to a low of 20¾.

When the dollar was devalued in 1971 and again in 1973, and the de facto price of gold rose from $42 an ounce to a high of $198 an ounce, gold shares zoomed as they did again in 1978 when gold rose to $245 an ounce. Dome Mines rose from a low of 17⅞ in the 1960s to 73 in 1971 and 155 in 1973. It fell to 30 in 1975 and was back up to 95 in 1978.

After the oil embargo and the OPEC cartel's sharp increases in oil prices, the spotlight in the United States turned to coal. Investors bid up the coal stocks rapidly, in 1975–77. North American Coal rose from 24¼ to 55¼; Pittston Company from 17⅞ to 47⅛; Westmoreland Coal, from 18⅛ to 65¾; and St. Joe Minerals, from 17⅛ to 50.

The legalization of gambling in 1978 saw Resorts International jump from a low of 6⅜ to an adjusted high of 84. The *Wall Street Journal* reported that on September 14 Resorts International Class B rose $54 a share to close at $266. Another similarly oriented company, Bally Manufacturing Corporation, rose from 15⅝ to 71¾ in 1978.

In recent years the term *concept stock* has become popular. If Wall Street believes the story behind the stock, the stock will go up—even if the *concept* ultimately proves to have been just puffery.

Keeping up with styles in stocks is, then, in many cases, an important part of the selection process. There has never been a time when some stocks were not advancing against a declining market. Spotting those stocks early and getting out before the usual collapse should be the goal of every intelligent investor. Sometimes riding *concepts* through their upswing is worth more in total return than fundamental analysis.

The penny mining and oil shares are perhaps the lowest level of speculative stocks. A broker specializing in such shares circulated his market report and offers extensively by mail, and his combination packets read almost like a stamp dealer's. In one report he plugged Trans-Mountain Uranium Company, Globe Hill Mining Company, and Santa Fe International. The mail-order broker's packet offer read:

> *Combination Offer*—Following combination orders will be filled for whatever number combinations desired while can locate stock in above 3 companies to fill at price shown below (bonus, 1000 United Empire Gold with each combination order):
> 1,000 Trans-Mountain, 1,000 Santa Fe and 5,000 Globe Hill Mining, $63.75.

Thus common stock investment can range from buying shares in the staid and stable Bank of New York, which has paid dividends uninterruptedly since 1785, to buying Trans-Mountain Uranium at two cents per share. Obviously, with so wide a diversity in common stock, generalizations are both difficult and hazardous.

BOND INVESTMENT

No more than one-fifth of the public considers itself knowledgeable about corporate bonds, Treasury bills, preferred stock or convertible securities. But these are perceived as relatively low-risk investments, and the public generally considers low-risk investments as appropriate for keeping up with inflation and meeting other important financial goals.[5]

Except for the affluent high-income families, who are acquainted with tax-free bonds, the general public knows practically nothing about bond investment. In recent years the high yields, 8½–10 percent offered on good or high-grade bonds have brought some additional interest in the bond market, but this has been mainly an institutional interest, not an individual interest. Several events have converged to make the bond market boom—and to make fools out of its doomsayers.

Corporate Bonds And The Small Investor

There are pitfalls for the small investor who puts his money into corporate bonds.

Corporations' fixed-income securities have a lot of investment appeal because their yields are higher than the current income of other securities.

---

[5] *Public Attitudes toward Investing,* New York Stock Exchange, June 1978.

In the winter of 1978, Mountain States Telephone (an AT&T subsidiary) triple-rated bonds—the highest quality—sold to yield 9.25 percent. Medium-grade corporate bonds, such as those of the Standard Oil Company of Ohio, sold to yield 8.5 percent.

What are the pitfalls? There is the difficulty and expense of trading small amounts. Corporate bonds are usually sold in units of $1,000 but they trade in the over-the-counter market in blocks of $100,000. Anything below this amount is considered an odd lot, takes time to trade, and is expensive. The spread between the buying price and the selling price is much wider on odd lots than on round lots.

Many corporate bonds may be called early, and the owner of a 25-year bond who thought that a yield of 8–8½ percent had been nailed down for a quarter of a century, found that when interest rates dipped lower a few years after purchase, the bond was called and replaced by one carrying an interest rate 1½ or 2 points lower.

Bond Investment Timing

When a bull market begins to near its peak, when blue chips begin to sag, when speculative highfliers and low-priced cats and dogs begin to get the play, when stock yields fall to 3 percent or less and the yield spread between stocks and high-grade bonds widens to 4 percent in favor of bonds, when business is booming and interest rates are tight—then the shrewd institutional investment manager who has choice and flexibility will quietly withhold funds from new common stock commitments and place the funds in high-grade bonds.

When prosperity tops out into recession, when business and common stock prices begin to slide, high-grade bonds come into favor. As interest rates decline, high-grade bond prices tend to rise. High-grade bond prices tend to vary inversely with interest rates and with common stock prices if inflation is not present. As recession turns into recovery, reverse trends set in. Interest rates and common stock prices which have fallen start to rise, and

"I know that's the correct term, Finley, but couldn't we call them something else beside 'Sinking Fund Bonds'?"

Reprinted by permission *The Wall Street Journal*

high-grade bond prices tend to weaken. Generally speaking, by high-grade bonds are meant those that are rated AAA or AA by the rating services.

The primary investment interest in bonds comes from institutions which must pay obligations in fixed numbers of dollars, such as banks and insurance companies. If you have a $50,000 life insurance policy, for example, at some point in the future—whether 5 years or 35 years hence—the insurance company will have to pay $50,000. If it invests in securities—bonds—which will return it a fixed number of dollars, it is in a position to meet its obligation. It does not matter in this case whether the dollars that the insurance company pays out buy half as little as they did when they were invested. The insurance company has a fixed dollar obligation, not a purchasing power obligation. The individual investor may shy away from high-grade bonds because of the purchasing power risk, but most institutional investors have less need to worry about this problem. Individual investors, particularly wealthier ones, have a special interest in certain types of bonds, particularly tax-exempts and convertibles. As a hedge against recession and deflation, however, switching from common stock to high-grade bonds as a boom tops out may be an excellent, profitable move for any investor who is clever enough to perceive the trend.

Bond Prices And Interest Rates

The principal price risk in high-grade bonds is related to the trend of interest rates. If a commercial bank holds high-grade bonds, and interest rates start to rise, and the bank must sell its bonds because funds are needed for some other purpose, such as expanding business loans, then a capital loss results. Why? If the bonds carry a coupon interest rate of, say 6 percent, and bonds of similar quality are now being issued with coupons of 7½ percent or higher, no one will be willing to purchase the 6 percent bonds at par value. The unwillingness of buyers to pay the previously prevailing prices, coupled with the actual selling pressure of investors who are seeking to raise funds for other investments, forces the price of the old 6 percent issue down.

However, if inflation rates accelerate during a recession, *as in 1973–74,* lenders will demand a premium and interest rates on new high-grade bonds may increase to provide a margin for inflation. The poor investment performance of bonds as compared to common stocks may be seen in Table 12–10.

Types of Bonds

Bonds may be either secured or unsecured, and they may range from first-mortgage bonds on the one hand to subordinated debentures on the other. The security behind a bond, although important, is not crucial. The earning power, financial condition, and quality of management are vital. Because of this, one company's unsecured bonds may be rated higher than another company's secured obligations. For example, the debentures of AT&T are rated higher than the first-mortgage bonds of Indianapolis Power and Light. The debentures of Southern Bell Telephone have a higher rating than the first-mortgage bonds of Missouri Power and Light.

Mortgage bonds are secured by a conditional lien on part or all of a company's property. If the company defaults (fails to pay interest or repay principal), the bondholders, through the trustee appointed to represent them and look after their rights, may foreclose the mortgage and take over the pledged property.

Debentures

Debentures are unsecured bonds protected only by the general credit of the borrowing corporation. If there are no mortgage bonds, and debentures are the senior issues, they may rate very high. AT&T, for example, has only debentures outstanding. There are no bonds senior to these. Debentures may contain a "covenant of equal coverage." Which means that if any mortgage bond is issued in the future, which ordinarily would take precedence over the debentures, the issuer agrees to secure the debentures equally. In some states the law requires that this be done. All direct domestic obligations of federal, state, and municipal governments in the United States are debentures.

Since debentures are protected only by the general promise to pay and the debenture holder is merely a general creditor in the event of default, debentures can usually be sold only by corporations enjoying very high credit standings. The value of a debenture must be judged wholly in terms of the overall financial status and earnings outlook of the issuer, which is the best basis for evaluating any bond.

Convertible Bonds

Convertible bonds are bonds which may be exchanged, at the option of the holder, for a specified amount of other securities (usually common stock) of the issuing corporation. Theoretically, the convertible bond would appear to be an ideal security, since it affords, on the one hand, the relative safety of a fixed-income creditor obligation and, on the other, an opportunity to share in the prospective profits of the company. Thus it would seem to provide both relative safety and a hedge against inflation.

TABLE 12–10
Securities Markets of the Years 1958–1977

	Jan. 1, 1958	Jan. 1, 1963	Jan. 1, 1968	Dec. 31, 1977	Percent Change 10 Years 1968–1977	Percent Change 15 Years 1963–1977	Percent Change 20 Years 1958–1977
Cost-of-living index	85.2	91.0	101.6	186.1	+83%	+105%	+118%
Value of the dollar	117.4	109.8	98.4	53.7	−45	−51	−54
Dow-Jones Industrial Average	435.69	652.10	905.11	831.17	−8	+27	+91
Standard & Poor's 500 Stock Index	39.99	63.10	96.47	95.10	−1	+51	+138
New York Stock Exchange index	21.11	33.81	53.83	52.50	−2	+55	+149
Value Line composite average	—	88.20	152.89	93.92	−39	+6	—
S&P utilities	32.14	61.09	66.08	54.24	−18	−11	+69
S&P railroads	20.95	32.73	43.71	47.44	+9	+45	+126
S&P high-grade corporate bonds	102.7	97.34	75.41	58.01	−23	−40	−44
S&P municipal bonds	107.5	113.0	93.33	80.27	−14	−29	−25
S&P long-term government bonds	99.17	90.06	75.29	56.55	−25	−37	−43
S&P preferred stocks	156.0	158.3	117.8	89.29	−24	−44	−43
Savings bank deposit	100.0	100.0	100.0	100.0	0	0	0

Source: *Johnson Charts*, 1978 edition.

The market value of convertible bonds tends to rise as the price of the common into which they are convertible rises. On the other hand, in a declining market, the price of a convertible bond declines until the conversion parity point is reached; that is, the conversion feature no longer has any value, and the bond, therefore, sells solely on the basis of its fixed-income and safety status. Thus you may conclude that two considerations affect the market value of a convertible bond: *(a)* its actual value as a fixed-income obligation and *(b)* its potential value in terms of the stock into which it may be converted.

Callable Bonds

Callable bonds are bonds which may be redeemed by the issuing company prior to the maturity date. Why should a corporation, when it has borrowed for a term of, say, 20 years, decide to retire its debt in a shorter period of time? Usually

"Well, if you consider a four-hour briefing on convertible subordinated debentures a good time—then I had a good time!"

The Commercial and Financial Chronicle

it does so because it finds that, due to a decline in interest rates, it can borrow more cheaply now. It therefore calls the old issue with the higher coupon rate and sells a new one at a lower rate. Some bonds are noncallable.

Financial Analysis and Bond Evaluation

Although the technical aspects of bonds which have been described thus far are all useful in judging the quality and soundness of an issue, the real basis for evaluation lies in the financial status and earning power of the borrowing corporation or government. The farsightedness and efficiency of the management, the outlook for the industry, the position of the particular firm in the industry, and the soundness of the company's internal finances as reflected in its balance sheet and income account must all be carefully considered.

The security behind a bond is, in itself, no guarantee of soundness, since the value of pledged property is often dependent on the earning power of a corporation. If the corporation fails, its fixed assets may prove to be worth very little. A good example is the Seaboard–All Florida Railway's first-mortgage 6's, which sold in 1931 at one cent on the dollar soon after completion of the road. In selecting bonds, it is best to try to choose a company that will avoid trouble rather than seek to protect yourself in the event of trouble (see Figure 12–3).

Tax Exempt Bonds

Wealthier investors find that the tax-exempt features of state and municipal bonds are quite attractive. If you or your parents are in this category, a simple formula will show you the percentage yield which a bond or other security, with fully taxable income, must give in order to provide an aftertax yield equivalent to that of a given tax-exempt yield. Find your tax bracket and then apply this formula:

Tax-exempt yield ÷ (100% − Tax bracket %)
= Taxable equivalent yield

FIGURE 12–3
Investment Yields and Interest Rates

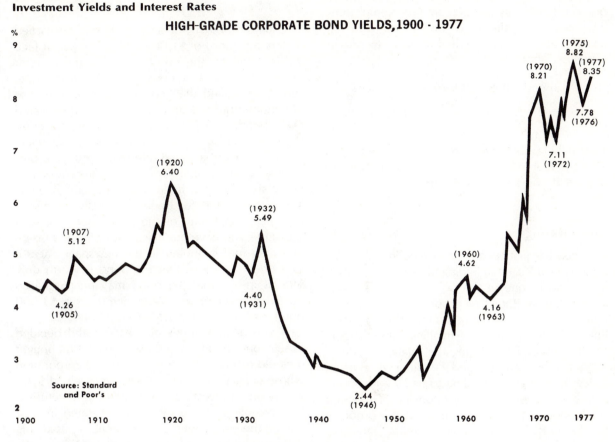

HIGH-GRADE CORPORATE BONDS

Bond yields in 1975 were the highest of the 20th century as shown by the chart. They were very likely the highest in our history, although Standard and Poor's Corporate Bond Yield Indexes only go back to 1900. Since bond prices fluctuate in inverse proportion to yields, high-grade bond prices in 1975 were the lowest on record. Many Bond Funds and Balanced Funds have been taking advantage of these low bond prices and commensurate high yields in 1974 through 1977. The following table shows major high and low points of bond yields and prices over the past 78 years.

Year	Yield	Price Index	Year	Yield	Price Index
1902	4.29%	96.13	1960	4.62%	91.97
1907	5.12	86.09	1963	4.16	97.79
1920	6.40	73.14	1970	8.21	59.00
1931	4.40	94.72	1972	7.11	67.10
1932	5.49	82.05	1975	8.82	55.53
1946	2.44	124.60			

Source: *Johnson's Charts,* 1978 edition.

Assume that you are in the 55 percent tax bracket. If you buy a 6 percent tax-exempt bond, what would an alternative investment with fully taxable income have to yield in order to provide 6 percent after taxes?

$$6\% \div (100\% - 55\%) = ?$$
$$\frac{6\%}{45\%} = 13.33\%$$

Your fully taxable investment would have to yield 13.33 percent to give you an aftertax return of 6 percent if you are in the 55 percent tax bracket.

Bond Ratings

When you first become interested in a particular bond, an initial step in finding out something about it is to go to one of the financial services, such as Standard & Poor's or Moody's, and see what rating it has assigned to the bond.[6] Although these financial services are not infallible, their experts are accustomed to judging the relative merits of fixed-income securities, and the rating will give you a clear idea of the approximate quality of the bond. It is a useful orientation for looking further into the merits, or the lack of merits, of the proposed purchase. Perhaps when you see the rating assigned, you will no longer be interested in the bond, since it may be classed as speculative; and you would have little interest in buying a speculative bond, which is really a contradiction in terms. While these services can be obtained in banks, brokerage houses, or large libraries, Standard & Poor's publishes a *Monthly Bond Guide*, which provides, among other information, the bond ratings. Thus, "General Tel. Co., Ohio, 1st 7⅝s 2001" means the first-mortgage bond issue of the General Telephone Company of Ohio paying 7⅝ percent interest per annum and maturing in 2001.

---

[6] For further detail, see Hugh C. Sherwood, *How Corporate and Municipal Debt Is Rated*, (New York: John Wiley & Sons, 1976); and *The Rating Game*, report of the Twentieth Century Fund Task Force on Municipal Bond Credit Rating (New York: The Twentieth Century Fund, 1974).

Bond Prices, Coupons, and Yields

Usually, though not always, bonds are issued in denominations of $1,000. This is the par or face value stated on the bond, and it is the amount on which interest is computed. The bond rate, sometimes called the "coupon rate" in the case of coupon bonds, is the simple interest rate, stated in the bond, at which the interest payment is computed. If you buy a bond which has a par value of $1,000 and the stated rate of interest is 10 percent, you will be paid $100 a year interest, or $50 every six months if interest is paid semiannually. The price quoted for bonds is usually expressed as a percentage rate of the par value. That is, a year after you have purchased your $1,000 bond, you may find it quoted in the newspaper at 98. This does *not* mean that the bond is worth only $98. It means that the bond may be purchased for 98 percent of par value: $980 for a $1,000 bond, or $98,000 for a $100,000 bond.

If you needed funds at the time and decided to sell your bond for $980, the person who bought it would receive $100 a year from the corporation whose obligation it was. When you received $100 a year on an investment of $1,000, your return—10 percent—was the same as the stated interest rate on the bond; but the new purchaser, assuming that he holds the bond just one year and then resells it to someone for $980, has received $100 for one year on an investment of $980. Clearly, he has received a return of more than 10 percent. His current yield is not the stated rate (the coupon rate) on the bond.

Investment officers of financial institutions and others dealing with bonds use an elaborate book of bond tables to determine the true yield when they know the coupon rate, the maturity, and the proposed purchase price of a bond. A page of a bond table is shown in Table 12–11.

Assume that you paid $971.80 for a bond with a 10 percent coupon and 13 years to run to maturity. If you had purchased the bond for $1,000, the coupon and the yield would have been identical—10 percent—as the table indicates; but since you purchased the bond at a considerable discount,

TABLE 12–11

A Page of a Bond Yield Table (10 percent coupon)

	11 YRS EVEN	11 YRS 6 MOS	12 YRS EVEN	12 YRS 6 MOS	13 YRS EVEN	13 YRS 6 MOS	14 YRS EVEN	14 YRS 6 MOS	15 YRS EVEN	15 YRS 6 MOS	16 YRS EVEN	16 YRS 6 MOS
YIELD												
7.00	122.75	123.43	124.09	124.72	125.34	125.93	126.50	127.05	127.59	128.10	128.60	129.09
7.10	121.89	122.54	123.16	123.77	124.35	124.92	125.47	125.99	126.50	126.99	127.47	127.93
7.20	121.03	121.65	122.25	122.83	123.38	123.92	124.44	124.94	125.43	125.90	126.35	126.78
7.30	120.18	120.77	121.34	121.89	122.42	122.94	123.43	123.91	124.37	124.81	125.24	125.66
7.40	119.34	119.90	120.44	120.97	121.47	121.96	122.43	122.88	123.32	123.74	124.15	124.54
7.50	118.50	119.04	119.56	120.05	120.53	121.00	121.44	121.87	122.29	122.69	123.07	123.44
7.60	117.68	118.19	118.68	119.15	119.60	120.04	120.46	120.87	121.26	121.64	122.01	122.36
7.70	116.86	117.34	117.81	118.25	118.68	119.10	119.50	119.88	120.25	120.61	120.95	121.28
7.80	116.05	116.51	116.94	117.37	117.77	118.17	118.54	118.91	119.25	119.59	119.91	120.22
7.90	115.25	115.68	116.09	116.49	116.87	117.24	117.60	117.94	118.27	118.58	118.89	119.18
8.00	114.45	114.86	115.25	115.62	115.98	116.33	116.66	116.98	117.29	117.59	117.87	118.15
8.10	113.66	114.04	114.41	114.76	115.10	115.43	115.74	116.04	116.33	116.61	116.87	117.13
8.20	112.88	113.24	113.58	113.91	114.23	114.53	114.83	115.11	115.38	115.63	115.88	116.12
8.30	112.11	112.44	112.76	113.07	113.37	113.65	113.92	114.18	114.43	114.68	114.91	115.13
8.40	111.34	111.65	111.95	112.24	112.51	112.78	113.03	113.27	113.50	113.73	113.94	114.15
8.50	110.58	110.87	111.15	111.41	111.67	111.91	112.14	112.37	112.58	112.79	112.99	113.18
8.60	109.83	110.10	110.35	110.60	110.83	111.06	111.27	111.48	111.68	111.87	112.05	112.22
8.70	109.09	109.33	109.56	109.79	110.00	110.21	110.41	110.60	110.78	110.95	111.12	111.28
8.80	108.35	108.57	108.78	108.99	109.19	109.37	109.55	109.72	109.89	110.05	110.20	110.34
8.90	107.62	107.82	108.01	108.20	108.37	108.54	108.71	108.86	109.01	109.15	109.29	109.42
9.00	106.89	107.07	107.25	107.41	107.57	107.73	107.87	108.01	108.14	108.27	108.39	108.51
9.10	106.17	106.34	106.49	106.64	106.78	106.92	107.04	107.17	107.29	107.40	107.51	107.61
9.20	105.46	105.60	105.74	105.87	105.99	106.11	106.23	106.34	106.44	106.54	106.63	106.72
9.30	104.76	104.88	105.00	105.11	105.22	105.32	105.42	105.51	105.60	105.69	105.77	105.85
9.40	104.06	104.16	104.26	104.36	104.45	104.54	104.62	104.70	104.77	104.85	104.91	104.98
9.50	103.37	103.45	103.54	103.61	103.69	103.76	103.83	103.89	103.96	104.01	104.07	104.13
9.60	102.68	102.75	102.81	102.88	102.94	102.99	103.05	103.10	103.15	103.19	103.24	103.28
9.70	102.00	102.05	102.10	102.15	102.19	102.23	102.27	102.31	102.35	102.38	102.41	102.44
9.80	101.33	101.36	101.39	101.42	101.45	101.48	101.51	101.53	101.55	101.58	101.60	101.62
9.90	100.66	100.68	100.69	100.71	100.72	100.74	100.75	100.76	100.77	100.78	100.79	100.81
10.00	100.00	100.00	100.00	100.00	100.00	100.00	100.00	100.00	100.00	100.00	100.00	100.00
10.10	99.34	99.33	99.31	99.30	99.28	99.27	99.26	99.25	99.24	99.22	99.21	99.20
10.20	98.70	98.66	98.63	98.60	98.58	98.55	98.53	98.50	98.48	98.46	98.44	98.42
10.30	98.05	98.01	97.96	97.92	97.88	97.84	97.80	97.77	97.73	97.70	97.67	97.64
10.40	97.41	97.35	97.29	97.24	97.18	97.13	97.08	97.04	96.99	96.95	96.91	96.88
10.50	96.78	96.71	96.63	96.56	96.50	96.43	96.37	96.32	96.26	96.21	96.16	96.12
10.60	96.16	96.07	95.98	95.90	95.82	95.74	95.67	95.61	95.54	95.48	95.42	95.37
10.70	95.54	95.43	95.33	95.24	95.15	95.06	94.98	94.90	94.83	94.76	94.69	94.63
10.80	94.92	94.80	94.69	94.58	94.48	94.38	94.29	94.20	94.12	94.04	93.97	93.90
10.90	94.31	94.18	94.05	93.93	93.82	93.71	93.61	93.52	93.42	93.34	93.25	93.18
11.00	93.71	93.56	93.42	93.29	93.17	93.05	92.94	92.83	92.73	92.64	92.55	92.46
11.10	93.11	92.95	92.80	92.66	92.52	92.40	92.27	92.16	92.05	91.95	91.85	91.76
11.20	92.52	92.35	92.18	92.03	91.88	91.75	91.62	91.49	91.38	91.26	91.16	91.06
11.30	91.93	91.75	91.57	91.41	91.25	91.10	90.96	90.83	90.71	90.59	90.48	90.37
11.40	91.35	91.15	90.97	90.79	90.63	90.47	90.37	90.18	90.05	89.92	89.80	89.69
11.50	90.77	90.56	90.37	90.18	90.01	89.84	89.68	89.53	89.39	89.26	89.14	89.02

LEHMAN BROTHERS HIGH YIELD TABLES   SEMI–ANNUAL INTEREST PAYMENTS   INTEREST RATE 10.000

Source: Lehman Brothers, *High Yield Tables*, p. 727.

your yield must obviously be higher than 10 percent. Looking down the 13-year column, you come to the figure $97.18. Looking across to the left, you find the exact yield—10.40 percent. In similar fashion, somewhere in the 1,200 pages of this particular set of tables, you would be able to find the effective yield of any bond with a maturity of from six months to 50 years bearing a coupon rate of from 7 to 11.95 percent. Other sets of tables cover rates below 7 percent; still others cover maturities of from 50 to 100 years; and there is a special set of tables covering maturities of less than six months. There is, therefore, no need to be concerned with the exact details of bond yield computations, since it is much easier to use prepared bond tables. Bond experts and investment specialists do.

PREFERRED STOCK

From an investment point of view, preferred stocks are more like bonds than common stocks. The return on the investment, if one gets it, is fixed and limited. Of course, preferred stock, unlike most bonds, has no maturity, and the preferred stockholder is a stockholder, that is, an owner, not a creditor. Preferred stocks are issued to attract investors who wish a safer and less changeable income than they can get from common stocks. For most of the last 30 years, high-grade preferred stocks have tended to yield more than high-grade bonds, but this extra payment is largely to compensate for extra risk.

The rights of the preferred stockholder are to be found in the corporation's charter. Dividends on preferred stock my be cumulative or noncumulative. Cumulative dividends which are not paid when they should regularly be paid (ordinarily once a quarter) accumulate for the benefit of the preferred stockholder, and as a matter of law they must be paid when the earnings of the corporation permit, *before* dividends can be paid on the common. If the preferred is noncumulative, the preferred stockholder has no special claim for dividends which have been passed.

Ordinarily the return on preferred stock is definite, and the owner of preferred stock does not share in earnings beyond his stated percent. In some cases, however, a special type of preferred stock, known as "participating preferred," is issued. Then the stock is permitted to share in earnings, if the earnings are large enough to so warrant, in excess of the stated rate of dividend, after the common stock holder has received his share. Some preferred stock is callable; that is, the issuing company can retire the stock, usually at a small premium.

Sometimes preferred stock is issued with a conversion feature which allows it to be exchanged for common stock at a given ratio. Convertible preferreds have been popular because they give the cautious investor a steady return but also provide a hedge against inflation, since conversion into common is possible. Such conversion proves advantageous when earnings increase and common stock rises in price. Ideally, the best preferred to buy would be cumulative, participating, convertible preferred, but there are few such animals. Indeed, for the small investor, preferred stock has the disadvantages of both bonds and common and the advantages of neither.

REAL ESTATE INVESTMENT

Over the last decade the lures of tax-free income, current returns ranging from 10 to 16 percent, substantial capital gains, and, in addition, an excellent hedge against inflation have combined to heighten interest in real estate investment and speculation.

Billion Dollar Trinkets

One last myth about Manhattan real estate deserves to be exploded. Every school kid knows that crafty Peter Minuit put one over on the Manhattoes Indians in 1626 by buying their island for $24 worth of doodads. But, Salomon Bros.' Sidney Homer, author of *The History of Interest Rates,* provides figures that show that the Indians got the best of the deal. Had they taken a boat to Holland, invested the $24 in Dutch securities returning 6% per year and kept the money invested at 6%, they would now have $13 billion. With that sum they could buy back all the land on the island, and still have $4 billion left for trinkets. Or the Indians could keep the money invested at 6%, so it could continue yielding $780 million a year, without the risk of doing business amid urban decay.

The question isn't who owns New York. It's who the hell wants to?

From "Who Owns New York?" *Forbes,* June 1, 1971.

There are a wide and unfortunately bewildering variety of ways to invest or speculate in real estate. Generally, the main channels are buying your own home, co-op, or condominium apartment; investing in raw land or in mortgages; participating in real estate syndicates; buying shares in real estate

FIGURE 12–4
U.S. Farm Real Estate Values: (per acre)

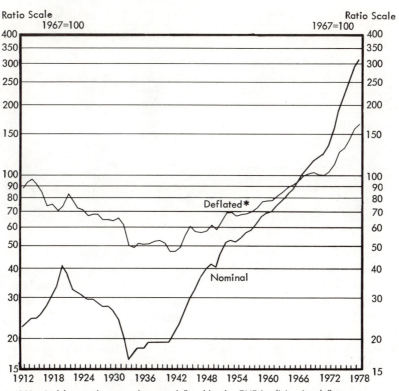

* Nominal farm real estate values are deflated by the GNP implicit price deflator.
Source: U.S. Department of Agriculture; and The Review of the Federal Reserve Bank of St.
Cour, May 1978, p. 17.

companies; and investing in real estate investment trusts.

Raw Land

On the average, an acre of U.S. farmland which sold for $200 as recently as 1971, has more than doubled in value. See Figure 12–4 and Table 12–12. Farmers today regularly increase their wealth more from the growing value of their land than from tilling the soil.

Amfac, Inc., is Hawaii's biggest company, rich in land and other valuable assets. It recently sold eight beachfront acres on the island of Maui for $1 million per acre. The land cost $10 an acre in 1893, when Amfac purchased it. Subsequently,

Amfac invested about $17,000 per acre for improvements. It owns 40 more acres next to the 8, and another 65,000 acres in all, not all of which is beachfront, however. All over Hawaii, buyers are competing in lotteries for the right to buy new one and two bedroom condos or town houses, still on the drawing board, and selling between $165,000–$270,000 apiece, that Barrons[7] describes in an article ironically entitled "Little Grass Shacks?" Typical of the phenomenon is a two bedroom town house in Maui sold in 1975, before building, for $159,000 and then some months before completion in 1977, for $230,000 and recently for $350,000.

---

[7] *Barrons,* December 4, 1978.

TABLE 12–12
Farm Real Estate Prices ($ per acre)

	Ala.	Fla.	Ga.	La.	Miss.	Tenn.	Average* District States	U.S.
1971	227	378	256	350	238	277	284	202
1972	238	404	292	382	242	303	306	218
1973	270	466	333	406	271	349	346	245
1974	337	613	432	474	344	421	436	303
1975	370	692	486	518	386	477	487	343
1976	410	732	488	545	388	507	509	390
1977	437	783	524	590	411	556	548	456

Note: Prices as of March 1 for 1971–75; as of February 1 for 1976 and 1977.
* Weighted by 1974 Census estimates of land in farms in each state.
Source: *Farm Real Estate Market Developments,* U.S. Department of Agriculture; and *Economic Review,* Federal Reserve Bank of Atlanta, March–April 1978, p. 46.

"Land speculators play Disney's money machine—the new Florida playland has pushed land values to 500 times their former worth," wrote *Business Week.* The 27,000-acre tract on which Disney World is located, some 25 miles southwest of Orlando, Florida, was assembled at an average price of $350 per acre. Land nearby rose to a range of $75,000 to $130,000 per acre for choice motel sites.

As cities grow and the urban pattern encroaches upon suburbia, land in the path of the expansion increases in value. Over time, the sheer growth of population tends to enhance the value of raw land. Seemingly, all you have to do is follow the bus line out, see where the vacant lots start, and buy a few. It isn't that easy, however. Towns don't necessarily grow in all directions, and you may pick the wrong end of town. You can't borrow money on land from banks, insurance companies, or savings and loan associations. You either sink your own cash, or you put up a down payment and give the seller a purchase money mortgage for the main amount. If you have to hold the lot or lots for a while, waiting for the growth of population and the enhancement of values to occur, this can cost you a good sum each year without bringing any return. Some experts estimate that your lots must increase in value 12 to 15 percent a year to provide a gain equal to the gain you could obtain in more conventional, forms of investment. Also you may be locked in. You may want to sell and find no one who wants to buy. Or, on the other hand, you may be one of the fortunate ones, and double or triple your money in a few years. It's a tricky operation.

The land rush has reached an almost ludicrous pitch. In some areas, there are more lots on the market than any conceivable housing demand can justify. New Mexico officials estimate that more than 1 million acres of the state have been laid out in small lot subdivisions—enough to house eight times the present population if the land were actually developed.

Prospective buyers can now avoid buying swampland or cliffs. The federal law that set up the Office of Interstate Land Sales Registration in the U.S. Department of Housing and Urban Development requires companies selling land to register with HUD and give each potential customer a factual property report on developments, under threat of criminal penalties. There, the prospect will find information on such things as water and sewer availability, the existence of liens on the property, the number of houses in the development that are currently sold or occupied, and the type of title that the buyer will receive. A seller who fulfills HUD requirements and provides a property report is in the clear, even if the property is worthless.

"If you designate the property for what it is," says the head of HUD's Office of Interstate Land Sales Registration, "you can sell it."

Not too long ago, a popular book warned that buying country property had pitfalls as well as pleasures. The gist of the author's message was that most people's dream of a cottage in the country is just that—a dream. The reality requires about twice as much time, money, and effort as the average buyer expects to expend. There are no bargains left within two or three hours of a major city. The buyer must decide either to go farther out—six or seven hours—or to make do with less land than desired. Raw land requires cash since it can rarely be financed. Country houses, too, present problems. Buyers often say, "I want a place that you can't see from the road and that I can't see the road from." What they forget is that this means they will probably be responsible for plowing a half mile of their own driveway when it snows. Despite the drawbacks, however, it is estimated that 2 to 3 million families own country homes.

Real Estate Syndicates

In the real estate syndicate you obtain the benefit of professional real estate judgment, at least in theory. The real estate syndicate is a limited partnership formed to offer participations to numerous nonprofessional investors. Very popular in the 1950s, it enabled the smaller investor to participate in ventures involving higher cost, higher yield properties that would otherwise have been available only to wealthier investors. Partnership shares were sold in units of from $500 to $5,000, and even higher in semiprivate syndicates. The yields ranged from 8 to 15 percent, much higher than the usual returns on stocks and bonds. The key advantage of the syndicate was the tax-free cash flow through accelerated depreciation.

> "Buy land," said Will Rogers. "They aren't making any more of it." Not true. At least 25 percent of Manhattan Island has been created by landfill.

Usually, half or more of syndicate yields came from depreciation and were therefore a return of capital that was taxable as income. This advantage needs to be understood clearly, because it lies at the bottom of the attractiveness of much real estate investment.

The use of depreciation to achieve tax free income may be seen in the following hypothetical example.

Assume that property has been bought for $1 million—$900,000 for the building and $100,000 for the land. The cash payment was $400,000, and a 6 percent mortgage was secured for the $600,000 balance. The annual payments on the mortgage are $45,000, including principal and interest. Rent comes in at $100,000 a year, and operating expenses, including insurance, repairs, real estate taxes, and management, are $19,000. Here is a statement showing how tax free income of $36,000 a year could be paid to the owners of the building.

Profit and Loss for Income Tax Purposes

Rent income		$100,000
Expenses:		
Mortgage interest	$36,000	
Depreciation (5 percent)	45,000	
Operating expenses	19,000	
Total expenses		$100,000
Net profit or loss		–0–

As you can see, here is a property that made no profit, and therefore paid no income tax, but was able to give its owners a 9 percent return on a cash investment of $400,000. This technique can be carried even further. If a faster rate of depreciation is used, the owners may not only get a tax-free distribution but receive a tax loss in addition, which they may use to reduce their other income.

The syndicate appeared to be a way in which a small investor could participate in a high-return, tax-free real estate investment, avoid the headaches of property management, and be in partnership with professional operators. Although some of the earlier syndicates worked out well, later ones paid excessively high prices for properties, underestimated maintenance, overestimated income, and proved disappointing after the first few years, when the accelerated depreciation fell off. The syndicates offered to the public, required extensive sales efforts and numerous small investors, were likely to be the least attractive, because if they had had really been excellent prospects they would have been absorbed by big professional investors and never offered to the public.

Disadvantages of Syndicates

Most of the syndicates owned a single property which, no matter how well chosen, was more risky than diversified real estate investment. Also, they provided little liquidity for the individual participant. No formal market existed for the sale of participating units of the syndicate. Usually the contract made no provision for the repurchase or retirement of the participation. Furthermore, the participants' property share in the syndicate could not be used for loans. Syndicators took much of the profit and made little financial investment. One proposed syndicate listed in its prospectus the following details: For forming the syndicate and financing the estimated $50,000 organizational expenses, the promoters were to collect $612,350 in profit. An additional $265,650 in sales commission would go to their sales subsidiary. The subsidiary had agreed to hire the sellers of the building as "management consultants" at an annual fee of $20,000 for 25 years, or $500,000. The prospectus conceded, "The services of the consultants may not be required more than one day each month nor more than 12 times in any fiscal year. No representation is made that there is any relationship between the consultants' services and the compensation they are to receive." Even if the sellers worked their full 12 days a year, their pay would be at the rate of $1,600 a day. Prospective investors shunned the deal, and the prospectus was revised. Supervision by the SEC was avoided by limiting investment eligibility to residents of a single state. Only a very few states regulate intrastate syndicates.

Investors became wary when a number of highly speculative syndicates collapsed in scandalous fashion in the early 60s. Before the Tax Reform Act of 1969, tax savings could be achieved by the use of accelerated depreciation to convert ordinary income into capital gains. Accelerated depreciation on residential real estate provided initial tax loss deductions and subsequent capital gains. The Tax Reform Act of 1969 reduced the tax benefit opportunities in commercial and industrial real estate by restricting the use of accelerated depreciation methods and recapturing 100 percent of post-1969 accelerated depreciation. *To encourage new residential rental property, however, the act granted such property exceptions to the new restrictions.* The revival of syndication therefore centered on new residential rental properties.

Real Estate Corporations

A number of real estate syndicates subsequently converted into publicly held companies to finance large property acquisitions. The owner of stock in a real estate corporation has all the advantages of the usual stockholder—liquidity, marketability, limited liability—plus the advantage which accrues because funds are invested in a diversified portfolio representing various properties whose blend of earnings is combined into a single earnings package.

There are a number of different types of real estate companies to choose from. There are diversified real estate companies such as City Investing; converted syndication corporations such as Arlen Realty; construction firms such as Diesel Engineering and Tishman, now part of Rockefeller Center, Inc.; hotel-motel firms such as Hilton, Sheraton and Loew's; and land development firms such as General Development, Deltona, and Arvida. Returns from investment in such companies are less than returns for syndicates, and have also proved vulnerable to required changes in the accounting practices of the nation's retail land sales companies in response to a vigorous controversy over how the industry's earnings should be reported.[8]

In evaluating such companies, it is more impor-

---

[8] See Abraham J. Briloff, *More Debits than Credits* (New York: Harper & Row, 1976), especially chap. 9, "Unrealities in Realty Accounting."

tant to look at their cash flow before taxes than at their net income after taxes. Cash flow is depreciation plus net income. Depreciation in industrial firms is plowed back to replace old and worn equipment, but in real estate operations well-constructed and well-maintained buildings have actually increased rather than decreased in value. Thus the depreciation allowed on such buildings represents nontaxable earnings which can be paid out to investors. This results in large tax-sheltered earnings and at times high dividends.

As a result of sharp and continued criticism of the accounting practices in the real estate field, the Accounting Principles Board of the American Institute of Certified Public Accountants issued a guide entitled *Accounting for Retail Land Sales.*

Real Estate Investment Trusts (REITs)

In recent years interest has shifted to the use of the real estate investment trust primarily for tax purposes. The trusts, which were incorporated, increased rapidly in numbers as a result of a 1960 law which permitted them to operate without paying taxes if they paid out 90 pecent of their income to shareholders and met certain other restrictions on operations and investments. The trusts, of which there were at one time over 200, were set up along the same lines as closed-end investment companies—they pooled the money of small investors for placement in real estate ventures. The REITs avoided making any promise on their return to shareholders and operated at a lower yield than syndicates. A number of REITs formed during the early 1970s were sponsored by commercial banks, insurance companies, or mortgage banking concerns.

To qualify as a real estate investment trust, there must be at least 100 shareholders and not more than 50 percent of the shares may be owned by five or fewer persons. These provisions are designed to ensure that every trust will be broadly owned and not serve as a personal holding company for a few investors. At least 75 percent of the gross income must be from investments related to real estate, and not more than 25 percent of the total assets can be invested in anything other than real estate.

The real estate investment trusts may not manage any of the property they own. Nor may they engage in developing land for sale. Thus the REITs must place their emphasis on longer term investments in office buildings, apartments, shopping centers, leases, mortgages and so on.

Types of REITs   Another way of looking at the REITs is as real estate mutual funds that are basically of two types—equity trusts and mortgage trusts. Equity trusts buy properties producing income, and after these trusts make outlays for expenses and mortgage payments, they pass the remaining income on to shareholders. Mortgage trusts invest in first mortgages rather than properties. These trusts have been more popular with investors than equity trusts.

Short-term or interim lenders write construction and development first mortgages with an average life of about 12 months. Once a building is completed and occupied, the interim lenders are repaid with the proceeds of the permanent mortgages, known as "takeout" mortgages.

The long-term mortgage trusts may make loans for up to 30 years, and such loans are made at lower rates than the loans for construction and development mortgages. The spread reflects the added risks of the short-term lender—that the project may flounder before it is completed or that the takeout money may not be forthcoming because of changes in economic conditions or because of contractual default by the builder. During 1973–75 the short-term trusts were particularly hard hit.

Procedures   All of the real estate investment trusts are users of borrowed capital. Some are permitted to mortgage up to two thirds of the total market value of their properties. Others have set lower limits for themselves.

The trusts also vary in their treatment of depreciation. A few use accelerated depreciation but not for the same reason that corporations do—that is, to defer taxes. The trusts, which are not taxed on distributed earnings, use depreciation to protect their shareholders from taxation. Because any distribution paid out of depreciation instead of net income is regarded as a return of capital, the shareholder owes little or no tax on it until the full investment in the shares is recovered or until the shares are sold—at which point a capital gains tax is paid instead of ordinary income taxes.

Most analysts believe that the REITs should be bought primarily on the basis of yield, not the promise of growth. Since the trusts cannot grow by retaining earnings because of the requirement that they distribute most of their income, they rely heavily on leverage to increase earnings. Mortgage trusts have no cash flow from depreciation, since they don't invest directly in real property. On the other hand, their investment in mortgages makes them more "liquid" than equity trusts.[9]

The REIT was designed as a vehicle by which the small investor could get into the real estate investing field with little know-how and less capital. The big operators were the organizers and the promoters, the managers and the financial executives: the small investors and the banks put up the funds.[10]

When the fallout came, in the mid-70s, the banks tried to bail out by one means or another, but suffered large losses. As you may have guessed, the little fellow was the one who lost his funds and his shirt. Many REITs went bankrupt; the price of REIT shares fell from $50–$100 to zero in one or two years. One wag suggested that a lending bank rename its REIT and call it RIP.

"Speculating in White Elephants," wrote *Forbes.* "Small investors lost billions in REIT stocks. Some very smart big investors now expect to make millions in them."[11]

Small investors suffered large losses in many REITs, largely because they were unacquainted with real estate values and because they believed that real estate values rise steadily and never come down. The shakeout in the industry was enormous and rough. It will be a long time, if ever, before REITs recover the confidence of the small investor.

As compared to direct investment in common stock or in the shares of investment companies, investing in REITs raises some difficult questions. Did insiders initially unload properties on the trust at inflated prices? Was the trust paying a reasonable price for the properties it acquired or the properties in which it invested? What kind of management fee was charged? Who are the trustees? Are they competent, experienced in real estate investment, and honest? You should have answers to all of these questions before you invest in a real estate investment trust.

Mortgage-Backed Securities

Investing in mortgage-backed securities is a newer choice that is available to those who were burned or singed by investments in REITs.

Brokerage firms and mutual funds have opened up a new field for investors in search of high income. One of the fastest-growing innovations in the credit markets has been mortgage-backed securities, a family of oddly nicknamed investments that includes Ginnie Mae and Freddie Mac. More than $50 billion of these securities are outstanding, and the total keeps rising as the avid investor in search of safety and yield moves into them. Mortgage-backed securities were first sold in 1970, but they really hit their stride in 1977.[12]

Mortgage-backed securities originate from two sources: the Government National Mortgage Association and the Federal Home Loan Mortgage Corporation. GNMA, or Ginnie Mae, is a federally chartered company set up to encourage the flow of funds into construction by increasing the flow of mortgage money. GNMA does not itself issue the mortgage-backed securities called Ginnie Maes. Rather, GNMA-approved firms pool mortgages and

[9] Additional material is available from Audit Investment Research, Inc., 230 Park Ave., New York, NY 10017. It publishes the *Realty Trust Review,* the only investment advisory service covering REITs. See also Kenneth G. Campbell, *The Real Estate Investment Trusts: America's Newest Billionaires* (New York: Audit Investment Research, 1971).

[10] The industry trade association, the National Association of Real Estate Investment Trusts, provides industry data, a yearbook of member trusts, and other information. Its address is 1101 17th St., N.W., Washington, D.C. 20036.

[11] *Forbes,* December 1, 1977, p 79.

[12] John H. Allan, "Boom in Mortgage-Backed Securities," *New York Times,* November 20, 1977. A move toward self regulation developed in 1979.

issue securities against the pools, in $25,000 units.

The securities are backed by single-family home mortgages, mobile home loans, and construction loans for multifamily projects. All of the loans are either insured by the FHA or guaranteed by the Veterans Administration. The company that pools the mortgages collects the monthly mortgage payments and passes them on to the Ginnie Mae owners. Even if the homeowners don't make their payments on time, the federal government guarantees the Ginnie Mae payments will be received on time.

The Federal Home Loan Mortgage Corporation (Freddie Mac) is also a U.S. government corporation. It buys and pools conventional, nonguaranteed mortgages and sells an interest in the pools through several types of securities. Freddie Mac securities are guaranteed by the FHLMC, not by the government, which is one reason why they yield a higher return than do Ginnie Maes.

Ginnie Maes and Freddie Macs are regularly traded in the open market. Brokerage houses organize unit trusts and they and the mutual funds assemble a portfolio of mortgage-backed securities—usually Ginnie Maes—and sell shares in the portfolio to the public. Interest and principal repayments are passed through to each shareholder.

There are differences in the way unit trusts and mutual funds operate. The *unit* trusts operate with a *fixed* portfolio. That portfolio is not replenished as the balance is reduced by amortization and repayments. Eventually the trust is dissolved, the remaining holdings sold off, and the proceeds distributed to the shareholders. However, you can get out before then by selling your shares in the open market or by selling them directly to the trust.

The mutual funds offer shares to the public continuously, and they manage their portfolios by frequently buying and selling securities. Two mutual funds appear to have been the first to specialize in mortgage-backed securities. They are Holdings of U.S. Government Securities, Inc. (HUSGSI), and Income Trust for U.S. Government Guaranteed Securities (InTrust Fund).

It's too early to say whether much will come of this new way to invest in mortgages. Again, the design is to lure the small investor.

INVESTING IN ART AND COLLECTOR'S ITEMS[13]

One of the earliest French impressionist paintings earned the artist, Claude Monet, only $80 in 1866. In 1926 the painting was purchased by a Pennsylvania minister, the Reverend Theodore Pitcairn, for $11,000. He sold it at auction in 1968 for $1.4 million.

In 1944 a Jackson Pollock could be bought for $100. In 1953 the price was $2,000; in 1960, $50,000; and in 1970, $100,000. In 1973 Pollock's *Blue Poles* was sold for $2 million.

The late Edward G. Robinson sold his collection (after 25 years) of 58 paintings and one sculpture to Stavros Niarchos, the Greek shipping magnate, through Knoedler & Co. for $3.2 million. The collection had cost him about $1 million to assemble.

Fashions and tastes change. Prices began soaring in the early 70s for the work of a group that had been largely neglected—20th-century American painters. A two-day auction by Sotheby Parke Bernet of 219 works from the estate of the late Edith Halpert, a leading New York gallery owner and a sponsor of U.S. artists since the 1920s, was expected to bring about $2.5 million. It brought $3.7 million. Japanese buyers developed a yen for works by Yasuo Kuniyoshi, a naturalized U.S. citizen who had been born in Japan. His *Little Joe with Cow,* which was painted in 1923 and sold for $300 at that time, went for a record $220,000.

Investments in art, antiques, rare books, and stamps have had greater appreciation over the years than have investments in common stocks.[14] Richard Rush, a leading art connoisseur and chronicler, advised: ''Between 1950 and 1955 art prices doubled. Then they tripled between 1955 and 1960 so that in a decade they went up six times. Between 1960 and 1970 they tripled again so in

---

[13] Collectively called collectibles.

[14] For extended discussion and detail, see Leo Barnes and Stephen Feldman (eds.), *Handbook of Wealth Management* (New York: McGraw-Hill, 1977), sect. 7, ''Special and Offbeat Investments,''; Richard H. Rush, ''Art as an Investment'' (chap. 37); Hauley Apfelbaum, ''Investment in Rare Coins'' (chap. 40); and Leona Seldow, ''Stamps as an Investment'' (chap. 41).

20 years they increased 18 times, despite the fact that 1970 was a recession year. From 1970 to 1975 they increased about 2½ times."

The London Times–Sotheby Index of Old Masters (overall) rose sevenfold between 1951 and 1969. Dutch landscapes increased 8 times, and Italian 18th-century works rose 9½ times. The index of impressionist paintings (overall) rose 15½ times between 1951 and 1970. Within this category, Monet's paintings increased 22½ times and Boudin's 19 times.

Some buy art as a status symbol, some as a hedge against inflation, some for capital gains—attempting to buy for a "song" today a painting that they hope to sell for a fortune tomorrow. Who does the buying? One survey shows that only 15 percent of the buyers in the United States are wealthy collectors. The largest percentage of buyers—about 50 percent—are high salaried, and 35 percent of those buying paintings are medium- or modest-salaried.

As you can see in the ten-year compound growth table, collectimania has paid off in double-digit appreciation. An investment in Chinese ceram-

Ten-Year Compound Growth Rate

Chinese ceramics	19.2%
Gold	16.3
Stamps	15.4
Old masters	13.0
Coins	13.0
Diamonds	12.6
Oil	11.5
Farmland	10.6
Housing	9.2
Silver	9.1
Foreign exchange	6.2
Consumer price index	6.1
Bonds	6.1
Stocks	2.8

Source: R. S. Salomon, Jr. "Stocks Are Still the Only Bargain Left," *Portfolio Planning*, Stock Research Department, Salomon Brothers, 1978.

ics has been even more profitable than an investment in oil. If continued over the long term at these high rates, the author of this study notes," such a process may mean that we are running the risk of immobilizing a substantial portion of the world's wealth in someone's stamp collection.[15]

Collectibles, remember, pay no interest or dividends, and they often entail costs for insurance and storage. They may be difficult to resell, and the commissions may largely wipe out profits. There are often organizations of collectors with the same interest. The *Encyclopedia of Associations,* available in most libraries, lists over 100 such groups, including the Society of Caddy-Spoon Collectors, the International Snuff Bottle Society, and the Beer Can Collectors of America.

Most paintings are sold for $1,000 or less. Finds are rare, but when they do occur they are usually so well publicized that the impression gets around that they occur all the time. A Frans Hals was sold in the Netherlands in 1963 for $7. It was bought by a Russian-born cabaret pianist, Leonid Hostinov,

"My investment portfolio? You're standing on it."

Reprinted by permission *The Wall Street Journal*

[15] R. S. Salomon, Jr., "Stocks Are Still the Only Bargain Left," Salomon Brothers, Stock Research Department, July 3, 1978. See also Benjamin Zucker, How to Invest in Gems (New York: Quadrangle/The New York Times Book Co., 1976).

at an auction in Arnhem, Holland. He resold it for $84,000, and the German woman who purchased it, resold it at auction two years later for $205,800. One of the world's wealthiest men, John Paul Getty, bought a heavily repainted Raphael at auction for £40 (worth about $200 at the time). When it was cleaned, restored, and identified, it was valued at $1 million.

Nevertheless, the *London Times*–Sotheby analysis of the art market warned investors against pulling out of the stock market and plunging into art. "Apart from the fact that pictures pay no dividends, it is not possible to buy a painting one day and sell it at auction the next," the *Times* said. "If a picture is resold too quickly in the salesroom it usually drops in price." It takes about five years for some schools to "mature" on the market, the analysis noted. The art market, it advised, is not for the short-term investor.

The Monet-Picasso Action

So popular has art investing become that a number of mutual funds for investment in art have been started. Typical of the pressure for art investment was the investor who told his broker: "Forget Polaroid and Burroughs. I want a piece of that Monet-Picasso action." One of the most noted of the some 20 mutual funds formed around the world for investment in art is *Artemis,* after the Greek goddess of hunting. Incorporated in Luxembourg, it was founded by two prestigious European bankers who went into it, part time, to get richer—its record purchase was of an 1888 oil painting by Seurat for $1,033,200, sold at auction by Christie's of London.

Rare Books

Rare books have appreciated even more than old masters. The *London Times*–Sotheby index for old books (overall) rose 11½ times between 1951 and 1969. For the last decade and a half, rare book prices, with few exceptions, have climbed at a startling rate. Franz Pick, who chronicles the yearly changes in auction prices of rare books and

manuscripts, found that the figures were up 40 to 50 percent in 1966, 50 to 60 percent in 1967, 60 percent in 1968, and 30 percent in 1969 and 1970, with a continuing spiral over the past ten years.

Most collectors hold onto their acquisitions. It is the disposal of private collections—usually after the collector's death—that makes up most of the rare book market. There are, however, occasions on which individuals do sell, affording added insight into the market. Thus, in 1970 Arthur A. Houghton, Jr., president of Steuben Glass and a book collector, sold a 15th-century Gutenberg Bible to a book dealer, H. P. Kraus, for which Mr. Kraus subsequently asked $2.5 million. Mr. Houghton acquired the Bible in the 1950s for a reported $150,000. His selling price was not disclosed.

Some price shifts on volumes seems inexplicable. A case cited by a prominent rare book dealer is Edward S. Curtis' *The North American Indian,* a 40-volume set published between 1907 and 1930, half of whose volumes consist of illustrations. The full set sold for $20,000 in 1972 and five years later was auctioned off for $50,000. Recently it went to $60,000.

Just as some paintings have declined in price due to the loss in popularity of a painter or a school of painting, books too at times decline in price. In the 1920s, for example, first editions of some of Bernard Shaw's works cost about $350. Today they can be purchased for $50. The prices for books by John Galsworthy went into the thousands then; $100 would be a common price now.

The Stamp Market

The stamp market is another interesting investment market. There are some 25 million stamp collectors, and the market is international in scope. Values are appreciating by as much as 20 to 30 percent a year. Over the last decade, collections of American stamps have increased in value an average of 10 percent a year, while a good Japanese stamp collection rose 1,000 percent over the decade. Two 1847 stamps from the island of Mauritius (in the Indian Ocean) sold for $380,000. A

New Orleans stamp dealer bought them. Only 14 such stamps were ever printed, and they contained a typographical error which added to their rarity and value. Consider the recent sale of a piece of reddish purple paper with a face value of one penny. This last surviving first British Guiana stamp sold at auction for $280,000. The buyer was a representative of a syndicate of investors who felt that the best place for spare funds was in stamps. A 24-cent 1918 U.S. airmail stamp with an upside-down airplane is worth some $25,000 today. The same stamp without the upside-down error is worth only $10. Watch out, however, for purposely manufactured errors. You can be taken. Postage stamps are a traditional hedge against inflation. It would be better to have a nest egg in the upside-down U.S. airmail than in the safest bond. The stamp would provide no current income, but its appreciation over a period of time would more than make up for this current shortcoming, if you can afford to do without the income.

You have to be very careful, however, There are shady dealers in the trade who have been known to counterfeit—who promise 25 percent off "prices" and sell inferior-quality stamps worth far less. There are auctioneers who hire shills to inflate the bidding. If you are going to invest in stamps on a serious scale, you must make an in-depth study of the philatelic market.[16]

All of these rather esoteric types of investments have one thing in common. You have to know the field to buy safely. If you don't, you can be taken badly.[17] This doesn't mean that you have to be an expert. Experts are available for consultation, but if you know little about the field, you run a substantial risk. Forgeries, imitations, fakes, and the like, abound. Each market is somewhat obscure and relatively unpublicized. And if you are among the uninitiated, you may not know how to locate a reputable expert. Study the field. Invest a minimum to start. Even the experts, especially in art and antiques, have sometimes been fooled.[18]

GOLD

In 1971, when the official U.S. price of gold was $35 an ounce, the world market price was $41 an ounce. In 1974, the official price was $42 an ounce and the market price reached $180 an ounce. Since Americans were forbidden to own gold until 1975, the pursuit of gold as an inflation hedge led to collecting gold coins and buying gold stocks (shares in gold mining companies). In response to rising gold prices, the price of the *London Financial Times* average of gold mining stocks increased sixfold between 1972 and 1974. With the rise in inflation in the United States, London and Zurich gold prices rose to a high of about $250 an ounce in late 1979.

For more than 3,500 years collecting gold or gold coins has been a fascinating pursuit, no less in ancient times than in contemporary times. As one writer has noted:

> Millions of people owe their lives to gold coins, secretly stashed away, which have enabled them to survive in times of famine, political upheaval, or natural disaster, to escape persecution or death; or to flee to safer lands by buying off guards, officials, or border sentinels. Gold has always opened myriads of doors, closed to those who had nothing, lost everything, or held only depreciating or worthless paper money.

In the 70s, hoarding gold has been popular worldwide, as fear of inflation and depreciated paper currencies has swept across nations. The French, mindful of 14 devaluations in this century, are estimated to be hoarding $6 billion in gold bars, jewelry, and coins. Among Swiss bankers, Indian merchants, Japanese industrialists, and now nervous Americans, holding gold or gold coins has become increasingly popular. The world-famous gold coins—napoleons, sovereigns, double eagles, Mexican 50 pesos, Dutch guilders—are in good

---

[16] See "Stamps—From High-School Hobby to Big-Time Investment," *Business Week,* June 12, 1978.

[17] See Gerald Reitlinger, *The Economics of Taste: The Rise and Fall of the Objets d'Art Market since 1750* (New York: Henry Holt, 1965), vol. 2.

[18] David L. Goodrich, *Art Fakes in America* (New York: Viking Press, 1973). See also W. Crawley, *Is It Genuine?* (New York: Hart Publishing Co. 1972).

supply, but their prices have risen more than 100 percent since the early 1970s.

It was illegal for Americans to own gold bullion from 1934 to the end of 1974, but legal to own gold coins of numismatic value that had been minted before 1934. The latent demand of Americans for gold spilled over into the gold coin market, and the prices of select coins rose to substantial premiums above the intrinsic gold content of those coins. The premiums on gold coins, which U.S. citizens, residents, or corporations could own legally for "numismatic purposes," kept changing all the time. The premium is the amount of extra money you pay for a coin over and above the current market value of its actual gold content.

In 1974 a $20 U.S. double eagle (1909 St. Gaudens) was worth about $500. A $20 U.S. double eagle (1863) had a value of $275, as compared with a value of about $65 in 1971. About 52,500 of the former and 966,570 of the latter had been minted. Hence the numismatic value of the former was higher. The $5 half eagle (1834) was valued at $550, and the $2.50 quarter eagle (1848), of which only 13,771 had been minted, sold for $425.

When at the end of 1974 it once again became legal for U.S. citizens to own gold bullion, the "gold rush of 1975" failed to materialize. A surge to gold was anticipated because of the widespread desire to preserve capital and hedge against inflation. In the flight from currency to goods which usually marks a period of sharp inflation, there is also an awareness that over the ages gold has been a store of value, independent of any governmental or monetary authority. Despite efforts in recent years to get away from the gold standard and to relegate gold to a place of no importance in monetary systems, for Europeans and Asians gold retained its age-old attraction as a means of preserving capital—bypassing depreciating paper money and the loss of purchasing power—and among them it has remained a traditional way of coping with inflation.

The Cost of Owning Gold

The failure of Americans to become excited about gold ownership when this became legally permissible was probably due to a variety of reasons. First, gold paid no return at all. Second, there are a bewildering variety of ways to buy it—gold bullion or bars, gold coins, gold commodity futures, shares in gold funds, and gold mining company stocks, to name the major ways. Third, it is costly to buy and own gold. Local sales and use taxes are payable in many states—they amount to 8 percent in New York City. Gold must be insured, shipped, and stored at the purchaser's expense. Premiums—fabrication charges—of 2 to 7 percent must be paid on the relatively small purchases within the reach of the typical investor, and before gold can be resold it must almost always be assayed, in order to determine its quality and fineness, a service for which charges begin at $30. The standard 400-ounce gold bars are expensive. They sell for about $77,000 at current world prices. As one banker put it: "We want every customer to realize that gold is expensive to buy, expensive to store, expensive to insure, and expensive to sell. Besides it pays no return." Finally the extent of the rise in gold bullion prices may be seen in Figure 12–5, both in dollars and Swiss francs. It also shows how clearly it serves as a hedge against inflation. As you can see, gold stocks outpaced the market, and also have the advantage over bullion of paying a dividend return instead of incurring storage and insurance costs.

SILVER

Citizens of the United States have been free to buy, sell, and hoard silver bullion or silver coins, and many U.S. citizens have sought to hedge against inflation or capital gains via silver. Silver is traded on both the New York Commodity Exchange and the Chicago Board of Trade. Silver coins in bags of $10,000 face value are traded on the New York Mercantile Exchange. People began to hoard silver coins extensively in the mid-1960s. In 1965 the U.S. government stopped minting coins of 90 percent silver. In 1967, the price of silver rose above the mint price of $1.29 an ounce and a free market in silver developed. In

FIGURE 12–5
Gold Catches Up

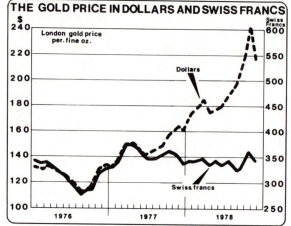

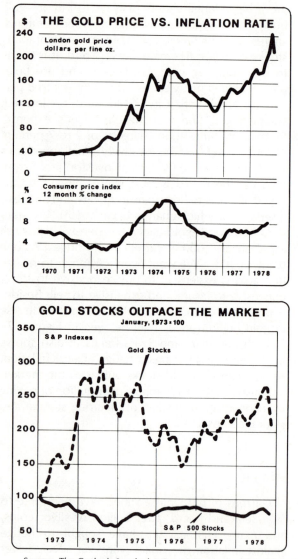

Source: *The Outlook,* Standard & Poor's Corporation, New York, 1978.

1968 the government no longer redeemed silver certificates (paper money) for silver bullion, and in 1969 the government sold over 2 billion ounces of silver from its stockpile. Unlike gold, silver has numerous industrial uses, and in the 1970s the industrial demand for silver tended to outrun supply, with the price rising to about $6 an ounce. Buying silver contracts on the commodity exchanges requires a knowledge of the mechanics and procedures of commodity trading, which is a compli-

TABLE 12–13
Comparative Changes in Asset Values, 1968–1978

	1968	1969	1970	1971	1972	1973	1974	1975	1976	1977	1978	Compound Rate of Return
Chinese ceramics	100	111	107	187	295	652	333	186	439	504	580	19.2%
Gold	$39.26	$41.09	$35.94	$40.81	$58.16	$97.32	$159.26	$161.02	$124.84	$147.72	$177.57	16.3
	100	105	92	104	148	248	406	410	318	376	452	
U.S. stamps	100	115	135	149	164	206	222	250	302	366	419	15.4
Old masters	100	107	107	114	135	175	181	206	255	301	340	13.0
U.S. nongold coins	100	101	106	107	111	112	135	174	241	285	339	13.0
Diamonds	100	104	—	108	122	176	178	184	194	261	327	12.6
U.S. crude oil ($ per barrel at wellhead)	$2.94	$3.09	$3.18	$3.39	$3.39	$3.89	$6.87	$7.67	$8.19	$8.57	$8.76	11.5
	100	105	108	115	115	132	233	261	278	291	298	
U.S. farmland ($ per acre)	$179	$188	$195	$203	$219	$246	$302	$341	$387	$450	$490	10.6
	100	105	109	113	122	137	169	191	216	251	274	
Housing	$20,000	$21,500	$22,900	$24,600	$26,300	$28,500	$31,700	$34,900	$37,700	$42,000	$48,200	9.2
	100	108	115	123	132	143	159	175	189	210	241	
Silver ($ per ounce)	$2.14	$1.79	$1.77	$1.55	$1.68	$2.56	$4.71	$4.42	$4.35	$4.62	$5.15	9.1
	100	84	83	72	79	119	220	206	203	216	240	
Foreign exchange (DM, yen, SF, and guilder)	100	100	102	100	117	139	142	138	146	155	183	6.2
Consumer price index	100	105	111	116	120	127	141	154	164	174	181	6.1
Salomon Brothers Bond Index (total return)	100	104	97	114	126	134	126	136	156	175	180	6.1
S&P Composite (total return)	100	102	81	109	120	120	108	115	128	130	132	2.8

For each of the tangible asset categories, figures have been obtained from reliable sources with special expertise in that category. The data, while appearing to be precise, are in fact only an indication of broad longer-term trends.

Source: R. S. Salomon, Jr., "Stocks Are Still the Only Bargain Left," *Portfolio Planning,* Stock Research Department, Salomon Brothers, 1978.

cated business. Numerous coin-dealing firms have sprung up that sell bags of silver coins to the public on margin (you put up only part of the purchase price) and at excessively high prices. When you buy bags of silver on margin you do not get delivery of the bags. The coin exchange holds them, and some coin exchanges have allegedly not used the margin money to buy coins but instead have speculated in silver futures.

Conclusion

The evidence seen in Table 12–13 supports the thinking that the last ten years have been good years to acquire anything but common stocks. As gold, coins, stamps, and other collectibles have all appreciated beyond average expectation, the relatively low cost of stocks in contrast has made them a "bargain." Although common stocks have been far outdistanced by more esoteric investments over the last decade, there is no reason to believe that they will decline over the long pull.

SUGGESTED READINGS

Barnes, Leo, and Feldman, Stephen (eds.). *Handbook of Wealth Management*. New York: McGraw-Hill, 1978.

Case, Fred E. *The Investment Guide to Home and Land Purchase*. Englewood Cliffs, N.J.: Prentice-Hall, 1977.

Cohen, Jerome B.; Zinbarg, Edward D.; and Zeikel, Arthur. *Investment Analysis and Portfolio Management*. 3d ed. Homewood., Ill.: Richard D. Irwin, 1977.

Darst, David M. *The Complete Bond Book: A Guide to All Types of Fixed-Income Securities*. New York: McGraw-Hill, 1975.

Dreyfus, Patricia A. "Investments You Can Love," Special Report on Collectibles, *Money,* August 1978.

Hayes, Douglas A., and Bauman, W. Scott. 3d ed. *Investments: Analysis and Management*. New York: Macmillan, 1976.

Henry, Rene A., Jr. *How to Profitably Buy and Sell Land*. New York: John Wiley & Sons 1977.

Leibowitz, Martin L.; Meyer, Kenneth R.; and Carter, Andrew M. *Bond Analysis and Selection*. Occasional Paper no. 6. Charlottesville, Va.: Financial Analysts Research Foundation, 1977.

Maisel, Sherman J., and Roulac, Stephen. *Real Estate Investment and Finance*. New York: McGraw-Hill, 1976.

Mendelsohn, Morris and Robbins, Sidney. *Investment Analysis and Securities Market*. New York: Basic Books Inc., 1976.

Seldin, Maury. *Land Investment*. Homewood, Ill.: Dow Jones-Irwin, 1975.

CASE PROBLEMS

Case Problems for Chapters 12, 13, and 14 will be found at the end of Chapter 14.

13

Buying and Selling Securities

All you do is buy a stock, wait till it goes up, and then sell it. And if it don't go up, don't buy it.

WILL ROGERS

The American economy and its growth are the underpinnings of stock market activity, whether on the Big Board or on the regional exchanges. If corporate earnings and dividends continue to rise steadily, after adjustment for inflation, then the securities markets will grow and expand over the long run.

But there are exceptions for shorter periods. Over the last decade, GNP, disposable income, corporate earnings, and corporate dividends all rose significantly (see Figure 13–1). *But the stock market did very poorly.* In fact, many stock investors had only bitter experiences and memories of the 1968–77 period.

That same decade saw a whole range of problems in a changing financial marketplace. The failure and disappearance of some leading brokerage houses, the paper glut, the antiquated stock certificate, back office problems, the advent of extensive automation, the computer and the role of the specialist, the central marketplace, the composite tape, the rise of institutional trading, the question of institutional membership on exchanges, negotiated commission rates, block positioning, the proposed automated book, the third market and the fourth market, members' capital requirements, SIPC (Se-

417

FIGURE 13–1
The Economy and the Market

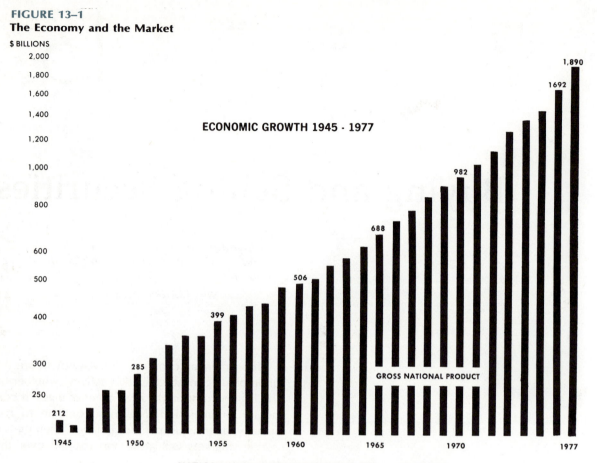

NATIONAL AND CORPORATE ECONOMY — 20 YEARS
1958 - 1977

	Population (millions)	Gross National Product (billions)	Disposable Income	Corporate Earnings After Taxes (billions)	Corporate Dividends (billions)	% of Net Earnings
1977	217.6	$1,890.4	$1,308.7	$102.3	$41.2	40.2%
1976	215.1	1,692.4	1,181.8	84.2	35.1	41.7
1975	213.5	1,516.3	1,080.9	72.5	32.1	45.2
1974	211.9	1,406.9	983.6	79.5	31.1	39.1
1973	210.4	1,306.3	903.1	68.8	27.8	40.4
1972	208.8	1,171.1	801.3	54.6	24.6	55.2
1971	207.0	1,063.4	742.8	44.3	23.0	51.9
1970	204.9	982.4	685.9	37.0	22.9	61.9
1969	202.7	935.5	630.4	43.8	22.6	51.6
1968	200.7	868.5	588.1	46.2	21.9	47.4
1967	198.7	796.3	544.5	44.9	20.1	44.8
1966	196.6	753.0	510.4	47.1	19.4	41.2
1965	194.3	688.1	472.2	44.3	19.1	43.1
1964	191.9	635.7	437.0	36.7	17.3	47.1
1963	189.2	594.7	402.8	31.5	15.5	49.2
1962	186.5	563.8	383.9	29.6	14.4	48.6
1961	183.7	523.3	362.9	25.8	13.3	51.6
1960	180.7	506.0	349.4	25.8	12.9	50.0
1959	177.8	486.5	336.1	28.0	12.2	43.6
1958	174.4	448.9	317.1	22.1	11.3	51.1
1957	172.0	442.8	306.9	25.5	11.5	45.1
1956	168.9	420.7	291.3	26.6	11.1	41.7
% Change	+27%	+327%	+326%	+301%	+258%	

Source: *Johnson's Chart's,* 1978 edition.

curities Investors Protection Corporation), box differences, disclosure, fails, give-ups, disintermediation, market governance and structure, the expansion of NASDAQ (National Association of Securities Dealers Automatic Quotation System)—these are some of the issues and subjects that have received attention in recent years, and many still remain unresolved.

The investment process encompasses a number of markets and many institutions. There is a money market and a capital market. There are primary markets and secondary markets. There are organized exchanges and over-the-counter markets. There are both borrowers and lenders of short- and long-term funds. There are now organized markets for options, for commodities, for futures, and for warrants and rights. There are corporations and individuals with surplus funds that may decide to invest, lend, or save those funds. There are a variety of financial intermediaries that facilitate the transfer of funds from those who have surpluses to those who need resources for a diversity of purposes, ranging from productive investment to speculative trading.

Money and Capital Markets

Short-term funds change hands in the money market. It is customary to distinguish between the money and capital markets by saying that the money market is the arena in which claims to funds change hands for from one day up to one year, but not beyond. Money market instruments include promissory notes and bills of exchange, commercial paper, banker's acceptances, Treasury bills, short-term tax-exempts, dealer paper, and negotiable time certificates of deposit. Institutions participating in the money market include the commercial banks, corporations (large and small), the Federal Reserve, U.S. government securities dealers, and indeed anyone who lends or borrows on short term, including those who borrow on the collateral of securities to speculate. Activities in the money market range from a one-day loan of several millions by one commercial bank with surplus reserve funds to another commercial bank which is short

of reserves—the federal funds market—to a loan by an investor who is borrowing to buy securities on margin. Corporations with a temporary surplus of funds may place the funds in Treasury bills for 91 or 182 days or in time certificates of deposit tailored to their financial time requirements. The money market is the vital arena in which the Federal Reserve influences the reserve positions of commercial banks, and therefore their capacity to lend, by engaging in open-market operations in U.S. government securities.[1]

In contrast, the capital market focuses on long-term funds. It is in the capital market that the demand for and the supply of investment funds are brought together. Here savings are converted into investments. The major supply of funds for the capital market is channeled through specialized financial institutions, such as insurance companies, pension and retirement funds, and savings institutions. At times, dealings between borrowers and lenders may be direct, but often transfers are effected through intermediaries, such as investment bankers, stockbrokers, and securities dealers. Instruments in the capital market include, of course, bonds, notes, mortgages, stock, and warrants.

Like the money market, the capital market has many facets. A large corporation borrowing directly from an insurance company is participating in the capital market, even though the whole transaction may be arranged by phone. Another corporation borrowing through the facilities of an investment banker, who in turn makes use of a selling organization that spans the country, is also participating in the capital market. There is a market for corpo-

---

[1] For further information, see Wesley Lindow, *Inside the Money Market* (New York: Random House, 1972); *Money Market Investments: The Risk and the Return* (New York: Morgan Guaranty Trust Co., latest edition); *Instruments of the Money Market* (Federal Reserve Bank of Richmond, latest edition); *Money Market Investments* (Federal Reserve Bank of Cleveland, latest edition); *Money Market Handbook for the Short-Term Investor* (New York: Brown Brothers, Harriman & Co., latest edition); *The U.S. Government Securities Market* (Chicago: Government Bond Division, Harris Trust and Savings Bank latest edition); also Marcia Stigum, *The Money Market: Myth, Reality, and Practice* (Homewood, Ill.: Dow Jones-Irwin, 1978).

rate bonds, a market for longer term U.S. government issues, a market for state and local bonds ("municipals"), a market for corporate equities, and a mortgage market.

Primary and Secondary Markets

There is an active primary or new issues market as well as large secondary securities markets. For mortgages, for example, the new issues market is significant and substantial, whereas the secondary market is negligible. For equities, on the other hand, the new issues market is relatively limited, but the secondary market is large and active. For bonds there are both a large and active new issues market and a substantial secondary market.

In recent years 70 to 80 percent of total new corporate issues have consisted of bonds. The percentage is even higher if U.S. government and state and municipal issues are included. The new issues market is therefore normally mainly a bond market. Securities in this market can be sold either through investment bankers or through private placements. About a third of all new corporate bond issues have been placed privately. Many of the largest firms with the best credit ratings have come to favor this quiet, relatively unobserved method of financing. For large companies the method offers a variety of advantages, though investment bankers claim that the interest cost is somewhat higher in private placement than in a public offering. A private placement frees a borrower from the uncertainties of market conditions for new issues. Market fluctuations are avoided. For example, as IBM's computer program unfolded, the company obtained a $500 million long-term credit from Prudential and drew down the funds from time to time as needed, without having to worry about changing conditions in the financial markets. Also, registration with the SEC was not necessary.

The Investment Banker and the Stockbroker

Investment bankers are, however, the traditional middlemen in the capital market. For the most part,

they buy the new issue from the borrower at an agreed-upon price, assume a market risk, and hope to resell the issue to the investing public at a higher price. In this respect, they differ from the stockbroker, who usually acts as an agent, earns a commission, and takes no risk. In the sale of certain issues, however, investment bankers may function more like stockbrokers. Instead of buying the issue, they may take it on a "best efforts" basis, accepting a commission for what they are able to sell but not buying the issue themselves. This type of arrangement can occur in the most diverse cases. The seller may be a small company whose securities are too unseasoned to warrant the investment bankers' assumption of the risk of purchase and redistribution. Or, on the other hand, the seller may be a very large corporation whose securities are so well known that it wants to pay the investment bankers only for their sales efforts and not for assuming the risks of distribution.

Prices set in the primary market when the new issue first appears may thus be negotiated prices, or competitive auction prices, or privately agreed-upon prices. Usually all three types take into consideration the prevailing prices for comparable or nearly comparable outstanding issues traded in secondary markets. Institutional investment managers are much more involved than individual investors in prices and purchases in the primary market. While the value analysis of the individual investor is directed almost entirely toward existing securities and secondary markets, institutional investment managers give substantial attention both to new-issue markets and to secondary markets.

Secondary Markets

Secondary markets for securities—the organized exchanges and the over-the-counter markets—provide the trading forums, the liquidity, the familiarity with issues and companies, and the price and value determinations which encourage public interest in security investment and facilitate new financing. When individuals or institutional investors buy securities, they buy claims to assets or future income, or both, and faith in these claims is enhanced or diminished, depending on the ease or difficulty of finding a ready market for the claims on short notice, if desired. No doubt, many would hesitate to buy securities if they could not count on a ready market if it were needed. Clearly the development of the now elaborate machinery for trading in existing securities came about in response to felt needs.

Measuring Stock Prices

The performance of the stock market is of vital interest to the trend of the economy. Changes in the level and direction of stock prices signal future economy directions. But there is no one single stock price index which is universally accepted. A number have developed over the years which claim to measure the market but each has its limitations. There follows a discussion of the more important indices.

The Dow-Jones Industrial Average

The Dow-Jones Industrial average published each day in the *Wall Street Journal* contains the most widely quoted and extensively used stock price average. The Dow-Jones Industrials consist of 30 blue-chip stocks. There are also additional averages of 20 transportation stocks, 15 utility stocks, and a composite average of the 65. The composite is almost never used.

The 30 stocks in the DJIA at present include: Allied Chemical, Aluminum Co. of America, American Brands, American Can, AT&T, Bethlehem Steel, Chrysler, Du Pont, Eastman Kodak, Esmark (Swift & Co.), Exxon (Standard Oil of New Jersey), General Electric, General Foods, General Motors, Goodyear, International Harvester, International Nickel, International Paper, Johns-Manville, Minnesota Mining & Manufacturing (3M), Owens-Illinois, Procter & Gamble, Sears Roebuck, Standard Oil of California, Texaco, Union Carbide, United States Steel, United Technology (United Aircraft), Westinghouse, and Woolworth. The only names in that group that appeared in the original list are American Tobacco (now American Brands) and General Electric. See Figure 13–2.

The way the DJIA is constructed tends to magnify changes in the market. For example, many people are perplexed when the headlines proclaim that the average rose 16 points and they cannot find on the quotation page a single "Dow" stock which increased so much as $16. Actually, all that was needed to get this rise was an average price advance of only 88 cents for each of the 30 stocks.[2]

There is, of course, a tremendous disparity between DJI points and dollars and cents, which has led to some highly misleading descriptions of the market. The DJI advances ten points, for example, and immediately there are reports that the market is soaring; the fact is that the stocks in the DJI have moved up an average of 55 cents a share. If the DJI declines 15 points, the market is said to have plunged; again the fact is that the stocks in the DJI have lost an average of only 83 cents a share. With a divisor of 1.443, a one-point change in the DJI equals about six cents in the arithmetic average of the stocks in the DJI.

In the light of the excitement about the DJI finally breaking through 1,000 in 1972–73, it is interesting to note that but for one substitution the DJI would have broken through the 1,000 level in December 1961. In 1939, IBM was removed from inclusion in the DJI 30 and AT&T was substituted. Had IBM remained, the DJI would have reached a December 1961 high of 1,017.39 instead of 734.91.

"It's *Catch-22*. Everyone looks at the Dow because it's prominently displayed. It's displayed because everyone looks at it," said one observer.

Standard & Poor's Stock Price Index

After the Dow-Jones Industrial Average, probably the most widely known market barometer is the index prepared by Standard & Poor's Corporation, which is based on 400 industrial stocks. Standard & Poor's also has a 40-stock financial index, a 20-stock transportation index, and a 40-stock utility index, making up a 500-stock composite.

---

[2] "The Dow Average: Its Makeup and History," *Weekly Staff Report,* David L. Babson & Co., Boston, January 15, 1976.

FIGURE 13–2

DOW-JONES INDUSTRIAL AVERAGE

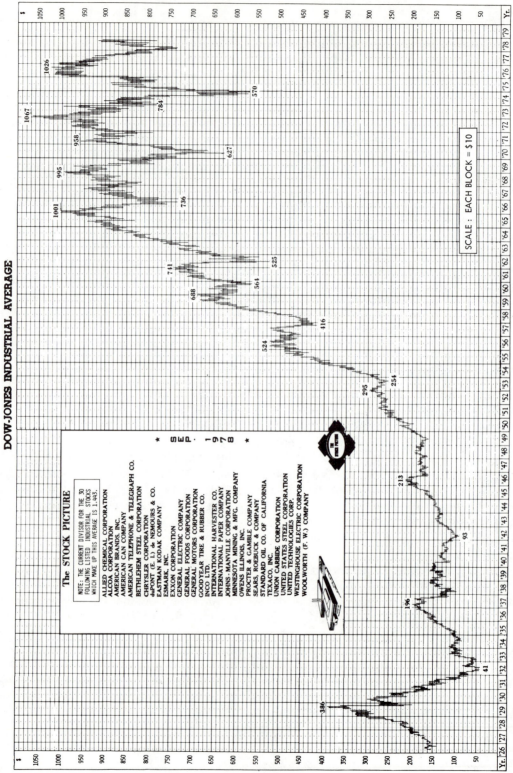

The STOCK PICTURE

NOTE: THE CURRENT DIVISOR FOR THE 30 FOLLOWING LISTED INDUSTRIAL STOCKS WHICH MAKE UP THIS AVERAGE IS 1.443.

ALLIED CHEMICAL CORPORATION
ALCOA CORPORATION
AMERICAN BRANDS, INC.
AMERICAN CAN COMPANY
AMERICAN TELEPHONE & TELEGRAPH CO.
BETHLEHEM STEEL CORPORATION
CHRYSLER CORPORATION
duPONT (E. I.) de NEMOURS & CO.
EASTMAN KODAK COMPANY
ESMARK, INC.
EXXON CORPORATION
GENERAL ELECTRIC COMPANY
GENERAL FOODS CORPORATION
GENERAL MOTORS CORPORATION
GOODYEAR TIRE & RUBBER CO.
INCO LTD.
INTERNATIONAL HARVESTER CO.
INTERNATIONAL PAPER COMPANY
JOHNS-MANVILLE CORPORATION
MINNESOTA MINING & MFG. COMPANY
OWENS ILLINOIS, INC.
PROCTER & GAMBLE COMPANY
SEARS, ROEBUCK & COMPANY
STANDARD OIL CO. OF CALIFORNIA
TEXACO, INC.
UNION CARBIDE CORPORATION
UNITED STATES STEEL CORPORATION
UNITED TECHNOLOGIES CORP.
WESTINGHOUSE ELECTRIC CORPORATION
WOOLWORTH (F. W.) COMPANY

SCALE : EACH BLOCK = $10

Source: *The Stock Picture*, M. C. Horsey & Co., Salisbury, Maryland, 1978.

The DJI 30 stocks represent about 25 percent of the market value of all NYSE-listed shares. Standard & Poor's index of 500 stocks accounts for between 75 and 80 percent of the market value of all listed shares. The S&P 500 Stock Index (Composite) is shown in Figure 13–3, and its performance in defined periods is shown in Figures 13–4A and 13–4B.

Of all the statistics available to investors, Standard & Poor's Composite of 500 Stocks spans almost 100 industry groups. It therefore provides a very useful large industry breakdown and a broad

FIGURE 13–3
Standard & Poor's Indexes of the Security Markets

Weekly Stock Price Indexes — 1941-43 = 10

	Feb. 28	Feb. 21	% Change	Feb. Avgs.	1978-79 High	Range Low
500 Stocks, Combined	96.28	99.07	− 2.8	98.23	106.99	86.90
400 Industrials	107.26	110.51	− 2.9	109.49	118.71	95.52
20 Transportation	12.90	13.21	− 2.3	13.08	16.20	12.40
40 Utilities	49.98	50.93	− 1.9	50.74	54.47	48.23
40 Financial	11.05	11.30	− 2.2	11.28	13.18	10.14
109 Capital Goods	108.99	112.37	− 3.0	110.66	117.09	92.72
190 Consumer Goods	80.31	82.55	− 2.7	81.80	93.83	77.33
*25 High Grade Common	71.55	73.77	− 3.0	72.79	77.97	64.22
*20 Low Price Common	185.83	194.11	− 4.3	191.41	245.84	138.55

INDUSTRIALS

	Feb. 28	Feb. 21	% Change	Feb. Avgs.	1978-79 High	Range Low
8 Aerospace	102.04	106.64	− 4.3	106.38	125.33	68.51
*3 Air Freight	27.45	30.57	−10.2	29.32	44.90	24.40
4 Aluminum	109.73	113.48	− 3.3	110.80	114.92	79.13
4 Automobile	68.21	69.81	− 2.3	69.35	84.03	68.21
Excl. General Motors	24.55	24.83	− 1.1	24.56	29.82	23.41
3 Auto Parts—After Mkt.	14.57	15.09	− 3.4	15.00	17.25	13.34
5 Auto Parts—Orig. Equip.	14.66	15.15	− 3.2	15.07	16.77	13.52
3 Auto Trucks & Parts	42.03	44.80	− 6.2	44.19	54.64	41.26
4 Beverages: Brewers	35.30	36.65	− 3.7	36.32	41.58	30.80
4 Distillers	133.84	136.79	− 2.2	134.37	139.86	108.41
5 Soft Drinks	107.11	109.00	− 1.7	108.10	127.59	98.58
Building Materials Composite	56.21	57.87	− 2.9	57.56	65.82	47.87
4 Air Conditioning	31.60	32.03	− 1.3	32.30	35.16	22.15
4 Cement	29.27	31.36	− 6.7	30.69	35.40	25.41
2 Heating & Plumbing	73.37	75.31	− 2.6	75.42	91.64	60.17
5 Roofing & Wallboard	62.20	63.80	− 2.5	63.21	77.45	57.27
7 Chemicals	52.02	54.02	− 3.7	52.82	59.62	46.05
4 Coal: Bituminous	312.46	322.91	− 3.2	319.40	391.74	271.49
10 Conglomerates	16.66	17.09	− 2.5	16.97	19.42	14.06
5 Containers: Metal & Glass	34.13	34.41	− 0.8	34.20	41.36	33.57
6 Paper Containers	163.41	166.11	− 1.6	160.23	167.73	124.75
5 Copper	30.28	31.10	− 2.6	30.83	31.66	22.03
6 Cosmetics	60.27	62.11	− 3.0	61.96	75.56	55.73
10 Drugs	157.28	160.74	− 2.2	159.54	180.43	140.72
7 Electrical Equipment	268.21	272.96	− 1.7	271.98	310.04	239.02
3 Major Electrical—Electronic	76.88	79.05	− 2.7	78.07	96.10	74.47
3 Household Appliances	128.82	129.07	− 0.2	128.79	163.45	123.53
4 Electronics (Instrumentation)	25.13	25.71	− 2.3	25.61	26.61	17.84
6 Electronics (Semi./Comp.)	18.21	18.54	− 1.8	18.55	22.90	15.13
6 Entertainment	153.14	160.82	− 4.8	158.11	181.21	111.78
4 Fertilizers	11.60	11.52	+ 0.7	11.50	12.55	9.44
22 Foods	68.65	70.49	− 2.6	68.90	79.51	68.65
7 Forest Products	21.12	21.91	− 3.6	21.58	24.08	16.66
*5 Gaming Cos.	15.63	14.31	+ 9.2	14.59	19.70	4.66
3 Gold Mining	107.30	107.89	− 0.5	108.03	121.22	86.99
3 Home Furnishings	22.81	23.05	− 1.0	23.47	25.65	22.34
3 Homebuilding	19.84	21.36	− 7.1	20.52	26.94	13.75
4 Hospital Management	11.85	12.62	− 6.1	12.24	14.38	6.58
6 Hospital Supplies	31.53	33.27	− 5.2	32.89	42.35	31.53
3 Hotel-Motel	47.85	47.76	+ 0.2	47.93	74.15	29.85
6 Leisure Time	25.66	26.90	− 4.6	26.64	35.94	21.74
6 Machine Tools	53.75	55.63	− 3.4	54.23	65.02	35.17
4 Machinery: Agricultural	71.15	74.77	− 4.8	73.02	78.30	51.27
5 Construction & Mat. Handl.	388.90	401.36	− 3.1	396.65	430.70	324.43
10 Industrial/Specialty	108.50	110.41	− 1.7	109.75	123.70	98.68
3 Metal Fabricating	134.47	138.79	− 3.1	137.92	162.55	102.82
8 Metals—Miscellaneous	53.16	55.66	− 4.5	54.48	55.66	38.87
3 Mobile Homes	46.51	48.03	− 3.2	48.00	73.03	45.09

	Feb. 28	Feb. 21	% Change	Feb. Avgs.	1978-79 High	Range Low
8 Office & Business Equipment	1206.82	1238.45	− 2.6	1223.67	1272.98	960.29
Excl. I.B.M.	227.10	240.09	− 5.4	236.05	264.17	180.09
4 Offshore Drilling	51.53	54.89	− 6.1	53.04	80.09	51.53
Oil Composite	164.01	167.46	− 2.1	164.66	170.59	144.50
5 Crude Producers	278.27	287.00	− 3.0	283.75	291.25	227.04
9 Integrated: Domestic	174.15	177.75	− 2.0	173.90	177.75	146.93
6 International	153.95	157.12	− 2.0	154.94	162.00	138.27
*4 Canadian Oil & Gas Exploration	13.32	13.51	− 1.4	13.22	13.51	9.09
6 Oil Well Equip. & Services	1026.22	1063.04	− 3.5	1031.61	1078.91	794.10
8 Paper	219.07	227.75	− 3.8	222.65	247.56	189.57
5 Pollution Control	26.02	27.61	− 5.8	26.45	32.71	22.88
6 Publishing	255.58	276.66	− 7.6	264.30	290.13	208.37
4 Publishing (Newspapers)	23.37	23.62	− 1.1	23.28	27.67	18.52
6 Radio-TV Broadcasters	424.13	444.08	− 4.5	439.86	502.92	325.41
4 Railroad Equipment	57.52	58.50	− 1.7	58.57	74.63	49.12
6 Restaurants	74.31	76.47	− 2.8	75.76	90.44	73.70
Retail Stores Composite	121.77	126.15	− 3.5	124.98	154.60	121.77
8 Department Stores	15.15	15.77	− 3.9	15.58	21.09	12.22
*3 Discount Stores	19.58	20.13	− 2.7	19.88	26.41	17.99
3 Retail Stores (Drug)	57.97	58.52	− 0.9	57.98	62.27	49.32
7 Food Chains	7.18	7.40	− 3.0	7.34	9.07	7.08
4 Gen. Merchandise Chains	47.75	49.19	− 2.9	48.18	56.55	44.53
3 Shoes	158.19	160.51	− 1.4	160.26	177.06	150.75
5 Soaps	41.93	43.94	− 4.6	43.32	50.10	39.94
9 Steel	43.80	45.49	− 3.7	45.04	50.17	41.12
Excl. U.S. Steel	18.38	18.54	− 0.9	18.06	22.34	16.57
3 Sugar Refiners	30.34	30.88	− 1.7	30.81	31.51	23.51
6 Textiles: Apparel Mfrs.	53.47	54.84	− 2.5	53.68	60.96	48.14
2 Synthetic Fibers	46.32	47.11	− 1.7	46.67	54.09	44.04
6 Textile Products	118.39	121.85	− 2.8	120.36	132.75	111.76
4 Tires and Rubber Goods	72.93	74.23	− 1.8	73.78	81.75	64.81
4 Tobacco	11.80	13.06	− 9.6	12.52	13.58	7.45
3 Toys	26.06	27.11	− 3.9	26.89	32.55	20.71
6 Vending & Food Service						

PUBLIC UTILITIES

	Feb. 28	Feb. 21	% Change	Feb. Avgs.	1978-79 High	Range Low
22 Electric Companies	32.29	33.00	− 2.2	32.78	35.52	31.38
8 Natural Gas Distributors	79.37	80.06	− 0.9	79.14	86.19	76.34
6 Pipelines	131.73	134.71	− 2.2	132.85	146.83	118.69
3 Telephone	27.54	28.56	− 3.6	28.28	28.95	26.08
Excl. A.T.&T.	40.33	40.82	− 1.2	40.86	43.54	39.56*

TRANSPORTATION

	Feb. 28	Feb. 21	% Change	Feb. Avgs.	1978-79 High	Range Low
5 Air Transport	40.23	42.79	− 6.0	42.18	65.18	36.38
10 Railroads	44.77	45.43	− 1.5	44.92	49.63	42.04
4 Truckers	78.12	77.23	+ 1.2	76.17	116.31	68.75

FINANCIAL

	Feb. 28	Feb. 21	% Change	Feb. Avgs.	1978-79 High	Range Low
6 New York City Banks	40.92	42.08	− 2.8	41.91	50.91	37.43
10 Banks, Outside N.Y.C.	96.06	98.46	− 2.4	97.54	116.96	87.95
6 Life Insurance	192.49	197.28	− 2.4	196.13	230.33	181.39
4 Multi-Line Insurance	14.71	14.98	− 1.8	14.77	16.67	11.71
4 Property-Casualty Insurance	107.44	108.41	− 0.9	108.22	120.26	97.84
3 Savings & Loan Holding Cos.	23.39	24.27	− 3.6	24.23	31.62	20.29
2 Finance Companies	58.80	59.85	− 1.8	59.00	67.85	54.78
2 Personal Loans	79.07	80.92	− 2.3	80.46	93.52	72.68
*8 Brokerage Firms	9.18	9.76	− 5.9	9.46	13.52	7.85
*3 Real Estate Investment Trust	2.01	2.00	+ 0.5	2.01	2.31	1.89
*8 Investment Cos. (Closed-End)	42.38	43.29	− 2.1	43.02	49.94	41.96
*5 Investment Cos. (Bond Funds)	9.54	9.66	− 1.2	9.49	10.65	8.97

*Indicates a new high or low. ‡Converted from average yield to maturity, assuming an appropriate coupon and maturity. *Not included in composite indexes. a1955 = 10; b1957 = 10; c1959 = 10; e1965 = 10; f1968 = 10; g1970 = 10; h1973 = 10; i1978 = 10. kAll composite bond yields on average of industrial and utility bond yields. pIndustrials also include 23 miscellaneous issues; Transportation and Financial each include one miscellaneous issue. Refer to latest Cumulative Index for lists of all issues included in the indexes. **Based on intraday high and low prices. ¹BLS Index (1967 = 100). ²Business Week Index (1967 = 100). ‡Appreciation plus dividends (reinvested); compound rate.

Source: *The Outlook,* Standard & Poor's Corporation, March 5, 1979, p. 896.

FIGURE 13–4A

PERFORMANCE STATISTICS
33 YEARS OF 10 YEAR PERIODS
1945 - 1977

Period	Dow-Jones Industrials	S. & P. 500 Stocks	Johnson Growth Funds	Johnson Stock Funds	Johnson Balanced Funds	Cost of Living	Savings Bank Deposit	U. S. Govt. Bonds	High-Grade Corporate Bonds	Preferred Stocks
1968 - 77	− 8%	− 1%	− 14%	− 8%	− 8%	+ 83%	0%	− 25%	− 23%	− 24%
1967 - 76	+ 28	+ 34	+ 28	+ 32	+ 10	+ 77	0	− 9	− 25	− 32
1966 - 75	− 12	− 2	+ 7	+ 6	− 15	+ 75	0	− 16	− 38	− 47
1965 - 74	− 30	− 19	+ 2	− 4	− 22	+ 66	0	− 25	− 41	− 53
1964 - 73	+ 12	+ 30	+ 56	+ 45	+ 9	+ 50	0	− 20	− 34	− 45
1963 - 72	+ 56	+ 87	+137	+113	+ 44	+ 40	0	− 19	− 32	− 36
1962 - 71	+ 22	+ 43	+ 72	+ 59	+ 22	+ 37	0	− 17	− 29	− 32
1961 - 70	+ 36	+ 59	+ 82	+ 69	+ 27	+ 33	0	− 25	− 32	− 31
1960 - 69	+ 18	+ 54	+125	+ 92	+ 26	+ 28	0	− 23	− 33	− 32
1959 - 68	+ 62	+ 88	+213	+154	+ 57	+ 23	0	− 21	− 27	− 23
1958 - 67	+108	+143	+264	+202	+ 78	+ 19	0	− 24	− 28	− 25
1957 - 66	+ 57	+ 72	+123	+ 93	+ 36	+ 19	0	− 13	− 19	− 12
1956 - 65	+ 99	+103	+142	+113	+ 52	+ 19	0	− 17	− 19	− 9
1955 - 64	+116	+136	+127	+111	+ 56	+ 17	0	− 17	− 18	− 7
1954 - 63	+172	+202	+201	+167	+ 85	+ 15	0	− 16	− 16	− 3
1953 - 62	+123	+138	+154	+122	+ 61	+ 14	0	− 12	− 15	− 7
1952 - 61	+172	+201	—	+178	+ 89	+ 13	0	− 15	− 17	− 7
1951 - 60	+162	+185	—	+163	+ 73	+ 19	0	− 16	− 22	− 19
1950 - 59	+239	+257	—	+213	+ 96	+ 24	0	− 25	− 25	− 21
1949 - 58	+229	+263	—	+215	+102	+ 20	0	− 16	− 17	− 11
1948 - 57	+141	+161	—	+112	+ 56	+ 21	0	− 7	− 11	− 6
1947 - 56	+182	+205	—	+138	+ 66	+ 28	0	− 13	− 16	− 23
1946 - 55	+153	+162	—	+142	+ 92	+ 47	0	− 6	− 8	− 11
1945 - 54	+165	+171	—	+115	+ 63	+ 50	0	− 2	− 2	− 1
Average of 24 Periods (1945 - 1977)	+ 96	+116	—	+111	+ 48	+ 35	0	− 17	− 23	− 21
Average of 16 Periods (1953 - 1977)	+ 54	+ 73	+107	+ 86	+ 32	+ 38	0	− 18	− 27	− 26

PERFORMANCE STATISTICS
15, 20, 25, 30 YEAR PERIODS
ENDING DECEMBER 31, 1977

Period	Dow-Jones Industrials	S. & P. 500 Stocks	Johnson Growth Funds	Johnson Stock Funds	Johnson Balanced Funds	Cost of Living	Savings Bank Deposit	U. S. Govt. Bonds	High-Grade Corporate Bonds	Preferred Stocks
15 Years 1963 - 1977	+ 27%	+ 51%	+ 97%	+ 80%	+ 18%	+105%	0%	−37%	−40%	−44%
20 Years 1958 - 1977	+ 91	+138	+227	+209	+ 70	+118	0	−43	−44	−43
25 Years 1953 - 1977	+185	+283	+409	+373	+121	+133	0	−45	−50	−47
30 Years 1948 - 1977	+359	+522	+720	+657	+136	+165	0	−47	−51	−47

STANDARD & POOR'S COMPOSITE 500 STOCK INDEX
VARIOUS PERIODS 1871 - 1977

Length of Periods	Total Number of Periods in 106 Years	Number of Periods in Which Stock Prices Rose	Number of Periods in Which Stock Prices Declined	No Change	Percentage Opportunity for Profit
1 year	106	62	43	1	58%
5 years	102	77	24	1	75
10 years	97	83	14	0	86
15 years	92	83	9	0	90
20 years	87	84	3	0	97
25 years	82	81	1	0	99
30 years	77	77	0	0	100

Source: *Johnson's Charts,* 1978 edition.

FIGURE 13–4B

INVESTMENT YIELDS AND INTEREST RATES
1958 - 1977

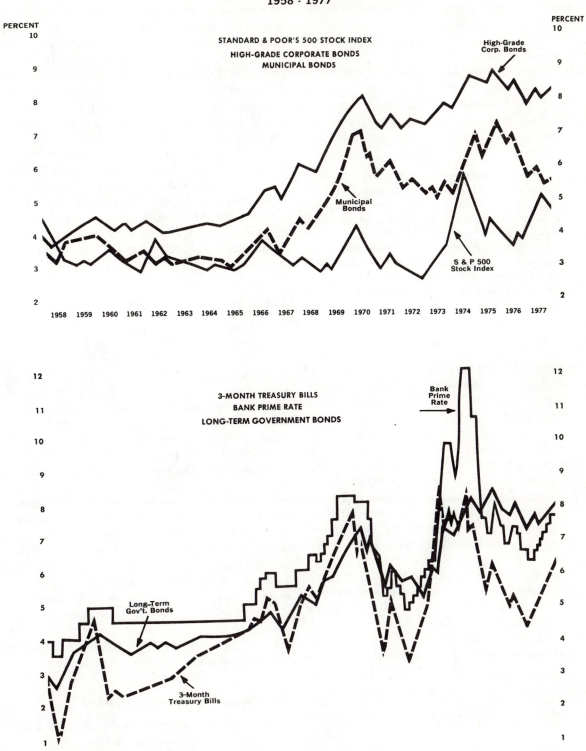

Source: *Johnson's Charts,* 1978 edition.

outlook on the market. These indexes are published weekly in the *Outlook*.

The Composite aims "to supply a dependable measure of the composite price pattern of the majority of stocks." The list of stocks is frequently changed, to keep it representative of the major industries and leading companies. Issues are weighted by their total market capitalizations, so the largest companies have the greatest influence over the movements of the index.

> Of late, there has been increasing interest in using the S&P 500, or some approximation of it, as a portfolio. By duplicating the index, the investor expects to achieve an average return (before transaction costs)—no more and no less. Others have taken the Composite's industry weightings as a starting point for portfolio diversification, deviating from it in areas where they felt confident of above-average results.[3]

Other Stock Price Indexes

In mid-1966 both the American Stock Exchange and the New York Stock Exchange developed and introduced their own stock price indexes. Since the AMEX index considers net price changes only, it gives no consideration to the relationship between the net change and a stock's price. This means that a $1 more in a $5 stock receives the same weight as a $1 change in a $100 stock.

The NYSE Common Stock Exchange Index is a composite index of all the equity issues listed on the exchange. It is weighted by the total market value of every common stock traded on the exchange.

Computers of the New York Stock Exchange's Market Data System calculate the new indexes throughout the trading day. The New York Stock Exchange Price Index reflects the trend in stock prices not only day to day, but hour to hour and even minute to minute. The composite index and

[3] See "The S&P 500: Price Index, Performance Yardstick or Portfolio?" *Weekly Staff Report,* David L. Babson & Co., Boston, January 13, 1977. As of February, the food and health care sectors of the Composite Index were restructured. See *The Outlook,* Feb. 12, 1979, p. 927.

its net change from the previous day's close are printed on the ticker tape every half hour along with the actual dollars-and-cents change in the average price of all common stocks. The 1,000-stock Industrial, the 76-issue Transportation, the 136-issue Utility, and the 75-stock Finance indexes, with net changes, are reported hourly. The final results for the day are printed on the tape after the close of the market.

There are other stock price averages or indexes, such as the Value Line Average of 1,600 stocks. Value Line computes its own stock averages and publishes a weekly chart. This may be seen in Figure 13–5. It should be noted that in the Value Line Composite, prices are not weighted by the number of outstanding shares, as in the case of the NYSE and S&P averages.

The Organized Exchanges

The organized exchanges provide physical marketplaces where trading in existing securities occurs. They furnish facilities "for the maintenance of a free, close, and continuous market for securities traded"—free in that the trading price of any security, in the absence of now illegal manipulation, is governed by the forces of supply and demand; close in that the spread between the bid price for a security and the price at which it is offered for sale is normally relatively narrow; and continuous in that successive sales are ordinarily made at relatively small variations in price, thus providing a liquid market. Organized exchanges are markets whose prices are set by thousands of buyers and sellers in numerous little auctions that occur daily on the floor of the exchange. The New York Stock Exchange is, of course, the most important exchange, and it accounts for about 80 percent of all trading on organized U.S. exchanges. The American Stock Exchange ranks next, with the Midwest, Pacific Coast, and PBW (Philadelphia, Baltimore, Washington) also exchanges of importance.

The Over-The-Counter Market

The over-the-counter market consists of a loose aggregation of brokers and dealers who make a

FIGURE 13–5
Value Line Index of 1600 Stocks

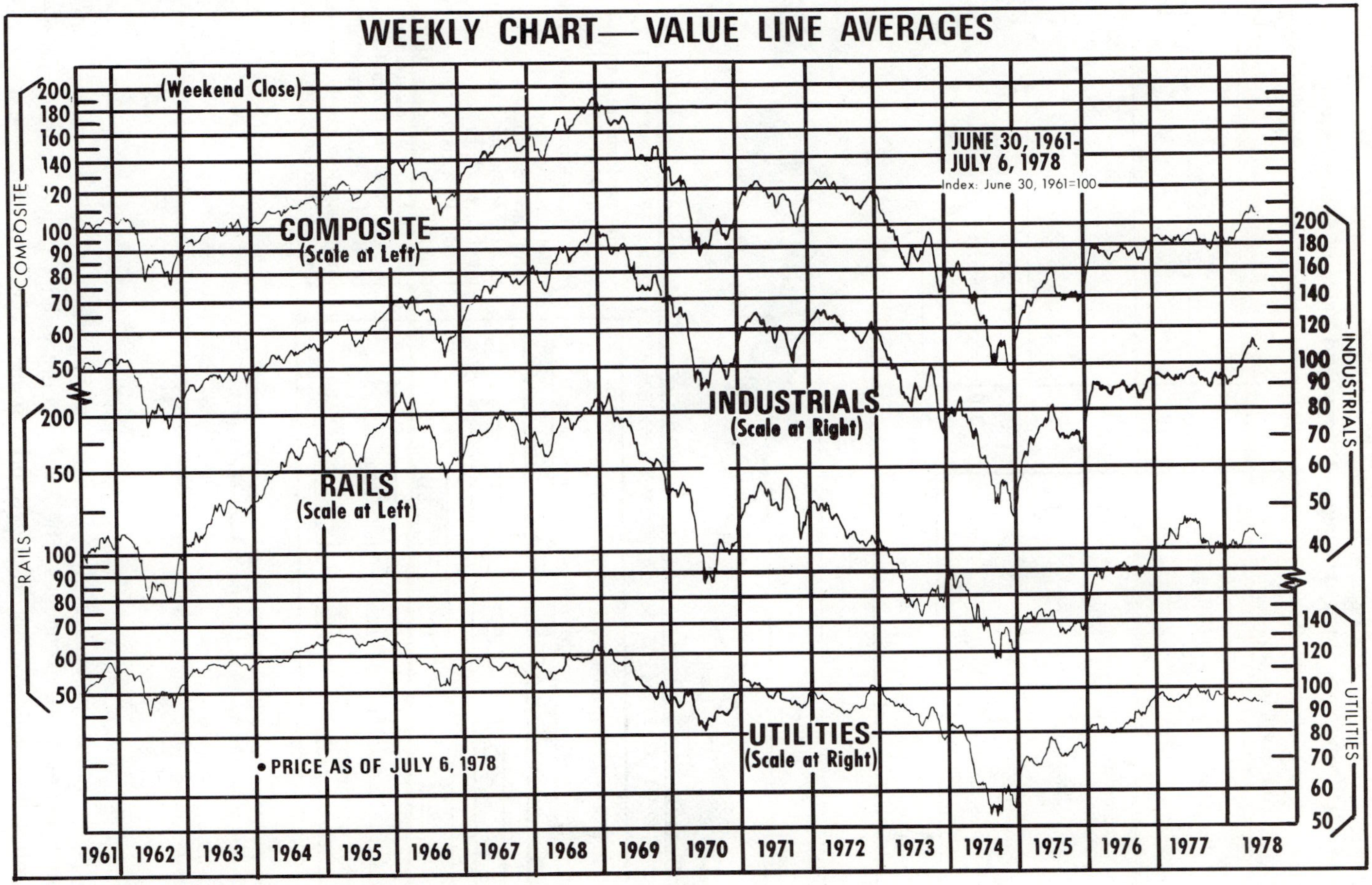

WEEKLY CHART — VALUE LINE AVERAGES

Source: Value Line Investment Service, Arnold Bernhard & Co.

FIGURE 13–6

The Equity Market: New York Stock Exchange—Volume and Value of Shares Traded

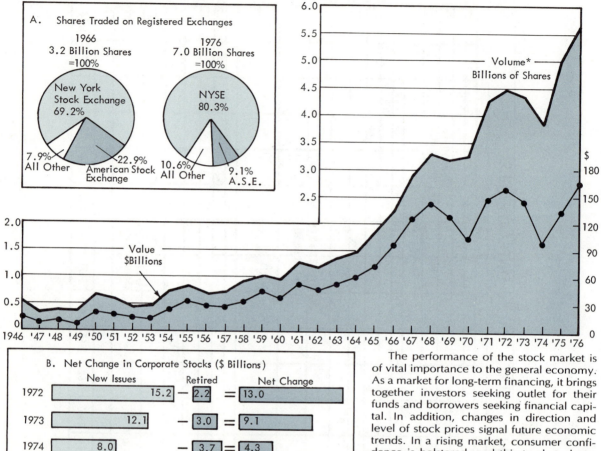

The performance of the stock market is of vital importance to the general economy. As a market for long-term financing, it brings together investors seeking outlet for their funds and borrowers seeking financial capital. In addition, changes in direction and level of stock prices signal future economic trends. In a rising market, consumer confidence is bolstered, and this tends to buoy personal consumption expenditures. Finally, the decision to purchase equities depends on the investors' expectation of the economy, its effect on the market, and the prospective earnings and dividends of the particular issue.

*Includes nonreported and odd lot transactions.

Source: *Road Map of Industry,* no. 1802, Conference Board, March 1977.

market principally, though not exclusively, for securities not listed on organized exchanges. The term *over-the-counter* itself is misleading. There are no counters, and there is no market in the sense of a given place where buyers and sellers meet to dispose of wares. The over-the-counter market is a complex network of trading rooms all over the country, linked by telephone and electronic communications. The phrase is a carry-over from the past, when shares were literally sold over the counter of private banking houses.

Securities transactions in the over-the-counter

market run about 60 percent of the volume on all of the organized exchanges. Most federal, state, and municipal securities, most bonds, and many bank and insurance company stocks are traded over the counter. There is also an over-the-counter market in exchange-listed securities, the so-called third market. Unlike the stocks traded on the organized exchanges, over-the-counter securities are traded in a negotiated rather than an auction market. The price at which a given security can be purchased or sold on the over-the-counter market is determined by bargaining, with the broker-dealer usually acting as a principal in the transaction, although sometimes asked to act as an agent.

THE REGISTERED EXCHANGES

The New York Stock Exchange

The New York Stock Exchange is almost as old as the country. Established in 1792, it wasn't until 1863 that its name was changed to New York Stock Exchange. The exchange is now a corporation, and it has 1,366 members who have bought "seats" (memberships) on the exchange. Only members of the exchange are permitted to trade on its "floor." A seat, or membership, has sold for as high as $625,000 (1929) and for as low as $17,000 (1942). Since 1950, the price of a membership has ranged from $40,000 to $515,000 (1969). The securities of more than 1,500 major companies are "listed" on the New York Stock Exchange, which means that they have been accepted for trading. Only those securities which have been accepted for listing may be traded on the exchange floor. Trading takes place between the hours of 10:00 A.M. and 4:00 P.M., New York time, Monday through Friday.

The New York Stock Exchange is located at the corner of Wall and Broad Streets. Its floor is almost the size of a football field. On the trading floor are 19 posts, at which some 2,000 listed stock issues are traded, and the "Bond Crowd," where 2,300 bond issues are bought and sold. Much more bond trading takes place in the over-the-counter market than on the floor of the New York Stock Exchange.

Automation has taken over at the Big Board, but it is in such a state of flux that what is true today may be obsolete tomorrow. A high-speed ticker now provides a "composite" tape that carries reports of trades in listed stocks wherever those stocks are traded, whether on the floor of the NYSE itself, or on the regional exchanges, or in the third market. There is also a composite quotation system. Your broker, using a desk-top electronic machine linked to remote computers, can know immediately the bid and asked prices of any listed security in all markets, by simply punching in the stock symbol. It takes only a matter of seconds to get a "quote" on a stock you are interested in.[4]

CLOB and SLOB

If you invest or trade you should learn the stock symbols. "T" stands for American Telephone & Telegraph, "A" for Anaconda Copper, "GE" for General Electric, and "GM" for General Motors; but "N" is for Inco, Ltd., and "NG" for National Gypsum; "X" is U.S. Steel, "Y" is Alleghany Corp., and "Z" is F. W. Woolworth & Co. When a broker asks, "How's Mickey Mouse?" he's referring to Disney (Walt) Productions (DIS), and if he says "Knockout" he means Coca-Cola Co. (KO). Some of the names derived from symbols—such as Slob for Schlumberger (SLB)—are abhorred by the listed companies themselves. By a logic that has nothing to do with the sound of their ticker symbols, Holiday Inns (HIA) is known as "Hot Beds" and Simmons Co. (SIM) as the "world's playground." What the brokers call two AMEX stocks, Fluke Manufacturing Corp. (FKM) and Shaer Shoe Corp. (SHS), you can imagine.

How does a transaction taking place on the floor of the exchange get onto the ticker tape in seconds or minutes? There is an optical scanner or card reader at each trading post on the floor of the exchange. The card reader scans optically the details of a transaction marked on a special IBM card by a reporter at the trading post, and it simultaneously

---

[4] See "Here Comes the New Stock Market," *Dun's Review,* April 1978, p. 65.

transmits this information electronically—stock symbol, number of shares, and price—to the exchange's computer center, where it is in turn automatically printed on thousands of stock tickers and display devices.

The pneumatic tubes which were formerly used to convey completed transaction information from the trading posts to the ticker room have gone the way of the horse and buggy and the trolley car. So also have the huge annunciator boards whose flashing or flapping numbers used to summon brokers from the trading posts to their phone or order booths lining the floor of the exchange. Brokers no longer need to keep their eyes on the annunciator call boards because radio paging is now in effect. Members now carry five-ounce pocket radio receivers which audibly beep and indicate with lights which booth or booths are paging them.

Automated equipment has begun to be used extensively, and vast changes are at hand in the coming central market system and certificateless society. The NYSE and AMEX have established a joint subsidiary, the Securities Industry Automation Corporation, which is now engaged in a variety of experimental programs and techniques. Perhaps just ahead is the Consolidated Limit Order Book (CLOB), the electronic "black box" which may some day supersede the specialist.

The Securities Industry Automation Corporation (SIAC) has developed a new automated bond trading system (ABS) and a Common Message Switch. It allows a broker, from his office, to send an order of up to 500 shares directly to the trading post of the market which is offering the best price. Orders for odd lots (that is, fewer than 100 shares) are routed through the Common Message Switch and executed automatically. This occurs at a price based on the first auction market round lot trade that follows receipt of the odd lot order at the trading post.[5] SIAC has also developed the Designated Order Turnaround (DOT) system to speed up the processing of orders directly to the specialist at the trading post. DOT maximizes automation

in order processing while adhering to auction market pricing. Even on high-volume days 86 percent of DOT orders were confirmed to the originating office in five minutes or less.

The Functions of Members

A member of the New York Stock Exchange may be a general partner or a holder of voting stock in one of the brokerage concerns which, by virtue of his or her exchange membership, is known as a member firm or a member corporation. There are 473 such member organizations—228 partnerships and 266 corporations. About half of the members of the New York Stock Exchange are partners or officers in member organizations doing business with the public—so-called *commission houses.* These members execute customers' orders to buy and sell on the exchange, and their firms receive negotiated commissions on those transactions. Many commission brokerage houses, particularly the larger ones such as Merrill Lynch, Pierce, Fenner & Smith; Bache Halsey Stuart; and Paine, Webber, Jackson & Curtis have more than one member.

The Specialists

About one fourth of the members of the New York Stock Exchange are *specialists,* so called because they specialize in "making a market" for one or more stocks.

What exactly do the specialists do? How do they help provide liquidity in the central marketplace? The specialists have two jobs.[6] First, they execute limit orders that other members of the exchange may leave with them. These orders are left with the specialists when the current market price is away from the prices of the limit orders, for instance, when a commission broker receives a limit order to buy at 55 a stock that is selling at

----

[5] Odd lot orders are now handled by specialists. There are no longer any odd lot dealers.

[6] Since the function of the specialist is difficult to describe briefly, you may wish to write to the New York Stock Exchange for the booklet *The Specialist* which will provide much more detail.

60. By executing limit orders on behalf of other exchange members when the market price reaches the price stated on the orders, the specialists make it possible for those members to transact other business elsewhere on the exchange floor. In handling these orders, the specialists act as brokers or agents.

The second, more complex role of the specialists is that of dealers or principals for their own accounts. As dealers, the specialists are expected, insofar as reasonably practical, to maintain continuous, fair, and orderly markets in the stocks assigned to them. When there is a temporary disparity, for example, between supply and demand, the specialists are expected to buy or sell for their own accounts in order to narrow the price changes between transactions and to give depth to the market. By doing this, the specialists maintain a more orderly price continuity than would otherwise exist and thus contribute to the liquidity of the market. In this way they usually make it possible for investors' orders to be executed at better prices when a temporary disparity exists.

In order to maintain the market the specialists usually purchase stock at a higher price than anyone else is willing to pay. For example, let's assume that a stock has just sold at 55. The highest price that anyone is willing to pay is 54¼ (the best bid), and the lowest price at which anyone is willing to sell is 55¼ (the best offer). The specialists, acting as dealers for their own accounts, may now decide to bid 54¾ for 100 shares, making the quotation 54¾–55¼, which narrows the spread between the bid and offer prices to one-half point. Now, if a prospective seller wishes to sell 100 shares at the price of the best bid, the specialist will purchase the stock at 54¾. By doing this, the specialist not only provides the seller with a better price, but also maintains better price continuity, since the variation from the last sale is only one quarter of a point.

On the other hand, here is an example of how the specialists may sell stock for their own accounts in order to maintain a market. Let's assume that with the last sale in a stock at 62¼ the best bid is 62 and the best offer 63. The specialist offers 500 shares at 62½ for his own account, changing the quotation to 62–62½. A buyer enters the market and buys the stock from the specialist. Thus the buyer purchased the stock one-half point cheaper than would have been the case without the specialist's offer.

Many times, when the specialists do not have sufficient stock in their inventories, they will sell "short" in order to maintain a market. In doing this, they must observe all the rules and regulations governing "short" selling (See pages 438–40).

The Specialist's Book

Specialists enter limit orders in their "books" under each price category in the sequence in which they are received. For each order the specialist shows the number of shares and from whom the order was received. He represents these orders in the market, frequently competing against other members representing other customers. As specialists succeed in executing the orders in their books, they send reports to the members for whom they have acted according to the sequence of listing in their books.

Most of the orders received by brokers on the floor before the opening of the market are left with specialists. Using these orders and also dealing for their own accounts in varying degrees, the specialists arrange the opening price in each of the stocks assigned to them. The opening is expected to be near the previous close unless some startling new development has taken place in the interim.

The exchange sets specific requirements for specialists concerning their market experience, their dealer function, and the amount of capital they must possess. Specialists are expected to subordinate their own interests in the market to the interests of the public. Specialists, for example, cannot *buy* in the exchange market for their own account at any given price until they have executed all public *buy* orders held by them at that price. The same rule also applies to *sales* by specialists. A specialist on the New York Stock Exchange must now be able to carry 5,000 shares of each stock handled, while a specialist on the American Stock Exchange must either have a capital of $100,000 or be able to carry 2,000 shares of each stock, whichever is larger.[7]

A specialist's business is concentrated in one or more stocks at one trading post. He "keeps the books" in these stocks. Specialists usually have associates or assistants, and one or the other is always at the post during trading hours. Thus specialists can also act for other brokers who cannot remain at one post until the prices specified by their customers' buy and sell orders—either purchases below or sales above the prevailing prices—are reached. The specialists must assume full responsibility for all orders turned over to them. Part of the commission that customers pay their own brokers goes to the specialists when their services are used, and much of the specialists' earnings comes from commissions on orders that they execute for other brokers.

Because the specialists keep the books in the stock and thus have advance notice of prospective buy and sell orders at varying prices, and because they can also deal for their own accounts, suspicion has always been raised concerning their objectivity and impartiality and doubts have been expressed about their conflict of interest between making a market and making money for themselves. The trading practices of the specialists are carefully supervised, but the supervisors—exchange officials or other members—are either their employees or associates of the specialists.

If and when the black box replaces the specialist's activities either in whole or in part, because a Central Limit Order File operated by computers is established, the role and functions of the specialist will be limited. Price competition on limit orders will, it is hoped, then be strengthened.

Other members of the New York Stock Exchange serve as *floor brokers,* assisting busy commission brokers to ensure the swift execution of orders. Investors complain if their orders are not handled rapidly and efficiently. Commission brokerage houses are very sensitive to this.

Smaller houses, which have only one member of the firm on the floor of the exchange, need

help when orders flow in rapidly or in bunches. They can call upon the floor brokers to take over some of their volume and by this means secure quick execution of orders which might otherwise be delayed. The commission brokerage houses which utilize the services of floor brokers share commissions with them.

Some 90 members of the New York Stock Exchange, use their privilege of being able to engage in transactions on the floor of the exchange simply to buy and sell for their own accounts. The transactions of these members, who are now known as *registered traders,* must meet certain exchange requirements and must contribute to the liquidity of the markets in the stocks in which they trade. Registered traders may also be called upon to help expedite the handling of blocks of stock bid for or offered on the exchange.

Listing Requirements

To be listed on the New York Stock Exchange, a company is expected to meet certain qualifications and to be willing to keep the investing public informed on the progress of its affairs. In determining eligibility for listing, particular attention is given to such qualifications as: (*a*) whether the company is national or local in scope; (*b*) its relative position and standing in the industry; and (*c*) whether it is engaged in an expanding industry, with prospects of at least maintaining its relative position.

Of the approximately 1,700,000 publicly and privately held corporations filing reports with the U.S. Treasury, 30,000 have their shares quoted over the counter; about 11,000 have sufficiently wide ownership to be considered publicly owned; and 2,900 are listed or traded on stock exchanges. The NYSE currently lists the common stock of 1,500 corporations, but these include most of the larger, nationally known companies. They earn about 90 percent of total corporate income.

The American Stock Exchange

AMEX, sometimes called the Little Big Board, is located a few blocks away from the NYSE.

---

[7] Or 20 trading units.

Founded in the 1850s, it was known as the New York Curb Exchange until its name was changed in 1953. Its earlier name resulted from the fact that it was an outdoor market from its origin until 1921, its members conducting trading along the curb on Broad and Wall streets. Brokers' clerks sat or leaned out of the second-story windows of office buildings lining the street and by the use of hand signals conveyed orders and messages to their brokers on the street below.

The brokers wore picturesque hats of various bright multicolored hues so that they could be distinguished from one another and recognized by their clerks in the second-story windows. Yet even today the hand signals survive, and a visitor to the American Stock Exchange can watch the rather esoteric hand signals between the telephone clerks in tiers around the floor of the exchange and brokers milling around the various trading posts.

Basically the procedures of the American Stock Exchange are much like those of the New York Stock Exchange. The listing requirements follow those of the NYSE but are not as stringent. Although some stable old-line companies are listed on the AMEX, generally the companies listed are less mature and seasoned than those listed on the NYSE. Indeed, the AMEX has served as a kind of proving ground for newer companies, many of which, as they grow and expand, transfer their listing to the NYSE. Thus, for example, both Du Pont and General Motors were first traded on the AMEX. Starting in 1976, dual listing of shares on both the NYSE and the AMEX was permitted in yet another move toward a central market system.

Many of the stocks on the AMEX are low priced (the average is about $15 per share versus approximately $55 on the Big Board), and many trade in round lots of 10, 20, and 50 shares, instead of the customary hundred. Unlike the New York Stock Exchange, the AMEX permits trading in some unlisted companies. The American Stock Exchange grants specialists the right to make a market in certain issues, even though the companies have not applied for listing privileges. There is also considerable trading in foreign securities on the AMEX. In fact, the AMEX originated the ADR—American De-

pository Receipts—by means of which American investors can trade in claims to foreign securities, the shares themselves being held by U.S. banks abroad. Many large commission brokerage houses hold membership on both the AMEX and the NYSE.

The Regional Exchanges

Over the last decade the regional exchanges expanded their proportion of the total shares sold on registered exchanges. By 1975, their share of the total volume traded was a little more than 11 percent and their proportion of the total value of the shares traded reached 12 percent.

The three principal regional exchanges are the Midwest Stock Exchange (MSE), the Pacific Coast Stock Exchange (PCSE), and the Philadelphia-Baltimore-Washington (PBWSE) exchange. Over a third of the member organizations of the MSE are also members of the NYSE, and over 90 percent of the issues traded on the MSE are also traded on either the NYSE or the AMEX.

The Pacific Coast Stock Exchange resulted from a consolidation in 1957 of the San Francisco and Los Angeles stock exchanges. The PCSE's two divisions, one in San Francisco and one in Los Angeles, each with its own trading floor, are interconnected by an extensive communications system. The PCSE has the largest volume of shares traded of all the regional exchanges. About one third of the PCSE member firms are members of the NYSE, and over 90 percent of the PCSE's stocks are traded on either the NYSE or the AMEX. Because of the time differential between the East Coast and the West Coast, the PCSE provides trading facilities after the close of the NYSE and the AMEX.

Generally the larger regional exchanges list some 600 to 900 companies each, while the smaller ones list about 100 companies each. The companies listed are for the most part regional or local concerns, but there is extensive trading in securities listed on the NYSE or the AMEX. Such shares usually enjoy unlisted trading privileges on the regional exchanges. Odd lots are a larger part of total trading volume on the regional exchanges than on the NYSE. For dually traded issues, transactions on the regional exchanges are usually based on the prices and quotations of the NYSE or the AMEX. The NYSE, AMEX, MSE, PCSE, and PBWSE account for 99 percent of the dollar volume and 99 percent of the share volume of the securities traded on all exchanges.

THE EXECUTION OF TRANSACTIONS ON THE EXCHANGES

Types of Orders

The most generally used type of order is the *market order*. When a customer places an order "at the market," this means that the commission broker is authorized to execute the order at the best possible price that can be obtained at the time the order reaches the post at which the stock is traded: in brief, at the then prevailing market price or close to it. Probably about 75–85 percent of all orders are market orders. Such orders can be executed very quickly. Market orders are perhaps more common in sales than in purchases, since the seller is usually more anxious to obtain action than the buyer.

When the buyer or the seller wishes to specify the price at which an order is to be executed, a *limit order* is placed. The broker is expected to execute such an order at the limit set or better. If it is a buy order, this means either at the price specified or lower, and if it is a sell order, either at the price specified or higher. It may be that at the time the order is given it cannot be executed at the price specified. In that case the customer will have to wait until the market gets around to that price. Naturally the floor member of the commission brokerage house that is given the order to execute cannot wait at the trading post until the market moves to the specified price. This may take days, or weeks, or it may never occur at all. Instead of waiting, the commission broker gives the order to the specialist in the stock, who immediately enters it in his book. If and when, minutes, or hours, or days, or weeks, or months later, the market price moves to the price specified in the limit order and the limit order is still in effect, the specialist will execute the order at the price specified and notify the commission broker, who in turn will notify the customer.

How an Order Is Handled

Perhaps routine auction market operations will be clearer if we trace a typical order. Assume that Anne Wilton of New Orleans decides to buy 100 shares of American Telephone & Telegraph. She asks the member firm's registered representative to find out for her what AT&T shares are selling for on the exchange. Employing an electronic interrogation device which has instant access to a computer center that receives current market data from the exchange, the representative reports that "Telephone" is quoted at "50 to a quarter." This means that, at the moment, the highest bid to buy AT&T stock is $50 a share and that the lowest offer to sell is $50.25 a share. Ms. Wilton thus learns that a round lot—100 shares—will cost her about $5,000 plus commission. She decides to buy. The registered representative writes out an order to buy 100 shares of T "at the market." This is transmitted to the New York office at once and phoned from the firm's New York office to its clerk in a phone booth on the floor of the exchange. The clerk summons the firm's member partner and gives him the order. Each stock listed on the exchange is assigned a specific location at one of the trading posts, and all bids and offers must take place at that location. The floor partner hurries over to Post 15 where T is traded.

About the same time a Minneapolis grain merchant, Edward Hardy, decides that he wants to sell his 100 shares of Telephone. He calls his broker, gets a "quote," and tells his broker to sell. That order, too, is wired or phoned to the floor. Hardy's broker also hurries to Post 15. Just as he enters the AT&T "crowd," he hears Ms. Wilton's broker calling out, "How's Telephone?" Someone—usually the specialist—answers, "50 to a quarter."

Ms. Wilton's broker could, without further thought, buy the 100 shares offered at 50¼, and Mr. Hardy's broker could sell his 100 at 50. In that event, and if their customers had been looking over their shoulders, the customers probably would have said, "Why didn't you try to get a better price for us?" And they would have been right. Ms. Wilton's broker should reason: "I can't buy my 100 shares at 50. Someone has already bid 50, and no one will sell at that price. I could buy at 50¼ because someone has already offered to sell at that price, but no one has come forward to buy. Guess I'd better try 50⅛." Mr. Hardy's broker reasons: "I can't sell my shares at 50¼ because someone has already tried, and no one will buy them. I could sell at 50, but why don't I try 50⅛?" At that moment he hears Ms. Wilton's broker bid 50⅛, and instantly he shouts: "Sold 100 at 50⅛." They have agreed on a price, and the transaction takes place.

The two brokers complete their verbal agreement by noting each other's firm name and reporting the transaction back to their phone clerks so that the respective customers can be notified. At the moment that the transaction took place, an exchange reporter noted it on a card and placed the card in the optical card reader at the post. This transmitted the report of the transaction to the exchange's computer center and to the ticker. In a few seconds it automatically appears as T 50⅛ on some 12,000 tickers and display devices all over the United States and Canada.

In two or three minutes the buyer in New Orleans and the seller in Minneapolis are notified of the transaction. In a transaction on an organized exchange, when you buy, you buy from another person. When you sell, you sell to another person. The exchange itself does not buy, or sell, or set prices. It merely provides the marketplace, the physical setting, and the equipment. Prices are determined in "double auction"—a number of prospective buyers and a number of prospective sellers bidding in an active market. Although the written description of the process may seem lengthy, the actual transaction could take two or three minutes.

Special Types of Orders

Do you know what a WOW order is? It is one of the numerous special types of orders, but you won't need to know about it until you buy your seat on the exchange. There are a few special types of orders, however, that are important.

Stop orders may be used in an effort to protect a paper profit or to try to limit a possible loss. There are stop orders to sell and stop orders to buy. These are essentially conditional market orders. They go into effect if something happens. For example, you bought IBM at 150 and now it is 300. You want to continue to hold it as long as it keeps going up, but you want to protect your gain in case the market turns down. You place a stop order to sell at, say, 290, 10 points below the current market. If the market turns down and goes to 290 or lower, your stock will be sold. Though you lose the last 10 points of your stock's climb, you preserve all the rest of the gain.

Or, to take another use, you note that General Motors is selling at 62. You think and hope that it will go up farther and then split. You buy 100 shares at 62, but at the same time you place a stop order to sell at 60. If your guess is incorrect and GM falls instead of rising, you will be out of it with a two-point loss, plus commissions.

The stop order to buy is used in a short sale to limit losses. You sell Celanese short at 60. You expect and hope that it will decline to 40. If it does, you will cover at that time and have a 20-point gain. But there is also the possibility that it may go up farther. To cut your possible loss, if it does, you place a stop order to buy at 65. Thus if the stock goes up contrary to your expectation, you will have bought back and covered at 65, and your loss will be held to five points.

The investor is not assured of getting the exact price designated by the stop order. If the market takes a sudden drop, the specialist sells the stock at whatever can be obtained; and that might be somewhat below the stop price. If you place a stop-loss order at 50, an accumulation of prior sell orders at this price, or a sharp drop in the market, may prevent the specialist from executing your order until the price is somewhere below 50. There is, however, a hybrid version called the *stop-limit order*. This enables the investor to stipulate the maximum or minimum price acceptable for purchase or sale. If the specialist cannot execute at that price or better, no transaction takes place.

At times the New York Stock Exchange has become worried about stop-loss orders in high-flying glamour stocks, because a downward dip in the market could set off a chain of stop orders and by enlarging sales cause a sharp break in the given stock or stocks. It has, therefore, from time to time, suspended the placement of stop orders in designated stocks to prevent undue market repercussions.

Both stop-limit and stop-loss orders may be day, week, month, or "open" (GTC) orders. A market order is always a day order, good until the close of trading on the day it is written. When you give your broker a limit or stop order, you can specify that it is to be good for only one day—or for a week—or for a month. If the order is not executed during the period designated, it automatically expires. An open or GTC order is one that holds good indefinitely. The order holds until either the broker executes it or the customer cancels it. GTC means "good till canceled."

A discretionary order is one which allows the broker to determine when to buy and when to sell, what to buy, what to sell, and in what volume. This is a complete discretionary order. It must be given in writing by the customer and approved by a member of the firm. A limited discretionary order permits the broker to determine only the price and the timing. Discretionary orders are used by those who are ill, aged, or off on a prolonged vacation. A long and close relationship with a reputable broker is a basic requirement for the use of such orders.

What It Costs to Buy and Sell Stocks

Until 1971–72 the NYSE was able to maintain a fixed rate structure for all transactions, regardless of their amount. Membership was limited, and the NYSE was able to require all members to charge *fixed rates* depending on the price of the stock and the number of shares involved. Pressure on the fixed-fee system came from Congress, from the SEC, and especially from institutional investors. Institutions have pressed either for membership on exchanges or for negotiated commissions. Obviously an order that is ten times as large as a round lot (a round lot is 100 shares) does not involve ten times as much overhead—telephoning, bookkeeping, execution, and delivery costs. Yet until 1975, commission charges on a 1,000-share order were ten times as large as the fees on the 100-share (round lot) order. As a result of institutional pressures commissions became competitive (negotiated) on transactions of $500,000 and over in 1971, and this was lowered to $300,000 or more in 1972. *On May 1, 1975, all fixed commission rates were abolished and commissions became competitive (negotiated).*

With the move to competitive rates in 1975 the chief beneficiaries at first were the institutional investors. Discounts of up to 60 percent off the old fixed rates were granted on large transactions, according to the financial press.

In its first report to Congress on changes in commission rates, the SEC noted that "rates paid by institutions are lower for each order size category, declining about 15 percent for small orders and about 28 percent for the largest orders. . . . In contrast, rates paid by individuals have changed relatively little. . . . rates remain relatively stable except on the very largest orders. Rates at first increased on small orders by about 4 percent and are down almost 44 percent for orders of 10,000 or more shares."

The small investor benefited from the rise of the retail discount house. Discounters offer less services and no or little research, but charge lower commission rates. For example, the pre–May Day (May 1, 1975) commission of $53.90 on 100 shares of a stock trading at $30 a share was $29.60. The president of the trade association of discount houses claims that rates are 20–50 percent off the old fixed rate.

Consumer Reports undertook a study of discount stockbrokers. The commissions for buying 100 shares of a $30 per share stock ranged from a high of about $59 at Merrill Lynch, Pierce, Fenner & Smith, Bache Halsey Stuart, and Dean Witter & Co., to a low of $23 at Burke, Christensen & Lewis Securities, Inc., a Chicago discounter.

Although the revenues of older brokerage firms have fallen, and many have merged to cut expenses and others have closed their doors, nonetheless Merrill Lynch raised its charges to the individual investor. Other firms likewise raised rates 4–7 percent. Merrill Lynch clients have been offered a way to save 20 percent on the new rates. If they agree to have their orders executed at the market opening on the day after they place the order, they are eligible for that discount.

It would seem that large brokerage houses are not pursuing the small investor to the extent that their public relations offices claim.

Settlement

After a transaction has taken place on the floor of the exchange, shares must be delivered from the seller to the buyer, and funds must pass the other way. The customary standard procedure in the absence of any agreement to the contrary is for the delivery of certificates and cash to be made by noon of the fifth business day following the day of the transaction. Thus, transactions on Tuesday require delivery by noon on the following Tuesday, since Saturday and Sunday are not counted, as they are not business days. Holidays are not counted either. Technically this is the requirement, but in fact many transactions take much longer to complete.

In addition to *regular way* settlements, there are two other principal forms, *cash contracts* and *seller's option*. A *cash contract* calls for immediate delivery. A transaction for cash made before 2:00 P.M. on a given day requires delivery before 2:30 P.M. on the same day. If the transaction occurs after 2:00 P.M., delivery must be made within a half hour. There are a variety of special circumstances which dictate a cash contract, but three are recurrent. These involve the expiration of tax years, rights, and conversion privileges. To establish a capital loss on December 30 or December 31, a cash transaction is required, because a regular way contract would bring delivery and settlement into the following year. A cash contract is necessary

to acquire rights on the last day of the period for which they run. *Seller's option* is a form of settlement contract which gives the seller, at his or her option, up to 60 days to deliver.

Recent Problems

The various rules and regulations regarding delivery and clearance are now quite complex, and conforming to the rules has been quite a problem in recent years.

The back office paper glut of 1968–69 was followed by a capital crisis in 1970 and again in 1973–74. More than 160 NYSE member organizations—and an undisclosed, but presumably large number of non-NYSE brokerage firms—went out of business. Most of the NYSE firms either merged with or were acquired by other NYSE firms—quite often through arrangements facilitated or initiated by the exchange itself. Almost 100 firms dissolved and retired from the securities business. A number of well-known brokerage houses disappeared.

To minimize the possibility of future bankruptcies, the NYSE raised the capital requirements of member firms. In addition, the government established the Security Investors Protection Corporation (SIPC; pronounced "Sipic") to cover certain investors' losses should it again become necessary to liquidate broker-dealer firms. Generally speaking, the corporation will protect customers against losses of up to $100,000 in securities held for them by a broker-dealer, but only $40,000 in cash. Where both are involved, and the claim is over $100,000, only $100,000 will be paid. The securities industry, through assessments by SIPC on its member firms, is the principal source of SIPC funds. However, SIPC may borrow up to $1 billion from the U.S. Treasury through the SEC if the commission determines that such a loan is necessary for the protection of customers and the maintenance of confidence in U.S. securities markets.[8]

---

[8] For a brochure entitled *An Explanation of the Securities Investor Protection Act of 1970,* write to Securities Investors Protection Corporation, 485 L'Enfant Plaza, S.W., Suite 2150, Washington, D.C. 20024.

BUYING ON MARGIN AND SELLING SHORT

Pay Cash or Buy on Margin?

Stock can be purchased for cash or on margin. When you buy on margin, you put up only part of the purchase price, and the broker lends you the remainder. What part you put up and what part you can borrow are not matters of negotiation. They are determined by the Federal Reserve System, but the New York Stock Exchange has its own requirements in addition. The Federal Reserve is involved because it is charged with the control and regulation of the volume of credit. It controls the initial extension of credit to customers by members of national securities exchanges and by other brokers or dealers, and it regulates loans by banks for the purpose of purchasing and carrying stocks registered on national securities exchanges. Most unregistered securities can only be purchased on a cash basis.

Since the Federal Reserve Board first set margin requirements in 1934, the amount of margin which a purchaser of listed securities has been required to deposit has ranged from 4 percent to 100 percent of the purchase price.

The purpose of buying on margin, of course, is to stretch your funds. With a given amount of funds, you can command more shares on margin than if you pay cash. If the stock rises in price, your profits are enhanced. On the other hand, if the stock goes down and you cannot put up more

margin, assuming that you are long, and you are forced to sell or you are sold out, you can lose more than you would have if you had used the same amount of money to buy the stock for cash. With a 50 percent margin you can buy twice as many shares as in a cash transaction. With a 25 percent margin you can buy four times as many. The principle of leverage comes into play. By operating with other people's money, you magnify opportunity for profit or loss. This may be seen in Table 13–1. Keep in mind, however, that if the chance for profit is increased two- or fourfold, the chance for loss also increases.

Bull or Bear: Long or Short?

Where the expressions first arose we don't know, but a bull market is a rising market and a bear market is a falling market. A "bull" in Wall Street is an optimist, one who expects the market to go up. A "bear" is, of course, just the opposite, a pessimist who expects stock prices to decline. To take advantage of his forecast, a bull buys stock today in the hope of selling it later at a higher price. He goes *"long."* The bear, on the other hand, expecting the market to go down, *"sells short"*; that is, he sells stock today in the hope of buying it back at a lower price, thus profiting from the decline.

Short selling in the securities market basically is selling shares you don't own and borrowing the same number of shares to deliver to the purchaser. When you buy the stock later to return to the

TABLE 13–1
Relative Gain or Loss under Different Margin Requirements

Requirement for Margin	Funds Advanced by Buyer	Amount of Credit Needed	Number of Shares Purchased at $50 each	Per Share Change in Market Value	Profit (+) or Loss (−) Involved
10%	$1,000	$9,000.00	200.00	±$5	±$1,000.00
20	1,000	4,000.00	100.00	±$5	± 500.00
50	1,000	1,000.00	40.00	± 5	± 200.00
75	1,000	333.33	26.67	± 5	± 133.33
100	1,000	0.00	20.00	± 5	± 100.00

lender, you hope to do so at a lower price, thus making a profit. How is it possible to sell something you don't own and buy it back later? In securities markets the short sale is possible as long as you can borrow the shares you have sold and deliver them to the buyer. You can almost always do this, because your broker can borrow the stock from some left in "Street names" with him, from some of his other customers, or from some other broker.

Why are these people willing to lend? Because it is usually to their financial advantage. When you sell short and borrow a hundred shares, say of General Motors, to deliver to the purchaser, he, in turn, pays for the stock. You, the short seller, receive payment. If General Motors was selling at 100, you receive $10,000 (less costs). But you can't keep this $10,000.[9] You have to give it to the person or firm that loaned you the 100 shares of General Motors as collateral for the loan. When you return the shares, you get your funds back. Meanwhile that person or firm can use the money— lend it out at short term and get the prevailing interest, or buy more stock, or use it for any other purpose.

There is usually no charge made by the lender of a stock involved in a short sale, but he requires that the cash derived from the sale of the stock be left with him. The use of the cash turned over as collateral and then loaned out at interest will bring a return, making it financially advantageous to lend stock. That is why short sellers can function. The loan can be "called" at any time by either side. At any time the borrower of the stock can ask for the return of his funds and give back the shares, or the lender of the stock can ask for the return of his shares and give back the funds.

If you were alert when you read the forgoing, several possible dilemmas may have suggested themselves. What, for example, if the lender of the stock wants his shares back, and you are not ready to close the short sale? Very simple. You borrow 100 shares of General Motors from someone else. Suppose that General Motors rises to 110

and thus the stock is worth $11,000, but the money collateral given was only $10,000. The lender of the shares will call for more money collateral to support the loan. This is called "mark to the market." You, the short seller, will have to provide an additional $1,000, either from your own resources or by borrowing it. Conversely, if the stock price falls to $90 from the original $100—the short seller can and will ask for the return of $1,000 of his cash collateral. Both sides must "mark to the market."

Another problem may have occurred to you. Suppose that a dividend is declared while the short sale is under way. Who is entitled to the dividend? It would seem that two parties are, since seemingly two parties "own" the shares—the party to whom you sold the shares and the lender from whom you borrowed the shares you sold. Actually, both parties get the dividend. General Motors pays the dividend to the registered owner, and the short seller pays the dividend to the lender. Usually this is not an extra cost to the short seller, because when the stock goes *ex-dividend,* the market price of the stock drops by an amount approximating the dividend, so that when the short seller covers later, it will be at a lower price than if the stock had not gone ex-dividend.

In a declining market, extensive short selling might cause a panic drop. Both the SEC and the exchange have been determined to prevent short selling from being used to depress security prices artificially. There are rules to enforce this. No short sale of a stock is permitted except on a rising price. One can sell short at the price of the last sale provided that the price was above the next preceding different price. For example, two sales of ZXY occur: the first at 44⅛, the second at 44. You cannot sell ZXY short at this point. You must wait for an uptick. The next transaction is at 44. You cannot sell short yet. The next price is 44⅛. Now you can sell short. The next transaction is also at 44⅛. You can sell short. As long as this price lasts, you can sell short, since the next preceding different price was lower. The market uses the terms *plus tick, minus tick,* and *zero plus tick* to indicate subsequent transactions. Dials at each post for each

---

[9] The short seller must also provide margin at the prevailing percentage.

stock indicate the last sale by + or −, that is, by whether it is a plus tick or a minus tick. You can sell short on a plus tick. You cannot sell short on a minus tick. You can sell short on a zero plus tick. The prices 44, 44⅛, and 44⅛ in succession provide an example of a zero plus tick.

Short selling is done mainly by professionals. The small investor seldom engages in short selling. The risk is very much greater here than in a long transaction. If you buy 100 shares of a stock at 30, the worst that can happen, if the company goes bankrupt, is that you can lose $3,000. But if you sell short at 30 and sit mesmerized and watch the stock go up to 70, 80, 90, 100, and so on, your potential loss is open-ended. It depends on your stubbornness and on your financial resources. If you engage in short selling, your resources should and must be very ample and your temperament should include a quick capacity to admit a mistake.

The Over-the-Counter Market

"The over-the-counter markets are large and important, they are heterogeneous and diffuse, they are still relatively obscure and even mysterious for most investors." This is the way the *Report of the Special Study of the Securities Markets* characterized the over-the-counter market.

Transactions in securities that take place elsewhere than on an exchange are referred to as over-the-counter transactions. The over-the-counter market, unlike the exchanges, has no centralized place for trading. There are no listing requirements for issues traded, and all registered broker-dealers are entitled to participate. The broker-dealers vary in size, experience, and function; the securities differ in price, quality, and activity. While the OTC market includes from 30,000 to 40,000 common stocks of public corporations, only about 10,000 to 12,000 issues trade with any regularity within a given year, and only 5,000 of these could be described as actively traded.

It is generally agreed that the over-the-counter market is the biggest securities market in the world—but exactly how big nobody knows. In a year's time, the National Quotation Bureau quotes prices on approximately 40,000 securities: 26,000 stocks and 14,000 bonds.

The over-the-counter market encompasses all securities not traded on national securities exchanges. Securities traded over the counter are quite diverse in kind, price, quality, and activity, reflecting the free entry of securities into the over-the-counter market. Most of the trading in government and municipal bonds, bank and insurance company stocks, and common and preferred stocks in some seasoned industrial companies, as well as in thousands of newer or smaller industrial companies, takes place in the over-the-counter market. The SEC Special Study estimated that $556 billion out of a total of $1,092 billion in securities outstanding in the United States were not listed on any national securities exchange. There is also an active over-the-counter market in exchange-listed securities.

The issues of corporate stocks traded over the counter vary considerably in asset size, number of shareholders, and shares outstanding. There are substantial numbers of over-the-counter companies that cannot be distinguished from companies with securities listed on exchanges. Many others, however, are small companies, often speculative ventures in the promotional stage which have recently obtained public financing.

Just as there is an unlimited right of entry of securities into the over-the-counter markets, there is also virtually free access of persons into the over-the-counter securities business. There are about 5,000 active broker-dealers registered with the SEC. By comparison, approximately 1,200 member firms participate in trading on the securities exchanges. There is a high concentration of over-the-counter business with a few large firms. Fifty-six broker-dealers, or less than 2 percent of the total number, account for half the dollar volume of over-the-counter sales.

NASDAQ

The over-the-counter market faced a special problem. The old system for obtaining quotations in this negotiated market necessitated a broker-dealer checking with several dealers by telephone in order to develop reasonably accurate bid and asked figures. Even then the broker couldn't be sure he had the correct range unless he checked all of the market members, and this often wasn't practicable. As volume reached record heights, the system which had worked for years reached its limits. It became saturated with more trading activity and more demand for quotes than it could handle effectively. Stockbrokers were having difficulty securing bid and asked prices for their clients. And the clients were becoming disillusioned with the inadequate service.

The National Association of Securities Dealers (NASD) set out to correct the situation. After much study and discussion the NASD signed a contract with the Bunker-Ramo Corporation to build an electronic communication system to tie the OTC segment of the industry into one vast electronic stock market, as can be seen in Figure 13–7. The result was NASDAQ, the NASD's automated quotation system, which became operative in February 1971 and drastically changed and modernized the OTC market.

Self-styled as "The Nation's No. 2 Stock Market," NASDAQ is a computerized communications system that collects, stores, and displays up-to-the-second quotations from a nationwide network of OTC dealers making markets in stocks which have been approved for inclusion in the NASDAQ system. NASDAQ companies must also meet the SEC reporting and disclosure standards that have been established for exchange-listed stocks.

Serving as an electronic link between almost all of the major retail firms and OTC market makers, NASDAQ made trading more efficient because it enabled the best market for a security, no matter where it was, to be located instantly. Because each dealer could see competitors' quotations, price spreads (the difference between bid and asked quotations) narrowed. With accurate and timely trading information, and with heightened competition narrowing spreads, the NASDAQ dealer market seemed to be a significant alternative to the exchange-listed auction market.

Market makers are, in effect, the trading sponsors of OTC securities. They stand ready to buy and sell as individual and institutional orders appear. A market maker's role is similar in many ways to that of a stock exchange specialist. An important difference, however, is that often only one specialist makes a market in an exchange-listed stock, whereas a half-dozen or more market makers may compete in a particular NASDAQ/OTC security.

Thus, with stocks in the NASDAQ system, you can call your broker for a quote, receive it immediately, and make your decision to buy or sell then and there, while you are still on the telephone.[10]

The Options Market

The options market is primarily a market of small investors attracted by the hope of making big money on a small stake—and of being able to gamble on a big win without the risk of a huge loss.

It is the newest of the financial markets and perhaps the most complicated. In April 1973, the CBOE (Chicago Board Options Exchange) was set up to deal in standardized options. Seldom has there been a more successful venture in finance. Trading in options grew so fast that in 1977 the SEC placed a moratorium on new listings. Its study of the options market (1979) made more than 75 recommendations for stiffer self regulation by the exchanges, especially the NYSE.

Call options that are traded on the exchange have certain common characteristics that make it possible for investors to trade in options in a more flexible and convenient manner than was possible in the prior over-the-counter market for puts and calls. The striking price or exercise price, the price per share at which the option buyer may purchase a call, is now standardized.

In contrast to the older put and call market, where it was possible to buy or write an option with practically any striking price or expiration date, the striking prices of listed options always end in

---

[10] See *The NASDAQ Revolution: How Over-the-Counter Securities Are Traded,* Merrill Lynch, Pierce, Fenner & Smith. For a free copy write to the firm at One Liberty Plaza, New York, NY 10006.

FIGURE 13–7

The Expanding NASDAQ System

The NASDAQ System—the nationwide, computerized communications facility for the NASDAQ/OTC Market—grew in usage and capability during 1977.

More Usage

The comparison between 1976 and 1977 NASDAQ System operating statistics is as follows:

	December 31, 1976	December 30, 1977
Terminals		
Level 1	31,750	34,680
Level 2	108	122
Level 3	953	977
Subscribers 1 (est.)	1,800	1,900
Subscribers 2 & 3	511	499
	1976	*1977*
Average calls processed per day	737,608	756,185

Level 1 terminals are located primarily in the retail branches of brokerage firms. They show the representative bid and asked price (RBA), the middle point of the quotes of all market makers in a given security. Level 1 terminals also provide market summary data.

Level 2 terminals are used by institutions and brokerage firms. They show the specific quotations by market makers in NASDAQ securities. They do not permit the entry of information into the NASDAQ System.

Level 3 terminals are used by the market makers in NASDAQ securities. They allow the market makers to enter, change or update their quotations and to see the quotations of all market makers.

Greater Capabilities

In 1977, the NASDAQ System leased UNIVAC 1100/22 computers to replace its UNIVAC 1108s in early 1978. The new computers have 516,000 words of memory, compared with the 258,000 words of the old ones.

The Scope of the System

The NASDAQ System proper consists of a Central Processing Complex in Trumbull, Connecticut; four regional concentrator sites in New York, Atlanta, Chicago and San Francisco; 20,000 miles of leased telephone lines; and the 1,099 Level 2 and Level 3 terminals.

☆   Central Processing Complex

⊕   Regional Concentrator Sites

▭   Trunk Lines

—   Telephone Lines

$5 or $0, unless a stock dividend or other capital change occurs after trading in the options has begun. If AT&T is selling at $64 a share at the time options for a new expiration month are being listed for trading, the new AT&T option will have a striking or exercise price of $65 per share. If the stock price closes above $67.50 for two consecutive days, the exchange will add $70 contracts for each expiration date beyond 60 days.

In addition to the standardized exercise price, listed options have standardized expiration dates—the third Friday of January, April, July, or October; or of February, May, August, or November. Each listed option with a common expiration date and striking price is interchangeable with any similar listed option. This standardization of both exercise prices and expiration dates made possible the development of a secondary market and is responsible in great part for the tremendous increase in option activity.

Call options give their holders the right to buy 100 shares of the underlying stock at a specified price at any time before the call expires. Call options are bought in anticipation of a price rise. If the stock goes up, so will the call, and it may be sold at a profit. Or the call holder may exercise the call by acquiring the stock. Through the use of options, buyers aim to make $1,000 do the work of $10,000.

Who would want to buy a call option—to pay $500 for the right to buy 100 shares of AT&T stock at $60 a share over the ensuing six months? Obviously it would be someone who expected AT&T to go up sharply in that six-month period. Second, it would be someone who would at that time rather pay a call premium of $500 than the cost of 100 shares of AT&T stock—namely $6,000. If the stock goes down, a call buyer would perhaps lose the premium, but that would be less dollars lost than if the stock had been owned outright. Also less capital would be involved. If he guessed right and exercises his option, he gets the stock at 60—even though it may have gone to 75 and may even have made profit on the rise in options. You buy the 100 shares at $60—but the market price is $75—which gives you a profit of $1,000 after you subtract the $500 cost of the call.

A put gives the holder the right to sell 100 shares of AT&T at a specified price within a certain time. Puts are bought by those who believe the stock's price will decline within that period. If it doesn't, the purchaser need not exercise his option. All that is lost is the premium.

Who would want to sell such options? The holder of stock who does not believe that in the specified period the underlying stock will move up (call) or down (put) and therefore believes that he will still own the stock plus the premium lost by the purchaser of the option. He has increased his income from the stock—or looked at differently, the successful sale of the call option could be viewed as decreasing the cost of his stock.

Toward a Central Market

The Securities Amendments Act of 1975 ordered the SEC to appoint a board to advise the commission on "steps to facilitate the establishment of a national central market system for the trading of securities." Under pressure from Congress and the SEC, the securities industry is now moving, or being pushed, toward a computerized automated national marketing system. The SEC hopes to have all major components of its proposed automated market in place by the end of 1982. Two of the three major parts of the new automated system are now functioning. These are the composite quotation system providing instant complete marketing information and a system for the execution of market orders known as the Intermarket Trading System. The remaining link will be a central file that will collect all *limit* orders from all brokers and will list them according to the price and time they were placed (see Figure 13–8). They will be available to all participants in the marketplace. There would thus be equal access to all in the market at competitive prices.

The Intermarket Trading System

The intermarket trading system electronically connects participating market centers in which listed stocks are bought and sold. Access to the linkage is through the facilities of the existing securi-

FIGURE 13–8

LIMIT ORDER

In the new national market system, limit orders will be computerized. According to the SEC blueprint, all limit orders will be collected in one giant "central file," so that they can be filled later in any market. Here's how:

1 Investor Smith tells his broker to sell 500 shares of XYZ Corp. at 52. The broker checks the market for XYZ Corp. It is 50½.

NO. SHARES
TIME
PRICE

CENTRAL FILE

2 Broker places a limit order to sell 500 shares of XYZ Corp. at 52 in the central file. It is filed by the time the order was placed, the price and the numbers of shares.

3 The orders in the central file are displayed to every market and exchange in the nation that deals in XYZ Corp.

4 **NO SALE** If no one is willing to buy at 52, the order remains in central file.

5 If price of XYZ Corp. rises, the first market that reaches 52 must buy Investor Smith's shares before the market maker can satisfy any other order.

CHI.
S.F.
L.A.
N.Y.C.

Source: Reprinted with the special permission of *Dun's Review,* April 1978. Copyright 1978, Dun & Bradstreet Publications Corporation.

ties industry self-regulatory organizations which have agreed to assure essential operational and regulatory quality for the intermarket trading system and a central computer facility.

The initial participants are the American, Boston, Midwest, New York, Pacific, and Philadelphia stock exchanges, each of which determines how and under what rules and regulations its own members may use the system's facilities. The ITS linkage enables a broker or market-maker who is physically present in one market center to represent his own or his customer's orders in listed stocks, electronically, in other market centers. The following example illustrates how brokers and market-makers in the participating market centers will actually use the intermarket trading system to transmit commitments to trade and to confirm executions.

A broker on the New York Stock Exchange has a market order to sell 100 shares of XYZ stock. The quotation display on the floor of the New York Stock Exchange shows that the best current bid for XYZ has been entered on the Pacific Stock Exchange, and he decides to meet that bid. He enters a commitment—a firm commitment—into the New York Stock Exchange terminal to sell 100 shares at the bid on the Pacific Stock Exchange. Within seconds, the commitment is flashed on the screen and also printed out at the PSE specialist's post, where it is executed against the PSE bid.

After the commitment is accepted, a short message is entered into the system and the system immediately reports an execution back to New York. This is the equivalent of the traditional "brokers' handshake"—stretching across the continent—signifying that a trade has taken place.

After the trade is executed, the appropriate market system reports it to the consolidated tape.

Brokers on both sides of the transaction receive an immediate confirmation, and a journal of all transactions is transmitted to the appropriate market centers at the end of the day.

Thereafter, each broker completes the clearance and settlement procedure through his own chosen clearing corporation.

No additional clearing process is required for brokers using ITS. All the systems necessary for fast and reliable clearance among the market centers involved are in place and are operating efficiently.

Following are two examples of how commitments to trade involving more than 100 shares are handled through the intermarket trading system (see Figure 13–9).

A broker on the NYSE has a market order to buy 500 shares of XYZ. The quotation display shows that the best current offer has been entered on the Philadelphia Stock Exchange and is firm for 1,000 shares.

He decides to enter a commitment to buy 500 shares at that quoted price. Within seconds, the commitment is flashed on the screen in Philadelphia and printed out on both the Philadelphia and New York trading floors. When the commitment is accepted, an execution report is transmitted back to New York and is printed out on both trading floors.

On the other hand, suppose that the best offer in Philadelphia is only firm for 300 shares. In that case, the NYSE broker may request a supplementary montage display of the quotes from other market centers. The montage may show that equivalent best offers, firm for 100 shares each, have been entered on both the Boston and Pacific exchanges.

Now the NYSE broker can elect to enter commitments to buy 300 shares in Philadelphia, 100 shares in Boston, and 100 shares on the Pacific Exchange—thereby fulfilling his order for 500 shares.

The new national market system is to be "fair and orderly," "in the public interest," for the "protection of investors," and "efficient." *Efficient* can have several meanings. "An economically efficient execution of securities transactions" can mean that the cost of transferring securities should be reasonable. Markets may be structured so as to secure an efficient allocation of scarce resources (capital). Or the term *efficient markets* may be used in the way that economists use it, to mean markets in which the prices respond quickly to new information.

A current pilot project involving the Cincinnati

FIGURE 13–9

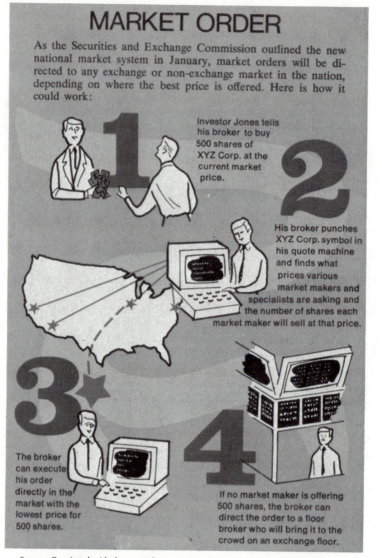

MARKET ORDER

As the Securities and Exchange Commission outlined the new national market system in January, market orders will be directed to any exchange or non-exchange market in the nation, depending on where the best price is offered. Here is how it could work:

1 Investor Jones tells his broker to buy 500 shares of XYZ Corp. at the current market price.

2 His broker punches XYZ Corp. symbol in his quote machine and finds what prices various market makers and specialists are asking and the number of shares each market maker will sell at that price.

3 The broker can execute his order directly in the market with the lowest price for 500 shares.

4 If no market maker is offering 500 shares, the broker can direct the order to a floor broker who will bring it to the crowd on an exchange floor.

Source: Reprinted with the special permission of *Dun's Review*, April 1978. Copyright 1978, Dun & Bradstreet Corporation.

Stock Exchange in an electronic trading test is going so well that it is being extended. Significant amounts of stock are being traded. Merrill Lynch, which accounts for 75 percent of the electronic transactions, is using these computers to fill 90 percent of its retail orders for 5 of the 40 stocks traded.

In the process the New York Stock Exchange has lost 10 percent of the volume it formerly had in these 5 stocks.[11]

---

[11] *Wall Street Journal*, February 2, 1979. This article suggests that many changes are more cosmetic than real and the program is being unduly delayed.

Under these systems, which should provide more information, the individual investor may gain a better advantage than he had previously vis-à-vis specialists or the institutions.

Conclusion

In the past, investment for individuals usually meant buying common stock. The experience of the common stock investor was so difficult and irritating, both pricewise and procedurally in the 1960s and early 1970s that some turned away from stocks and sought other forms of investment. A number of brokerage houses developed operational difficulties, including a shortage of capital, and a number failed or merged with stronger houses.

A variety of problems led Congress and the SEC to intervene. First they investigated, and then they suggested reforms. They especially urged more automation.

It seems likely that the next decade will witness significant changes in trading procedures and rules.

SUGGESTED READINGS

Merrill Lynch, Pierce, Fenner & Smith. *Proposal for a National Market System.* New York, 1975.

Regan, Donald T. *A View from the Street.* New York: New American Library, 1972.

Securities Industries Association. *Report of the National Market Systems Committee.* New York, 1976.

Stigum, Marcia. *The Money Market.* Homewood, Ill.: Dow Jones-Irwin, 1978.

Welles, Chris. *Last Days of the Club.* New York: E. P. Dutton, 1975.

The Merrill Lynch Guide to Writing Options. For a free copy write to Merrill Lynch, Pierce, Fenner & Smith, One Liberty Plaza, New York, N.Y. 10006.

Option Writing Strategies. A free copy may be obtained from the Chicago Board Options Exchange, La Salle at Jackson, Chicago, Illinois 60604.

The Versatile Option. New York: American Stock Exchange, 1975. A free copy may be obtained by writing to the American Stock Exchange, 86 Trinity Place, New York, N.Y. 10006.

The following are publications available from the New York Stock Exchange, *without charge.* If you wish to obtain a copy of any of these publications, write to the Director of Educational Relations, New York Stock Exchange, 11 Wall St., New York, NY 10005.

Does It Make Sense for Me to Buy Stocks? Helps prospective investor decide whether to invest. Answers ten questions most often asked, such as Why do people buy stocks? Which stocks should I choose? Should everybody own stocks?

Growth Leaders on the Big Board. 32-page investment guide. Groups top-growth listed common stocks by industry. Gives price range, five-year and one-year growth rates, earnings per share, yields, dividends, and other records. Includes convertible preferred stocks.

How Is the Health of Your Portfolio? 16-page booklet, illustrated with cartoons, emphasizing need for investors to review their portfolios periodically; includes three handy checklists.

How to Get Help When You Invest. Primer for prospective and new investors; basic information on investing; clear, nontechnical description of the services of NYSE member firms.

Income Leaders on the Big Board. Lists common stocks, preferred stocks, and bonds that yield 6 percent or more and meet specified quality standards.

Individual Retirement Program. Booklet points out the importance of financial planning for retirement and explains how to set up an individual retirement investment program.

The Language of Investing, a Glossary. 245 stock market terms defined in clear, concise language.

Low Prices on the Big Board. Booklet includes statistical data on all common stocks priced $20 or less that have paid dividends in every one of the past five years and have been growing in earnings per share over the same period.

Margin. How margin accounts are handled; potential advantages and risks.

Understanding Bonds and Preferred Stocks. Explanation of investment characteristics of senior securities and of the role of senior securities in a balanced investment program.

Understanding Convertible Securities. Characteristics of convertible stocks and bonds; what is likely to happen to a convertible when the related common stock fluctuates in value; roster of NYSE convertible securities.

Understanding Financial Statements. Seven "keys" to evaluate financial reports; an aid for those who want to make their own studies of financial statements.

Understanding the New York Stock Exchange. Description of the functions of the NYSE and member firms.

CASE PROBLEMS

Case Problems for Chapters 12, 13, and 14 will be found at the end of Chapter 14.

14

Managing Your Investments

Investigate before you invest.
BETTER BUSINESS BUREAU

The Bawl Street Journal comes out once a year. In it many a true word is said in jest. "We sincerely hope the market catches up with our predictions before the SEC does," advertised one brokerage house specializing in growth stock recommendations. "Now that logical reasoning is no longer required in this crazy market we have more confidence in our recommendations," announced another large firm. "Let us review your holdings with an aim at increasing our commissions," suggested another jokingly. "If you're looking for laughs come in and see us! Some of our offerings are hilarious," said a new-issue house. "Get our research bulletin: Rarely do so many who know so little say so much," advertised another firm.

Fundamental Analysis

In investments there are at least four basic questions which you have to ask yourself: *first,* "What to Buy?"; *second,* "When to Buy?"; *third,* "When to Sell?"; and *fourth,* "What to Sell?" Sounds simple, perhaps, but it's very difficult to follow through a full cycle. Various techniques have been developed to cope with these questions.

Fundamental analysis is the basic process of evaluating common stock by studying earnings, dividends, price-earnings multiples, economic outlook

449

for the industry, financial prospects for the company, sales penetration, market share, and quality of management. Selecting the industry or industries which are likely to do best over the next three to five years and then choosing the company or companies within the selected industries which are likely to outperform their competitors—this is the essence of both fundamental and security analysis.

In general terms there are four aspects of any competent analysis: *(a)* the sales analysis and forecast, *(b)* the earnings analysis and forecast, *(c)* the multiplier analysis and forecast, and *(d)* the analysis of management, a qualitative consideration.

The heart of the investment process, known as *fundamental analysis,* may well be seen in Figure 14–1. It shows the stocks of 50 industries classified by their investment performance over the past ten years. Do you perceive much difference between machinery and machine tool stocks? Superficially not, perhaps, but over the period from January 1, 1968, through December 31, 1977, machinery stocks *rose* 141 percent while over the same period machine tool stocks *lost* 46 percent of their value.

One would hardly guess that restaurants were so efficient and well run that they would emerge in third place, while discount stores lost 73 percent of their value and were at the bottom of the heap. They shared the cellar with air transport companies, while the gold mining companies led the 50-industry list.

The difficulty of choosing the "right" investment, the "right" industry, the "right" company, may be seen by contrasting Figures 14–1 and 14–2. The wide range of investment results for different industries over a ten-year period are shown in Figure 14–1. Some industries flourished and expanded. Others dragged along with dull and unattractive profit records.

But the variations over time are startling! One industry, Coal Mining (Bituminous), is a good example. Over the 10-year period shown in Figure 14–I, it was seventh in performance; in 1978 (see Figure 14–2) it ranked 109 in the stock group (S&P) performance.

Industry selection is one of the most difficult and complicated aspects of fundamental analysis.

Industry Analysis

Generally, after examining the state of business and corporate profits and the condition of the market, investors make industry-to-industry comparisons to select those industries whose growth and profitability outlook is most favorable.

To secure data for industry studies and comparisons, investors may either research an industry in depth, using a variety of sources, or if they have less time available and wish compact and concise information, they may turn to one of the investment services. Standard & Poor's issues an excellent series of industry surveys, covering 45 industries. For each industry a *Basic Analysis* is issued, usually annually. This is followed by supplementary sections, entitled "Current Analysis and Outlook," which are issued at varying intervals, usually quarterly. The *Basic Analysis* contains a wealth of data, which would require much time by individual investors if they were to attempt to gather it themselves. In the report on the container industry, for example, the *Basic Analysis* includes:

The outlook	Ecology
Paper	Financial
Packaging	Composite industry data
Metal containers	Company analysis
Glass containers	Market action
Plastic packaging	Statistical data
Closures	

Where an industry is more homogeneous, as with the automobile industry, the contents of the *Basic Analysis* will reflect more internal operational data. Thus the automobile industry survey contains:

The outlook	Imports-exports
Sales and production	Financial
Technology	Composite industry data
Auto parts	Comparative company
Market action	analysis
	Statistical data

In most of the S&P industry surveys, data are provided for forecasting purposes. For example, in the electronics-electrical equipment *Basic Analysis,* a line of average relationship, or least squares line, has been fitted to show the relationship be-

FIGURE 14–1
Selection

The wide range of investment results for the past 10 years of 50 different industries as shown by Standard & Poor's reveals the difficulty of selecting common stocks. During this period 21 of the 50 industries shown below declined in market value, and three of the groups actually lost over 50%. However, investment of equal amounts in each industry would have resulted in a profit of 13% because of the broad diversification.

STOCKS OF FIFTY INDUSTRIES
JANUARY 1, 1968 — DECEMBER 31, 1977

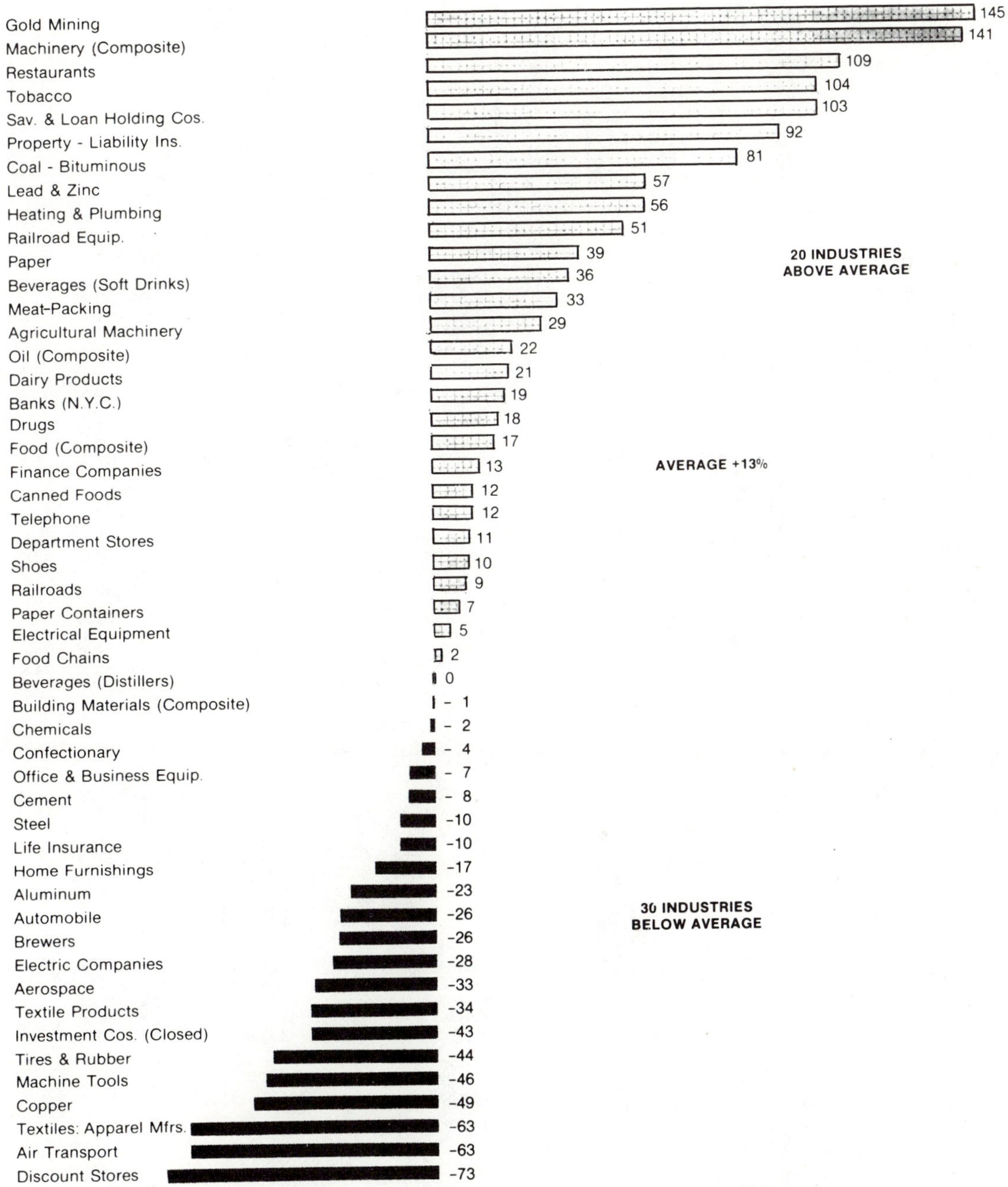

Industry	Value
Gold Mining	145
Machinery (Composite)	141
Restaurants	109
Tobacco	104
Sav. & Loan Holding Cos.	103
Property - Liability Ins.	92
Coal - Bituminous	81
Lead & Zinc	57
Heating & Plumbing	56
Railroad Equip.	51
Paper	39
Beverages (Soft Drinks)	36
Meat-Packing	33
Agricultural Machinery	29
Oil (Composite)	22
Dairy Products	21
Banks (N.Y.C.)	19
Drugs	18
Food (Composite)	17
Finance Companies	13
Canned Foods	12
Telephone	12
Department Stores	11
Shoes	10
Railroads	9
Paper Containers	7
Electrical Equipment	5
Food Chains	2
Beverages (Distillers)	0
Building Materials (Composite)	– 1
Chemicals	– 2
Confectionary	– 4
Office & Business Equip.	– 7
Cement	– 8
Steel	–10
Life Insurance	–10
Home Furnishings	–17
Aluminum	–23
Automobile	–26
Brewers	–26
Electric Companies	–28
Aerospace	–33
Textile Products	–34
Investment Cos. (Closed)	–43
Tires & Rubber	–44
Machine Tools	–46
Copper	–49
Textiles: Apparel Mfrs.	–63
Air Transport	–63
Discount Stores	–73

20 INDUSTRIES ABOVE AVERAGE

AVERAGE +13%

30 INDUSTRIES BELOW AVERAGE

Source: *Johnson's Charts,* 1978 edition.

FIGURE 14–2
Stock Group Performances in 1978

*Rank	1977 Dec. 31	1978 Dec. 31	% Change	1978 Range High	Low
1 Aerospace	74.39	110.76	+ 48.9	125.33	68.51
2 Machine Tools	38.50	53.79	+ 39.7	65.02	35.17
3 Hotel-Motel	32.93	45.73	+ 38.9	74.15	29.85
4 Air Conditioning	23.47	32.41	+ 38.1	35.16	22.15
5 Homebuilding	15.20	20.13	+ 32.4	26.94	13.75
6 Toys	8.32	10.78	+ 29.6	13.58	7.45
7 Electronics (Instrum.)	20.40	25.85	+ 26.7	25.94	17.84
8 Mach.: Agricultural	56.44	70.13	+ 24.3	78.30	51.27
9 Entertainment	128.55	159.50	+ 24.1	181.21	111.78
10 Radio-TV Broadcasters	353.66	428.14	+ 21.1	502.92	325.41
11 Air Transport	38.77	46.64	+ 20.3	65.18	36.38
12 Air Freight	26.14	31.32	+ 19.8	44.90	24.40
13 Vending & Food Service	21.79	25.92	+ 19.0	32.55	20.71
14 Canned Foods	91.93	107.72	+ 17.2	112.74	87.20
15 Low-Price Stocks	144.90	169.32	+ 16.9	245.84	138.55
16 Leisure Time	23.58	27.22	+ 15.4	35.94	21.74
17 Office & Bus. Equip.: Excl. IBM	205.17	235.44	+ 14.8	264.17	180.09
18 Textiles: Apparel Mfrs.	25.06	28.60	+ 14.1	31.51	23.51
19 Beverages: Distillers	114.12	128.79	+ 12.9	136.62	108.41
20 Oil Well Equip. & Svce.	911.85	1029.12	+ 12.9	1078.91	794.10
21 Aluminum	92.90	103.30	+ 11.2	114.92	79.13
22 Office & Bus. Equip.	1095.44	1209.57	+ 10.4	1247.78	960.29
23 Conglomerates	14.92	16.46	+ 10.3	19.42	14.06
24 Electronics (Semi./Comp.)	16.83	18.55	+ 10.2	22.90	15.13
25 Containers: Paper	129.50	142.62	+ 10.1	167.73	124.75
26 Multi-Line Insurance	13.02	14.34	+ 10.1	16.67	11.15
27 Publishing (Newspapers)	20.82	22.83	+ 9.7	27.67	18.52
28 Publishing	234.29	256.34	+ 9.4	289.18	208.37
29 Metal Fabricating	109.30	119.34	+ 9.2	162.55	102.82
30 Tobacco	70.10	76.02	+ 8.4	81.75	64.81
31 Drugs	149.93	162.44	+ 8.3	180.43	140.72
32 Crude Oil Producers	244.29	264.32	+ 8.2	291.25	227.04
33 Discount Stores	12.89	13.94	+ 8.1	21.09	12.22
34 Cosmetics	60.29	64.49	+ 7.0	75.56	55.73
35 Beverages: Soft Drinks	105.28	112.51	+ 6.9	127.59	98.58
36 Banks: Outside N.Y.C.	94.52	100.64	+ 6.5	116.96	87.95
37 Pollution Control	24.78	26.30	+ 6.1	32.71	22.88
38 Railroad Equipment	56.72	60.11	+ 6.0	74.63	49.12
39 Building Composite	51.83	54.70	+ 5.5	65.82	47.87
40 Copper	24.40	25.54	+ 4.7	31.66	22.03
41 Metals: Miscellaneous	44.71	46.68	+ 4.4	53.10	38.87
42 Heating & Plumbing	67.59	70.53	+ 4.3	91.64	60.17
43 Capital Goods	103.54	107.58	+ 3.9	117.09	92.72
44 Auto Parts—Orig. Equip.	14.47	15.02	+ 3.8	16.77	13.52
45 Constr. & Mat. Handling	375.45	389.19	+ 3.7	430.70	324.43
46 Food Chains	53.25	55.15	+ 3.6	62.27	49.32
47 Auto Parts—After Mkt.	14.94	15.40	+ 3.1	17.25	13.34
48 Oil: Integr. Domestic	165.63	170.76	+ 3.1	177.74	146.93
49 High Grade Stocks	70.39	72.48	+ 3.0	77.97	64.22
50 Oil Composite	156.68	161.43	+ 3.0	170.59	144.50
51 Oil: Integr. Intl.	148.12	152.26	+ 2.8	162.00	138.27
52 Retail Stores (Drug)	20.59	21.10	+ 2.5	26.41	17.99
53 **400 INDUSTRIALS**	104.71	107.21	+ 2.4	118.71	95.52
54 Hospital Supplies	34.09	34.77	+ 2.0	42.35	31.75
55 Electrical Equipment	266.80	271.63	+ 1.8	310.04	239.02
56 Cement	28.09	28.51	+ 1.5	35.40	25.41
57 **500 COMPOSITE**	95.10	96.11	+ 1.1	106.99	86.90
58 Gold Mining	96.54	97.61	+ 1.1	121.22	86.99
59 Beverages: Brewers	33.90	34.14	+ 0.7	41.58	30.80
60 Life Insurance	197.90	199.27	+ 0.7	230.33	181.39
61 **40 FINANCIAL**	11.15	11.22	+ 0.6	13.18	10.14
62 Personal Loans	78.09	78.53	+ 0.6	93.52	72.68
63 Banks: New York City	42.11	42.18	+ 0.2	50.91	37.43
64 Soaps	166.56	166.62	0	177.06	150.75
65 Telephone	27.47	27.25	− 0.8	28.95	26.08
66 Sav. & Loan Hold. Cos.	24.19	23.53	− 2.7	31.62	20.29

*Rank	1977 Dec. 31	1978 Dec. 31	% Change	1978 Range High	Low
67 Finance Cos.	59.80	57.91	− 3.2	67.85	54.78
68 Roofing & Wallboard	61.71	59.36	− 3.8	77.45	57.27
69 Property-Casualty Insur.	108.76	104.07	− 4.3	120.26	97.84
70 Synthetic Fibers	54.30	51.97	− 4.3	60.96	48.14
71 Steel: Excl. U.S. Steel	44.25	42.21	− 4.6	50.17	41.12
72 Electronic Major Cos.	82.42	78.35	− 4.9	96.10	74.47
73 Forest Products	20.03	18.95	− 5.4	24.08	16.66
74 Restaurants	25.20	23.74	− 5.8	30.07	22.71
75 Food Composite	74.35	69.90	− 6.0	79.51	68.75
76 Home Furnishings	24.69	23.22	− 6.0	25.65	22.34
77 Indus./Spec. Mach.	107.52	100.92	− 6.1	123.70	98.68
78 **20 TRANSPORTATION**	13.65	12.79	− 6.3	16.20	12.40
79 Auto Trucks & Parts	45.28	42.24	− 6.7	54.64	41.26
80 Tel.: Excl. A.T.&T.	42.78	39.87	− 6.8	43.54	39.56
81 Paper	219.08	204.02	− 6.9	247.56	189.57
82 Chemicals	54.79	50.94	− 7.0	59.62	46.05
83 Investment Cos. (Closed-End)	47.66	44.28	− 7.1	49.94	41.96
84 Processed Foods	104.05	95.58	− 8.1	109.26	94.12
85 Sugar Refiners	19.42	17.81	− 8.3	22.34	16.57
86 Dairy Products	92.97	84.66	− 8.9	99.61	84.38
87 Shoes	50.90	46.02	− 9.6	56.55	44.53
88 Natural Gas Distributors	87.44	78.73	−10.0	86.19	76.34
89 Auto: Excl. Gen. Motors	27.40	24.59	−10.3	29.82	23.41
90 Offshore Drilling	61.24	54.68	−10.7	80.09	51.59
91 Railroads	47.51	42.22	−11.1	49.63	42.04
92 **40 UTILITIES**	54.73	48.47	−11.4	54.47	48.23
93 Containers: Metal & Glass	38.74	34.16	−11.8	41.36	33.57
94 Electric Companies	35.67	31.38	−12.0	35.52	31.38
95 Automobiles	78.72	68.82	−12.6	84.03	68.28
96 Textile Products	50.84	44.36	−12.7	54.09	44.04
97 Meat Packing	56.91	49.11	−13.7	59.22	48.07
98 Elec. Household Appl.	149.35	126.69	−15.2	163.45	123.53
99 Tire & Rubber	133.74	113.09	−15.4	132.75	111.76
100 Natural Gas Pipelines	141.58	119.65	−15.5	146.83	118.69
101 Fertilizers	11.43	9.63	−15.7	12.55	9.44
102 Mobile Homes	56.86	47.70	−16.1	73.03	45.09
103 Steel	47.64	39.98	−16.1	50.10	39.94
104 Retail Stores Comp.	89.18	73.70	−17.4	90.44	73.70
105 Department Stores	151.23	123.80	−18.1	154.60	121.90
106 Real Estate Inv. Trust	2.35	1.91	−18.7	2.31	1.89
107 General Mdse. Chains	9.21	7.08	−23.1	9.07	7.08
108 Truckers	95.69	73.31	−23.4	116.31	68.75
109 Coal: Bituminous	384.33	285.21	−25.8	391.74	271.49

Source: *The Outlook,* Standard & Poor's, January 8, 1979.

FIGURE 14–3
Corporate Profits and Stock Prices

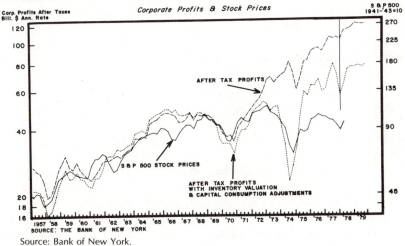

Source: Bank of New York.

tween electrical appliance sales production and disposable personal income, a component of gross national product. Using a GNP and DPI estimate for the next five years, a forecast can be obtained for electrical appliance sales, and this in turn can be used to arrive at an earnings-per-share estimate for the forecast period.

The "Current Analysis and Outlook" updates the figures in the basic survey, provides a short-run forecast, gives brief analyses of representative companies in the industry, and provides updated data on the comparative statistical position of leading common stocks in the industry.

Forbes publishes an "Annual Report on American Industry" at the beginning of each year. The report covers each of the major industries, and within each industry it makes comparisons of companies based on two yardsticks of performance: growth (five-year compounded rate for both sales and earnings) and profitability (five-year average for return on equity and on total capital). Each of the industries reviewed is analyzed for both past and prospective performance. The close relationship between stock prices and corporate aftertax profits may be seen in Figure 14–3.

For the investor who wishes to do an industry study in depth, a variety of sources are available. The trade journals covering different industries in-

clude *Chemical Week, Drug and Cosmetic Industry, Modern Plastics, Computer Age, Coal Mining, Mining Journal, Electrical World, Electrical Week, Electronics, Food Industries, The Timberman, Iron Age, Paper Trade Journal, Oil and Gas Journal, Petroleum Times, Ward's Auto World, Airline Management & Marketing, Airline Newsletter, Brewers Digest, Textile World, Automotive News, Ocean Oil Weekly Report,* and *Metals.* The *Business Periodicals Index* and the *Science and Technology Index* list the articles that appear in all of the trade journals. In addition, each industry has one or more trade associations which maintain specialized libraries and issue books, bulletins, and monographs on industry developments.

The deeper investors dig into a given industry, the more likely they are to find a superabundance rather than a paucity of information. Selecting, organizing, and analyzing the information may become a major task. The economy and usefulness of the financial services will become apparent in the course of the process.

Company Analysis

After industry analysis comes *company* selection within the chosen *industry* or *industries.* Company selection is more complex than industry selection, as can be seen in the following examples. The most obvious source of information about a company is its own annual reports, including its balance sheets and income accounts. Frequently the annual reports are not as informative as they might be, and the investor may also wish to look at various company reports filed with regulatory agencies.

In addition, the various investment services publish individual company reports. Standard & Poor's covers both listed and unlisted companies. An example of an S&P individual company report is shown in Figure 14–4.

As a result of the rise in the price of gold, the stock of Dome Mines increased in price 238 percent, but that of Homestake Mining increased only 16 percent. In soft drinks, Pepsico went up 110 percent, but Coca Cola fell 12 percent. Liggett & Myers fell 24 percent, while Philip Morris rose 456 percent. CBS, Inc., went down 1 percent, while the American Broadcasting System rose 84 percent. The many startling contrasts in common stock performance over the period between January 1, 1968, and December 31, 1977, as seen in Figure 14–5, suggest the need for careful security analysis before selecting companies.

The S&P reports provide, in capsule form, much of the relevant information that the investor seeks. They provide data on sales, operating revenues, common share earnings, recent developments, fundamental position, dividends, prospects, finances, capitalization, and pertinent balance sheet and income account statistics for the prior ten years. In addition, the investment service recommendation is given. The individual company reports are dated and revised every three or four months or more often, as developments require.

Extensive sources of company data and information are to be found in the registration statements, prospectuses, proxy statements, and other reports that result from the "full disclosure" philosophy of the SEC, ICC, FPC, FCC, CAB, and NYSE. SEC filings, for example, contain much essential information that may be omitted in voluntary reports.

The registration statement is the basic disclosure document in connection with a public distribution of securities registered under the Securities Act of 1933. The registration statement has two parts. The prospectus, the first part, is the only part which is generally distributed to the public. The second part contains information of a more technical nature.

The Securities and Exchange Act of 1934 has disclosure requirements relating to registration, periodic reporting, proxy solicitation, and insider trading. Listed and OTC-registered companies are required to file certain periodic reports. The most important of these are Forms 8-K, 10-K, and 10-Q, of which 10-K is the most useful.

Form 10-K is an annual report which is due 90 days after the end of the company's fiscal year. The Form 10-K report contains certified financial statements, including a balance sheet, a profit and loss statement for the fiscal year covered by the report, and an analysis of surplus and supporting schedules. A new and tougher set of disclosure requirements was stipulated for all 10-K filings on or after December 31, 1970.

But not everything that is now contained in a 10-K finds its way into a company's annual report to its shareholders. Thus the careful investor must work more closely with a company's 10-K than with its annual report.

Forms, publications, and reports may be consulted at the SEC's main and regional offices.[1] A vast array of data on individual companies can be found in official filings with governmental agencies. Increasingly this information is being made available to the public in accordance with the SEC's full-disclosure concept.

The Sales and Earnings Forecasts

Basic to any estimate of earning power is a sales analysis and forecast. The growth of demand for a company's products is essential for common stock appreciation. While expanding production and sales do not guarantee increased profits, rising demand or the introduction of new products at least gives a company an opportunity to earn a growing profit.

[1] Regional offices (and branches of regional offices) are maintained in New York City, Boston, Atlanta (Miami), Chicago (Cleveland, Detroit, St. Paul, St. Louis), Fort Worth (Houston), Denver (Salt Lake City), San Francisco (Los Angeles), Seattle, and Arlington, Virginia.

FIGURE 14–4

American Tel. & Tel.

182

Stock—	Price Jun. 13'78	*P-E Ratio	Dividend	Yield
COMMON...	61¾	9	[2]$4.60	[2]7.4%
$4 CONV. PREFERRED	65⅝		4.00	6.1

SUMMARY: AT&T is dominant in communications, not only through its telephone subsidiaries but also through Western Electric and Bell Telephone Laboratories. The Justice Department filed an antitrust suit in 1974 charging AT&T with monopolizing the market for telecommunications services and equipment, and seeking the break-up of the company. The quality of the company's earnings is high owing to the use of conservative accounting; nevertheless, continuing rate relief will be needed to maintain long-term share earnings progress.

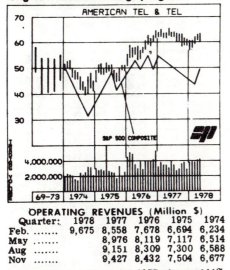

OPERATING REVENUES (Million $)

Quarter:	1978	1977	1976	1975	1974
Feb.	9,675	8,558	7,678	6,694	6,234
May		8,976	8,119	7,117	6,514
Aug		9,151	8,309	7,300	6,588
Nov		9,427	8,432	7,504	6,677

Operating revenues for 1977 advanced 11%, from those of 1976, reflecting gains of 4.3% for telephones in service and 9.9% for toll call volume, and rate increases. The operating ratio moved up to 82.4%, from 82.1%, and operating income rose 9.1%. After 63% larger other income and only 1.8% higher interest charges, net income moved ahead 19%. Following 19% lower preferred dividend requirements, earnings amounted to $6.97 a share ($0.78 from Western Electric and $0.13 from state rate increases subject to refund) on 5.2% more shares, versus $6.05 ($0.37 and $0.09).

For the three months ended March 31, 1978 revenues and net income showed year-to-year gains of 13% and 21%, respectively. Share earnings were $1.91 on 6.5% more shares, against $1.65 (restated).

COMMON SHARE EARNINGS ($)

Quarter:	1978	1977	1976	1975	1974
Feb.	1.80	[4]1.52	1.33	[3]1.13	[3]1.26
May		1.80	1.51	[3]1.32	[3]1.39
Aug.		[4]1.79	1.60	[3]1.33	[3]1.31
Nov.		1.77	1.61	1.30	[3]1.32

PROSPECTS

Rising demand for telephone services, rate increases, and technological advances should lead to share earnings progress in 1978 from 1977's $6.97. Partially limiting are likely to be higher employment costs. The dividend was recently raised to $1.15 quarterly, from $1.05.

Long-term prospects point to continued growth in operations. However, some erosion of revenue gains is expected from increasing competition in the terminal equipment and private line communications markets.

RECENT DEVELOPMENTS

In June, 1978 the House Communications Subcommittee proposed legislation which included: (1) The barring of telephone companies from manufacturing telecommunications equipment (which would mean the divestiture of Western Electric) within three years of passage of the bill . (2) The opening of private line communications to competition. (3) The permitting of telephone companies to offer both computer and television transmission services (the latter in competition with both cable TV firms and broadcasters). (4) The establishment of a new commission which would determine to what extent one telephone service should subsidize another.

In May, 1978 the Supreme Court refused to stay a Federal Appeals Court ruling requiring AT&T to provide additional local telephone connections for competing long distance service such as Execunet (provided by MCI Communications Corp.). The Appeals Court had overturned an FCC ruling that AT&T did not have to provide the local connections pending the outcome of an FCC inquiry (not yet completed) to determine whether competition would be in the public interest.

DIVIDEND DATA

A dividend reinvestment plan is available.

Amt of Divd $	Date Decl	Ex div Date	Stock of Record	Payment Date
1.05...	Aug. 17	Aug. 25	Aug. 31	Oct. 1'77
1.05...	Nov. 16	Nov. 23	Nov. 30	Jan. 3'78
1.15...	Feb. 15	Feb. 22	Feb. 28	Apr. 1'78
1.15...	May 17	May 23	May 31	Jul. 1'78

[1]Listed N.Y.S.E.; com. also listed Boston, Midwest, Pacific & Philadelphia S.Es. & traded Cincinnati S.E.; pfd. also listed Philadelphia S.E. [2]Indicated rate. [3]Restated to reflect revised depr. rates. [4]Reflects revised depr. rate (retroactive to Jan. 1, 1977) for 3 mos. Feb. & 5 mos. Aug. *Based on latest 12 mos. earns.

STANDARD N.Y.S.E. STOCK REPORTS   **STANDARD & POOR'S CORP.**

© Copyright 1978 Standard & Poor's Corp.

Published at Ephrata, Pa. Editorial & Executive Offices, 345 Hudson St., New York, N.Y. 10014

FIGURE 14–4 *(continued)*

182 AMERICAN TELEPHONE & TELEGRAPH COMPANY

[1]INCOME STATISTICS (Million $) AND PER SHARE ($) DATA

Year Ended Dec. 31	Revenues Local	Revenues Toll	[3]Gross	% of Gr. Revs. Depr. & Maint.	% of Gr. Revs. Oper. Taxes	[2]Oper. Ratio	[7]Fxd. Chgs. & Pfd. Divs. Tms. Earns.	[8]Net Inc.	Common Share ($) Data [4][8]Earns.	Divs. Paid	Price Range	Earns. Ratios HI LO
1978--	------	------	------	---	---	---	---	-----	---	3.35	63½-56⅞	-----
1977--	17,070.9	18,093.8	36,494.8	34.3	18.0	82.4	2.70	4,543.9	6.97	4.10	65⅝-58⅜	9- 8
1976--	15,609.0	16,065.5	32,815.6	33.9	18.0	82.1	2.41	3,829.2	6.05	3.70	64¾-50⅞	11- 8
1975--	14,027.8	13,925.2	28,957.2	34.6	17.5	82.3	2.18	3,147.7	5.13	3.40	52 -44¾	10- 9
1974--	12,812.8	12,460.9	26,174.4	34.6	18.2	82.1	2.31	3,169.9	[9]5.27	3.16	53 -39⅝	10- 8
1973--	11,418.5	11,278.5	23,527.3	34.7	18.5	82.2	2.47	2,946.7	4.98	2.80	55 -45⅜	11- 9
1972--	10,362.9	9,771.4	20,904.1	35.1	18.2	82.9	2.50	2,532.1	4.34	2.65	53½-41⅛	12- 9
1971--	9,135.5	8,632.8	18,442.1	35.5	18.0	83.4	2.66	2,202.0	3.92	2.60	53⅞-40¾	14-10
1970--	8,456.0	7,874.1	16,954.9	34.8	19.3	83.4	3.25	2,192.2	3.99	2.60	53⅞-40⅜	14-10
1969--	7,774.4	7,297.8	15,683.8	33.5	22.3	83.6	4.70	2,198.7	4.00	2.40	58⅛-48⅛	15-12
1968--	7,184.1	6,341.2	14,100.0	32.7	23.4	83.3	5.34	2,051.8	3.75	2.40	58⅜-48	16-13

[1]PERTINENT BALANCE SHEET STATISTICS (Million $)

Dec. 31	Gross Prop.	Capital Expend.	%Depr. of Gross Prop.	[6]%Earn. on Net Prop.	[5]Long Term Debt	% Long Term Debt of— Net Prop.	Gross Rev.	Invest. Cap.	Total Invest. Cap.	[6][7]%Earn. on Inv. Cap.	Net Inc. per Tel.	($) Book Val. Com. Sh.
1977--	101,859	11,293	19.1	7.8	32,500	39.4	89.1	38.3	84,756	8.4	35.36	75.32
1976--	94,167	9,747	19.4	7.8	32,525	42.8	99.1	41.3	78,684	8.0	31.11	69.81
1975--	87,621	9,329	19.6	7.3	31,793	45.1	109.8	43.5	73,172	7.5	26.57	64.46
1974--	81,146	10,074	20.0	7.2	32,308	49.8	123.4	46.4	69,575	7.6	27.69	59.74
1973--	74,005	9,322	20.9	7.1	28,371	48.4	120.6	45.2	62,748	7.6	26.71	55.08
1972--	67,082	8,306	21.6	6.8	26,020	49.5	124.5	45.7	56,969	7.2	24.05	50.95
1971--	60,568	7,564	22.1	6.5	22,828	48.4	123.8	44.7	51,112	7.0	21.96	47.36
1970--	54,813	7,159	22.4	6.6	20,454	48.1	120.6	44.2	46,286	7.0	22.70	45.53
1969--	49,244	5,731	22.8	6.8	15,868	41.7	101.2	38.9	40,792	7.1	23.72	43.96
1968--	44,975	4,742	22.7	6.8	13,430	38.8	95.2	36.0	37,366	7.0	23.31	42.24

[1]Data for 1973 & thereafter as originally reported; data for each yr. prior to 1973 as taken from subsequent yr.'s Annual Report. [2]After depr. & taxes. [3]Aft. deduct. uncollectible revs. [4]Based on avge. shs. [5]Incl. interim debt to be refinanced. prior to 1975. [6]Based on bk. value, may differ from return on rate base. [7]Fixed chgs. only prior to 1971. [8]Bef. spec. cr. of $0.08 a sh. in 1973. [9]As restated to reflect 1975 elimination of provisions for certain contingencies sh. earns. were $5.28.

Fundamental Position

A holding company, American Telephone & Telegraph, through its telephone subsidiaries comprising the Bell System, controlled 128.5 million phones at year-end 1977, about 80% of the U. S. total. Noncontrolling interests are held in other telephone operating companies. The parent directly operates long-distance lines connecting regional units and independent systems. Of 1977 revenues, toll accounted for 49%, local 46% and other 4%.

Equipment is purchased largely from 100%-owned Western Electric Co., an important contributor to earnings. Research is done for AT&T and Western Electric on a non-profit basis by Bell Telephone Laboratories.

Auxiliary services of AT&T include private line telephone services, and transmission of data and radio and TV programs. Overseas service to over 235 countries is provided through cable, radio, and satellite circuits.

Rapid depreciation is used for tax purposes with normalization. Savings from investment tax credits are amortized.

In November, 1974 the Justice Department filed an antitrust suit charging AT&T with monopolizing the market for telecommunications services and equipment through the use of illegal methods against competitors, mainly in the area of business services. The suit sought divestiture of Western Electric and its division into two or more companies, and the divestiture of AT&T's Long Lines Department or the sale of some or all of the 23 local telephone companies served by Long Lines. Legal proceedings may continue for many years.

Dividends paid in each year since 1885, averaged 60% of earnings in 1973-77.

Employees: 950,000. Stockholders: 2,960,-200.

Finances

Capital outlays for 1978 are estimated at $13-$13.4 billion (about 75% to be generated internally), up from $11.6 billion (on a comparable basis) spent in 1977. Subsidiaries are expected to raise $2.6 billion through outside financing in 1978. New money financing in 1977 totaled $2.7 billion.

At 1977 year-end common equity per share was $57.78 and the 1977 return thereon 11.7%. For 1977 the Federal income tax rate was 38.8% and construction credits were 5% of common earnings.

Institutional Holdings

Institutions: 940. Shares: 81,084,000 (12% of the total outstanding).

CAPITALIZATION

LONG TERM DEBT: $32,448,188,000.
MINORITY INTEREST: $1,269,614,000.
$4 CUM. CONV. PREFERRED STOCK: 11,-323,000 shs. ($1 par; $50 stated value); red. at $50; conv. into approx. 1.05 com.
$77.50 PREFERRED STOCK: 600,000 shs. ($1 par; $1,000 stated value). Privately held.
$3.74 CUM. PREFERRED STOCK: 10,000,000 shs. ($1 par; $50 stated value).
$3.64 CUM. PREFERRED STOCK: 10,000,-000 shs. ($1 par; $50 stated value).
COMMON STOCK: 652,884,000 shs. ($16 2/3 par).

Incorporated in N.Y. in 1885. **Office**—195 Broadway, NYC 10007. **Tel**—(212) 393-9800. **Chrmn & Chief Exec Officer**—J. D. deButts. **Pres**—C. L. Brown. **Secy**—F. A. Hutson, Jr. **VP-Treas**—W. G. Burns. **Dirs**—W. M. Batten, C. L. Brown, E. W. Carter, W. S. Cashel, Jr., C. B. Cleary, A. K. Davis, J. D. deButts, W. M. Ellinghaus, J. H. Evans, P. E. Haas, E. B. Hanify, W. A. Hewitt, J. A. Holland, B. K. Johnson, D. S. MacNaughton, W. J. McGill, J. I. Miller, E. B. Speer, R. Warner, Jr. **Transfer Offices**—Company's offices, 180 Fulton St., NYC; 444 Hoes Lane, Piscataway, N.J.; 140 New Montgomery St., San Francisco. **Registrars**—Bankers Trust Co., NYC; First National Bank, Boston; First National Bank, Chicago; Wells Fargo Bank, San Francisco.

FIGURE 14–5
Selected Individual Stocks

The diverse range of results for the ten year period 1968-1977 for individual stocks is even greater than for industrial groups. This is illustrated by the market performance of the broad range of over 400 stocks which follow:

SELECTED INDIVIDUAL STOCKS
January 1, 1968 — December 31, 1977

Stock	+/−	%
ACF Industries, Inc.	+	15%
Adams Express	−	19
Addressograph-Multigraph	−	80
Airco	−	0
Air-Products & Chemicals	+	48
Akzona, Inc.	−	57
Alabama Gas Corp.	−	50
Alberto Culver	−	82
Alcan Aluminum Ltd.	−	0
Alcon Labs	+	357
Allegheny Ludlum Industries	−	61
Allegheny Power System	−	9
Allied Stores	+	18
Allied Supermarkets	−	88
Allis-Chalmers	−	31
Alpha Portland	+	33
Amax Corp.	+	19
American Airlines	−	69
American Bakeries	−	35
American Broadcasting	+	84
American Cyanamid	−	5
American Distilling	−	63
American Electric Power	−	33
American Express	+	97
American Greetings Corp.	+	13
American Home Products	+	44
American Hospital Supply	−	11
American Invest. Co. of Ill.	−	72
American Motors	−	73
American Natural Gas	+	26
American Seating	−	40
American Standard	+	25
American Stores	+	2
American Waterworks	+	8
AMF Corp.	−	19
AMP, Inc.	+	118
Ampex Corp.	−	71
Amstar Corp.	−	22
Amsted Industries	+	115
Anchor Hocking Glass	+	25
Anderson, Clayton	+	28
Anheuser-Busch, Inc.	−	6
Archer, Daniels, Midland	+	314
Aristar, Inc.	−	76
Arizona Public Service	−	9
Arkansas Louisiana Gas	+	14
Armco Steel	−	17
Armstrong Cork	−	35
ASA, Ltd.	−	28
Asamera Oil	+	70
Asarco	−	45
Ashland Oil	−	15
Associated Dry Goods	−	47
Atlantic City Electric	−	13
Atlantic Richfield	+	96
Atlas Corp.	−	51
Avco Corp.	−	73
Avon Products	−	32
Babcock & Wilcox	+	23
Baker Industries	+	40
Baker International	+	435
Baltimore Gas & Elec.	−	9
Bankamerica Corp.	+	82
Bank of N.Y. Co.	−	18
Bankers Trust	−	0
Bausch & Lomb	+	48
Baxter Travenol Labs	+	85
Beatrice Foods	+	60
Beckman Instruments	+	7
Becton Dickinson	+	21
Beech Aircraft	+	59
Bell & Howell	−	83
Bendix Corp.	+	10
Beneficial Corp.	+	1
Black & Decker	+	39
Boeing	−	39
Borden Co.	−	13
Borg Warner Corp.	−	7
Boise Cascade	−	33

Stock	+/−	%
Braniff Int'l	−	34%
Briggs & Stratton	+	91
Bristol Myers	−	9
Brooklyn Union Gas	−	31
Brown Group	−	47
Brunswick Corp.	−	15
Bucyrus Erie	+	132
Budd Co.	−	6
Burlington Ind.	−	47
Burlington Northern, Inc.	−	26
Burroughs Corp	+	57
Campbell Red Lake Mines	+	159
Campbell Soup	−	19
Canadian Pacific	+	46
Cannon Mills	−	81
Carborundum	+	157
Carnation Co.	−	80
Carolina Power & Light	−	43
Carrier Corp.	−	18
Carter-Wallace	−	53
Caterpillar Tractor	+	90
CBS, Inc.	−	1
Celanese	−	33
Central and Southwest Corp.	−	31
Central Illinois Public Service	−	27
Central Maine Power	−	13
Central Soya Co.	+	10
Certain-Teed Corp.	+	202
Charter New York Corp.	−	21
Chase Manhattan Bank	−	27
Chemical New York Corp.	−	17
Chesebrough Ponds	+	9
Chessie System	+	5
Chicago Pneumatic Tool	−	42
Chock Full O'Nuts	−	70
Cincinnati Gas and Elec.	−	14
Cincinnati Milacron	−	25
CIT Financial	−	0
Cities Service	+	16
Clark Equipment	+	28
Cleveland Electric Illum.	−	8
Cluett Peabody	−	57
Coastal States Gas Corp.	−	77
Coca-Cola Co.	−	12
Colgate Palmolive	+	46
Columbia Gas System	+	14
Combustion Engineering	+	50
Commonwealth Edison	−	39
Communications Satellite Corp.	−	40
Cone Mills	+	193
Connecticut General	+	87
Consolidated Edison of N.Y.	−	19
Consolidated Foods Corp.	−	44
Consolidated Natural Gas	+	54
Consumers Power	−	44
Continental Group	+	4
Continental Oil	+	61
Control Data	−	79
Cooper Industries	+	88
Copperweld Corp.	+	69
Corning Glass	−	62
CPC Products	−	14
Crane Corp.	+	164
Crown Cork & Seal	+	104
Crown Zellerbach	+	11
Culbro Corp.	−	16
Curtis Wright Corp.	−	16
Cutler Hammer	+	7
Dana Corp.	+	109
Dan River Mills	−	47
Dayton Power & Light	−	35
Deere & Co.	+	85
Delmarva Power & Light	−	43
Delta Airlines	−	17
Dentsply Int'l	−	39
Detroit Edison Co.	−	37
Diamond Shamrock	+	87

Stock	+/−	%
Digital Equipment	+	189%
Disney (Walt)	+	288
Dome Mines	+	238
Dover Corp.	+	195
Dow Chemical	+	84
Dresser Industries	+	131
Dr. Pepper	+	79
Duquesne Light Co.	−	37
Eagle Picker Industries	+	104
Eastern Airlines	−	87
Eastern Gas & Fuel	+	37
Eaton Corp.	+	11
EG&G Inc.	−	67
ElPaso Natural Gas	−	20
Emerson Electric	+	35
Emery Air Freight	+	68
Engelhard Minerals & Chem.	+	9
Enserch Corp.	−	0
Equitable Gas Corp.	+	7
Ex-Cell-O	−	32
Fairchild Camera	−	72
Fairmont Foods	−	48
Federal Mogul Corp.	−	46
Federal Paperboard	−	40
Federated Dept. Stores	+	6
Ferro Corp.	+	75
Firestone Tire & Rubber	−	42
First Charter Financial	+	134
Flintkote	−	18
Florida Power & Light	−	29
Florida Power Corp.	−	27
Fluor Corp.	+	121
FMC Corp.	−	39
Food Fair Stores	−	33
Ford Motor Corp.	−	14
Franklin National Bank	−	100
Freeport Minerals	+	73
Fruehauf Corp.	−	32
Gamble Skogmo	+	10
Gardner Denver	+	43
GATX	−	29
General Cable	−	69
General Dynamics	−	31
General Host	+	76
General Instrument	−	56
General Mills	+	77
General Portland Cement	−	21
General Public Utilities	−	24
General Refractories	−	47
General Signal	+	138
General Tel. & Tel.	−	26
General Tire & Rubber	−	7
Genesco Inc.	−	91
Georgia Pacific	+	98
Gerber Products	+	4
Gillette Co.	−	61
Goodrich (B.F.) Tire & Rubber	−	56
Grace (W.R.) Co.	−	36
Grant (W.T.)	−	100
Great Atlantic & Pacific Tea Co.	−	69
Great Northern Iron	+	40
Greyhound Corp.	−	43
Gulf Oil Corp.	−	30
Gulf States Utilities Co.	−	46
Gulf & Western Ind.	−	45
Halliburton Co.	+	526
Hanover Insurance	−	57
Harcourt, Brace & Jovanovich	−	62
Hart Schaffner & Marx	−	61
Heinz (H.J.) Co.	+	125
Heller International	+	41
Hercules, Inc.	−	30
Hershey Foods	−	20
Heublein	−	21
Hewlett-Packard	+	104
Hoffman Electronics	−	43

Source: *Johnson's Charts,* 1978 edition.

FIGURE 14–5 *(continued)*

SELECTED INDIVIDUAL STOCKS
January 1, 1968 — December 31, 1977

Holiday Inns ....– 41%	Melville Corp. ....+ 160%	Revlon ....+ 57%
Holly Sugar ....– 53	Merck and Co. ....+ 32	Rio Grande Industries ....+ 100
Homestake Mining ....+ 16	Mesta Machine ....– 24	Robertshaw Controls ....+ 15
Honeywell, Inc. ....– 58	Metro Goldwyn Mayer ......+ 76	Royal Dutch Petroleum ......+ 62
Household Finance ....– 12	Middle South Utilities ....– 36	
Howard Johnson ....+ 11	Missouri Pacific Corp. ....+ 168	Safeway Stores ....+ 71
	Mobil Oil Corp. ....+ 49	St. Joe Minerals ....+ 58
IBM ....+ 9	Monarch Machine Tool .....– 47	St. Regis Paper ....+ 52
Idaho Power Co. ....– 10	Monsanto Corp. ....+ 22	Santa Fe Industries ....+ 41
Ideal Basic Ind. ....+ 28	Montana Power Co. ....– 17	Schering Plough ....+ 70
Illinois Power ....– 28	Murphy (G.C.) Co. ....– 23	Schlumberger ....+ 1453
Indianapolis Power & Light ..– 14		Scott Paper ....– 48
Ingersoll Rand Co. ....+ 30	Nabisco ....+ 9	Shell Oil ....+ 2
Inland Steel ....+ 14	Nalco Chemical ....+ 17	Sherwin Williams ....– 42
Inspiration Cons. Copper ....– 44	National Distillers ....+ 5	Simmons Co. ....– 4
Interco, Inc. ....+ 22	National Fuel Gas ....+ 4	Singer Corp. ....– 71
Interlake, Inc. ....– 2	National Gypsum ....– 26	Smith, A.O. Corp. ....– 19
Int'l Flavors & Fragrances ...+ 27	National Steel ....– 29	Smithkline Corp. ....– 1
International Minerals ....+ 41	National Tea ....– 70	Southern California Edison ..– 28
International Te. & Tel. ......– 45	NCR Corp. ....– 39	Southern Company ....– 37
Interstate Power Co. ....– 16	New England Elec. System ..– 11	Southern Natural Resources .+ 53
Iowa Beef Processors ....– 2	Newmont Mining ....– 33	Southern Pacific Co. ....+ 14
Iowa Power & Light ....– 15	N.Y. State Electric & Gas ...– 53	Southern Railway ....+ 116
Itek Corp. ....– 85	Niagara Mohawk ....– 21	Southwestern Public Service + 12
	NL Industries ....– 48	Sperry Rand ....– 43
Jewel Companies ....– 11	Norfolk & Western R.R. ......– 11	Square D Co. ....– 13
Johnson & Johnson ....+ 151	North American Coal ....+ 24	Standard Brands ....+ 42
Joy Mfg. Co. ....+ 86	Northern Natural Gas ....+ 68	Standard Oil (Indiana) ....+ 83
	Northern States Power .....– 2	Standard Packaging ....– 57
Kaiser Aluminum & Chem. ...– 37		Stauffer Chemical ....+ 62
Kansas City Power & Light ..– 10	Ohio Edison ....– 23	Stewart Warner ....– 9
Kansas City Southern Ind. ...– 12	Oklahoma Gas & Elec. Co. ...– 29	Sunbeam Corp. ....– 40
Kellogg Co. ....+ 129	Oklahoma Natural Gas ......+ 60	Superior Oil of Cal. ....+ 74
Kennecott Copper ....– 52	Olin Corp. ....– 65	
Kerr, McGee ....+ 12	Outboard Marine ....– 31	Tandy Corp. ....+ 409
Kimberly Clark ....+ 50	Owens Corning Fiberglass ..+ 101	Texas Gas Transm. ....+ 23
K-Mart ....+ 180		Texas Gulf Inc. ....+ 54
Koppers Co. ....– 153	Pacific Gas & Electric ....– 33	Texas Instruments ....+ 36
Kraftco ....+ 26	Pacific Lighting Corp. ....– 24	Texas Utilities ....– 24
Kroger Co. ....+ 17	Pacific Tel. & Tel. ....– 24	Textron ....– 49
	Panhandle Eastern Pipeline ..+ 37	Thiokol Chemical ....– 36
Laclede Gas Co. ....– 8	Penney, J.C. ....+ 8	Time, Inc. ....– 19
Lear Siegler ....– 31	Pennwalt Corp. ....– 33	Timken Co. ....– 26
Lehigh Portland Cement .....– 40	Peoples Gas Co. ....+ 1	Trans World Airlines ....– 80
Libbey Owens Ford Glass ...– 46	Pepsico ....+ 110	Tricontinental Corp. ....– 35
Liggett & Myers ....– 24	Perkin, Elmer ....– 1	TRW, Inc. ....– 37
Lincoln National Corp. ....+ 21	Pfizer, Inc. ....+ 9	Twentieth Century Fox ......– 31
Lockheed Aircraft ....– 72	Phelps Dodge Corp. ....– 40	
Loews Corp. ....– 92	Philadelphia Electric ....– 34	Union Electric ....– 32
Lone Star Ind. ....+ 11	Philip Morris ....+ 456	Union Pacific R.R. ....+ 141
Long Island Lighting ....– 30	Phillips Petroleum ..!.......– 10	Uniroyal ....– 67
Louisiana Land & Explor. ....– 26	Pillsbury Co. ....+ 100	Upjohn Co. ....+ 43
Louisville Gas & Elec. ....– 9	Pitney Bowes ....– 44	U.S. Fidelity & Guarantee ....+ 25
Lowenstein (M.) & Sons .....– 32	Pittston Co. ....+ 237	U.S. Gypsum ....– 33
Lukens Steel ....– 18	Polaroid ....– 79	Utah Power & Light ....– 35
	Potomac Electric Power Co. ..– 9	
Macy (R.H.) Co. ....+ 11	PPG Industries ....– 17	Varian Assoc. ....– 37
Mallory Products ....+ 26	Public Service Co. of Colorado– 11	Virginia Electric & Power ....– 56
MAPCO ....+ 454	Public Service Electric & Gas – 30	
Maremont Corp. ....– 18	Puget Sound Power & Light .– 46	Washington (D.C.) Gas & Light– 14
Marine Midland Bank ....– 58		Western Pacific R.R. ....– 23
Marshall Field & Co. ....+ 2	Quaker Oats ....+ 33	Western Union ....– 52
Martin Marietta ....– 18		Weyerhaeuser Co. ....+ 178
Masco Corp. ....+ 281	Ralston Purina ....– 38	Williams Companies ....– 3
Masonite Corp. ....+ 93	Rapid America Corp. ....– 57	Winn-Dixie Stores ....+ 90
May Dept. Stores ....– 0	Raybestos-Manhattan ....– 33	Wisconsin Electric Power ....+ 25
Maytag ....+ 60	Raytheon ....+ 29	Wrigley (Wm. Jr.) ....+ 36
McDonalds ....+ 617	RCA Corp. ....– 50	
McGraw Edison ....– 27	Republic Steel ....– 49	Xerox ....– 54
McGraw Hill ....– 59	Revere Copper & Brass ....– 55	
Mead Corp. ....+ 66	Reynolds Industries ....+ 34	Zenith Radio ....– 75
	Reynolds Metals ....– 36	

Source: *Johnson's Charts,* 1978 edition.

What the investor is seeking is an analysis of a sales forecast in order to determine the profit implications. The starting point of an effective industry and company forecast may be a GNP forecast, with a breakdown of components. For example, a forecast of automobile industry sales may be tied to the growth of real GNP by using historic figures on the number of cars sold per billion dollar increase in real GNP.

Having obtained an estimate or a range of estimates of prospective sales growth rates, the next step is to proceed to obtain an estimate, or a range of estimates, of prospective earnings growth rates. To achieve this, an analysis of earnings is necessary. One approach is to start with the GNP forecast and to derive from it a prospective corporate profits trend for all industry. Then, factor out a profits trend for the particular industry under review, making adjustments for special industry characteristics that may suggest a greater or lesser rate of growth than that of the total corporate profits series. Finally, develop from this a company estimate, again making adjustments for special company characteristics.

Of all factors, the growth rate of earnings is perhaps the most significant. There seems to be a consensus that in general the higher the growth rate of earnings, the higher the P/E ratio.

From this brief summary of fundamental analysis, it should be clear that the modern approach to common stock evaluation centers on a two-part question: What is the potential growth of earnings and dividends of a company whose stock is being analyzed, and what is a reasonable price to pay for that potential?

Of Random Walks and Efficient Markets

Before attempting to plumb the depths of common stock analysis, the aspiring investor must carry the perils of two widely held academic concepts—the efficient market and the random walk. Both concepts combined imply that the security analyst and the portfolio manager are engaged in futile exercises, for their services can avail little.

According to one terse glossary, "an efficient market is one in which prices always fully reflect all available relevant information. Adjustment to new information is virtually instantaneous," while "a random walk implies that there is no discernible pattern of travel (of a drunk wandering in the woods—or of stock prices). The size and direction of the next step cannot be predicted from the size and direction of the last or even from all the previous steps. . . . Random walk is a term used in mathematics and statistics to describe a process in which successive changes are statistically independent."[2]

In the words of another authority, "There are two forms of random walk—narrow and broad. Thus, an accurate statement of the narrow form of the random-walk hypothesis goes as follows: The history of stock price movements contains no useful information that will enable an investor consistently to outperform a buy-and-hold strategy in managing a portfolio."[3] If this is correct, then technical analysis (predicting future stock prices based on analysis of past stock prices and other internal market factors, such as volume, breadth, highs, and lows) is about as scientific and useful as astrology.

Nor does fundamental analysis escape and survive. It is demolished by the broad form. Malkiel says:

> The broad form states that fundamental analysis is not helpful either. It says that all that is known concerning the expected growth of the company's earnings and dividends, all of the possible favorable and unfavorable developments affecting the company that might be studied by the fundamental analyst, are already reflected in the price of the company's stock. Thus throwing darts at the financial page will produce a portfolio that can be expected to do as well as any managed by professional security analysts. In a nutshell, the broad form of the random-walk theory states: Fundamental analysis of publicly available information cannot produce investment recommendations that will enable an investor consistently to outperform a buy-and-hold

---

[2] See James H. Lorie and Mary T. Hamilton, *The Stock Market: Theories and Evidence* (Homewood, Ill.: Richard D. Irwin, 1973), pp. 270, 273.

[3] Burton G. Malkiel, *A Random Walk down Wall Street* (New York: W. W. Norton, 1973), p. 121.

strategy in managing a portfolio. The random-walk theory does not, as some critics have proclaimed, state that stock prices move aimlessly and erratically and are insensitive to changes in fundamental information. On the contrary, the point of the random-walk theory is just the opposite: the market is so efficient—prices move so quickly when new information does arise—that no one can consistently buy or sell quickly enough to benefit.[4]

What does the random walk mean for the investor who wants to operate in the market?[5] To many investors it may suggest that they are pursuing a program that has no real purpose or function. Why? Because, in an efficient market, buyers and sellers factor into their buying and selling decisions all known influences and knowledge—public and private, past, present, and future—that will have an impact on the price of a security.

The poor results achieved by the money managers of 87 percent of the 3,000 largest pension funds in the country, as reported in the A. G. Becker study,[6] would seem to be supportive of the random walk and efficient market theories. The study found that the S&P 500 outperformed the managers over the 1962–75 period. The funds were said to be running $13 billion behind the S&P Index during this period.

Some money managers turned to the Index as a guideline. The idea is that if you can't do as well as the averages, the way to be sure of at least keeping up with the averages is in the index fund approach. If the professional turns to the index, why not the investor?

[4] Ibid., p. 168. In fact, there are three forms of the efficient market-random walk hypothesis: the weak, the semistrong, and the strong. See Charles D. Kuehner, "Efficient Markets and Random Walk," in *Financial Analyst's Handbook* (Homewood, Ill.: Dow Jones-Irwin, 1975), vol. 1, chap. 43. pp. 1226–95.

[5] For a lucid discussion of the random walk theory, see Neil S. Berkman, "A Primer on Random Walks in the Stock Market," *New England Economic Review,* Federal Reserve Bank of Boston, September–October 1978.

[6] See "Must Be a Beta Way: Random Walk, An Analyst Argues, Is an Idea Whose Time Has Gone," *Barron's,* April 18, 1977.

Investment Timing

Perhaps as important as the choice of what stocks to buy is the decision as to when to buy—and when to sell. Investment timing may be an even more difficult task than investment choice. But the competent investor must constantly make a judgment as to the trend and level of the market as a whole in order to provide the appropriate environmental setting for portfolio additions or deletions. The level and trend of the market may be considered in three time dimensions: the secular, the cyclical, and the seasonal.

The secular trend is the long-run course of the market over a 20-, 25-, 40-, or 50-year period. Generally the trend has been upward because of the continuing decline in the purchasing power of the dollar, the gradual inflation in the economy, the rise in the demand for common stock as compared to the relatively limited supply, and the relatively steady growth in gross national product and corporate profits. The secular trend in common stock prices may be seen in Table 14–1.

In 1898 the Dow-Jones Industrials registered a low of 42 and a high of 60.97. By 1903 the high was 103; in 1916 it reached 110.15, and in 1919, 119.62. There followed a postwar setback, but from 81.50 in 1921 the DJIA rose to a peak of 381.17 in 1929. During the Great Depression, in 1932, the index fell to a low of 41.22, back to the 1898 level. It recovered to a peak of 194 in 1937, fell thereafter, and did not regain this level again until it reached 195 in 1945. Then it rose sharply to a peak of 995 in 1966. This postwar bull market far outshone anything in our history. The market remained on a plateau until a sharp setback occurred in 1969–70, the DJIA falling to a low of 631 in May 1970. The years 1971 and 1972, particularly 1972, saw a resurgence with the DJIA piercing the 1,000 level in 1972 and attaining a peak of 1,051 in January 1973. Then the average fell about 45 percent, touching a low of 577 in December 1974. Anticipating the economic recovery of 1975–76, it rose sharply, reaching 1,014 in September 1976. But once again the falling dollar, sharply rising inflation, and skyrocketing interest

TABLE 14–1
Dow-Jones Industrial Average 43-Year Performance, 1935–1977

Year	Market High	Market Low	Market Close	Market Yearly Change	Earnings	Dividends	Yield High	Yield Low	P/E Multiple High	P/E Multiple Low	Book Value	Consumer Price Index (Annual Average) 1967=100
1935	148.44	96.71	144.13	38.5	6.34	4.55	4.7%	3.1%	23½	15	80.42	41.1
1936	184.90	143.11	179.90	24.8	10.07	7.05	4.9	3.8	18	14	83.20	41.5
1937	194.40	113.64	120.85	− 32.8	11.49	8.78	7.7	4.5	17	10	86.48	43.0
1938	158.41	98.95	154.76	28.1	6.01	4.98	5.0	3.1	26	16½	87.38	42.2
1939	155.92	121.44	150.24	− 2.9	9.11	6.11	5.0	3.9	17	13	90.20	41.6
1940	152.80	111.84	131.13	− 12.7	10.92	7.06	6.3	4.6	14	10	92.39	42.0
1941	133.59	106.34	110.96	− 15.4	11.64	7.59	7.1	5.7	11½	9	95.45	44.1
1942	119.71	92.92	119.40	7.6	9.22	6.40	6.9	5.3	13	10	97.94	48.8
1943	145.82	119.26	135.89	13.8	9.74	6.30	5.3	4.3	15	12	101.68	51.8
1944	152.53	134.22	152.32	12.1	10.07	6.57	4.9	4.3	15	13	105.40	52.7
1945	195.82	151.35	192.91	26.6	10.56	6.69	4.4	3.4	18½	14	110.29	53.9
1946	212.50	163.12	177.20	− 8.1	13.63	7.50	4.6	3.5	15½	12	119.22	58.5
1947	186.85	163.21	181.16	2.2	18.80	9.21	5.6	4.9	10	9	126.65	66.9
1948	193.16	165.39	177.30	− 2.1	23.07	11.50	7.0	6.0	8	7	148.12	72.1
1949	200.52	161.60	200.13	12.9	23.54	12.79	7.9	6.4	8½	7	160.33	71.4
1950	235.47	196.81	235.41	17.6	30.70	16.13	8.2	6.9	7½	6½	186.11	72.1
1951	276.37	238.99	269.23	14.4	26.59	16.34	6.8	5.9	10½	9	197.05	77.8
1952	292.00	256.35	291.90	8.4	24.78	15.48	6.0	5.3	12	10	207.50	79.5
1953	293.79	255.49	289.90	− 3.8	27.23	16.11	6.3	5.5	11	9½	218.76	80.1
1954	404.39	279.87	404.39	44.0	28.18	17.47	6.2	4.3	14½	10	248.96	80.5
1955	488.40	388.20	488.40	20.8	35.78	21.58	5.6	4.4	13½	11	271.77	80.2
1956	521.05	462.35	499.47	2.3	33.34	22.99	5.0	4.4	15½	14	284.78	81.4
1957	520.77	419.79	435.69	− 12.8	36.08	21.61	5.1	4.2	14½	11½	298.69	84.3
1958	583.65	436.89	583.65	34.0	27.95	20.00	4.6	3.4	21	15½	310.97	86.6
1959	679.36	574.46	679.36	16.4	34.31	19.38	3.4	2.9	20	17	339.02	87.3
1960	685.47	566.05	615.89	− 9.3	32.21	20.46	3.6	3.0	21	17½	369.87	88.7
1961	734.91	610.25	731.14	18.7	31.91	21.28	3.5	2.9	23	19	385.82	89.6
1962	726.01	535.76	652.10	− 10.8	36.43	22.09	4.1	3.0	20	15	400.97	90.6
1963	767.21	646.79	762.95	17.0	41.21	23.20	3.6	3.0	18½	15½	425.90	91.7
1964	891.71	766.08	874.13	14.6	46.43	25.38	3.3	2.8	19	16½	417.39	92.9
1965	969.26	840.59	969.26	10.9	53.67	28.61	3.4	2.9	18	15½	453.27	94.5
1966	995.15	744.32	785.69	− 18.9	57.68	31.89	4.0	3.0	17	13	475.92	97.2
1967	943.08	786.41	905.11	15.2	53.87	30.19	3.8	3.2	17½	14½	467.50	100.0
1968	985.21	825.13	943.75	4.3	57.89	31.34	3.8	3.2	17	14	521.08	104.2
1969	968.85	769.93	800.36	− 15.2	57.02	33.90	4.2	3.3	17	13½	542.25	109.8
1970	842.00	631.16	838.92	4.8	51.02	31.53	5.0	3.7	16½	12½	573.15	116.3
1971	950.82	797.97	890.20	6.1	55.09	30.86	3.9	3.2	17	14½	607.61	121.3
1972	1,036.27	889.15	1,020.02	14.6	67.11	32.27	3.6	3.1	15½	13	642.87	125.3
1973	1,051.70	788.31	850.86	− 16.6	86.17	35.33	4.5	3.4	12	9	690.23	133.1
1974	891.66	577.60	616.24	− 27.6	99.04	37.72	6.5	4.2	9	5.8	746.95	147.7
1975	881.81	632.00	852.41	38.3	75.66	37.46	5.9	4.2	12	8	783.61	161.2
1976	1,014.79	858.70	1,004.65	17.9	96.72	41.40	4.8	4.1	10½	9	798.20	170.5
1977	999.8	800.85	831.17	−17.3	89.10	45.84	5.7	4.6	11.2	9.0	842.00E	181.5
Increase from 1935 to 1977	+574%	+727%	+477%	—	+1,305%	+907%	—	—	—	—	+947%	+342%

Note: Book values are based on net tangible assets per share. All data are adjusted to a basis consistent with the average.

Source: *Johnson's Charts,* 1978 edition.

rates brought still another setback to the market. The DJI dropped to a low of 742 in 1978.

Cyclical Trends

Investment timing is mostly concerned with the *cyclical* dimension of the stock market. In due course, despite possible temporary deviations or psychological pulls, stock prices tend to anticipate and reflect basic economic trends and may anticipate or respond to corporate profits, earnings per share, and dividends. Analysis of these fundamentals is a guide to whether the market is in a buying (low) or selling (high) range.

Common stock prices are one of the 12 leading indicators that were developed during the course of years of business cycle study by the National Bureau of Economic Research (NBER). Leading indicators are economic series, such as new orders for durable goods, commercial and industrial building contracts, and business failures, whose basic changes or direction tend, on the average, to precede and signal cyclical changes in business activity as a whole. Based on a study of past business cycles from 1873 to date, it has been found that cyclical changes in common stock prices tend to precede cyclical changes in business as a whole by about five to nine months.

Seasonal Trends

There has been considerable debate over whether there is a discernible seasonal pattern in the market. Financial writers speak of the traditional "summer rally" and "year-end rally." To a lesser extent there is a widespread impression that February and September are generally—but not always—poor months in the market. These impressions of financial writers and observers of the market are based upon tabulations of advances and declines, by months, of long past periods of time. A recent study covering the 23-year period May 1951–April 1974 found pronounced seasonal strength in January, March–April, July–August, and November–December, with weakness in February, May, June, and October (see Figure 14–6).

Statistical analysts have taken issue with these conclusions on seasonality. Using a sophisticated technique for examining economic time series, two experts found very little evidence of a seasonal

FIGURE 14–6
Market Performance Each Month of the Year, May 1951–April 1977

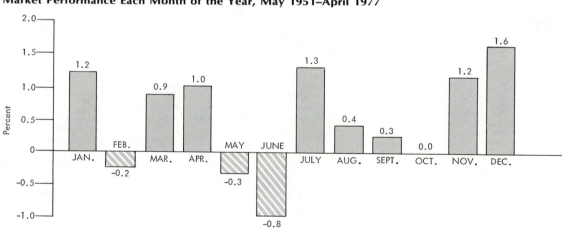

Average Month-to-Month Change in Standard & Poor's Composite Index (monthly average)

Source: *The 1978 Stock Traders Almanac* (Old Tappan, N.J.: The Hirsch Organization, Inc., 1978).

pattern. They declared: "In general, the seasonal components, although just observable, are of no financial significance."

The folklore of the market refuses to die, however, and any practitioner will tell you that the professors are wrong—that there usually is a summer and end-of-year rally. Some will go even further and tell you that Friday morning trading is the strongest of the week; that Fridays rise 54 percent more than Mondays; that when the market is down on Fridays, the chances are three to one that it will be down on Monday as well. Figure 14–7 records what really happened over a period of several years. Perhaps most bizarre is the notion that what happens in the first five days of a calendar year is predictive of the market for that year.

The Technical Approach

Some analysts do attempt to forecast changes in stock prices, including turning points in the market. They study the movements of stock prices themselves, past and present, and other technical data, in order to forecast future stock price trends. They are the "technical analysts."

The tools of the technical analyst are numerous,

and an elaborate and exotic jargon has been evolved. Technical factors examined and interpreted include odd lot trading, the short interest, the volume of trading, breadth-of-market, advance-decline lines, high-low indexes, and moving average lines. The complete market technician's and chartist's kit would also have to include chart jargon involving support and resistance, heads and shoulders, double tops and bottoms, line and saucer formations, V formations, gaps, islands, bear traps, bull traps, fulcrums, duplex horizontals, inverse fulcrums, delayed endings, saucers, inverse saucers, compound fulcrums.

An example from a market letter reads as follows:

> The question is, of course, what we are to make of this phenomenon. The lows of mid-February and late February are, in all cases, close enough to each other so that if a rally were to continue from these levels, we would have a potential for a so-called "double bottom." The upside implications of that double-bottom base formation are not, at the moment, too terribly exciting, and we, for one, would prefer to see backing and filling around current levels so that a base suggesting a

FIGURE 14–7
Market Performance Each Day of the Month, May 1952–April 1975*

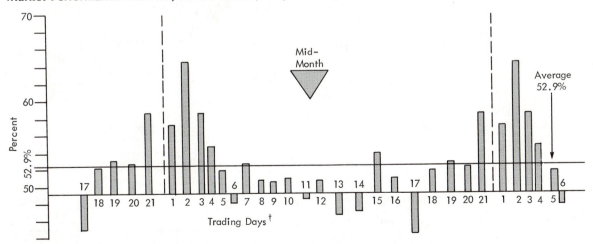

* Based on number of times S&P composite index closed higher than previous day.
† Excluding Saturdays, Sundays, and holidays.
Source: *The 1978 Stock Traders Almanac* (Old Tappan, N.J.: The Hirsch Organization, 1978).

meaningful advance might be formed. The likelihood of such an event is strengthened by the fact that most of the averages have now moved above the downtrend channels projected from the year-end highs to their lows of last month.

This sort of jargon has convinced many observers that technical analysis is just nonsense. Many academicians believe that short-term stock price movements are *random,* and that no amount of analysis of historical data on prices, volume, and the like, can enable one to forecast future stock prices. On the other hand, large numbers of Wall Street practitioners are equally convinced that price movements are not random and that technical analysis can improve one's chances of making correct timing decisions.

No one analyst uses all of the technical approach methods. If he did he would be hopelessly confused. A more interesting approach, however, is that of the indicator consensus technique. Since individual technical indicators have given false signals from time to time in the past, the idea occurred to use a consensus of indicators for greater reliability.

A number of services now use this technique. One of the more widely known is the Indicator Digest, which achieved some prominence as a result of performance.

Indicator Digest, Inc., uses a composite index that consists of 12 technical indicators at any one time. It varies several of them, depending on whether a bull market or a bear market is under way. The indicators are given weights for a total of ten. Whenever the composite total is six or more, a favorable signal is given. If the score sinks to four or less, the signal is unfavorable. The 40–60 percent range is regarded as neutral. (See Figure 14–8.)

Mechanical Timing Techniques

The limitations of the technical approach cause some investors to use mechanical timing techniques. Three varieties of mechanical timing techniques can be distinguished, of which the most

used is dollar cost averaging. There are also formula plans (constant dollar, constant ratio, or variable ratio); and there is automatic trend following.

Dollar cost averaging involves the regular purchase of securities—monthly or quarterly—in equal dollar amounts. The very obvious fact that the same amount of money will buy a greater number of shares of any stock when the price is low than it will when the price is high is the basis for the success of dollar averaging. You put the same fixed amount of money periodically into the same stock or stocks, regardless of the price. Your fixed amount of money buys more shares when the stock is low, less shares when it is high—as can be seen in Figure 14–9. The important thing is to stick to your schedule—to buy even though the price keeps falling, which, psychologically, is usually hard to do. This brings your average cost down, so that any subsequent rise will yield a significant capital gain. To engage in dollar cost averaging successfully, you

"No annual report, no net earnings, no dividends—what a chance to get in on the ground floor!"

Edgar Allen, Jr., The Commercial and Financial Chronicle

FIGURE 14–8

The Indicator Digest Composite Index

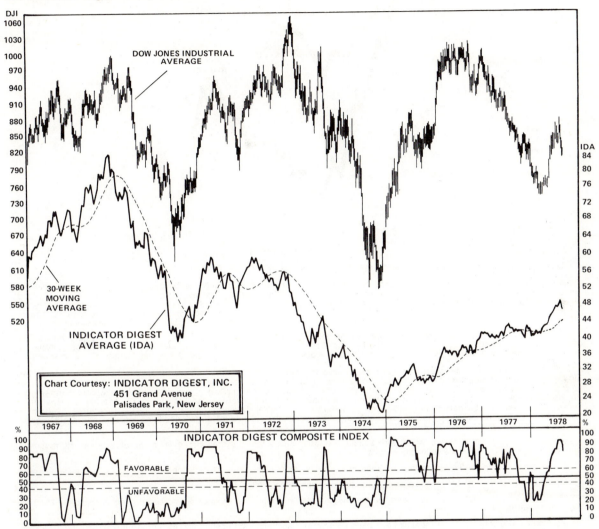

must have both the funds and the courage to continue buying in a declining market, when prospects may seem bleak.

In a bull market, investors hate to sell and take a profit, both because they do not want to pay the capital gains tax and because they are afraid that the market will continue to rise and that they will forgo added gains by selling. Thus they miss the top, the goal which most investors aim for but rarely achieve, and continue to hold well into the downturn. Then they are reluctant to sell during the early stages of the downturn because they mourn the profits they missed by not selling at or near the peak (which only hindsight reveals as a peak), and they hold, hoping that the market will reverse itself and return to the peak. It usually does not, but they continue to hold until, well on the downside, they lose their patience and sell. In this way emotion and bad judgment play a real role in a lack of investment success. Dollar cost averag-

FIGURE 14–9
Dollar Cost Averaging

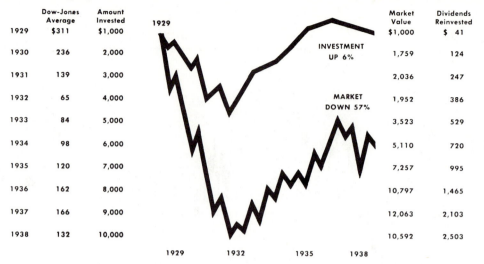

	Dow-Jones Average	Amount Invested		Market Value	Dividends Reinvested
1929	$311	$1,000		$1,000	$ 41
1930	236	2,000		1,759	124
1931	139	3,000		2,036	247
1932	65	4,000		1,952	386
1933	84	5,000		3,523	529
1934	98	6,000		5,110	720
1935	120	7,000		7,257	995
1936	162	8,000		10,797	1,465
1937	166	9,000		12,063	2,103
1938	132	10,000		10,592	2,503

TIME, NOT TIMING

Time itself, rather than timing, or guessing market action, is the secret of investment success.

A regular program of investing equal sums of money at regular intervals of time produces a pattern in the mathematics of investment of reducing the average cost of investments. This is called "dollar cost averaging." It requires that the investor's disposition and financial ability will allow him to continue the program through good and bad markets over reasonably long periods of time. Let us presume that we started to buy the Dow-Jones Industrial Average at the average of the high 1929 prices, and continued to invest $1,000 at the beginning of each year for the next ten years — irrespective of market forecasts:

At the end of the ten years, the market was worth only 43% of its original value, but dollar cost averaging had actually resulted in a profit of about 6%, in a market that had lost 57%. This would have been the result of the mathematics of dollar cost averaging of the Dow-Jones Industrial Stocks during the worst crash of securities' prices in the history of our markets.

The practice of dollar cost averaging does not remove the possibility of loss when the market is below the average cost, but it clearly demonstrates that the successful prosecution of the method will lessen the amount of loss in declining markets and increase the opportunities for greater profit in rising markets. The accompanying table of a hypothetical dollar cost averaging pattern demonstrates that (1) the average dollar-cost will be below the average market price, (2) the fluctuations of the average dollar cost will be narrow in comparison with the actual market fluctuations, (3) the lower dollar cost average will continually work toward increasing investment yield, and that (4) losses are limited during declining markets and profits accelerated during rising markets.

Instead of buying 120 shares of stock with $1,200, the table illustrates a systematic investment of $100 at 12 reasonably regular intervals of time with the following results:

(1) At point (3) the market value has declined 50%, but a loss of only 29% is sustained.

(2) At point (4) the market is down 60%, but the loss has been limited to 32.5%.

(3) At point (7) the market has recovered to the original starting point, but instead of just being even, a profit of 57% could be realized.

(4) Finally, at point (12) the purchases have been completed but the market is still 20% lower than the starting point. A single purchase of 120 shares with $1,200 would have a loss of $240, but the systematic purchases of $100 twelve times would have resulted in the purchase of 200 shares with a profit of $400.

DOLLAR COST AVERAGING

	Invest-ment	Total Invested	Market Price	Shares Bought	Total Shares	Average Price	Average Cost	Market Value	Profit (Loss)
1.	$100	$ 100	$10	10.0	10.0	$10.00	$10.00	$ 100.00	$ —
2.	$100	200	8	12.5	22.5	9.00	8.89	180.00	(20.00)
3.	$100	300	5	20.0	42.5	7.67	7.06	212.50	(87.50)
4.	$100	400	4	25.0	67.5	6.75	5.93	270.00	(130.00)
5.	$100	500	5	20.0	87.5	6.40	5.71	437.00	(67.50)
6.	$100	600	8	12.5	100.0	6.67	6.00	800.00	200.00
7.	$100	700	10	10.0	110.0	7.14	6.36	1,100.00	400.00
8.	$100	800	8	12.5	122.5	7.25	6.53	980.00	180.00
9.	$100	900	5	20.0	142.5	7.00	6.32	712.50	(187.50)
10.	$100	1,000	4	25.0	167.5	6.70	5.97	670.00	(330.00)
11.	$100	1,100	5	20.0	187.5	6.55	5.87	937.50	(167.50)
12.	$100	1,200	8	12.5	200.0	6.67	6.00	1,600.00	400.00

Source: *Johnson's Charts*, 1978 edition.

ing has been designed to overcome such human failings.

Sources of Investment Information

No one invests in a vacuum. We act on some type of information, whether it be a tip from a friend, advice from a banker, a broker's recommendation, a newspaper report, or a magazine article.

Individual investors are in a difficult position. They don't usually have the facilities, the resources, or the time to research a stock in depth before making their investment decision. They have a business life, a family life, a social life, and the time remaining from these pursuits, if any, is likely to be very limited. What they read, what they look into, must be most judiciously selected, because it can't, by definition, be very extensive. For the small investor, selection may become almost a hit-and-run operation.

Although small investors may not be able to devote the time necessary to answer many questions in depth, they must spend some time with one or more sources of information in order to come to investment decisions. Which source or sources should they choose? Reliance on a broker, on the financial press, and on one or more investment services seems to be a minimal requirement.

Brokerage Houses

Brokerage houses with research departments provide information for both individual and institutional investors. Some large brokerage houses maintain substantial research staffs. They publish market letters or market reviews. They provide company analyses and recommendations. They undertake portfolio reviews. They provide industry studies. If you tell them the approximate amount you wish to invest, they will provide a suggested portfolio in line with the investment objective you have indicated.

These are services which full line brokers generally provide, free of charge, in contrast to the newer discount houses which seldom offer any of them and charge for them when they do. This is a major reason for the differences in commissions charged.

The largest brokerage house, Merrill Lynch, Pierce, Fenner & Smith, has a huge research department, as might be expected. Merrill Lynch has published extensively, and it will readily mail out samples of its reports.[7] A few other large brokerage houses issue similar material. Smaller brokerage houses which do not have research departments of their own sometimes buy their "research" from "wholesale" organizations such as Argus Research and Data Digests, or else obtain it from large houses through which they clear.

The Financial Press

The intelligent investor and the professional analyst generally browse through, read, or study a part of the financial press each week, ranging from the financial section of a large metropolitan daily newspaper or the *Wall Street Journal,* to the *Financial Analysts Journal* (published every two months) or the *Journal of Finance* (published quarterly). The financial section of a newspaper can range from the elaborate and informative pages of the *New York Times* to a mere listing of daily stock quotations.

The *Wall Street Journal* is a daily, published every weekday by Dow Jones & Co. in New York, Chicago, San Francisco, and Los Angeles. It provides full coverage of business and financial news, including special news of companies, corporate profits reports, new issues, bond financing, national and local over-the-counter quotations, NYSE and AMEX stock prices, and CBOE option quotations.

Barron's is a financial weekly published by Dow Jones & Co. It usually may be viewed as having three categories: leading in-depth articles; departments, such as "The Trade," "Up & Down Wall Street," "Investment News & Views," "Capital Markets," "The Striking Price" (options), and "Market Laboratory"; and a substantial statistical section which includes "new highs and lows in stocks," "mutual funds," "short interest," "stock

---

[7] For Merrill Lynch research reports, write to the firm at One Liberty Plaza, 165 Broadway, New York, N.Y. 10006.

quotations," "over-the-counter market," "bond quotations," and "pulse of trade and industry." The market laboratory section contains a wealth of basic figures on the Dow-Jones averages, price-earnings ratios, odd lot trading, stock and bond yields, and the 20 most active stocks of the week.

Forbes is published twice monthly. It features articles on industry and company financial developments and trends. Its regular columns include "The Market Outlook," "Stock Analysis," "Investment Pointers," "Market Comment," and "Technician's Perspective." Each year the January 1 issue is devoted to rating companies within industries, comparing and contrasting profitability and performance. The August 15 issue contains the *Forbes* evaluation and rating of comparative mutual fund performance. It is one of the better tools for mutual fund evaluation.

The *Media General Financial Weekly,* published in Richmond, Virginia, covers the financial waterfront. In addition to a number of feature articles and columns, it provides financial and statistical data on 3,300 common stocks, including 800 OTC issues, and indicator charts on every NYSE and AMEX common stock plus 800 OTC issues. Its "Stocks in the Spotlight" lists the 40 leading and lagging issues in six major price categories and 40 leading issues in six volume categories. Two pages of charts show the performance of all 60 major industrial groups, compared with *Media General's* Composite Market Index. Long series of fundamental and technical indicators are shown in both charts and figures. This too, like the *Wall Street Transcript,* published weekly at $10 a copy, is a publication that is intended primarily for the security analyst and the professional money manager.

The *Financial World,* published weekly, and the *Magazine of Wall Street,* published biweekly, both feature articles on the trend of the market, industry evaluations, and individual company analyses.

The *Financial Analysts Journal* is published every two months by the Financial Analysts Federation, an association devoted to the advancement of investment management and security analysis. Each issue features 7 to 12 articles on varying phases of investment analysis and portfolio management.

The *Institutional Investor* is a monthly journal published for professional money managers. Like the *Financial Analysts Journal,* it features articles on investment analysis and portfolio management, but it places more emphasis on the personalities of money managers, and its articles are often grouped about such themes as "Wall Street's Search for Leadership." Its more learned and academic counterpart is the *Journal of Portfolio Management.*

The *Journal of Finance* is published quarterly by the American Finance Association. It is much more academically and theoretically oriented than the *Financial Analysts Journal.* In recent years it has attempted to cover not only all phases of finance but monetary and economic theory as well.

Even more mathematical and theoretically oriented is the *Journal of Financial and Quantitative Analysis,* published quarterly. Other publications of possible interest include *Finance, The Financial Executive, Financial Management, Investment Dealer's Digest, Journal of Commerce, Money, Trusts and Estates,* and *Wall Street Letter.*

Direct Financial Information

To the average person who has not had an accounting course, the mere sight of a balance sheet or an income statement inspires awe and fear. Yet, to invest wisely, you should know how to read and understand a financial statement. It is not at all difficult. This ability to read and understand a financial report is a "must" today for anyone going into business; and for the average investor, putting in a few hours to study the subject may pay dividends in the future.[8]

Information Sources on Business Conditions and Corporate Profits

If the investor's starting point is an examination of business trends, including a forecast of the out-

---

[8] A free copy of *How to Read a Financial Report* may be obtained by writing to Merrill Lynch, Pierce, Fenner & Smith, One Liberty Plaza (165 Broadway), New York, N.Y. 10006. You may also obtain a free copy of *Understanding Financial Statements* by writing to the Publications Division of the New York Stock Exchange, 11 Wall St. New York, N.Y. 10005.

look for business, the economy, and corporate profits, it is not difficult to find material. Indeed, the real problem may be choosing from among the multiplicity of sources. A number of the leading banks publish monthly reports or surveys dealing with the business outlook and other topics. Citibank of New York publishes a *Monthly Economic Letter.* The leading article is always on "General Business Conditions." The *Morgan Guaranty Survey* is published monthly by the Morgan Guaranty Trust Company of New York. The first article always covers "Business and Financial Conditions." The Bank of New York issues *General Business Indicators,* a statistical tabulation of selected economic indicators. It provides the bank's forecast of prospective gross national product, disposable personal income, the index of industrial production, corporate profits, and the earnings of the Dow-Jones Industrials, over the coming year. The Chase Manhattan Bank's *Business in Brief* is a bimonthly by its Economic Research Division. The first article is usually an analysis of the business outlook.

The 12 Federal Reserve banks publish monthly or quarterly bulletins devoted to banking, economic, and financial topics. The Federal Reserve Bank of New York, for example, publishes the *Quarterly Review,* which always includes an article on "The Business Situation." The Federal Reserve Bank of Philadelphia publishes the *Business Review,* a monthly. The Federal Reserve banks of Chicago and St. Louis also issue excellent monthly reviews. The Board of Governors of the Federal Reserve System in Washington, D.C., publishes the *Federal Reserve Bulletin,* a monthly. This contains a "National Summary of Business Conditions." The "National Summary" can be obtained as a separate monthly release.

For economic forecasting purposes, perhaps the most useful government publication is *Business Conditions Digest,*[9] issued monthly by the Bureau of the Census of the U.S. Department of Commerce. This report brings together many of the available economic indicators in convenient form for analysis and interpretation. The presentation

and classification of the series follow the business indicator approach of the National Bureau of Economic Research (NBER). The classification of series and business cycle turning dates are those designated by the NBER, which has been the leader in this field of investigation in recent years. About 90 principal indicators and over 300 components are included in the report.

Overall trends in corporate profits can be seen in the *Quarterly Financial Report for Manufacturing Corporations,* which is published jointly by the Federal Trade Commission and the Securities and Exchange Commission. Profitability is reported in two ways—"profits per dollar of sales" and "annual rate of profit on stockholders' equity at end of period." The quarterly summaries may be used to measure efficiency and appraise costs by comparing a company's operating results with the average performance of companies of similar size or in the same line of business.

Each year, in the April issue of its *Monthly Economic Letter,* the Citibank (of New York) publishes the results of its survey of the profit performance of almost 4,000 U.S. corporations in manufacturing, trade, transportation, utilities, services, real estate, and banking. Profits are reported for the two prior years on two bases—as "percent return on net worth" and as "percent margin on sales." The detailed industry classification and breakdown permits an investor or a securities analyst to compare a given company with the reported industry average.

If in the future you are too busy professionally making money in your own specialty and do not have the time to investigate each proposed investment opportunity, you may want to use professional services. You may be knowledgeable in your own field and despite reading all the suggested sources, assuming you have the time, you can still hesitate to risk your savings on your own.

There are many professionals, be they advisory services, investment counselors, bank investment officers, brokerage houses, or mutual fund managers, all eager to help you—at a price.

The following pages will attempt to acquaint you with some of the services of these professional money managers.

---

[9] It is urged that the student become thoroughly familiar with the latest issue of *Business Conditions Digest.* This is a basic economic source.

Investment Advisory Services

A wealth of information is available in the publications of the investment advisory services. The major services are:

Moody's Investor Services (owned by Dun
& Bradstreet)
99 Church Street
New York, N.Y. 10007

Standard & Poor's Corporation (owned by
McGraw-Hill)
345 Hudson Street
New York, N.Y. 10014

The Value Line Investment Survey (owned
by Arnold Bernhard & Co.)
5 East 44th Street
New York, N.Y. 10017

A comprehensive and copious flow of bulletins and reports emerges daily, weekly, and monthly from these services. It is possible to subscribe to part or all of the publications. The annual cost of any of the services is a properly deducted expense from investors' income under the personal income tax regulations. A well-stocked college or universtiy library will have one or more of these services, and the larger public libraries also make them available.

A basic part of both the Moody's and the Standard & Poor's services are the reference volumes: Moody's *Manuals* and Standard & Poor's *Corporation Records*. Moody's *Manuals* are six, thick volumes published each year and issued for various fields—industrials, OTC industrials, public utilities, transportation, municipals and governments, and banks and finance. Each volume contains reports on thousands of corporations (or governmental bodies), giving the financial history and full investment data for a period of years. Standard & Poor's six-volume *Corporation Records* are continuous and alphabetical, regardless of field. Both Moody's *Manuals* and Standard & Poor's *Corporation Records* are kept up to date by current supplements. The *Corporation Records* are augmented by a daily bulletin, and the *Manuals* are kept up to date by a semiweekly report. Most large

brokerage offices will have one or the other of these basic services.

Standard & Poor's issues a weekly magazine, the *Outlook,* while Moody's issues the weekly *Stock Survey.* Both publications review market conditions and recommend investment choices in common stock. The *Outlook* generally contains an overall market forecast and policy recommendation, a list of the ten best-performing and the ten poorest-performing groups of the week, an occasional "Stock for Action" recommendation, discussion of stocks in the limelight, on-the-spot reports on individual companies, a report on business, and special articles, such as "Stocks with Tax Exemption on Dividends," "Portfolio for New Investors," "Low-Priced Speculations," and "A Special Study on Municipal Bonds." A Master List of recommended issues is maintained. These are classified as follows: "Group 1—Foundation Stocks for Long-Term Gain"; "Group 2—Stocks with Promising Growth Prospects"; "Group 3—Cyclical/Speculative Stocks"; and "Group 4—Liberal Income with Inflation Protection." The annual forecast of the *Outlook* features ten stocks for action in the year ahead, the industries best situated for the year ahead, speculative stocks for aggressive investors, candidates for dividend increases, and stocks to outrun inflation.

The Standard & Poor's *Stock Guide* is a monthly pocket-size condensed handbook containing a thumbnail sketch of essential facts about some 5,000 common and preferred stocks, listed and unlisted. Most of the 5,000 stocks are rated for earnings and dividend stability and growth.

Each issue the S&P *Stock Guide* also contains a list of "stocks for potential price appreciation" and list of "stocks for good income return." At the back of each issue are to be found "quality ratings of utility preferred stocks" and a section on the performance of 400 mutual funds. In addition, there is one feature article, such as "Cyclical Buys Offering Sound Values" or "Electronics-Electrical Prospects Brighter."

Both Moody's and Standard & Poor's publish compendiums on individual companies. Moody's *Handbook of Common Stocks,* first published in

1964, is issued quarterly. It covers over 1,000 companies. For each company it has a chart, showing the industry group stock price trend and the company's stock price performance for the years 1953 to date. Basic financial statistics for the past decade are given. The written analysis covers the company's financial background, recent financial developments, and prospects. The Standard & Poor's compendium is called *Standard N.Y.S.E. Stock Reports*. It covers about 1,850 stocks. Each report gives the full financial facts about a company. A chart shows the market performance of the stock, the average performance of the stocks in its industry, the trading volume of the stock, and the performance of the stock market as a whole. Each report carries Standard & Poor's opinion of the investment merits of the stock.

Both Standard & Poor's and Moody's publish weekly and monthly bond guides. Standard & Poor's publishes a weekly *Bond Outlook,* Moody's a weekly *Bond Survey.* Each issue of these publications discusses new offerings in the corporate and municipal markets, opportunities in convertibles, changes in bond ratings, new-issue ratings, and bonds called for payment. Both services issue one-page summaries of individual bond situations.

The extensive nature of the many services provided for individual investors and for security analysts may be seen from the following list of publication services provided by Standard & Poor's.[10]

Analysts Handbook	Earnings Forecaster
Bond Guide	Fixed Income Investor
Called Bond Record	
Compmark Data Services	Industry Surveys
	International Stock Report
Convertible Bond Reports	Investment Advisory Survey
Corporation Records	
Daily Stock Price Records	Municipal Bond Selector

Dividend Record	The Review of Securities Regulation
Opportunities in Convertible Bonds	Security Dealers Directory
Outlook	Statistical Service
Poor's Register of Corporations, Directors, and Executives	Stock Guide
	Stock Reports
	Stock Summary
Registered Bond Interest Record	Transportation Service
	Trendline Charts

Of particular interest are the *Analysts Handbook* and the *Earnings Forecaster.* The *Analysts Handbook* provides composite corporate per share data on a true comparison basis. It maintains the best possible continuity since 1946 for 95 industries and the S&P 400 Industrial Index, making possible a great variety of significant per share comparisons. It is available annually with monthly updatings. The *Earnings Forecaster* provides weekly new and revised earnings estimates on 1,800 companies, prepared by S&P and other leading investment organizations and brokerage firms. Continuously updated, this 40–52-page summary offers an at-a-glance comparison of the various estimates. Each company listing includes an identification of the sources of the estimates, per share earnings for the past full year, and where possible, for the next year.

The *Value Line Investment Survey* covers 1,640 stocks in 75 industries. It is essentially a reference and current valuation service. Each stock in the list is reviewed in detail once every three months. Weekly supplements provide interim reports on any new developments that take place between the time of the regular quarterly reports. Each week the *Value Line Investment Survey* covers four to six industries on a rotating basis. Each industry report contains full-page reports on individual stocks. About 125 stocks are covered every week. After all 1,640 stocks have been covered in 13 weeks, the cycle starts again.

Investment Counseling Services

There is an easy and relatively inexpensive "out" for well-to-do investors who want to avoid the bur-

---

[10] A booklet describing these services—*Standard & Poor's Services and Publications Cover Every Financial Information Need*—may be obtained by writing to Standard & Poor's at 345 Hudson St., New York, N.Y. 10014. Moody's comparable services are described in a booklet entitled *How Moody's Can Help You.* A copy may be obtained by writing to Moody's Investor Service, 99 Church St., New York, N.Y. 10007.

densome and often time-consuming chore of digging up facts for themselves, following industry and company trends, and judging the state of the economy and the market. Such investors can use an investment counselor, or the investment counseling department of a bank, or one of the large investment services. Under the Investment Advisers Act of 1940, independent (nonbank) investment counseling firms must be registered with the SEC. In general, the clientele of the professional money managers consists of busy professional people, active business executives who have little or no time to do the digging involved in managing their own investments, or widows or widowers who have no knowledge of finance and investments.

The usual annual fee charge by an investment counselor is 0.5 percent of the value of the portfolio being managed. For a $200,000 portfolio this means an annual fee of $1,000. Most of the larger investment counseling firms will not take accounts with portfolios of less than $100,000. The largest firms in the business—Scudder, Stevens & Clark; Loomis-Sayles; Lionel D. Edie; Calvin Bullock; Stein, Roe & Farnham; Fayez Sarofim, & Co.; Eaton & Howard, Inverness Counsel—maintain professional staffs of security analysts and portfolio managers to assist clients. These staffs do the investment research and make recommendations to customers.

Some of the large investment counselors manage their own mutual funds. Others advise corporate pension funds or college or university endowment funds. The mutual funds are for investors whose assets are nowhere near the $100,000 minimum level. It has been estimated that the investment counselors' average client has a portfolio of about $250,000. Since investment counselors publish no records of performance, selecting a firm is usually an act of faith based on someone's recommendation or on the firm's general reputation.

Banks provide investment advisory services, sometimes on a formal, fee basis, sometimes on an informal, complimentary customer-relations basis. A wealthy individual who wants investment help from a bank can usually obtain it without formally turning over funds to the bank's trust department. An investment officer in the trust department or in the investment advisory department, if the bank has one, will serve as an investment counselor to those with portfolios of $100,000 and over. The investment officer ascertains the client's investment objectives and attempts to tailor recommendations to the objectives. The account may be discretionary or nondiscretionary—that is, the securities may be placed in the custody of the bank, or the customer may retain possession of them. Although the customer's portfolio is reviewed regularly, the customer usually receives a monthly or quarterly report from the bank on it. The investment officer makes recommendations, and in the case of the discretionary account he arranges portfolio changes. For wealthier investors who wish to be free from money-management problems and are comfortable in conservative investment hands, this is a useful arrangement. In the discretionary account the owners do not surrender title to their own securities. The bank acts only as their agent. This is in contrast to the more formal trust arrangement.

Bank-Administered Trusts

There are individual trusts and common trust funds. The common trust fund, akin to a mutual fund, is gaining in popularity. It is designed to appeal to smaller investors, persons with from $5,000 to $75,000 to invest, but some accounts go up to $100,000 and more. You set up a trust and name the bank as trustee, and the bank, in turn, mixes or pools your funds with other small individual trust accounts for investment in a common portfolio of securities. In a common trust fund, investments are spread far more widely than would be possible in an individual trust. Also, the cost is lower.

Banks offer several types of common trust funds. If you set up a trust without specifying the type of investment you want, the bank is required by law to put you into what is called a legal investment fund. This is a conservative type, consisting of about 65 percent bonds and 35 percent stock. But if you give the bank discretion, you may be placed in one of four types of funds: the balanced fund (about 60 percent common stock, 40 percent bonds), the

100 percent common stock fund; the tax-exempt bond fund (a rapidly growing type); or a taxable corporate bond and preferred stock fund designed for income. Thus banks have developed greater flexibility in serving investors. When you establish your trust, you can name the type of fund you want.

Mutual Funds

For the investor, large or small, who has no desire to "do-it-yourself," an incredible variety of mutual funds are available to assist or relieve him entirely of the burden of choosing appropriate investments.

An investment company is simply a financial institution whose aim is to gather the savings of many individuals and invest them in a diversified portfolio of securities. If the investments were made chiefly in bonds and mortgages, the portfolio would not be unlike that of mutual savings banks, savings and loan associations, or life insurance companies. However, investment companies typically invest more extensively in common stocks than do these other institutions. The exceptions, however, are the numerous bond funds that have been formed in the 1970s and the money market funds.

It cannot be emphasized too much that all sorts of investment companies exist. Some of them have as their prime purpose investment in relatively new and untried undertakings, which by their very nature can be only speculative. At the other extreme, some investment companies invest only in high-grade bonds. Investors can find investment companies which limit their investments to the type of securities in which they wish to participate, be these securities blue-chip common stocks, speculative common stocks, preferred stocks, high-grade bonds, more speculative bonds, a balanced fund of stocks and bonds, or a short-term liquid asset current income fund. Some investment companies can be found which emphasize as objectives high income or capital appreciation; others stress primarily the preservation of principal; some attempt to combine both.

Not only do investment companies vary widely in their investment objectives and policies, but very great disparities exist in their investment results. In many cases, the management more than earns its fee; in some instances, it would seem that the managers should pay the investors for the privilege of learning how to invest. Indeed, the most difficult problem for the small investor is to learn how to distinguish the competent, ably managed funds from the less effective ones.

Open-End Investment Companies

There are two principal types of investment companies—open end and closed end. An open-end investment company is one whose shares are redeemable at any time at their approximate asset value. In most cases, new shares are offered for sale by the fund continuously at asset value plus a fixed percentage as the selling charge.

The large majority of open-end investment companies appraise the market value of portfolios daily—after the close of the markets in New York—and thus arrive at a figure for net asset value per share on which the published bid and offered prices are based. Net asset value, then, is the worth of a mutual fund share as determined by dividing the total market value of its portfolio by the number of its outstanding shares.

A surcharge of 6 to 9 percent is levied by some mutual funds. When he sells, he usually receives the net asset value of his shares without deduction. But even this cost could wipe out earnings of 3 or 4.5 percent per year for a couple of years, should the investor decide not to retain the investment. If there is doubt as to whether the investment can be retained for at least five years, the investor might well consider whether it might not be more profitable to accept the current per annum return from a savings bank or a savings and loan association than to buy shares in an open-end investment company. It is the surcharge of 6 to 9 percent which encourages brokerage firms to push the sale of some open-end investment company shares.

If a mutual fund has a surcharge—or a "loading charge," as it is usually called in the trade—of, say, 8 percent, this means that if you invest $10,000 in the fund, you get only $9,200 of net asset value, while $800 of your money goes to

FIGURE 14–10

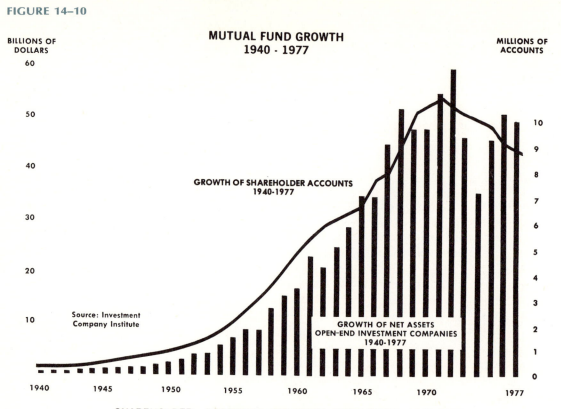

MUTUAL FUND GROWTH
1940 - 1977

BILLIONS OF DOLLARS

MILLIONS OF ACCOUNTS

GROWTH OF SHAREHOLDER ACCOUNTS 1940-1977

Source: Investment Company Institute

GROWTH OF NET ASSETS OPEN-END INVESTMENT COMPANIES 1940-1977

SHAREHOLDER ACCOUNTS AND TOTAL NET ASSETS, 1940-1976
(Assets in 000's of Dollars)

Calendar Year-End	No. of Reporting Funds	No. of Accounts	Assets	Calendar Year-End	No. of Reporting Funds	No. of Accounts	Assets
1940	68	296,056	447,959	1959	155	4,276,077	15,817,962
1941	68	293,251	401,611	1960	161	4,897,600	17,025,684
1942	68	312,609	486,850	1961	170	5,319,201	22,788,812
1943	68	341,435	653,653	1962	169	5,910,455	21,270,735
1944	68	421,675	882,191	1963	165	6,151,935	25,214,436
1945	73	497,875	1,284,185	1964	160	6,301,908	29,116,254
1946	74	580,221	1,311,108	1965	170	6,709,343	35,220,243
1947	80	672,543	1,409,165	1966	182	7,701,656	34,829,353
1948	87	722,118	1,505,762	1967	204	7,904,132	44,701,302
1949	91	842,198	1,973,547	1968	240	9,080,168	52,677,188
1950	98	938,651	2,530,563	1969	269	10,391,534	48,290,733
1951	103	1,110,432	3,129,629	1970	361	10,690,312	47,618,100
1952	110	1,359,000	3,931,407	1971	392	10,900,952	55,045,328
1953	110	1,537,250	4,146,061	1972	410	10,635,287	59,830,646
1954	115	1,703,846	6,109,390	1973	421	10,330,862	46,518,535
1955	125	2,085,325	7,837,524	1974	431	10,174,191	35,776,793
1956	135	2,580,049	9,046,431	1975	423	9,876,551	45,823,404
1957	143	3,110,392	8,714,143	1976	445	9,055,271	50,941,900
1958	151	3,630,096	$13,242,388	1977	469	8,826,939	48,548,100

NOTE: Figures for shareholder accounts represent combined totals for member companies. Duplications have not been eliminated.

Source: *Johnson's Charts,* 1978 edition.

the broker or other financial middleman who solicited and obtained your order. A share in an investment company, some argue, is not an ordinary "security." In addition to representing a pro rata share of ownership in a fund, it is in effect, they contend, a service contract for which you also pay, out of the dividends earned and due you, an annual management fee for this service.

A number of funds—for example, Loomis-Sayles and Scudder, Stevens and Clark, both of Boston; the T. Rowe Price Growth Stock Fund of Baltimore; and Stein, Roe & Farnham—have no loading charges at all.

The actual percentage sales charges of the "load" funds are, in fact, somewhat higher than stated. This is because the sales charge is stated as a percentage of the total purchase price, including the sales charge, or "load," itself. Thus, the mutual fund purchaser who buys $10,000 in mutual funds and pays an 8.5 percentage load or $850 is paying 8.5 percent on $10,000, but the net asset value of the shares he receives is only $9,150. A charge of $850 for $9,150 in mutual fund shares is 9.3 percent, not 8.5 percent. New mutual funds with scaled charges now make such differences explicit.

Types of Open-End Companies

It is the open-end investment companies which have enjoyed the greatest growth in the past. Mutual fund objectives are often so broadly stated as to defy classification. Mutual funds portfolio holdings change over time with changing conditions. The simplest classification of mutual funds is: *(a)* balanced funds, *(b)* growth (including performance) funds, *(c)* growth and income funds, and *(d)* income funds.

Usually the bond-stock fund is called a *balanced fund*. A balanced fund has been described as any fund which at all times holds at least 20 to 25 percent (although never more than 75 to 80 percent) of its assets in cash and good-grade or high-grade bonds for defensive purposes and the remainder in common stocks or other equity-type securities. Balanced funds appear suitable for investors who want to turn over to investment company management fairly complete responsibility for their invested capital.

Diversified bond-stock, or balanced, funds normally invest some portion of their assets in bonds or preferred stocks, or both, in addition to a portion which is invested in common stocks. On the average, the funds in the bond-stock classification follow more conservative investment policies than do the funds which normally limit their holdings to common stocks. They tend to have a lower average return, less capital gain in a rising market, less volatility, better defenses in a falling market, more stability of income, and greater safety of principal than do the stock funds.

The largest group of mutual funds—over 50 percent by net assets—are the *diversified common stock funds*. These invest all, or almost all, of the money they hold in common stock, but they are by no means alike, either in investment objectives or in performance. Some invest primarily in the better-known stocks of large corporations—the standard type of good-quality shares that are frequently described as blue chips. Others specialize in "growth company" shares. Some concentrate on the shares of less well known firms, where greater opportunities for profits are believed to exist. Some *performance* funds provide a means of buying into a diversified list of low-priced or highly volatile shares. Some diversified common stock funds place greater stress on growth with stability, while others emphasize volatile capital appreciation. Generally, diversified common stock funds appeal to investors who concentrate funds in common stock, taking risks to achieve capital gains.

Closed-End Investment Companies

The closed-end investment company is one with a fixed amount of capital, generally all raised when the company is formed. Its securities are traded on an organized securities exchange or in the over-the-counter market in the same way as ordinary corporate securities. Closed-end investment companies issue authorized stock at a given time and wait before they float another issue, if at all. They do not usually redeem the stock for their shareholders. Investors who wish to purchase the issued shares of a closed-end company must purchase those shares from persons who are already stockholders, through brokers on the exchanges (if the stock is listed) or via the over-the-counter market.

Shares of closed-end companies are priced differently from those of open-end companies. The shares of open-end companies are bought and sold on the basis of their net asset value, whereas the prices of closed-end shares are governed entirely by the supply of and the demand for the shares in the open market. The shares of closed-end companies are usually traded at discounts from their asset value, though a few command premiums.

The resale market for the shares of open-end investment companies lies primarily in the companies themselves, for they are pledged to redeem their shares. In good times, when the sale of their new shares to the public is producing more money than is needed to buy in old shares offered for redemption, there is apt to be no problem; but in times when investment company shares are difficult to sell, the only way that open-end investment companies can secure the money with which to redeem their own outstanding shares is by selling investments in their portfolio. Selling at such times may upset dollar averaging and automatic formula timing. In addition, the large-scale selling of good securities by many investment companies can only serve to depress the prices at which those securities can be sold.

The closed-end investment companies do not have this problem, because they do not, and cannot be required to, repurchase their shares. Some closed-end investment companies are listed on the security exchanges, where active trading secures a market for them. Some closed-end companies have a multiple capital structure. Besides common stock, they may have preferred stocks, bonds, or bank loans (or all three) outstanding. In such cases, the common stock possesses a special quality, generally known as "leverage." At one time a number of closed-end investment companies were highly leveraged and therefore speculative. In recent years leverage has declined in importance as closed-end

companies have reduced or eliminated senior capital. Also the interest in closed-end companies has fallen sharply.

Withdrawal Plans

Many mutual funds provide withdrawal plans for those who desire a regular quarterly or monthly income, especially for retirement purposes. A minimum amount, usually $5,000 or $10,000, is customarily required to start a withdrawal plan. As with an annuity, this may be paid in gradually via either regular payments or an accumulation plan, or it may be paid in as a lump sum at a given time, say, when the individual decides to retire. The monthly or quarterly payments made by the mutual fund to the individual may be drawn from capital as well as from investment income and capital gains. It may be more or less per month, per quarter, or per annum than the capital earns via income and capital gains. How fast or slowly you use up your capital depends on the monthly or quarterly payment specified and on the performance of the fund.

The advantage of a withdrawal plan is that in a successful fund you can obtain steady income and preserve or enhance your capital as well or that in retirement you can eat into capital to maximize your drawing. The limitation is that if you select a poorly performing fund, your capital will melt away rapidly and you will outlive your capital. Unlike an annuity, which guarantees you either a fixed or a variable income for life, a mutual fund withdrawal plan will give you income only as long as your capital lasts. If the underlying stocks in the mutual fund decline in value, your capital can eventually be used up.

Thus the risk of outliving your capital makes a mutual fund withdrawal plan more suitable as a supplement to a pension or an annuity rather than as the sole source of retirement income. Such a plan is also useful for paying for a college education or for helping to pay off a mortgage.

The most important ingredient of a successful withdrawal plan is having the "right" mutual fund. The "right" fund, of course, is a fund that will keep your money growing fast enough so that your shares will never be worth any less than when you started. Some mutual fund 6 percent withdrawal plans started a decade ago showed capital appreciation of 50 percent or more despite monthly withdrawals. Others had sharp decreases in assets, in some cases 50 percent or more.

Portfolio Changes

Most mutual funds publish a quarterly list showing their security holdings; and the portfolio and operations of mutual funds are perhaps more open to public scrutiny than those of any other type of financial institution. The securities that a mutual fund holds, as of the most recent quarter, can usually be easily ascertained, either by writing to the fund itself or by consulting such sources as *Vickers Guide to Investment Company Portfolios* as can be seen in Figures 14–12 and 14–13. Observation of changes in portfolios over a period of years will provide interesting insights into changing investment patterns and will tell the smart amateur investor what the investment managers are thinking and doing.

Measuring Performance

There are generally two views of the performance record of investment companies, especially of the mutual funds. The salesperson's view is that mutuals are incomparable. This view is usually buttressed by a formidable chart that shows a ten-year rise in per share asset value. However, the chart is normally unaccompanied by an explanation that rising stock prices over the prior decade caused a swelling book value for many investment portfolios. Nor does the salesperson for a mutual fund provide any indication that a given sum of money, such as $10,000, invested at compound interest over a decade would appreciate significantly solely by reason of the compounding process. You can see in Figure 14–11 that $10,000 invested at 6 percent compound interest for 20 years would amount to about $33,000 by the end of the 20th year just as a result of the compounding.

A second, more sober view was expressed by *Forbes* magazine when it declared: "Some mutuals have achieved results far better than the average small investor could accomplish for himself. Others just equal blind chance. And a third and sizable group show few results but expensive managements."

The customary presentation assumes that $10,000 was invested in a given fund 15 or 20 years ago, or when the fund was started, and then shows what happened to the investment by the end of the selected period. For example, in the case of a leading no-load fund, an assumed investment of $10,000 made when the fund started in April 1950 would, by June 1978, with dividends reinvested and with capital gains accepted in additional shares, have amounted to $177,097.

Another view compares the performance of a given fund with the investment results which would have been produced by placing the same amount of money across the board directly into the stocks comprising the Dow-Jones Industrial Average. In 1949 one of the longest and greatest bull markets in U.S. history began. From December 31, 1949, to January 11, 1973, the Dow-Jones Industrial Average rose from 200 to 1051, a 425 percent increase. Only a minority of the mutual funds equaled or exceeded that performance. Many of the funds, despite their professional management, did not do as well.[11]

This type of comparison—contrasting, for example, the performance of the Standard & Poor's Stock Index and that of any given fund—can be made at a glance by using *Johnson's Charts*. This volume has a chart for each major fund as well as overlays of the Standard & Poor's Stock Index and of the performance of a number of individual stocks, such as General Motors or Exxon or Xerox. By simply placing any of these overlays on the chart of a given fund, you can compare the performance of the two at a glance. It helps materially in the difficult process of deciding which fund to select. The results achieved by individual funds can

[11] See Patricia Dreyfus, "Mutual Funds That Have Beaten Inflation," *Money,* April 1978.

FIGURE 14–11
Quarterly Compounding Table

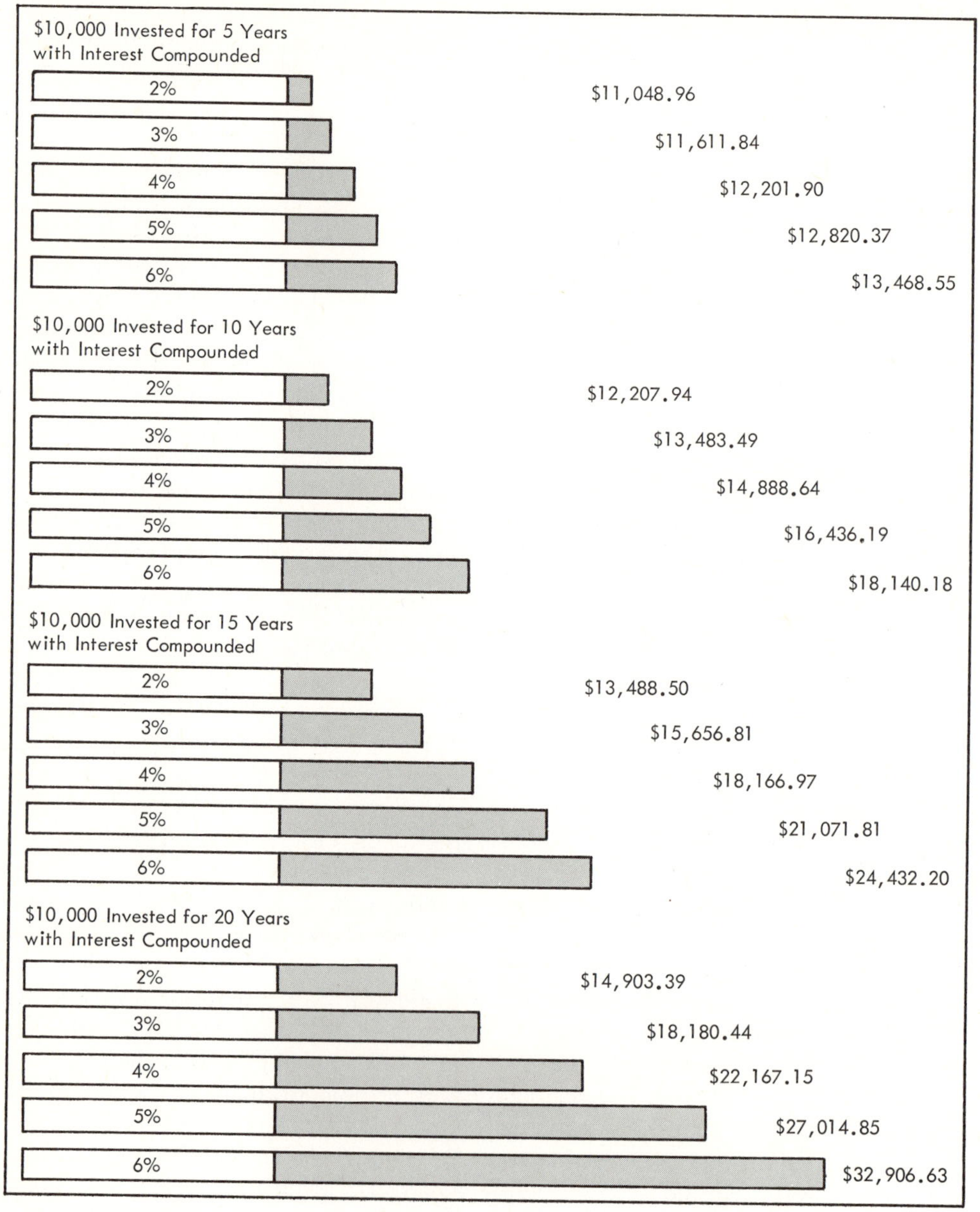

$10,000 Invested for 5 Years
with Interest Compounded

2%	$11,048.96
3%	$11,611.84
4%	$12,201.90
5%	$12,820.37
6%	$13,468.55

$10,000 Invested for 10 Years
with Interest Compounded

2%	$12,207.94
3%	$13,483.49
4%	$14,888.64
5%	$16,436.19
6%	$18,140.18

$10,000 Invested for 15 Years
with Interest Compounded

2%	$13,488.50
3%	$15,656.81
4%	$18,166.97
5%	$21,071.81
6%	$24,432.20

$10,000 Invested for 20 Years
with Interest Compounded

2%	$14,903.39
3%	$18,180.44
4%	$22,167.15
5%	$27,014.85
6%	$32,906.63

be compared to the average results of all balanced funds or the average results of all growth stock funds or of all income funds.

A quarterly list of the stocks most popular with mutual fund managers can be seen in Vickers Favorite 50 (see Figures 14–12 and 14–13).

Invest in Common Stock Directly or Buy Mutual Fund Shares?

Well-managed investment companies may be in a position to handle the selection, timing, and diversification of security purchases and sales more

FIGURE 14–12

VICKERS FAVORITE 50

RANK BY $ VALUE				STOCKS	$ Value (Mil.)	No. Funds Holding	No. of Shares Held	Net Chng. in Holdings	Net Chng. by Insiders	% Outst. Stk. Held by Funds
9/30 1973	9/30 1977	6/30 1978	9/30 1978							
1	1	1	1	International Business Machines	1,658.29	321	5,994,727	+62,477	4.1	-2,398
4	2	2	2	American Telephone & Telegraph	628.23	169	10,091,969	-235,865	1.5	+26
2	3	3	3	Exxon Corporation	578.94	179	11,106,813	-839,339	2.5	+1,414
8	5	4	4	Philip Morris	469.02	132	6,480,373	+210,990	10.5	-900
-	8	5	5	Schlumberger Ltd.	395.2	121	4,373,486	+150,538	5.1	-8,900
6	4	6	6	General Motors Corporation	350.76	115	5,578,720	-314,678	2.0	-7,663
9	6	7	7	Ford Motor Company	328.13	87	7,394,504	+165,685	6.2	- 0 -
14	7	8	8	General Electric Co.	297.16	138	5,580,426	-204,107	2.5	+757
-	34	10	9	Boeing Co.	294.47	67	4,628,200	-317,900	10.8	-3,918
13	12	9	10	Atlantic Richfield Co.	281.57	102	5,178,249	-191,800	5.0	- 0 -
3	9	11	11	Xerox Corp.	278.49	129	5,040,555	+214,841	6.3	+3,093
15	17	12	12	Du Pont (E.I.) De Nemours Co.	275.15	70	2,124,720	+83,263	4.4	-350
10	50	17	13	Polaroid Corp.	269.23	62	5,439,006	-123,000	16.6	- 0 -
-	16	16	14	NCR Corp.	265.42	79	4,378,038	+357,038	16.5	-1,027
-	46	14	15	SmithKline Corp.	241.37	66	2,681,850	+126,835	8.9	-2,816
26	13	13	16	Phillips Petroleum Co.	235.01	81	6,836,703	159,050	4.4	+200
38	19	19	17	Halliburton Co.	219.58	83	3,076,370	+73,200	5.2	+400
18	27	15	18	Avon Products Inc.	215.87	93	3,951,898	+8,320	6.8	-2,440
7	14	20	19	Burroughs Corp.	199.81	86	2,599,145	+56,200	6.4	-3,000
-	41	24	20	Northwest Airlines	187.67	56	6,127,961	-92,111	28.3	-850
33	35	21	21	Travelers Corp.	184.54	72	4,888,433	-120,800	11.3	-176
12	18	18	22	McDonalds Corp.	181.64	82	3,641,980	+20,700	9.0	-12,680
20	21	27	23	Mobil Corp.	179.96	92	2,512,531	169,310	2.4	+2,500
21	37	25	24	Minnesota Mng. & Mfg. Co.	178.21	82	3,039,760	+13,709	2.6	- 0 -
27	10	23	25	Digital Equipment Corp.	171.43	74	3,543,793	-144,440	9.0	-12,127
-	28	28	26	Merck & Co.	170.77	95	2,864,068	-24,930	3.8	-11,039
34	20	26	27	General Tel & Electronics	167.70	90	5,498,503	-229,921	3.9	+250
-	-	-	28	**UAL INC.	167.00	71	4,227,804	+221,600	17.1	-200
-	43	35	29	Amer. Broadcasting Co.	161.88	58	4,360,510	-149,550	16.1	-9,175
-	30	39	30	Union Oil Co. of California	160.89	47	2,860,250	-29,500	6.5	- 0 -
-	-	-	31	**Alcan Aluminum	159.53	93	4,834,114	+510,934	12.0	+188
-	-	-	32	**Eastman Kodak Co.	158.82	127	2,614,373	+505,035	1.6	+190
5	40	-	33	Standard Oil of Calif.	157.36	75	3,348,137	-560,643	2.0	- 0 -
28	15	30	34	Standard Oil Co. (Indiana)	153.95	74	2,870,851	-28,131	2.0	+3,551
-	42	38	35	Pepsico Inc.	153.50	75	5,293,260	-806,324	5.7	-5,150
-	36	29	36	Bristol-Myers Co.	151.56	71	4,507,411	+96,285	6.9	+1,600
-	-	41	37	Martin-Marietta Corp.	151.20	53	4,634,415	-35,585	19.4	-3,000
-	22	32	38	Tenneco Inc.	148.91	68	4,690,221	-131,180	4.9	+254
-	49	37	39	Johnson & Johnson	148.79	73	1,784,559	+71,910	3.0	- 0 -
-	-	33	10	Pfizer Inc.	144.66	78	4,074,904	-274,700	5.8	-14,500
-	-	36	41	General Dynamics Corp.	142.98	34	1,738,300	-201,600	16.3	-201
-	-	49	42	Caterpillar Tractor	141.33	75	2,463,245	+276,930	2.9	-6,134
-	-	-	43	*MCA Inc.	141.24	28	2,690,308	-277,775	11.6	-4,831
-	-	44	44	Abbott Laboratories	139.71	69	4,020,492	-4,300	6.7	+36,433
39	26	34	45	International Tel. & Tel.	136.49	62	4,315,907	-378,497	4.1	-55,709
-	32	-	46	**Standard Oil Co. (Ohio)	134.75	50	3,593,220	+347,800	3.1	-300
11	11	31	47	Texaco Inc.	134.09	79	5,445,178	-873,600	2.0	-10,000
17	31	-	48	**K mart Corp.	133.16	75	4,909,180	405.958	4.0	-2,133
-	-	-	49	*Great Western Financial Corp.	132.12	45	4,385,775	+91,500	29.4	-4,100
-	29	-	50	**Continental Oil Co.	130.12	68	4,506,373	+130,900	4.2	-100

DISPLACED STOCKS:

Aetna Life & Casualty Co. - Federal Natl. Mortgage Assn. - Motorola Inc. - Reynolds (R.J.) Industries - Schering-Plough - Union Carbide Corp. - United Technologies Corp. - Warner-Lambert Co.

*NEWCOMER **RETURNEE

Source: Vickers Associates, Huntington, New York.

FIGURE 14–13

DOW-JONES INDUSTRIAL AVERAGES and VICKERS FAVORITE 50 AVERAGES

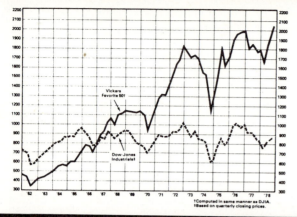

†Computed in same manner as DJIA.
‡Based on quarterly closing prices.

September 30, 1978

The Vickers Favorite 50 Index, which is a composite of the 50 stocks (ranked by dollar value) that were most popular with investment companies during the quarterly period covered, was up to 2050.6 on a 10.4% rise for the period versus a corresponding 5.7% rise for the DJIA.

A comparison of the VFFI and the DJIA for a 5-year period shows that the VFFI fared better than the DJIA in 12 out of 20 quarters and is up 17.3% versus a decrease of 8.6% for the DJIA over the same period.

SUMMARY OF FAVORITE 50 BY INDUSTRY

DOLLAR VALUE OF STOCKS BY INDUSTRY TO TOTAL VALUE OF FAVORITE 50

Industry	9/30/78	6/30/78	9/30/77	9/30/73
Oil & Natural Gas	23.7%	21.3%	27.1%	17.6%
Office Equipment	20.9	20.6	22.1	20.7
Chemicals & Drugs	12.1	15.5	12.8	13.4
Leisure	7.4	4.7	5.0	7.9
Utilities	6.5	6.9	7.8	5.3
Motors	5.5	6.0	6.5	5.8
Aerospace	4.8	5.9	1.3	--
Miscellaneous	19.1	19.1	17.4	29.3
	100.0%	100.0%	100.0%	100.0%

CANDIDATES FOR THE FAVORITE 50

STOCKS	Value ($Mil.)	No.Funds Holding	Number of Shs. Held	STOCKS	Value ($Mil.)	No.Funds Holding	Number of Shs. Held
Dome Petroleum Corp.	129.86	54	1,583,700	Hospital Corp. of America	105.95	47	3,531,771
Gulf Oil Corp.	129.17	64	5,090,280	Celanese Corp.	105.18	34	2,446,140
Kaiser Alum. & Chem.	127.16	34	6,920,464	Coca Cola Co.	105.13	62	2,369,045
Champion Int'l Corp.	126.57	56	5,012,645	RCA Corp.	104.57	62	3,500,413
Reynolds (R.J.) Inds. Inc.	125.51	55	2,036,691	Honeywell Inc.	104.06	59	1,610,154
Schering Plough Co.	123.73	65	3,763,604	International Paper Co.	99.89	57	2,263,840
United Technologies Corp.	123.08	63	2,821,387	Capital Cities Comm.	99.73	28	2,381,700
Fed. Nat'l Mortgage Assn.	123.00	44	6,929,635	American Home Products	98.69	64	3,374,062
Hewlett Packard Co.	120.29	46	1,372,816	Dart Industries	97.10	38	2,271,449
Warner Lambert Co.	120.22	55	4,411,903	Reynolds Metals Co.	96.37	34	2,705,172
Delta Airlines Inc.	120.06	46	2,507,750	Colonial Penn Group Inc.	94.84	38	2,999,015
CBS	119.53	59	2,168,310	Sears Roebuck & Co.	93.75	78	4,166,709
Union Carbide Corp.	119.13	88	3,006,493	Upjohn Co.	93.72	58	1,912,635
Monsanto Co.	117.92	64	2,059,685	Revlon Inc.	93.44	45	1,763,025
Citicorp	117.61	56	4,480,368	Marathon Oil Co.	92.94	39	1,813,372
Warner Comm. Inc.	116.50	37	2,353,508	Squibb Corp.	92.73	34	2,842,368
Raytheon Co.	113.99	59	2,399,790	Sperry Rand Corp.	91.22	46	2,102,949
Aetna Life & Casualty Co.	113.13	58	2,750,880	Times Mirror Co.	90.46	35	2,794,236
Motorola, Inc.	112.94	44	2,545,201	Getty Oil Co.	88.43	22	2,150,152
St. Regis Paper Co.	112.64	32	3,533,732	Deere & Co.	87.68	36	2,478,700
First Charter Fin'l Corp.	111.30	36	6,016,219	Lilly (Eli) & Co.	86.81	57	1,789,851
INA Corp.	109.86	35	2,489,652	Weyerhaeuser Co.	86.64	44	2,949,375
Baxter Travenol Labs.	109.62	65	2,549,384	Norton Simon Inc.	86.59	43	4,610,409
Procter & Gamble Co.	109.34	65	1,265,925	American Express Co.	86.36	60	2,449,835
Georgia Pacific Corp.	107.06	50	3,644,476	Union Pacific Corp.	85.91	43	1,583,563

Source: Vickers Associates, Huntington, New York.

effectively than an individual with moderate resources. Which securities to buy and which to sell are difficult problems that can perhaps be best answered by analysts who have had sufficient training in such areas as accounting, economics, and finance. Not only do investment companies have their own staffs, accustomed to such work, but they can use outside research whenever it is deemed necessary.

Even with the best of facilities at one's command, the wise selection of securities is not easy. Not only is it necessary to choose the right securities to buy or sell, but it is equally important to time the purchases and sales correctly. If you feel unable to do this for yourself, you can pass the problem along to an investment company to do it for you. In this way you may secure the advantages of such techniques as dollar averaging and automatic formula timing.

But even if you turn to an investment company to solve your investment problems, there still remains one major problem which you cannot unload in this fashion. You must make at least one major judgment and decision yourself: you must decide which of the many and diverse investment companies, with their very different objectives and their very unequal performance, you wish to choose. This is a decision that you should not let a salesperson make for you. If you do decide to buy mutual fund shares, don't let yourself be sold; decide for yourself after you have all the facts.

Forbes declared:

> To invest intelligently, therefore, the investor must make a choice. Does he want a "growth" stock for the long pull? A diversified commitment in a single promising industry? A changing approach which gives management full power to switch money around as conditions change? Or a low geared stake in stocks through a balanced fund?

Bear in mind that the no-load funds, some of which have performed well, have no salespeople. The better no-load funds may never come to your attention. You do not need an intermediary to buy no-loads. You can order shares yourself by mail or telephone.

Mutual Funds Adapt to Change

Mutual funds have adapted to changing economic times and conditions. New forms have been developed to meet current needs. For example, when interest rates shot up in 1973 and 1974 and disintermediation took place—that is, investors shifted their money from savings institutions to short-term, high-yield, partially tax-exempt instruments, such as U.S. Treasury bills or short-term municipals—the mutuals developed money market funds. These were designed to buy those high-yield money market instruments which the small investor could not buy. At one time there were almost 50 money market funds in the field.[12] Most of the new money market and tax-exempt municipal bond funds came out as "no-loads," since the mutual fund managers had learned that the public was much more receptive to such arrangements.

Mutual fund organizations have developed families of funds. That is, they will have a growth stock fund, a speculative stock fund, a conservative bond fund, a money market fund, a tax exempt bond fund, and several others.

When stock prices fell and interest rates rose, investors switched out of their stock funds into new tax-exempt bond funds, which offered small investors attractive tax-exempt yields.[13] The move toward fund switching has been growing and appears now to be replacing the "accumulate and hold philosophy."

One method of investing for the amateur is to observe the switches in mutual fund purchases and sales as market conditions change and to follow suit as soon as the action is known. This lets the expert do your investing for you and at no cost to you. By following fund leadership and observing portfolio changes much valuable information can be gained. While past performance does not guarantee future results, the top funds tend to remain at the top for some time as Table 14–2 shows.

---

[12] See John H. Allan, "The Lure of the Money Market Funds," *New York Times*, February 3, 1978.

[13] Phyllis Feinberg, "The Bouncing New Tax Exempt Funds," *Money*, January 1977. See also "Yes, Virginia, Bonds Fluctuate Too," *Forbes*, October 2, 1978, p. 106.

TABLE 14–2
Best Performance Scores 1974–1978

Net Assets 9/29/78 (Mil. $)	Fund	†Principal Objective	1976	1977	1978	‡1974–1978 Performance Score
17.0	V. L. Leveraged Growth	G	+46.9	+51.3	+27.3	312-B
36.2	44 Wall Street	G	+46.5	+16.5	+32.9	308-C
60.8	Sequoia Fund	G	+67.4	+17.3	+21.7	302-A
52.4	Mutual Shares Corp.	GIS	+63.1	+13.2	+16.1	279-B
4.2	Sherman Dean	G	+31.3	+ 2.5	+28.3	259-B
34.7	20th Century Growth	G	+61.1	+13.8	+41.7	256-B
7.8	Sigma Venture	G	+24.4	+39.8	+21.3	252-B
52.2	Pennsylvania Mutual	G	+49.0	+23.4	+14.4	251-B
207.0	Templeton Growth	G	+44.6	+18.0	+17.7	232-A
16.3	Lexington Growth Fund	G	+46.8	+10.9	+29.8	231-A
18.4	Pace Fund	R	+27.8	+28.6	+23.5	230-A
124.0	Pioneer II	IG	+57.4	+20.3	+ 2.5	218-A
4.5	20th Century Income	I	+23.4	+25.0	+32.8	216-B
16.9	Over-The-Counter Secs.	G	+33.6	+18.3	+27.5	215-B
11.8	Amer. General Venture	R	+25.3	+25.6	+22.4	213-B
106.9	V. L. Special Situation	G	+51.5	+11.8	+20.3	210-A
N.A.	Comstock	R	+31.8	+ 7.3	+13.5	209-A
30.0	Magellan Fund	G	+36.0	+12.7	+29.5	204-A
32.2	Safeco Growth Fund	GI	+54.2	+14.2	+14.5	203-B
107.7	Fidelity Destiny	G	+29.4	+ 8.3	+19.0	197-A
50.0	Acorn	G	+62.2	+16.1	+14.3	196-B
17.2	Dreyfus No. Nine	GIS	+37.8	+ 6.3	+19.1	186-B
56.0	Vance Sanders Special	G	+34.0	+18.1	+20.9	183-B
28.4	Amer. Nat'l Growth	G	+33.7	+10.7	+16.1	181-A
45.1	Value Line Fund	G	+39.8	+ 7.7	+17.3	181-A
74.5	AMCAP	G	+28.4	+14.2	+20.0	180-B
N.A.	Hartwell Leverage	G	+34.6	+16.6	+11.3	179-A
10.2	General Securities	GSI	+32.7	− 5.0	+12.6	178-A
102.8	Mathers	G	+41.1	+11.4	+11.4	178-B
N.A.	Cardinal Fund	G	+27.9	+ 0.9	+20.8	177-A
48.5	Nicholas Fund	G	+22.2	+19.3	+23.2	174-B
74.7	Growth Fund of Amer.	G	+17.8	+19.2	+25.6	173-B
17.7	Charter Fund	G	+40.4	+ 3.7	+24.8	171-B
12.5	Tudor Hedge	G	+23.8	+ 6.6	+19.9	171-B
4.9	Hartwell Growth	G	+24.0	+17.0	+18.9	170-B
37.9	Union Capital	G	+26.4	+ 3.9	+14.2	170-B
29.7	Partner's Fund	G	+26.4	+ 4.4	+13.3	167-B
20.0	Security Ultra	R	+54.4	+ 2.3	− 1.4	166-B
48.2	Kemper Summit	G	+30.7	+10.8	+16.2	165-B
574.8	Windsor	GI	+40.3	− 3.3	+ 3.6	165-A
29.8	Dreyfus Third Century	GIS	+21.5	+11.2	+ 8.9	162-B
14.6	Pilgrim Fund	G	+26.8	+10.9	+18.4	162-B
94.9	Philadelphia	G	+28.9	+ 1.4	+21.5	160-B
76.7	Oppenheimer Time	G	+32.4	+14.9	+17.2	157-B
13.5	Plitrend	G	+32.2	+14.3	+19.7	157-B
22.6	Sigma Capital Shares	G	+32.0	+ 4.2	+ 5.5	155-B
55.3	Putnam Voyager	G	+28.0	+ 4.3	+12.7	154-A
18.0	Weingarten Equity	G	+14.8	+18.7	+26.0	153-C
564.9	Pioneer Fund	IG	+31.8	− 0.1	+ 7.6	150-A
43.1	Putnam Equities	G	+23.3	− 1.3	+20.7	150-A
72.9	Fidelity Equity Inc.	IG	+38.2	− 0.6	+ 4.8	148-A
12.8	Naess & Thomas Special	G	+14.9	+ 8.7	+ 5.5	148-C
9.7	Paramount Mutual	G	+32.1	− 1.0	+ 8.5	147-A
117.9	State Farm Growth	G	+34.6	+ 1.3	+ 5.8	144-A
2.8	Investment Guidance	G	+28.4	+ 4.9	+ 4.0	143-B
123.4	Kemper Growth	G	+26.6	+ 0.5	+15.1	143-B
17.7	St. Paul Growth	G	+27.5	+ 1.2	+25.7	143-B
24.9	Columbia Growth	G	+29.0	− 1.7	+ 5.7	140-A
26.3	Farm Bureau Growth	G	+24.8	− 0.5	+ 2.3	140-A
23.7	Afuture Fund	G	+19.0	+ 3.2	+19.3	139-C
99.8	Guardian Mutual	G	+29.8	− 4.9	+ 4.2	139-A
50.3	Salem Fund	G	+34.1	0.0	+ 2.7	139-A
32.9	Safeco Equity	GI	+30.3	+ 1.7	+ 6.5	138-B
380.0	Technology	GI	+22.3	− 4.5	+18.5	138-B
4.6	Constellation Growth	G	+20.6	− 5.2	+21.2	137-A
N.A.	Explorer	G	+16.3	+27.8	+18.7	137-D
194.2	New Perspective	G	+13.5	− 0.5	+15.6	137-B
1.8	Rainbow Fund	G	+28.7	+19.9	0.0	137-D
1.9	Planned Investment	GIS	+25.8	+ 1.9	− 1.0	136-C
47.7	Contrafund	G	+32.6	−12.5	+ 1.7	135-B
19.5	Mass. Cap. Develop.	G	+20.0	+13.0	+17.2	134-C
171.4	Financial Indus. Income	IG	+33.5	− 1.6	− 4.3	133-C
N.A.	Morgan (W.L.) Growth	G	+17.4	+ 5.2	+15.7	133-C
355.7	Amer. Mutual	IGS	+27.6	− 3.1	+ 6.8	132-B
3.5	Eagle Growth	G	+37.1	+ 7.2	−11.4	132-B
14.6	Schuster	G	+29.1	+13.6	+16.2	132-C
67.0	Value Line Income	G	+26.9	− 3.6	+ 5.1	132-A
40.9	New York Venture	G	+18.5	+ 2.3	+16.7	131-C
107.4	Security Equity	G	+31.2	− 2.5	+ 9.3	131-B
16.9	Amer. Growth	G	+25.5	+ 8.7	+ 4.1	130-B
1,399.9	Investment Co. Amer.	GI	+25.3	− 5.9	+10.7	130-B
45.9	Kemper Total Return	I	+27.8	− 1.0	+ 4.6	130-B
185.2	Energy	G	+27.7	− 0.9	+ 1.9	129-B
38.5	Edie Spec. Growth	G	+ 5.6	+ 7.8	+22.5	128-C
157.2	Penn Square Mutual	G	+28.7	− 9.8	− 1.1	128-B
59.1	Putnam Vista	G	+22.1	− 3.2	+16.0	128-B
3.0	Capamerica	G	+21.1	+ 2.8	− 0.7	127-C
1,533.9	Dreyfus Fund	GIS	+23.4	− 3.5	+ 7.2	127-B
287.8	Income Fund Amer.	I	+27.6	− 6.2	− 2.3	127-C
470.3	Key. Cust.: Spec. Com.	G	+31.1	+ 7.2	+18.2	127-B
244.6	National Secur.: Stock	IGS	+27.9	− 7.7	+ 0.3	127-B
102.4	Scudder Special	G	+22.0	+ 5.8	+18.8	127-C
343.3	Washington Mutual Inv.	IG	+25.1	− 8.4	+ 2.5	126-A
28.7	Fairfield	G	+31.0	−10.6	+ 7.6	125-A
26.1	Omega	G	+46.3	− 2.4	+ 4.5	125-B
48.7	Amer. Birthright Trust	GIS	+20.9	− 1.8	+ 0.5	124-C
4.4	Sierra Growth	G	+25.9	+ 1.6	+ 8.9	124-B
N.A.	Beacon Hill Mutual	G	+10.1	+ 0.1	+ 7.6	123-B
5.6	Centennial Cap. Spl.	R	+25.6	+ 5.0	+ 5.9	123-B
252.0	Decatur Income	I	+30.0	− 4.4	− 3.8	123-C
97.7	Key. Cust.: Grth. Com. S-3	G	+20.8	− 0.3	+ 6.1	123-B
59.8	Life Insur. Investors	G	+39.1	+11.0	+10.9	123-C
93.4	National Secs.: Dividend	IGS	+31.6	− 2.2	− 1.5	123-C
64.4	National Secs.: Income	ISG	+28.2	− 1.1	− 1.1	123-C
21.6	Sigma Trust Shares	G	+23.4	− 0.5	− 1.0	123-C
474.9	Price (T. Rowe): N. Hor.	G	+ 9.9	+11.6	+19.3	122-C
1,516.6	Affiliated	GIS	+28.8	−11.0	− 1.8	121-B
47.1	Financial Dynamics	G	+29.2	+ 5.9	+ 3.2	121-B
2.2	Herold	G	+16.2	− 1.9	+ 6.1	121-B
18.6	Bondstock	GI	+20.0	− 5.6	+11.4	120-B
31.3	Capital Shares	G	+41.3	+ 5.1	+ 1.4	120-C
290.0	Delaware Fund	GI	+28.8	− 7.5	− 2.7	120-C
286.3	Dreyfus Leverage	GIS	+21.8	+ 4.9	+ 6.7	120-B
259.6	Financial Indus. Fund	GI	+25.3	− 0.7	+ 1.7	120-B
24.0	National Industries Fund	G	+26.4	− 3.9	+ 5.5	120-B
2.5	Nat. Securities: Balanced	SIG	+27.3	− 5.6	− 2.8	120-B
14.3	Sentry Fund	G	+13.8	+ 0.4	+11.6	120-C
3.3	Smith Barney Inc. & Gr.	I	+31.3	− 3.5	− 3.4	120-C
44.4	Vance Sanders Cm. Stk.	G	+18.2	+ 0.5	+20.4	120-C
S&P 500 Composite			**+19.1**	**−11.5**	**+ 1.1**	**99**

†Principal objective: G-Growth; I-Income; R-Return on capital; S-Stability, in order of importance. *Percent change derived by taking net asset value (NAV) at end of period, less NAV at the beginning of the period, divided by NAV at the beginning of the period.

‡Performance Score computed by compounding annual performance data with Jan. 1, 1974, as 100. Letter after Score indicates number of periods in 1974–1978 in which fund outperformed S&P 500 Index (A—5 out of 5 periods; B—4 out of 5 periods; C—3 out of 5 periods; D—2 out of 5 periods).

Source: *The Outlook*, Standard and Poor's, January 15, 1979, p. 975. © Copyright 1979.

Conclusion

If you are financially successful you will have an investment problem with you all your life. You can leave it to others, or you can take time out to "do it yourself." The probability is that you will compromise; a busy career won't allow the time for real investment results. The more successful you are, the more you will have to depend on others. But you'll want to know and understand what is suggested for you and to reserve the right of approval or disapproval. It's more fun to "do-it-yourself," but if you don't have the time, then you must depend on others, and in selecting them you face the same problems as you did in selecting a mutual fund. Ultimately you have to know enough to depend on your own judgment.

SUGGESTED READINGS

Ambachtsheer, Keith P. "Investment Scenarios for the 1980s," *Financial Analysts Journal,* November–December 1977.

Blume, Marshall E., and Friend, Irwin. *The Changing Role of the Individual Investor. A Twentieth Century Fund Report.* New York: Wiley-Interscience, 1978.

Business Week. "How the New Tax Law Changes Your Investment Planning," A Personal Business Supplement, November 13, 1978.

Forbes. "The Nifty Fifty, the Shifty Fifty," December 15, 1977.

———. "How the Investment Game Is Changing," June 12, 1978.

Helms, Gary B. "Toward Bridging the Gap," *Financial Analysts Journal,* January–February 1978.

Miller, Edward M. "Portfolio Selection in a Fluctuating Economy," *Financial Analysts Journal,* May–June 1978.

Money. "Amateur Investors Who Outperformed the Pros," February 1977.

———. "Mutual Funds That Beat Inflation," April 1978.

———. "Taking Stock of the Investment Advisory Services," January 1978.

The Outlook. "Women's Guide to Investment."

New York: Standard & Poor's, March 27, 1978.

CASE PROBLEMS
(for Chapters 12, 13, and 14)

1 Richard Naylor is 30, married, and earns $18,000 a year. His wife has inherited $75,000, and they are debating how to invest it. He favors real estate. She prefers blue-chip common stocks for their safety and marketability. He argues that returns over time are higher in real estate and that it is a better hedge against inflation. How would you invest the $75,000? do you agree with either of them, or do you have a completely different view point?

2 Steve Rome believes in improving the environment. He has $10,000 to invest and would like to put his money into companies that would be supportive of his beliefs. How does he obtain the necessary information?

3 Jim Jefferson, age 23, is advised by his father to buy a few shares in the stock market in order to learn about investments. He recently graduated from college and is earning $9,000 per year. In school he majored in liberal arts and had no investment training. His savings are such that he feels that he can invest $1,000 initially in stock. How would you suggest he should proceed?

4 Max Kugelfuss is a young bachelor, a teacher with a Ph.D., and a man earning a moderately good income. Since he has no outstanding financial obligations, he decides to invest some of his savings. He hears about some oil stock in a Canadian company which is for sale at 50 cents a share. Before he decides to buy 1,000 shares, what facts do you think he should consider? How can he find out more facts about the company?

5 Elinore Bush has been a college professor for ten years. Her retirement fund is with the Teachers Insurance and Annuity Association in New York and has been invested (along with the funds of other teachers) in bonds. The association has also set up an organization (CREF) which invests its funds in common stock. She is asked whether she wants part of her retirement contributions invested by that organization or whether she prefers to have her entire retirement fund invested in bonds as heretofore. What are your thoughts on the subject?

6   Robert and Alice Quint have one son (age eight), for whose education they are building a college fund. Whenever they can afford it, they buy a share of the common stock of the American Telephone and Telegraph Company and add it to the fund. What do you think of their plan? Should the stock be in their son's name?

The John Dohertys, who live next door to the Quints, have a daughter (age six) whom they want to be able to send to college. They make regular monthly payments to a savings and loan association with an eye to building a fund of $20,000 for their daughter's education. Do you like this plan more than that of the Quints? Why? Why not?

7   Bert (35), an alumnus of a graduate school of business, has a secure job with a manufacturing firm. He is married and has two children (ages five and three). His home and automobile are paid for. Ten years ago Bert inherited a dryland wheat farm, which for years, because of drought and poor crops, barely produced a sufficient income to cover taxes and cost of operation. Three years ago oil was discovered on his farm, and it is now yielding an annual net income of $25,000. Bert wants to invest this extra income in securities. What would you advise him to do?

8   Jane and Ted Lyons have been married six years. They live in a rented, furnished apartment and carry no insurance. They have saved about $3,000. Both work and are covered by social security and pension plans. Jane wants to invest their savings in shares of the stock of IBM. What do you think about this idea?

9   You are young and have a good job and no dependents. You saved $5,000 and want your money "to make money." Should you think of a gambling stock, a current fad, or a substantial growth stock such as Kodak, or a new small company such as New England Nuclear?

15

Your Estate and How You Will It

*If your riches are yours, why don't you take
them with you to the other world?*
BENJAMIN FRANKLIN

Residing in a small village was a lawyer who was famous throughout the state for drawing up wills. When a wealthy man died, there was much speculation as to the value of his estate, and the town gossip set about to find out. He went to see the lawyer, and after a few preliminary remarks about the deceased he said rather bluntly:

"I understand you made his will. Would you mind telling me how much he left?"

"Not at all," answered the attorney, resuming his writing. "He left everything he had."

ESTATE PLANNING

Estate planning has been called "an old trade with a new name." At one time it appeared to involve merely will making, but today it is recognized that making a will is just one part of a more elaborate process that should take place for most of a person's adult lifetime.

Talk of estates and estate planning is regarded as irrelevant by the young, since they lack both age and assets. Such thinking is not valid, however; age is not the only cause of death, and you may have more assets than you think.

If you work for a company that provides group insurance based on three times your annual salary, your financial estate could begin with $45,000 (assuming that your salary is $15,000). Other items, even without counting all of your personal possessions, might bring the total up to $63,000:

Insurance on job	$45,000
Personal insurance	10,000
Car	3,000
Bank savings	5,000
Total	$63,000

Surely you would want to plan where that $63,000 should go?

Estate planning is the process of arranging your affairs to produce the most effective disposition of your capital and income. It is an attempt to work out an arrangement which passes along your assets to those whom you wish to have them, and to do so with the least possible cost in taxes and administration. The tools of estate planning include:

1. *Passing property by will.* Personal property that is passed is called a "bequest"; real property that is passed is called a "devise."
2. *Giving outright gifts during the owner's lifetime.* Too often this aspect of estate planning is ignored. Gifts may include cash, securities, real estate, life insurance, and annuities.
3. *Creating gifts in trust during the owner's lifetime.* This is a particularly useful device for endowing minor children.
4. *Creating trusts at death.* Just as you can create trusts during your lifetime, you can also create them by will at death.
5. *Annuities.* The annual payments are determined by the amount of money and the number of years involved.
6. *Life insurance.* Contrary to popular belief, life insurance proceeds, except under certain circumstances, are part of one's taxable estate.
7. *Social security benefits.* These provide goodly sums to the surviving parent with dependent children and again at age 60.
8. *Pensions at retirement.* These include the Keogh plan for the self-employed through U.S. government securities, savings accounts, mutual funds, or life insurance.

Social security, annuities, insurance, Keogh, and IRA have been discussed separately. You can now see how they each fit into an integrated scheme for retirement. You saw that each had to be started at an early age—to be planned for either casually or carefully—so that you would have an estate when it was needed. Having life insurance or a home makes your estate substantial even though you are now struggling to make payments on the policy or pay off the mortgage. A **now** advantage of estate planning is the security that this will give you about the future during your working years.

You can either use these resources wisely, or you can do nothing. Not making an estate plan is making an estate plan, in a way, but it may be an estate plan that you do not really want to make. If you do nothing, the state takes over.

What Happens if You Do Not Leave a Will

If you die and leave no will, you are said to have died "intestate."[1] In effect, the state in which you are domiciled makes your will for you, and your property passes in accordance with the fixed provisions of the law of that state. For example, the inheritance struggle over Howard Hughes' multi-million dollar estate was complicated by the jurisdictional tangle between Texas and California, because that state which could claim him could also claim a fortune in taxes. Although born in Houston, Texas, he left when he was 21, never to live there again. But he paid taxes as a Texan for 30 years, and registered for the draft in World War II as a Texan. During the decades he lived in Los Angeles he paid California taxes under protest, noting he was a Texan. To complicate matters further he lived outside the U.S. in the last eight years of his life.

---

[1] If your spouse dies and leaves a mass of papers, perhaps entitling you to funds—workmen's compensation, union benefits, stocks and bonds, profit-sharing funds, veterans' insurance, annuities, insurance payments—you can turn to SOS—Special Organizational Services—for assistance. This program is available at more than 1,000 banks in 32 states. Write Special Organizational Services, P.O. Box SOS, Athens, TX 75751.

Seven out of ten people in the United States die without leaving wills. Single persons are the most numerous among those who fail to leave wills. According to a recent American Bar Association study, only 1 percent of adults under 25 make wills.

But, you may say, no one would be interested in a small estate, and why does a person with very little to leave have to make a will? Assume that you are married, have one small child, and leave $18,000—but no will. Under the laws of many states, your wife will receive only one third of your estate. The child will inherit two thirds, but since it is a minor, a guardian will have to be appointed by the probate (or surrogate's) court. It may very well be that your wife will be that guardian; yet she will be anything but a free agent in the handling of your child's money. She will have to provide a bond; she will be under the constant supervision of the court; she will have to file annual accountings. All told, guardianship is an expensive and cumbersome procedure.

Your failure to leave a will would have the following undesirable consequences:

1. Your family would find itself unnecessarily involved in certain court procedures of which it will probably have little or no knowledge.
2. Your knowledge of the property that you own and your advice as to its disposition would not be passed on. These would die with you.
3. You would lose the privilege of naming your executor—and this might be a very costly loss indeed.
4. You would lose the privilege, afforded by the laws of most states, of naming a guardian for your minor children. Such a guardian is vital, particularly if your spouse should not survive you.
5. In some instances, if you leave no immediate family, it might result in the passage of your property to persons in whom you have no particular interest, or even in the property's reversion to the state.
6. The procedures involved in intestacy are likely to result in a greater shrinkage of your estate than would otherwise be the case.

7. You would lose the opportunity of minimizing estate and inheritance taxes, as can often be done by means of a carefully planned will.

How Property Passes if There Is No Will

Although the states have varying statutes of descent and distribution which govern the disposition of one's estate if there is no will, it is possible to give a general impression of what is usually found in those statutes, as follows:

1. On the death of an unmarried person (or widow or widower).
   a. In the absence of children or their descendants, one half of the property goes to each parent or the entire property goes to the surviving parent.
   b. In the absence of children or their descendants and of parents, the property goes equally to brothers and sisters. The children of a deceased brother or sister divide their parent's share equally.
   c. In the absence of children or their descendants, of parents, and of brothers and sisters or their descendants, the property is divided among the next of kin.
   d. In the absence of all relatives, the property escheats to the state of the deceased person's domicile.
2. On the death of a married person.
   a. In the absence of children or their descendants, a stipulated amount (perhaps $5,000 or $10,000) and half of the remaining balance go to the surviving spouse, with the remainder going to the parents of the deceased; in the absence of parents, the surviving spouse is apt to take the entire estate.
   b. In the presence of children or their descendants, either one third or one half goes to the surviving spouse, and the balance is divided equally among the children, the descendants of a deceased child dividing their parent's share equally. The amount herein stipulated for the surviving spouse is in addition to the life interest in real estate granted by the homestead statutes.

The surviving spouse may be given the option of taking an amount mentioned in a will or provided by rights of dower and curtesy, if that amount is larger than the amount that would be secured under the statutes of descent and distribution. Dower is the wife's right to one third of the income for life from her husband's real estate after his death; curtesy is a like right giving a husband one third of the income for life from his wife's real estate after her death. In some states these rights no longer exist; in other states they have been written into law in the form of a wife's (or a husband's) right to elect to take the intestate share against the will rather than accept the share provided in the will.

3. On the death of a widow or a widower with children or their descendants, the children take the property equally, the descendants of deceased children dividing their parents' share equally.

In the absence of a will, the state, whose laws of intestacy are inflexible and cannot be adapted to your dependents' needs, will distribute your property in a manner which you might not think desirable.

Assume that your father is age 65 and your mother 59 and that you have a 30-year-old brother who is earning a good income but likes a good time and spends money easily. You like to be independent, and you have accumulated a number of college debts which you are gradually paying off. Your father dies without leaving a will. Your mother, who has no other means of support and who has not worked since you were a child, gets only one third of the $60,000 estate. Your brother, who does not need the money and will probably squander it, shares the remaining two thirds with you.

Another example might interest you. Tom and Ethel Parker have no children and have made no wills. They are young teachers who have been saving every dollar to buy a home. They are killed in a car crash. Ethel dies immediately, Tom one day later. Tom's father is quite wealthy. Ethel's mother has few resources. Yet on Tom's death, since there was no will, Ethel's mother receives nothing, Tom's father everything.

The Young Family and "Guardianship"

You are young and carefree, and nothing could be further from your mind than death, wills, and estates. Who cares—why bother? But consider one young and carefree family.

Jim and Mary Fantini had been married for three years. They had a son, aged one. On a family summer vacation, Jim drowned in a sudden storm. He had no will. With the house that Jim and Mary owned jointly, the estate amounted to about $70,000. They lived in a state whose law said that if a husband died without leaving a will, one third of his estate must go to the widow, two thirds to the child.

When Mary recovered, she was shocked to learn that she could not administer her child's money or even act as her child's guardian without the consent of the court. She had to apply to the court to administer the estate and to post a bond, the premium cost of which was $210. Then she had to apply for the legal guardianship of her son and to post another bond, at an additional cost of $380. She had to secure court approval to sell the house. As a result there were additional fees, including payments to lawyers, totaling $750. The first year after her husband's death, then, her expenses because of his failure to leave a will came to almost $1,400.

That isn't the end, however, for Mary's lengthy legal involvement with the court will continue until the boy reaches 18. Each year she will have to post bonds, and the fees will be about $500 per year. Altogether, Mary and her son will have to spend about $10,000 of a modest estate because Jim did not draw up a will. That amount could have financed the boy's college education. And it was all so unnecessary. A simple will drawn by Jim, leaving everything to Mary and naming her as the executor to serve without bond, would have avoided most of Mary's involvement with the court and eliminated almost all of the cost. A will drawn by Mary leaving everything to Jim under the same circumstances would have been useful had fate decreed the reverse and had Mary died before Jim.

YOUR "LAST WILL AND TESTAMENT"

The expression "last will and testament" is historical. It comes from the time when a distinction was drawn between a *testament* (a term derived from the Latin), which disposed of personal property, and a *will* (a term derived from the Anglo-Saxon), which disposed of real property. The word *will* is the current equivalent of both terms, although the heading of a will customarily employs the longer form. Some states distinguish between the descent of real property and the descent of personal property. You need not list all your assets item by item in a will. Even though you have left a particular property to an heir in your will, you can sell it at any time. You can change your will as often as you like, if you don't mind paying a lawyer's fee each time you do so.

The Disposition of Property by Will

Usually a person may dispose of his property by will as he wishes. One possible exception to this rule is that if one spouse leaves the other spouse less in the will than that spouse would have received under the statutes of descent and distribution or under the laws of dower and curtesy, the surviving spouse may elect to take the larger amount granted by the statutes or laws. One spouse may not usually, in most states, disinherit the other, though it is possible to disinherit children. Another exception to the unrestricted disposition of property by will is provided by the homestead laws, which are found in nearly every state. The purpose of such laws is to see that a wife has a roof over her head in spite of her husband's possible desire to deprive her of it.

Certain provisions or bequests in wills may be invalidated because they are against "public policy." For example, a man who had lived in a certain house during his entire adult life provided that it be boarded up for 20 years after his death and then be given free of charge for two years to any deserving young married couple. The probate court held that, though it appreciated the man's sentimental purpose, the closing of a needed dwelling for 20 years was against public policy. Also, a condition in a will to the effect that a person who has never married shall receive a bequest only if he or she remains unmarried for life is usually regarded as against public policy, since it is thought that marriage and the founding of families are in the best interests of society. Although you are not permitted to prevent a person who has never married from getting married, you are usually permitted to restrict a person from remarrying a second or a third time on pain of losing the legacy set forth in your will.

Certain property passes automatically on death and is not subject to disposition by will. This may be because of the nature of the property or because of the technical legal title by which the property is held; because the testator is married; or because of a combination of reasons. For example, if property is held by two persons as joint tenants with right of survivorship, or by husband and wife as tenants by the entirety, and one of them dies, the survivor becomes the sole owner of the property, regardless of the will of the decedent. This does not mean that such property automatically escapes the federal estate tax.

The Validity of Wills

It is the generally accepted rule that the validity of a will which bequeaths personal property depends upon the law of the state or country in which the deceased had his domicile (home), whereas the validity of a will which devises real estate depends on the law of the state or country in which the real estate is located (its "situs"). Most states have loosened the principles of local sovereignty in order to give validity to wills made in other states or in another country. Many states have adopted the Uniform Wills Act or similar statutes. The power to dispose of property by will is neither a natural nor a constitutional right. It depends wholly upon statute; that is, it may be given, revoked, or circumscribed by legislative action.

"Domicile" is a very important concept in wills, especially from a tax standpoint. A person may have a number of residences, but there is usually only one domicile. The location of the domicile is based on intent, and it is judged by such things as where the person voted and paid taxes. In the famous *Dorrance* case, both New Jersey and Pennsylvania claimed that John T. Dorrance (the sole stockholder of the Campbell Soup Company) had been domiciled in their respective states. The U.S. Supreme Court refused to take jurisdiction, and both states assessed and collected death taxes on Dorrance's estate—New Jersey, $12 million; Pennsylvania, $14 million.

Formalities in Wills

There are several steps in the ritual that is required to make a valid will. Although these steps may seem excessively precise to you, remember that the law insists on them in order to prevent fraud, as safeguards for the protection of all concerned. A will must be in writing, and the more important aspects of the ritual with which the maker must comply are outlined in the following paragraphs.

The Signature of the Testator A valid will must be signed by the maker. Although the signature may be made satisfactorily by pen, pencil, or typewriter, it is only common sense to write it in ink, by hand. The signature should be placed right after the last sentence of the will itself. The will must be signed at the end to prevent fraud—to eliminate the possibility that someone might add a typed paragraph either before or after the signature and thus change the terms and intent of the will. A surprisingly large number of cases are brought to court to determine whether the signature was at the end of a will, particularly where a rather confusing printed form was used by a testator (the maker of a will) who tried to write his own will. Where the signature of the decedent was not at the end, the will was denied "probate." That is, it was held not to be a valid will, and the testator's property was divided up when he died, as if he had died intestate. It is a further legal requirement that the signature be written in the presence of the subscribing witnesses. Confusion is avoided if the testator's signature agrees in all respects with his name as given elsewhere in the will. To avoid question as to other pages of the will, the testator's signature, or at least his initials, should be written on each of the other pages, customarily in the margin. This is also done to prevent fraud—to prevent the substitution of a new typed page for one of the original pages.

Witnesses State statutes generally require at least two or three witnesses to a will. The witnesses, like the testator, should be of full age and of sound mind. It is also a good idea to use witnesses who are healthy and younger than the testator. Usually a will is not needed for some years after it is made. In case of later dispute, it is helpful if the witnesses are still living and still mentally competent, so that they can give any necessary testimony. Neither a beneficiary under a will nor the spouse of a beneficiary should sign as a witness, since the beneficiary may lose any bequest provided for in the will if this is done.

Witnesses should see the testator write his signa-

"As a firm believer in reincarnation, I'm leaving everything to me."

Reprinted by permission *The Wall Street Journal*

ture or be told by the testator that the signature on the will is his. They should see one another sign, and the will itself should state that all of the witnesses signed in one another's presence. Adding the addresses of witnesses may help later in locating them. Although the witnesses need not read the will, and the testator may not want them to read it, the testator should tell the witnesses that he wants them to witness his signature to his last will and testament.

The Absence of Alterations Alterations should not be made in a will after it has been signed and witnessed. Any alterations made prior to the signing of a will should be incorporated in a fair copy, free of erasures or any other changes which might later be the cause of misunderstanding. Once a will has been completed, changes can be effected through a codicil, or addition, executed with all the formalities of the will itself.

A few examples of errors will serve to show the importance of the ritual. An intelligent, literate woman bought a will form at a stationery store, on which she wrote her wishes for the disposal of her property. There was not enough room for her to write all she wanted to above the dotted lines for the signatures of the will maker and the witnesses, so she continued to write below those lines. She and the witnesses signed on the dotted lines. Everything seemed to be in order. There was no question but that she was of sound mind when she wrote and signed her will; no doubt as to how she wished to dispose of her property; no dispute over the fact that the witnesses had seen her sign, that they knew she had meant the document to be her will, and that they had signed as witnesses. Nor was there anything necessarily wrong with a will made out on a printed form. But she hadn't signed the will at the end; and in the state where she lived, the law required that a will be signed at the end. The court would not permit the document to be given effect as her will. It could not consider the writing above the signature as a will and ignore what followed inasmuch as she had written the entire will as a single, consecutive expression of her wishes.

Mr. Thomas asked two friends if they would come over to the home of his sister, Mrs. Conway, to witness the signing of her will. Two or three days later he drove them to her house. They waited in the living room while Mr. Thomas went into the dining room. In a few minutes the two witnesses were called into the dining room; then Mrs. Conway was wheeled in. Mr. Thomas told her to "sign this paper here," and she did. Then the witnesses signed. Later, after Mrs. Conway's death, the paper was offered for probate; but the court would not accept it as her will. The witnesses testified that, at the time of signing, Mrs. Conway had not shown, either by word or deed, that she knew the paper was her will. Neither she nor anyone else in her presence had asked the witnesses to sign as witnesses to her will.

Thus a will is not valid unless the maker of the will, in the presence of the witnesses and at the time they sign, "declares" or gives a definite indication that it is his will. The example given illustrates the reason for this requirement: Mrs. Conway was age 85 and infirm at the time she signed. The requirement—like the other requirements for a valid will—is intended to protect anyone from being imposed upon in making what may be a last, and hence irrevocable, will.

From 1919 to 1962 the well-known commentator Drew Pearson wrote seven wills by hand on hotel stationery, telegraph paper, and university letterhead, but only one of those wills was witnessed. It was that will—written in 1938 in Council Bluffs, Iowa—which the District of Columbia Register of Wills accepted as valid. Drew Pearson's family and friends were convinced that the 1962 will represented what he really wanted, but it was the 1938 will that was probated.

The Terminology of Wills

Occasionally a student will complain, "I do not understand why such unintelligible terms as *intestate, testamentary, corpus, issue, per stirpes, power of appointment,* and the like, have to be used in talking—or writing—about wills and trusts. Why don't you use language that is easily understood?"

There is a good reason why lawyers use legal terms in legal situations, such as wills and trusts represent. Over the years, through definition by statute and interpretation by the courts, those terms have acquired precise meanings—meanings that might take pages of words to explain fully. Technical terms are a means of exact and comprehensive expression; and when properly used in wills and trust agreements, they protect the people whose interests are served by such documents, and can also be an economy in the avoiding of litigation. You should, therefore, understand at least a few of the terms that are used in wills.

Administrator. The person (or persons) appointed by the court to administer the estate of someone who died intestate.

Administration expenses. The costs of settling an estate—court costs; the fees of executors, attorneys, and appraisers; and other expenses.

Beneficiary. A person who is named in a will as a recipient of property under it.

Bequeath. In connection with wills, this word means the giving of a bequest of personal property (as contrasted with real property), the recipient being a *legatee.*

Codicil. An addition to a will or a change executed in a will with the same formalities as those required for the will itself.

Decedent. The deceased person.

Devise. The gift of real property (not personal property) to a person known as the "devisee."

Estate. Your estate is all you own—real estate, cash, stocks, bonds, and other property. You can pass these on by will, subject to the deduction of debts, estate and inheritance taxes, and administration expenses.

Exculpatory clause. "None of my Executors or Trustees shall be liable for any act or omission in connection with the administration of my estate or any of the trusts or powers hereunder nor for any loss or injury to any property held in or under my estate or any of said trusts or powers, except only for his or her actual fraud; and none of my Executors or Trustees shall be responsible for any act or omission of any other Executor or Trustee."

Executor. The person appointed in a will to administer an estate according to the provisions of the will.

Holographic will. A will written entirely in the handwriting of the person who made it.

Intestate. Refers to a person who dies without leaving a valid will.

Legatee. A person who receives personal property under a will (as contrasted with a "devisee," who receives real property).

Letters testamentary. The court's certificate of the probate of a will and the executor's authority to act under it.

Personal property. All property which is not real estate.

Probate. The name of a court having jurisdiction over wills and the name of the procedure for proving the validity of wills. "Probating a will" refers to the process by which proof of the legality of your last will and testament is presented to a probate court after your death, whereupon the probate court grants authority to the executor to carry out your intentions as expressed in the will.

Real estate. Land and the buildings thereon.

Surrogate. A term used in New York which has the same meaning as "probate judge."

Testator. A person who makes and leaves a will.

Trust. A trust puts your money or other property into the hands of a trustee (either a financial institution or an individual, or both) for the management and disposition of the income and principal as you direct in your will or trust agreement. There are "living trusts," "insurance trusts," and "testamentary trusts," to be described later. A person who receives the income from a trust during his or her lifetime is known as a "life tenant" or a "life beneficiary," while a person who receives the principal of the trust after the death of the life tenant is a "remainderman."

What Is in a Will?

There are five principal sections to a will.

The opening section tells who you are and where you live, says that you are of sound mind and competent to make a will, revokes all previous wills, and directs that all just debts and funeral expenses be paid.

The dispositive clauses are the heart of a will. They indicate who is to get what. There are four types of legacies: specific, general, demonstrative, and residuary. There are also lapsed and preferred legacies. A *specific* legacy sets aside a particular piece of property in an estate and gives it to a named individual: you bequeath your gold watch to your son, Thomas. A *general* legacy leaves a given sum of money, say $5,000, to an individual. A cash bequest is payable out of the general assets of an estate. When a testator does not leave sufficient property to pay all of the general legacies, the specific legatees would nevertheless receive the particular items bequeathed to them, whereas the general legacies would be proportionately diminished and may be abated (or disappear).

A *demonstrative* legacy is usually one of a stated amount of money coupled with a specification in the will of a source of funds for its payment. If the indicated source of funds is nonexistent—or to the extent that it is insufficient,—the legacy is payable out of general assets, like a general legacy. This has, however, occasioned considerable litigation, so that many lawyers prefer to avoid demonstrative legacies.

A *residuary* legacy, as the term implies, is payable after administration expenses, debts, and specific, general, and demonstrative legacies have been paid. Danger exists if you make a will with a number of specific and general legacies and then leave the remainder—which you believe to be the bulk of your estate—as a residuary legacy to your spouse or child inasmuch as a shrinkage of the assets of the estate may sharply reduce the residuary legacy without impairing or touching the specific and general bequests. You can guard against this eventuality by inserting an abatement clause which provides that if the entire net estate, or residuary estate, is less than a certain amount, or shrinks a certain percentage from the value of the estate when the will was drawn, then the general legacies shall be reduced proportionately or eliminated altogether. When you leave your residuary estate to your nearest and dearest, you should always use such an abatement clause.

A *lapsed* legacy occurs when the legatee predeceases the testator. To provide for such contingencies, the will should make provision for alternative disposition. A *preferred* legacy is one in which the testator's will indicates that preference shall be given in the event that the estate is insufficient to satisfy all legacies in full.

The third major part of a will is the section that contains the administrative clauses. These clauses set up the machinery for carrying out your instructions. Here you name your executor and your guardian (if you have any minor children). The executor is the person (or persons) or the institution (since the executor can be a trust company) responsible for having the will approved by the court, for locating heirs and property, for paying bills, and distributing bequests. You may select anyone—your spouse, a business partner, your brother or sister, your lawyer, your banker, a friend—as your executor; but you will want to ask the persons you select whether they will accept, and you will want to be reasonably sure that they are able to handle the complicated business of settling an estate and are young enough so that they are not likely to predecease you. You may also wish to name an alternate or substitute executor in case your first choices decline to serve or die. The guardian you appoint for your minor child may, of course, be your spouse, in which case you will want to provide that this service be without bond and with absolute discretion in the handling of any funds that you may leave to the child. If you own and operate a business and you want the business continued, you should give your executor very broad powers because otherwise the business may be liquidated as there may not be sufficient authority to operate it efficiently. These are all highly technical matters, the settlement of which should never be attempted without the advice of a lawyer.

The fourth part of a will ends the will and says that, in approval of the foregoing, you are signing your name. Do not sign your name, however, until the witnesses are present. This clause is likely to read: "In witness whereof, I have hereunto set my hand [and seal, in some states] this 5th day of May 1979."

Mr. Kelly's "Humorous" Will

"For years I have been reading Last Wills and Testaments, and I have never been able to clearly understand any of them at one reading. Therefore, I will attempt to write my own Will with the hope that it will be understandable and legal. Kids will be called 'kids' and not 'issue' and it will not be cluttered up with 'parties of the first part,' 'per stirpes,' 'perpetuities,' 'quasi judicial,' 'to wit' and a lot of other terms that I am sure are only used to confuse those for whose benefit it is written."

So begins the Last Will of John B. Kelly of Philadelphia, onetime bricklayer, founder of two of the country's largest brick contracting firms, former Olympic rowing champion, and father of H.S.H. Princess Grace of Monaco.

It was typed on 12 full-sized legal sheets, prompting his parting observation: "If I don't stop soon, this will be as long as Gone with the Wind."

Finally, there is what the lawyers call the "attestation clause." This is the clause for witnesses, so that a record will exist reciting the circumstances under which the signing of the will was witnessed and who witnessed it. Remember that the witnesses must hear you announce that this is your will, must see you sign it, and must then sign both in one another's presence and in your presence.

Probate

The purpose of probate is to ensure that the will which has your signature is genuine and that its execution will carry out your precise intent. But before that can be done, the executor must satisfy the probate court that your debts and your state and federal taxes have been paid and that any one who has a claim against the estate has been notified. Please note in Figure 15–1 all the other time-consuming duties that the executor must handle. Creditors have from four months to a year to make a claim. Although the executor must settle federal estate taxes within nine months after the testator's death, the Internal Revenue Service and the state tax authorities may take several months to a year to indicate their acceptance. Only then can distribution be made from the estate. Any contest creates delay. And while taxes and legal and court costs shrink an estate, the need for cash mounts during the time that probate freezes funds. Studies have shown that the average time spent in probate is 12 to 15 months—on estates averaging about $30,000.

Uniform Probate Code

It has been suggested that if the states adopted the Uniform Probate Code, a proposed model law that was fashioned by legal experts over a ten-year period, uncontested wills could be put into effect as quickly as five days after death. The Uniform Probate Code would free the executor to pay bills, taxes, and legacies without the probate court's formalities. It would simplify legal procedures for unchallenged small estates and for estates administered by members of the family. Fewer than one third of the states have adopted this code.

Before an estate can be settled, every asset owned by the deceased must be fully inventoried, and when and how it was acquired must be noted. Determining the original value of the deceased's home and the value of subsequent improvements, as well as the market value of securities, automobiles, jewelry and artwork, and personal possessions, such as furniture, might require an executor to spend days or weeks in locating canceled checks, invoices, title records, brokerage slips, and other papers.

Executors are, of course, compensated for such services, but an inexperienced person would either spend an excessive amount of time at the task or perform it inadequately. For this reason, if you appoint your spouse as executor, you may wish to name your lawyer as coexecutor in order to take adequate care of such involved matters as probating the will, settling the estate, meeting claims, providing for estate taxes, and filing an accounting with the court. Choose your executors carefully—not on the basis of friendship alone, but on the basis of competence and ability to handle money matters. When you have chosen your executors tell them where you keep your will and give each executor an unsigned copy of it.

Fees for independent executors, such as those appointed by courts, are fixed by state law. A typical example of the sliding scale that is generally used would be the following:

4 percent on the first $25,000 of the estate.

3.5 percent on the next $125,000.

3 percent on the next $150,000.

2 percent on any amount in excess of $30,000.

Executors are held legally responsible for their actions, as the lengthy tangled litigation involving the Rothko estate illustrates.

For six years after his suicide, three executors of the estate of Mark Rothko, a leading abstract expressionist painter, were involved in a $32 million estate suit with international art galleries and famous art centers, a phalanx of lawyers, a guardian for a minor child, and the attorney general of New York State taking sides. One of the executors opposed the other two. Rothko's daughter, when she came of age several years ago, brought suit to dismiss the executors because they had sold all 800 of her father's paintings to one gallery in an exclusive deal. She alleged that two of the executors had a relationship with the gallery and they had thereby "wasted the assets" of the estate. One art dealer testified that 100 paintings bought by the gallery for $1.8 million were worth $6,420,000 at the artist's death and had since risen in value to $14,613,000.

In the final settlement, the New York Court of Appeals called the conduct of the executors "manifestly wrongful and indeed shocking" and upheld a ruling that damages and fines of $9.2 million against the executors and the art gallery were to be paid to the estate.

Simultaneous Deaths (Common Disasters)

You often read about a husband and wife dying in the same accident. In the absence of a will, all of their property would probably pass to their children. If they had no children, there would probably be an argument as to which of the two died first. The same sort of difficulty could arise if each of them had left a will. If it were established that the husband had died first, the wife would have inherited whatever property her husband had willed her; and this property, together with any other property that she owned, would pass as stipulated in her will, except that her husband, of course, would not receive anything that had been left to him in that will. In the absence of a will, any property that she left would go to her relatives, to the exclusion of his.

To prevent unwanted results as far as possible, it may be helpful for a will to state how the property is to be disposed of if both a husband and wife die in a common disaster. A well-drawn will usually contains a *common disaster clause*. Such a clause may read: "Any person who shall have died at the same time as I, or in a common disaster with me, or under such circumstances that it is difficult or impossible to determine which died first, shall be deemed to have predeceased me."

The Review of Wills

Here is a streamlined statement of the facts in a court case: Mrs. J. owned 75 shares of General Electric stock when she executed her will. The will gave a niece "Seventy five (75 sh.) of common stock of General Electric Company." Between the time that the will was signed and the time that Mrs. J. died, General Electric effected a three for one stock split. As a result, there were 225 shares of General Electric in Mrs. J's estate at the time of her death.

In the same will Mrs. J bequeathed "ninety (90) shares of International Paper Company stock" to a nephew. After the will was signed, the company paid dividends in its own stock. As a consequence, there were 104 shares in Mrs. J's estate at her death.

Was the niece entitled to 75 shares of General Electric or to 225?

Was the nephew entitled to 90 shares of International Paper or to 104?

Figure 15–1

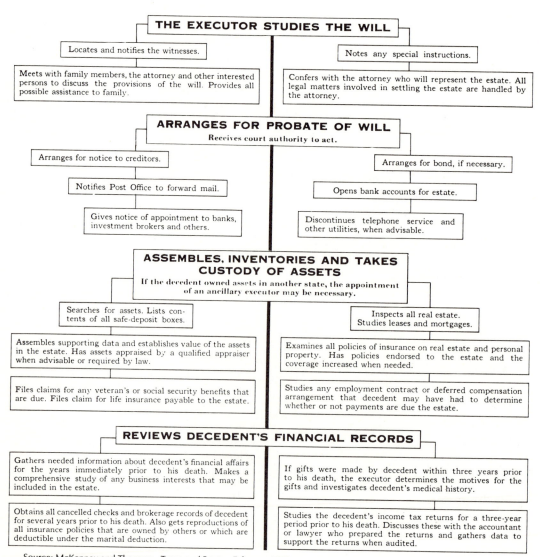

A CHART OF THE DUTIES OF AN EXECUTOR

This chart is a generalized presentation of some of the more common problems that confront an executor. It is not intended to be exhaustive or technical. The specific details of an executor's duties often vary from state to state, but the chart is not intended to cover these in depth. Furthermore, many of the steps that an executor must take in settling an estate depend on the provisions of the decedent's will and the composition of the assets comprising the estate.

THE EXECUTOR STUDIES THE WILL

Locates and notifies the witnesses.

Notes any special instructions.

Meets with family members, the attorney and other interested persons to discuss the provisions of the will. Provides all possible assistance to family.

Confers with the attorney who will represent the estate. All legal matters involved in settling the estate are handled by the attorney.

ARRANGES FOR PROBATE OF WILL
Receives court authority to act.

Arranges for notice to creditors.

Arranges for bond, if necessary.

Notifies Post Office to forward mail.

Opens bank accounts for estate.

Gives notice of appointment to banks, investment brokers and others.

Discontinues telephone service and other utilities, when advisable.

ASSEMBLES, INVENTORIES AND TAKES CUSTODY OF ASSETS
If the decedent owned assets in another state, the appointment of an ancillary executor may be necessary.

Searches for assets. Lists contents of all safe-deposit boxes.

Inspects all real estate. Studies leases and mortgages.

Assembles supporting data and establishes value of the assets in the estate. Has assets appraised by a qualified appraiser when advisable or required by law.

Examines all policies of insurance on real estate and personal property. Has policies endorsed to the estate and the coverage increased when needed.

Files claims for any veteran's or social security benefits that are due. Files claim for life insurance payable to the estate.

Studies any employment contract or deferred compensation arrangement that decedent may have had to determine whether or not payments are due the estate.

REVIEWS DECEDENT'S FINANCIAL RECORDS

Gathers needed information about decedent's financial affairs for the years immediately prior to his death. Makes a comprehensive study of any business interests that may be included in the estate.

If gifts were made by decedent within three years prior to his death, the executor determines the motives for the gifts and investigates decedent's medical history.

Obtains all cancelled checks and brokerage records of decedent for several years prior to his death. Also gets reproductions of all insurance policies that are owned by others or which are deductible under the marital deduction.

Studies the decedent's income tax returns for a three-year period prior to his death. Discusses these with the accountant or lawyer who prepared the returns and gathers data to support the returns when audited.

Source: McKenney and Thomsen, *Taxes and Estates,* February 1978.

Figure 15–1 (*continued*)

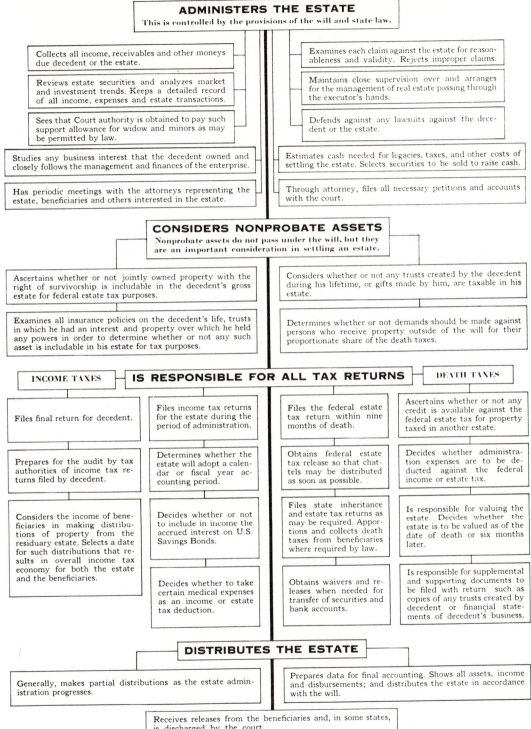

ADMINISTERS THE ESTATE
This is controlled by the provisions of the will and state law.

Collects all income, receivables and other moneys due decedent or the estate.

Reviews estate securities and analyzes market and investment trends. Keeps a detailed record of all income, expenses and estate transactions.

Sees that Court authority is obtained to pay such support allowance for widow and minors as may be permitted by law.

Studies any business interest that the decedent owned and closely follows the management and finances of the enterprise.

Has periodic meetings with the attorneys representing the estate, beneficiaries and others interested in the estate.

Examines each claim against the estate for reasonableness and validity. Rejects improper claims.

Maintains close supervision over and arranges for the management of real estate passing through the executor's hands.

Defends against any lawsuits against the decedent or the estate.

Estimates cash needed for legacies, taxes, and other costs of settling the estate. Selects securities to be sold to raise cash.

Through attorney, files all necessary petitions and accounts with the court.

CONSIDERS NONPROBATE ASSETS
Nonprobate assets do not pass under the will, but they are an important consideration in settling an estate.

Ascertains whether or not jointly owned property with the right of survivorship is includable in the decedent's gross estate for federal estate tax purposes.

Examines all insurance policies on the decedent's life, trusts in which he had an interest and property over which he held any powers in order to determine whether or not any such asset is includable in his estate for tax purposes.

Considers whether or not any trusts created by the decedent during his lifetime, or gifts made by him, are taxable in his estate.

Determines whether or not demands should be made against persons who receive property outside of the will for their proportionate share of the death taxes.

INCOME TAXES — **IS RESPONSIBLE FOR ALL TAX RETURNS** — **DEATH TAXES**

Files final return for decedent.

Prepares for the audit by tax authorities of income tax returns filed by decedent.

Considers the income of beneficiaries in making distributions of property from the residuary estate. Selects a date for such distributions that results in overall income tax economy for both the estate and the beneficiaries.

Files income tax returns for the estate during the period of administration.

Determines whether the estate will adopt a calendar or fiscal year accounting period.

Decides whether or not to include in income the accrued interest on U.S. Savings Bonds.

Decides whether to take certain medical expenses as an income or estate tax deduction.

Files the federal estate tax return within nine months of death.

Obtains federal estate tax release so that chattels may be distributed as soon as possible.

Files state inheritance and estate tax returns as may be required. Apportions and collects death taxes from beneficiaries where required by law.

Obtains waivers and releases when needed for transfer of securities and bank accounts.

Ascertains whether or not any credit is available against the federal estate tax for property taxed in another estate.

Decides whether administration expenses are to be deducted against the federal income or estate tax.

Is responsible for valuing the estate. Decides whether the estate is to be valued as of the date of death or six months later.

Is responsible for supplemental and supporting documents to be filed with return such as copies of any trusts created by decedent or financial statements of decedent's business.

DISTRIBUTES THE ESTATE

Generally, makes partial distributions as the estate administration progresses.

Prepares data for final accounting. Shows all assets, income and disbursements; and distributes the estate in accordance with the will.

Receives releases from the beneficiaries and, in some states, is discharged by the court.

A court proceeding was necessary to decide what Mrs. J intended. It was finally held that the niece was entitled to all 225 shares of General Electric. But it was also held that the nephew was entitled to only 90 shares of the International Paper stock; the balance went to the person to whom Mrs. J willed her residuary estate.

Here trouble and expense could have been avoided by wording the will in a way that would have anticipated the possibility of stock splits and dividends. A review of the will after the extra stock had been received should have revealed its weakness.

We live in a dynamic—not a static—world. A will which makes a sensible distribution of property at one time may result in a foolish distribution at a later time. When a will has been made, therefore, it should not be put aside and overlooked for many years. Its stipulations should be reviewed at regular intervals to determine whether any of its provisions require change. A variety of causes may signal the need for review, such as changes in the size of the estate or changes in the family—marriage, a birth, a death, a significant change in the assets of a family member, or the move of a family member to another state.

A husband may have drawn a will leaving everything to his wife, explaining that he is leaving nothing to his little daughter because he is confident that his wife will provide for her. Several years later a son is born. Then the husband dies. The son may be entitled to one third of his father's estate. The widow receives two thirds. The daughter gets nothing. Why? Because the law in most states provides that when a child is born after a will is made, that child is entitled to take his "intestate share" as if no will existed—unless some provision has been made in advance for after-born children, or unless it is clear from the language of the will that no provision for such children is intended. A useful rule for every family is: whenever a child is born, have both parents' wills checked by the family lawyer.

If individual pieces of property are left to each of several children, there is always the question of whether some pieces of property may increase in value and others decline in value by the time

of the testator's death, thus effecting an unequal distribution. It might be better to give each child an equal interest in all properties or in the proceeds from the sale of all properties. Some years ago, a certain wealthy individual left stipulated amounts to several charities, thinking that he was leaving such a substantial estate that there would be plenty left over for his family. A depression in the stock market, however, so depleted the assets that after the designated amounts were distributed to the charities, little remained for the family.

The safest way to make changes is to have a new will drawn, though a codicil to the old will may be effective.

A *codicil* is an instrument which amends or changes a will. An example will indicate how it is drawn. Assume that you want to change your executor:

> I, Joseph F. Tarren, of the County of Confusion, City of Confusion, State of Confusion, do hereby make, publish, and declare this Codicil to my Last Will and Testament:
>
> I hereby ratify each and every provision of my will executed the 24th day of September, 1974, except insofar as such will is inconsistent with the terms of this instrument.
>
> I hereby direct that Henry Takelittle be substituted as my executor, in place of Thomas Graball.
>
> In witness whereof I have hereunto set my hand (and seal) this 20th day of January, 1979.

Names Clipped from Will Restored by Surrogate

BUFFALO, N.Y. (UPI)—Surrogate Thomas J. O'Donnell recently told nine persons they could not be cut out of the will of a relative even though they literally were.

One paragraph of the will of Mrs. Lillian G. Briggs of suburban Kenmore, who died Feb. 21, 1962, was scissored out. It provided for bequests to nine relatives. The will was contested.

In what Surrogate O'Donnell called "a rare move," he accepted a carbon copy of the will and awarded $6,000 to the relatives. It was not determined who did the cutting.

The same formality must be employed in executing and witnessing a codicil as was employed with the will itself. You need not have the same witnesses, but you must have the same number of witnesses. You must announce to the witnesses that the instrument is a codicil to your will. Then you must sign, and they must sign, all in the presence of one another. You should then fasten the codicil securely to the will itself.

The Revocation of Wills

The safest way to revoke a will is to tear it up and burn the pieces in the presence of informed witnesses. If the will is burned, canceled, torn, or otherwise destroyed by the testator or by another person in the testator's presence and at his order, the law will consider the will revoked. A new will signed under a later date and stating the testator's intention to revoke prior wills is sufficient to do so. Those provisions of the later will which are not consistent with any of the earlier ones replace them.

Where to Keep a Will

Being valuable documents, wills should be kept with other important papers. Above all, they should be left where they will come into the hands of persons who will see that they are presented to the court for probate. Wills are frequently left for safekeeping with one's attorney; logically, they should be left with one's executor-to-be.

A safe deposit box is not recommended as a place to keep a will, because when a person dies, his safe deposit box is sealed. It may be opened only upon application to the probate court, and then only in the presence of a representative of the estate tax division of the state's tax department. It must then be resealed, and the contents may not again be touched until the will is probated and the executor is given authority and access to the box. It is better, therefore, to keep your will either in a strongbox at home or with your lawyer or your executor. Of course, if your spouse also has a personal safe deposit box, you can keep your wills in each other's box.

The Letter of Last Instructions

You should give your executor or your lawyer a letter of last instructions, which is separate and apart from your will. This letter, to be opened upon your death, should contain the following:

1. A statement as to where your will may be found.
2. Instructions as to your funeral and burial. You may wish to specify for example, that, as a veteran, you be buried in a certain national cemetery rather than in the family burial plot.
3. Where your birth or baptismal certificate, social security card, marriage or divorce certificate, naturalization and citizenship papers, and discharge papers from the armed forces may be found. The last is important if you wish to be buried in a national cemetery, which is the privilege of any veteran.
4. Where your membership certificates in any lodges or fraternal organizations which provide death or cemetery benefits may be found.
5. A list of the locations of any safe deposit boxes that you have, and where the keys may be found.
6. A list of your insurance policies, and where they may be found.
7. A statement concerning any pension systems to which you belonged and from which your estate may be entitled to receive a death benefit.
8. A list of all your bank accounts, checking and savings, and their locations.
9. A list of all the stocks and bonds you own, and where they may be found.
10. A statement of all the real property owned by you.
11. A list of all your other property—personal, business, and other.
12. Instructions or directions concerning your business in the event that your will suggests or provides that it be continued.
13. A statement of the reasons for the actions taken in your will, such as disinheritances. It is sometimes better to place the explanation in a separate letter available to the court,

rather than in your will, to avoid a complicated will and expensive litigation in connection therewith.

THE FEDERAL ESTATE TAX

For the first time in over 40 years, Congress in 1976 and again in 1978 made important changes in the estate and gift tax law. The Internal Revenue Service has estimated that by 1981, when the law is fully effective, 98 percent of all estates will escape the tax. "That lets me out," you say—with relief. Maybe. Just in case, take a quick look at the highlights of these tax acts, so that you can think about how they might relate to you.

The estate and lifetime gift exemptions are now unified and will become effective over a transitional period affecting the amount of gross estate that requires a tax.

The unified tax credit, which increases over those five years, explains why there is this increasing amount of an estate free from taxation.

Unified Estate and Gift Tax Credit

Estates

For decedents dying in 1977 and thereafter, the credit is phased in as follows:

Year	Credit	Equivalent Exemption
1977	$30,000	$120,667
1978	34,000	134,000
1979	38,000	147,333
1980	42,500	161,563
After 1980	47,000	175,625

Gifts

The credit is phased in, as follows, for gifts made after:

December 31, 1976, and before July 1, 1977	$ 6,000
June 30, 1977, and before January 1, 1978	30,000
December 31, 1977, and before January 1, 1979	34,000
December 31, 1978, and before January 1, 1980	38,000
December 31, 1979, and before January 1, 1981	42,500
December 31, 1980	47,000

The Gift Tax

The law allows anyone to give up to $3,000 a year tax-free to as many people as desired. The parents of three children, for example, could each give $3,000 to each child, or $18,000 a year. Husbands and wives can give each other $3,000 a year as gifts tax-free. The first $100,000 given by one spouse to another during their lifetime is tax-free, with the unified tax credit applied to gifts between $100,000 and $200,000 and to 50 percent of such gifts over $200,000.

All other gifts are taxable. The annual gift tax required is calculated on a graduated rate schedule based on the taxable gifts made during a given year and during the donor's lifetime, minus the applicable year's unified credit.

Since the unified tax credit applies toward gifts made during a lifetime and on the estate at the time of death, credits previously taken and gift taxes previously paid are both subtracted from the final estate tax.

All gifts (less the allowed annual $3,000), including those made three years prior to death are included in the estate at the value of the property at the time of the donor's death or at the alternative valuation date, if used.

Formerly gift giving was used by the wealthy to lower their estate and income taxes, because funds could be shifted to members of the family in lower tax brackets and be taxed at lower rates. The new unified gift and estate tax credit now minimizes the use of gifts as a tax-saving technique.

The federal estate tax is neither a property tax nor an inheritance tax, but a tax on the right to transfer property.

The executor or administrator has the option of valuing the estate either at the date of the decedent's death or six months after the date of death. Estate taxes due the federal government, which are much heavier than those due the state where you live, are payable within nine months after death. State estate and inheritance tax laws vary but usually require that estate taxes be paid over a period extending from one year to 18 months after death.

The settlement of an estate generates a need for immediate cash for taxes, estate administration expenses, and funeral costs, and it may be necessary to sell assets (stocks, business, property) in order to realize the necessary funds. It has been estimated by the Internal Revenue Service that the expenses of probating an estate of $50,000–$250,000 are about 6 percent of the value of the estate.

Your Gross Estate—What Is Included?

Estate tax laws refer to the "gross estate." This means the fair market value of all the real and personal property which you own at your death—of your house and its contents, your cash stocks, bonds, mortgages (owned by you), notes (held by you), jewelry, automobile, and all other such property. Your executor can exclude $10,000 of personal and household effects. The following are also included in the gross estate:

1. Life insurance on your life is taxable if you pay the premiums on the policy directly or indirectly or if you possess "incidents of ownership in the policies," such as the right to change the beneficiaries, to borrow on the policies, or to collect cash surrender values. If your wife pays the premiums out of money you give her for household expenses, you are considered to have paid indirectly. Most people labor under the illusion that because life insurance proceeds are not taxable under the personal income tax, they are also exempt from the federal estate tax. This is not the case.

If you do not retain any "incidents of ownership," then at your death the principal may not be taxed to your estate, even if you continued to pay all the premiums on the policy directly.

2. Another illusion is that if all your property is in joint ownership with rights of survivorship, your estate will not have to pay taxes on it. The property passes outside your will, just as does insurance to a named beneficiary, but both are subject to the federal estate tax.

Before 1976 the government presumed that jointly owned property belonged completely to the first owner to die. Under the new rules married couples are given a chance to change their property ownership to conform to the 50–50 arrangement. These joint property arrangements must have property titles legally changed to qualify—even if this involves the payment of a gift tax.

Only one half of property created after 1976 which you own jointly with a spouse with rights of survivorship can now be taxable, since the law now allows the joint owners to use gifts to each other (which may be subject to the gift tax) to equalize the contributions.

3. If you have created a trust in your lifetime wherein you have reserved certain rights or powers or wherein the enjoyment of the trust property by the beneficiaries depends on their surviving you, that trust is taxable. For example, bank accounts which you establish in trust for your children are taxable, since you can add to them or withdraw from them at will. For tax purposes, it is the same as if the bank accounts were solely in your name.

4. Funds in a Keogh or IRA retirement plan are excluded from estate or gift taxes if the survivor receives the payments over a period of not less than 36 months.

Your Net Estate—What Is Included?

The federal estate tax laws allows certain exemptions and deductions in determining the "net estate," which is the base on which the estate tax is computed. Among the permissible deductions are funeral expenses and claims, loans, and mortgages against your property. Expenses for the administration of your estate, including fees for legal services and the commissions of your executor,

The Estate Tax—How It Might Work

Robert Brown's estate	$380,000
Estate expenses	10,000
Adjusted gross estate	$370,000
Marital deduction	250,000
Net estate	$120,000
Exemption and unified tax credit	120,000
Federal Tax	$

are deductible, and this reduces the net cost of these services to your estate. Bequests to qualified charities and other tax-exempt institutions are deductible. The most important deduction, if your wife or your husband survives you, is the "marital deduction." One spouse may leave the surviving spouse one half of the estate or up to $250,000 (whichever is *greater)* tax-free.

Capital Gains

A fundamental change in the Tax Reform Act of 1976 refers to the capital gains calculations that take place if you want to sell any of the assets you inherited. Previously the gain or loss on such a sale was calculated from the value of the assets at date of death (or as an alternative, six months afterward), and therefore the heir paid no capital gains tax on any increase in the value of the assets that might have taken place since the assets were purchased. Under the Tax Reform Act of 1976 marketable securities owned at death are to be valued on two bases. If bought before December 31, 1976, they are valued as of that date. If those assets were bought after January 1, 1977, they are valued at their original cost.

The Tax Law of 1978 postponed until 1980 the carry-over provision of the Tax Reform Act of 1976. The "carry-over" refers to the required use of the original cost basis of assets acquired before December 31, 1976. Congress provided for a "fresh start" and allowed the value of such property to be "stepped up" to reflect a value as of December 31, 1976. This means that property bought in 1960 and inherited in 1980 would, when sold, be taxed on the appreciation in value since January 1, 1977. There are many modifications to this rule which only a tax expert should explain.

Deferring the effective date of the 1976 provision until 1980 means that the heirs of an estate of anyone dying in 1978 or 1979 have a choice in determining the capital gains tax basis, because the fair market value can still be used as a tax basis for sold assets until 1980.

TRUSTS

A trust is an agreement whereby the person who establishes the trust—the grantor—gives property to a trustee or trustees for the benefit of the beneficiary or beneficiaries of the trust. Those beneficiaries who receive income from trusts during their lifetime only are known as "life tenants"; those beneficiaries who get the principal of the trust upon the death of the life tenants are called "remaindermen." Individuals and such institutions as trust companies and banks act as trustees. According to the desire of the grantor, a trust may be revocable or irrevocable. The advent of the trust company brought a continued life beyond that enjoyed by individuals as trustees. Sooner or later an individual is sure to die; however, a trust company usually enjoys a perpetual charter. Furthermore, the large volume of trust business handled by such institutions gives them an experience and organization beyond the scope of individuals. By teaming an institution and an individual as cotrustees, many of the advantages of each may be secured for a trust.

Living Trusts

A living trust, or trust *inter vivos,* or voluntary trust, is in effect while the grantor is still living; in fact, he may be the beneficiary of the trust. Any person having enough property to warrant it can set up such a trust for his own protection. Unless there is a minimum of $10,000 or $20,000, there will be difficulty in finding competent persons who are willing to undertake the responsibility of acting as trustees. The trustee takes the legal title to the property and administers it with a view to preserving the principal and earning a relatively safe income from it, although both principal and income may be distributed currently under the agreement, in which case the beneficiary would be very much like an annuitant.

In addition to the advantage of putting the property into skillful hands, living trusts also provide some tax advantages. If the settlor really parts definitely with the property put into the trust by (1) making the trust irrevocable, (2) receiving no income, and (3) not retaining the power to change the beneficiary, although he will be answerable for gift taxes when the trust is established, no estate or inheritance taxes will be levied on this property when he dies. Should the settlor retain the power to revoke the trust, receive income from it, or change the beneficiary, he has in important respects not really parted with his property at all. He still has it under his control and cannot reasonably expect to obtain an estate tax advantage from it. Important income tax advantages may still result, however. That is because the income produced by the capital is taxable to the beneficiary, who normally would be in a lower bracket. The living trust, also known as a Clifford trust, must run a minimum of ten years.

There would by no tax advantage in setting up a living trust for the education of children because the tax laws state that any money spent to take care of one's legal obligations is taxed to the person who has that obligation. A trust created through a will is regarded differently from a tax viewpoint.

Testamentary Trusts

A testamentary trust is a trust established under the will of a deceased person, becoming effective at death. The trustee and the executor may or may not be the same person. The purpose of such a trust is to lodge the property of the deceased person in skillful hands, so that it may be advantageously administered for the beneficiaries. If the same money were handled by an inexperienced person, the chances of doing as well with it, either from the viewpoint of income or of the safety of the principal, would probably not be bright.

A testamentary trust is often set up so that the surviving parent (a life tenant) may receive the income for life and so that the children (the remaindermen) may have the principal upon death. In the absence of a parent, the income may be left to the children for a number of years, usually during their minority, at the end of which time the principal of the trust is to be paid to them. It is possible to incorporate a provision in the trust agreement whereby the trustee may use part of the principal

to supplement the beneficiaries' income should the income alone be inadequate. Testamentary trusts are often useful as a means of reducing taxes.

It is obviously undesirable to bequeath or devise property directly to a minor, because a minor cannot receive or manage the property. Such a gift requires the appointment of a guardian. A guardian is usually required to file a bond; must make an annual accounting to the court; has to obtain a court order before any property can be used for the minor's maintenance; and is limited to so-called legal investments in investing any of the minor's funds. Then, too, the sale of a minor's real estate requires the approval of the court, and it is an expensive and lengthy proceeding to obtain the necessary permission. All of these difficulties can be avoided by creating a trust.

The Power of Invasion

Future developments cannot be foreseen, especially during a trust term which may run for many years. Furthermore, no one can predict whether the investments of a trust will retain their value or will depreciate. Hence, inadequacy of income is a contingency which must be faced and covered in the drafting of the trust, particularly if the initial corpus of the trust is not large and if the purpose of the trust is to support the testator's immediate family.

For example, assume that a married man with children (the testator) has accumulated $100,000 and that up to the time of his death he is earning $15,000 a year. When he dies he leaves a widow and young children. In his will he has directed that his entire estate be held in trust, with the income to be paid to his wife during her life and the principal to be divided among his children on her death. Assume that his net estate is $90,000 and that this forms the principal of the trust. On the basis of the present yield of so-called trust investments, that amount might produce no more than $5,000 per year. From this there must be deducted trustee's commissions and any income tax payable by the widow, which means that the amount available for the support of her family will be only a small proportion of her husband's income at the time of his death.

In this hypothetical example the principal, although much needed for the support and education of the young children, cannot be used by the trustee because the will contains no permissive language to that effect. The hardship which would arise in this situation is obvious, and it might have been avoided by appropriate language allowing an invasion of the principal.

There are many ways of avoiding such a situation. The testator can provide that if the income from the trust fund is less than a stated amount in any year, the deficiency is to be made up out of the principal. However, the testator may prefer to leave it to the discretion of the trustee to determine how much of the principal shall be paid over to the wife from time to time, in order to enable her to support her family. Or, alternatively, the testator may wish to vest this discretion in his wife, giving her the right to require the trustee to pay over whatever amounts of principal she may request. Various combinations are also possible.

Tax Advantages of the Trust

If the testator leaves an estate outright to the surviving spouse, an estate tax may have to be paid. When the surviving partner dies, another estate tax is payable, frequently on the same property—now doubly taxed. If part of the property had been left in trust in the first instance, taxes on it would be avoided. Life income could have been paid from it, and the capital could have gone untaxed to the children on the death of the surviving parent.

Formerly trust funds were not taxed when a child died and passed the trust capital to the grandchildren. This generation-skipping trust is no longer allowed, although a limited sum is allowed to pass tax-free in this manner.

State Inheritance Taxes and Estate Taxes

An inheritance tax differs from an estate tax in that an inheritance tax is levied on the right of the beneficiary to receive a bequest and is based on his or her share, but an estate tax is levied on all the property of the deceased and must be paid out of the estate by the executor.

All states, except Nevada, levy either inheritance or estate taxes. In some states these are known as succession taxes. Don't hurry to Nevada. It won't help. The federal estate tax is constructed to equalize state practices by allowing a credit against the federal tax for the amount paid to the state. Thus, if you pay nothing to the state, you receive no credit and your federal estate tax is just that much higher.

Most states—Colorado, Illinois, Indiana, Kansas, Maine, Pennsylvania, Texas, Virginia, West Virginia, and Wisconsin, for example—have inheritance taxes. Only a few—New York, for example—have estate taxes. Some states, such as Ohio, have both.

The state inheritance tax is usually levied at a much lower rate than the federal estate tax—1 to 20 percent in most cases. The rate varies with (a) the degree of relationship between the decedent and the beneficiary and (b) the size of the bequest. In Kansas, for example, a widow is given a $75,000 personal exemption, a child only a $15,000 exemption. In Ohio a widow or a child under 21 receives a $5,000 exemption and a son or daughter over 21 receives only a $3,500 exemption. The practices of the various states vary so widely that it is useless to attempt to generalize. This is especially true of rates, the kinds of property taxed, and those that are exempt. Usually the states are not only lower in their rates but they are also more generous than the federal government in their exemptions on the kinds of property that they tax. The chief tax officer of your state can provide you with a copy of your state inheritance or estate tax law.

Gifts to Children

Sentiment, dreams, and tax savings all combine to make this a popular form of gift giving. The procedure for giving securities or money to minors is regulated by law in each of the 50 states, the District of Columbia, the Virgin Islands, and the

Canal Zone. These factors must be remembered in making such a gift.

1. It is irrevocable—and the custodian must act for the minor and not for himself.
2. There is no way that the donor can reclaim the gift before the minor comes of age. The property is the minor's.
3. All that is required is registration of the securities in the name of the custodian for the minor. There is no other legal technicality.

The custodial property may be used for the support, maintenance, education, and general use of the minor as the custodian with discretion deems suitable and proper.

The tax benefits allow the donor to shift income to a lower bracket and are therefore taxable at lower rates. The parents of the minor continue to enjoy tax exemptions for the minor, regardless of his income, if they contribute more than half of his support and he is under 19 or a full-time student. However, if income from the gift is used to discharge the legal obligation of any person to support the minor, the sum used is taxable to that person as income.

Conclusion

Of the many complex and involved financial problems inevitably faced through life—insurance, debts, mortgage financing, taxes, investments—(all of which we have now surveyed)—none are more difficult or technical than wills, trusts, estates, and death and gift taxes. Nowhere will you save more time and trouble by paying the fee of a lawyer or other expert for careful, competent, precise, and correct advice. Invariably, a shortsighted attempt to save a fee will result in a much more serious loss.

All that this book has attempted to do is to provide the framework and background that will enable you to talk more intelligently about your personal financial problems with the various experts—lawyers, accountants, insurance agents, bank mortgage officers, internal revenue agents, trust officers, and others—whom you will encounter during the course of your "three score and ten." It would be a real disservice to yourself to attempt to deal with all of these complicated matters on your own. Remember "Many persons might have attained to wisdom had they not assumed that they already possessed it" (Seneca).

SUGGESTED READINGS

Ashley, Paul. B. *You and Your Will.* New York: McGraw-Hill, 1975.

Beckman, Gail McKnight. "Estate Planning: A Woman's Perspective," *Trusts and Estates,* March 1975.

Chemical Bank, New York. "Taxes and Estates," *Monthly Bulletin.*

Commerce Clearing House, Inc. *Federal Estate and Gift Taxes Explained.* Chicago, 1978.

Forbes. "The Art of Willmaking," October 16, 1978.

Irving Trust Company. "How to Do More for Your Family," *Monthly Bulletin.* New York, 1976.

Money. "Wills That Keep Your Heirs from Turning Grey," December 1976.

Securities Industry Association. *Gifts of Securities or Money to Minors: A Guide to Laws in 50 States.* Write to the association at 120 Broadway, New York, NY 10005; annual.

CASE PROBLEMS

1 Norman Roberts is 28 years old and an employee of a large advertising concern. He is married and the father of a year-old son. He has life insurance payable to his wife, owns a car, and recently his parents gave him a small ranch house worth about $45,000. He has stock in his name totaling about $10,000, and has a joint savings account with his wife in which they have deposited about $4,000. It has not occurred to him to make a will, but his wife suggests that he should do so. Norman is not impressed, saying that what he has would automatically go to her. How would you advise them?

2 John Smith, aged 26, was killed in an accident, leaving a wife and two children (ages one and three). Having just begun his career, John left very little money. His father, Fred Smith, a widower, has cancer, and the doctors give him only a year to live. His will, as it stood at the time of the accident, named his son as sole heir. His estate amounts to about $400,000. Fred Smith now wishes to rewrite the will so as to aid his daughter-in-law and his grandchildren. What are your suggestions?

3 Allen Rubens has a large income and pays heavy income taxes. Besides his wife, he supports his daughter-in-law and her three children by sending them $800 monthly, since his son was killed in Vietnam. How can he reduce his tax liability and accomplish the same goals?

4 Peter Tompkins inserted in his will a specific legacy of old gold coins, worth $3,000, to a local museum; a legacy of $8,000 to his grandson, to be taken from $10,000 deposited in a savings bank; and residuary legacies of $57,000, all to be taken from his estate, which he believed was worth $68,000. After his death it was found that burial expenses, debts, and taxes absorbed $10,000. At his death he still owned the gold coins, and his savings account amounted to $14,000. The balance of his estate consisted of stocks and bonds, which brought $32,000 upon their sale. The residuary legacies were for $20,000 to his grown, successful son and $37,000 to his elderly wife. Tompkins and his wife had been living for years on his $28,000 annual salary. How did the will affect the way the money left was distributed?

5 Branch Burlingame (age 59) is a successful account executive in an advertising agency. He makes $55,000 a year and has a wife (age 47) and three children: a son, age 27, and two daughters, ages 18 and 16. In addition to a mortgage-free home worth $70,000, which will go to his wife upon his death, and substantial annuities and insurance coverage of $400,000 to send his daughters to college and provide himself and his family with a comfortable income after his retirement, he has other assets of $300,000. He made gifts of $3,000 each to each of his children for the last three years. If he were to die in 1981, how much would you estimate his estate tax to be?

Index

C

T

U

This book has been set CAP, in 10 point and 9 point Roma, leaded two points. Part numbers are 64 point Compano; chapter numbers are 66 point Weiss Series I; part and chapter titles are 28 point Compano. The size of the type page is 37 by 48 picas.